The Zohar

by
Rav Shimon bar Yochai
From The Book of Avraham

with
The Sulam Commentary

by
Rav Yehuda Ashlag

The First Ever Unabridged
English Translation with Commentary

Published by
The Kabbalah Centre International Inc.
Dean Rav S. P. Berg Shlita

Edited and Compiled by
Rabbi Michael Berg

שבזכות ספר הזהר
יזכו לרפואה שלמה
חיים ארוכים של ברכה
זוגיות וילדים בריאים ורוחניים

רינת ויואב ברמץ

לעילוי נשמת אברהם בן עזיז
תבדל לבריאות ושמחה רינה (זרין)
פרנסה ובריאות לאחי עוזי, חיים, אסתר וחנה
זיווג מתאים וזרע בר קיימא לחיים בת שבע וחנה
לרפאל יציאה מן המיצר
לגיסי וגיסתי מרים וגונטר
אליהו, שרה, אופיר, מיכל, עמית, דניאל ומיכאל
זכות רבי שמעון והפצת ספרי הזהר יגן עליהם, לברכה, והצלחה בכל
אשר יפנו

לשפע רוחני וכלכלי, בריאות שלמה, חיבור תמידי לאור והגנה מעין הרע , מציאת והגשמת היעוד ולחיים
ארוכים עבור:
מיכאל בן יהושע, יעל בת יהושע
דנה בת ברוך ויהושע בן יעקב
לאה בת שלמה
אבא בן צבי
ולמשפחות הדני, נאור ובלוך

בזכות רבי שמעון בר יוחאי וספר הזוהר
לברכה, הצלחה, לחיבור לאור אינסוף ולעץ החיים, פרנסה, רפואות הנפש
ורפואת הגוף
לבני משפחת כץ
יהושע דוד, גלית יהודית מלכה, אדווה דינה, ושונית
מהאם
רחל

לברכה, לבריאות, שמחה והצלחה
לבני :
נדב ואיתי בני טובי בילה
לנעמה בת יעל
ולעידו בן נעמה
שהאור ידריך אתכם כל ימי חייכם

לברכה, להצלחה, לפרנסה, לבריאות,
לכל טוב ומכל טוב
שפע של אור
להלינה בת סבינה ויצחק
לאלכסנדר בן נחמה וגרשון
לרוזה בת נחמה וגרשון
לאביטל בת הלינה ויוסף
ליהודית בת הלינה ויוסף
לנויה שחר ורז בני אביטל ואמנון
לאמנון בן רבקה וקופל

לעלוי נשמת הורי
ישראל ושרה
לברכת פרנסה טובה ובריאות
ליהודית בת שרה
ועידו בן שרה
וחיבור לעץ החיים

To elevate the soul of my beloved Mother
Zarin Bat Rabie

May the Light of the Zohar protect her soul

With love and appreciation for having the light of the Zohar
in my life

In love and memory of

CORINA (BRAFMAN) GRAJDEANU

for the elevation of her soul to the highest level

Dear Mom, thank you for being a perfect mother.

In Sweet Memory and Honor of

Paul Perry Schwartz
"The Boss Man"

May your Big Bright Light continue to shine forever!

Thank you for your devotion to the very end.

Always Love,

Your Beloved Family

APPLYING THE POWER OF THE ZOHAR

The Zohar is a book of great mystical power and wisdom. It is Universally recognized as the definitive work on the Kabbalah – and it is also so Much more.

The Zohar is a wellspring of spiritual energy, a fountainhead of metaphysical power that not only reveals and explains, but literally brings blessing, protection, and well-being into the lives of all those who read or peruse its sacred texts. All that is required is worthy desire, the certainty of a trusting heart, and an open and receptive mind. Unlike other books, including the great spiritual texts of other traditions, The Zohar is written in a kind of code, through which metaphors, parables, and cryptic language at first conceal but ultimately reveal the forces of creation.

As electrical current is concealed in wire and cable before disclosing itself as an illuminated light bulb, the spiritual Light of the Creator is wrapped in allegory and symbolism throughout the Aramaic text of the Zohar. And while many books contain information and knowledge, the Zohar both expresses and embodies spiritual Light. The very letters on its pages have the power to bring spiritual wisdom and positive energy into every area of our lives.

As we visually scan the Aramaic texts and study the accompanying insights that appear in English, spiritual power is summoned from above – and worlds tremble as Light is sent forth in response.

It's primary purpose is not only to help us acquire wisdom, but to draw Light from the Upper Worlds and to bring sanctification into our lives. Indeed, the book itself is the most powerful of all tools for cleansing the soul and connecting to the Light of the Creator. As you open these pages, therefore, do not make understanding in the conventional sense your primary goal.

Although you may not have a knowledge of Aramaic, look first at the Aramaic text before reading the English. Do not be discouraged by difficulties with comprehension. Instead, open your heart to the spiritual transformation the Zohar is offering you.

Ultimately, the Zohar is an instrument for refining the individual soul – for removing darkness from the earth – and for bringing well being and blessing to our fellow man.

Its purpose is not only to make us intellectually wise, but to make us spiritually pure.

Torah

Also known as the Five Books of Moses, the Torah is considered to be the physical body of learning, whereas the Zohar is the internal soul. The literal stories of the Torah conceal countless hidden secrets.` The Zohar is the Light that illuminates all of the Torah's sublime mysteries.

Beresheet	Genesis
Shemot	Exodus
Vayikra	Leviticus
Bemidbar	Numbers
Devarim	Deuteronomy

Prophets

Amos	Amos
Chagai	Haggai
Chavakuk	Habakkuk
Hoshea	Hosea
Malachi	Malachi
Melachim	Kings
Michah	Micah
Nachum	Nahum
Ovadyah	Obadiah
Shmuel	Samuel
Shoftim	Judges
Tzefanyah	Zephaniah
Yechezkel	Ezekiel
Yehoshua	Joshua
Yeshayah	Isaiah
Yirmeyah	Jeremiah
Yoel	Joel
Yonah	Jonah
Zecharyah	Zechariah

Writings

Daniel	Daniel
Divrei Hayamim	Chronicles
Eicha	Lamentations
Ester	Esther
Ezra	Ezra
Nechemiah	Nehemiah
Iyov	Job
Kohelet	Ecclesiastes
Mishlei	Proverbs
Rut	Ruth

Sir Hashirim	Songs of Songs
Tehilim	Psalms

The Ten Sfirot – Emanations

To conceal the blinding *Light* of the Upper World, and thus create a tiny point into which our universe would be born, ten *curtains* were fabricated. These ten *curtains* are called Ten Sfirot. Each successive Sfirah further reduces the emanation of *Light*, gradually dimming its brilliance to a level almost devoid of *Light* – our physical world known as *Malchut*. The only remnant of Light remaining in this darkened universe is a *pilot light* which sustains our existence. This Light is the life force of a human being and the force that gives birth to stars, sustains suns and sets everything from swirling galaxies to busy ant hills in motion. Moreover, the Ten Sfirot act like a prism, refracting the Light into many *colors* giving rise to the diversity of life and matter in our world.

The Ten Sfirot are as follows:

Keter	Crown
Chochmah	Wisdom
Binah	Understanding
Da'at	Knowledge
Zeir Anpin	Small Face,
	(includes the next six Sfirot):
Chesed	Mercy (Chassadim - plural)
Gvurah	Judgment (Gvurot - Plural)
Tiferet	Splendor
Netzach	Victory (Eternity)
Hod	Glory
Yesod	Foundation
Malchut	Kingdom

The Partzufim - Spiritual forms

One complete structure of the Ten Sfirot creates a *Partzuf* or Spiritual Form. Together, these forces are the building blocks of all reality. As water and sand combine to create cement, the Ten Sfirot combine to produce a Spiritual Form [*Partzuf*]. Each of the Spiritual Forms below are therefore composed of one set of Ten Sfirot.

These Spiritual Forms are called:

Atik	Ancient
Atik Yomin	Ancient of Days
Atika Kadisha	Holy Ancient
Atik of Atikin	Anceint of Ancients
Aba	Father
Arich Anpin	Long Face
Ima	Mother
Nukva	Female
Tevunah	Intelligence
Yisrael Saba	Israel Grandfather
Zachar	Male

These names are not meant to be understood literally. Each represents a unique spiritual force and building block, producing a substructure and foundation for all the worlds make up reality.

The Five Worlds

All of the above Spiritual Forms [*Partzufim*] create one spiritual world. There are Five Worlds in total that compose all reality, therefore, five sets of the above Spiritual Forms are required.

Our physical world corresponds to the world of: Asiyah – Action

Adam Kadmon	Primordial Man
Atzilut	Emanation
Briyah	Creation
Yetzirah	Formation
Asiyah	Action

The Five Levels of the soul

Nefesh	First, Lowest level of Soul
Ruach	Second level of Soul
Neshamah	Third level of Soul
Chayah	Fourth level of Soul
Yechidah	Highest, fifth level of Soul

Names of God

As a single ray of white sunlight contains the seven colors of the spectrum, the one Light of the Creator embodies many diverse spiritual forces. These different forces are called *Names of God*. Each Name denotes a specific attribute and spiritual power. The Hebrew letters that compose these Names are the interface by which these varied Forces act upon our physical world. The most common Name of God is the Tetragrammaton (the four letters, *Yud Hei Vav Hei* יהוה.) Because of the enormous power that the Tetragrammaton transmits, we do not utter it aloud. When speaking of the Tetragrammaton, we use the term *Hashem* which means, *The Name*.

Adonai, El, Elohim, Hashem, Shadai, Eheyeh, Tzevaot, Yud Hei Vav Hei

People

Er	The son of Noach
Rabbi Elazar	The son of Rabbi Shimon bar Yochai
Rabbi Shimon bar Yochai	Author of the Zohar
Shem, Cham, Yefet	Noach's children
Shet	Seth
Ya'akov	Jacob
Yishai	Jesse (King David's father)
Yitzchak	Isaac
Yosef	Joseph
Yitro	Jethro
Yehuda	Judah

Angels

Angels are distinct energy components, part of a vast communication network running through the upper worlds. Each unique Angel is responsible for transmitting various forces of influence into our physical universe.

Adriel, Ahinael, Dumah (name of Angel in charge of the dead), Gabriel, Kadshiel, Kedumiel, Metatron, Michael, Rachmiel,

Raphael, Tahariel, Uriel

Nations

Nations actually represent the inner attributes and character traits of our individual self. The nation of Amalek refers to the doubt and uncertainty that dwells within us when we face hardship and obstacles. Moab represents the dual nature of man. Nefilim refers to the sparks of Light that we have defiled through our impure actions, and to the negative forces that lurk within the human soul as a result of our own wrongful deeds.

Amalek, Moab, Nefilim

General

Aba	Father
	Refers to the male principle and positive force in our universe. Correlates to the proton in an atom.
Arvit	The Evening prayer
Chayot	Animals
Chupah	Canopy (wedding ceremony)
Et	The
Avadon	Hell
Gehenom	Hell
Sheol	Hell
	The place a soul goes for purification upon leaving this world.
Ima	Mother
	The female principle and minus force in our universe. Correlates to the electron in an atom.
Kiddush	Blessing over the wine
Klipah	Shell (negativity)
Klipot	Shells (Plural)
Kriat Sh'ma	The Reading of the Sh'ma
Mashiach	Messiah
Minchah	The Afternoon prayer
Mishnah	Study
Mochin	Brain, Spiritual levels of Light
Moed	A designated time or holiday
Negev	The south of Israel
Nukva	Female

Partzuf	Face
Shacharit	The Morning prayer
Shamayim	Heavens (sky)
Shechinah	The Divine presence, The female aspect of the Creator
Tefilin	Phylacteries
The Dinur river	The river of fire
Tzadik	Righteous person
Zion	Another name for Jerusalem
Yisrael	The land of Israel
	The nation of Israel or an individual Israelite
Zohar	Splendor

The Hebrew vowels

Chirik אָ, Cholam אֹ א, Kamatz אָ, Patach אַ, Segol אֶ, Sh'va אְ, Shuruk אֹ א, Tzere אֵ.

The Twelve Tribes

Asher, Dan, Ephraim, Gad, Issachar, Judah, Levi, Menasheh, Naphtali, Reuben, Shimon, Zebulun

Jewish Holidays

Rosh Hashanah	The Jewish New Year
Yom Kippur	Day of Atonement
Sukkot	Holiday of the Booths
Shmini Atzeret	The day of Convocation
Simchat Torah	Holiday on which we dance with the Torah
Pesach	Passover
Shavout	Holiday of the Weeks

כרך יח

פרשת שלח לך, קרח, חקת

Vol. XVIII

Shlach Lecha, Korach, Chukat

A Prayer from The Ari

To be recited before the study of the Zohar

Ruler of the universe, and Master of all masters, The Father of mercy and forgiveness, we thank You, our God and the God of our fathers, by bowing down and kneeling, that You brought us closer to Your Torah and Your holy work, and You enable us to take part in the secrets of Your holy Torah. How worthy are we that You grant us with such big favor, that is the reason we plead before You, that You will forgive and acquit all our sins, and that they should not bring separation between You and us.

And may it be your will before You, our God and the God of our fathers, that You will awaken and prepare our hearts to love and revere You, and may You listen to our utterances, and open our closed heart to the hidden studies of Your Torah, and may our study be pleasant before Your Place of Honor, as the aroma of sweet incense, and may You emanate to us Light from the source of our soul to all of our being. And, may the sparks of your holy servants, through which you revealed Your wisdom to the world, shine.

May their merit and the merit of their fathers, and the merit of their Torah, and holiness, support us so we shall not stumble through our study. And by their merit enlighten our eyes in our learning as it stated by King David, The Sweet Singer of Israel: "Open my eyes, so that I will see wonders from Your Torah" (Tehilim 119:18). Because from His mouth God gives wisdom and understanding.

"May the utterances of my mouth and the thoughts of my heart find favor before You, God, my Strength and my Redeemer" (Tehilim 19:15).

SHLACH LECHA

Names of the articles

1. "Send you men"

A Synopsis

Rabbi Chiya says that when the sun begins to set, the energy of the sun, Zeir Anpin, is less powerful, and that is when the left dominates and judgments pertain. At that time one must pray.

١. וַיְדַבֵּר יְיָ' אֶל מֹשֶׁה לֵאמֹר, שְׁלַח לְךָ אֲנָשִׁים וְיָתוּרוּ אֶת אֶרֶץ כְּנַעַן וְגוֹ'. רִבִּי חִיָּיא פָּתַח, הֲמִיָּמֶיךָ צִוִּיתָ בֹּקֶר יִדַּעְתָּ הַשַּׁחַר מְקוֹמוֹ. שַׁחַר כְּתִיב, הֵ"א אִתְרַחֲקָא מִשַּׁחַר. מ"ט. אֶלָּא א"ר חִיָּיא, בְּשַׁעֲתָא דְּנָטֵי עֶרֶב, וְשִׁמְשָׁא נָטֵי לְמֵיעַל, כְּדֵין אִתְחֲלָשׁ תּוּקְפֵּיה, כְּדֵין שַׁלְטָא שְׂמָאלָא, וּמִשְׁתְּכַח דִּינָא בְּעָלְמָא, וְאִתְפָּשַׁט. וּכְדֵין בָּעֵי ב"נ לְצַלָּאָה, וּלְכַוְּנָא רְעוּתָא קַמֵּי מָארֵיה.

1. "And Hashem spoke to Moses, saying, 'Send you men, that they may spy out the land of Canaan...'" (Bemidbar 13:1). Rabbi Chiya opened the discussion saying, "Have you commanded the morning since your days began; and caused dayspring to know its place" (Iyov 38:12). It is written "dayspring" WITHOUT THE HEI (DEFINITE ARTICLE). Hei has been far from dawn. What is the reason? Rabbi Chiya said: When the evening shadows lengthen and the sun – THAT IS, ZEIR ANPIN – begins to set, MEANING AFTER MIDDAY, the strength OF THE SUN is less powerful, WHICH IS ZEIR ANPIN. This is when the left rules and Judgment prevails and spreads over the world. Then a person is required to pray and direct his desire to his Master.

2. The name that rules after midnight

A Synopsis
Rabbi Yesa describes what happens when night falls and midnight comes. We read a detailed description of the thirteen carved letters in the Holy Name that dominates from midnight onward.

2. דְּאָמַר רִבִּי יֵיסָא, כַּד נָטֵי שִׁמְשָׁא, וְאִתְחַלָּשׁ, כְּדֵין אִתְפְּתַח חַד פִּתְחוּ בְּשִׁמְשָׁא, וְאִתְכְּנִישׁ חֵילֵיהּ, וּשְׂמָאלָא שַׁלִּיט. וְיִצְחָק כָּרֵי בֵּירָא תְּחוֹתֵיהּ.

2. As Rabbi Yesa said, when the sun is about to set, THAT IS ZEIR ANPIN, and is losing its strength, MEANING PAST MIDDAY, an aperture in the sun opens – THE DOOR OF THE DOMINATION OF THE LEFT – AND THE SUN'S power is gathered in, THAT IS ZEIR ANPIN AND THE CENTRAL COLUMN, and the left reigns. Isaac, WHO IS THE LEFT COLUMN, digs a well underneath it, WHICH IS MALCHUT THAT SUCKLES FROM THE LEFT, AND THEN HE ESTABLISHES HER.

3. כֵּיוָן דְּעָאל לֵילְיָא, פִּתְקָא דְּקוּטְפָא בְּאַחֲמָתֵיהּ שְׁכִיחַ. וְכַמָּה חֲבִילִין טְרִיקָן אִתְפָּשְׁטוּ בְּעָלְמָא, וְכֻלְּהוּ שָׁטָאן בְּעַרְבּוּבְיָא, וְאָזְלֵי וְחַיְיכָאן בְּנַפְשָׁן דְּרַשִׁיעַיָּיא, וּמוֹדְעִין לוֹן מִלִּין, מִנְּהוֹן כְּדִיבָן, וּמִנְּהוֹן קְשׁוֹט, וּמַאן דְּאִשְׁתְּכַח בֵּינַיְיהוּ, אִתְיְיהִיב לוֹן רְשׁוּ לְחַבָּלָא, וְכֻלְּהוּ בְּנֵי עָלְמָא נַיְימִין, וְטַעֲמִין טַעֲמָא דְּמוֹתָא, וְהָא אוֹקִימְנָא.

3. When the night falls, the written edicts are in their pockets. Many harmful demons spread out in the world, which all roam around in confusion. They go about and mock at the souls of the wicked and inform them of various matters, some false and some true. If any PERSON is found among them, they are given permission to do harm. Everyone is sleeping and tasting the taste of death, as we have already explained.

4. ת"ח, כַּד אִתְּעַר רוּחַ צָפוֹן, כְּדֵין אִתְקַבְּלָא כְּנֶסֶת יִשְׂרָאֵל בִּשְׂמָאלָא, וְאִתְחַבָּרוּ כַּחֲדָא וְשַׁרְיָא בִּדְרוֹעָא בְּאַתְרָהָא. וְקוּדְשָׁא בְּרִיךְ הוּא אָתֵי

לְאִשְׁתַּעְשְׁעָא עִם צַדִּיקַיָּיא דִּבְגִנְתָּא דְּעֵדֶן, וּכְדֵין כָּל מַאן דְּיִתְּעַר לְמִלְעֵי בְּאוֹרַיְיתָא בְּהַהוּא שַׁעֲתָא. הָא אִשְׁתַּתָּף בַּהֲדָהּ, בְּגִין דְּהִיא וְכָל אֲכְלוּסִין דִּילָהּ, מְשַׁבְּחָן לְמַלְכָּא עִלָּאָה, וְכָל אִינוּן דְּאִשְׁתְּכָחוּ בְּתוּשְׁבַּחְתָּא דְּאוֹרַיְיתָא, כֻּלְּהוּ כְּתִיבִין בְּבְנֵי הֵיכָלָא, וְאִקְרוּן בִּשְׁמֵהוֹן, וְאִלֵּין רְשִׁימִין בִּימָמָא.

4. Come and see: When the north wind stirs, the Congregation of Yisrael WHICH IS MALCHUT, is received by the left OF ZEIR ANPIN. They join together and she rests in her place in the LEFT arm and the Holy One, blessed be He, comes to delight Himself with the righteous who are in the Garden of Eden. Whoever is awakened to study the Torah during that period is participating WITH MALCHUT, because she and all her multitudes praise the High King, WHO IS ZEIR ANPIN. All who are present at the praising of the Torah are registered among the inhabitants of the temple, and are proclaimed there by their names. These are recorded during the daytime; THAT IS, THEY ARE REGISTERED TO RECEIVE CHASSADIM, WHICH IS THE QUALITY OF DAY, WHICH IS ZEIR ANPIN.

ת״ח שְׁמָא חֲדָא קַדִּישָׁא אִית בְּגִלּוּפֵי אַתְוָון, דְּהוּא שַׁלְטָא מִפַּלְגּוּ **5.** לֵילְיָא וְאֵילָךְ, וְאִינוּן אַתְוָון כל״ך סעפ״ה יאעוצ״ה ס״ן דְּמַנְצַפָּ״ךְ כָּלִיל לוֹן, ם אוּקְמוּהָ, לְסַרְבֵּהּ הַמִּשְׂרָה. נ׳ הֲוָה אַסְתִּים לְהַאי וּלְהַאי, כְּדֵין כְּתְרִין כְּלִילָן הוּא ו׳ דְּשְׁמָא קַדִּישָׁא אַתְקִין לֵיהּ. וְסָתִים מַבּוּעָהָא. בָּתַר דְּאוֹלִידַת, פְּתִיחָא הֲוַת בְּחַד רֵישָׁא דְּפִתְחָא.

5. Come and see that there is a Holy Name of carved letters that rules from midnight onward. It is of these letters: Caf-Lamed-final Caf, Samech-Ayin-Pe-Hei, Yud-Aleph-Ayin-Vav-Tzadi-Hei. Final Mem-final Nun of 'final Mem-final Nun-final Tzadi-final Pe-final Caf' include them. Final Mem was explained in accordance with the secret of: "For the increase (Heb. *lemarbeh*) of the realm" (Yeshayah 9:6), WHICH IS SPELED WITH A CLOSED FINAL MEM IN THE MIDDLE OF THE WORD, WHICH ALLUDES TO BINAH DURING THE DOMINATION OF THE LEFT WHEN THE LIGHTS ARE ENCLOSED WITHIN HER. Nun was hiding the one and the other, MEANING THE BENT NUN IN THE SECRET MEANING OF, "THE VIRGIN OF YISRAEL IS FALLEN (HEB. *NAFLAH*); SHE SHALL NO MORE RISE" (AMOS 5:2),

WHICH CONCEALS BINAH AND MALCHUT. For then the Sfirot were included, MEANING THAT MALCHUT AND BINAH WERE INCLUDED ONE WITHIN THE OTHER, AND BINAH WAS FALLEN LIKE MALCHUT. The Vav of the Holy Name restored MALCHUT, WHICH IS THE SECRET OF NUN, AND DREW THE LEFT COLUMN UPON HER IN THE FORM OF VAV. AT THAT POINT, SHE RISES FROM HER FALL. HOWEVER, it closed up her springs, SINCE, DUE TO THE DOMINATION OF THE LEFT, THE LIGHTS WERE CONGEALED AND FROZEN. THROUGH THIS, BINAH WAS CONCEALED BY THE DOMINATION OF THE LEFT COLUMN. THAT IS WHY BINAH IS THEN CONSIDERED A CLOSED MEM. After BINAH gave birth TO THE VAV OF YUD HEI VAV HEI – WHICH IS ZEIR ANPIN, THAT IS THE SECRET OF THE CENTRAL COLUMN – OR MALCHUT GAVE BIRTH TO THE SOUL, it became open in one end, MEANING THE CLOSED FINAL MEM WAS OPENED AT THE BOTTOM AND BECAME AN OPEN MEM.

6. כַּד אִתְחֲרִיב בֵּי מַקְדְּשָׁא, אַסְתִּימוּ מַבּוּעִין מִכָּל סִטְרִין. וְאַכְלִיל אַתְוָון אַחֲרָן, וְאִינּוּן שַׁבְעָה. תְּלַת מֵהַאי סִטְרָא, וְאַרְבַּע מֵהַאי סִטְרָא. כל״ך. יָפָה וְסִימָן כֶּלָּךְ יָפָה רַעְיָתִי וּמוּם אֵין בָּךְ, ז׳ דְּכַר וְנוּקְבָּא כָּלִיל כַּחֲדָא, דָּא כָּלִיל תְּלַת מִכָּאן וּתְלַת מִכָּאן וְאִינּוּן שִׁית. וְאוֹקִימְנָא בְּאִלֵּין תְּרֵין אַתְוָון ם׳ ן׳ אִתְכְּלָלוּ תְּלֵיסָר אַתְוָון סָלִיק מִנַּיְיהוּ תְּרֵי. חַד לְאָת חַד, וְחַד לְאָת חַד.

6. When the Temple was destroyed, MEANING WHEN THERE WAS NO UNION BETWEEN ZEIR ANPIN AND MALCHUT, WHEN THE TEMPLE WAS DESTROYED, WHICH IS MALCHUT, the springs OF MALCHUT were blocked from all sides. THAT MEANS, IT BECAME A CLOSED MEM IN THAT ALL HER LIGHTS WERE FROZEN. THE CLOSED MEM is comprised of other letters, which are seven LETTERS FROM THE HOLY NAME MENTIONED ABOVE. Three are from one side, WHICH ARE SAMECH-AYIN- VAV, and four are from another side, WHICH ARE ALEPH-AYIN-TZADI-HEI. Caf-Lamed-Final Caf, Yud-Pe-Hei REMAIN FROM THE HOLY NAME. This is derived from: "You are all fair (Heb. kulach [Kuf-Lamed-Final Caf] yafah [Yud -Pe-Hei]), my love; there is no blemish in you" (Shir Hashirim 4:7). THAT IS THE SECRET OF FINAL NUN ALLUDING TO male and female in one composition. FINAL NUN is composed of three letters from this side, WHICH ARE CAF-LAMED-FINAL CAF, and three from that side, WHICH ARE YUD- PE-HEI, so there are six LETTERS. We have explained that these two

letters, final Mem and final Nun, include the thirteen letters OF THE HOLY NAME – CAF-LAMED-FINAL CAF, SAMECH-AYIN-PE-HEI, YUD-ALEPH-AYIN-VAV-TZADI-HEI, since two ASPECTS result from them, one ASPECT in one letter, WHICH IS FINAL MEM, and one in another letter, WHICH IS FINAL NUN.

7. כל"ךְ סעפ"ה יאע"וצה, הָכִי אִתְגְּלִיפוּ אַתְוָון, וְרָזָא דָּא בְּכִי תֵצֵא לַמִּלְחָמָה, קְרָא דִּכְתִּיב, כִּי יִהְיֶה נַעֲרָה בְתוּלָה. נַעַר כְּתִיב, בָּתַר דְּאִסְתָּלַּק לֵילְיָא, וְצַפְרָא נָהִיר, כְּדֵין ה' סַלְקָא וְאִתְכְּלִילַת בְּנְהוֹרָא עִלָּאָה. וּכְדֵין יְדַעְתָּ הַשַּׁחַר מְקוֹמוֹ, דְּיָדַע שַׁחַר מְקוֹמוֹ דְּהֵ"א, וְאִתְכְּלִילַת בְּגַוֵּיהּ.

7. Caf-Lamed-final Caf, Samech-Ayin-Pe-Hei, Yud-Aleph-Ayin-Vav-Tzadi -Hei: Thus were the letters engraved. That is the secret meaning, in the portion of Ki Tetzeh, of the words, "If a girl (Heb. *na'arah*) that is a virgin" (Devarim 22:23), which is spelled "*naara*" WITHOUT HEI. After the night is gone and the morning light shines, the Hei ascends and is included in the letter above. Then IT IS SAID: "And caused dayspring to know its place" (Iyov 38:12). Dawn, WHICH IS ZEIR ANPIN, knows the place of the Hei, and the latter is composed in it.

3. The moon shines only when the sun sets

A Synopsis

We are told that God told Moses he could not enter the promised land because he was the sun, and the sun and the moon could not stand together since the moon would not shine while the sun was around. God suggested that Moses send men to spy out the land if he wanted to know about it. Moses was shown the land from Mount Avarim and he was also shown all the leaders who would arise in every successive generation. Finally we are told that Moses asked his spies to find out whether there was a tree in the land, and he was looking to see if it contained the Tree of Life.

‏8. ת״ח, מֹשֶׁה הֲוָה שִׁמְשָׁא, וּבָעָא לְאַעֲלָאָה לְאַרְעָא. אָ״ל קוּדְשָׁא בְּרִיךְ הוּא, מֹשֶׁה, כַּד אָתֵי נְהוֹרָא דְשִׁמְשָׁא, אִתְכְּלִיל סִיהֲרָא בְּגַוֵּוֵיהּ, הַשְׁתָּא דְאַנְתְּ שִׁמְשָׁא, הֵיךְ יְקוּמוּן כַּחֲדָא שִׁמְשָׁא וְסִיהֲרָא, לָא נְהִיר סִיהֲרָא אֶלָּא בְּשַׁעֲתָא דְאִתְכְּנִישׁ שִׁמְשָׁא, אֲבָל הַשְׁתָּא לֵית אַנְתְּ יָכִיל. אִי תִּבְעֵי לְמִנְדַּע מִנָּה שְׁלַח לְךָ אֲנָשִׁים, לְגַרְמָךְ, בְּגִין לְמִנְדַּע.‏

8. Come and see, Moses was THE ASPECT OF the sun, WHICH IS ZEIR ANPIN, and he wished to enter the land of Yisrael. The Holy One, blessed be He, told him, 'Moses, when the sunlight arrives, the moon, WHICH IS MALCHUT, is included in it AND HER QUALITY IS INVISIBLE. Now, you are the sun, AND IF YOU ENTER THE LAND WHICH IS THE SECRET OF THE MOON, MEANING MALCHUT, how can the sun and the moon stand together if the moon shines only when the sun is gathered in? However, now you can not ENTER THE LAND, and if you wish to know about it, "send you men" (Bemidbar 13:1), MEANING for your sake, so that you shall know.'

‏9. ת״ח, מֹשֶׁה, אִי תֵּימָא דְּהוּא לָא יָדַע דְּלָא יֵיעוּל לְאַרְעָא בְּזִמְנָא דָּא. לָאו הָכִי, אֶלָּא יָדַע, וַהֲוָה בָּעֵי לְמִנְדַּע מִנָּה, עַד לָא יִסְתַּלַּק, וְשָׁלַח לְאִלֵּין מְאַלְּלֵי, כֵּיוָן דְּלָא אֲתִיבוּ מִלָּה כַּדְקָא יָאוֹת, לָא שָׁלַח זִמְנָא אַחֲרָא, עַד דְּקוּדְשָׁא בְּרִיךְ הוּא אַחֲזֵי לֵיהּ, דִּכְתִּיב עֲלֵה אֶל הַר הָעֲבָרִים הַזֶּה וּרְאֵה אֶת הָאָרֶץ. וּכְתִיב וַיַּרְאֵהוּ יְיָ׳ אֶת כָּל הָאָרֶץ. וְלָא דָּא בִּלְחוֹדוֹי, אֶלָּא כָּל אִינּוּן דִּזְמִינִין לְמֵיקַם בְּכָל דָּרָא וְדָרָא, כֻּלְּהוּ אַחֲזֵי לֵיהּ לְמֹשֶׁה. וְאִתְּמַר, וְאוֹקְמוּהָ חַבְרַיָּיא.‏

9. Come and see: If you think Moses did not know at that time that he would not enter the land of Yisrael, it is not so. He most certainly knew and he wished to know about it before he departed; therefore, he sent spies. Since they did not report to him properly, he did not send more until the Holy One, blessed be He, showed IT to him, as it is written: "Go up into this mount Avarim...and behold the land" (Devarim 32:49), and: "And Hashem showed him all the land" (Devarim 34:1). Not only WAS HE SHOWN this, but Moses was shown all those LEADERS who were destined to arise in each successive generation, as we have learned. This was already explained by the friends.

10. כֵּיוָן דְּשָׁאֲרֵי מֹשֶׁה לְמִשְׁלַח, מַה אָמַר לוֹן. הֲיֵשׁ בָּהּ עֵץ. וְכִי מַה הוּא דְּקָאָמַר, וְאִי תֵּימָא דְּלָא יָדַע. אֶלָּא הָכִי אָמַר מֹשֶׁה, אִם יֵשׁ בָּהּ עֵץ, הָא יְדַעְנָא דַּאֲנָא אִיעוּל לְתַמָּן. מַאי עֵץ. דָּא אִילָנָא דְּחַיֵּי. וְתַמָּן לָא הֲוָה אֶלָּא בְּג"ע דְּאַרְעָא. אָמַר אִם יֵשׁ בָּהּ עֵץ דָּא, אֲנָא אִיעוּל לְתַמָּן. וְאִי לָא, לָאו אֲנָא יָכִיל לְמֵיעַל.

10. As soon as Moses began to send out the spies, what did he say to them? "Whether there is a tree in it" (Bemidbar 13:20). What is the reason that he said this? Do you think that he did not know IF THERE WAS A TREE THERE? However, this is what Moses said: If "there is a tree in it," I know that I will enter the land. What tree? That is the Tree of Life. It was not there, but rather in the terrestrial Garden of Eden. MOSES said to himself: If that tree is in it, I will enter there and if not, I cannot enter.

4. Zelophehad was gathering sticks

A Synopsis

Rabbi Chiya and Rabbi Shimon talk about the sin of the man who gathered sticks on the Shabbat. and who died in his own sin. Since he received his punishment of death, his sin was forgiven; this made it difficult for Moses to know what sentence to give his daughters. We learn that a person must never exchange the Tree of Life for the world, and that the Ark, Malchut, and the Torah, Zeir Anpin, exist as one. The Ark is the abode for the Torah. Moses had wanted to find out if the Tree of Life existed in the promised land, but his spies brought him only fruits from regular trees. Rabbi Yitzchak says that faithful messengers refresh the soul of their master.

11. אָמַר רְבִּי חִיָּיא, כְּתִיב וַיִּמְצְאוּ אִישׁ מְקוֹשֵׁשׁ עֵצִים בְּיוֹם הַשַּׁבָּת. מַאן עֵצִים הָכָא. וּמַאן הוּא דָא. אֶלָּא דָא צְלָפְחָד, וַהֲוָה דָּיֵיק עַל אִלֵּין אִילָנִין, הֵי מִנַּיְיהוּ רַב עַל אַחֲרָא, וְלָא חָשַׁשׁ לִיקָרָא דְּמָארֵיהּ, וְאַחֲלַף שַׁבָּת לְשַׁבָּת. הה"ד, כִּי בְחֶטְאוֹ מֵת, בְּחֶטְא ו' מֵת. בְּגִין כַּךְ, הֲוָה דִּינֵיהּ סָתִים, וְלָא אִתְפְּרָשׁ דִּינֵיהּ. כִּדְינִין אַחֲרָנִין. בְּגִין דְּמִלָּה דָא בָּעֵי בַּחֲשַׁאי וְסָתִים וְלָא גַּלְיָיא. וע"ד לָא אִתְּמַר בְּאִתְגַּלְיָיא, וְקוּדְשָׁא בְּרִיךְ הוּא עֲבַד יְקָר לִיקָרֵיהּ.

11. Rabbi Chiya said that it is written: "They found a man gathering sticks (also: 'trees') upon the Shabbat day" (Bemidbar 15:32). What are the trees involved here and who is THAT MAN? HE RESPONDS: That must be Zelophehad, who was particular IN KNOWING exactly about these trees, WHICH ARE ZEIR ANPIN AND MALCHUT, which of them was greater than the other. He did not care for the glory of his Master and exchanged the Shabbat to the other Shabbat. This is what is written: "But he died in his own sin (Heb. *chet'o* – Chet Tet Aleph Vav)" (Bemidbar 27:3), MEANING in the sin (Chet Tet Aleph) of Vav, SINCE HE MADE A BLEMISH IN ZEIR ANPIN, WHICH IS REFERRED TO BY THE VAV OF YUD HEI VAV HEI, he died. Therefore, his sentence was left unsaid and not explained as other sentences. HE IS DESCRIBED SIMPLY AS A GATHERER OF STICKS, because this matter had to be in secrecy and NEEDED TO BE veiled and not made known. Therefore, it was not mentioned openly and the Holy One, blessed be He, glorified His own glory.

12. רִבִּי יוֹסֵי אָמַר, שְׁאַר עֵצִים בַּהֲדֵי שַׁבָּת הֲוָה מְקוֹשֵׁשׁ, וְקַבִּיל עוֹנְשָׁא לְפוּם שַׁעֲתָא, וְאִתְכַּפַּר חוֹבֵיהּ. וע״ד אִתְקַשֵּׁי מֹשֶׁה בְּדִינָא דִּבְנָתָא, דְּלָא יָדַע אִי אִתְכַּפַּר לְמֶהֱוֵי לִבְנָתֵיהּ חוּלָק וְאַחֲסָנָא אִי לָאו. כֵּיוָן דְּדָכַר שְׁמֵיהּ קוּדְשָׁא בְּרִיךְ הוּא, דִּכְתִּיב כֵּן בְּנוֹת צְלָפְחָד דּוֹבְרוֹת, אִתְיְדַע דְּהָא אִתְכַּפַּר חוֹבֵיהּ.

12. Rabbi Yosi said: He was gathering other trees, INDICATING THE SEVENTY EXTERNAL CHIEFS, together with the Shabbat, AND WAS COMPARING AND MATCHING THE LEVEL OF THE SEVENTY CHIEFS TO THE LEVEL OF THE SHABBAT DAY. He received his timely punishment and his iniquity was forgiven. Therefore, Moses had difficulty in judging the sentence of his daughters, since he was not sure if HIS SIN was forgiven, and if his daughters would take their lot and inheritance IN THE LAND OF YISRAEL or not. As soon as the Holy One, blessed be He, mentioned his name, as is written: "The daughters of Zelophehad speak right" (Ibid.), it became known that his sin was forgiven.

13. ת״ח, ב׳ אִילָנִין אִינּוּן, חַד לְעֵילָא, וְחַד לְתַתָּא, בְּדָא חַיִּין, וּבְדָא מוֹתָא. מַאן דְּאַחְלָף לוֹן, גָּרִים לֵיהּ מוֹתָא בְּהַאי עָלְמָא, וְלֵית לֵיהּ חוּלָקָא בְּהַהוּא עָלְמָא. וע״ד אָמַר שְׁלֹמֹה, דְּבַשׁ מָצָאתָ אֱכֹל דַּיֶּיךָ וְגוֹ׳.

13. Come and see that there are two trees: One above, WHICH IS THE TREE OF LIFE, ZEIR ANPIN, and one below, WHICH IS THE TREE OF KNOWLEDGE OF GOOD AND EVIL, THE NUKVA. In the one there is life and in the other death. Whoever exchanges them – MEANING THAT HE CONSIDERS THE FEMALE WHEN SHE IS SEPARATE MORE THAN ZEIR ANPIN, WHO IS THE TREE OF LIFE – causes himself death in this world, and has no part in the World to Come. About this, Solomon said, "Have you found honey? eat as much as is sufficient for you" (Mishlei 25:16).

14. אָרוֹן וְתוֹרָה בְּחַד קַיְימֵי. תּוֹרָה עִקָּרָא, אָרוֹן בֵּיתָא. וע״ד, אָרוֹן חָסֵר בְּלָא וָא״ו בְּכָל אֲתָר, אֲרוֹן הַבְּרִית, אֲרוֹן הָעֵדוּת. בְּכָל אֲתָר אַהֲרֹן דְּרוֹעָא יְמִינָא, בַּר בְּחַד, דִּכְתִּיב כָּל פְּקוּדֵי הַלְוִיִּם אֲשֶׁר פָּקַד מֹשֶׁה וְאַהֲרֹן, נָקוּד לְעֵילָא.

14. The Ark and Torah, THAT ARE MALCHUT WHICH IS CALLED ARK AND ZEIR ANPIN THAT IS CALLED TORAH, are as one, MEANING IN UNITY. The Torah THAT IS IN THE ARK is primary and the Ark is the abode FOR THE TORAH. Therefore, the Ark is spelled without Vav wherever it is mentioned; that is, the Ark of the Covenant, the Ark of Testimony, SINCE THE TORAH INSIDE THE ARK IS THE SECRET OF VAV. Aaron is always the right arm, except once where it is written: "All that were numbered of the Levites, whom Moses and Aaron numbered" (Bemidbar 3:39), which has dots above it TO INDICATE THAT HERE HE WAS NOT THE RIGHT ARM, WHICH IS CHESED, BUT RATHER AN ASPECT OF MALCHUT CALLED ARK, AS MENTIONED.

15. א״ר יִצְחָק, מֹשֶׁה אִילָנָא דְחַיֵּי נָקַט, וע״ד בָּעָא לְמִנְדַּע, אִי הֲוָה שְׁכִיחַ בְּאַרְעָא, אִי לָאו, ובג״כ אָמַר, הֲיֵשׁ בָּהּ עֵץ אִם אַיִן וְהִתְחַזַּקְתֶּם ולְקַחְתֶּם מִפְּרִי הָאָרֶץ. דְּהָא אִילָנָא דְחַיֵּי אִתְחֲמַד לְכֹלָּא. וְאִינּוּן לָא אַיְיתִיאוּ אֶלָּא עֲנָבִים וְרִמּוֹנִים וּתְאֵנִים, בְּאִילָנָא אַחֲרָא תַּלְיָין וַאֲחִידָן.

15. Rabbi Yitzchak said: Moses was attached to the Tree of Life and therefore he wanted to find out if he existed in the land or not. Therefore, he said, "Whether there is a tree in it, or not. And be of good courage, and bring of the fruit of the land" (Bemidbar 13:20), since the Tree of Life is pleasant to all. But they brought only grapes, pomegranates and figs, which are attached to another tree, MEANING THE NUKVA, AND NOT IN ZEIR ANPIN, WHICH IS THE TREE OF LIFE.

16. ת״ח, שְׁלַח לְךָ אֲנָשִׁים: בִּגִינָךְ. רִבִּי יְהוּדָה פָּתַח, כְּצִנַּת שֶׁלֶג בְּיוֹם קָצִיר צִיר נֶאֱמָן לְשׁוֹלְחָיו וְנֶפֶשׁ אֲדוֹנָיו יָשִׁיב. כְּצִנַּת שֶׁלֶג בְּיוֹם קָצִיר, דְּאַהֲנֵי לְגוּפָא ולְנַפְשָׁא. צִיר נֶאֱמָן לְשׁוֹלְחָיו, אֵלּוּ כָּלֵב וּפִנְחָס דַּהֲווֹ שְׁלִיחֵי מְהֵימְנֵי לְגַבֵּי יְהוֹשֻׁעַ. וְנֶפֶשׁ אֲדוֹנָיו יָשִׁיב, דְּאַהֲדְרוּ שְׁכִינְתָּא לְדַיְירָא בְּהוּ בְּיִשְׂרָאֵל, וְלָא אִסְתַּלָּקָא מִנַּיְיהוּ.

16. Come and see that in "send you men," "you" MEANS for your sake. Rabbi Yehuda opened the discussion saying, "Like the cold of snow in the time of harvest, so is a faithful messenger to those who send him: for he refreshes the soul of his master" (Mishlei 25:13). "Like the cold of snow in the time of harvest": BECAUSE THEN THE CHILL is good for the body and soul. "A faithful messenger to those who send him": these are Caleb and Pinchas, who were faithful messengers of Joshua AT THE TIME WHEN HE SENT THEM TO SPY ON JERICHO. "For he refreshes the soul of his master": they returned the Shechinah to rest on Yisrael, and She did not part from them.

17. וְאָלֵּין דְּשָׁדַר מֹשֶׁה, גְּרִימוּ בְּכִיָּיה לְדָרִין בַּתְרָאִין, וְגָרִימוּ לְאִסְתַּלְּקָא מִיִשְׂרָאֵל כַּמָּה אֶלַף וְרִבְבָן. וְגָרִימוּ לְסַלְּקָא שְׁכִינְתָּא מֵאַרְעָא מִבֵּינַיְיהוּ דְּיִשְׂרָאֵל. אִינּוּן דְּשָׁדַר יְהוֹשֻׁעַ, וְנֶפֶשׁ אֲדוֹנָיו יָשִׁיב.

17. These SPIES, whom Moses sent, caused grief for latter generations, SINCE ON THAT DAY, THE FIRST AND SECOND TEMPLES WERE DESTROYED. This caused thousands and tens of thousands of Yisrael to die and furthermore caused the Shechinah to depart from the land and from the midst of Yisrael. IT SAYS ABOUT those whom Joshua dispatched: "For he refreshes the soul of his master."

5. "That which befalls the sons of men befalls the beasts"

A Synopsis

The rabbis encounter a traveler who they think knows nothing of the Torah, and yet he invites them to place their difficulty before him, which is the verse from Kohelet, "For that which befalls the sons of men befalls the beasts." The traveler tells the rabbis that Solomon was only repeating what the foolish people of the world say, and Solomon was calling those ignorant people beasts. He explains that the following verse tells that the spirit of man goes upwards to a holy place to be sustained by the supernal light, and the spirit of the beast does not go to the place designated for humans. The fools who believe men and beasts go to the same place will remain in Gehenom. The traveler continues talking about the wicked who lack faith, and who will not dwell with God. After the traveler leaves the rabbis discover that he is Rabbi Chagai who has been sent to find out things from Rabbi Shimon and the friends, and Rabbi Chiya says that through his modesty Rabbi Chagai is a faithful messenger. Rabbi Chiya tells about Eliezer who was a faithful messenger to his master Abraham.

18. רְבִּי חִזְקִיָּה וְר' יֵיסָא הֲווֹ אָזְלֵי בְּאָרְחָא, אָמַר רִבִּי יֵיסָא לר' חִזְקִיָּה. חֲמֵינָא בְּאַפָּךְ דְּהִרְהוּרָא אִית בְּגַוָּוךְ. אָמַר לֵיהּ, הָא וַדַּאי הַאי קְרָא אִסְתַּכַּלְנָא בֵּיהּ, כֵּיוָן דְּאָמַר שְׁלֹמֹה, כִּי מִקְרֶה בְּנֵי הָאָדָם וּמִקְרֶה הַבְּהֵמָה וּמִקְרֶה אֶחָד לָהֶם וְגוֹ'. וְתָנֵינָן, דְּכָל מִלּוֹי דִּשְׁלֹמֹה מַלְכָּא, כֻּלְּהוּ סְתִימִין מִדַּרְגִּין דְּחָכְמְתָא. אִי הָכִי, הַאי קְרָא אִית בֵּיהּ לְאִסְתַּכְּלָא, דְּהָא פִּתְחָא לְאִינוּן דְּלָאו בְּנֵי מְהֵימָנוּתָא אִשְׁתְּכַח בֵּיהּ.

18. Rabbi Chizkiyah and Rabbi Yesa were traveling along the road. Rabbi Yesa said to Rabbi Chizkiyah: I see by your face that you are thoughtful. He said: Certainly so, I read this verse, where Solomon said, "For that which befalls the sons of men befalls the beasts; even one thing befalls them both..." (Kohelet 3:19). We have learned that King Solomon's sayings are made unclear with grades of wisdom. If so, we must contemplate it, since we find an opening here for non believers.

19. אָ"ל וַדַּאי הָכִי הוּא, וְאִית בֵּיהּ לְמִנְדַּע וּלְאִסְתַּכְּלָא. אַדְהָכִי חָמוּ חַד ב"נ דַּהֲוָה אָתֵי, שָׁאַל לוֹן מַיָּיא, דַּהֲוָה צָחֵי, וַהֲוָה לָאֵי בְּתוּקְפָּא

דְּשִׁמְשָׁא. אָמְרוּ לֵיהּ, מַאן אַתְּ. אָמַר לוֹן יוּדָאי אֲנָא, וַאֲנָא לָאֵי
וְצָחֵינָא. אָמְרוּ לָעֵית בְּאוֹרַיְיתָא, אָמַר לוֹן, עַד דַּאֲנָא עִמְכוֹן בְּמִלִּין,
אֶסְלַק לְהַאי טוּרָא, וְתַמָּן אֶסַּב מַיָּיא וְאִשְׁתֵּי.

19. He answered him: It is most certainly true THAT THERE EXISTS AN
OPENING TO NON-BELIEVERS. It is important to be aware of it and pay
attention to it. While talking, they noticed a man who approached them and
asked for water, since he was thirsty and tired from the sun's strong heat.
They said to him: Who are you? He responded: I am Jewish and I'm tired
and thirsty. They asked him: Do you study Torah? He said to them, Before I
engage in a conversation with you, let me climb this mountain. There I will
take water and drink.

20. אַפִּיק רִבִּי יֵיסָא חַד זְפִירָא מָלֵי מַיָּין, וְיָהַב לֵיהּ. בָּתַר דְּשָׁתָה, אָמַר
נִסַּלֵק עִמָּךְ לְמַיָּיא. סָלִיקָא לְטוּרָא, וְאִשְׁתְּכָחוּ חַד חוּטָא דְּמַיָּיא דְּקִיק,
וּמָלֵי קַטְפּוֹרָא חַד. יָתְבוּ. אָמַר לוֹן הַהוּא ב״נ, הַשְׁתָּא שָׁאִילוּ, דְּהָא
אֲנָא אִשְׁתְּדַּלְנָא בְּאוֹרַיְיתָא, עַל יְדוֹי דְּחַד בְּרִי, דַּאֲנָא עַיְילִית לֵיהּ לְבֵי
רַב, וּבְגִינֵיהּ רָוַוחְנָא בְּאוֹרַיְיתָא. אָמַר רִבִּי חִזְקִיָּה אִי עַל יְדָא דִּבְרָךְ, טַב
הוּא. אֲבָל מִלָּה דַּאֲנַן בֵּיהּ, אֲנָא חֲמֵינָא דְּלְאַתָר אַחֲרָא בָּעֵי
לְאִסְתַּלְּקָא. אָמַר הַהוּא ב״נ, אֵימָא מִלָּךְ, דְּלְזִמְנִין בְּאַפְרַקְסָתָא דְּעַנְיָיא
תִּשְׁכַּח מַרְגָּנִיתָא.

20. Rabbi Yesa took out a skin-hide full of water and presented it to him.
After he drank, he said: Let us ascend with you TO THE MOUNTAIN for
water. They climbed the mountain and found a narrow stream of water and
filled a container. They sat down. That man said to them: Ask now, since I
strive in the Torah through one of my sons that I have enrolled in the school,
AND HE TAUGHT ME TORAH. For his sake, I have made gains in the Torah.
Rabbi Chizkiyah said: If YOU MADE GAINS IN TORAH through your son, it
is nice. However, I must elevate what we are discussing at present to
another height, MEANING THAT HE IS NOT WISE ENOUGH TO EXPLAIN
THEIR QUESTION. That man spoke: Speak up, since sometimes in the
grain-receiver of the poor, THAT IS THE VESSEL ON TOP OF THE
MILLSTONE, you will find a precious stone.

21. אָ"ל הַאי קְרָא דְּאָמַר שְׁלֹמֹה, סַח לֵיהּ. אָמַר לֵיהּ. וְכִי בְּמָה אַתּוּן
פְּרִישָׁן מִשְּׁאַר בְּנֵי נָשָׁא דְּלָא יַדְעֵי. אָמְרוּ לֵיהּ וּבְמָה. אָמַר לוֹן, עַל דָּא
אָמַר שְׁלֹמֹה הַאי קְרָא, וְלָא אָמַר הַאי מִגַּרְמֵיהּ, כִּשְׁאַר אִינּוּן מִלִּין.
אֶלָּא אַהֲדַר אִינּוּן מִלִּין דְּטִפְּשָׁאֵי עָלְמָא דְּאַמְרֵי כָּךְ, וּמַאי אַמְרֵי. כִּי
מִקְרֶה הָאָדָם וּמִקְרֶה הַבְּהֵמָה וְגוֹ', טִפְּשָׁאֵי דְּלָא יַדְעֵי וְלָא מִסְתַּכְּלָן
בְּחָכְמְתָא אַמְרֵי דְּהַאי עָלְמָא אָזִיל בְּמִקְרֶה, וְקוּדְשָׁא בְּרִיךְ הוּא לָא
אַשְׁגַּח עֲלַיְיהוּ, אֶלָּא מִקְרֶה הָאָדָם וּמִקְרֶה הַבְּהֵמָה מִקְרֶה אֶחָד וְגוֹ'.

21. He quoted the verse that Solomon spoke, and related to him THE ENTIRE DILEMMA. He asked him: How are you different from other people who do not know? They replied to him: How DO YOU EXPLAIN THE VERSE? He said to them: Regarding it, Solomon said this verse, but he did not say it from his own IDEAS as HE SAID the rest; he simply repeated what the fools of the world say. What do they say? That is: "for that which befalls the sons of men befalls the beasts..." The fools who are not aware and do not see things with wisdom say that this world is led by chance. The Holy One, blessed be He, is not paying attention to them, but "that which befalls the sons of men befalls the beasts; even one thing befalls them both..."

22. וְכַד שְׁלֹמֹה אִסְתָּכַּל בְּאִלֵּין טִפְּשָׁאִין דְּקָאַמְרֵי דָּא קָרָא לוֹן בְּהֵמָה,
דְּאִינּוּן עַבְדִין גַּרְמַיְיהוּ בְּהֵמָה מַמָּשׁ, בְּגִין דְּאַמְרֵי מִלִּין אִלֵּין. וּמְנָלָן.
קְרָא דְּעֲלֵיהּ אוֹכַח, דִּכְתִּיב אָמַרְתִּי אֲנִי בְּלִבִּי עַל דִּבְרַת בְּנֵי הָאָדָם
לְבָרָם הָאֱלֹהִים וְלִרְאוֹת שֶׁהֶם בְּהֵמָה הֵמָּה לָהֶם. אָמַרְתִּי אֲנִי בְּלִבִּי
וַחֲשִׁיבְנָא בְּהַאי לְאִסְתַּכְּלָא עַל מָה, עַל דִּבְרַת בְּנֵי הָאָדָם. עַל הַהוּא
מִלָּה דְּטִפְּשׁוּתָא, דְּאִינּוּן אַמְרֵי לְבָרָם הָאֱלֹהִים בִּלְחוֹדַיְיהוּ, וְלָא
יִתְחַבְּרוּן בַּהֲדֵי בְּנֵי נָשָׁא אַחֲרָנִין דְּאִית לוֹן מְהֵימְנוּתָא, וְלִרְאוֹת שֶׁהֶם
בְּהֵמָה הֵמָּה לָהֶם. וְלִרְאוֹת בְּהוּ אִינּוּן בְּנֵי מְהֵימְנוּתָא, שֶׁהֶם בְּהֵמָה
מַמָּשׁ, וְדַעְתַּיְיהוּ כִּבְעִירָא. הֵמָּה לָהֶם בִּלְחוֹדַיְיהוּ, וְלָא לְאַעֲלָאָה לִבְנֵי
מְהֵימְנוּתָא בְּדַעְתָּא דְּטִפְּשׁוּתָא דָּא, וע"ד הֵמָּה לָהֶם, וְלָא לַאֲחֲרָנִין.
וּמָה דַּעְתָּא דִּלְהוֹן. כִּי מִקְרֶה בְּנֵי הָאָדָם וּמִקְרֶה הַבְּהֵמָה וּמִקְרֶה אֶחָד
לְכֻלָּם וְגוֹ'. תִּיפַּח רוּחֵיהוֹן דְּאִינּוּן בְּעִירֵי. אִינּוּן טִפְּשָׁאֵי. אִינּוּן מְחוּסְרֵי

מְהֵימְנוּתָא. וַוי לוֹן וַוי לְנַפְשַׁיְיהוּ. טַב לְהוּ דְּלָא יֵיתוּן לְעָלְמָא.

22. When Solomon gazed at the fools who said this, he called them beasts, since they made themselves actual beasts by what they said. From where do we derive this? The preceding verse proves it, since it is written: "I said in my heart, after the speech of the sons of men, that the Elohim has chosen them out, but only to see that they themselves are but as beasts" (Kohelet 3:18). "I said in my heart" and I planned to observe. Observe what? "The speech of the sons of men" and the foolish sayings that they utter, THAT THE WORLD CONTINUES BY CHANCE. "That the Elohim has chosen them out," MEANING THAT ELOHIM HAS PICKED THEM OUT to be separated and they should not join with other people that have faith, "but only to see that they themselves are but as beasts." "TO SEE" MEANING that those who have faith will see that these are really beasts, and they think like animals. "They themselves" MEANS THAT they are on their own and they shall not bring these foolish ideas to those who are faithful. Therefore, it is "they themselves" and not others. What is their idea? ABOUT THIS, THE VERSE CONCLUDES: "That which befalls the sons of men befalls the beasts; even one thing befalls them both..." Let these beasts die, these foolish ones who are faithless. Woe to them and woe to their souls. It would have been better to them if they would not have come into this world.

23. וּמַה אָתִיב לוֹן שְׁלֹמֹה עַל דָּא. קְרָא אֲבַתְרֵיהּ, וְאָמַר, וּמִי יוֹדֵעַ רוּחַ בְּנֵי הָאָדָם הָעוֹלָה הִיא לְמַעְלָה וְרוּחַ הַבְּהֵמָה הַיּוֹרֶדֶת הִיא לְמַטָּה לָאָרֶץ. מִי יוֹדֵעַ בְּאִינּוּן טִפְשָׁאֵי, דְּלָא יַדְעֵי בִּיקָרָא דְּמַלְכָּא עִלָּאָה, וְלָא מִסְתַּכְּלֵי בְּאוֹרַיְיתָא, רוּחַ בְּנֵי הָאָדָם הָעוֹלָה, הִיא לְמַעְלָה, לַאֲתָר עִלָּאָה, לַאֲתָר יְקָר, לַאֲתָר קַדִּישָׁא, וּלְאִתְזָנָא מִנְּהִירוּ עִלָּאָה, מִנְּהִירוּ דְּמַלְכָּא קַדִּישָׁא, לְמֶהֱוֵי צְרוֹרָא בִּצְרוֹרָא דְּחַיֵּי, וְאִשְׁתְּכַחַת קַמֵּי מַלְכָּא קַדִּישָׁא עוֹלָה תְּמִימָה וְדָא הוּא הָעוֹלָה הִיא לְמַעְלָה.

23. And what did Solomon respond to them? This FOLLOWS in the next verse and says: "Who knows whether the spirit of man goes upwards, and the spirit of the beast goes downwards to the earth" (Ibid. 21). "Who knows" these foolish who are not cognizant in the reverence of the High King and do not look into the Torah. "The spirit of man goes upwards," MEANING to a higher place, to a precious place, to a holy place. It goes upward to be sustained by the supernal light, by the light of the Holy King, to be bound in the bundle of life and to be in the presence of the Holy King as a pure burnt offering (Heb. *olah*). That is the meaning of "goes upwards (Heb. *olah*)."

24. וְרוּחַ הַבְּהֵמָה הַיּוֹרֶדֶת הִיא לְמַטָּה לָאָרֶץ, וְלָאו לְהַהוּא אֲתָר דְּהֲוָה כָּל ב״נ, דִּכְתִיב בֵּיהּ בְּצֶלֶם אֱלֹהִים עָשָׂה אֶת הָאָדָם, וּכְתִיב נֵר יְיָ' נִשְׁמַת אָדָם. הֵיךְ אַמְרֵי אִינוּן טִפְּשָׁאֵי דְּלָאו מִבְּנֵי מְהֵימְנוּתָא, וְרוּחַ אֶחָד לַכֹּל, תִּיפַח רוּחֵיהוֹן, עָלַיְיהוּ כְּתִיב, יִהְיוּ כְּמוֹץ לִפְנֵי רוּחַ וּמַלְאַךְ יְיָ' דּוֹחֶה. אִלֵּין יִשְׁתַּאֲרוּן בַּגֵּיהִנָּם, לְאִינוּן דַּרְגִּין תַּתָּאִין, וְלָא יִסְתַּלְקוּן לְדָרֵי דָרִין. עָלַיְיהוּ כְּתִיב יִתַּמּוּ חַטָּאִים מִן הָאָרֶץ וּרְשָׁעִים עוֹד אֵינָם בָּרֲכִי נַפְשִׁי אֶת יְיָ' הַלְלוּיָהּ. אָתוּ רַבִּי חִזְקִיָּה וְרַבִּי יֵיסָא, וְנַשְׁקוּ רֵישֵׁיהּ, אָמְרוּ וּמַה כָּל כָּךְ הֲוָה עִמָּךְ וְלָא יְדַעְנָא, זַכָּאָה הַאי שַׁעֲתָא דְּאַעַרְעָנָא בָּךְ.

24. "And the spirit of the beast goes downwards to the earth": It is not to the same place designated for all the humans, about whom it is written: "For in the image of Elohim made He man" (Beresheet 9:6), and: "The soul of man is the candle of Hashem" (Mishlei 20:27). How could these fools, those who are not of the Faithful, say, "They have all one breath" (Kohelet 3:19)? Let them breathe their last. About them, it is written: "Let them be as chaff before the wind; the angel of Hashem thrusting them" (Tehilim 35:5). They shall remain in Gehenom, in its lower levels, and shall not ascend from there for generations to come. About them, it is written: "They will be consumed out of the earth, and the wicked will be no more. Bless you Hashem, O my soul, Haleluyah" (Tehilim 104:35). Rabbi Chizkiyah and Rabbi Yesa approached and kissed his head. They said: there is so much in you, yet we did not know. Happy is this time that we have met with you.

25. תוּ אָמַר, וְכִי עַל דָּא בִּלְחוֹדוֹי תָּוָה שְׁלֹמֹה, וְהָא בַּאֲתָר אַחֲרָא אָמַר בְּגוֹוְנָא דָּא, פָּתַח וְאָמַר, זֶה רָע בְּכֹל אֲשֶׁר נַעֲשָׂה תַּחַת הַשָּׁמֶשׁ. זֶה רָע וַדַּאי. מַאי זֶה רָע. דָּא הוּא מַאן דְּאוֹשִׁיד זַרְעָא בְּרֵיקַנְיָא, וְחָבִיל אוֹרְחוֹי, בְּגִין דְּהַאי לָאו מָדוֹרֵיהּ בְּקוּדְשָׁא בְּרִיךְ הוּא, וְלָא יְהֵא לֵיהּ חוּלָקָא בְּעָלְמָא דְּאָתֵי. הה״ד כִּי לֹא אֵל חָפֵץ רֶשַׁע אָתָּה לֹא יְגוּרְךָ רָע.

עַל דָּא אָמַר, זֶה רָע, דְּלָא יְהֵא לֵיהּ מָדוֹרָא לְעֵילָא. כִּי מִקְרָא אֶחָד לַכֹּל וְגַם לֵב בְּנֵי הָאָדָם מָלֵא רָע וְהוֹלֵלוֹת בִּלְבָבָם. בְּחַיֵּיהֶם שְׁטוּתָא תָּקִיע בְּלִבַּיְיהוּ, וְאִינּוּן מְחוּסְרֵי מְהֵימְנוּתָא, וְלֵית לוֹן חוּלָקָא בְּקוּדְשָׁא בְּרִיךְ הוּא, וּבְאִינּוּן בְּנֵי מְהֵימְנוּתָא, לָאו בְּעָלְמָא דֵין, וְלָא בְּעָלְמָא דְאָתֵי, הה"ד וְאַחֲרָיו אֶל הַמֵּתִים.

25. Furthermore, he said: Did Solomon wonder about this alone? We find him saying something similar on another occasion. He opened the discussion with the verse: "This is an evil in all things that are done under the sun" (Kohelet 9:3). "This is an evil": Certainly, what is evil? That is one who spills his seed in vain and destroys his path, since he does not reside with the Holy One, blessed be He, and will not have a part in the World to Come. This is what is written: "For you are not an El that has pleasure in wickedness: nor shall evil dwell with You" (Tehilim 5:5). About this, he said, "This is an evil," for he will have no dwelling above, "that there is one event to all: yea, also the heart of the sons of men is full of evil, and madness is in their heart" (Kohelet 9:3). While they live, foolishness is stuck in their heart. They are lacking faith and have no part in the Holy One, blessed be He, or in these faithful ones, not in this world and not in the World to Come, as is written: "And after that they go to the dead" (Ibid.).

26. ת"ח, קוּדְשָׁא בְּרִיךְ הוּא אַזְהַר לִבְנֵי עָלְמָא וְאָמַר, וּבָחַרְתָּ בַּחַיִּים לְמַעַן תִּחְיֶה, וְחַיִּין דְּהַהוּא עָלְמָא נִינְהוּ. אִינּוּן חַיָּיבִין מְחוּסְרֵי מְהֵימְנוּתָא מַאי קָא אַמְרֵי. כִּי מִי אֲשֶׁר יְבָחַר וְגוֹ'. אע"ג דְּיִבְחַר בַּר נָשׁ בְּהַהוּא עָלְמָא כְּמָה דְאָמַר, לָאו הוּא כְּלוּם, דְּהָא מְסִירָא דָא בִּידָנָא, אֶל כָּל הַחַיִּים יֵשׁ בִּטָּחוֹן, וּמְסִירָא דָא בִּידַיְיהוּ, כִּי לְכֶלֶב חַי הוּא טוֹב מִן הָאַרְיֵה הַמֵּת. הֵיךְ יְהֵא לָן חַיִּין בְּהַהוּא עָלְמָא. וע"ד זֶה רָע וַדַּאי, דְּלָא יְדוּרוּן בְּמַלְכָּא עִלָּאָה, וְלָא יְהֵא לוֹן חוּלָקָא בֵּיהּ. ואע"ג דְּכָל הָנֵי קְרָאֵי תִּשְׁכַּח סְמִיכִין חַבְרַיָּיא בְּמִלִּין אַחֲרָנִין, אֲבָל וַדַּאי שְׁלֹמֹה קָא אָתָא לְגַלָּאָה עַל אִינּוּן חַיָּיבִין מְחוּסְרֵי מְהֵימְנוּתָא, דְּלֵית לוֹן חוּלָקָא בְּקוּדְשָׁא בְּרִיךְ הוּא בְּעָלְמָא דֵין וּבְעָלְמָא דְאָתֵי.

26. Come and see that the Holy One, blessed be He, warns the people and says, "Therefore choose life, that both you and your seed may live" (Devarim 30:19). That is the life of that world. And these wicked who lack Faith, what do they say? "For to him that is joined (choose) TO ALL THE LIVING THERE IS HOPE" (Kohelet 9:4). Although the man will choose that world, as he says, it means nothing, as we have this tradition handed to us. "To all the living there is hope," MEANING THE LIFE IN THIS WORLD. They have that tradition handed to them, "for a living dog is better than a dead lion" (Ibid.). How can we have life in that world? Therefore, "this is an evil" and certainly they will not dwell by the King up high and will have no part in Him. And although you could find other supports to the friends, NAMELY INTERPRETATIONS, for all these verses, yet most certainly Solomon came to reveal to the wicked lacking Faith that they have no part in the Holy One, blessed be He, not in this world nor in the World to Come.

27. אָ״ל, תִּבְעֵי דְנִתְחַבֵּר בַּהֲדָךְ וְתֵזִיל בַּהֲדָן. אָמַר לְהוּ, אִי עֲבִידְנָא הָכִי, אוֹרַיְיתָא יִקְרֵי עָלַי כְּסִיל, וְלֹא עוֹד אֶלָּא דְּאִתְחַיַּיבְנָא בְּנַפְשַׁאי. אָמְרוּ לֵיהּ לָמָּה. אָמַר לוֹן דְּהָא שְׁלִיחָא אֲנָא, וְשַׁדְּרוּ לִי בִּשְׁלִיחוּתָא, וּשְׁלֹמֹה מַלְכָּא אָמַר, מְקַצֶּה רַגְלַיִם חָמָס שׁוֹתֶה שׁוֹלֵחַ דְּבָרִים בְּיַד כְּסִיל. ת״ח, מְרַגְּלִים עַל דְּלָא אִשְׁתְּכָחוּ בְּנֵי מְהֵימָנוּתָא וּשְׁלוּחֵי מְהֵימָנוּתָא, אִתְחַיָּיבוּ בְּנַפְשַׁיְיהוּ בְּעָלְמָא דֵּין וּבְעָלְמָא דְאָתֵי. נָשַׁק לוֹן, וְאָזַל לֵיהּ.

27. They said to him: Would you like us to join you so that you will go with us? He replied to them: If I do this, the Torah calls me a fool and not only that, I would be risking my life. They asked him why. He replied to them: Since I am a messenger sent on a mission, and King Solomon said, "He that sends a message by the hand of the fool cuts off his own feet, and drinks in damage" (Mishlei 26:6). Come and see: The spies, because they were found to be unfaithful and untrustworthy messengers, risked their lives in this world and the World to Come. He kissed them and left.

28. אַזְלוּ רִבִּי חִזְקִיָּה וְר׳ יֵיסָא, עַד דַּהֲווֹ אָזְלֵי פָּגְעוּ בְּאִינּוּן בְּנֵי נָשָׁא. שָׁאִילוּ ר׳ חִזְקִיָּה וְרִבִּי יֵיסָא עָלֵיהּ, אָמְרוּ מַה שְׁמֵיהּ דְּהַהוּא ב״נ. אָמְרוּ, ר׳ חַגַּי הוּא, וְחַבְרָא דְּבֵין חַבְרַיָּיא הוּא, וְשַׁדְּרוּ לֵיהּ חַבְרַיָּיא דְּבָבֶל, לְמִנְדַּע מִלִּין מֵר׳ שִׁמְעוֹן בֶּן יוֹחָאי וּשְׁאַר חַבְרַיָּיא. א״ר יֵיסָא,

וַדַּאי דָא הוּא ר' חַגַּי, דְּכָל יוֹמוֹי לָא בָּעָא לְאַחֲזָאָה גַּרְמֵיהּ בְּמַה דְּיָדַע,
וְעַל דָא אָמַר לָן דִּבְרֵיהּ זָכָה לֵיהּ בְּאוֹרַיְיתָא, בְּגִין דְּאָמַר קְרָא,
רָאִיתָ אִישׁ חָכָם בְּעֵינָיו תִּקְוָה לִכְסִיל מִמֶּנּוּ. וַדַּאי שְׁלִיחָא מְהֵימָנָא
אִיהוּ, וְזַכָּאָה אִיהוּ מַאן דְּשָׁדַר מִלּוֹי בִּידָא דִשְׁלִיחָא מְהֵימָנָא.

28. Rabbi Chizkiyah and Rabbi Yesa continued traveling along. As they went, they met some people. Rabbi Chizkiyah and Rabbi Yesa asked about him. They said: What is the name of that person? They replied: That is Rabbi Chagai and he is a friend among the friends. The friends sent him from Babylon to find out about things from Rabbi Shimon bar Yochai and the rest of the friends. Rabbi Yesa said: That must be the Rabbi Chagai who all his life did not wish to show off what he knows and, therefore, he told us that his son has merited the gain of his Torah knowledge. Since he said: "See you a man wise in his own eyes? There is more hope of a fool than of him" (Mishlei 26:12). He most certainly is a faithful messenger and praised is he who dispatches his matters by the hand of a faithful messenger.

29. ת"ח, אֱלִיעֶזֶר עֶבֶד אַבְרָהָם מִבְּנֵי כְּנַעַן הֲוָה, כד"א, כְּנַעַן בְּיָדוֹ
מֹאזְנֵי מִרְמָה. וּכְנַעַן כְּתִיב עָלֵיהּ, אָרוּר כְּנָעַן עֶבֶד עֲבָדִים יִהְיֶה לְאֶחָיו.
וּבְגִין דַּהֲוָה שְׁלִיחָא מְהֵימָנָא, מַה כְּתִיב בֵּיהּ. בֹּא בְּרוּךְ יְיָ'. בְּרוּךְ יְיָ'
מַמָּשׁ. וְעַל דָּא אִכְתִּיב הָכִי בְּאוֹרַיְיתָא, בְּגִין דְּנָפַק מֵהַהִיא קְלָלָה,
וְאִתְבְּרַךְ. וְלָא דִי לֵיהּ דְּנָפִיק מִנָּהּ, אֶלָּא דְּאִתְבְּרַךְ בִּשְׁמֵיהּ דְּקוּדְשָׁא
בְּרִיךְ הוּא. וְאוֹלִיפְנָא דְּאָתָא מַלְאָךְ, וְאָעִיל מִלָּה דָא בְּפוּמֵיהּ דְּלָבָן.

29. Come and see that Eliezer, the servant of Abraham, was from the children of Canaan, as is written: "As for the merchant (Heb. knaan), the balances of deceit are in his hands" (Hoshea 12:8). About Canaan, it is written: "Cursed be Canaan; a servant of servants shall he be to his brethren" (Beresheet 9:25). Because Eliezer was a faithful messenger, it is written about him: "Come in, you blessed of Hashem" (Beresheet 24:31), really blessed of Hashem. Therefore, it is written so in the Torah since he has emerged from the curse OF CANAAN, and became blessed. He was not only excluded FROM THE CURSE, but he was also blessed it the name of the Holy One, blessed be He. And I learned that an angel came and inserted this – THAT HE SHOULD CALL HIM "BLESSED OF HASHEM" – into the mouth of Laban.

6. Joshua and Caleb

A Synopsis

The rabbis examine the scriptures concerning the behavior of the spies who Moses sent into the Promised Land. We hear how Moses, when he sent him to Yisrael, changed Oshea's name to Joshua to indicate that he was attached to the Shechinah. Rabbi Shimon talks about Moses' need to distinguish if the land was worthy of the Tree, Zeir Anpin, or of Ayin Ayin, Arich Anpin: thus he would know if there was a tree in it, or not (ayin). We are told about Caleb, who went to pray on the graves of the patriarchs in Hebron in order to be rescued from the misguided decisions of the rest of the spies. Rabbi Shimon says that the Shechinah was robed in Caleb to bring tidings to the Patriarchs, and that the three spies were descendants of the Nefilim.

30. וַיִּשְׁלַח אוֹתָם מֹשֶׁה וְגו', כֻּלָם אֲנָשִׁים. כֻּלְהוּ זַכָּאִין הֲוֹו, וְרֵישֵׁי דְיִשְׂרָאֵל הֲוֹו. אֲבָל אִינּוּן דִּבְרוּ לְגַרְמַיְיהוּ עֵיטָא בִּישָׁא. אֲמַאי נַטְלֵי עֵיטָא דָא. אֶלָּא אָמְרוּ, אִי יֵיעֲלוּן יִשְׂרָאֵל לְאַרְעָא, נִתְעֲבַר אֲנָן מִלְמֶהֱוֵי רֵישִׁין, וִימַנֵּי מֹשֶׁה רֵישִׁין אַחֲרָנִין, דְּהָא אֲנָן זַכֵּינָן בְּמַדְבְּרָא לְמֶהֱוֵי רֵישִׁין, אֲבָל בְּאַרְעָא לָא נִזְכֵּי. וְעַל דְּנַטְלֵי עֵיטָא בִּישָׁא לְגַרְמַיְיהוּ, מִיתוּ אִינּוּן, וְכָל אִינּוּן דְּנַטְלָן מִלַּיְיהוּ.

30. "And Moses...sent them...all those men" (Bemidbar 13:3), MEANING THAT all were righteous and chiefs of Yisrael. However, they took bad counsel for themselves. Why did they take this counsel? It was because they thought: if Yisrael entered the land, we would be removed as chiefs and Moses would appoint other chiefs; since we deserved to be chiefs only in the desert, in the land we would not deserve TO BE CHIEFS. Due to having taken bad counsel for themselves, they died, as did all those who accepted their counsel.

31. אֵלֶּה שְׁמוֹת הָאֲנָשִׁים אֲשֶׁר שָׁלַח מֹשֶׁה וְגו', אָמַר רִבִּי יִצְחָק, מֹשֶׁה אִסְתָּכַּל וְיָדַע דְּלָא יִצְלְחוּן בְּאָרְחַיְיהוּ, כְּדֵין צַלֵּי עֲלֵיהּ דִּיהוֹשֻׁעַ. כְּדֵין כָּלֵב הֲוָה בְּדוֹחֲקָא, אָמַר, מַה אַעֲבִיד, הָא יְהוֹשֻׁעַ אָזִיל בְּסִיַּיעְתָּא עִלָּאָה דְּמֹשֶׁה, דְּשָׁדַר בֵּיהּ נְהִירוּ דְּסִיהֲרָא, וְהוּא אַנְהִיר עֲלֵיהּ

בִּצְלוֹתֵיהּ, בְּגִין דְּאִיהוּ שִׁמְשָׁא. מָה עֲבַד כָּלֵב. אִשְׁתְּמִיט מִנַּיְיהוּ, וְאָתֵי לְגַבֵּי קִבְרַיָּיא דַּאֲבָהָן, וְצַלֵּי תַּמָּן צְלוֹתֵיהּ.

31. "These are the names of the men whom Moses sent... " (Ibid. 4). Rabbi Yitzchak said: Moses observed and was aware that they, THAT IS THE SPIES, would not succeed in their mission, and he then prayed about Joshua. Caleb was then in distress. He said: What shall I do, since Joshua goes forth with the utmost help of Moses, who inspired in him the illumination of the moon, WHICH IS MALCHUT. He shone upon him with his light in his prayer, since he is THE ASPECT OF the sun, WHICH IS ZEIR ANPIN. So what did Caleb do? He dropped back from THE SPIES, and came to the burial place of the patriarchs, and prayed his prayer there.

32. א״ר יְהוּדָה, אֹרַח אַחֲרָא נָטִיל, וְעָקִים שְׁבִילִין, וּמָטָא עַל קִבְרֵי דַּאֲבָהָן, וְאִסְתַּכַּן בְּגַרְמֵיהּ, דְּהָא כְּתִיב וְשָׁם אֲחִימָן שֵׁשַׁי וְתַלְמַי יְלִידֵי הָעֲנָק. אֲבָל מַאן דְּאִיהוּ בְּדוֹחֲקָא, לָא אִסְתַּכַּל מִדִּי. כַּךְ כָּלֵב, בְּגִין דַּהֲוָה בְּדוֹחֲקָא, לָא אִסְתַּכַּל מִדִּי, וְאָתָא לְצַלָּאָה עַל קִבְרֵי אֲבָהָן, לְאִשְׁתְּזָבָא מֵעֵיטָא דָא.

32. Rabbi Yehuda said: Caleb went a different way and took winding paths, MEANING THAT HE FOLLOWED TWISTED PATHS. He reached the burial plots of the patriarchs and endangered himself, as is written: "Where Ahiman, Sheshai, and Talmai, the children of Anak, were" (Ibid. 22). However, just as someone in distress does not pay attention to anything, so too it was with Caleb. Because he felt distress, he was not observant, and came to pour his prayers upon the burial plots of the patriarchs, in order to be saved from the counsel OF THE SPIES.

33. וַיִּקְרָא מֹשֶׁה לְהוֹשֵׁעַ בֶּן נוּן יְהוֹשֻׁעַ. רִבִּי יִצְחָק אָמַר, וְכִי הוֹשֵׁעַ קְרָאֵיהּ קְרָא, וְהָא כְּתִיב וַיֹּאמֶר מֹשֶׁה אֶל יְהוֹשֻׁעַ. וִיהוֹשֻׁעַ בֶּן נוּן נַעַר. וַיַּחֲלוֹשׁ יְהוֹשֻׁעַ. אֶלָּא א״ל מֹשֶׁה, יָהּ יוֹשִׁיעֲךָ מִנַּיְיהוּ.

33. "And Moses called Hosea son of Nun, Joshua" (Bemidbar 13:16). Rabbi Yitzchak said: Did the scripture ever call him Hosea? Is it not written: "And Moses said to Joshua" (Shemot 17:9) and "Joshua, the son of Nun, a young man" (Shemot 33:11) and "Joshua harried" (Shemot 17:13)? HE RESPONDS: However, Moses told him Yud-Hei will save you (Heb. *yoshia*) from them, SINCE JOSHUA (HEB. *YEHOSHUA*) IS SPELLED WITH THE LETTERS YUD AND HEI, AND YOSHIA (LIT. 'WILL SAVE').

34. רִבִּי אַבָּא אָמַר, כֵּיוָן דְּשַׁדְרֵיהּ לְמֵיעַל לְתַמָּן, אִצְטְרִיךְ לְמֶהֱוֵי שְׁלִים. וּבַמָּה. בִּשְׁכִינְתָּא. דְּעַד הַהִיא שַׁעֲתָא נַעַר אִקְרֵי, כְּמָה דְּאוֹקִימְנָא. וּבְהַהִיא שַׁעֲתָא קָשִׁיר לֵיהּ מֹשֶׁה בַּהֲדָהּ, וְאע״ג דְּאַשְׁכְּחָן יְהוֹשֻׁעַ בְּקַדְמֵיתָא, קְרָא קַרְיֵיהּ הָכִי עַל הַהוּא דְּזַמִּין לְמִקְרְיֵיהּ. אָמַר מֹשֶׁה, וַדַּאי לָא אִצְטְרִיךְ דָּא לְמֵיעַל תַּמָּן, אֶלָּא בִּשְׁכִינְתָּא, וְהָכִי אִתְחֲזֵי.

34. Rabbi Aba said: As soon as MOSES sent JOSHUA to go there, TO THE LAND OF YISRAEL, he needed to be perfect. And in what way? With the Shechinah, SINCE THE LAND OF YISRAEL IS THE SECRET OF THE SHECHINAH. Until that time, he was considered a young man, as we have explained, MEANING THAT HE WAS ATTACHED TO METATRON REFERRED TO AS YOUNG MAN. At that time, Moses tied him to THE SHECHINAH. He was referred to in the scriptures prior to that as Joshua because the scriptures referred to him according to what he was destined to be called. Moses said: Most certainly, it is not proper for him to arrive there except by the Shechinah and that is appropriate. THEREFORE, HE CALLED HIM JOSHUA ADDING THE YUD TO HIS NAME, WHICH IS THE SECRET OF THE SHECHINAH.

35. הֲיֵשׁ בָּהּ עֵץ אִם אַיִן וְגוֹ', רִבִּי חִיָּיא אָמַר, וְכִי לָא הֲוָה יָדַע מֹשֶׁה דְּאִית בָּהּ כַּמָּה אִילָנִין מְשַׁנְיָין דָּא מִן דָּא, וְהָא הוּא שַׁבַּח לָהּ לְיִשְׂרָאֵל בְּכַמָּה זִמְנִין, וְהוּא אִסְתָּפַּק בְּדָא. וְהָא קוּדְשָׁא בְּרִיךְ הוּא קָאָמַר לֵיהּ לְמֹשֶׁה בְּקַדְמֵיתָא, דְּהִיא אֶרֶץ זָבַת חָלָב וּדְבָשׁ. אָמַר רִבִּי יוֹסֵי, הָא אִתְּעֲרוּ חַבְרַיָּיא, דִּכְתִיב אִישׁ הָיָה בְאֶרֶץ עוּץ אִיּוֹב שְׁמוֹ.

35. "Whether there is a tree in it, or not..." (Bemidbar 13:20). Rabbi Chiya said: Did Moses not know that there are a variety of trees there, different one from the other? Isn't he the one who praised the land several times

WITH ITS OLIVES, GRAPES, POMEGRANATES, and was satisfied with it. Didn't the Holy One, blessed be He, tell Moses originally that this was a land flowing with milk and honey? Rabbi Yosi said the friends already noted that it is written: "There was a man in the land of Utz, whose name was Job" (Iyov 1:1), MEANING THAT HE WISHED TO INQUIRE OF THEM WHETHER JOB WAS THERE TO PROTECT THEM. AND TREE (HEB. *ETZ*) IS LIKE UTZ.

36. אָמַר רִבִּי שִׁמְעוֹן, רָמַז לָהֶם רְמִיזָא דְּחָכְמְתָא, עַל מַה דְּשָׁאִילוּ בְּקַדְמֵיתָא. דִּכְתִיב הֲיֵשׁ יְיָ' בְּקִרְבֵּנוּ אִם אָיִן. אָמַר, תַּמָּן, תֶּחֱמוּן, אִי הִיא אִתְחֲזִיָּא לְהַאי, אוֹ לְהַאי. אָמַר לוֹן, אִי תֶחֱמוּן דְּאִיבָא דְּאַרְעָא כִּשְׁאַר אַרְעֵי דְּעָלְמָא, יֵשׁ בָּה עֵץ אִילָנָא דְּחַיֵּי, וְלָא מֵאֲתָר עִלָּאָה יַתִּיר. וְאִי תֶחֱמוּן דְּאִיבָא דְּאַרְעָא יַתִּיר וּמְשַׁנְיָיא מִכָּל אֲתָר דְּעָלְמָא, תִּנְדְּעוּן, דְּהָא מֵעַתִּיקָא קַדִּישָׁא קָא נָגִיד וְאִתְמְשַׁךְ הַהוּא שִׁנּוּיָיא עִלָּאָה, מִכָּל אֲתָרֵי דְּעָלְמָא. וּבְדָא תִּנְדְּעוּן, הֲיֵשׁ בָּה ע"ץ, אִם אַיִ"ן, וְדָא בָּעִיתוּן בְּקַדְמֵיתָא לְמִנְדַּע דָּא, דִּכְתִיב הֲיֵשׁ יְיָ' בְּקִרְבֵּנוּ. בְּקִרְבֵּנוּ דַּיְיקָא, אוֹ אִם אַיִן. וע"ד וְהִתְחַזַּקְתֶּם וּלְקַחְתֶּם מִפְּרִי הָאָרֶץ, לְמִנְדַּע שִׁנּוּיָיא דִּילֵיהּ.

36. Rabbi Shimon said: He gave them a wise allusion regarding to what they asked before, as is written: "Is Hashem among us, or not (Heb. *ayin*)" (Shemot 17:7) – BEING THE QUESTION OF WHETHER ZEIR ANPIN, REFERRED TO BY YUD HEI VAV HEI, IS STAYING WITH THEM, OR ARICH ANPIN IS AMONG THEM, REFERRED TO BY *AYIN* (LIT. 'NOT'). He said: There IN THE LAND, you will recognize if it is worthy of this, OF ZEIR ANPIN WHO IS REFERRED TO AS TREE, or of this, OF ARICH ANPIN WHO IS REFERRED TO BY *AYIN* (LIT. 'NAUGHT'). He further told them, if you notice that the fruits of the land are similar to those in the other countries in the world, then "there is a tree in it," which is the Tree of Life, MEANING ZEIR ANPIN, but not from a higher place. However, if you notice that the fruits of the land are decidedly different from other fruits in other countries of the world, you will know that the supernal difference flows and comes out from Atika Kadisha and THAT IT CONTAINS rather than all the places in the world. Through this, you will be able to recognize if there is a tree in it – THAT IS, ZEIR ANPIN – or not (Heb. *ayin*), ATIKA KADISHA, THAT IS ARICH ANPIN. That is what you set out to discern in the beginning, as is

written: "Is Hashem among us" – and "among us" is specific SINCE THEY INQUIRED IF ZEIR ANPIN RESTS AMONG THEM, or not – *Ayin* REFERRING TO ARICH ANPIN. Therefore, "And be of good courage, and bring of the fruit of the land" (Bemidbar 13:20), to know the difference in them, MEANING TO BE AWARE IF THERE IS A DIFFERENCE IN THEM OR NOT.

37. וְהַיָּמִים יְמֵי בִּכּוּרֵי עֲנָבִים. וְהַיָּמִים, מַאי קָא מַיְירֵי, דְּהָא וְאָז בִּכּוּרֵי עֲנָבִים סַגִּי לֵיהּ. אֶלָּא וְהַיָּמִים, אִינּוּן דְּאִשְׁתְּמוֹדְעָן, כֻּלְּהוּ הֲווֹ מִתְחַבְּרָן בְּהַהוּא זִמְנָא בְּהַהוּא אִילָנָא דְּחָטָא בֵּיהּ אָדָם הָרִאשׁוֹן. כְּמָה דְּתָנֵינָן עֲנָבִים הָיוּ וְעַל דָּא, וְהַיָּמִים: אִינּוּן דְּאִשְׁתְּמוֹדְעָן, יְמֵי בִּכּוּרֵי עֲנָבִים דַּיְיקָא.

37. "Now the time (days) was the time of the firstripe grapes" (Ibid.). HE INQUIRES: "Now the days": What is it meant to convey, since it would have been sufficient TO SAY, "Now was the time of the firstripe grapes." HE RESPONDS: However, "now the days" are those that are known, MEANING THE SIX DAYS WHICH ARE CHESED, GVURAH, TIFERET, NETZACH, HOD AND YESOD OF ZEIR ANPIN. All were attached at that time to the tree against which the first man sinned, WHICH IS MALCHUT, and we have learned that it was the grapes (tree). THEREFORE, WE SEE THAT GRAPES IS MALCHUT. As a result, the days that were already known TO BE THE SIX ENDS OF ZEIR ANPIN are the season of firs tripe grapes, WHICH IS MALCHUT; THAT IS, THE SIX ENDS OF ZEIR ANPIN WERE JOINED AT THAT TIME WITH MALCHUT.

38. וַיַּעֲלוּ בַנֶּגֶב וַיָּבֹא עַד חֶבְרוֹן. וַיָּבֹאוּ מִבָּעֵי לֵיהּ. אֶלָּא אָמַר רִבִּי יוֹסֵי, כָּלֵב הוּא דְּאָתָא לְצַלָּאָה עַל קִבְרֵי אֲבָהָתָא. אָמַר כָּלֵב, יְהוֹשֻׁעַ הָא בִּרְכֵיהּ מֹשֶׁה בְּסִיּוּעָא עִלָּאָה קַדִּישָׁא, וְיָכִיל לְאִשְׁתְּזָבָא מִנַּיְיהוּ, וַאֲנָא מַה אַעֲבִיד. אִימְלָךְ, לְמִבָעֵי בְּעוּתָא עַל קִבְרֵי אֲבָהָתָא, בְּגִין דְּיִשְׁתְּזִיב מֵעֵיטָא בִישָׁא דִּשְׁאַר מְאַלְלִין.

38. "And they ascended into the Negev, and (he) came to Hebron" (Bemidbar 13:22). HE INQUIRES: It should have said, 'And they came' in plural. HE ANSWERS: However, Rabbi Yosi said it refers to Caleb, who came to pray upon the graves of the patriarchs IN HEBRON. Caleb thought

to himself: Joshua, indeed! Moses blessed him with the highest, holy help and he could extricate himself and save himself from them; what shall I do? He took counsel to pray a prayer by the graves of the patriarchs, in order to be rescued from the misguided decisions of the rest of the spies.

39. רִבִּי יִצְחָק אָמַר, מַאן דְּהֲוָה רָשִׁים מִכֻּלְּהוּ דָּא עָאל בְּגַוֵּויה דְּבֵיהּ תַּלְיָא כֹּלָּא. וְתָ"ח, מַאן הוּא מִשְּׁאָר אָחֲרִי דְּיָכוּל לְאַעֲלָא תַּמָּן, דְּהָא כְּתִיב וְשָׁם אֲחִימָן שֵׁשַׁי וְתַלְמַי, וּמִדְּחִילוּ דִּלְהוֹן מַאן יָכִיל לְאַעֲלָאָה בִּמְעַרְתָּא. אֶלָּא שְׁכִינְתָּא עָאלַת תַּמָּן בְּכָלֵב, לְבַשְׂרָא לַאֲבָהָן, דְּהָא מָטָא זִמְנָא לְאַעֲלָא בְּנַיְיהוּ לְאַרְעָא, דְּאוֹמֵי לוֹן קוּדְשָׁא בְּרִיךְ הוּא, וְדָא הוּא וַיָּבֹא עַד חֶבְרוֹן.

39. Rabbi Yitzchak said, "AND (HE) CAME" MEANS whoever is more important than the rest, it enters into him; THAT IS, THE SHECHINAH ENTERED AND WAS CLOTHED IN CALEB since upon it, ON THE SHECHINAH, everything depends. Come and see: Who has the advantage over the rest, to be able to come there, TO HEBRON, since it is written: "And there were Ahiman, Sheshai, and Talmai." As a result of fearing them, who would be able to come EVEN TO HIDE in the cave? But the Shechinah was clothed there in Caleb to bring tidings to the Patriarchs. The time has arrived for their children to enter the land which the Holy One, blessed be He, had sworn to them, and that is why he: "came to Hebron." IT DOESN'T SAY, "AND THEY CAME," SINCE IT ALLUDES TO THE SHECHINAH.

40. תָּאנָא, אֲחִימָן שֵׁשַׁי וְתַלְמַי, מִמַּאן נַפְקוּ. זַרְעָא הֲווֹ מֵאִינּוּן נְפִילִין, דְּאֲפִיל לוֹן קוּדְשָׁא בְּרִיךְ הוּא בְּאַרְעָא, וְאוֹלִידוּ מִבְּנַת אַרְעָא, וּמִנַּיְיהוּ נַפְקוּ גִּיבְּרֵי עָלְמָא, כְּמָה דִּכְתִיב, הֵמָּה הַגִּבּוֹרִים אֲשֶׁר מֵעוֹלָם אַנְשֵׁי הַשֵּׁם. אֲשֶׁר מֵעוֹלָם, מִדְּאִתְבְּרֵי עָלְמָא מִשְׁתַּכְּחֵי. אַנְשֵׁי הַשֵּׁם אֲחִימָן שֵׁשַׁי וְתַלְמַי.

40. From whom were Ahiman, Sheshai and Talmai descended? They were the offspring of the Nefilim (lit. 'fallen ones') that the Holy One, blessed be He, dropped FROM THE HEAVEN to the earth, and they produced offspring from the daughters of the earth. From them emerged the mighty men of old, as is written: "The same were mighty men of old, men of renown"

(Beresheet 6:4). "Of old" MEANS they were present from the time the world was created and "men of renown" are Ahiman, Sheshai and Talmai, MEANING THAT THEIR NAMES WERE WELL KNOWN IN THE WORLD.

41. וַיָּבֹאוּ עַד נַחַל אֶשְׁכּוֹל וְגוֹ', רַבִּי יְהוּדָה פָּתַח, כֹּה אָמַר הָאֵל יְיָ' בּוֹרֵא הַשָּׁמַיִם וְנוֹטֵיהֶם וְגוֹ'. כַּמָּה אִית לְהוּ לִבְנֵי נָשָׁא לְאִסְתַּכְּלָא בְּפוּלְחָנָא דְקוּדְשָׁא בְּרִיךְ הוּא, כַּמָּה אִית לְהוּ לְאִסְתַּכְּלָא בְּמִלֵּי דְאוֹרַיְיתָא, דְכָל מַאן דְּאִשְׁתְּדַּל בְּאוֹרַיְיתָא, כְּאִילוּ מְקָרֵב כָּל קוּרְבָּנִין דְעָלְמָא לְקַמֵּי קוּדְשָׁא בְּרִיךְ הוּא. וְלָא עוֹד אֶלָּא דְקוּדְשָׁא בְּרִיךְ הוּא מְכַפֵּר לֵיה עַל כָּל חוֹבוֹי, וּמְתַקְּנִין לֵיה כַּמָּה כּוּרְסָיִין לְעָלְמָא דְאָתֵי.

41. "And they came to the wadi of Eshkol (cluster valley)..." (Bemidbar 13:23). Rabbi Yehuda opened the discussion with the verse: "Thus says the El, Hashem, He that created the heavens, and stretched them..." (Yeshayah 42:5). How much do people need to observe the worship of the Holy One, blessed be He. How much need there is to inquire in matters of Torah, for it is as if everyone that studies Torah brings all the offerings in the world to the Holy One, blessed be He. Not only that, but the Holy One, blessed be He, also wipes away all his iniquities, and prepares many thrones for him in the World to Come.

7. Before the world was created, how could it be written: "And... died"

A Synopsis

Rabbi Yehuda wonders why God created Adam if He knew that Adam would sin and that He would have to sentence him to death. He wonders why those who study the Torah die in this world just like those who don't. Rabbi Yehuda and Rabbi Aba discuss why they are permitted to seek out the mysteries in the Torah but they have no right to inquire about the ways of God, as for example when it pertains to things like the question above. The conclusion is that there are things that are secret to God and that no one should even ask about them, except for Rabbi Shimon who can explain things to his generation openly.

42. ר' יְהוּדָה הֲוָה אָזִיל בְּאָרְחָא בַּהֲדֵי ר' אַבָּא, שָׁאַל לֵיהּ, אָמַר מִלָּה חַד בָּעֵינָא לְשָׁאֲלָא, כֵּיוָן דְּיָדַע קוּדְשָׁא בְּרִיךְ הוּא דְּזַמִּין ב״נ לְמֶחֱטֵי קַמֵּיהּ, וּלְמִגְזַר עֲלֵיהּ מִיתָה, אֲמַאי בָּרָא לֵיהּ. דְּהָא אוֹרַיְיתָא הֲוָה תְּרֵי אַלְפִין שְׁנִין עַד לָא אִיבְרֵי עָלְמָא. וּכְתִיב בָּהּ בְּאוֹרַיְיתָא, אָדָם כִּי יָמוּת בְּאֹהֶל. אִישׁ כִּי יָמוּת. וַיָּמֹת. וַיְחִי פְּלוֹנִי וַיָּמֹת. מַאי קָבָעֵי קוּדְשָׁא בְּרִיךְ הוּא לב״נ בְּהַאי עָלְמָא, דַּאֲפִילוּ אִי אִשְׁתַּדַּל בְּאוֹרַיְיתָא יְמָמָא וְלֵילְיָא יְמוּת, וְאִי לָא אִשְׁתַּדַּל בְּאוֹרַיְיתָא יְמוּת, כֹּלָּא בְּחַד אָרְחָא, בַּר פְּרִישׁוּתָא דְּהַהוּא עָלְמָא, כד״א כַּטּוֹב כַּחוֹטֵא.

42. Rabbi Yehuda was walking along the way with Rabbi Aba. He said to him: I wish to ask you one thing. Since the Holy One, blessed be He, was aware that Adam was going to commit sin in His presence and that He would sentence him to death, why did He create him? Didn't the Torah exist 2,000 years prior to the creation of the world, MEANING BEFORE THE SIN OF ADAM? And in the Torah it is written: "When a man dies in a tent" (Bemidbar 19:14), "if a man die," "and...died" and "such and such lived and died." What did the Holy One, blessed be He, want from man in this world? If man studies Torah day and night he will die, and if he does not study Torah he will die. The same course applies to all, except that THE SINNER is removed from the World to Come. HOWEVER, IN THIS WORLD ALL ARE EQUAL, as it is written: "As is the good, so is the sinner" (Kohelet 9:2).

43. א״ל, אוֹרְחוֹי דְּמָארָךְ, וְגִזְרֵי דְּמָארָךְ, מַה לָךְ לְמִטְרַח בְּהוּ. מַה

דְּאִית לָךְ רְשׁוּ לְמִנְדַע וּלְאִסְתַּכְּלָא שָׁאִיל, וּדְלֵית לָךְ רְשׁוּ לְמִנְדַע,
כְּתִיב אַל תִּתֵּן אֶת פִּיךָ לַחֲטִיא אֶת בְּשָׂרֶךָ, דְּאוֹרְחוֹי דְּקוּדְשָׁא בְּרִיךְ
הוּא וְסִתְרִין, גְּנִיזִין עִלָּאִין, דְּהוּא סָתִים וְגָנִיז לֵית לָן לְשַׁאֲלָא. אָ"ל,
אִי הָכִי, הָא אוֹרַיְיתָא כֹּלָּא סָתִים וְגָנִיז, דְּהָא הִיא שְׁמָא קַדִּישָׁא עִלָּאָה
הֲוֵי, וּמַאן דְּמִתְעַסָּק בְּאוֹרַיְיתָא כְּאִלּוּ אִתְעַסָּק בִּשְׁמֵיה קַדִּישָׁא, וְאִי
הָכִי, לֵית לָן לְשַׁאֲלָא וּלְאִסְתַּכְּלָא.

43. He said to him: Why do you need to toil in the ways of your Master and the edicts of your Master? Ask about that which you have permission to know and gaze at, and about that which you have no permission to know, it is written: "Do not let your mouth cause your flesh to sin" (Kohelet 5:5), since we have no right to inquire about the ways of the Holy One, blessed be He, and His mysteries, the utmost high secrets that He covered and hid. He said to him: If so, the entire Torah is concealed and hidden, since it is the most Holy Name and whoever studies the Torah, it is as if he deals in His Holy Name. If so, we are not permitted to inquire and gaze IN THE TORAH.

44. אָ"ל אוֹרַיְיתָא כֹּלָּא סָתִים וְגַלְיָיא, וּשְׁמֵיה קַדִּישָׁא סָתִים וְגַלְיָיא,
וּכְתִיב הַנִּסְתָּרֹת לַה' אֱלֹהֵינוּ וְהַנִּגְלֹת לָנוּ וּלְבָנֵינוּ, לָנוּ, הַנִּגְלוֹת דְּאִית
רְשׁוּ לְשַׁאֲלָא, וּלְעַיְּינָא וּלְאִסְתַּכְּלָא בְּהוּ וּלְמִנְדַע בְּהוּ. אֲבָל הַנִּסְתָּרוֹת
לַייָ' אֱלֹהֵינוּ, דִּילֵיה אִינוּן, וְלֵיה אִתְחַזְיָין, דְּמַאן יָכִיל לְמִנְדַע
וּלְאִתְדַּבְּקָא דַּעְתּוֹי סְתִימָא, וְכ"ש לְמִשְׁאַל.

44. He said to him: The entire Torah is both concealed and revealed and the Holy Name is both concealed and revealed, as it is written: "The secret things belong to Hashem our Elohim: but those things which are revealed belong to us and to our children" (Devarim 29:28). "But those things which are revealed belong to us," meaning that we have permission to inquire and observe and gaze at them to know them. However, "the secret things belong to Hashem our Elohim": They are His and to Him they are proper, since who could know and comprehend His concealed mind, let alone ask about it.

45. ת"ח, לֵית רְשׁוּ לִבְנֵי עָלְמָא לְמֵימַר מִלִּין סְתִימִין וּלְפָרְשָׁא לוֹן, בַּר
בּוֹצִינָא קַדִּישָׁא, ר"ש דְּהָא קוּדְשָׁא בְּרִיךְ הוּא אִסְתַּכַּם עַל יְדוֹי. וּבְגִין

דְּדָרָא דִּילֵיהּ רְשִׁימָא הוּא לְעֵילָא וְתַתָּא, וע״ד מִלִּין אִתְּמָרוּ
בְּאִתְגַּלְיָיא עַל יְדוֹי, וְלָא יְהֵא דָּרָא כְּדָרָא דָּא דְּאִיהוּ שָׁארֵי בְּגַוֵּיהּ, עַד
דְּיֵיתֵי מַלְכָּא מְשִׁיחָא.

45. Come and see, people are not permitted to talk about concealed matters and explain them, besides the Holy Luminary, Rabbi Shimon, since the Holy One, blessed be He, acceded to him. Since his generation is distinguished above and below, the matters are therefore said through him openly. There will be no other generation like the generation that he resides in, until the coming of King Messiah.

8. The Holy One, blessed be He, has three worlds

A Synopsis

We are told the secret that God has three worlds in which He is concealed. The first is the uppermost world of which nothing is known. The second is the world by which God is known. The third is the world below them where division exists, and it consists of Briyah, Yetzirah and Asiyah; this constitutes the world within which the highest angels dwell and where God is sometimes present and sometimes not. We also hear about three realms, the first of which is the realm of division, meaning this world. The second world, the terrestrial Garden of Eden, is the realm that is connected to the highest realm. The third world is the higher world that is hidden and secret. We hear that the children of God merit all three worlds. The Torah warns that people should not mutilate themselves in grief for the dead because the righteous dead are not lost and they exist in high and precious realms in a state of happiness. We hear that because of Adam's sin man does taste the taste of death prior to entering into the other realms. The conclusion is that God tells people that if they follow His paths and do His work He will bring them to good worlds and higher realms.

46. אֲבָל ת״ח, כְּתִיב וַיִּבְרָא אֱלֹהִים אֶת הָאָדָם בְּצַלְמוֹ בְּצֶלֶם אֱלֹהִים בָּרָא אוֹתוֹ רָזָא דְמִלָּה, תְּלַת עָלְמִין אִית לֵיה לְקוּדְשָׁא בְּרִיךְ הוּא, דְּאִיהוּ גָּנִיז בְּגַוַּוייהוּ. עָלְמָא קַדְמָאָה, הַהוּא עִלָּאָה טְמִירָא דְכֹלָּא, דְּלָא אִסְתְּכַּל בֵּיה, וְלָא אִתְיְדַע בֵּיה, בַּר אִיהוּ, דְּאִיהוּ גָּנִיז בְּגַוֵּיה.

46. Come and see, it is written: "So Elohim created man in His own image, in the image of Elohim He created him" (Beresheet 1:27). The secret of the matter is that the Holy One, blessed be He, has three worlds in which He is concealed. The first world is the uppermost world that is concealed from all, at which we should not gaze. Nothing is known of it except that He is concealed in it. THIS IS THE WORLD OF ZEIR ANPIN OF ATZILUT.

47. עָלְמָא תִּנְיָינָא, דְּאִיהוּ קָשִׁיר בְּהַהוּא דִּלְעֵילָּא, וְדָא הוּא דְקוּדְשָׁא בְּרִיךְ הוּא אִשְׁתְּמוֹדַע מִנֵּיה, כְּמָה דִכְתִיב פִּתְחוּ לִי שַׁעֲרֵי צֶדֶק, זֶה הַשַּׁעַר לַיְיָ'. וְדָא הוּא עָלְמָא תִּנְיָינָא.

47. The second world, which is tied to that WORLD above, is the one by which the Holy One, blessed be He, is known, as it is written: "Open to me the gates of righteousness" (Tehilim 118:19) and "This is the gate of Hashem" (Tehilim 118:20). AND THAT IS THE WORLD OF MALCHUT IN ATZILUT, WHICH IS THE GATE TO ZEIR ANPIN and constitutes the second world.

48. עָלְמָא תְּלִיתָאָה, הַהוּא עָלְמָא תַּתָּאָה מִנַּיְיהוּ, דְּאִשְׁתְּכַח בֵּיה פֵּרוּדָא, וְדָא הוּא עָלְמָא, דְּמַלְאֲכֵי עִלָּאֵי שַׁרְיָין בְּגַוֵויה, וְקוּדְשָׁא בְּרִיךְ הוּא אִשְׁתְּכַח בֵּיה, וְלָא אִשְׁתְּכַח. אִשְׁתְּכַח בֵּיה הַשְׁתָּא, כַּד בָּעָאן לְאִסְתַּכְּלָא וּלְמִנְדַע לֵיה, אִסְתַּלָק מִנַּיְיהוּ, וְלָא אִתְחֲזֵי, עַד דְּכַלְּהוּ שָׁאֲלֵי אַיֵּה מְקוֹם כְּבוֹדוֹ. בָּרוּךְ כְּבוֹד יְיָ' מִמְּקוֹמוֹ. וְהַאי הוּא עָלְמָא דְּלָא אִשְׁתְּכַח בֵּיה תְּדִירָא.

48. The third world is the world below them, where division exists. THAT IS BRIYAH, YETZIRAH AND ASIYAH, ABOUT WHOM IT IS SAID: "AND FROM THENCE IT WAS PARTED… " (BERESHEET 2:10). It constitutes the world within which the highest angels dwell, and the Holy One, blessed be He, is present yet and not so present in it. Now He seems in it, yet when one wishes to observe and to know Him, He disappears from them and is not visible until all ask: "Where is the place of His glory?" "Blessed be the glory of Hashem from His place" (Yechezkel 3:12), and that is the realm where He is not always present.

49. כְּגַוְונָא דָא, בְּצֶלֶם אֱלֹהִים עָשָׂה אֶת הָאָדָם. כְּדֵין אִית לֵיה תְּלַת עָלְמִין. עָלְמָא קַדְמָאָה: הַאי עָלְמָא דְּאִקְרֵי עָלְמָא דְּפֵירוּדָא, וב"נ אִשְׁתְּכַח בֵּיה וְלָא אִשְׁתְּכַח. כַּד בָּעָאן לְאִסְתַּכְּלָא בֵּיה, אִסְתַּלָק מִנַּיְיהוּ וְלָא אִתְחֲזֵי.

49. In the same manner: "For in the image of Elohim made He man" (Beresheet 9:6). Then he has the three realms. The first realm is that world that is referred to as the world of division, MEANING THIS WORLD. The man is existent and not existent in it, since when you wish to look at him, he departs from there and is no longer visible.

50. עָלְמָא תִּנְיָינָא, עָלְמָא דְּאִיהוּ קָשִׁיר בְּהַהוּא עָלְמָא עִלָּאָה, וְדָא הוּא ג"ע דִּי בְאַרְעָא, דְּדָא הוּא קָשִׁיר בְּעָלְמָא אַחֲרָא עִלָּאָה, וּמֵהַאי אִתְיְדַע וְאִשְׁתְּמוֹדַע עָלְמָא אַחֲרָא.

50. The second world is the realm that is connected to the highest realm. That is the terrestrial Garden of Eden, which is tied to another higher world, and from that REALM another world is known and conceived.

51. עָלְמָא תְּלִיתָאָה, עָלְמָא עִלָּאָה טְמִירָא, גְּנִיז וְסָתִים, דְּלֵית מַאן דְּיָדַע לֵיהּ, כְּמָה דִּכְתִיב עַיִן לֹא רָאָתָה אֱלֹהִים זוּלָתְךָ יַעֲשֶׂה לִמְחַכֵּה לוֹ. וְכֹלָּא כְּגַוְונָא עִלָּאָה, דִּכְתִיב בְּצֶלֶם אֱלֹהִים עָשָׂה אֶת הָאָדָם.

51. The third world is the higher world that is concealed, hidden and secret. There is nobody that knows it, as is written: "Neither has the eye seen, that Elohim, beside You, should do such a thing for him that waits for Him" (Yeshayah 64:3). All is similar to the above, as is written: "For in the image of Elohim made He man."

52. עַל דָּא כְּתִיב, בָּנִים אַתֶּם לַיְיָ' אֱלֹהֵיכֶם וְגוֹ', כְּמָה דְּאוּקְמוּהָ. וְאִלֵּין אִינּוּן בְּצֶלֶם אֱלֹהִים, וְאִלֵּין יַרְתִין יְרוּתָא עִלָּאָה כְּגַוְונָא דִּילֵיהּ. וְע"ד אַזְהַר בְּאוֹרַיְיתָא, לָא תִּתְגּוֹדְדוּ וְלֹא תָשִׂימוּ קָרְחָה. דְּהָא לָא אִתְאֲבִיד, וְהָא שְׁכִיחַ בְּעָלְמִין טָבִין עִלָּאִין וְיַקִּירִין, לְהֱווֹן חַדָן כַּד אִסְתָּלַק צַדִּיקָא מֵהַאי עָלְמָא.

52. SINCE THEY MERIT THE THREE WORLDS, about this it is written: "You are children of Hashem your Elohim..." (Devarim 14:1), as we have explained. These are in the image of Elohim and these inherit the highest legacy, similar to His – THAT IS, THREE WORLDS. Therefore, it was warned in the Torah that "you shall not gash yourselves, nor make any baldness between your eyes for the dead" (Ibid.) since one is not lost after his death and he exists in good realms, supernal and precious, and they should be in a state of happiness when a righteous one departs from this world.

53. ות"ח, אִלְמָלֵי לָא חָב אָדָם, לָא יִטְעַם טַעֲמָא דְּמוֹתָא בְּהַאי עָלְמָא,

בְּזִמְנָא דְּעָיֵיל לְעָלְמִין אַחֲרָנִין. אֲבָל בְּגִין דְּחָב, טַעַם טַעֲמָא דְּמוֹתָא,
עַד לָא יֵיעוּל לְאִינּוּן עָלְמִין, וְאִתְפְּשַׁט רוּחָא מֵהַאי גוּפָא, וְאַשְׁאַר לֵיהּ
בְּהַאי עָלְמָא, וְרוּחָא אִסְתַּחְיָא בִּנְהַר דִּינוּר לְקַבְּלָא עוֹנְשָׁא. וּלְבָתַר
עָיֵילָא לְגִ״ע דִּבְאַרְעָא, וְאִזְדַּמְּנָא לֵיהּ מָאנָא אַחֲרָא דִּנְהוֹרָא, כְּהַאי
פַּרְצוּפָא דְּגוּפָא דְּהַאי עָלְמָא מַמָּשׁ. וְאִתְלָבָּשׁ וְאִתְתַּקָּן בֵּיהּ. וְתַמָּן הוּא
מָדוֹרֵא דִּילֵיהּ תָּדִיר. וְאִתְקְשַׁר בְּרֵישׁ יַרְחֵי וְשַׁבַּתֵּי בְּנִשְׁמָתָא. וְסָלִיק
וְאִתְעַטָּר לְעֵילָא לְעֵילָא, הה״ד וְהָיָה מִדֵּי חֹדֶשׁ בְּחָדְשׁוֹ וְגוֹ׳.

53. Come and see: If man (Adam) would not have sinned, he would not have tasted the taste of death in this world during his passing into the other realms. However, due to his sinning, he does taste the taste of death prior to entering into these realms. The spirit gets divested from this body and leaves it in this world. The Ruach is cleansed in the Dinur River to receive its punishment and then enters into the terrestrial Garden of Eden. Another vessel of light that is precisely similar to the form of the body which it previously had on this world is ready for it. It vests and prepares itself in it and there, IN THE GARDEN OF EDEN, is its permanent residence. On the first of each month and Shabbat, the Ruach connects to the Neshamah and ascends to be crowned very high, IN THE MOST HIGH GARDEN OF EDEN. This is what is written: "And it shall come to pass, that every new moon" (Yeshayah 66:23).

54. מִדֵּי חֹדֶשׁ בְּחָדְשׁוֹ אֲמַאי. אֶלָּא רָזָא דְּמִלָּה, בְּגִין חַדְתּוּתֵי דְּסִיהֲרָא,
דְּאִתְעַטְּרָא לְאַנְהָרָא מִן שִׁמְשָׁא בְּהַהוּא זִמְנָא. וְכֵן מִדֵּי שַׁבָּת בְּשַׁבַּתּוֹ,
מִדֵּי שַׁבָּת דָּא סִיהֲרָא. בְּשַׁבַּתּוֹ דָּא שִׁמְשָׁא. דִּנְהוֹרָא אַתְיָא לָהּ מִן תַּמָּן.
וְעַל דָּא כֹּלָּא חַד מִלָּה. וְדָא הוּא בְּרִירָא דְּמִלָּה, בַּר לְחַיָּיבַיָּא דִּכְתִיב
בְּהוּ מִיתָה לְכֻלְּהוּ עָלְמִין, כָּרַת מִכֻּלְּהוּ עָלְמִין. וְאִשְׁתְּצִיָּין מִכֹּלָּא, כַּד
לָא עָיֵילֵי בִּתְשׁוּבָה. אָמַר רִבִּי יְהוּדָה, בְּרִיךְ רַחֲמָנָא, דְּשָׁאִילְנָא
וְרַוַוחְנָא מִלִּין אִלֵּין, וְקָאִימְנָא עֲלַיְיהוּ.

54. "That every new moon": HE INQUIRES: Why SPECIFICALLY ON THE FIRST OF THE MONTH? HE RESPONDS: The secret of the matter is due to the renewal of the moon that is adorned to illuminate from the sun at that time, MEANING THAT THEN IS THE TIME OF THE SUPERNAL UNION OF ZEIR ANPIN AND THE NUKVA CALLED SUN AND MOON. Similarly on "every Shabbat," "every" is the moon, WHICH IS MALCHUT and "Shabbat" is the sun, WHICH IS ZEIR ANPIN, since the light comes to her from him. Therefore, it is all the same thing, THAT THE FIRST OF THE MONTH AND THE SHABBAT ARE INDICATIVE OF THE SAME, THAT IT IS THE TIME OF THE UNION OF ZEIR ANPIN AND MALCHUT. HOWEVER, THERE IS A DEGREE OF DIFFERENCE IN THE ELEVATION, THAT ON THE NEW MOON, THEY ARE IN THE LEVEL OF YISRAEL-SABA AND TEVUNAH, AND ON THE SHABBAT IN THE LEVEL OF ABA AND IMA. That is the clear definition of this matter, except for the sinners who are sentenced to death in all the realms, which means being cut off from all the realms and losing all if they have not come to repentance. Rabbi Yehuda said: Blessed is the All Merciful that I asked and gained these, and came to understand THESE MEANINGS.

55. אָמַר ר' שִׁמְעוֹן, מִפַּרְשָׁתָּא דָּא אוֹלִיפְנָא רָזָא דְּחָכְמְתָא, וְאִשְׁתְּמָעוּ מִנָּה רָזִין עִלָּאִין וְיַקִּירִין. ת"ח, קוּדְשָׁא בְּרִיךְ הוּא מְשַׁבַּח בְּאוֹרַיְיתָא, וְאָמַר אֲזִילוּ בְּאוֹרְחַי, אִשְׁתַּדְלוּ בְּפוּלְחָנִי, וְהָא אֲנָא מְעַיֵּיל לְכוֹן לְעָלְמִין טָבִין, לְעָלְמִין עִלָּאִין. בְּנֵי נָשָׁא דְּלָא יַדְעֵי, לָא מְהֵימְנֵי, וְלָא מִסְתַּכְּלֵי, קוּדְשָׁא בְּרִיךְ הוּא אָמַר, אֲזִילוּ אֲלִילוּ הַהוּא עָלְמָא טָבָא, הַהוּא עָלְמָא עִלָּאָה דְּכְסוּפָא. אִינּוּן אַמְרֵי, אֵיךְ נֵיכוּל לְאַלְלָא לֵיהּ, וּלְמִנְדַּע כָּל הַאי.

55. Rabbi Shimon said: From this portion, I have learned the secret meaning of wisdom, from which are derived lofty and precious secrets. Come and see that the Holy One, blessed be He, praises the Torah and says, 'Go in My paths and labor in My service, and I will bring you to good worlds and higher realms.' To those people who do not know, or have no faith and do not look, the Holy One, blessed be He, says, 'Go seek out and and look at that better world, that supernal and exquisite realm.' They reply: How could we possibly do that and how could we know all this?

9. "Go up this way by the south"

A Synopsis

We learn that God tells people to strive in the Torah and they will then recognize that it is available to support them, and they will be able to see if the just that live in the Garden of Eden got there by having overpowered their inclinations with strong effort, or if they studied the Torah day and night. They will be able to see what type of world it is and whether the Tree of Life is present forever. We hear warnings against those who think they can achieve the Garden of Eden with a lazy attitude and meaningless effort.

56. מַה כְּתִיב. עֲלוּ זֶה בַּנֶּגֶב, אִשְׁתַּדְּלוּ בְּאוֹרַיְיתָא, וְתֶחֱמוּן דְּהָא הִיא קַיְּימָא קַמַּיְיכוּ, וּמִנָּה תִּנְדְּעוּן לֵיהּ. וּרְאִיתֶם אֶת הָאָרֶץ מַה הִיא וְגוֹ'. תֶּחֱמוּן מִנָּה הַהוּא עָלְמָא, דְּהָא יְרוּתָא דְּאַחֲסָנָא, דַּאֲנָא עָיֵיל לְכוּ בָּהּ. וְאֶת הָעָם הַיּוֹשֵׁב עָלֶיהָ, אִינּוּן צַדִּיקַיָּיא דִּבְגִנְתָּא דְעֵדֶן, דְּקַיְימָן שׁוּרִין שׁוּרִין בִּיקָרָא עִלָּאָה, בְּדַרְגִּין עִלָּאִין.

56. It is written THAT THE HOLY ONE, BLESSED BE HE, TELLS THEM: "'Go up this way by the south" (Bemidbar 13:17), MEANING strive in the Torah and you will then recognize that it stands in good stead for you. Through it, you will know that WORLD "and see the country, what it is..." (Ibid. 18), MEANING you will recognize through it that world, which is an inheritance and a legacy, to which I bring you.' "And the people who dwell in it" (Ibid.): these are the righteous in the Garden of Eden, who stand row by row in the highest glory on the highest grades.

57. הֶחָזָק הוּא הֲרָפֶה, בָּהּ תֶּחֱמוּ אִי זָכוּ לְכָל הַאי כַּד אַתְקְפוּ עַל יִצְרֵיהוֹן, וְתַבְרוּ לֵיהּ, אִי לָא. אוֹ כַּד אַתְקְפוּ בְּאוֹרַיְיתָא, לְמִלְעֵי בָּהּ יְמָמָא וְלֵילְיָא. אוֹ אִי אַרְפּוּ יְדַיְיהוּ מִנָּהּ. וְזָכוּ לְכָל הַאי. הַמְעַט הוּא אִם רָב, אִי סַגִּיאִין אִינּוּן דְּאִשְׁתַּדְּלוּ בְּפוּלְחָנִי, וְאַתְקִיפוּ בְּאוֹרַיְיתָא, בְּגִין דְּזָכוּ לְכָל הַאי אִי אִי לָא.

57. "Whether they are strong or weak..." (Ibid.) MEANING you will see in her if they gained all these due to having overpowered their inclination WITH STRONG EFFORT and broken it, or whether they did it WEAKLY

WITHOUT ANY EFFORT. Or see if they enhanced their strength in Torah by studying it day and night or if they have loosened their hands of it, AND YET IN SPITE OF THAT they merited all these. "Are they few or are they many" (Ibid.): Are there many who are involved in My service and getting stronger by the Torah, so that they therefore merit all these, or not?

58. וּמָה הָאָרֶץ הַשְּׁמֵנָה הוּא אִם רָזָא. מִדְּאוֹרַיְיתָא תִּנְדְּעוּן מַה הָאָרֶץ. מַה הַהוּא עָלְמָא אִי אַסְגֵּי טִיבוּ עִלָּאָה לְיָתְבָהָא, אוֹ אִי אַזְעֵיר מִנֵּהּ כְּלוּם. הֲיֵשׁ בָּהּ עֵץ אִם אַיִן, הֲאִית בָּהּ אִילָנָא דְחַיֵּי, לְעָלַם וּלְעָלְמֵי עָלְמִין, אוֹ אִי צְרוֹרָא דְחַיֵּי אִשְׁתְּכַח בְּגַוַּוהּ, אִם לָא.

58. "And what the land is, whether fat or lean" (Ibid. 19): through the Torah, you will know what the land is, MEANING what type of world it is – whether there is a great deal of beneficial good from above to its dwellers, or whether it is lacking anything. "Whether there is a tree in it, or not" (Ibid. 20): is the Tree of Life – THAT IS, ZEIR ANPIN – present forever and ever? And does it contain the bundle of life, WHICH IS YESOD, or not?

59. וַיַּעֲלוּ בַנֶּגֶב וַיָּבֹא עַד חֶבְרוֹן. וַיַּעֲלוּ בַנֶּגֶב, בְּנֵי נָשָׁא סַלְקִין בְּגַוַּוהּ בַנֶּגֶב, בְּלִבָּא עֲצֵלָא, כְּמַאן דְּאִשְׁתְּדַל בְּמַגָּנָא, בְּנִגּוּבוּ, דְּחָשִׁיב דְּלֵית בָּהּ אֲגַר, חָמֵי דְּהָא עוּתְרָא דְּהַאי עָלְמָא אָבִיד בְּגִינָהּ, חָשִׁיב דְּכֹלָּא הוּא. בַנֶּגֶב: כד"א חָרְבוּ הַמַּיִם, וּמִתַּרְגְּמִינָן נְגִיבוּ.

59. "And they ascended into the Negev, and (he) came to Hebron" (Ibid. 22). "And they ascended into the Negev" MEANS that people elevate themselves within her, THE TORAH, and "into the Negev" means with a lazy heart, as one whose effort is dry and meaningless, because he believes that there is no recompense in that. He sees that he has lost the world's riches due to her and thinks that everything is LOST. "Into the Negev" is as written: "The face of the ground was dry" (Beresheet 8:13), "dry" being translated into Aramaic as negivu.

60. לְבָתַר וַיָּבֹא עַד חֶבְרוֹן, עַד דְּאָתֵי לְאִתְחַבְּרָא בָּהּ, קָאֵרֵי וְשַׁאֲנֵי בָּהּ. וְשָׁם אֲחִימָן שֵׁשַׁי וְתַלְמַי, תַּמָּן חָמֵי פְּלִיגָן סַגִּיאִין, טָמֵא וְטָהוֹר, אָסוּר

וּמוּתָּר, עוֹנָשִׁין וְאַגְרִין. אִלֵּין אִינוּן אָרְחֵי דְאוֹרַיְיתָא, דְּקְדוּקֵי
אוֹרַיְיתָא. יְלִידֵי הָעֲנָק, דְּאִתְיְלִידוּ מִסְטְרָא דִּגְבוּרָה.

60. Following that: "and (he) came to Hebron," MEANING that he has come
to adhere to the Torah, and he reads and studies it. "Where Ahiman, Sheshai
and Talmai..." (Bemidbar 13:22), MEANING he sees there many divisions:
unclean and clean, forbidden and permitted, punishment and recompense.
These are the paths of the Torah, the specifics of the Torah. "The children of
Anak" (Ibid.): MEANING THAT they were born from the side of Gvurah.

10. The spies

A Synopsis

We are told that Hebron is the Oral Torah because whoever strives in her is referred to as Chaver, or comrade; it emerges from the written Torah, Zeir Anpin. Reference is made to homiletical interpretations and Agadah that surround the Torah like grapes in a cluster. Those who do not study the Torah for its own sake cause a flaw in the faith because they consider the written and oral Torahs to be two rather than one; this leads to the separation of Zeir Anpin and Malchut. People recant from the true path, saying that the world above might indeed be good, as the Torah says, but who could possibly deserve it? It takes too much work. We read of the difficulties of poverty and weakness of body among those who study the Torah, but of the great reward that comes to them and the great connection they make with God. We are told the inner meaning of Joshua and Caleb who carried between them the branch with the cluster of grapes. The rabbis talk about the giants who came against them, and Rabbi Shimon tells of the slanderous spies who told lies about the promised land. It was as if by speaking slanderously about the Holy Land they spoke badly about God, and God later caused the destruction of both temples on the anniversary of that day. Had Moses not prevailed with his prayer the children of Yisrael would have been destroyed from the world.

61. וְחֶבְרוֹן שֶׁבַע שָׁנִים נִבְנְתָה, אִלֵּין אִינּוּן שַׁבְעִין אַנְפִּין, דְּאוֹרַיְיתָא, שַׁבְעִין פָּנִים אִית לָהּ, לְכָל סִטְרָא עֲשָׂרָה. וְחֶבְרוֹן, דָּא אוֹרַיְיתָא, מַאן דְּאִשְׁתְּדַל בָּהּ אִקְרֵי חָבֵר. לְפְנֵי צוֹעַן מִצְרַיִם, תְּנֵינָן אוֹרַיְיתָא אִית לְקַבֵּל אוֹרַיְיתָא. וְהַיְינוּ תּוֹרָה שֶׁבִּכְתָב, וְתוֹרָה שבע״פ. וְהַאי חֶבְרוֹן. מִתּוֹרָה שֶׁבִּכְתָב נַפְקַת. כד״א אֱמוֹר לַחַכְמָה אֲחוֹתִי אָתְּ. וְהַאי נִבְנְתָה שֶׁבַע שְׁנִין, דבג״כ אִקְרֵי בַּת שֶׁבַע. לְפְנֵי צֹעַן מִצְרַיִם, כד״א וַתֵּרֶב חָכְמַת שְׁלֹמֹה מֵחָכְמַת כָּל בְּנֵי קֶדֶם וּמִכָּל חָכְמַת מִצְרָיִם.

61. "Now Hebron was built seven years" (Bemidbar 13:22): These are the seventy faces of the Torah. The Torah contains seventy aspects, WHICH ARE THE SECRET OF ZEIR ANPIN THAT HAS SIX ENDS AND CHESED, GVURAH, TIFERET, NETZACH, HOD, YESOD AND MALCHUT THAT TOTAL SEVEN SFIROT. Each aspect haas ten, MEANING THAT EACH ONE IS COMPRISED

OF TEN SFIROT, TOTALLING SEVENTY. Hebron is the Torah, because whoever strives in her is referred to as *Chaver*, or friend. "Before Zoan in Egypt" (Ibid.): We learned that a Torah corresponds to a Torah, namely the written Torah, WHICH IS ZEIR ANPIN, and the oral Torah, WHICH IS MALCHUT. That Hebron, WHICH IS THE ORAL TORAH THAT IS MALCHUT, comes out from the written Torah, ZEIR ANPIN, as it says: "Say to wisdom, 'You are my sister'" (Mishlei 7:4). And it was built seven years, MEANING THE SEVEN SFIROT – CHESED, GVURAH, TIFERET, NETZACH, HOD, YESOD AND MALCHUT. Therefore, it was referred to as Bathsheba, daughter of seven. "Before Zoan in Egypt" as it says: "Solomon's wisdom" – THAT IS MALCHUT - "excelled of all the children of the east country, and all the wisdom of Egypt" (I Melachim 5:10).

62. וַיָּבֹאוּ עַד נַחַל אֶשְׁכּוֹל, אַלֵּין אִינּוּן מִלֵּי אַגָּדָה, דְּרָשָׁה, דְּתַלְיָין מִסִּטְרָא דִּמְהֵימְנוּתָא. וַיִּכְרְתוּ מִשָּׁם זְמוֹרָה וְגוֹ', אוֹלְפִין מִתַּמָּן רָאשֵׁי פִּרְקִין. רָאשֵׁי מִלִּין, אִינּוּן דִּבְנֵי מְהֵימְנוּתָא, חַדָּאן בְּמִלִּין, וּמִתְבָּרְכָן מִלִּין בְּגַווַיְיהוּ, וּמִסְתַּכְּלָן שָׁרְשָׁא חַד וְעִקָּרָא חַד, וְלָא אִשְׁתְּכַח בְּהוּ פֵּרוּדָא. אִינּוּן דְּלָא מִשְׁתַּכְּחֵי בְּנֵי מְהֵימְנוּתָא, וְלָא אוֹלְפֵי אוֹרַיְיתָא לִשְׁמָהּ, שַׁוְיָין לֵיהּ לִמְהֵימְנוּתָא בִּפְרוּדָא, הה"ד וַיִּשָּׂאוּהוּ בַמּוֹט בִּשְׁנָיִם, בִּפְרוּדָא. מַהוּ בַּמּוֹט. כד"א אַל יִתֵּן לַמּוֹט רַגְלֶךָ. וּמִן הָרִמּוֹנִים וּמִן הַתְּאֵנִים, כֹּלָּא שָׁוְיָין לְהָנֵי מִילֵי לְסִטְרָא אַחֲרָא, לְסִטְרָא דְּמִינָאֵי, לְסִטְרָא דִּפְרוּדָא.

62. "And they came to the wadi of Eshkol (lit. 'cluster')" (Bemidbar 13:23): these refer to matters of Agadah and homiletical interpretation that are derived from the aspect of Faith, WHICH IS MALCHUT, SINCE HOMILETICAL INTERPRETATIONS AND AGADAH ARE DEPENDENT ON TORAH AND SURROUND HER LIKE GRAPES IN A GRAPE CLUSTER. "And cut down from thence a branch..." (Ibid.): they learned from there the headings of the chapters and the highlights of the matters. The faithful rejoice with these matters, which are blessed within them. They notice that they stem from one source and principal and there is no division that divides them. Those who are not of Faith and do not study the Torah for its own sake cause the Faith, WHICH IS MALCHUT, to be separated FROM ZEIR ANPIN, SINCE THEY CAUSE A FLAW IN THE UNION OF ZEIR ANPIN AND MALCHUT – WHICH ARE THE WRITTEN TORAH AND THE ORAL TORAH. THEY DO NOT ACCEPT

THE BELIEF THAT THEY ARE ONE ESSENCE AND ONE SOURCE. This is what is written: "And they carried it between two on a pole (Heb. *mot*)" (Ibid.), WHICH MEANS THEY CAUSED a division BETWEEN THE WRITTEN AND ORAL TORAH AND CONSIDER THEM, HEAVEN FORBID, AS TWO. What is the meaning of "*mot*"? It is as is written: "He will not suffer your foot to be moved (Heb. *lamot*)" (Tehilim 121:3) and "of the pomegranates (Heb. *rimonim*), and the figs (Heb. *te'enim*)" (Bemidbar 13:23). They have placed these matters entirely into the Other Side, to the side of heretics, and the side of separation, SINCE *RIMONIM* IS DERIVED FROM *MINIM* (LIT. 'HERETICS'). AND *TE'ENIM* IS DERIVED FROM: "BUT ELOHIM ALLOWED IT (HEB. *INAH*) TO HAPPEN TO HIM" (SHEMOT 21:13), MEANING THAT IT HAPPENED BY CHANCE, AS THEY DO NOT BELIEVE IN PROVIDENCE AND SAY EVERYTHING IS BY CHANCE, AND SEPARATE THE BLESSED HASHEM FROM THE WORLD.

63. הה״ד וְיָשׁוּבוּ מִתּוּר הָאָרֶץ. וְיָשׁוּבוּ, תַּיְיבִין לְסִטְרָא בִּישָׁא, וְתַיְיבִין מֵאָרְחָא דִּקְשׁוֹט. אַמְרֵי, מַאי אִכְפַּת לָן. עַד יוֹמָא לָא חֲמֵינָא טַב לְעָלְמָא, אַעֲמַלְנָא בָּהּ, בֵּיתָא רֵיקָם. יָתִיבְנָא בְּקִלָנָא דְעַמָּא, וּלְהַהוּא עָלְמָא מַאן יִזְכֵּי וּמַאן יֵיעוֹל לְגַוְוֵיהּ, טַב לָן דְּלָא אַטְרַחְנָא כּוּלֵי הַאי. וַיְסַפְּרוּ לוֹ וַיֹּאמְרוּ וְגוֹ', הָא אַעֲמַלְנָא וְלָאֵינָא, בְּגִין לְמִנְדַּע חוּלָקָא דְּהַהוּא עָלְמָא. וְגַם זָבַת חָלָב וּדְבַשׁ הִיא, טַב הוּא הַהוּא עָלְמָא עִלָּאָה, כְּמָה דְּיַדְעָנָא בְּאוֹרַיְיתָא, אֲבָל מַאן יָכִיל לְמִזְכֵּי בֵּיהּ.

63. This is what is written: "And they returned from searching the land" (Bemidbar 13:25). "And they returned" means they returned to the Evil Side and recanted from the true path, saying, What result did we get, to this day we have not experienced any worldly benefits for our labor in the Torah. The house was empty and we were settled among the lower class of the people. Who will merit that world and who will reach to enter into it? It might be better for us not to work so hard. "And they told him, and said..." (Ibid. 27), Here we labored and studied in order to know that part of the world, AS YOU ADVISED US: "And indeed it flows with milk and honey" (Ibid.). That world above is indeed good, as we were informed in the Torah, but who could deserve it?

64. אֶפֶס כִּי עַז הָעָם, תַּקִּיף הוּא, דְּלָא יַחֲשִׁיב כָּל עָלְמָא כְּלָל, בְּגִין

דִּיהֵא לֵיהּ עוּתְרָא סַגִיא לְאִשְׁתַּדְּלָא בֵּיהּ, מַאן הוּא דְּיִזְכֵּי בָּהּ. וַדַּאי
אֶפֶס כִּי עַז הָעָם הַיּוֹשֵׁב בָּאָרֶץ, מַאן דְּבָעֵי לְמִזְכֵּי בָּהּ, בָּעֵי לְמֶהֱוֵי
תַּקִיף בְּעוּתְרָא, כד"א וְעָשִׁיר יַעֲנֶה עַזּוֹת. וְהֶעָרִים גְּדוֹלוֹת בְּצוּרוֹת.
בָּתִּין מַלְיָין כָּל טוּבָא, דְּלָא יַחְסְרוּן מִכֹּלָא. וְעִם כָּל דָּא וְגַם יְלִידֵי
הָעֲנָק רָאִינוּ שָׁם, בָּעֵי גוּפָא תַּקִיף, גִּיבָּר כַּאֲרִי. בְּגִין דְּהִיא מַתָּשַׁת
חֵילֵיהּ דב"נ לְאִשְׁתַּדְּלָא בְּהַהוּא אִיסוּר וְהֶתֵּר, טָמֵא וְטָהוֹר, כָּשֵׁר
וּפָסוּל. מַאן יֵיכוּל לְזַכָּאָה בָּהּ.

64. "But the people are strong" (Ibid. 28). Powerful is THE NATION THAT
MERITED THE WORLD ABOVE, which did not value the whole world at all
to strive in it so as to acquire great wealth. Who is he THAT COULD ACT
THAT WAY to gain merits in the world above? Certainly, "but the people are
strong that dwell in this land." Whoever wishes to make gains in her must
be wealthy and strong as it says: "But the rich answers with impudence (lit.
'strength')" (Mishlei 18:23) INDEED HE MUST BE SO. "and the cities are
fortified and very great" (Bemidbar 13:28), MEANING nothing will be
lacking in homes filled with all goodness. "And moreover we saw the
children of Anak there" (Ibid.), meaning it requires a firm body strong as a
lion, since the Torah diminishes the strength of a person when he deals in
the forbidden and the permissible, the defiled and the cleansed, the fit and
the rejected. Who could merit her?

65. וְעוֹד, עֲמָלֵק יוֹשֵׁב בְּאֶרֶץ הַנֶּגֶב. אִי יֵימָא בַּר נָשׁ, דַּאֲפִילוּ בְּכָל דָּא
יִזְכֵּי. עֲמָלֵק יוֹשֵׁב בְּאֶרֶץ הַנֶּגֶב, הָא יִצְרָא בִּישָׁא, קַטֵיגוֹרָא, מְקַטְרְגָא
דְּבַר נָשׁ, דְּיִשְׁתְּכַח תָּדִיר בְּגוּפָא. וְהַחִתִּי וְהָאֱמוֹרִי וְגוֹ', כַּמָּה מְקַטְרְגֵי
מִשְׁתַּכְּחֵי תַּמָּן. דְּלָא יָכִיל בַּר נָשׁ לְמֵיעַל בְּהַהוּא עָלְמָא כְּלָל, מַאן יִזְכֵּי
לֵיהּ, וּמַאן יֵיעוּל בְּגַוֵּיהּ, בְּמִלִּין אִלֵּין, וַיָּנִיאוּ אֶת לֵב בְּנֵי יִשְׂרָאֵל. בְּגִין
דְּאַפִּיקוּ שׁוּם בִּישׁ עֲלָהּ, כד"א וַיּוֹצִיאוּ אֶת דִּבַּת הָאָרֶץ.

65. Furthermore, "Amalek dwells in the land of the Negev" (Ibid. 29). If a
person should think to himself that even with all this, he will deserve TO BE
STRENGTHENED, "Amalek dwells in the land of the Negev." Here is the
Evil Inclination that prosecutes the person, always present in the body.
"And the Hittites...and the Amorites..." (Ibid.). How many prosecutors exist

there to prevent a person from ever entering that world at all? Who will have merit for it and who will enter into it? With these words, "they disheartened the children of Yisrael" (Bemidbar 32:9), since they have implicated it in bad rumors, as it says: "They spread an evil report of the land" (Ibid.).

‎66. אִינּוּן בְּנֵי מְהֵימְנוּתָא מַאי קָא אָמְרֵי, אִם חָפֵץ בָּנוּ יְיָ' וּנְתָנָה לָנוּ. כֵּיוָן דְּיִשְׁתַּדַּל בַּר נָשׁ בִּרְעוּתָא דְּלִבָּא לְגַבֵּי קוּדְשָׁא בְּרִיךְ הוּא, לָא בָּעֵי מִנָּן אֶלָּא לִבָּא, וְיִסְתַּמְּרוּן הַהוּא רְשִׁימָא קַדִּישָׁא, דִּכְתִּיב וְעַמֵּךְ כֻּלָּם צַדִּיקִים לְעוֹלָם יִירְשׁוּ אָרֶץ.

66. What did these faithful say? "If Hashem delights in us...and give it us" (Bemidbar 14:8), MEANING THAT if a person strives with a willing heart for the Holy One, blessed be He, HE WILL MERIT HER, since He only wants his heart. And they will preserve that Holy Sign, THAT IS THE HOLY COVENANT, as is written: "Your people also shall be righteous: they shall inherit the land for ever" (Yeshayah 60:21), MEANING THOSE WHO PRESERVE THE COVENANT, WHO ARE CALLED RIGHTEOUS.

‎67. אֲבָל, אַךְ בַּיְיָ' אַל תִּמְרוֹדוּ, בָּעֵי דְּלָא יִמְרְדוּן בְּאוֹרַיְיתָא, דְּאוֹרַיְיתָא לָא בָּעֵי עוּתְרָא, וְלָא מָאנֵי דְכַסְפָּא וְדַהֲבָא. וְאַתֶּם אַל תִּירְאוּ אֶת עַם הָאָרֶץ, דְּהָא גּוּפָא תְּבִירָא, אִי יִשְׁתַּדַּל בְּאוֹרַיְיתָא, יִשְׁכַּח אַסְווֹתָא בְּכֹלָּא. הה"ד, רִפְאוּת תְּהִי לְשָׁרֶךְ וְשִׁקּוּי לְעַצְמוֹתֶיךָ. וּכְתִיב וּלְכָל בְּשָׂרוֹ מַרְפֵּא. וְכָל אִינּוּן מְקַטְרְגֵי, אִינּוּן מַכְרְזָאן וְאָמְרֵי, פְּנוּ אֲתָר לִפְלַנְיָיא עַבְדָּא דְמַלְכָּא.

67. However, "only rebel not against Hashem" (Bemidbar 14:9). It is necessary not to rebel against the Torah, since Torah neither requires wealth, nor utensils of silver and gold. "Nor fear the people of the land" (Ibid.), for if a broken body will engage to study the Torah, it will find a remedy in everything. This is what is written: "It shall be a health to your navel, and marrow to your bones" (Mishlei 3:8). And: "And health to all their flesh" (Mishlei 4:22). All the prosecutors AGAAINST THE PERSON BECOME HELPFUL TO HIM. They proclaim and make room for so-and-so, servant of the King, MEANING THAT NO ONE WILL DETER HIM FROM

COMING TO THE KING TO SERVE HIM.

‏68. בְּגִין כַּךְ אַל תִּירָאוּ, כִּי לַחְמֵנוּ הֵם, אִינּוּן בְּגַרְמַיְיהוּ מְזַמְּנָן מְזוֹנֵי בְּכָל יוֹמָא לְאִינּוּן דְּמִשְׁתַּדְּלֵי בְּאוֹרַיְיתָא. כד"א וְאֶת הָעוֹרְבִים צִוִּיתִי לְכַלְכֶּלְךָ. וּכְתִיב וְהָעוֹרְבִים מְבִיאִים לוֹ לֶחֶם וּבָשָׂר. סָר צִלָּם מֵעֲלֵיהֶם. מַאן צֶלֶם. דָּא תּוּקְפָּא דְּדִינָא קַשְׁיָא. מַאי טַעְמָא אַעְדֵּי. מִשׁוּם דַּיְיָ' אִתָּנוּ אַל תִּירָאוּם. כֹּלָּא אַעְדִּיאוּ בְּגִין אוֹרַיְיתָא. זַכָּאָה חוּלָקֵהוֹן דְּאִינּוּן דְּמִשְׁתַּדְּלֵי בְּאוֹרַיְיתָא לִשְׁמָהּ, דְּהָא מִתְקַשְּׁרֵי בְּקוּדְשָׁא בְּרִיךְ הוּא מַמָּשׁ. וְאִקְרוּן אַחִים וְרֵעִים. הה"ד לְמַעַן אַחַי וְרֵעָי אֲדַבְּרָה נָא שָׁלוֹם בָּךְ.‏

68. Therefore, "nor fear the people of the land; for they are bread for us" (Bemidbar 14:9). THE PROSECUTORS themselves prepare food daily for those who study Torah, as it says: "And I have commanded the ravens to feed you there" (I Melachim 17:4). It is further written: "And the ravens brought him bread and meat" (Ibid. 6). ALTHOUGH THE RAVENS ARE UNCLEAN BIRDS, FROM THE OTHER SIDE, STILL THEY WERE FEEDING HIM. "Their defense (shadow) is departed from them" (Bemidbar 14:9): What is meant by shadow? That is the strength of harsh Judgment IN THEM THAT WAS DEPARTED AND VOIDED. What is the reason that it was gone? "And Hashem is with us: fear them not" (Ibid.): All their power was voided as a result of the Torah. Praised is the lot of those who deal with and study Torah for its own sake, because they really get connected to the Holy One, blessed be He. They are considered brethren and friends and this is what is written: "For my brethren and friends' sakes, I will now say, 'Peace be within you'" (Tehilim 122:8).

‏69. וַיָּבֹאוּ עַד נַחַל אֶשְׁכֹּל וְגוֹ'. רִבִּי אַבָּא אָמַר, כָּרְתוּ הַהוּא אֶשְׁכֹּל, אָתוּ לְסַלְּקָא לֵיהּ לָא יָכִילוּ. אָתוּ לְנַטְלָא לֵיהּ, לָא יָכִילוּ. אָתוּ כָּלֵב וִיהוֹשֻׁעַ, נַטְלוּ לֵיהּ, וּסְלִיקוּ לֵיהּ, וְאִזְדְּקַף עַל יְדַיְיהוּ. הה"ד וַיִּשָּׂאוּהוּ בַמּוֹט בִּשְׁנָיִם. בִּשְׁנַיִם בְּאִינּוּן שְׁנַיִם יְחִידָן. זְמוֹרָה מַאי קָא בָּעָאן. אֶלָּא אֶשְׁכּוֹל הֲוָה תַּלְיָיא בֵּיהּ, וּבְעוֹד דַּהֲוָה מִתְחַבַּר בְּאַתְרֵיהּ, אִקְרֵי זְמוֹרָה. לְבָתַר קַרְיֵיהּ מוֹט, דִּכְתִיב וַיִּשָּׂאוּהוּ בַמּוֹט. הַהוּא דְּאִשְׁתְּמוֹדַע. הַהוּא דְּכָרְתוּ.‏

69. "And they came to the wadi of Eshkol." Rabbi Aba said, They cut off the cluster (Heb. *eshkol*) of grapes, which they tried to lift up, but could not. They tried to move it FROM ITS PLACE but could not. Joshua and Caleb came, took hold of it, raised it and it was upright through them. This is what is written: "And they carried it between two on a pole" MEANS by the only two WHO DID NOT SIN, WHICH ARE JOSHUA AND CALEB. HE ASKS: What purpose did "a branch" serve? HE RESPONDS: It is only that the cluster was attached hanging to it and, while it is attached on location, it is called a branch. After THEY CUT IT OFF, it is called pole, as is written: "And they carried it...on a pole," MEANING that specific one, the one they severed FROM THE TREE.

70. מִכָּאן יָדְעוּ יְהוֹשֻׁעַ וְכָלֵב, דְּאִינוּן אִתְחַזְיָין לְמֵיעַל לְאַרְעָא, וּלְמֶהֱוֵי לוֹן בָּהּ חֵלֶק וְאַחֲסָנָא. עַד דַּהֲווֹ אַתְיָין אַמְלִכוּ עָלַיְיהוּ כֻּלְּהוּ, קָאִים כָּלֵב בְּאִיבָא, אָמַר אִיבָא אִיבָא, אִי בְּגִינָךְ אֲנָן מִתְקַטְלִין, מַה אֲנָן בְּחוּלְקָךְ. מִיַּד קָלִיל גַּרְמֵיהּ. וְיָהֲבוּ לוֹן.

70. From this, SEEING THAT THEY ARE ABLE TO TAKE THE CLUSTER AND YET THE OTHERS WERE UNABLE TO DO IT, Joshua and Caleb realized that they deserved to enter the promised land and that they would have a part and an inheritance. While THE SPIES were still traveling, they made a decision in council about them – JOSHUA AND CALEB – SINCE THE OTHERS WERE JEALOUS OF THEM THAT THEY WERE ABLE TO CARRY THAT CLUSTER. AND THEY DECIDED IN COUNCIL TO MURDER THEM. Caleb stood up over the fruit and said, Fruit, fruit, if for your sake we are killed, why are we in your part? Immediately, THE CLUSTER made itself lighter, SO THAT ALL COULD CARRY IT. And they passed it on to them.

71. ר' אֶלְעָזָר אָמַר, לָא יָהֲבוּ לְאָחֳרֵי, דְּהָא כְּתִיב וַיִּשָּׂאֻהוּ בַמּוֹט, וּכְתִיב בִּשְׁנַיִם, וּבְכֻלְּהוּ לָא הֲווֹ שְׁנַיִם כְּוָותַיְיהוּ. וּמִכָּאן אוֹלִיף יְהוֹשֻׁעַ לְבָתַר, דִּכְתִּיב וַיִּשְׁלַח יְהוֹשֻׁעַ בִּן נוּן מִן הַשִּׁטִּים שְׁנַיִם אֲנָשִׁים מְרַגְּלִים. וְהָנֵי שְׁנַיִם הָא אוּקְמוּהָ קַדְמָאֵי. וְכַד מָטוּ לְגַבַּיְיהוּ דְּיִשְׂרָאֵל, יָהֲבוּ לוֹן, וְאִינוּן אִשְׁתָּאֲרוּ, וְעַבְדוּ גַּרְמַיְיהוּ שִׁירַיִים.

71. Rabbi Elazar said, They did not give THE CLUSTER to others, since it is clearly written: "And they carried it between two on a pole," INDICATING

THE TWO INDICATED. Among all of them, there were no other two like them. From this, Joshua took a lesson at a later date, TO SEND JUST TWO SPIES, as is written: "And Joshua the son of Nun sent out of Shittim two men to spy secretly" (Yehoshua 2:1). Those two have already been explained by the ancient ones. When JOSHUA AND CALEB reached back to Yisrael and handed to them THE CLUSTER, they remained silent AND SAID NOTHING TO YISRAEL AT FIRST. IT WAS ONLY THE REST OF THE SPIES WHO SAID, "AND THIS IS THE FRUIT OF IT" (BEMIDBAR 13:27) and they pretended themselves to be the least.

72. ר' יִצְחָק אָמַר, כַּד הֲווֹ מָטָאן לְגַבַּיְיהוּ דְּאִינוּן עֲנָקִים, הֲווֹ שַׁוְּויִין הַהוּא חוּטְרָא דְמֹשֶׁה קַמַּיְיהוּ, וְאִשְׁתְּזִיבוּ. וּמְנָלָן דְּהַהוּא חוּטְרָא יָהִיב לוֹן. הה"ד, וַיֹּאמֶר אֲלֵיהֶם עֲלוּ זֶה בַּנֶּגֶב. כְּתִיב הָכָא עֲלוּ זֶה, וּכְתִיב הָתָם וְאֶת הַמַּטֶּה הַזֶּה וְגו', וּבְגִינֵיה אִשְׁתְּזִיבוּ. דְּאִי תֵּימָא הָנֵי עֲנָקַיָּיא שַׁבְקֵי לוֹן. אֶלָּא אָתוּ לְנַסְבָּא לוֹן, וַהֲווֹ שַׁוְּויִין לְקַמַּיְיהוּ הַהוּא חוּטְרָא, וּמִשְׁתְּזִיבֵי מִקַּמַּיְיהוּ. רִבִּי יְהוּדָה אָמַר, מָסוֹרֶת שְׁמָא קַדִּישָׁא מָסַר לוֹן מֹשֶׁה, וּבְגִינֵיה אִשְׁתְּזִיבוּ מִנַּיְיהוּ.

72. Rabbi Yitzchak said, When the spies reached those giants, they put in front of them the staff of Moses and were saved. How do we know that he gave them the staff? Since it is written: "And he said to them, 'Go up this way (Heb. zeh) by the south'". It is written here: "Zeh" or this and it is written there: "This (Heb. hazeh) rod..." (Shemot 4:17). AND WE HAVE LEARN THAT THE SAME MEANING IS DERIVED FROM THE SAME WXPRESSION, ZEH- THIS, IN BOTH SENTENCES. Due to this staff, they were saved. If you think that those giants simply left them alone, IT WAS NOT SO. The giants in fact came to capture them, but they put the staff in front of the giants and saved themselves. Rabbi Yehuda said, Tradition is that Moses passed on to them the Holy Name. Due to this, they were saved and survived.

73. רִבִּי חִיָּיא אָמַר, תְּלַת שְׁמָהָן אִקְרוּן, נְפִילִים. עֲנָקִים. רְפָאִים. וְכֻלְּהוּ אוֹרְכֵי יוֹמֵי. נְפִילִין אִקְרוּן בְּקַדְמֵיתָא, לְבָתַר כַּד אִתְחַבְּרוּן בִּבְנַת בְּנֵי נָשָׁא, וְאוֹלִידוּ מִנַּיְיהוּ, אִקְרוּן עֲנָקִים. לְבָתַר דַּהֲווֹ אָזְלֵי וְשָׁטָאן בְּהַאי עָלְמָא, וּמִתְרַפְּיָין מֵהַהוּא דִּלְעֵילָא, אִקְרוּן רְפָאִים.

73. Rabbi Chiya said, They were referred to by three names – *Nefilim* (lit. 'fallen ones'), *Anakim* (lit. 'giants'), *Refaim* (lit. 'lax ones') – and all of them lived long. First they were called Nefilim, the fallen, AT THE TIME THEY WERE DROPPED DOWN FROM HEAVEN. After they joined up with the daaughters of man and had children from them, THE CHILDREN were called Anakim. Later on, when they continued to spread about the world and become lax, and let go of the WORLD above, they were referred to as Refaim.

74. אָמַר ר' יְהוּדָה, וְהָא כְּתִיב הָרְפָאִים יְחוֹלָלוּ, רְפָאִים יֵחָשְׁבוּ אַף הֵם כָּעֲנָקִים. אָ"ל, הָכִי הוּא, בְּגִין דַּעֲנָקִים אָתוּ מֵהַאי סִטְרָא וּמֵהַאי סִטְרָא, וְאִתְיָאֲשׁוּ יַתִּיר בְּאַרְעָא. כְּגַוְונָא דָא רְפָאִים, וּמִנַּיְיהוּ נָפְקֵי, וַהֲווֹ אוֹרְכֵי יוֹמֵי. וְכַד מִתְחַלְּשֵׁי אִתְחֲלָשׁ פַּלְגוּת גּוּפָא, וּפַלְגוּת קַיָּים. כֵּיוָן דְּפַלְגוּת גּוּפָא הֲוָה מִית, הֲווֹ נַסְבֵּי עִשְׂבֵּי מֵעִשְׂבֵּי בָרָא וְשַׁדְיָין לְפוּמַיְיהוּ, וּמֵתוּ. וּבְגִין דְּאִינּוּן בָּעָאן לְקַטְלָא גַּרְמַיְיהוּ, אִקְרוּן רְפָאִים. אָמַר ר' יִצְחָק, שַׁדְיָין גַּרְמַיְיהוּ בְּיַמָּא רַבָּא, וְטָבְעָן וּמֵתִין. הַה"ד הָרְפָאִים יְחוֹלָלוּ מִתַּחַת מַיִם וְשׁוֹכְנֵיהֶם.

74. Rabbi Yehuda said, Behold, it is written: "The shades (Heb. *refaim*). tremble" (Iyov 26:5) and "who also were considered Refaim as the Anakim" (Devarim 2:11). HOW CAN YOU SAY THAT "REFAIM" IS FROM THE LINGUISTIC ROOT OF LAX, WEAK? RABBI CHIYA said to him: It is so. The explanation is because those giants were from two sides, MEANING FROM AN ANGELIC SOURCE AND A HUMAN FEMALE SOURCE, AND WERE MADE more hopeless TO EXIST on the earth. Similarly, the Refaim that resulted and were born FROM ANAKIM WERE EVEN MORE DESPAIRING UNTIL THEY RELEASED THEMSELVES ALTOGETHER FROM THE ABOVE and were living long lives. When they became weaker, half their body became weakened AND DIED and half their body remained LIVING – SINCE THEY WERE COMPOSED HALF OF ANGELS THAT DO NOT DIE, AND HALF OF HUMANS THAT DO EVENTUALLY DIE. When half of their body was deceased, they used to pick herbs from the wild grasses, MEANING POISONOUS HERBS, swallowed them and died. Because they wished to kill themselves, they were called Refaim, or lax ones, SINCE THEY LET THEMSELVES LOOSE FROM LIFE. Rabbi Yitzchak said, They used to throw themselves into the great sea and drown, and they died. That is what it is written: "The shades (Heb. *refaim*) tremble; the waters beneath with the inhabitants thereof."

75. ר' שִׁמְעוֹן אָמַר, אִלְמָלֵא הֲווֹ עַיְילִין יִשְׂרָאֵל לְאַרְעָא, בְּסִימָנָא דְלִישָׁנָא בִישָׁא, לָא הֲוָה קָאֵים עָלְמָא רִגְעָא חַד. מַאן אוּמָנָא דְלִישָׁנָא בִישָׁא, נָחָשׁ. וְרָזָא דְמִלָּה, מִדְּאָתָא נָחָשׁ עַל חַוָּה אַטִּיל בָּהּ זוּהֲמָא. אָמַר ר' שִׁמְעוֹן, וְעַל כֹּלָּא מָחַל קוּדְשָׁא בְּרִיךְ הוּא, בַּר מִן לִישָׁנָא בִישָׁא. בְּגִין דִּכְתִיב, אֲשֶׁר אָמְרוּ לִלְשׁוֹנֵנוּ נַגְבִּיר שְׂפָתֵינוּ אִתָּנוּ מִי אָדוֹן לָנוּ.

75. Rabbi Shimon said, Had Yisrael entered the promised land under the stigma of THE SPIES' slanderous speech, the world could not have withstood it even for a moment. Who is the artisan of slanderous speech, MEANING ITS SOURCE? The serpent. The secret of the matter is that when the serpent violated Eve, REFERRING TO THE SIN OF THE TREE OF KNOWLEDGE OF GOOD AND EVIL, he inflicted her with impurity, MEANING HIS UNCLEANNESS, FROM WHICH COME ALL HUMAN SINS. Rabbi Shimon said the Holy One, blessed be He, forgave everything except for slanderous speech, since it is written: "Who have said, 'With our tongue we will prevail; our lips are our own: who is lord over us'" (Tehilim 12:5).

76. ת"ח, כַּמָּה עָבֵד הַהוּא לִישָׁנָא בִישָׁא, גָּזַר עַל אֲבָהָתָנָא דְלָא יֵיעוּל לְאַרְעָא וּמִיתוּ אִינוּן דְּאָמְרוּ. וְאִתְגְּזַר בְּכִיָּה לְדָרֵי דָרִין. כִּבְיָכוֹל כֵּיוָן דְּאַפִּיקוּ עַל אַרְעָא קַדִּישָׁא, כְּאִילּוּ אַפִּיקוּ עֲלֵיהּ. בְּגִין כָּךְ קַנֵּי קוּדְשָׁא בְּרִיךְ הוּא עַל דָּא, וְקָאֵימוּ יִשְׂרָאֵל כֻּלְּהוּ לְאִשְׁתֵּצָאָה מֵעָלְמָא, אִלְמָלֵא בָּעוּתֵיהּ דְּמֹשֶׁה.

76. Come and see, the slanderous language OF THE SPIES caused that decree that our ancestors not enter the land. Those who spoke SLANDEROUSLY died, and weeping for generations to come was decreed, SINCE ON THE ANNIVERSARY OF THAT DATE WAS ALSO THE DESTRUCTION OF BOTH TEMPLES. It was as if, by speaking SLANDEROUSLY about the Holy Land, they spoke badly about Him. Therefore, the Holy One, blessed be He, zealous about it, and Yisrael would have perished had not Moses prevailed with his prayer.

77. וַיְסַפְּרוּ לוֹ וַיֹּאמְרוּ וְגוֹ'. אָמַר רבִּי חִיָּיא, מ"ש הָכָא וַיְסַפְּרוּ, וְלָא כְּתִיב וַיַּגִּידוּ, אוֹ וַיֹּאמְרוּ. אֶלָּא כָּל חַד אוֹלִיף מִלָּה בִּלְחוֹדוֹי. וַיַּגִּידוּ,

בְּכָל אֲתָר רֶמֶז קָא רָמִיז בְּחָכְמְתָא, וְהָא אִתְּמַר. וַיֹּאמֶר, אֲמִירָה
בְּעָלְמָא. וַיֹּאמְרוּ, הַרְהוּרָא דְלִבָּא. וַיֹּאמְרוּ, תַּפְקִידְתָּא. וְהָא אוֹקִימְנָא
בְּכַמָּה אֲתָר. וַיְסַפְּרוּ, פְּרִישׁוּתָא דְמִלָּה בְּכָל אֲתָר.

77. "And they told to him and said to him..." (Bemidbar 13:27): Rabbi Chiya said, What is the change here THAT IT IS WRITTEN: "And they told"? It is not using the words 'speak' or 'say'? HE RESPONDS: Each one interpreted the matters separately: "And spoke": wherever IT IS WRITTEN "THEY SPOKE" it is alluding to wisdom and we already learned that. "And he said" simply MEANS the thoughts of the heart IN THE SAME LINE OF SPEECH, AS IS WRITTEN: "NOW HAMAN THOUGHT (LIT. 'SAID') IN HIS HEART" (ESTER 6:6). "And they said" MEANS giving an order, as we already defined it in several places. "And they told" always MEANS relating matters, THAT EACH ONE LAID OUT HIS EXPLANATION OF THE MATTERS.

78. בָּאנוּ אֶל הָאָרֶץ, הָלַכְנוּ מִבָּעֵי לֵיהּ. אֶלָּא בָּאנוּ, עָאלָנָא לְתַמָּן
לְהַהִיא אַרְעָא דַּהֲוֵית מְשַׁבַּח בְּכָל יוֹמָא, וַהֲוֵית אַמְרַת דְּלֵית דִּכְוָותָהּ.
וְגַם זָבַת חָלָב וּדְבַשׁ הִיא. רִבִּי יִצְחָק אָמַר, מַאן דְּבָעֵי לְמֵימַר כְּדִיבָא,
אָמַר מִלָּה דִּקְשׁוֹט בְּקַדְמֵיתָא, בְּגִין דִּיְהֵימְנוּ לֵיהּ כְּדִבוֹי.

78. "We came to the land": HE ASKS: It should have said, 'We went TO THE LAND'. HE RESPONDS: Yet "we came" MEANS we entered that land that you praised daily, and said that there is nothing like it. "And indeed it flows with milk and honey" (Ibid.): Rabbi Yitzchak said, Whoever wants to lie about something starts first with some truthful matters, in order to have them believe his deceptions. THEREFORE, THEY BEGAN FIRST: "AND INDEED IT FLOWS WITH MILK AND HONEY."

79. רִבִּי חִיָּיא אָמַר, הָכִי אָמְרוּ, עָאלָנָא לְהַהִיא אַרְעָא דַּהֲוֵית מְשַׁבַּח
לָהּ כָּל יוֹמָא וְאָמְרַת דְּלֵית דִּכְוָותָהּ, גַּם זָבַת חָלָב וּדְבַשׁ הִיא, וַאֲרִימַת
שְׁבָחָא עַל כֹּלָּא. וְלָאו הָכִי, דְּהָא זֶה פִּרְיָהּ, אִתְכְּלָא חַד מֵאִינּוּן זְעִירִין
קַטְפוּ. אָמְרוּ, אִי לְדָא אַחֲסִין קוּדְשָׁא בְּרִיךְ הוּא לְיִשְׂרָאֵל, וְסָבְלוּ כָּל
אִינּוּן עֲקָתִין וְלֵיאוּתִין, הָא בְּאַרְעָא דְמִצְרַיִם אִית אִתְכְּלִין וְאֵיבִין
דְּאַרְעָא יַתִּיר, עַל חַד תְּרֵין.

79. Rabbi Chiya said, This is what they said: We came to the land which you were praising every day. You said that there is nothing like it "and indeed it flows with milk and honey," and you exaggerated its praise above all THE LANDS. It is not so, since "this is the fruit of it" (Ibid.). In fact, they cut down one of the smallest clusters AND SHOWED IT TO THEM. They said, If this is the land that the Holy One, blessed be He, wishes as an inheritance for Yisrael, and for which they suffered all these hardships and troubles, we find in the land of Egypt clusters of fruits that are doubly finer than these.

80. אֶפֶס כִּי עַז הָעָם, אוֹרְחֵיה דְּעָלְמָא דְּאִינּוּן גִּבָּרִין מַגִּיחֵי קְרָבָא יַתְבִין לְבַר, לְאִסְתַּמְּרָא אָרְחִין. וְהָכָא אֲפִילוּ אִינּוּן בְּנֵי מָתָא, תַּקִּיפִין גִּבּוֹרִין. וְהֶעָרִים בְּצוּרוֹת, דַּאֲפִילוּ כָּל מַלְכִין דְּעָלְמָא יִתְכַּנְּשׁוּ עֲלַיְיהוּ. לָא יַעַבְדוּן בְּהוּ פְּגִימוּתָא. א"ר יוֹסֵי, כָּל מַה דְּאָמְרֵי, בְּלִישָׁנָא בִּישָׁא אָמְרוּ, וְקַשְׁיָא מִכֻּלְּהוּ, דִּכְתִּיב עֲמָלֵק יוֹשֵׁב בְּאֶרֶץ הַנֶּגֶב. לְבַר נָשׁ דְּנִשָׁכֵיה חִוְיָא, כַּד בָּעָאן לְאַגְזְמָא לֵיה, אַמְרֵי הָא חִוְיָא הָכָא.

80. "But the people are strong" (Ibid. 28): THEY SAID, It is the custom of the world that the strong ones, who do battles, stay outside THE CITIES to guard the roads. Here, even the city dwellers are powerful and strong. "and the cities are fortified," even if all the kings of the world gather against them, they will not be able to make a dent in their defenses. Rabbi Yosi said, Everything they said was with evil speech, and the harshest of all is what is written: "Amalek dwells in the land of the Negev" (Ibid. 29). This is like a person who was bitten by a snake. When they wish to threaten him, they say to him, Here comes the snake.

81. ר' אַבָּא אָמַר, וַדַּאי דָא קַשְׁיָא מִכָּל מַה דְּאָמְרֵי, כְּלוֹמַר, הַהוּא דְּאַגָּח קְרָבָא בְּכֹלָּא, הָא הָכָא זַמִּין. וּבְאָן אֲתָר. בְּאֶרֶץ הַנֶּגֶב, דְּהָא הוּא אֲתָר לְאַעֲלָאָה בֵּיה. מִיַּד וַתִּשָּׂא כָּל הָעֵדָה וַיִּתְּנוּ אֶת קוֹלָם. קָבִיעוּ בְּכִיָּה לַדּוֹרוֹת, לְעָלְמִין, בְּהַהוּא לֵילְיָא.

81. Rabbi Aba said, This certainly posed more difficulty than everything else they said, meaning to say THAT THEY SAID that the one who wages battle with everyone lives here. Where? In the land of the Negev, which is an area THROUGH WHICH entrance is gained TO THE LAND. Immediately, "all the congregation lifted up their voice, and cried" (Bemidbar 14:1). They set a weeping pattern for generations to come that night, SINCE IT WAS THE EVENING OF THE NINTH OF AV, AT WHICH DATE BOTH TEMPLES WERE DESTROYED.

82. א"ר יוֹסֵי, עֵיטָא נָסִיבוּ עַל כֹּלָּא, לְאַפָּקָא שׁוּם בִּישׁ. מַאי עַל כֹּלָּא. עַל אַרְעָא, וְעַל קוּדְשָׁא בְּרִיךְ הוּא. א"ר יִצְחָק, עַל אַרְעָא תִּינַח. עַל קוּדְשָׁא בְּרִיךְ הוּא מְנַיִן. אָ"ל מַשְׁמַע דִּכְתִּיב, אֶפֶס כִּי עַז הָעָם. מַאן יָכִיל בְּהוּ. כִּי עַז הָעָם דַּיְיקָא. וּכְתִיב עֲמָלֵק יוֹשֵׁב בְּאֶרֶץ הַנֶּגֶב, כְּדֵין גָּרְמוּ כָּל הַאי, כְּמָה דְּאִתְּמַר. וּבָעָא קוּדְשָׁא בְּרִיךְ הוּא לְשֵׁיצָאָה לוֹן מִן עָלְמָא, הה"ד וַיֹּאמֶר לְהַשְׁמִידָם לוּלֵי מֹשֶׁה בְחִירוֹ עָמַד בַּפֶּרֶץ לְפָנָיו וְגוֹ'.

82. Rabbi Yosi said, They have conspired among themselves to spread an evil report about everything. What is about everything? Meaning, about the land and the Holy One, blessed be He. Rabbi Yitzchak said, about the land it is correct. About the Holy One, blessed be He, where do we know that from? He told him that is derived from what is written: "But the people are strong," MEANING TO INDICATE there might be no one who could possibly vanquish them. "The people are strong" is exact, MEANING TO SAY THAT EVEN THE HOLY ONE, BLESSED BE HE, COULD NOT GO AGAINST THEM, AND THAT IS SLANDERING THE HOLY ONE, BLESSED BE HE. It is further written: "Amalek dwells in the land of the Negev." They then caused everything, as we learned, and the Holy One, blessed be He, wished to annihilate them from the world. This is what is written: "Therefore He said that He would destroy them, had not Moses His chosen one stood before Him in the breach..." (Tehilim 106:23).

11. A man in the world is similar to above

A Synopsis
The rabbis tell us that the world was only created for the sake of
the children of Yisrael so that they could study the Torah, since
Zeir Anpin and Malchut are united through it. They compare the
body of man with its heart and brain to the body of the world.

83. וְעַתָּה יִגְדַּל נָא כֹּחַ יְיָ'. ר' אֲחָא וְר' יוֹסֵי אַמְרֵי, זַכָּאי אִינּוּן יִשְׂרָאֵל
מֵעַמִּין עכו"ם דְּעָלְמָא. דְקוּדְשָׁא בְּרִיךְ הוּא אִתְרְעֵי בְּהוּ, וְאִתְכְּנֵי בְּהוּ,
וְאִתְפָּאַר בְּהוּ, דְּהָא עָלְמָא לָא אִבְרֵי אֶלָּא בְּגִינֵיהוֹן דְּיִשְׂרָאֵל,
דְּיִשְׁתַּדְּלוּן בְּאוֹרַיְיתָא, בְּגִין דְּחַד בְּחַד אִתְקַשְׁרָן. וְיִשְׂרָאֵל לְתַתָּא בְּהַאי
עָלְמָא, אִינּוּן קִיּוּמָא דִּילֵיהּ, וְקִיּוּמָא דְּכָל שְׁאַר עַמִּין, אֵימָתַי בִּזְמַן
דְּעַבְדֵי רְעוּתָא דְּמָארֵיהוֹן.

83. "And now, I pray You, let the power of Hashem be great" (Bemidbar
14:17). Rabbi Acha and Rabbi Yosi say, Praised are Yisrael over all the
nations in the world that the Holy One, blessed be He, favored them, called
them by His Name and was glorified in them. The world was only created
for the sake of Yisrael, so they could study the Torah, since one is united
with one, MEANING ZEIR ANPIN AND MALCHUT. Yisrael below in this
world are His existence, SINCE THROUGH THEIR GOOD DEEDS THEY
ELEVATE MAYIN NUKVIN (LIT. 'FEMALE WATERS') FOR THEIR UNION.
They maintain all the nations, MEANING THEY EXIST DUE TO YISRAEL
SAKE. When is this? It is when they do their Master's will.

84. ת"ח, כַּד בָּרָא קוּדְשָׁא בְּרִיךְ הוּא בַּר נָשׁ בְּעָלְמָא, אַתְקִין לֵיהּ
בְּגַוְונָא עִלָּאָה, וְיָהַב לֵיהּ חֵילֵיהּ וְתוּקְפֵּיהּ בְּאֶמְצָעִיתָא דְּגוּפָא, דְּתַמָּן
שַׁרְיָא לִבָּא. דְּהוּא תוּקְפָּא דְּכָל גּוּפָא, וּמִתַּמָּן אִתְזָן כָּל גּוּפָא. וְהָא
לִבָּא אָחִיד וְאִתְקַף בַּאֲתָר עִלָּאָה דִּלְעֵילָא. דְּאִיהוּ מוֹחָא דְּרֵישָׁא,
דְּשָׁארֵי לְעֵילָא, וְדָא אִתְקְשַׁר בְּדָא.

84. Come and see, when the Holy One, blessed be He, created man in the
world, He prepared him in the likeness of the above. He gave him strength
and power in the midst of his body, where the heart lies, which is the

strength of the entire body. From there, the entire body is sustained and the heart is attached and strengthened in the high area above, which is the brain in the head that rests above, and one is connected to the other.

85. וּבְגַוְונָא דְּדָא, אַתְקִין קוּדְשָׁא בְּרִיךְ הוּא עָלְמָא. וְעֲבַד לֵיהּ חַד גוּפָא, וְאַתְקִין שַׁיְיפֵי דְגוּפָא סַחֲרָנֵיהּ דְּלִבָּא, וְלִבָּא שָׁארִי בְּאֶמְצָעִיתָא דְּכָל גוּפָא. וְכָל אִינּוּן שַׁיְיפִין אִתְּזָנוּ מֵהַהוּא לִבָּא, דְּהוּא תּוּקְפָּא דְּכֹלָּא, וְכֹלָּא בֵּיהּ תַּלְיָין. וְהַהוּא לִבָּא, אִתְקְשַׁר וְאִתְאֲחָד בְּמוֹחָא עִלָּאָה דְּשַׁרְיָא לְעֵילָּא.

85. In a similar pattern, the Holy One, blessed be He, has prepared the world. He made it one body and He assembled the body organs around the heart, the heart in the center of the whole body, and all the organs take their nourishment from that heart that provides the strength to all of them. Everything is dependent on it. And that heart is connected and united to the high brain that rests above, as was explained before.

12. This world is similar to those above

A Synopsis

This section tells how the Temple courts of Yisrael are inside the temple mount which is inside Jerusalem which is inside the settlement of all seventy nations which is inside the oceanic sea that God created to surround the whole inhabitable planet. The description goes deeper into the Temple treasures and the altar area and the front entrance hall and the temple and the Holy of Holies and eventually the Ark itself; here is the heart of the land and the world – from here all the organs of the body of the world get their nourishment. The heart and the brain unite. All this is parallel to the structure above in the world of Atzilut. The body organs receive from the heart and the heart receives from the brain. Next the Zohar explains the Chariot of Malchut in its three aspects. Rabbi Chiya concludes by saying that with the same measure that a person measures, he gets measured from above.

86. ת״ח, כַּד בָּרָא קוּדְשָׁא בְּרִיךְ הוּא עָלְמָא, אַשְׁרָא לְיַמָּא דְּאוֹקְיָנוּס דְּאַסְחַר כָּל יִשּׁוּבָא דְּעָלְמָא. וְיִשּׁוּבָא דְּכָל שַׁבְעִין אוּמִין כֹּלָּא אַסְחַר לִירוּשְׁלֵם. וִירוּשְׁלֵם בְּאֶמְצָעִיתָא דְּכָל יִשּׁוּבָא שַׁרְיָא. וְהִיא אַסְחָרָא לְהַר הַבַּיִת. וְהַר הַבַּיִת אַסְחַר לַעֲזָרוֹת דְּיִשְׂרָאֵל. וְאִינּוּן עֲזָרוֹת סָחֲרָן לְלִשְׁכַּת הַגָּזִית, דְּתַמָּן סַנְהֶדְרֵי גְדוֹלָה יַתְבִין. וְתָנֵינָן, לֵית יְשִׁיבָה בַּעֲזָרָה, אֶלָּא לְמַלְכֵי בֵּית דָּוִד בִּלְחוֹדַיְיהוּ.

86. Come and see, when the Holy One, blessed be He, created the world, He installed the ocean that surrounds the whole inhabitable world, and the settlement of all seventy nations surrounding Jerusalem. Jerusalem is situated in the center of all this settled area and it surrounds the Temple mount. The Temple mount surrounds all the Temple courts of Yisrael, and these Temple courts encircle the Temple treasuries for congregational sacrifices, MEANING TO SAY, IN TERMS OF IMPORTANCE, which compartments also include the seat of the high court of the Sanhedrin. We have learned that there were no seating privileges in these Temple courts, with the exception made to the kings of the house of David. IN SPITE OF ALL THESE, THEY SURROUNDED THE TEMPLE TREASURIES, WHERE THE SEAT OF THE SANHEDRIN ABIDES. AND HE COUNTS HERE SEVEN ASPECTS, ONE MORE IMPORTANT THAN THE ONE BEFORE, IN PARALLEL

WITH THE SEVEN SFIROT.

87. וְלִשְׁכַּת הַגָּזִית אַסְחַר לַמִּזְבֵּחַ. וְהַמִּזְבֵּחַ אַסְחַר לְבֵית הָאוּלָם. וְהָאוּלָם לְהֵיכָל. וְהֵיכָל לְבֵית קֹדֶשׁ הַקֳּדָשִׁים, דְּתַמָּן שְׁכִינָה שַׁרְיָא, וְכַפֹּרֶת וּכְרוּבִים וַאֲרוֹן. וְהָכָא הוּא לִבָּא, דְּכָל אַרְעָא וְעָלְמָא. וּמֵהָכָא אִתְּזָנוּ כָּל אִינּוּן אַתְרֵי דְּיִשׁוּבָא, דְּאִינּוּן שַׁיְיפֵי דְּגוּפָא. וְלִבָּא דָּא אִתְּזָן מִמּוֹחָא דְּרֵישָׁא, וְאִתְאֲחִיד דָּא בְּדָא, הַה"ד מָכוֹן לְשִׁבְתְּךָ פָּעַלְתָּ יְיָ'. כְּגַוְונָא דָּא לְעֵילָא לְעֵילָא, וְאִיהוּ בְּרָזָא דְּמַלְכָּא עִלָּאָה, בְּרָזָא יַקִּירָא סְתִימָאָה.

87. The Temple treasuries for congregational sacrifices surround the altar, and the altar area surrounds the front entrance hall. That hall surrounds the sanctuary and the sanctuary the Holy of Holies, wherein are found the Shechinah and the Ark cover and the Cherubs and the Ark. Here is the heart of the land and the world. From here, all the settled areas, which are the organs of this body – MEANING OF THE WORLD – get their nourishment. This heart, WHICH IS THE SHECHINAH, gets its nourishment from the brain in the head, WHICH IS MALCHUT OF ATZILUT, and they unite with each other. This is what is written: "In the sanctuary, Hashem, which Your hands have established" (Shemot 15:17). It is similar to this high above, IN THE WORLD OF ATZILUT, and THE HEART is in the secret of the supernal King, WHICH IS ZEIR ANPIN. THE BRAIN ABOVE IS in the secret OF THE BRAIN, the precious and concealed, MEANING THE CONCEALED BRAIN OF ARICH ANPIN, FROM WHICH ZEIR ANPIN, THE SECRET OF THE HEART, RECEIVES THROUGH ABA AND IMA.

88. יַמָּא עִלָּאָה לָקֳבֵיל דָּא. דְּאִית יַמָּא לְעֵילָא מִן יַמָּא, וְיַמָּא מִן יַמָּא. תָּא חֲזֵי, נְהַר דִּינוּר אַסְחַר לְכַמָּה מַשִׁרְיָין. מְקַבְּלֵיהּ שַׁבְעִין סְטְרִין, גְּלִיפִין מִשַּׁבְעָה דְּלִיקִין, וְאִינּוּן סָחֲרָן, לְאִינּוּן שַׁמָּשֵׁי דִּלְגוֹ מִנַּיְיהוּ. וְאִינּוּן סָחֲרִין לְאַרְבַּע רְתִיכִין. וְאִינּוּן סָחֲרָן לְהַהִיא קַרְתָּא דְּקַדִּישָׁא דִּרְבִיעָא עֲלַיְיהוּ.

88. The upper sea, WHICH IS MALCHUT OF ATZILUT, corresponds to that.

IT ALSO CONTAINS THE SAME MENTIONED THREE ASPECTS IN ITS
CHARIOT, WHICH ARE THE ASPECT OF THE BODY ORGANS, THE HEART
IN THEIR CENTER – FROM WHICH THE BODY ORGANS RECEIVE – AND
THE BRAIN IN THE HEAD, FROM WHICH THE HEART RECEIVES. There is a
sea above the sea OF THIS WORLD – MEANING TO SAY, JUST LIKE THERE
IS A SEA IN THIS WORLD, SO THERE IS ABOVE IN ATZILUT A SEA, WHICH
IS MALCHUT. There is also a sea from the sea, THERE IS ADDITIONALLY
EVEN A HIGHER SEA ABOVE THE HIGH SEA THAT IS MALCHUT, SINCE
BINAH IS ALSO CALLED SEA. NOW THE ZOHAR EXPLAINS THE CHARIOT
OF MALCHUT IN ITS THREE ASPECTS, EACH ASPECT INCLUDING SEVERAL
ASPECTS. AND HE SAYS, Come and see, the Dinur River (lit. 'of fire').
surrounds several camps OF ANGELS. Across from it emerge seventy
aspects OF ANGELS, inscribed with seven torches, WHICH ARE SEVEN
SFIROT – CHESED, GVURAH, TIFERET, NETZACH, HOD, YESOD AND
MALCHUT – OF THE FLAME OF GVURAH, WHERE EACH ONE IS
COMPRISED OF TEN THAT GUARD THE SHECHINAH. They encircle those
who serve on the interior of them, and they surround the four Chariots,
WHICH ARE THE SECRET OF THE FOUR ANGELS – MICHAEL, GABRIEL,
URIEL, RAPHAEL – WHERE EACH ONE IS COMPRISED OF THREE THAT
CARRY MALCHUT. AND UP TO HERE IS THE ASPECT OF THE BODY AND
THE EXTERIOR ASPECT OF MALCHUT. They encircle this holy city that
reclines over them, WHICH IS MALCHUT OF ATZILUT, THAT IS THE
SECRET OF THE HEART IN THEM. EXCEPT THAT SHE TOO SPLITS UP TO
SEVERAL ASPECTS, AS HE CONTINUES ON TO SAY.

89. וְתָאנָא, תַּמָּן עֲזָרוֹת לְגוֹ מֵעֲזָרוֹת. וְלֵית יְשִׁיבָה בַּעֲזָרָה דְּתַמָּן, אֶלָּא
לְמַלְכֵּיהוֹן דְּבֵית דָּוִד בִּלְחוֹדַיְיהוּ, וְתַמָּן מִשְׁתַּכְחֵי וְיָתְבֵי. וְסַהֲדָרֵי
גְדוֹלָה, מִשְׁתַּכְחֵי תַּמָּן בְּלִשְׁכַּת הַגָּזִית. וְהַהוּא בֵּי דִּינָא עֲלַיְיהוּ,
דִּמְשַׁמֵּשׁ לַאֲתַר דִּמְשַׁמֵּשׁ. וְדִינָא אִתְיְהִיב מִתַּמָּן, לְקַדִּישִׁין עֶלְיוֹנִין, עַד
דְּמָטָא לַאֲתַר דְּאִקְרֵי קֹדֶשׁ הַקֳּדָשִׁים, דְּבֵיהּ כֹּלָּא, וְתַמָּן הוּא לְבָא
שַׁרְיָיא, וְדָא אִתְזָן מִן מוֹחָא דִּלְעֵילָּא, וְאִתְאֲחִיד דָּא בְּדָא.

89. NOW HE EXPLAINS THAT MALCHUT HERSELF IS DIVIDED UP INTO
SEVERAL ASPECTS AND JUST THE INNERMOST PART, THAT IS THE HEART,
RECEIVES FROM THE BRAIN, WHICH IS ZEIR ANPIN. HE SAYS, We
learned that there, IN MALCHUT, there are Temple courts within Temple
courts. There is no seating in that court, except for the kings of the house of

David that reside and sit there, MEANING TO SAY THAT THE KINGS OF THE HOUSE OF DAVID ARE ATTACHED TO IT. The High Court of the Sanhedrin is located in the Treasury Chambers, and the courthouse above them that serves that place, MEANING TO SAY THAT THEY ARE SERVING MALCHUT EXCLUSIVELY AND NOTHING OF THEM IS CARRIED FURTHER DOWN FOR THE LOWER GRADES. Judgment is carried from there to the uppermost holy, MEANING TO SAY THAT THE JUDGMENTS IN THERE THAT FLOW DOWN OVER THE HEADS OF THE WICKED ALONE ARE CONCEIVABLE TO THE MOST HOLY IN THE SECRET MEANING OF WHAT IS WRITTEN: "AND THEY SHALL GO FORTH, AND LOOK UPON THE CARCASSES OF THE MEN..." (YESHAYAH 66:24) until it reaches the area considered the Holy of Holies, WHICH IS THE INNERMOST INTERIOR OF MALCHUT; THAT IS, YESOD OF HER GREATNESS in which everything exists. The heart lies there – that is, the one which is nourished from the upper brain – WHICH IS ZEIR ANPIN, and they unite with each other.

90. כְּגַוְונָא דָא לְעֵילָא לְעֵילָא, וְאִיהוּ בְּרָזָא דְמַלְכָּא עִלָּאָה, בְּרָזָא יַקִּירָא סְתִימָאָה. עַד דְּאִשְׁתְּכַח, דְּכֹלָא אִתְּזָן מִמּוֹחָא עִלָּאָה, סְתִימָאָה דְּכֹלָא. וְכַד יִסְתַּכְּלוּן מִלֵּי, כֹּלָא אִתְקְשַׁר דָּא בְּדָא וְדָא בְּדָא.

90. HE RETURNS TO THE MATTERS MENTIONED AND DEFINES THEM MORE THOROUGHLY. It is similar up above, IN ATZILUT; and this, THE HEART, accords with the secret meaning of the supernal King THAT IS ZEIR ANPIN, AND THE BRAIN with the secret of the precious concealed BRAIN OF ARICH ANPIN FROM WHICH ZEIR ANPIN RECEIVES THROUGH ABA AND IMA. Consequently, everything is nourished from the higher brain OF ARICH ANPIN, that is hidden from everything. When attention is paid to these matters, IT IS APPARENT that all things are connected to each other.

91. ת"ח, כַּד אַנְהִיר עַתִּיקָא סְתִימָא בְּמוֹחָא, וּמוֹחָא אַנְהִיר לְלִבָּא, בְּדֶרֶךְ נֹעַם יְיָ'. וְהָא אוֹקִימְנָא, וְדָא הוּא כֹּחַ יְיָ'. הַהוּא חֵילָא דְּאָתֵי מֵעַתִּיקָא קַדִּישָׁא. סְתִימָא דְּכָל סְתִימִין. יִגְדַּל נָא, דְּיִתְרַבֵּי וְיִסְגֵּי לְעֵילָא לְעֵילָא. וְיִתְנְגִיד וְיִתְמְשַׁךְ לְתַתָּא. כַּאֲשֶׁר דִּבַּרְתָּ, כְּמָה דְּאוּקְמוּהָ. לֵאמֹר, לְמֵילַף מֵהָכָא כָּל דָּרִין בַּתְרָאִין, לְעָלַם וּלְעָלְמֵי עָלְמִין. לֵאמֹר, לְמֵימַר לְדָא בְּשַׁעֲתָא דְעָקְתָא. לְמֵימַר דָּא, בְּשַׁעֲתָא

-59-

דִּרְוָוחָא. וּמַאי הוּא. יְיָ' אֶרֶךְ אַפַּיִם וְגוֹ', וְהָא אוֹקִימְנָא מִלֵּי.

91. Come and see: When the concealed Atika – THAT IS THE CONCEALED BRAIN OF ARICH ANPIN – shines in the brain – THAT IS ABA – then the brain illuminates the heart – THAT IS ZEIR ANPIN – in the pleasant path of Hashem; THAT IS, THROUGH BINAH CALLED THE PLEASANTNESS OF HASHEM. We have explained that this is "the power of Hashem" (Bemidbar 14:17). Meaning that power flows from Atika Kadisha, who is the most concealed. "Be great" (Ibid.) MEANS that it will grow and increase high above and flow and run down. "According as you have spoken" (Ibid.) is as was explained THAT HE IS LONGSUFFERING BOTH TO THE JUST AND THE WICKED. "Saying" (Ibid.), meaning that the later generations should take lessons from this forever and meaning that they should mention this in times of trouble, and say it in times of abundance. Say what? That is: "Hashem is longsuffering..." (Ibid. 18), and we have already defined these things.

92. אָמַר ר' יִצְחָק, אֱמֶת אֲמַאי סָלִיק מִכָּאן. אָמַר רַבִּי חִיָּיא, אִינּוּן גָּרְמוּ לֵיהּ דְּאִסְתָּלִיק מִכָּאן, דְּהָא בְּשִׁקְרוּ דִּבְרוּ גַּרְמַיְיהוּ בְּהַהוּא מִדָּה דִּב"נ מוֹדֵד בָּהּ, מוֹדְדִין לֵיהּ. וְכֵן שְׁאַר אָחֲרֵי אִסְתְּלָקוּ, דְּלָא יָכִיל מֹשֶׁה לְמֵימְרִינְהוּ, בְּגִין דְּאִינּוּן גָּרְמוּ. סָלַחְתִּי כִּדְבָרֶיךָ, כִּדְבָרֶיךָ מַמָּשׁ, וְהָא אִתְּעֲרוּ חַבְרַיָּיא, וְהָא אִתְּמַר.

92. Rabbi Yitzchak said, Why is "truth" missing here, MEANING THAT "AND ABUNDANT IN LOVE AND TRUTH" (SHEMOT 34:6), IS NOT MENTIONED HERE AS IT IS MENTIONED AT THE THIRTEEN MEASURES IN THE PORTION OF KI TISA. Rabbi Chiya said, THE SPIES caused it to be removed from here – HASHEM AND TRUTH – since they carried on with deception, and with the same measure that a person measures, he is measured FROM ABOVE. Likewise, the other measures were gone, so that Moses could not mention them, SINCE WE FIND HERE ONLY NINE MEASURES OF COMPASSION AND NOT THIRTEEN. This was brought about BY THE SPIES. "I have pardoned according to your word" (Bemidbar 14:20). means actually your word. This was already commented on by the friends and we have learned it.

13. The head of the Yeshivah (Torah academy)

A Synopsis

This section records the start of a supernal experience of the rabbis. They hear a mysterious saying that is eventually explained to them. They heard a voice saying that whoever stops shall be stopped, whoever curtails shall be curtailed and whoever curtails shall be prolonged. The rabbis hear many secrets and are then deemed worthy of going to a higher level. They are given a rose and inhale its fragrance, as the illumination of wisdom is called scent. They learn from the Mishnah scholars thirty laws that they hadn't known and other secret meanings in the Torah. They see people digging graves and dying and immediately reincarnating with bright holy bodies. They hear another set of riddles full of hidden meanings. We hear of the heads of the Yeshivot and how they travel with Aaron and fly like eagles to the Yeshivah of light, the Yeshivah of Moses. The face of Moses is radiant so that it cannot be looked upon, and there is a curtain between him and the wise men. Acting as an intermediary, Aaron takes Moses' explanations to the heads of the Yeshivot. We also hear how all the virtuous women of the desert generation came to Miriam to study about God. The generation of the desert is the most blessed because they left the Yeshivah of Moses and flew to the Yeshivah of the firmament, Metatron; those who are worthy take flight to the highest Yeshivah, the Yeshivah of God.

93. דָּא עִם דָּא, מַה דְּלָא הֲווֹ יַכְלִין לְמַלְּלָא מִקַּדְמַת דְּנָא. נַפְקוּ מֵהַהִיא פִּתְחָא, וְיָתְבוּ בְּגִנְתָּא תְּחוֹת אִילָנִין. אָמְרוּ דָּא לְדָא, כֵּיוָן דַּאֲנָן הָכָא, וְחָמֵינָן כָּל דָּא, אִי נְמוּת הָכָא, וַדַּאי נֵיעוּל לְעָלְמָא דְּאָתֵי. יָתְבוּ. שִׁינָתָא נַפְלַת עֲלַיְיהוּ. וְדָמְכוּ. אַדְּהָכִי, הָא הַהוּא מְמָנָא אָתָא, וְאִתְּעַר לוֹן, אָמַר לוֹן, קוּמוּ פוּקוּ לְגוֹ פַּרְדֵּס דְּאַבְרָא. נַפְקוּ, חָמוּ לְאִלֵּין מָארֵי מִקְרָא, דַּהֲווֹ אַמְרֵי בְּהַהוּא קְרָא, בַּמִּדְבָּר הַזֶּה יִתַּמּוּ, הָא בַּאֲתַר אַחֲרָא לָא. וְשָׁם יָמוּתוּ, הָא בַּאֲתַר אַחֲרָא לָא, וְדָא בְּגוּפִין, אֲבָל בְּנִשְׁמָתִין לָא, כְּגַוְונָא דִּבְנֵי גִנְתָּא.

93. THE BEGINNING OF THIS ARTICLE IS MISSING. They spoke with each other what they could not speak before this. They emerged from that opening and sat in the garden underneath the trees. They said to each other, Since we were here and saw all this, if we die here, we will most certainly

attain the World to Come. They sat down. A sleep fell upon them. In the meanwhile, the one appointed came and woke them up. He told them to get up and go into the orchard outside, MEANING TO THE EXTERIOR LEVEL. They went out. They noticed the scholars of the scriptures, who talked of this verse: "In this wilderness shall they be consumed" (Bemidbar 14:35), but not in another place, THAT IS, THEY WILL MERIT THE WORLD TO COME. "And there they shall die" (Ibid.), but not in another place, MEANING THAT THEY WILL HAVE THE LIFE OF THE WORLD TO COME. That concerns the bodies – THAT EVEN IN THIS WORLD, THEY WILL ONLY DIE FROM THE ASPECT OF THE BODY – but not the souls, WHICH WILL BE similar to the denizens of the Garden, MEANING THE SOULS WILL MERIT THE GARDEN OF EDEN.

94. אָמַר לוֹן הַהוּא מְמָנָא, פּוּקוּ. נָפְקוּ בַּהֲדֵיהּ, אָמַר לוֹן, שְׁמַעְתּוּן מִדֵּי לְגוֹ הַהוּא דַּרְגָּא. אָמְרוּ, שְׁמַעְנָא דְּהָא חַד קָלָא הֲוָה אָמַר, מַאן דְּפָסַק, יִתְפְּסַק. מַאן דְּקָצַר, יִתְקְצַר. מַאן דְּקָצַר, יִתְאֲרַךְ. אָמַר לוֹן, יְדַעְתּוּן מַאי הַאי. אָמְרוּ לָא. אָמַר לוֹן, חֲמִיתּוּן הַהוּא נִשְׁרָא רַבְרְבָא, וְהַהוּא יְנוֹקָא דְּקָא מְלַקֵּט עֲשָׂבִין, ר' אִילָאִי דִּנְצִיבִין הֲוָה. הוּא וּבְרֵיהּ, וּמָטָא הָכָא, וְחָמָא הוּא וִינוֹקָא בְּרֵיהּ מְעַרְתָּא דָּא, כֵּיוָן דְּעָאלוּ לְגוֹ חֲשׁוּךְ, לָא יָכִילוּ לְמִסְבַּל, וּמִיתוּ.

94. The appointed one told them to leave. They left with him. He asked them, Did you hear something on that level? They said, We heard that a voice was saying that whoever stops shall be stopped, whoever curtails shall be curtailed and whoever curtails shall be prolonged. He said to them, Do you understand what this means? They said no. He said to them, Did you see that great eagle and that child that picks grasses? This was Rabbi Ila'i from Netzivin, he and his son. They arrived here and they saw him and his boy and this cave. As soon as they entered into this darkness, they were not able to stand it and died.

95. וְהַהוּא יְנוֹקָא בְּרֵיהּ, קַיְימָא בְּכָל יוֹמָא קַמֵּיהּ דִּבְצַלְאֵל, בְּשַׁעֲתָא דְּנָחִית מִמְּתִיבְתָּא עִלָּאָה, וְאָמַר קַמֵּיהּ תְּלַת מִלִּין, עַד לָא יִפְתַּח בְּצַלְאֵל בְּרָזִין סְתִימִין דְּחָכְמְתָא, דְּכָל מִלּוֹי רָזִין סְתִימִין אִינּוּן, דְּעַיִן לֹא רָאָתָה אֱלֹהִים זוּלָתְךָ. הַאי דְּאָמַר, מַאן דְּפָסַק יִתְפְּסַק. מַאן דְּפָסַק

מִלִּין דְּאוֹרַיְיתָא, עַל מִלִּין בְּטֵלִין, יִתְפַּסְקוּן חַיּוֹהִי מֵהַאי עָלְמָא, וְדִינֵיהּ
קַיְּימָא בְּהַהוּא עָלְמָא. מַאן דְּקָצַר יִתְקְצַר, מַאן דְּקָצַר אָמֵן, וְלָא
מַאֲרִיךְ בֵּיהּ גּוֹ נַיְיחָא, יִתְקְצַר מֵחַיִּין דְּהַאי עָלְמָא. מַאן דְּקָצַר יִתְאֲרָךְ,
מַאן דְּאָמַר אֶחָד, אִצְטְרִיךְ לְחַטְפָא אָלֶף, וּלְקַצְרָא קְרִיאָה דִּילֵהּ, וְלָא
יְעַכֵּב בְּהַאי אָת כְּלָל. וּמַאן דְּעָבֵיד דָּא, יִתְאַרְכוּן חַיּיו.

95. That child, his son, stands daily in front of Betzalel, when he descends from his high Yeshivah, and says to him three things, prior to Betzalel's divulgence of the concealed secrets of wisdom. All his sayings are concealed secrets, since "neither has the eye seen, that Elohim, beside You" (Yeshayah 64:3). That is what is said: 'Whoever stops, shall be stopped meaning that whoever ceases from the sayings of Torah in order to speak of vain matters, his life will be ended from this world. His judgment remains for the World to Come. 'Whoever curtails shall be curtailed' means that whoever cuts short the Amen and does not extend it leisurely, BUT SAYS IT ABRUPTLY, shall have his life shortened in this world. Whoever curtails shall be prolonged means that whoever said *Echad* (Eng. 'one') must hurry with the Aleph OF *ECHAD* and shorten its pronunciation, and not dally with this letter at all. Whoever acts this way shall have his life extended.

96. אָמְרוּ לֵיהּ, תּוּ אָמַר, תְּרֵין אִינּוּן, וַחֲדָא אִשְׁתְּתַּף בְּהוּ, וְאִינּוּן
תְּלָתָא. וְכַד הֲווֹ תְּלָתָא, אִינּוּן חַד. אָמַר לוֹן, אִלֵּין תְּרֵין שְׁמָהָן דִּשְׁמַע
יִשְׂרָאֵל, דְּאִינּוּן יְיָ' יְיָ'. אֱלֹהֵינוּ אִשְׁתְּתַּף בְּהוּ, וְאִיהוּ חוֹתָמָא
דְּגוּשְׁפַּנְקָא, אֱמֶת. וְכַד מִתְחַבְּרָן כַּחֲדָא אִינּוּן חַד בְּיִחוּדָא חֲדָא.

96. They said to him: He further said: They are two and one joins them. They become three and when they are three, they are one. He told them, These are the two names, Yud Hei Vav Hei and Yud Hei Vav Hei in Sh'ma Yisrael (the Kriat Sh'ma). "Our Elohim" was united with them and that is the seal of the ring, truth. When they are joined together, they are one in one union.

97. תּוּ אָמַר, תְּרֵין אִינּוּן וְחַד אִתְהַדָּר. כַּד שַׁלִּיט. טָאס עַל גַּדְפֵי רוּחָא,
וְשָׁאט בִּמְאתָן אָלַף, וְאִתְטָמַּר. אָמַר לוֹן, אִלֵּין תְּרֵין כְּרוּבִים, דְּהֲוָה

רָכִיב בְּהוּ קוּדְשָׁא בְּרִיךְ הוּא. וּמִן יוֹמָא דְּאַגְנִיז יוֹסֵף מֵאֲחוֹי, אַגְנִיז חַד,
וְאִשְׁתְּאַר חַד לְגַבֵּי בִּנְיָמִין, הה"ד וַיִּרְכַּב עַל כְּרוּב וַיָּעֹף וַיֵּדֶא עַל כַּנְפֵי
רוּחַ. וְאַגְנִיז בְּמָאתָן אֶלֶף עָלְמִין וְאִתְטַמַּר, הַהוּא דְּרָכִיב עָלֵיה, דְּאִינוּן
מָאתָן אֶלֶף גְּנִיזִין, אִינוּן דִּילֵיה, בְּרִיךְ הוּא.

97. He said more: They are two and to one he returned. When he dominates, he flies on the wings of the wind and loiters and wanders into a group of two hundred thousand ones and hides there. He said to them, These are the two Cherubs upon which the Holy One, blessed be He, was riding. From the day that Joseph was hidden from his brothers, one was stored away and one remained with Benjamin as it is written: "And He rode upon the Cherub, and did fly: He soared on the wings of the wind" (Tehilim 18:11). AND WHAT HE SAID, And was hidden in two hundred thousand and was hidden, that refers to the one who rides on it, THAT IS CONCEALED IN TWO HUNDRED THOUSAND, that those two hundred thousand that are stored away are His, blessed is He.

98. פּוּקוּ מֵהָכָא, זַכָּאִין אַתּוּן, נַפְקוּ, יָהַב לוֹן הַהוּא מְמָנָא וַורְדָּא חֲדָא
וְנַפְקוּ. כַּד נָפְקוּ אַסְתִּים פּוּם מְעַרְתָּא, וְלָא אִתְחֲזֵי כְּלַל. חָמוּ הַהוּא
נִשְׁרָא, דְּהֲוָה נָחִית מֵהַהוּא אִילָנָא, וְעָאל גּוֹ מְעַרְתָּא אַחֲרָא. אַרְחוּ
אִינוּן בְּהַהוּא וַורְדָּא, וְעָאלוּ תַּמָּן, אַשְׁכָּחוּ הַהוּא נִשְׁרָא אַפּוּם מְעַרְתָּא,
אָמַר לוֹן עוּלוּ זַכָּאֵי קְשׁוֹט חַבְרִין, דְּהָא לָא חֲמֵינָא חֶדְוָה דְּחַבְרוּתָא,
מִן יוֹמָא דַּאֲנָא הָכָא, אֶלָּא בְּכוּ.

98. THE APPOINTED ONE told them, Go out from here. You are righteous AND DESERVING A HIGHER LEVEL. They emerged. The appointed one presented them with a lily, WHICH IS THE SECRET OF MALCHUT IN THE ASPECT OF LOWER CHOCHMAH and they left. When they left, the opening of the cave was shut and was not visible at all. They noticed the eagle, WHICH IS THE SECRET OF THE FACE OF AN EAGLE, which descended from a tree and entered into a different cave. They inhaled the scent of the lily, AS THE ILLUMINATION OF CHOCHMAH IS CALLED SCENT, and entered there. They discovered the eagle on the mouth of the cave. He told them, Enter friends, the truly righteous, since I have not felt the gladness of having company since the day that I have been here, except through you.

99. עָאלוּ מָאטוּ לְפַּרְדֵּס אַחֲרָא, וְהַהוּא נִשְׁרָא בַּהֲדַיְיהוּ, כַּד מָטוּ לְגַבֵּי אִינּוּן מָארֵיהוֹן דְּמַשְׁנָה, אִתְהַדָּר הַהוּא נִשְׁרָא בְּדִיּוּקְנָא דְּאָדָם, בִּלְבוּשׁ יְקָר, מְנַהֲרָא כְּוָותַיְיהוּ, וְיָתִיב עִמְּהוֹן כַּחֲדָא, אָמַר לְאִינּוּן דְּיַתְבֵי, הָבוּ יְקָר לְמָארֵי מַתְנִיתָא דְּאָתוּ הָכָא, דְּהָא מָארֵיהוֹן אַחֲמֵי לוֹן פְּלִיאָן רַבְרְבָן הָכָא. אָמַר חַד מִנַּיְיהוּ, אִית בְּכוּ סִימָנָא. אָמְרוּ הִין. אַפִּיקוּ תְּרֵין וְרָדִין, וְאָרַחוּ בְּהוּ. אָמְרוּ, תִּיבוּ מָארֵי מְתִיבְתָּא, תִּיבוּ זַכָּאֵי קְשׁוֹט, אֲחִידוּ בְּהוּ, וְיָתְבוּ. בְּהַהִיא שַׁעֲתָא, אוֹלִיפוּ תַּמָּן תְּלָתִין הֲלָכוֹת, דְּלָא הֲווֹ יַדְעֵי מִקַּדְמַת דְּנָא, וְרָזִין אַחֲרָנִין דְּאוֹרַיְיתָא.

99. They entered another orchard, MEANING TO ANOTHER LEVEL, and the eagle was with them, THAT IS THE SECRET OF THE FACE OF AN EAGLE. When they arrived at those scholars of the Mishnah, the eagle converted back to the shape of a man, MEANING TO THE SECRET OF THE FACE OF A MAN with a precious glowing robe like them, and sat together with them. He said to THE MISHNAH SCHOLARS that were seated, Give honor to the Mishnah scholars that arrived here, since their Master shows them great wonders. One of them said to them, Have you a sign THAT YOU ARE WORTHY OF BEING HERE? They replied, Yes. They slipped out two lilies and smelled them, THEREBY ALLUDING TO MALCHUT AND BINAH THAT ARE COMBINED TOGETHER IN THE SECRET OF THE TWO LILLIES. They said, Be seated, heads of the Yeshivah. Be seated, truly righteous men. They held on to them and they sat. At that time, they learned from them thirty Halachot (lit. 'laws') that they did not know of before, and other secret meanings in the Torah.

100. אַהֲדרוּ לְגַבֵּי אִינּוּן מָארֵי מִקְרָא, אַשְׁכָּחוּ דַּהֲווֹ אַמְרֵי, אֲנִי אָמַרְתִּי אֱלֹהִים אַתֶּם וּבְנֵי עֶלְיוֹן כֻּלְּכֶם. אֲנִי אָמַרְתִּי, בְּשַׁעֲתָא דְּאַקְדִּימְתּוּן עֲשִׂיָּה לַשְׁמִיעָה. דְּהָא אֱלֹהִים אַתֶּם וְגוֹ'. כֵּיוָן דְּאַמְשִׁכְתּוּן בָּתַר יֵצֶר הָרָע, אָכֵן כְּאָדָם תְּמוּתוּן וְגוֹ'. מַה מִיתָתוֹ שֶׁל אָדָם אָחִית לֵיהּ לְעַפְרָא, בְּגִין דְּיִתְמַחֵי הַהוּא יֵצֶר הָרָע דִּי בְּגַוֵּיהּ, וְהַהוּא יֵצֶר הָרָע אִיהוּ דְּמִית, וְאִתְעֲכַל בְּגַוֵּיהּ.

100. They then returned to the scholars of the scripture, and they found them studying and saying: "I had said, 'You are angels (Heb. *Elohim*), all of

you sons of the most High'" (Tehilim 82:6), MEANING "I had said" during the time when you acted before listening, for "You are Elohim..." However, since you were drawn after your Evil Inclination, "nevertheless, you shall die like a man..." (Ibid. 7), just like the death of man brings him to dust in order to erase the Evil Inclination in his corpse. It is that Evil Inclination that dies and decays within.

101. אָמַר הַהוּא סָבָא דְּעָלַיְיהוּ, אוֹף הָכָא כְּתִיב, וּפִגְרֵיכֶם אַתֶּם יִפְּלוּ בַּמִּדְבָּר הַזֶּה. מַאי פִּגְרֵיכֶם. דָּא יֵצֶר הָרָע, כָּלִיל דְּכַר וְנוּקְבָּא. חֶסְרוֹנִין דְּאִית בְּכוּ, דְּיֵצֶר הָרָע נָחִית תָּדִיר לְחֶסְרוֹנָא, וְלָא סָלִיק. בַּקֹדֶשׁ מַעֲלִין וְלָא מוֹרִידִין, בִּמְסָאֲבוּ מוֹרִידִין תָּדִיר, וְלָא מַעֲלִין. וע״ד אִקְרוּן פִּגְרֵיכֶם, חֶסְרוֹנִין דִּלְכוֹן. כד״א אֲשֶׁר פִּגְּרוּ מֵעֲבוֹר אֶת הַנַּחַל וְגו׳, סוֹפָא דִּקְרָא אוֹכַח, דִּכְתִיב יִפְּלוּ, וְלָא תִּפְּלוּ. וע״ד, בַּמִּדְבָּר הַזֶּה יִתַּמּוּ אִינּוּן פְּגָרִים וְשָׁם יָמוּתוּ, בְּגִין דִּרְעוּתָא דְּקוּדְשָׁא בְּרִיךְ הוּא לְשֵׁיצָאָה לְהַנֵּי פְּגָרִים מֵעָלְמָא, לְעָלַם.

101. The older man in charge over them said, It is also written here: "But as for you, your carcasses (Heb. *pigreichem*) shall fall in this wilderness" (Bemidbar 14:32). IF IT WAS JUST THE DEMISE OF THE BAD INCLINATION, what is the meaning of "your carcasses" IN PLURAL FORM? IT IS ONE EVIL INCLINATION THAT APPLIES TO ALL OF THEM. HE RESPONDS: That Evil Inclination is combined of male and female, AND "YOUR CARCASSES" MEANS the things lacking in you, since the Evil Inclination IS CALLED LACK, AS IT always descends to an area that is lacking IN THE PERSON and does not ascend. Hence, we always promote things pertaining to holiness, not to decrease. In defilement, there is always a decrease and never an increase. Therefore, THE EVIL INCLINATION IS REFERRED TO AS, "your carcasses," MEANING those things lacking within you, as is written: "Who were too weak (Heb. *pigru*) to go over the wadi" (I Shmuel 30:10). The final sequence of the verse is proof THAT IT REFERS TO THE EVIL INCLINATION, since it is written: "(they) shall fall" (Bemidbar 14:39) and IT IS not WRITTEN: '(you) shall fall'. So, too, "in this wilderness they shall be consumed" (Ibid. 35) these carcasses, MEANING, THE EVIL INCLINATIONS, "and there they shall die," since it is the wish of the Holy One, blessed be He, to eliminate these carcasses from the world forever.

102. אָמַר לְהוּ רִבִּי אִילָאִי, זַכָּאֵי קְשׁוֹט, עוּלוּ וְתֶחֱמוּ, דְּהָא רְשׁוּ
אִתְמְסַר לְכוּ, לְמֵיעַל עַד הַהוּא אֲתָר דְּפָרוֹכְתָּא פְּרִיסָא. זַכָּאָה
חוּלָקְכוֹן. קָמוּ וְעָאלוּ גוֹ דוּכְתָּא חֲדָא, וַהֲווֹ תַּמָּן מָארֵיהוֹן דְּאַגָּדָה,
וְאַנְפַּיְיהוֹן מְנַהֲרָן כְּנְהִירוּ דְּשִׁמְשָׁא. אָמְרוּ מַאן אִלֵּין. אָמַר לְהוֹן, אִלֵּין
מָארֵיהוֹן דְּאַגָּדָה. וְחָמָאן בְּכָל יוֹמָא נְהִירוּ דְּאוֹרַיְיתָא כִּדְקָא יֵאוֹת.
קַיְימוּ, וּשְׁמָעוּ כַּמָה מִלִּין חַדְתִּין בְּאוֹרַיְיתָא, וְלָא אִתְיְהִיב לוֹן רְשׁוּ
לְמֵיעַל לְגַוַוייהוּ.

102. Rabbi Ila'i said to them: truly righteous men, enter and see, since permission is given to you to proceed to the area where the veil is spread. Praised is your lot. They rose and entered a place where there were scholars of Agadah, whose faces were bright as the sunlight. They said: Who are these? He said to them: These are the Agadah scholars, and they properly see the light of the Torah, daily. They remained and listened to several new illuminations in the Torah, but were not given authority to join with them.

103. אָ"ל ר' אִילָאִי, עוּלוּ לְדוּכְתָּא אַחֲרָא וְתֶחֱמוּ. עָאלוּ לְגוֹ גִּנְתָּא
אַחֲרָא, וְחָמוּ אוֹף הָכִי כְּרָאן קִבְרִין, וּמִיַּד מֵתִין. וּמִתְהַדְּרִין חַיִּין בְּגוּפִין
מְנַהֲרָן קַדִּישִׁין. אָמְרֵי לֵיהּ, מַאי הַאי. אָ"ל, דָּא עַבְדֵי בְּכָל יוֹמָא, וּמִיַּד
דְּשַׁכְבֵי מִתְעַכְּבְלָא הַהוּא זוּהֲמָא בִּישָׁא דְּקַבִּילוּ בְּקַדְמֵיתָא, וְקָיְימִין מִיַּד
בְּגוּפִין חַדְתִּין מְנַהֲרִין, בְּאִינּוּן גוּפִין קַדִּישִׁין דְּקָיְימֵי עַל טוּרָא דְּסִינַי,
כְּגַוְונָא דְּאַתּוּן חָמָאן, קַיְימוּ כֻּלְּהוּ עַל טוּרָא דְּסִינַי, בְּגוּפִין בְּלָא לִכְלוּכָא
כְּלָל, כֵּיוָן דְּאַמְשִׁיכוּ עֲלַיְיהוּ יצה"ר, אִתְהַדְּרוּ בְּגוּפִין אַחֲרָנִין, דְּגוּפִין
קַדְמָאִין, גוּפִין נוּכְרָאִין, הה"ד וַיִּתְנַצְּלוּ בְנֵי יִשְׂרָאֵל אֶת עֶדְיָם מֵהַר
חוֹרֵב.

103. Rabbi Ila'i told them to enter another area and look around. They entered into another garden and also saw, BESIDES OTHER THINGS, people digging graves. Immediately they die, and immediately reincarnate with bright holy bodies, SINCE THESE WERE THE DECEASED OF THE DESERT. They said to him, What is this? He replied to them, They do this every day and, when they die, the evil filth which they received before immediately decays. They quickly rise up with bright new bodies, with these holy bodies that they had when they stood on Mount Sinai, exactly as you see THEM, since all stood on Mount Sinai with bodies totally free of dirt. As soon as they drew upon themselves the Evil Inclination, they again had other bodies other than the bodies they had prior to that, strange bodies – MEANING THAT THE FILTH OF THE SERPENT WAS AGAIN UPON THEM. About this, it is written: "And the children of Yisrael stripped themselves of their ornaments by the Mount Horeb" (Shemot 33:6).

104. קָלָא אִתְּעַר, זִילוּ אִתְכְּנָשׁוּ, הָא אָהֳלִיאָב קָאִים עַל קִיּוּמֵיהּ, וְכָל אִינּוּן קַתֶּדְרָאִין קַמֵּיהּ. לְשַׁעֲתָא פַּרְחוּ כֻּלְּהוּ, וְלָא חָמוּ מִדִי, אִשְׁתְּאָרוּ בִּלְחוֹדַיְיהוּ תְּחוֹת אִילָנִין דְּגִנְּתָא. חָמוּ פִּתְחָא אַחֲרָא, עָאלוּ תַּמָּן, חָמוּ הֵיכְלָא חֲדָא, עָאלוּ וְיָתִיבוּ תַּמָּן. תְּרֵין עוּלֵימִין הֲווֹ תַּמָּן. זָקְפוּ עַיְינִין, וְחָמוּ חַד מַשְׁכְּנָא מְרֻקְמָא בְּכָל זִינֵי צִיּוּרִין וּגְוָונִין דְּעָלְמָא, וַעֲלֵיהּ פָּרֵיס פְּרִיסָא דִּנְהוֹרָא מְנַצְצָא, דְּלָא יַכְלִין עַיְינִין לְאִסְתַּכְּלָא, מִתַּמָּן וּלְהָלְאָה לָא חָמוּ כְּלוּם.

104. A voice stirred and said, Go and congregate there. Aholiav stands on his spot and there are chairs before him. Suddenly, everything disappeared and they saw nothing. They remained alone under the trees in the garden. They noticed another door. They entered there, saw a chamber and sat down there. There were two youths there. They raised their eyes and saw a dwelling that was embroidered in all the kinds of artistry and colors existing in the world. On it was spread a curtain of sparkling light, at which the eyes were not able to gaze. Beyond that, they saw nothing.

105. אַרְכִּינוּ אוּדְנִין, וְשָׁמְעוּ חַד קָלָא דַּהֲוָה אָמַר, בְּצַלְאֵל רְבִיעָאָה אִיהוּ לִנְהוֹרִין עִלָּאִין. יוֹסֵף רְבִיעָאָה אִיהוּ גּוֹ נְהוֹרִין דְּאָדָם קַדְמָאָה. סְלִיקוּ דִּלְעֵילָּא, חֲבִיבָא דְּכֹלָּא. עֲלֵיהּ כְּתִיב, וַנִסְכּוּ רְבִיעִית הַהִין בַּקֹּדֶשׁ וְגוֹ'. מַאן דְּיִסְתְּכַּל וְחָמֵי, יִסְמוּן עֵינֵיהּ. מַאן דְּלָא יִסְתְּכַּל, חָמֵי וְאִתְפְּתַח. אִילָנָא דְּתַמָּנֵי סְרֵי, כַּד כָּפִיף, יִזְקוֹף וְיִתְקַיָּים. אִי לָא כָּפִיף, חִוְיָא בִּישָׁא אָכִיל לֵיהּ. מַאן דְּעָאל תְּרֵין כְּרוּבִין לְגוֹ, רְעוּתֵיהּ אִתְעֲבֵיד. מַאן דִּמְעַיֵּין, רָחִיק מִרְעוּתֵיהּ. קָרְבְּנָא דְּרַבְיָא, שְׁלִים לְאִתְקַבְּלָא. פָּסַק הַהוּא קָלָא.

105. They inclined their ears and heard a voice that was saying, Betzalel is the fourth to the supernal lights. Joseph is the fourth in the lights of Adam. HE IS the elevation above, most beloved of all. About him, the verse is written: "And its drink offering shall be the fourth part of a hin...in the holy place..." (Bemidbar 28:7). Whoever gazes and looks, his eyes will be blinded. Whoever does not gaze will be open-eyed and see. A tree of eighteen, when it bends itself, will return upright and endure. If it does not bend itself, the evil snake will consume it. Whoever enters two Cherubs forward, his wish will be accomplished. Whoever contemplates is far from his will. The offering of a youth is perfect to be accepted. And the voice stopped. ALL THOSE POINTS WILL BE EXPLAINED IN THE ZOHAR FURTHER ON.

106. אָמְרוּ אִינּוּן תְּרֵין עוּלֵימִין, סִימָנָא אִית בְּגַוַויְיכוּ. אָמְרוּ הִין. אֲפִיקוּ אִינּוּן תְּרֵין וְרָדִין, אַרְחוּ בְּהוּ, אָמְרוּ תִּיבוּ, עַד דְּתִשְׁמְעוּן תְּרֵין מִלִּין, בְּרָזִין עַתִּיקִין, מִגּוֹ מָארֵי מְתִיבְתָּא, וְיהוֹן תָּדִיר בְּרָזָא בְּגַוַויְיכוּ. אָמְרוּ הֵן.

106. Those two youths asked, Have you a sign with you? They answered, Yes. They took out the two lilies and smelled them. They were told to be seated while they heard two of the ancient secrets from the head of the Yeshivah, which they shall keep forever secret. They agreed.

107. אָמַר רִבִּי שִׁמְעוֹן, כָּל הָנֵי מִלִּין, וְכָל מַה דְּחָמוּ, כַּתְבוּ. וְכַד מָטוּ הָכָא, הֲוָה כְּתִיב אֶשְׁמְרָה דְרָכַי מֵחֲטוֹא בִלְשׁוֹנִי. וַאֲנָא שָׁאִילְנָא לְאַבָּא אַבָּא, כַּמָּה הֲווֹ אִינּוּן תְּרֵין מִלִּין, וְאָמַר לִי חַיֶּיךָ בְּרִי, אִינּוּן תְּרֵין מִלִּין, בָּאנוּ עָלְמִין, וְחָרִיבוּ עָלְמִין, מַאן דְּאִשְׁתַּמָּשׁ בְּהוּ.

107. Rabbi Shimon said, All these points and all that they observed, they wrote down. When they reached here, AS THEY WERE TOLD TO KEEP THESE THINGS SECRET, it was written, MEANING IT WAS WRITTEN ABOUT THEM: "I will take heed to my ways, that I sin not with my tongue" (Tehilim 39:2). I inquired of my father, Father, what was referred to by these two items? He said to me, Your life, my son. These two matters have built worlds and destroyed worlds, for whoever made use of them.

108. כֵּיוָן דְּשַׁמְעוּ אֵלֵּין תְּרֵין מִילִין, אָמְרוּ אִינּוּן יְנוּקֵי, פּוּקוּ פּוּקוּ, לֵית

לְכוּ רְשׁוּתָא יַתִּיר לְמִשְׁמַע. אַפִּיק חַד מִנַּיְיהוּ, תַּפּוּחַ אֶחָד, וְיָהַב לוֹן. וְאָמַר, אֲרִחוּ בְּדָא, אֲרִחוּ בֵּיה, וְנַפְקוּ, וּמִכָּל דְּחָמוּ לָא אַנְשׁוּ כְּלוּם. נַפְקוּ.

108. As soon as they heard these two items, the youths told them, Leave, leave, for you have no permission to listen to more. One of them then took out an apple, gave it to them and said, Smell this. They smelled it and left. And of all that they saw, they forgot nothing. They left.

109. הָא מִמְנָא אַחֲרָא, אָתָא אָמַר לוֹן, חַבְרַיָּיא, ר' אִילָאי שָׁדַרְנִי לְכוּ, תּוֹרִיכוּ לֵיה הָכָא אַפּוּם מְעַרְתָּא, וְהוּא יֵיתֵי וְיוֹדַע לְכוּ מִלִּין עִלָּאִין דְּלָא יְדַעְתּוּן. דְּאִיהוּ תָּבַע מִגּוֹ מְתִיבְתָּא, דִּיהֵא לֵיה רְשׁוּ לְגַלָּאָה לְכוּ מִלִּין. נַפְקוּ בַּהֲדֵיה וְאוֹרִיכוּ אַפּוּם מְעַרְתָּא, וַהֲווֹ מְהַדְרִין מִלֵּי דָא לְדָא, מִכָּל מַה דְּחָמוּ וְאוֹלִפוּ תַּמָּן.

109. Another appointed one came and he said to them, Friends, Rabbi Ila'i has sent me to you. Wait for him here at the entrance of the cave and he will come and tell you about supernal matters of which you knew nothing, for he asked permission from the Yeshivah to have authority to reveal the matters to you. They came out with him and waited at the entrance of the cave and they were repeating the points to each other, of all that they beheld and learned there.

110. אַדְּהָכִי, הָא ר' אִילָאי אָתָא, נָהִיר כְּשִׁמְשָׁא. א"ל אוֹרַיְיתָא חַדְתָּא שְׁמַעְתָּא. אָמַר לוֹן וַדַּאי, וּרְשׁוּ יָהֲבוּ לִי לְמֵימַר לְכוּ מִלֵּי. אִתְחַבְּרָא כַּחֲדָא אַפּוּם מְעַרְתָּא, וְיָתְבוּ. אָמַר לוֹן זַכָּאִין אַתּוּן, דְּאָחֲמֵי לְכוֹן מָארֵיכוֹן כְּגַוְונָא דְּעָלְמָא דְּאָתֵי, וְהָא לֵית לְכוּ דְּחִילוּ וְאִמְתָנוּ, אָמְרוּ וַדַּאי הָא אִתְנַשֵׁי מִנָּן אָרְחָא דִּבְנֵי נָשָׁא, וּתְוּוֹהָא אִיהוּ עַל כָּל מַה דַּחֲמֵינָן בְּהַאי טוּרָא.

110. In the meantime, Rabbi Ila'i arrived and was shining like the sun. They inquired of him, Have you heard anything new in the Torah? He told them, Certainly. I have been granted permission to relate it to you. They joined together at the cave entrance and sat down. He told them, You are worthy that your Master has revealed to you the likeness of the World to Come, and you have no fear nor awe. They responded, Certainly, we have already forgotten the way of people, and is it any wonder, after all that we observed on this mountain?

111. אָמַר לוֹן, חֲמֵיתוּן אָלֵין טוּרַיָּא, כֻּלְּהוּ רָאשֵׁי מְתִיבְתֵּי לְעַמָּא דָּא דִּבְמַדְבְּרָא. וְזָכוּ הַשְׁתָּא, מַה דְּלָא זָכוּ כַּד הֲווֹ בַּחַיִּין. וְאָלֵין רֵישֵׁי מְתִיבְתֵּי, כֻּלְּהוּ בְּרֵישׁ יַרְחֵי וְשַׁבַּתֵּי וּמוֹעֲדַיָּא, מִתְכַּנְּשֵׁי לְגַבֵּי טוּרָא דְאַהֲרֹן כַּהֲנָא, וּמִתְעָרֵי לְגַבֵּיה, וְעָאלִין גּוֹ מְתִיבְתָּא דִּילֵיה, וּמִתְחַדְּשָׁן תַּמָּן, בִּדְכִיוּ דְטַלָּא קַדִּישָׁא דְּנָחִית עַל רֵישֵׁיה, וּמְשַׁח רְבוּ דְּנָגִיד עָלֵיה, וְעִמֵּיה מִתְחַדְּשָׁן כֻּלְּהוּ בְּחִדּוּשִׁין דִּרְחִימִין דְּמַלְכָּא קַדִּישָׁא, עַד דְּאִקְרֵי הָכָא מְתִיבְתָּא דִּרְחִימוּתָא.

111. He said to them, Have you seen all these mountains? All are heads of Yeshivot to this nation OF PEOPLE WHO DIED in the desert. They now achieve what they had not merited while they were alive. And these heads of the Yeshivot all gather on new moons, on Shabbat and holidays, at the mountain of Aaron the priest, awakened toward him and enter his Yeshivah. They are renewed there with the purity of the holy dew that flows down on the head of Aaron and the anointing oil that flows down on him. With him, all become renewed with the new interpretations of the Holy King's love, so that it is called here the Yeshivah of love.

112. וְאִיהוּ נָטִיל בְּכָל מְתִיבְתָּא, בִּטְמִירוּ דָקִיק מִתְעָטְּפָן כְּנִשְׁרִין גּוֹ מְתִיבְתָּא דִּנְהוֹרָא, וְאִיהִי מְתִיבְתָּא דְמֹשֶׁה, וְכֻלְּהוּ קַיְּמֵי לְבַר, וְלָא עָאלִין לְגוֹ, בַּר אַהֲרֹן בִּלְחוֹדוֹי וּכְפוּם שַׁעֲתָא אִקְרוּן בִּשְׁמָא.

112. He, AARON, travels with the entire Yeshivah and secretly and lightly they fly like eagles to the Yeshivah of light, which is the Yeshivah of Moses. Everyone stays outside and does not enter inside, except for Aaron alone, EXCEPTING only those that are called by name on specific times, MEANING, ON SHABBAT AND NEW MOON.

113. וְלֵית מַאן דְּחָמֵי לֵיה לְמֹשֶׁה, דְּהָא הַהוּא מַסְוֶה דְּאַנְפּוֹי, פָּרִיס

קַמֵּיהּ. וּשְׁבַע עֲנָנֵי יְקָר סַחֲרָנֵיהּ. אַהֲרֹן קָאִים גּוֹ פַּרְגּוֹדָא דִלְתַתָּא מִן מֹשֶׁה. וּפַרְגּוֹדָא פָּסִיק, וְלָא פָּסִיק בְּגַוַּיְיהוּ. וְכָל רֵישֵׁי מְתִיבָתֵּי, לְבַר מִפָּרוֹכְתָּא דְּפַרְגּוֹדָא דָא. וְכָל שְׁאָר, לְבַר מֵאִינּוּן עֲנָנִין. וּכְפוּם חִדּוּשֵׁי דִּנְהִירוּ דְּאוֹרַיְיתָא דְּאִתְנַהֲרָא, הָכִי מִנַּהֲרָן אִינּוּן עֲנָנִין.

113. No one can see Moses, since a veil is drawn over his face and seven clouds of glory surround him. Aaron stands within the surrounding curtain, WHICH IS THE PARTITION, below Moses. That fence is separating and not separating between them, MEANING THAT IT DOES NOT SERVE AS A COMPLETE SEPARATION. All the heads of the Yeshivot are on the outside of that curtain, which is this partition, MEANING THAT IN FACT, IT IS A COMPLETE SEPARATION. And all the rest OF THE WISE MEN are beyond the seven clouds THAT SURROUND HIM. The brightness of these clouds is in accordance with the new Torah illuminations that are revealed.

114. וְאִתְקְלִישׁוּ בִּדְקִיקוּ דִּנְהוֹרָא, עַד דְּאִתְחֲזֵי הַהוּא מַסְוֶה, וּמִגּוֹ הַהוּא מַסְוֶה, חָמָאן נְהוֹרָא דְּנָהִיר יַתִּיר מִכָּל נְהִירִין דְּעָלְמָא. וְאִינּוּן אַנְפֵּי מֹשֶׁה. אַנְפּוֹי לָא אִתְחַזּוּן כְּלָל, וְלֵית מַאן דְּחָמֵי לוֹן, בַּר הַהוּא נְהִירוּ דְּנָפִיק מִגּוֹ הַהוּא מַסְוֶה, בָּתַר כָּל אִינּוּן עֲנָנִין.

114. They were refined in the fineness of that light until MOSES' mask was visible to them. From that mask, they were able to see a light that is brighter than any light in the world. And that, THE MASK, IS the face of Moses, since his face is not at all visible. There is nobody who could see it, except for that light that emanates from this mask from behind all these clouds.

115. מֹשֶׁה אָמַר מִלָּה סְתָם לְאַהֲרֹן, וְאַהֲרֹן פָּרִישׁ לְרַבְרְבֵי מְתִיבָתֵּי. בְּמָה פָּרִישׁ. בְּכָל אִינּוּן מַבּוּעִין דְּאַסְתִּימוּ מִנֵּיהּ, כַּד מָטָא זִמְנֵיהּ דִּיהוֹשֻׁעַ. וְהַשְׁתָּא אִיהוּ מְהַדָּר לוֹן. בְּכַמָּה פְּלִיאָן, וּמְקוֹרִין וּמַבּוּעִין וְנַחֲלִין דְּנַבְעִין מִכָּל מִלָּה וּמִלָּה.

115. Moses told Aaron the matter simply, WITHOUT EXPLANATIONS, and Aaron then explained it to the heads of the Yeshivot. In what way did he explain THE MATTERS? With all these streams, THAT IS THE LEVELS, that were blocked FROM JOSHUA AND THE REST OF YISRAEL, when Joshua's time came TO LEAD THE GENERATION, MEANING THE THREE HUNDRED LAWS AND EIGHT HUNDRED DOUBTFUL MATTERS THAT HAD BEEN CONCEALED FROM HIM. Now, Moses returned them to them through many wonders and sources, and springs and streams that flow from each and every matter.

116. כָּל נָשִׁין זַכְיָין דְּהַאי דָּרָא, אָתָאן לְמִרְיָם אוֹף הָכָא בְּהָנֵי זִמְנִין. וּכְדֵין סַלְּקִין כֻּלְּהוּ, כִּתְמָרוֹת עָשָׁן גּוֹ מַדְבְּרָא דָּא. וְהַהוּא יוֹמָא, אִקְרֵי יוֹמָא דְּהִלּוּלָא. נָשִׁין בְּלֵילֵי שַׁבָּתוֹת וּבְלֵילֵי יוֹמִין טָבִין, כֻּלְּהוּ אָתָאן לְגַבֵּי מִרְיָם, וְיַדְעִין אִשְׁתַּדְּלוּתָא בִּידִיעָה דְּמָארֵי עָלְמָא. זַכָּאָה דָּרָא דָּא, מִכָּל דָּרִין דְּעָלְמָא. נָפְקֵי מִמְּתִיבְתָּא דְּמֹשֶׁה, וּפָרְחֵי לְגַבֵּי מְתִיבְתָּא דִּרְקִיעָא, וְאִינּוּן דְּאִתְחֲזוֹן פָּרְחֵי לְגַבֵּי מְתִיבְתָּא עִלָּאָה. עַל הַהוּא דָּרָא כְּתִיב, אַשְׁרֵי הָעָם שֶׁכָּכָה לּוֹ אַשְׁרֵי הָעָם שֶׁיְיָ' אֱלֹהָיו.

116. All the virtuous women of that generation, MEANING THE DESERT GENERATION, also came to Miriam in those times and they all ascended TO HER like smoke columns from the desert. That day is referred to as feast day. On Shabbat and holiday evenings, all the women came to Miriam and engaged in trying to understand the world's Master. Praised is this generation – THAT IS, THE GENERATION OF THE DESERT – from all the rest of the generations in the world. They left the Yeshivah of Moses and flew to the Yeshivah of the firmament, WHICH IS THE YESHIVAH OF METATRON. Those that are worthy take flight to the highest Yeshivah, WHICH IS THE YESHIVAH OF THE HOLY ONE, BLESSED BE HE. About that generation, it is written: "Happy is that people, that is in such a case: happy is that people whose Elohim is Hashem" (Tehilim 144:15).

14. The difference between Tam and Tamim

A Synopsis

Rabbi Ila'i explains why Abraham was referred to as Tamim, perfect, while Jacob was referred to as Tam, perfect, and says that the difference has to do with the fact that Jacob was more perfect, being circumcised. With the wholeness of male and female together, Tam takes the letter aleph to become Emet, truth, as in "You will show truth to Jacob." When Abraham circumcised himself he entered into Tam and also into its levels that are together called Yam, ocean, thus becoming Tamim that combines the letters of both; thus he was connected with the right. Everyone should contain the holy levels and be Tam Yam in order to be able to accept the aleph, the secret of Jacob, to become Emet or truth. Rabbi Ila'i tells us how Malchut is covered on the outside with blue that was taken from the ocean so that those who look at her with the evil eye will draw the blue color that is judgment; internally, however, all the colors sparkle in her and are embroidered with the light of Chochmah. Similarly the man who wears the blue tzitzit becomes Tamim every day. He becomes elevated afterward to higher levels by the wearing of the Tefilin, to the levels of Zeir Anpin. It now appears that seven days have passed since the righteous rabbis began their supernal experience, and Rabbi Ila'i now tells them the explanation of the six sections of the mysterious riddle they heard earlier.

117. פָּתַח ר׳ אִילָאִי וְאָמַר, תָּמִים תִּהְיֶה עִם יְיָ׳ אֱלֹהֶיךָ. מַה בֵּין תָּם לְתָמִים. בְּאַבְרָהָם כְּתִיב, הִתְהַלֵּךְ לְפָנַי וֶהְיֵה תָמִים. יַעֲקֹב דְּאִשְׁתְּלִים יַתִּיר, כְּתִיב בֵּיה, וְיַעֲקֹב אִישׁ תָּם. אֲמַאי אִקְרֵי אִישׁ תָּם. בְּגִין דְּלָא אִשְׁתְּאַר בֵּיה פְּסוֹלֶת כְּלָל, דְּהָא פְּרִיעָה הֲוָה בֵּיה.

117. Rabbi Ila'i opened the discussion saying, "You shall be perfect (Heb. *tamim*). with Hashem your Elohim" (Devarim 18:13). HE ASKS: What is the difference between Tam (lit. 'perfect') and Tamim (lit. 'perfect'). HE RESPONDS: By Abraham, it is written: "Walk before Me, and be perfect (Heb. *tamim*)" (Beresheet 17:1). By Jacob, who was more perfected, it is written: "And Jacob was a plain (perfect – *tam*) man" (Beresheet 25:27). Why was he called a perfect man? Since no refuse was left with him, as the uncovering of the membrane at circumcision was performed on him.

118. בְּמָה אִתְפְּרַע, וְאִתְדְּכֵי מֵהַהוּא פְּסוֹלֶת בְּגִין דְּהַהוּא אֲתָר דְּאַתְקִיף לִפְסוֹלֶת, דִּלְגוֹ אֲתָר דִּפְרִיעָה שָׁארֵי, אִיהוּ שׁוֹר, דְּיוּקְנָא דִּשְׂמָאלָא דְּכֻרְסְיָא דִּילֵיהּ. וְהַהוּא שׁוֹר, אִקְרֵי שׁוֹר תָּם. דְּהָא רְתִיכָא דְכֻרְסְיָא, רְשִׁימָא דִּבְרִית אִית בֵּיהּ. וע״ד, הַאי שׁוֹר אִקְרֵי תָּם. וְיַעֲקֹב אָחִיד בֵּיהּ בִּגְוַויהּ, וּבְהַאי שׁוֹר עָבֵיד פְּרִיעָה, וְאַעֲבַר זוּהֲמָא דִּפְסוֹלֶת כֹּלָּא.

118. HE INQUIRES: How did he perform that membrane uncovering and become cleansed from that refuse? HE RESPONDS: That area that strengthens the refuse within – THAT EXISTS where the membrane is – is an ox, WHICH IS the left image of His throne. FOR IN THE CHARIOT OF THE THRONE ARE THE FACE OF THE LION TO THE RIGHT AND THE FACE OF THE OX TO THE LEFT. That ox is referred to as an ox that has not gored (Heb. *tam*), since there exists an impression of that Covenant of circumcision in the Chariot of that throne. Therefore, this ox is called an unblemished ox. Jacob is connected with it and with this ox, he has performed the membrane uncovering and has removed the soil of that refuse entirely.

119. בְּמַתְנִיתָא דִּבְצַלְאֵל כְּתִיב, וַיִּזְכֹּר אֱלֹהִים אֶת רָחֵל. בְּשָׂרָה כְּתִיב פְּקִידָה, וּבְרָחֵל כְּתִיב זְכִירָה, אֲמַאי. בְּגִין דְּזָכוֹר אִתְרְשִׁים בְּיַעֲקֹב, דְּאִיהוּ בְּרִית שָׁלִים, כַּד אִתְיְילִד יוֹסֵף. וּבְמָה. כַּד נָטַל שׁוֹר בַּהֲדֵיהּ, דְּלָא יַתְקִיף לְסִטְרָא אַחֲרָא. וּבג״כ, אִתְקְרֵי יוֹסֵף בְּכוֹר שׁוֹר, בְּכוֹר דְּהַהוּא שׁוֹר דְּנָטַל יַעֲקֹב בְּכוֹר שׁוֹרוֹ, וְדָחֵי לְהַהוּא שׁוֹר.

119. In the Baraita of Betzalel, it is written: "And Elohim remembered Rachel" (Beresheet 30:22). HE INQUIRES: About Sarah, it is written "visited," as in: "AND HASHEM VISITED SARAH" (BERESHEET 21:1), but about Rachel, it is written "remembered." Why? HE RESPONDS: "Remember," WHICH IS THE SECRET OF YESOD, is impressed on Jacob, who was a complete Covenant, when Joseph was born. How WAS THIS PERFECT COVENANT ACHIEVED? It is when he took with him the ox that assails the Other Side, WHICH ASSAILS AND DESTROYS THE SOILED REFUSE OF THE OX THAT GORED THRICE THAT DWELLS WITHIN THAT

MEMBRANE TO BE REMOVED, AS MENTIONED NEARBY. Therefore, Joseph is referred to as "the firstling of his herd" (Devarim 33:17), meaning the ox's firstborn that Jacob took and that pushed aside that ox OF THE OTHER SIDE, WHICH IS THE OX THAT GORED THRICE.

120. שׁוֹר תָּם, וְיַעֲקֹב אִישׁ תָּם. רִבּוֹן וְשַׁלִּיט, מָארֵיהּ דְּבֵיתָא, דְּהַהוּא שׁוֹר תָּם שָׁארֵי בְּגַוְוִיהּ. בְּגִין דְּאִית שׁוֹר מוּעָד בְּסִטְרָא עָרְלָה פְּרִיעָה. וְכַמָּה גַרְדִּינֵי נִימוּסִין נַפְקִין מִנֵּיהּ, עַד דַּרְגָּא בַּתְרַיְיתָא דְּאִקְרֵי שְׁאִי"ה. הַהוּא דְּאָפִיל בֵּיתִין דְּעָלְמָא, דְּלָא דַּיְירִין בְּהוּ בְּנֵי נָשָׁא. וְכֻלְּהוּ נַפְקָא מֵהַהוּא שׁוֹר מוּעָד. וְדָא בְּחַבּוּרָא דַּחֲמוֹר בִּישָׁא. ובג"כ לֹא תַחֲרוֹשׁ בְּשׁוֹר וּבַחֲמוֹר יַחְדָּיו. בְּגִין דְּלָא לְאִתְעָרָא לְהוּ.

120. The unblemished (Heb. *tam*) ox, MEANING "and Jacob was a plain (Heb. *tam*) man" MEANS a sovereign ruler, the master of the house within which that unblemished ox dwells; THAT IS, MALCHUT FROM WHICH IS DRAWN THE UNBLEMISHED OX. Because there exists an ox that has gored thrice on the side of the foreskin and the skin of the uncovered membrane, MEANING THE ENTIRE FORESKIN AND THE REFUSE THAT IS ABSORBED IN THE SKIN OF THE MEMBRANE THAT GETS UNCOVERED, many prosecutors emanate and result from it down to the lowest level that is referred to as 'She'iyah', that HARMFUL DEMON, which fells the houses that are empty of people. All result from that ox who gored thrice when joined with the evil donkey. Therefore, "you shall not plow with an ox and an donkey together" (Devarim 22:10) in order not to incite them.

121. וּבְהַהוּא מְתִיבְתָּא דִּבְצַלְאֵל, וְכֵן בִּתְרֵין מְתִיבְתָּא, וְיַעֲקֹב אִישׁ תָּם. בַּעֲלָהּ דְּהַהוּא תָּם. וּמַאן אִיהוּ א' רָזָא דְּו"ו. וְכַד הֲווֹ כְּלָל דְּכַר וְנוּקְבָא כַּחֲדָא, כְּדֵין נָטִיל כָּל אַתְוָון אִלֵּין את"ם, וְאִיהוּ אמ"ת. תִּתֵּן אֱמֶת לְיַעֲקֹב, כְּלָל דְּכַר וְנוּקְבָא כַּחֲדָא, שְׁלִימוּ דְּכֹלָא.

121. In the Yeshivah of Betzalel and also in the two Yeshivot, MEANING IN THE YESHIVAH OF METATRON AND THE YESHIVAH OF THE HOLY ONE, BLESSED BE HE, THEY SAID THAT "And Jacob was a plain (Heb. *tam*) man" MEANS the husband of that Tam, WHICH IS MALCHUT. Who is he,

THE HUSBAND OF TAM? That is the Aleph, which is part of the secret of Vav, FULLY SPELLED VAV-ALEPH-VAV, SINCE JACOB IS THE SECRET OF ALEPH AND MALCHUT IS THE SECRET OF TAM. When they include male and female together, Jacob takes all these letters – ALEPH, TAM – THE SECRET of Aleph Tav Mem. These are THE LETTERS OF *emet* (Eng. 'truth') and it is written: "You will show truth to Jacob" (Michah 7:20), SINCE TRUTH combines the male and female together, AND THEN they are in complete perfection.

122. אַבְרָהָם לָא אִתְפְּקַד עַל פְּרִיעָה, וְכַד עָאל, עָאל לְהַאי תָּם, וְלִגוֹ דַּרְגִּין דִּילֵיהּ, דְּאִקְרוּן כַּחֲדָא יָם. וְהַיְינוּ תָּמִים. לְבָתַר אִסְתְּלַק אַבְרָהָם, וְעָאל לְגוֹ, וְאִתְקְשַׁר עִם יְמִינָא עִלָּאָה.

122. Abraham was not commanded about the uncovering of the membrane. When he entered, MEANING HE CIRCUMCISED HIMSELF, he entered into Tam and into its levels that are called in combination *Yam* (Eng. 'ocean'). This is Tamim, WHICH CONTAINS THE LETTERS IN TAM YAM. Following this, Abraham was elevated and entered the innermost interior, and was connected with the uppermost right.

123. תָּמִים תִּהְיֶה עִם יְיָ' אֱלֹהֶיךָ וַדַּאי, כְּמָה דְּאִיהוּ תָּמִים כְּלָלָא חֲדָא, אוֹף אַנְתְּ תְּהֵא עִמֵּיהּ תָּמִים, עִמֵּיהּ וַדַּאי. בְּמָה אִתְעֲבֵיד בַּר נָשׁ תָּמִים, דְּיְהֵא תָּ״ם יָם. תָּם כְּמָה דְּאִתְּמַר. יָ״ם כָּל אִינוּן דַּרְגִּין קַדִּישִׁין דִּילֵיהּ אִקְרוּן יָ״ם, וְלָא אִתְפְּרְשָׁן מִנֵּיהּ לְעָלְמִין. אוֹף אַנְתְּ כְּגַוְונָא דָא, לְאַעֲדָאָה מִנָּךְ דַּרְגִּין נוּכְרָאִין, וּלְאִתְקַשְּׁרָא בְּתָמִים, לְמֶהֱוֵי בָּךְ דַּרְגִּין קַדִּישִׁין, רָזָא דְּיָם, וְדַרְגָּא קַדִּישָׁא, תָּ״ם. לְקַבְּלָא א' רָזָא דְּיַעֲקֹב. ב״ן אִצְטְרִיךְ לְמֶהֱוֵי בְּכָל יוֹמָא, תָּ״ם יָ״ם. כְּגַוְונָא דָא מַמָּשׁ.

123. "You shall be perfect (Heb. *tamim*) with Hashem your Elohim," certainly. Just like He is Tamim in one principle, SINCE YAM WAS INCLUDED IN TAM, AS MENTIONED. You, too, be perfect (Heb. *tamim*) with Him, with Him certainly. Through what does a person become Tamim? – THAT IS by being Tam Yam IN ONE COMBINATION. As we explained about Tam, all the holy levels OF MALCHUT THAT IS REFERRED TO AS TAM are called Yam and never separate from it. You likewise remove from

yourself all the foreign levels, and connect yourself with Tamim. Thus you shall have in you the holy levels, which are the secret of Yam and the holy level Tam, THAT SHOULD BE READY to accept AFTERWARDS the Aleph, which is the secret of Jacob. AND THE COMBINATION, *Emet*, WILL BE MADE, AS WE MENTIONED PREVIOUSLY. Every day man must be Tam Yam, in exactly the same way.

124(1). הַשְׁתָּא פָּרִישׁ מַאן דְּפָרִישׁ, בְּמַתִיבְתָּא, דְּסִיהֲרָא קַדִּישָׁא שַׁפִּירָא, אִיהוּ בְּחִוָּורוּ, וְכָל גַּוּונִין מְנַצְצָן בָּהּ וּמְרֻקָּמָן, וְאִיהוּ כְּהַהוּא שַׁפִּירוּ וְחִוָּורוּ דְּשִׁמְשָׁא מַמָּשׁ. וּבְהַהוּא יַמָּא דִּילָהּ, גּוֹ שַׁבְעִין שְׁנִין, נָפְקָא נוּנָא חֲדָא, וְאַפִּיק מִנֵּיהּ גָּוֶון תְּכֵלֶת, וְאִיהִי נַטְלָא גָּוֶון דָּא, וְתַקִּינַת לֵיהּ, וְאִתְחַפְּיָיא לְבַר בְּהַאי גָּוֶון.

124a. Someone explained in the Yeshivah that the holy moon, WHICH IS THE SECRET OF MALCHUT, is white in color, WHICH IS THE SECRET OF THE LIGHT OF CHESED. All the colors sparkle within her and get embroidered, MEANING ALSO THE LIGHT OF CHOCHMAH, and she has the same as that actual beauty and whiteness of the sun, WHICH IS THE SECRET OF ZEIR ANPIN. In that ocean OF MALCHUT within a period of seventy years, a certain fish emerges and takes out from it the color blue, and she takes this dye and prepares it and covers herself from outside with that color.

124(2). לָאו דְּהַאי גָּוֶון לְבוּשָׁא דִּילָהּ, דְּהָא שֵׁשׁ וְאַרְגָּמָן לְבוּשָׁהּ. אֲבָל חוּפָאָה דִּלְבַר הַאי גָּוֶון הוּא. כְּגַוְונָא דָּא הֲוָה מַשְׁכְּנָא, דְּכוּלֵּיהּ בִּשְׁפִּירוּ מְרֻקָּמָא לְגוֹ, וּלְבָתַר וּפָרְשׂוּ בֶגֶד כְּלִיל תְּכֵלֶת. מ״ט. בְּגִין דִּתְחוֹת יָם דָּא, אִית מְצוּלוֹת יָ״ם, כְּלָל דְּכַר וְנוּקְבָא, וְאִית לוֹן עֵינָא בִּישָׁא לְאִסְתַּכְּלָא, וְכַד מִסְתַּכְּלִין, זַמִּין לְעֵינַיְיהוּ גָּוֶון תְּכֵלֶת, וְלָא יַכְלָא עֵינַיְיהוּ לְשַׁלְטָאָה, וְאִיהִי אִתְתַּקְנַת לְגוֹ, בְּכָל גַּוְונִין מְרֻקָּמָן כְּדְקָא יָאוּת, מִתְתַּחֲמָן לְד׳ סִטְרִין דְּעָלְמָא.

124b. It is not that the blue color is her dress, WHICH IS WHY SHE WEARS IT AS AN OUTER GARMENT, since IT IS WRITTEN: "Her clothing is fine linen and purple" (Mishlei 31:22), BUT BLUE IS NOT APPROPRIATE FOR HER

DRESS. However, this color IS ONLY an exterior cover OVER MALCHUT. Similar to this, it was at the Tabernacle that is entirely of beautiful embroidery internally and after that: "And shall spread over it a cloth wholly of blue" (Bemidbar 4:6) ON THE OUTSIDE. What is the reason? It is because below this ocean, WHICH IS MALCHUT, there are depths of the sea, WHICH ARE KLIPOT that are comprised of male and female. They have an evil eye with which to stare and, when they stare AT MALCHUT – MEANING THAT THEY WISH TO DRAW ILLUMINATION OF CHOCHMAH FROM HER FROM ABOVE DOWNWARD IN THE MANNER OF THE KLIPOT – the blue color is ready for their eyes. Their eyes cannot affect MALCHUT AND THAT IS ONLY EXTERNALLY. HOWEVER, she is fixed internally by all embroidery colors, WHICH IS THE SECRET OF WHITE, RED AND GREEN, as is proper FOR CONTINUATION OF CHOCHMAH. They spread to the four sides of the world.

125. כְּגַוְונָא דָּא ב״נ דְּלָבִישׁ צִיצִית, אִתְעֲבֵיד בְּכָל יוֹמָא תָּמִים. תָּ״ם, בְּד׳ כְּנָפַים מְתְקְנָן כַּדְקָא יָאוּת. יָ״ם, בְּהַהוּא תְּכֵלֶת דְּנוּנָא, דְּשַׁבְעִין דַּרְגִּין דְּיַמָּא, סִטְרָא בִּישָׁא כַּד אִסְתָּכַּל בְּהַאי בַּר נָשׁ לָא יָכִיל לְאַבְאָשָׁא לֵיהּ בְּעֵינָא בִּישָׁא. וּכְדֵין אִיהוּ תָּם יָ״ם, עִם יְיָ׳ אֱלָהָיו מַמָּשׁ, בְּתִקּוּנָא חֲדָא, אִיהִי לְעֵילָא, וְאִיהוּ לְתַתָּא.

125. Likewise, a man who wears *Tzitzit* (lit. 'fringed garment') becomes *tamim* every day. HE RECEIVES THE ASPECT OF Tam OF MALCHUT with the four corners OF THE GARMENT that are properly made. THE ASPECT OF Yam HE RECEIVES FROM MALCHUT with the blue OF THE TZITZIT THAT IS THE SECRET of the fish of seventy levels in the sea, AS MENTIONED, so that the Evil Side will not be able to harm him with the evil eye when it stares at this person, MEANING HE WILL NOT BE ABLE TO DRAW HIM TO THE DOMINION OF THE OX THAT GORED THRICE, SINCE THE BLUE PREVENTS THEM. Then he is Tam Yam with Hashem his Elohim in one preparation, SINCE MALCHUT TOO IS ESTABLISHED AND COVERED EXTERNALLY WITH THE BLUE COLOR, AS MENTIONED – she above and he below.

126. לְבָתַר אִסְתָּלְּקַת אִיהִי גּוֹ דַּרְגִּין עִלָּאִין. אוּף הָכִי בַּר נָשׁ, אִסְתַּלָּק אִיהוּ לְבָתַר בִּתְפִלִּין, גּוֹ דַּרְגִּין עִלָּאִין. וְעַ״ד תָּמִים תִּהְיֶה עִם יְיָ׳ אֱלָהֶיךָ, עִמֵּיהּ וַדַּאי. וַדַּאי בְּשַׁעְתָּא חֲדָא, בְּרִגְעָא חֲדָא, אִיהִי אִתְּתַּקְנַת

לְעֵילָא, וב״נ אִתָּקָן לְתַתָּא.

126. Following this, MALCHUT ascends to higher levels, THAT IS, TO THE LEVELS OF ZEIR ANPIN. So, the person also is elevated afterward with the Tefilin to higher levels OF ZEIR ANPIN. About this, it is said: "You shall be perfect (Heb. *tamim*) with Hashem your Elohim," with Him definitely. Certainly at once, at one moment MALCHUT is fixed above – FIRSTLY, BY TAM YAM, AND AFTERWARDS, IN A UNION WITH ZEIR ANPIN. A person is prepared likewise below. FIRSTLY, HE IS MADE READY BY THE TZITZIT, WHICH IS THE LEVEL OF TAM YAM, AND THEN BY THE TEFILIN, WHICH IS THE LEVEL OF ZEIR ANPIN.

127. א״ר אִילָאי, כָּל אִלֵּין דְּהָכָא, כְּגַוְונָא דָּא מִתַקְּנָן, לְמֶהֱוֵי כָּל חַד תָּמִים עִם יְיָ'. וְעַל רָזָא דָּא, בַּמִּדְבָּר הַזֶּה יִתַּמּוּ. אִי תֵּימְרוּן דְּכַד אִתְּמַר לְבִישׁ אִתְּמַר, הָכִי הוּא וַדַּאי, דַּהֲוָה לוֹן לְמֶהֱוֵי כָּל חַד תָּמִים עִם יְיָ' בְּאַרְעָא קַדִּישָׁא, אֲתַר דְּיְיָ' שָׁארֵי תַּמָּן, לְמֶהֱוֵי אַפִּין בְּאַפִּין כַּחֲדָא עִמֵּיהּ, וְהַשְׁתָּא כָּל חַד הֲוֵי תָּמִים בְּמַדְבְּרָא דָּא לְבַר, אֲתַר רָחִיק מִתַּמָּן, דְּלָא יִסְתַּכַּל אַנְפִּין בְּאַנְפִּין בַּהֲדֵיהּ לְמֶהֱוֵי עִם יְיָ' כַּדְקָא יָאוּת. וְשָׁם יָמוּתוּ, כְּמָה דַּחֲמִיתוּן דְּעַבְדִין בְּכָל יוֹמָא.

127. Rabbi Ila'i said, All these over here, MEANING THE GENERATION OF THE WILDERNESS, prepare in a similar way, so each one is Tam Yam with Hashem. About this secret, IT IS SAID, "In this wilderness they shall be consumed (Heb. *yitamu*)" (Bemidbar 14:35), MEANING THAT THEY WILL RECEIVE THE ASPECT OF TAM. If you shall think that when this was said it meant for ill, AND NOT TO PRAISE THEM, most certainly this is so. IT IS NO PRAISE TO THEM, since they should have each striven to be Tamim with Hashem in the Holy Land, in a place where the Holy One, blessed be He, dwells face to face together WITH MALCHUT. And now, there, each one is Tamim in this wilderness outside, a place distant FROM THE HOLY LAND, where MALCHUT does not look face to face to be with Hashem as required. "And there they shall die" means as you saw them doing every day, THAT THEY DIE AND ARE REVIVED.

128. זַכָּאָה חוּלָקְכוֹן חַבְרַיָּיא קַדִּישִׁין, דְּזַכִּיתוּן לְכָל הַאי. הָנֵי תְּרֵי

מְעַרְתֵּי אַחֲרָנִין דִּילְכוּ, דְּלָא תִּשְׁכְּחוּ כָּל דָּא תַּמָּן, דְּאִינּוּן גּוֹ מְתִיבְתָּא דְּמֹשֶׁה, יַתְבֵי מֵרָחִיק. וע״ד כְּתִיב בְּמֹשֶׁה, עָנָו מְאֹד מִכָּל הָאָדָם. וּנְבִיאָה עִלָּאָה, קַבִּיל לוֹן לִמְתִיבְתָּא דִּילֵיהּ, מִיּוֹמָא דְּשָׁארֵי לְמֶחֱמֵי כָּל דָּא, עַד הַהִיא שַׁעֲתָא שִׁבְעָה יוֹמִין. וְהָא לָא הֲווֹ מִסְתַּכְּלִין בְּהַאי עָלְמָא כְּלוּם.

128. Praised is your lot, holy friends, that you have merited all this. You will not find anyone there in those other two caves of yours, because they are in the Yeshivah of Moses. They sit from afar and, therefore, it says about Moses: "Very meek, more so than all the men" (Bemidbar 12:3), since the greatest prophet saw fit to receive them into his Yeshivah. Behold, from the day THAT THOSE RIGHTEOUS began to see all this to that time, seven days had already passed. They have not looked at this world at all, MEANING TO SAY THAT THEY WERE COMPLETELY REMOVED FROM ALL THAT IS MATERIAL.

129. אָמַר לוֹן רִבִּי אִילָאִי, זַכָּאִין קַדִּישִׁין, אֵימָא לְכוּ מִלִּין דִּשְׁמַעֲתּוּן. וּמִלָּה קַדְמָאָה כַּד תִּנְדְּעוּן מְדִידוּ דִּמְשִׁחֲתָא, בִּשְׁמָא גְּלִיפָא מְפָרָשׁ, תִּנְדְּעוּן דִּבְצַלְאֵל רְבִיעָאָה אִיהוּ, דִּנְהוֹרִין עִלָּאִין. דִּכְתִיב, וָאֲמַלֵּא אוֹתוֹ רוּחַ אֱלֹהִים בְּחָכְמָה וּבִתְבוּנָה וּבְדַעַת. מַאן דְּלָא אִסְתָּכַל חָמֵי וְאִתְפְּתַח.

129. Rabbi Ila'i said to them: Holy righteous men, I will list the things that you have heard, MEANING THOSE WORDS MENTIONED ABOVE. The first thing is when you will understand the measuring of the measure of the inscribed fully pronounced Name, YUD HEI VAV HEI. You will understand that Betzalel is the fourth of the high lights, since it is written: "And I have filled him with the spirit of Elohim, in wisdom, and in understanding, and in knowledge" (Shemot 31:3).

130. מַאן דְּלָא אִסְתָּכַל, בְּאִינּוּן תְּלַת מִלִּין טְמִירִין, מַה לְעֵילָא, מַה לְתַתָּא וְכוּ'. זַמִּין אִיהוּ לְאִתְפַּתְּחָא בְּאוֹרַיְיתָא, וּלְפַקְחָא עַיְינִין בָּהּ. אִילָנָא דְּתַמְנֵי סְרֵי, שְׁדַרְתּוֹ דב״נ, כַּד כָּפִיף קַמֵּי מָארֵיהּ, יִזְקוֹף

וְיִתְקַיֵּים לִתְחַיַּית מֵתַיָּיא. אִי לָא כָּפִיף בְּמוֹדִים, אִתְעֲבֵיד חִוְיָא, וְלֵית לֵיהּ תְּקוּמָה לְהַהוּא זִמְנָא.

130. NOW HE EXPLAINS THE SECOND POINT THAT IS MENTIONED ABOVE, SAYING WHOEVER DOES NOT GAZE SEES, AND HIS EYESIGHT IS RESTORED WITH GREAT CLARITY. Whoever does not look at these three concealed matters – what is above, what is below, what is before and what is after – IT SEEMS THAT HE COUNTS WHAT WILL BE AND WHAT WAS AS ONE ITEM – he is destined to regain sight in the Torah and open his eyes through it. THE THIRD ITEM: A tree of eighteen, as it bends, so it will stand upright and endure, MEANING the man's spine, THAT CONSISTS OF EIGHTEEN VERTEBRAE, when he bends it before his Master, MEANING WHEN HE STOOPS IN THE PRAYER OF MODIM (WE GIVE THANKS), he will stand upright and will endure at the revival of the dead. If he does not stoop at Modim, he becomes a snake and has no resurrection in the future to come. THAT IS WHAT IS SAID THERE: 'AND IF HE DOES NOT BEND, AN EVIL SNAKE CONSUMES HIM.'

131. מַאן דְּעָאל בֵּין תְּרֵין כְּרוּבִים לְגוֹ. מַאן דְּעָאל שִׁיעוּר תְּרֵין פִּתְחִין, לְגוֹ בֵּי כְּנִשְׁתָּא, אִתְדַּבָּק בְּמָארֵיהּ, וּרְעוּתֵיהּ אִתְעֲבֵיד. מַאן דִּמְעַיֵּין בִּצְלוֹתֵיהּ, וְאִסְתָּכַּל בָּהּ, רָחִיק מֵרְעוּתֵיהּ דְּשָׁאִיל. קָרְבְּנָא דְּרַבְיָא, כַּד קָרֵב ב"נ בְּרֵיהּ לְבֵי סַפְרָא, אוֹ לְמִילָה, דָּא קָרְבְּנָא שְׁלִים לְאִתְקַבְּלָא. מִכָּאן וּלְהָלְאָה רְחִימִין, זִילוּ.

131. THE FOURTH POINT: Whoever proceeds between the two Cherubs inward, THAT IS, whoever enters a measure of two doors inside the synagogue is attached to his Master, and his wishes are fulfilled. THE FIFTH POINT: Whoever contemplates his prayer and searches it – THAT IS TO SAY, HE THINKS IN HIS HEART THAT HIS REQUEST MUST BE GRANTED SINCE HE PRAYS WITH INTENTION – is far from being granted the wish he requested. THE SIXTH POINT: A child offering is the most perfect to be accepted, MEANING when a person brings his son to school and to circumcision, which is an acceptably perfect offering. From here on, my beloved, go your way.

15. The cave of the Machpelah

A Synopsis

Rabbi Elazar is told about how all the patriarchs are buried with their wives in the Cave of Machpelah, and exactly how they were laid out in the cave, women next to women and men next to men. And as these pairs were buried, so they will rise in the exact same manner; then Leah will rejoice with Messiah the son of David, who is her offspring and Rachel will rejoice with Messiah the son of Joseph, who is her offspring.

132. אֶלְעָזָר בְּרִי, שַׁפִּיר קָאַמְרַת, כְּפוּם מַה דְּאוֹלִיפַת. אֲבָל ח״ו, דְּאע״ג דְּרָחֵל הֲוַת עֲקָרָא בְּהַהוּא זִמְנָא, יַעֲקֹב חַכִּים הֲוָה. וְאִלְמָלֵא לָא יָדַע יַעֲקֹב, דְּלֵאָה אִנְתְּתֵיה, לָא קָבִיר לָה בִּמְעַרְתָּא, לְאִתְחַבְּרָא בַּהֲדֵיה, בְּחִבּוּרָא חֲדָא, וְיהֵא קָבִיר לָה לְבַר מֵאַרְעָא. אֲבָל לְלֵאָה אָעִיל לָה גּוֹ אַרְעָא, וּלְרָחֵל שַׁוֵּי לְבַר. מִית יַעֲקֹב, אִתְקְבַר בְּגַוַּוֵיה, בְּחִבּוּרָא חֲדָא.

132. (THE BEGINNING IS MISSING HERE.) Elazar, my son, according to what you have learned, you speak intelligently. However, heaven forbid, even though Rachel was barren during that period, Jacob was wise. And if he would not have known that Leah was his wife, he would not have buried her in the cave OF MACHPELAH to be continuously next to her. Instead, he would have buried her outside of the cave. However, he brought Leah to the land, THAT IS THE CAVE OF MACHPELAH, and Rachel he interred outside OF THE CAVE OF MACHPELAH. When Jacob died, he was buried inside THE CAVE OF MACHPELAH, jointly WITH LEAH.

133. כְּמָה דְּעָבְדוּ כָּל שְׁאַר אֲבָהָן, אוֹף הָכִי אָדָם. מֵתָה חַוָּה בְּקַדְמֵיתָא, אִתְקַבְּרַת תַּמָּן. וְתַמָּן יָדַע אָדָם, דְּהַאי דּוּכְתָּא אִתְחֲזֵי לֵיה. מִית אָדָם, אִתְקְבַר בְּגַוַּוֵיה בְּחִבּוּרָא חֲדָא. מֵתָה שָׂרָה אִתְקַבְּרַת תַּמָּן, וְחַוָּה חֲמָאת, וְחַדְאת לְקַבְּלָה, וְקָמַת וְקַבְּלָה לָה. שִׁעוּרָא דְּחַוָּה לְגַבֵּי שָׂרָה, שִׁעוּרָא דִּתְרֵין אַמִּין, וְלָא יַתִּיר. מֵת אַבְרָהָם, אִתְקְבַר לְגַבֵּי שָׂרָה, בְּחִבּוּרָא חֲדָא. מֵתָה רִבְקָה, אִתְקַבְּרַת תַּמָּן, וְשָׂרָה חֲמָאת, וְקָמַת וְקַבְּלַת לָה. מֵת יִצְחָק, אִתְקְבַר בַּהֲדָה בְּחִבּוּרָא חֲדָא. מֵתָה לֵאָה,

אִתְקַבְּרַת תַּמָּן, וְרִבְקָה חָמָאת, וְקַמַת, וְקַבְּלָה לָהּ. מֵת יַעֲקֹב, אִתְחַבָּר
בַּהֲדָהּ בְּחִבּוּרָא חֲדָא. וְכֻלְּהוּ דְכַר וְנוּקְבָּא כַּחֲדָא, בְּחִבּוּרָא חֲדָא.

133. As the rest of the patriarchs did, so did Adam. Eve died first and was buried there, IN THE CAVE OF MACHPELAH, and there Adam became aware that this place was appropriate for him. When Adam died, he was buried there jointly WITH EVE. When Sarah died, she was buried there. Eve saw her and was glad, and she rose and welcomed her. The measured DISTANCE of Eve from Sarah is two cubits and not more. Abraham died and was buried next to Sarah, jointly connected WITH HER. Rivkah died and she was buried there. Sarah saw this, and rose and welcomed her. When Isaac died, he was jointly buried with her jointly. When Leah died, she was buried there and Rivkah rose and welcomed her. When Jacob died, he joined her to be together. And all were male and female together, jointly united.

134. סִדּוּרָא דִּלְהוֹן הֵיךְ שְׁכִיבֵי. נָשִׁין לְגַבֵּי נָשִׁין, וּדְכוּרִין לְגַבֵּי דְכוּרִין.
אָדָם בְּרֵישָׁא, חַוָּה סָמִיךְ לֵיהּ. שָׂרָה לְגַבֵּי חַוָּה. אַבְרָהָם סָמִיךְ לְשָׂרָה.
יִצְחָק סָמִיךְ לְאַבְרָהָם. רִבְקָה סָמִיךְ לְיִצְחָק. לֵאָה סָמִיךְ לְרִבְקָה. יַעֲקֹב
סָמִיךְ לְלֵאָה. אִשְׁתְּכַח אָדָם בְּסִטְרָא דָא, יַעֲקֹב בְּסִטְרָא דָא, דָא רֵישָׁא,
וְדָא סֵיפָא.

134. HE INQUIRES: In what order were they laid out? HE RESPONDS: Women next to women and men next to men. Adam at first and, next to him, Eve. Sarah is next to Eve, Abraham is close to Sarah, Isaac is close to Abraham, Rivkah is close to Isaac, Leah is close to Rivkah and Jacob is next to Leah. The result leaves Adam on this side and Jacob on the other side, one at the beginning and one at the end.

135. בְּסִפְרָא דִשְׁלֹמֹה מַלְכָּא אִיהוּ כַּדְקָא יָאוּת וְהָכִי הוּא, אָדָם וְחַוָּה
בְּקַדְמֵיתָא. וְשָׂרָה וְאַבְרָהָם סָמִיךְ לוֹן. יִצְחָק וְרִבְקָה לְזִוְיָא אַחֲרָא,
בְּאֹרַח מֵישָׁר בְּשׁוּרָה חֲדָא. יַעֲקֹב וְלֵאָה בְּאֶמְצָעִיתָא. וְאִינּוּן נָשִׁין לְגַבֵּי
נָשִׁין. וּדְכוּרִין לְגַבֵּי דְכוּרִין. וְאָדָם וְחַוָּה, שָׂרָה וְאַבְרָהָם, יַעֲקֹב וְלֵאָה,
רִבְקָה וְיִצְחָק. אָדָם בְּסִטְרָא דָא, וְיִצְחָק בְּסִטְרָא דָא, וְיַעֲקֹב

בְּאֶמְצָעִיתָא. יִצְחָק לְגַבֵּי אֲבוּהָ לָאו אֹרַח עָלְמָא. וְעכ״ד יַעֲקֹב אִצְטְרִיךְ בְּאֶמְצָעִיתָא.

135. In the book of King Solomon, it is properly set. So it is Adam and Eve at first, Sarah and Abraham nearby, Isaac and Rivkah in the other corner OPPOSITE in a straight line and Jacob and Leah in the middle. They are women next to women and men next to men; that is Adam and Eve, Sarah and Abraham, Jacob and Leah and Rivkah and Isaac. THE RESULT IS that Adam is in one end and Isaac is in the other far end. Jacob is in the middle, as for Isaac to be next to his father is not the custom. Therefore, it was necessary for Jacob to be in the middle.

136. וּבְכָל אִינּוּן זוּגִין, כְּמָה דְּאִתְקְבָרוּ, הָכִי יְקוּמוּן, וְהָכִי יִשְׁתַּכְּחוּן. לֵאָה תֶּחֱדֵי בַּהֲדֵי מָשִׁיחַ, בְּרֵיהּ דְּדָוִד, דְּנָפִיק מִנָּהּ לְגוֹ. רָחֵל תֶּחֱדֵי בַּהֲדֵי מָשִׁיחַ, בְּרֵיהּ דְּיוֹסֵף, דְּנָפִיק מִנָּהּ לְבַר מִירוּשְׁלֵם. וְכֹלָּא לְדוּכְתַּיְיהוּ.

136. And all these pairs, as they were buried, in the same manner they will rise AT THE RESURRECTION OF THE DEAD. And so it will happen. Leah will rejoice with Messiah, the son of David, who is her offspring, inside THE CAVE OF MACHPELAH. Rachel will rejoice with Messiah, the son of Joseph, who is her offspring, outside of Jerusalem – MEANING WHERE SHE WAS BURIED, ON THE WAY TO EFRAT – and each one in his place.

16. Reading of the Torah

A Synopsis

We hear about a tower of precious stone in the midst of other towers; it rises to the high firmament and is not yet visible. Upon it the head of the Yeshivah inscribed: "The name of Hashem is a strong tower: the righteous runs to it, and is safe." We are given an analogy whereby the tower is the ark in which the Torah scroll is kept. From here it is derived that the cantor of the synagogue must be righteous and of the form of the supernal righteous, Yesod, and that the sixth person called up to read the Torah must be righteous, as the sixth alludes to Yesod. We hear more marvelous details about the tower, and are told that in it there is a light in the form of a Torah scroll that will be read in the future by King Messiah. He will explain all the Torah matters to the students of the Yeshivah, and they will then be elevated to the Yeshivah of Metatron. We are told that no one could withstand seeing that Torah scroll except Messiah, as its letters are sparkling flames of four colors that are from a higher world.

137. אֵלֵּין הָכָא וְאִלֵּין הָכָא. דְּאִינוּן מִגְדָּלִין דְּאֶבֶן טָבָא כֻּלְּהוּ. בֵּין כֻּלְּהוּ מִגְדָּלִין אִית חַד מִגְדָּל דְּאֶבֶן טָבָא בְּאֶמְצָעִיתָא. וְדָא סָלִיק לְרוּם רְקִיעָא, וְלָא אִתְחֲזֵי הַשְׁתָּא, עַד הַהוּא זִמְנָא דְּיִתְגַּלֵּי. רַב מְתִיבְתָּא חָמָא לֵיהּ, וַהֲוָה רָשִׁים בֵּיהּ לְעֵילָא הַאי קְרָא, מִגְדַּל עֹז שֵׁם יְיָ' בּוֹ יָרוּץ צַדִּיק וְנִשְׂגָּב. וּפָרִישׁ רַב מְתִיבְתָּא קְרָא דָא, מִגְדַּל עֹז: דָּא כְּנֶסֶת יִשְׂרָאֵל. בּוֹ יָרוּץ צַדִּיק: בֵּיהּ רְעוּתֵיהּ דְּצַדִּיק תָּדִיר. וע"ד, וְנִשְׂגַּב הַהוּא מִגְדַּל, דְּלָא יִנְפּוֹל לְעָלְמִין, כְּמָה דַּהֲוָה.

137. (THE BEGINNING OF THE ARTICLE IS MISSING) these here and these there, since all are towers of precious stone. Among the towers, there is a tower of precious stone in its midst. That one reaches to the lofty firmament and is not visible at present, until that time when it will appear. The head of the Yeshivah saw it and inscribed on it above this verse: "The name of Hashem is a strong tower: the righteous runs to it, and is safe" (Mishlei 18:10). This scriptural verse was explained by the head of the Yeshivah this way: "A strong tower" refers to the Congregation of Yisrael, MEANING MALCHUT; "the righteous runs (Heb. *yarutz*) to it," MEANING THAT the desire of the Righteous, WHICH IS YESOD, is always for it. SINCE *YARUTZ*

IS FROM THE SAME DERIVATION AS *RATZON* (ENG. 'DESIRE'), therefore, it is a tower of strength "and is safe," so that it will never AGAIN fall as it did.

138. וְרִבִּי כְּרוּסְפְּדָאי חָמִיד לִבָּא, פָּרִישׁ הַאי קְרָא עַד לָא אִסְתַּלָּק, וּפָרִישׁ שַׁפִּיר. מִגְדַּל עֹז: דָּא תֵּיבָה, וּסְ״ת דְּאִיהוּ עֹז, לְשַׁוָּאָה בֵּיהּ, וּלְאַפָּקָא לֵיהּ מִגּוֹ הֵיכָל, דְּיוּקְנָא דְּהֵיכָל פְּנִימָאָה, דְּמִנֵּיהּ נָפְקָא תוֹרָה, וְהַהוּא מִגְדָּל שֵׁם יְיָ׳ אִיהוּ, וּדְיוּקְנָא דִּילֵיהּ וְאִצְטְרִיךְ בְּשִׁית דַּרְגִּין.

138. And Rabbi Cruspedai, who delights the heart, explained this scriptural verse before his death and explains it well. "A strong tower" is the ark, to insert in it the Torah scroll, which is strong, and to take it out of the chamber, which is in the form of the inner chamber. THAT IS THE SECRET OF IMA from which the Torah comes out, WHICH IS ZEIR ANPIN. That tower, WHICH IS THE ARK, is the name of Hashem and His form, MEANING MALCHUT, and it needs to have six steps, CORRESPONDING TO CHESED, GVURAH, TIFERET, NETZACH, HOD AND YESOD IN MALCHUT.

139. בּוֹ יָרוּץ צַדִּיק, בְּמַאן. בְּמִגְדַּל, אוֹ בסְ״ת. אֶלָּא קְרָא דָּרִישׁ בְּהַאי וּבְהַאי. כַּד דָּרַשׁ בְּמִגְדָּל, אִצְטְרִיךְ צַדִּיק דָּא דְּלִיהֱוֵי חֲזַן הַכְּנֶסֶת, זַכָּאָה דְּקַשׁוֹט, וּדְיוּקְנָא דְּצַדִּיק עֶלָּאָה. כַּד דָּרִישׁ לסְ״ת, מַאן דְּסָלִיק לסְ״ת לְמִקְרֵי אוֹרַיְיתָא, אִצְטְרִיךְ צַדִּיק. וְצַדִּיק אִקְרֵי. מַאן אִקְרֵי צַדִּיק מִכֻּלְּהוּ. שְׁתִיתָאָה, דְּסָלִיק מֵאִינּוּן שִׁבְעָה. א״ר שִׁמְעוֹן, וַדַּאי, דְּאִיהוּ לָא סָלִיק כָּל יוֹמוֹי, אֶלָּא שְׁתִיתָאָה לְאִינּוּן דְּסַלְּקִין. בּוֹ יָרוּץ צַדִּיק, בסְ״ת יָרוּץ דִּבְרֵי צַדִּיק דָּא. וְנִשְׂגָּב מִמַּאן. מִדְּחִילוּ דְּמַלְאַךְ הַמָּוֶת, דְּהָא אוֹרִיךְ יוֹמִין. וְנִשְׂגָּב דְּלָא יִתְנְזַק לְעָלְמִין.

139. "The righteous runs to it." HE ASKS: To what WILL HE RUN? To the tower or the Torah scroll? HE RESPONDS: He explained this verse both ways, BOTH THE TOWER AND THE TORAH SCROLL. When he explained it as 'the tower', the righteous one needs to be the cantor of the synagogue AND BE truly righteous and of the form of the supernal Righteous, THAT IS YESOD. When he explained it to mean 'the Torah scroll', then whoever goes up to read the Torah should be righteous and be called righteous. Of all SEVEN THAT ARE CALLED UP TO THE READING OF THE TORAH, who is called righteous? THAT IS the sixth one to be called up for the reading among those seven, SINCE THE SIXTH READING PORTION ALLUDES TO YESOD THAT IS CALLED RIGHTEOUS. Rabbi Shimon said, Definitely, IT IS SO since RABBI CRUSPEDAI has always been called up to rise only for the sixth READING PORTION throughout his life, among the others who were also called for the reading OF THE TORAH. THAT WAS ALLUDING TO THE RIGHTEOUS, YESOD. "The righteous runs to it" MEANS THEN, the words of this righteous will run to the Torah scroll. HE ASKS: "And is safe" from whom? HE ANSWERS: From fearing the Angel of Death, since he shall have an extended life and he will never be hurt.

140. בְּהַהוּא מִגְדָּל דְּסַלְקָא בֵּין אִינוּן מִגְדָּלִין, קַיְימָא נְהִירוּ חַד, בְּדִיּוּקְנָא דס״ת, כַּד אָתֵי הַהוּא צִיפָּרָא, נַטְלָא הַהוּא מִגְדָּל מֵאַתְרֵיה, וְקָאִים גּוֹ אֶמְצָעִיתָא דַּעֲזָרָה, גּוֹ גַּדְפֵּי דִכְרוּבִים. וּמַה דַּהֲוָה. רוּמֵיה לְרוּם שְׁמַיָּא מָאִיךְ וְעָאל תְּחוֹת אִינוּן כְּרוּבִים, וְשׁוּרוֹי בֵּין רֵישֵׁי כְּרוּבִים.

140. In that tower that rises among the towers stands a light in the form of a Torah scroll. When a bird arrives, it takes the tower from its place and places it to stand in the middle of the court within the wings of the Cherubs. And what was high as the lofty heavens lowered and entered under the Cherubs, and the walls OF THE TOWER stood between the heads of the Cherubs.

141. תְּלַת מֵאָה פִּתְחִין תַּמָּן, בְּפִתְחָא דְּאֶמְצָעִיתָא, קַיְימָא נְהִירָא דָא, דְּיוּקְנָא דס״ת, בֵּיה זַמִּין מֶלֶךְ יִשְׂרָאֵל לְמִקְרֵי בְּפָרָשַׁת הַקְהֵל. וְדָא לִיהֱוֵי מַלְכָּא מְשִׁיחָא, וְלָא אַחֲרָא.

141. There are three hundred openings IN THAT TOWER. In the central opening is this light in the form of a Torah scroll standing, in which the king of Yisrael is destined to read in the portion of "Hak'hel (Eng. 'gather')." That will be King Messiah, and no other.

142. וּבְהַהוּא ס״ת דְּהַהוּא נְהִירוּ, אִי חֲסִידָא קַדִּישָׁא, זַכָּאָה אִיהוּ דְּמִפּוּמֵיה יִשְׁמְעוּ, קַל נְעִימוּ דְּמִלּוּי מֵאִינוּן מִלִּין סְתִימִין דְּפָרִישׁ

בְּאוֹרַיְיתָא. בְּכָל רֵישׁ יַרְחֵי, וְשַׁבַּתֵּי וּמוֹעֲדַיָּיא וְזִמְנַיָּיא, כַּד בָּעָאן כָּל
בְּנֵי מְתִיבְתֵּי לְסַלְּקָא לְעֵילָא לְגוֹ מְתִיבְתָּא דִּרְקִיעָא, כֻּלְּהוּ מִתְכַּנְפֵי
לְגַבֵּי מַלְכָּא מְשִׁיחָא, וְאִיהוּ פָּרִישׁ מִלִּין, וּמִגּוֹ מְתִיקוּ דְּמִלּוֹי
בְּתִיאוּבְתָּא, סַלְּקִין. כֻּלְּהוּ עֲשַׂר מִלִּין, גְּנִיזִין לָךְ מֵאִינּוּן מִלִּין דְּאִיהוּ
פָּרִישׁ, לְיוֹמָא דִּשְׁאֶלְתָּן דִּילָךְ.

142. With the Torah scroll of this light, THE AUTHOR TURNS TO THE LISTENER AND SAYS, Oh, holy pious one, glad is the one who will hear from the mouth OF MESSIAH, the sweet voice of his discourse is in the concealed matters of the Torah that he will explain. THAT IS, WITH THE LIGHT OF THAT TORAH SCROLL, every new moon, Shabbat and holiday and festival. When all the students of the Yeshivah wish to ascend high to the heavenly Yeshivah, THAT IS THE YESHIVAH OF METATRON, all congregate around King Messiah, who explains to them the TORAH matters. Through the sweetness of his words and through desire, they are elevated TO THE HEAVENLY YESHIVAH. AND THE AUTHOR OF THIS ARTICLE TURNS AGAIN TO THE LISTENER AND SAYS TO HIM, All the ten points of the matters, THAT MESSIAH DEFINED, will be stored for you for that day of your petitions, MEANING FOR THAT DAY WHEN YOU WILL PRAY FOR IT.

143. כַּד קַיְּימָא הַהוּא מִגְדָּל בְּאֶמְצָעוּ דַּעֲזָרָה, וּפִתְחָא דָּא פָּתַח,
פַּתְחִין אִינּוּן כְּרוּבִין פּוּמַיְיהוּ, וּפַרְשֵׂי גַּדְפַּיְיהוּ, וְנָהִיר נְהִירוּ עִלָּאָה עַל
הַהוּא פִּתְחָא. וְהַהוּא ס"ת פָּתִיחַ, וְאִינּוּן כְּרוּבִים פָּתְחֵי וְאַמְרֵי מָה רַב
טוּבְךָ אֲשֶׁר צָפַנְתָּ לִירֵאֶיךָ וְגוֹ'. סָגִירוּ פִּתְחִין, וְס"ת אִתְגְּלִיל.

143. When that tower stands in the middle of the court and that door is open, MEANING THE DOOR THAT IS IN THE CENTRAL COLUMN OF THE TOWER, the Cherubs open their mouths, and spread their wings. They illuminate with the higher light on that opening and that Torah scroll is open, and the Cherubim started to say: "Oh how great is Your goodness, which You have laid up for those who fear You..." (Tehilim 31:20). AFTER THAT, they close the doors and the Torah scroll is rolled up.

144. מַאן חָמָא, נְהִירוּ דְּנַהֲרָא דְּהַהוּא ס"ת, כּוּלֵּיהּ נְהוֹרָא דְּנָהִיר,
אַתְוָון דִּילֵיהּ, שַׁלְהוֹבֵי דְּאֶשָּׁא מֵד' גַּוְונֵי, דְּאִינּוּן דְּעָלְמָא עִלָּאָה, כֻּלְּהוּ

בַּלְטֵי וּמְנַצְצֵי, לֵית מַאן דְּיָכִיל לְמֵיקָם בְּהוּ, בַּר מָשִׁיחַ.

144. Who has witnessed the illuminating light of that Torah scroll? It is a bright light in its entirety, its letters are flames of fire of four colors, which are from a higher world and all stand out sparkling. Nobody could withstand seeing that except Messiah.

145. סָגִיר פִּתְחָא דָא, כְּרוּבִים מִשְׁתַּכְּכֵי. וְהַהוּא מִגְדָּל פָּרַח, וְקַיְּימָא בְּאַתְרֵיה בֵּין שְׁאַר מִגְדָּלִין.

145. When that door IN THE TOWER is closed, the Cherubs are still. That tower flies and takes its place among the rest of the towers.

17. The crown of Messiah

A Synopsis
The (unknown) author of this section tells of what will happen when King Messiah receives from a dove His magnificent crown of gold that is hidden in the tower.

146. בְּהַהוּא פִּתְחָא דְּאֶמְצָעִיתָא, אִית עֲטָרָה דְּפָז עִלָּאָה וְיַקִּירָא גְּנִיזָא, דְּלָא אִתְחֲזֵי הַשְׁתָּא, גְּלִיפָא וּמְחַקְּקָא בְּכָל זִינֵי אַבְנֵי יְקָר, וְזַמִּינָא לְמֶהֱוֵי עַל רֵישָׁא דְּמַלְכָּא מְשִׁיחָא, כַּד סָלִיק בְּהַהוּא מִגְדָּל, וּתְרֵין נִשְׁרִין, דָּא מִסִּטְרָא דָּא, וְדָא מִסִּטְרָא דָּא, נַטְלֵי לֵיהּ בִּידַיְיהוּ.

146. At that door in the center OF THE TOWER'S APERTURES, AS MENTIONED ABOVE, there is a most magnificent crown of gold hidden, which is presently invisible, elaborately engraved and embellished with all kinds of precious stones. It is destined to be installed upon the head of King Messiah, when the time comes and he will ascend that tower. And two eagles on each side will take this CROWN in their hands.

147. כַּד סָלִיק מַלְכָּא מְשִׁיחָא, מִתְתַּקְּנִין נִשְׁרִין, וְנַטְלֵי עֲטָרָא דָּא, בְּשַׁעֲתָא דְּיִשְׁרֵי לְמִקְרֵי, יִתְפְּתַח פִּתְחָא אַחֲרָא, וּמִתַּמָּן תִּפּוֹק הַהִיא יוֹנָה, דְּשָׁדַר נֹחַ בִּימֵי טוֹפָנָא, דִּכְתִיב וַיְשַׁלַּח אֶת הַיּוֹנָה, הַהִיא דְּאִשְׁתְּמוֹדְעָא, וְלָא מַלִּילוּ בָּהּ קַדְמָאֵי, וְלָא יָדְעוּ מַה הִיא, אֶלָּא מֵהָכָא נַפְקַת, וְעָבְדַת שְׁלִיחוּתָא.

147. When King Messiah, ascends THIS TOWER, the eagles will get ready and take this crown. When he begins to read THE TORAH, another aperture will open. From there will emerge the dove that Noah sent in the days of the flood, as is written: "Also he sent forth the dove" (Beresheet 8:8), the dove WITH THE DEFINITE ARTICLE, meaning the renowned dove that the ancient ones have not discussed and were not aware of. However, it is from here that she goes out on her mission.

148. וּבְשַׁעֲתָא דִּכְתִיב וְלָא יָסְפָה שׁוּב אֵלָיו, עוֹד לָא יָדַע בַּר נָשׁ לְאָן

אַזְלַת, וְהִיא תָּבַת לְאַתְרָה, וְאִתְגְּנִיזַת בְּפִתְחָא דָא וְאִיהִי תִּטּוֹל עֲטָרָה בְּפוּמָהָא, וּתְשַׁוֵּי עַל רֵישֵׁיה דְּמַלְכָּא מְשִׁיחָא, מָטֵי וְלָא מָטֵי, וּכְדֵין כְּתִיב, תָּשִׁית לְרֹאשׁוֹ עֲטֶרֶת פָּז.

148. During the time that it says: "Which returned not again to him any more" (Ibid. 12), no person knew where she went. She returned to her assigned place and was stored in this opening. She will take the crown in her mouth and place it on the head of King Messiah, touching yet not touching. Then, it is written: "You set a crown of pure gold on his head" (Tehilim 21:4).

149. וְכֵיוָן דְּיִקְרֵי מַלְכָּא מְשִׁיחָא בס״ת. יְקוּמוּן תְּרֵין נְשָׁרִין, דָּא מִכָּאן וְדָא מִכָּאן, וְיוֹנָה מָאִיךְ, וּמַלְכָּא מְשִׁיחָא נָחִית, וְעֲטָרָה עַל רֵישֵׁיה, עַד דַּרְגָּא בַּתְרָאָה. וּתְרֵין נְשָׁרִין פַּרְחִין לְעֵילָא עַל רֵישֵׁיה, וְיוֹנָה תָּבַאת וַעֲטָרָה בְּפוּמָה, וִיקַבְּלוּן לָה אִלֵּין תְּרֵין נְשָׁרִין.

149. As soon as King Messiah reads in the Torah scroll, the two eagles will rise from each side and the dove will lower HERSELF TO DESCEND. King Messiah will step down with the crown on his head to the last level and two eagles will fly above his head. The dove will return with the crown in her mouth, and the two eagles will welcome her.

150. דָּוִד מַלְכָּא, זַיִת רַעֲנָן אִקְרֵי קַמֵּיה קוּדְשָׁא בְּרִיךְ הוּא, דִּכְתִיב וַאֲנִי כְּזַיִת רַעֲנָן בְּבֵית וְגוֹ׳. עֲלֵה זַיִת, דָּא מַלְכָּא מְשִׁיחָא בְּרֵיה דְּדָוִד. וְדָא אִיהוּ דְּרָמִיז יוֹנָה דָּא בְּיוֹמוֹי דְּנֹחַ, דִּכְתִיב וְהִנֵּה עֲלֵה זַיִת טָרָף בְּפִיהָ. הַהוּא עֲלֵה זַיִת, טָרָף וְחָטַף לִיקָרָא דִּילֵיה. בַּמֶּה. בְּפִיהָ. דְּקַיְימָא עַל רֵישֵׁיה, וּמְקַבְּלָא יְקָר מֵהַאי יוֹנָה וְהַאי דִּכְתִיב טָרָף, וְלָא טָרְפָה, כִּדְכוּרָא דָא, דְּעָבִיד חֵילָא וְנָצַח. בִּמְתִיבְתָּא דִּרְקִיעַ, יוֹנָה דְּכַר הוּא, מִגּוֹ דְּאִקְרֵי יוֹנָה, כְּתִיב כְּנוּקְבָּא, וּכְתִיב כִּדְכוּרָא, בְּזִמְנָא דִּמְקַבְּלָא יְקָר דָּא.

150. King David is called a fresh olive in the presence of the Holy One, blessed be He, as is written: "But I am like a green olive tree in the house..." (Tehilim 52:10). A leaf of an olive tree is King Messiah, son of David. That is what the dove indicated during the time of Noah, as is written: "And, lo, in her mouth was an olive tree plucked off" (Beresheet 8:11). THE DOVE plucked off that olive leaf, WHICH IS MESSIAH, and grabbed his glory, MEANING THE CROWN. How? With her mouth, SINCE THE CROWN stands on his head and receives glory from the dove. That is why it says, "plucked off" IN MASCULINE FORM and not in feminine form, SINCE IT INDICATES that she is like a male gaining strength and she prevails. In the heavenly Yeshivah, THEY SAID this dove is a male because the NAME *Yonah* (Eng. 'dove'), by which it is called, is sometimes written female, IN FEMININE FORM AND SOMETIMES as male, IN MASCULINE FORM. When she receives this glory, SHE IS REFERRED TO IN MALE FORM. (THE END IS MISSING HERE).

151. מִגְדָּל דָּא כַּד תָּב לְאַתְרֵיהּ, נָהִיר כִּנְהִירוּ דְעֵינָא דְשִׁמְשָׁא, דִּכְתִיב, כְּסֵאוֹ כַּשֶּׁמֶשׁ נֶגְדִּי. וְאַף דִּכְרְסַיָּיא אַחֲרָא לִיהֱוֵי לֵיהּ בְּנִסִּין וְאָתִין רַבְרְבִין. בְּרֵישׁ מִגְדָּל דָּא, אִית עוֹפִין דְּנוּר דְּקָא מְצַפְצְפָאן, כַּד סָלִיק צַפְרָא, צִפְצוּפָא דִּנְעִימוּ, דְּלֵית נְעִימוּ וְנִגּוּנָא כְּהַהוּא נְעִימוּ.

151. When this tower returned into its place, MEANING AFTER THE TORAH READING, it is bright like the light of the sun – MEANING, LIKE THE LIGHT OF ZEIR ANPIN THAT IS CALLED SUN, WHICH IS COVERED CHASSADIM. It is written: "And his throne shall be like the sun before Me" (Tehilim 89:37). MALCHUT THAT IS REFERRED TO AS THE THRONE IS LIKE THE SUN, AS ZEIR ANPIN although he has another throne also, with great miracles and marvels. At the top of this tower there are birds of flame which chirp. When the bird ascends, THEY CHIRP with a pleasant sound, for there is no delight and song like this delight.

18. Letters soaring

A Synopsis

We hear of the birds that rise and descend, rise and descend, and are told that these are the great and the small letters. When the letters fly, a person sees written in the air temporarily, in great letters, "In the beginning Elohim created...", followed by the other sayings in the acts of creation. The author says that whoever preserves the covenant places himself to follow the Shechinah and is guarded from behind by the supernal righteous, with great love. We hear that when the firmament revolves it performs music from the sound of the waters that flow, but the lower grades are not capable of hearing it. Whoever deserves to receive from those waters stands there in happiness and in awe, since both come from serving God.

152. לְעֵילָא מִכֻּלְּהוּ, זִינִין אַחֲרָנִין, וְשַׁפְנִינִין אַחֲרָנִין, דְּקָא פַּרְחִין בַּאֲוִירָא, סַלְקֵי וְנַחְתֵּי, נַחְתֵּי וְסַלְקֵי, לָא מִשְׁתַּכְּכִין לְעָלְמִין. אַתְוָון רַבְרְבָן, וְאַתְוָון זְעִירָן, פַּרְחִין בֵּינַיְיהוּ.

152. Above them all, THAT IS IN BINAH, there are other varieties and other turtledoves that fly in the air IN THE SECRET OF THE ASCENSION OF MALCHUT TO BINAH. Rising and descending, descending and rising, they never rest quietly. AND HE EXPLAINS WHY IT IS SO. IT IS BECAUSE great letters THAT ARE BINAH and small letters THAT ARE MALCHUT fly between them, SINCE SOMETIMES THE SMALL LETTERS RISE TO THE GREAT LETTERS – THAT IS, MALCHUT TO BINAH – AND SOMETIMES THE SMALL LETTERS RETURN AND EMERGE FROM THE GREAT LETTERS, THAT IS, MALCHUT COMES BACK AND EMANATES FROM BINAH.

153. אִי חֲסִידָא קַדִּישָׁא, בְּשַׁעֲתָא דְּאַתְוָון פַּרְחִין, חָמֵי ב"נ בְּאַתְוָון רַבְרְבָן. כְּתִיב בַּאֲוִירָא לְפוּם שַׁעֲתָא, בְּרֵאשִׁית בָּרָא אֱלֹהִים אֵת הַשָּׁמַיִם וְאֵת הָאָרֶץ בַּטְשֵׁי אַתְוָון זְעִירָן בְּהוּ, וּפַרְחִין, וְאִתְחֲזֵי מִנַּיְיהוּ כְּתִיב, וַיֹּאמֶר אֱלֹהִים יְהִי אוֹר וְגוֹ', וַיַּרְא אֱלֹהִים אֶת הָאוֹר וְגוֹ'. לְבָתַר מַהַדְרֵי אַתְוָון זְעִירָן, וּבַטְשֵׁי בְּאַתְוָון רַבְרְבָן, וּמִתְחֲזֵי מִנַּיְיהוּ דִכְתִּיב, וַיֹּאמֶר אֱלֹהִים יְהִי רָקִיעַ וְגוֹ'. וְכֵן כָּל עוֹבָדָא דִּבְרֵאשִׁית, פְּלִיאָן

רַבְרְבָן, וְחֶדוּ לְעַיְינִין עוֹבָדָאן דְּאַתְוָון אִלֵּין, זַכָּאָה עַמָּא דְּכָל דָּא מְחַכָּאן.

153. Oh, holy pious one. When the letters fly, a person sees written in great letters, WHICH ARE BINAH, in the air temporarily: "In the beginning Elohim created..." (Beresheet 1:1), SINCE THESE WORDS ARE FROM BINAH; THAT IS, THE SECRET OF GREAT LETTERS. THEN the small letters strike them, MEANING MALCHUT RISES AND IMPACTS IN BINAH; THAT IS TO SAY THAT SHE REDUCES HER. Then they fly and it is seen written through them: "And Elohim said, 'Let there be light'... And Elohim saw the light..." (Beresheet 1:3-4). Then the small letters again strike the large letters, MEANING THAT AGAIN MALCHUT RISES TO BINAH AND DIMINISHES HER. It is seen through them that it is written: "And Elohim said, 'Let there be a firmament...'" (Ibid. 6) and so on in all of the acts of Creation. The acts of these letters are great marvels and gladness to the eyes. Praised is the nation for whom all this awaits.

154. אִי חֲסִידָא קַדִּישָׁא, מַאן דְּנָטִיר בְּרִית, שַׁוֵּי לֵיהּ אֲבַתְרוֹי, וְאִיהִי לְקַמָּא. וְאִי תֵּימָא, מַאן נָטִיר לַאֲחוֹרָא. הָא נְטִירוּ רַב וְעִלָּאָה מִכֹּלָּא, דְּנָטִיר לֵיהּ. וּמַאן אִיהוּ. צַדִּיק עִלָּאָה בִּרְחִימוּ סַגִּי. עָאל בֵּין צַדִּיק וְצֶדֶק. וְאִשְׁתְּכַח נָטִיר מִכָּל סִטְרִין. זַכָּאָה מַאן דְּנָטִיר בְּרִית דָּא. וְעַ"ד יִשְׂרָאֵל, אִתְחֲזוֹן כָּל דְּכוּרִין, דְּנַטְרִין אֶת קַיָּימָא דָּא, קַמֵּי מַלְכָּא קַדִּישָׁא. מַאן אִיהוּ דְּיָכִיל לְנַזְקָא לִבְרָא, דְּאִיהוּ בְּאֶמְצָעוּ אֲבוּהָ מִכָּאן, וְאִמֵּיהּ מִכָּאן, וְאִיהוּ בֵּינַיְיהוּ. וְדָא כַּד אִיהוּ אַחֲרֵי יְיָ'.

154. Oh, holy, pious one. Whoever preserves the Covenant places himself to follow THE SHECHINAH, AND THE SHECHINAH is in the lead. If you inquire as to who will guard him from behind, HE RESPONDS, There is a higher greater protection that protects him from everything. What is it? It is the supernal Righteous, THAT IS YESOD OF ZEIR ANPIN THAT PROTECTS HIM, with great love. Consequently, he enters between the Righteous, THAT IS YESOD, and righteousness, THAT IS MALCHUT, and is thus protected on all sides – YESOD FROM BEHIND AND MALCHUT IN FRONT. Praised is the one who preserves this Covenant. Therefore, Yisrael, all the males that uphold this Covenant, shall be seen in the presence of the Holy One, blessed be He, AS IS WRITTEN: "THREE TIMES IN THE YEAR ALL YOUR MALES SHALL APPEAR" (SHEMOT 23:17). Who is it that can harm a son whose father is on one side and his mother is on the other side, and he is in the middle between them? That is when he follows Hashem, MEANING ONLY BEHIND MALCHUT, AS MENTIONED ABOVE.

155. ת"ח הַהוּא רָקִיעַ כַּד סָחֲרָא בְּגִלְגּוּלָא מְנַגְּנָא בְּנִגּוּנָא, וּמִקָּל נְהִימוּ דְּמַיִין דְּנַבְעִין, לָא יְדִיעַ הַהוּא נִגּוּנָא. כָּל אִינּוּן אַגָּנִין דִּי בְּאַרְבַּע סִטְרִין, מַלְיָין מִנְּבִיעוּ דְּמַיִין דְּנַבְעִין. מַאן דְּאִיהוּ לְגוֹ, בִּתְרֵין סִטְרִין קַיְימָא תַּמָּן. חַד בְּחֶדְוָה, דְּלֵית חֶדְוָה כְּהַהִיא חֶדְוָה בְּעָלְמָא, לְקַיְימָא עַבְדוּ אֶת יְיָ' בְּשִׂמְחָה. וְחַד בִּירְאָה, דְּלֵית דְּחִילוּ כְּהַהוּא דְּחִילוּ בְּעָלְמָא, לְקַיְימָא עַבְדוּ אֶת יְיָ' בְּיִרְאָה.

155. Come and see that firmament, WHICH IS ZEIR ANPIN, when it revolves in the circle. It performs music, and from the sound of the waters that flow that song is not known. All of these basins on the four sides OF ZEIR ANPIN, IN THE SECRET OF WHAT IS WRITTEN: "YOUR NAVEL IS LIKE A ROUND GOBLET" (SHIR HASHIRIM 7:4), are filled with flowing waters. Whoever is inside – THAT IS, WHO MERITS TO RECEIVE FROM HIM – stands there in two aspects. One in happiness, since there is no other happiness in the world like fulfilling: "Serve Hashem with gladness" (Tehilim 100:2). And one is with awe, since there no other awe in the world like fulfilling: "Serve Hashem with fear" (Tehilim 2:11).

19. The spring of water

A Synopsis

We are told about the spring that was mentioned by Ezekiel. When the waters flow and rise all kinds of gems in the world, the grades referred to as gems, rise. The gems and the colors of a button and blossom that surround the spring are described in glowing terms, and the author says that since one cannot look at the button and blossom the importance of their activities can not be known. Many marvelous things are outlined for our contemplation. We read a description of a branch that emerges at the center of a spring; the branch covers worlds, and it is not possible to know about its fruit. The author concludes by telling us about a firmament from which dew flows to this spring; the dew produces fruit on the branch, and the firmament circles faster than the eye can see.

156. חַד מַעְיָינָא דְּמַיָּיא, דְּנָבִיעַ מִסְטַר מִזְרָח, דָּא הוּא דְּאָמַר יְחֶזְקֵאל נְבִיאָה. מֵהַאי מַעְיָינָא, לָא יַכְלִין לְסַיְּימָא שְׁבָחָא כָּל בְּנֵי עָלְמָא. בַּאֲתַר דְּאִתְיְלִיד תַּמָּן לִסְטַר מִזְרָח, לֵית עוּמְקָא וְרוּמָא דִּילֵיהּ, אֶלָּא זַרְתָּא וְלָא יַתִּיר.

156. One spring of water flows from the east side, WHICH IS TIFERET – THE CENTRAL COLUMN OF ZEIR ANPIN THAT INCLUDES RIGHT AND LEFT – the one that the prophet Ezekiel mentioned (YECHEZKEL 41:1). The entire world cannot give enough praise for that spring, SINCE IT COMBINES RIGHT AND LEFT, UNRAVELS ALL THE LIGHTS IN BINAH, CHASSADIM AND CHOCHMAH TOGETHER, AND DRAWS THEM TO THE LOWER LEVELS. At the place where it was born, that is, to the east side, the measure of its depth and height is no more than a span.

157. כַּד נַבְעִין מַיָּא וְסַלְקִין, סַלְקִין כָּל זִינֵי מַרְגְּלָאן דְּעָלְמָא, וְלָא נַפְלִין לְבַר, הַשְׁתָּא אִתְחָזוּן בְּגַוְון חַד, לְפוּם שַׁעֲתָא נַפְלִין אִלֵּין, וְהָא סַלְקִין, אַחֲרָנִין, בְּגַוְון אַחֲרָא, בְּכָל זִינֵי גַּוְונִין דְּעָלְמָא. נַפְלֵי אִינּוּן מַרְגְּלָאן, וְלָא נַפְלֵי לְבַר.

157. When the waters flow and rise, all kinds of gems come up, and they do not fall outside. For a while, they appear in one color and temporarily they

fall, MEANING THAT THIS COLOR IS TEMPORARILY REMOVED. Then other GEMS ascend of another color AND SIMILARLY in all other colors existing in the world, MEANING ALL COLORS OF MALCHUT REFERRED TO AS THE WORLD, WHOSE ESSENCE IS WHITE, BLACK AND RED. These gems fall outside ONE AFTER THE OTHER, ONE SINKING AND ONE FLOATING UP, but they do not fall outward.

158. סַחֲרָנִין דְּהַהוּא נְבִיעוּ, חֵיזוּר וְשׁוּשָׁן סָחֲרִין. וְלָא יַכְלִין כָּל בְּנֵי עָלְמָא לְמֵיקָם עַל אִינּוּן גַּוְונִין, כֻּלְּהוּ שַׁלְהוֹבִין מְלָהֲטָאן, וְלָא יַכְלִין לְאִסְתַּכְּלָא בְּהוּ. לָא יְדִיעַ חֲשִׁיבוּ דְעוֹבָדָא. טַרְפִּין דִּלְהוֹן מְנַצְצָן בְּכַמָּה גַּוְונִין.

158. Surrounding that spring is a button and blossom. No one can comprehend the variety of colors that is in them, SINCE all are glowing flames and it is not possible to gaze at them. THEREFORE, the importance of their activities is not known. The petals THAT ARE IN THE FLOWER BLOSSOM sparkle with a variety of colors.

159. עוֹבֵד צִיּוּר, אוּמָנוּ דְּמָארֵי עָלְמָא, חַפְיָין עַל תְּלַת מְאָה וְשַׁבְעִין וַחֲמִשָּׁה כְּרוּבִין דִּתְחוֹתַיְיהוּ, בָּתַר שְׁבָכִין אַחֲרָנִין לְגוֹ. וְאִינּוּן שְׁבָכִין סְחוֹר דַּעֲזָרָה לְגוֹ.

159. Embroidery, which is the artistry of The Creator of the world, covers over the 375 Cherubs below them over other covering tapestry layers that are inside, since these layers surround the inside of the court.

160. וּלְעֵילָא מִנְּהוֹן, אִינּוּן גּוּפִין פְּרִישָׁאן, תְּחוֹת גּוּפָנִין אִינּוּן כְּרוּבִין, כֻּלְּהוּ גַּדְפִין פְּרִישָׁן, מְשַׁלְּבָן אִלֵּין בְּאִלֵּין. הָכָא אָמַר רַב מְתִיבְתָּא, דְּכָל מַאן דְּאִסְתַּכַּל בְּאִינּוּן גּוּפָנִין, מְנַהֲרִין אַנְפּוֹי כִּנְהִירוּ דְשִׁמְשָׁא.

160. Grapevines are spread above THE CHERUBS, since the Cherubs are underneath the grapevines, all spreading out their wings and intertwined one into the other. Here, the head of the Yeshivah said that whoever gazes at these grapevines, his face shines like sunlight.

161. אִינּוּן שְׁבָכִין דְּאִתְחַמָן סָחוֹר סָחוֹר דַּעֲזָרָה, כֻּלְּהוּ מְרֻקְמָן, בְּחוּטִין דִּנְהִירִין בִּגְוָונִין סַגִּיאִין, מְלַהֲטָן בַּד׳ מִינֵי זְהוֹרִין דְּאֶשָּׁא. שַׁלְהוֹבִין סַלְקִין, וּגְוָונִין מְנַצְצָן, וּלְזִמְנִין שַׁלְהוֹבִין מִשְׁתַּכְּכֵי, וּנְהוֹרִין וּגְוָונִין סַלְקִין, וּבַטְשֵׁי אַלֵּין בְּאִלֵּין.

161. These tapestry grid covers are unfurled round about in the courtyard. FROM INSIDE, all are embroidered in strands of lights in multitudes of colors. They flame with four kinds of fiery glows of brightness. The flames rise, and the hues sparkle. Sometimes, the flames are soothed and the lights and colors rise. Then they clash one with the other.

162. שִׁית אֶלֶף אַגָּנִין, לְגַבֵּי אִינּוּן שְׁבָכִין, ד׳ גְּוָונִין, לְד׳ סִטְרִין דַּעֲזָרָה, אִלֵּין אִינּוּן רַבְרְבִין, וּנְבִיעוּ דְּמַיִין חַיִּין בְּכָל סִטְרֵי. וְאִינּוּן נַפְלֵי בְּאִינּוּן אַגָּנִין, וּבַלְעֵי בְּאַתְרַיְיהוּ וְאִלֵּין מַיִּין לָא יַדְעֵי לְאָן אַזְלִין.

162. And 6,000 basins lie next to these networks. There are four hues to the four sides of the courtyard. These are large, and a spring of living water is found on each side. They drop into these basins and get absorbed there. These waters do not know where they are flowing to.

163. בְּאֶמְצָעוּ דַּעֲזָרָה, יְקוּמוּן כֻּלְּהוּ יִשְׂרָאֵל, וְיִתְחֲזוּן קַמֵּי מַלְכָּא קַדִּישָׁא. בְּסְטַר דָּרוֹם בַּעֲזָרָה דָּא, אִתְיְילִיד חַד מַעְיִינָא דְּמַיָּא, וְאִתְדְּמֵי דְּקָא יִשְׁטְפוּן מַיָּא כָּל עָלְמָא. מַאן דְּיֵיעוּל בְּהוּ, יְהוֹן עַד בִּרְכַּיִם, יֵיעוּל בְּהוּ גִּבָּר רַב יֵיעוּל בְּהוּ עַד בִּרְכַּיִם, אִי תִּינוֹק בַּר יוֹמָא עַד בִּרְכַּיִם. מַאן דְּשָׁתֵי מִנַּיְיהוּ יִתְחַכַּם, וְיִתְפְּקַח בְּחָכְמְתָא.

163. In the center of the court, all Yisrael will stand and be seen in the presence of the Holy King, FROM WHOM YISRAEL RECEIVES CHOCHMAH THAT IS ALSO CALLED SIGHT. On the South side of the court, a new water spring is born and it seems that the waters will flood the whole world. Whoever enters into them will enter to his knees. If a mighty man enters, he will enter to his knees, and if a baby no older than a day ENTERS THEM, he shall still enter to his knees. Whoever drinks of them shall become filled with wisdom.

164. מַעְיָינָא דָּא נָפִיק מִגּוֹ מַרְגְּלָא חֲדָא זְעֵירָא, בְּכוֹתָלָא דְּדָרוֹם. אִינּוּן מַיִין בַּלְעֵי גּוֹ אַתְרָא, וּמִתַּמָּן יִפְּקוּן לְבַר מִמַּקְדְּשָׁא, עַד דְּיַעֲלוּ לְנַחַל שִׁטִּים, יְשַׁטְפוּן הַהוּא זִמָה, דְּאוֹלְדִין מַיָּא דְּשִׁטִּים. וע"ד מַיִין אִלֵּין בַּעֲזָרָה, בְּגִין אִינּוּן דְּאִתְחֲזוּן תַּמָּן דְּכוּרִין. הֲווֹ שָׁתָאן מִן מַיָּא, לָא חַיְישֵׁי בְּנוּקְבֵי, בְּמֵיתַיְיהוּן לְאִתְחֲזָאָה קַמֵּי מַלְכָּא קַדִּישָׁא. תּוּ, דְּהָא יִתְפַּקְּחוּן לְמִנְדַּע מִלִּין סְתִימִין דְּמַלְכָּא עִלָּאָה, גּוֹ מַקְדְּשָׁא דָּא כָּל הִרְהוּרִין יִשְׁתַּכְּחוּן, בַּר הִרְהוּרָא דְּחֶדְוָה דְּמַלְכָּא קַדִּישָׁא.

164. This spring emerges from one small gem in the south wall. These waters get absorbed in their area and from there, they will continue to flow out of the Temple until they reach up to the spring of Shitim. They will rinse away that obscenity that the waters of the spring of Shitim brought about. Therefore, once the males that came to be seen at the waters in the court drank from them, they had no fear of the females who came to be seen before the Holy King. Moreover, THROUGH THE WATER, they would become more knowledgeable about the concealed matters of the Supernal King. In this temple, all thoughts must be forgotten except for the thought of the Holy King's rejoicing.

165. עַנְפָּא חַד נָפִיק, גּוֹ אֶמְצָעוּ דְּהַהוּא מַעְיָינָא. אָמַר רַב מְתִיבְתָּא, כַּד קָרִיבְנָא לְהַהוּא עַנְפָּא גּוֹ מַעְיָינָא, אִסְתַּלַּק עַנְפָּא לְעֵילָּא לְעֵילָּא, כָּל מַה דְּקָרִיבְנָא, הָכִי אִסְתַּלַּק, יְסוֹדָא וְשָׁרְשָׁא דְּהַהוּא עַנְפָּא לָאו אִיהוּ אֶלָּא בְּמַיָּא. הַהוּא עַנְפָּא חָפֵי עָלְמִין. כָּל גַּווֹנִין דְּעָלְמָא בְּאִינּוּן טַרְפִּין דִּילֵיהּ. אִיבָּא דִּילֵיהּ, לָא יְדִיעַ מַהוּ. וְלָא יַכְלִין לְמִנְדַּע, וְאָמַר, דְּקָא שָׁאִיל לְמָשִׁיחַ עַל הַהוּא אִיבָּא, וְאָמַר, אִיבָּא דָּא גָּנִיז, לְאִישׁ מַשְׂעֶנְתּוֹ בְּיָדוֹ מֵרוֹב יָמִים. מַאן דְּזָכֵי לְמִנְדַּע דָּא, לִינְדַּע.

165. One branch emerges at the center of that spring. The head of the Yeshivah said, When I approached that branch in the spring, the branch went high above. The closer I approached, THE HIGHER it went. The foundation and the root of that branch are only in the water. This branch covers worlds and all the hues in the world ARE VISIBLE in its leaves. What kind of fruit it bears is unknown, and it is not possible to find out. THE

HEAD OF THE YESHIVAH said that he asked Messiah about this fruit and was told that this fruit is stored away for "every man with his staff in his hand for very age" (Zecharyah 8:4). Whoever deserves to experience this will understand.

166. רָקִיעַ חַד אִית עַל הַהוּא עַנְפָּא, פָּרִישׂ לְעֵילָא. מֵהַהוּא רְקִיעַ, אָזִיל טַלָּא ע"ג מַעְיָינָא דָא, וְלָא יַתִּיר. כַּד אִסְתַּכַּל ב"נ לְהַהוּא רְקִיעַ מֵרָחִיק, דָּמֵי תִּכְלָא קָרִיב יַתִּיר, דָּמֵי סוּמָקָא. קָרִיב יַתִּיר, דָּמֵי יָרוֹק, קָרוֹב יַתִּיר, דָּמֵי חִוָּור, דְּלֵית חִוָּור בְּעָלְמָא כְּגִינֵיה. טַלָּא דְּקָא אָזִיל מִנֵּיה, אִשְׁתְּאִיב בְּהַהוּא עַנְפָּא, וְעָבֵיד אִיבָּא דָא, וְאִתְרַבֵּי. הַהוּא רְקִיעָא, אִיהוּ אָזִיל בְּגִלְגּוּלָא יַתִּיר, מִמָּה דְּעַיְינִין יַכְלִין לְאִסְתַּכְּלָא.

166. There is one firmament above this CENTRAL branch, FROM THE RIGHT ASPECT that is spread over it from above. From that firmament dew flows to this spring and no further. When a person gazes at this firmament from a distance, it looks similar to blue. When he approaches nearer, it seems reddish and when he approaches even closer, it seems greenish. When he draws even nearer, it seems white and no other white in the world is like it. The dew that flows from it gets drawn into the branch and produces the fruit, and it grows. The firmament circles faster than the eye can see.

20. "All your males shall appear"

A Synopsis

We read about the requirement for all circumcised males to appear before God three times a year for the honor of the three patriarchs who accepted the covenant upon themselves. As soon as a man is circumcised and perfected, he is fit to walk behind the Shechinah instead of in front of her. Because Noah was circumcised and perfect but his membrane was not uncovered, he walked with the Elohim rather than in front of the Shechinah. We read that God traveled before Yisrael in the pillar of cloud and fire until they sinned and weakened, at which time the angel of God moved behind them. This section concludes with an incomplete fragment about the two Messiahs.

167. כָּל אִינוּן נְטוּרֵי קַיְּימָא קַדִּישָׁא, בָּעוּן לְאִתְחֲזָאָה קַמֵּי מַלְכָּא, דְּהָא לָא אִתְחֲזוּן, אֶלָּא בְּגִין לְאַחֲזָאָה דְּאִינוּן בְּנֵי גְזִירוּ קַדִּישָׁא. וע"ד יֵרָאֶה כָּל זְכוּרְךָ, אִינוּן בְּנֵי קַיְּימָא קַדִּישָׁא. דָּיֵיק רַב מְתִיבְתָּא, זְכוּרְךָ, וְלָא זְכָרְךָ. דְּהָא זָכָר כְּתִיב, וְלָא זָכוּר, מַאי זְכוּרְךָ אֶלָּא כָּל אִינוּן דְּנַטְרִין קַיְּימָא קַדִּישָׁא, וְלָא חָבָאן בֵּיה, אִינוּן הֲווֹ בְּנֵי מַלְכָּא, דְּבְכֹל יוֹמָא מִשְׁתַּבַּח בְּהוּ וְדָכִיר לוֹן תָּדִיר. וע"ד זְכוּרְךָ, הַהוּא דְּאִית בֵּיה קַיְּימָא קַדִּישָׁא, דְּדָכִיר לוֹן מַלְכָּא בְּכָל יוֹמָא, דְּלֵית שְׁבָחָא קַמֵּי מַלְכָּא עִלָּאָה, אֶלָּא כְּמַאן דְּנָטִיר קַיְּימָא דָא.

167. All those who preserve the holy covenant must show themselves in the presence of the Holy King, since they are there to be seen only for the purpose of showing that they are members of the holy covenant. Therefore, "all your males shall appear" (Shemot 23:17), who are members of the holy covenant. The head of the Yeshivah points out that it says *"Zechurcha"* (Eng. 'your males') and not *'Zecharcha'* (Eng. 'your memory'), since the word "*zachar*" is written, NAMELY MALE, and not *'zachor'* or memory, SINCE IT DOES NOT MEAN 'YOUR MEMORY'. Why "your males," – WHY JUST MALES? It is only those who preserve the holy covenant and do not sin with it who are worthy children of the King, who gets praised through them daily and always remembers them. Therefore, THE SCRIPTURE SAYS: "your males," MEANING the King remembers those who have a holy covenant every day, since there is no praise before the sublime King as the

one who preserves this covenant.

168. וע"ד בָּעֵי דְּיִתְחֲזוּן תְּלַת זִמְנִין בְּשַׁתָּא קַמֵּיהּ. תְּלַת זִמְנִין אֲמַאי. אֶלָּא בְּגִין אֲבָהָן קַדְמָאֵי, דְּקַבִּילוּ לְהַאי בְּרִית, קַדְמָאָה לְכָל פִּקּוּדִין דְּאוֹרַיְיתָא, וּבג"כ תְּלַת זִמְנִין אִינּוּן בְּשַׁתָּא. אַבְרָהָם קַבִּיל בְּרִית. יִצְחָק קַבִּיל בְּרִית. יַעֲקֹב הֲוָה שְׁלִים מִכֻּלְּהוּ, וע"ד כְּתִיב בֵּיהּ, וְיַעֲקֹב אִישׁ תָּם, שְׁלִים מִכֹּלָא.

168. Therefore, there is a requirement to be seen in His presence three times a year. Why exactly three times? It is only for the honor of the three patriarchs that accepted upon themselves this covenant as before all other commandments in the Torah. Therefore, it is three times a year. Abraham accepted the covenant and Isaac accepted the covenant. Jacob was most perfect of all, SINCE ABRAHAM AND ISAAC CORRESPOND TO THE RIGHT AND LEFT AND JACOB CORRESPONDS TO THE CENTRAL COLUMN THAT IS COMPOSED OF THE OTHER TWO. Therefore it is written by him: "And Jacob was a plain (*tam*: perfect) man" (Beresheet 25:27), MEANING MORE PERFECT THAN THE OTHERS.

169. אַבְרָהָם תָּמִים אִקְרֵי, וְלָא הֲוָה כ"כ שְׁלִים, אֲבָל תָּם: שְׁלִים מִכֹּלָא. מַה כְּתִיב בְּנֹחַ, אִישׁ צַדִּיק תָּמִים הָיָה בְּדוֹרוֹתָיו. הֲוָה רְשִׁים בִּרְשִׁימוּ קַדִּישָׁא בֵּינַיְיהוּ. וְאָמַר רַב מְתִיבְתָּא, בְּכָל אֲתָר דִּכְתִיב תָּמִים, דְּרָשִׁים בִּרְשִׁימוּ קַדִּישָׁא, בְּאָת קַיְּימָא דִּבְרִית, וּבְגִין דְּנָטַר בְּרִית, אִקְרֵי תָּמִים בְּדוֹרוֹתָיו. מַה דְּלָא הֲוֵי כֻלְּהוּ הָכִי, דְּאִינּוּן מְחַבְּלָן אָרְחַיְיהוּ.

169. Abraham was called *Tamim* (Eng. 'perfect'), but he was not all that perfect. However, *Tam* is most perfect. It is written about Noah: "A just man and perfect (Heb. *tamim*) in his generations" (Beresheet 6:9), for he was impressed with a holy mark among them. The head of the Yeshivah said, Anywhere that is written *Tamim*, ITS MEANING IS that he is inscribed with the holy mark of the sign of circumcision. Since he preserved the covenant, he was called *Tamim* in his generation, while all the others were not so, MEANING THAT THE OTHERS DID NOT KEEP THE COVENANT, as they corrupted their paths.

ס170. וע״ד כְּתִיב, אֶת הָאֱלֹהִים הִתְהַלֶּךְ נֹחַ. וְכִי מַאן יָכִיל לְמֵיהַךְ
עִמֵּיה. אֶלָּא כָּל מַאן דְּנָטִיר בְּרִית קַדִּישָׁא, אִזְדַּוְוגַת בֵּיה שְׁכִינְתָּא,
וְשַׁרְיָאת עֲלֵיה. וּבג״כ, תָּמִים תִּהְיֶה עִם יְיָ׳ אֱלֹהֶיךָ. תָּמִים תִּהְיֶה,
וּלְבָתַר עִם יְיָ׳ אֱלֹהֶיךָ. בְּזִוּוּגָא חֲדָא. דְּכֵיוָן דְּנָטִיר בְּרִית דָּא, עִם יְיָ׳
לֶהֱוֵי, וְלָא אִתְפְּרַשׁ מִנֵּיה.

170. Therefore, it is written: "And Noah walked with the Elohim" (Ibid.). HE ASKS: Who could possibly walk with THE ELOHIM? HE REPLIES: The Shechinah joins anyone that keeps the holy covenant. Therefore, it says, "You shall be perfect (Heb. *tamim*) with Hashem your Elohim" (Devarim 18:13), WHICH MEANS to first be perfect and then you will be joined "with Hashem your Elohim." If he preserves this covenant, he will be with Hashem and not separate from Him.

171. בְּאַבְרָהָם כְּתִיב, הִתְהַלֵּךְ לְפָנַי וֶהְיֵה תָמִים, גְּזִירוּ דְּאַתְּ קַיָּימָא.
הִתְהַלֵּךְ לְפָנַי, מֵהָכָא, דְּלָא יְהַךְ גְּבַר בָּתַר אִתְּתָא, אֶלָּא קַמָהָא, אֹרַח
כְּשֵׁר אִיהוּ וְהָא כְּתִיב, הִנֵּה אָנֹכִי שֹׁלֵחַ מַלְאָךְ לְפָנֶיךָ. וְשָׁלַחְתִּי לְפָנֶיךָ
מַלְאָךְ. לְאַבְרָהָם דְּלָא הֲוָה גָזִיר, דָּחָה לֵיה לְקַמָּה. וע״ד לָא כְּתִיב הֲוֵה
תָמִים, וְהִתְהַלֵּךְ לְפָנַי. אֶלָּא הִתְהַלֵּךְ לְפָנַי, דְּלָא יָאוֹת אַנְתְּ, עַד שֶׁתְּהֵא
תָמִים. וְכֵן בְּכֻלְּהוּ, כֵּיוָן דב״נ תָּמִים, וְנָטִיר לֵיה, מִיַּד הִיא לְקַמֵּיה,
וְאִיהוּ אֲבַתְרָה, כְּשֵׁר אִיהוּ לְדָא. לִגְרִעוֹנָא מַה כְּתִיב, כִּי שָׁב מֵאַחֲרַי.

171. Of Abraham, it says, "Walk before Me, and be perfect (Heb. *tamim*)" (Beresheet 17:1), MEANING the sign of circumcision THAT IS CALLED *TAMIM*: "Walk before Me." From here, we take it that a male should not walk behind a woman but rather in front of her, which is the fit way. HE INQUIRES: It is written: "Behold, I send an angel before you" (Shemot 23:20), WHICH MEANS THE SHECHINAH REFERRED TO AS ANGEL and also: "And I will send an angel before you" (Shemot 33:2). HENCE, THE SHECHINAH WAS GOING IN FRONT OF THEM AND THEY BEHIND HER. HE REPLIES: Abraham, who was not circumcised, was pushed in front of Her, AND SHE DID NOT ALLOW HIM TO WALK BEHIND HER. Therefore, it is not written: 'Be perfect and walk before Me', but rather "Walk before Me" AS LONG AS YOU HAVEN'T YET BEEN CIRCUMCISED, since you are not worthy yet TO GO BEHIND ME until you will be perfected, MEANING UNTIL YOU ARE CIRCUMCISED. It is the same with everybody. As soon as the person is perfected and preserves his perfection, the Shechinah immediately is in front of him and he is behind Her, since he is now fit for it. It is to one's detriment that it is written, "for he is turned back from following me" (I Shmuel 15:11), WHICH MEANS HE IS NOT WORTHY OF RECEIVING FROM THE BACK OF THE SHECHINAH.

172. נֹחַ גְּזִיר הֲוָה, וְתָמִים, פְּרִיעָה לָא הֲוָה בֵּיהּ, וּבְגִין דְּלָא הֲוָה בֵּיהּ פְּרִיעָה מַה כְּתִיב, אֶת הָאֱלֹהִים, וְלָא אַחַר הָאֱלֹהִים, לְקַמָּא לָא הֲוָה, בְּגִין דַּהֲוָה גְּזִיר, לַאֲחוֹרָא לָא הֲוָה, בְּגִין דְּלָא אִתְפְּרַע. אֵיךְ הֲוָה. אֶת הָאֱלֹהִים, סָמִיךְ לֵיהּ, וְלָא יָכִיל לְאִסְתַּכְּלָא בֵּיהּ, דְּלָאו כָּשֵׁר כ"כ.

172. Noah was circumcised and perfect, but his membrane was not uncovered. Because he did not perform this act of uncovering the membrane, it is written: "AND NOAH WALKED with the Elohim" and not behind the Elohim. He wasn't in front of the Shechinah, because he was circumcised and he wasn't behind the Shechinah, because he didn't perform this act of uncovering the membrane. How was it with him? "With the Elohim," meaning close to Him, but unable to observe HIS BACK since he was not that worthy – AND ALL THIS, SINCE HE DIDN'T PERFORM THE ACT OF UNCOVERING THE MEMBRANE (HEB. *PRIAH*).

173. בְּיִשְׂרָאֵל כְּתִיב, וַיְיָ' הוֹלֵךְ לִפְנֵיהֶם יוֹמָם בְּעַמּוּד עָנָן וְלַיְלָה בְּעַמּוּד אֵשׁ וְגוֹ'. כֵּיוָן דְּאָמְרוּ יִשְׂרָאֵל, הַמִבְּלִי אֵין קְבָרִים בְּמִצְרַיִם וְגוֹ'. כִּי טוֹב לָנוּ עֲבוֹד אֶת מִצְרָיִם. כִּבְיָכוֹל, אִתְחֲלַשׁ דַּעְתָּא. כְּתִיב וַיִּסַּע מַלְאַךְ הָאֱלֹהִים הַהוֹלֵךְ לִפְנֵי מַחֲנֵה יִשְׂרָאֵל וַיֵּלֶךְ מֵאַחֲרֵיהֶם, וַיִּסַּע לְמֶעְבַּד בְּהוּ נוּקְמִין.

173. About Yisrael, it says: "And Hashem went before them by day in a pillar of a cloud...and by night in a pillar of fire..." (Shemot 13:21), MEANING THAT THEY TRAVELED BEHIND HASHEM. As soon as Yisrael said, "Because there were no graves in Egypt...for it had been better for us to serve Egypt" (Shemot 14:11-12), their minds seemingly weakened. THEREFORE, it is written: "And the angel of Elohim who went before the

camp of Yisrael, removed and went behind them" (Ibid. 19), MEANING
THEY WERE PUSHED IN FRONT OF HASHEM. He "removed" to do
vengeance on them. (THE CONTINUATION IS MISSING).

174. וע"ד חֲדֵי מָשִׁיחַ, וְחַדֵי רַב מְתִיבְתָּא, דְּקָא אִתְבַּשַּׂר בְּדָא. וְאָמַר
רַב מְתִיבְתָּא, דְּהָא דָּיֵיק לְמָשִׁיחַ וְאָמַר, מְנָא הֲוָה לְדָנִיֵּאל דְּקָאָמַר,
פְּרֵיס פְּרִיסַת מַלְכוּתָךְ וִיהִיבַת לְמָדַי וּפָרָס. מֵאִינּוּן אַתְוָון דּוּפַרְסִין
אִשְׁתְּמַע לֵיהּ. וְהָכָא מַאי הוּא. א"ל, הָכִי הוּא וַדַּאי, פְּרֵיס פְּרִיסַת
מַלְכוּתָךְ חַיָּיבָא, ע"י דִּמְשִׁיחַ אַחֲרָא, וּלְבָתַר יִשְׁלוֹט מֶלֶךְ פְּרַס, וְיִטּוֹל
מַלְכְּוָון סַגִּיאִין, וְהוּא יִשְׁלַט עַל אַרְעָא קַדִּישָׁא תְּרֵיסָר יַרְחֵי, וְהוּא
יִשְׁלוֹט וְיִקְטוֹל סַגִּיאִין, וְהַהוּא מְשִׁיחָא, וּלְבָתַר יִפּוֹל, וִיקַבְּלוּן מַלְכוּתָא
קַדִּישֵׁי עֶלְיוֹנִין. וע"ד, וּפַרְסִין, מַלְכָּא דְּפָרַס, אִשְׁתְּמַע הָכָא.

174. (THE BEGINNING IS MISSING) and about this, Messiah was glad and
the head of the Yeshivah rejoiced when told of this. The head of the
Yeshivah, who was being precise, inquired of Messiah and said, From
where did Daniel know that he said, "Your kingdom is divided and given to
Media and Persia" (Daniel 5:28)? He learned it from these letters of
"*ufarsin*" (Ibid. 25. THAT WAS WRITTEN. Why is this here, MEANING TO
SAY WHAT CAN WE LEARN FROM THIS REGARDING MESSIAH? He said to
him, Certainly it is so, THAT HE IS ALLUDING HERE TO KING MESSIAH,
your (Belshazzar's) evil Kingdom shall be divided through the other
Messiah, MEANING MESSIAH THE SON OF JOSEPH. Following that, the
king of Persia will dominate and conquer many kingdoms and rule the Holy
Land for twelve months. And he will rule and kill many, AMONG THEM
Messiah, THE SON OF JOSEPH. After that, THE KING OF PERSIA will fall
and holy supernal ones will receive the kingdom. Therefore, here too, the
word "ufarsin" indicates the King of Persia.

21. The spring of water

A Synopsis

We hear about the trees that grow in the spring of water, all the parts of which are destined for healing; there is no hunger, worry nor sorrow among them. The author tells Rabbi Shimon about the river Jordan that is drawn yearly into the river that emerges from Eden. Then the flow from Eden spreads to the earth of the Temple, and when it withdraws after three days it leaves behind in the earth of the tabernacle all kinds of paintings that God produces in the Garden of Eden.

175. אִי חֲסִידָא קַדִּישָׁא, כַּמָּה חֶדְוָה עַל חֶדְוָה, בְּהַהוּא מַעְיָינָא. בְּהַהוּא מַעְיָינָא, מִגַּדְּלָא כָּל זִינֵי אִילָנִין, דְּנָצִיב קוּדְשָׁא בְּרִיךְ הוּא בג״ע, וְכֻלְּהוּ קַיְימֵי לְאַסְוָותָא, טַרְפִּין וְאֵיבִין וְעַנְפִין, וּלְחֶדּוּ לִבָּא תָּדִיר. וְלֵית בֵּינַיְיהוּ כַּפְנָא, וּדְאָגָה, וַאֲנָחָה, לְעָלְמִין. זַכָּאָה עַמָּא דְּכָל דָּא מְחַכָּאן, וְכָל דָּא גָּנִיז לוֹן.

175. Oh, holy pious one, how much happiness upon happiness is in that spring? In that spring grow all kinds of trees that the Holy One, blessed be He, planted in the Garden of Eden. All are made for healing, the leaves, the fruits and the branches, and always to the gladness of the heart. There is no hunger, worry nor sorrow among them. Praised is the nation for whom all this awaits and is stored up.

176. אר״ש, בְּקַרְקַע דְּהַאי מַקְדְּשָׁא, אִית מֵאֵלֵין פְּלִיאָן, אָ״ל, אִי רַבִּי, אִי ר׳, זַכָּאָה חוּלְקָךְ דְּכָל הַאי. בְּהַהוּא. ע״ג הַהוּא מַעְיָינָא רְקִימָא, אֲבָל לֵית מַאן דְּיָכִיל לְאִסְתַּכְּלָא בֵּיהּ, לְזִמְנִין נְהִירוּ דִילֵיהּ נְהוֹרָא. לְזִמְנִין חֲשׁוֹכָא, לְזִמְנִין גַּוֶון אַרְגְּוָונָא. מִנַּצְצָן דְּלָא יַכְלִין עַיְינִין לְאִסְתַּכְּלָא לְעֵילָא. הַהִיא דִּשְׁאַלְתְּ חֲסִידָא קַדִּישָׁא, מֵהַהוּא קַרְקַע דְּמַקְדְּשָׁא, רַב מְתִיבְתָּא לָא פָּרִישׁ מִנֵּיהּ, דְּהָא גָּנִיז אִיהוּ גּוֹ יַרְדְּנָא, וְהָא אֲמֵינָא לָךְ מַה דַּאֲמֵינָא, אֲבָל נִשְׁאַל מִלָּה דָּא, וְתִנְדַּע מַה דְּתִנְדַּע.

176. Rabbi Shimon said, All these wonders are available in the earth of the Temple. He said to him, Oh, my teacher. Praised is your lot that...(PART IS

MISSING HERE)...it is fashioned on that spring, but there is no one that could look at it. Sometimes its light is bright and sometimes it is dim, and sometimes it is in the color purple. It sparkles until the eyes can not look up. The head of the Yeshivah did not define any of that which you asked, holy pious one, about that Temple's earth, since it is stored in the Jordan River, and what I already told is said here. However, this has been asked and you shall know what you can.

177. יַרְדֵּן דָּא, עָאל וְאִתְמְשַׁךְ זִמְנָא חֲדָא בְּשַׁתָּא, גּוֹ הַהוּא נָהָר דְּנָפִיק מֵעֵדֶן, לָאו מֵאִינּוּן אַרְבַּע נַהֲרִין דְּאִתְמַשְׁכָן מִנֵּיה, אֶלָּא בֵּיה מַמָּשׁ. כֵּיוָן דְּמָטֵי לְגַבֵּיה, אִיהוּ אִתְמְשַׁךְ וְאִתְפָּשַׁט וְעָאל גּוֹ יַרְדְּנָא. וְכֵיוָן דְּמָטֵי גּוֹ קַרְקַע דְּמַקְדְּשָׁא, אִשְׁתְּכַח תַּמָּן תְּלַת יוֹמִין, וְלָא אִתְפָּשַׁט וְלָא אִתְמְשַׁךְ לְאֲתָר אַחֲרָא. וְאָמַר רַב מְתִיבְתָּא, דְּכַד אַהֲדָר הַהוּא נָהָר לְאַתְרֵיה, שָׁבִיק תַּמָּן, כָּל זִינֵי צִיּוּרִין, דְּקָא עָבֵיד קוּדְשָׁא בְּרִיךְ הוּא בג"ע, דְּאִינּוּן צִיּוּרִין גְּנִיזִין, דִּתְחוֹת דּוּכְתַּיְיהוּ.

177. The Jordan, WHICH IS YESOD OF MALCHUT, enters and flows once a year, MEANING ONE TIME WHICH IS THE SECRET OF ONE COLUMN, FROM THREE TIMES A YEAR, WHICH IS THE SECRET OF THREE COLUMNS AND THAT IS IN THE SECRET OF THE LEFT COLUMN, into that river that emerges from Eden, THAT IS YESOD OF ZEIR ANPIN, BECAUSE THE START OF THE UNION IS IN THE ASPECT OF THE LEFT COLUMN, not into the four rivers that spread out from it, but actually in it, INTO THE RIVER THAT EMANATES FROM EDEN ITSELF. As soon as it reaches it, it spreads and expands and enters into the Jordan, FROM THE ASPECT OF THE LEFT COLUMN FIRST, IN THE SECRET OF RECONCILIATION. AS SOON as it reaches the earth of the Temple, WHICH IS THE SECRET OF MALCHUT OF MALCHUT, it remains there three days – THAT IS, IN THE SECRET OF THE THREE COLUMNS – and does not spread and extend to another area. The head of the Yeshivah said, When that river, WHICH EMANATES FROM EDEN, returns to its original place, it leaves behind IN THE EARTH OF THE TABERNACLE all kinds of paintings that the Holy One, blessed be He, produces in the Garden of Eden, which are drawings stored underneath their area...(THE END IS MISSING).

22. Pillars and eagles

A Synopsis

We are told about the pillars that drip incense into basins, and how the incense will be burned daily in the presence of God in the time to come. We read about the flight of the eagles and the letters that fly from their mouths and the lamps suspended between the pillars; the candles in those lamps burn every day and are put out at night because of the pain of Yisrael. When morning comes they light up spontaneously. Next Rabbi Shimon is told that on the next day he will be granted the revelation of the rest of the secrets, and his teachers fly away.

178. אִלֵּין הָכָא וְאִלֵּין הָכָא, וְסַלְקֵי וְנַחֲתֵי כִּדְקַדְמֵיתָא. בְּהַהוּא סְטַר דָּרוֹם, אִית תְּלַת מְאָה וְחַמְשִׁין עַמּוּדִין, מִכָּל זִינֵי מַרְגְּלָאן. וְאִלֵּין אִינוּן דִּנְהִירִין תָּדִיר, וְנַטְפִין בּוּסְמִין טְמִירִין, דְּלָא אִתְגַּלּוּ לְעָלְמִין. אַרְבַּע אַגָּנִין בְּכָל עַמּוּדָא וְעַמּוּדָא נְעִיצִין. וְכַד אִינוּן בּוּסְמִין נַטְפִין, מֵאִינוּן עַמּוּדִין, נַפְלֵי בְּהוּ, וְאִתְמַלְיָין כֻּלְּהוּ אֲגָנוֹת, וְלָא נָפְקִין בּוּסְמִין לְבַר.

178. (THE BEGINNING IS MISSING) these here and those there, and they ascend and descend as at first. On the south side, WHICH IS THE RIGHT COLUMN THAT IS ALL CHESED, there are 350 pillars of all kinds of gems, and those are the ones that are always bright. They drip spices that are concealed and are never visible. Four basins are inserted in every pillar and when the fragrant droplets flow down from the pillars, they drip INTO THE BASINS. All the basins get filled and the spices do not flow out.

179. מֵאִינוּן בּוּסְמִין, זְמִינִין לְזִמְנָא דְּאָתֵי, לְאַקְטְרָא בְּכָל יוֹמָא קְטוֹרְתָּא, קַמֵּי מַלְכָּא קַדִּישָׁא. דְּלָא יְהֱווּ מִכְּתִישׁוּ דִּבְנֵי נָשָׁא. אִינוּן בּוּסְמִין לָא יְדִיעַ עִקָּרָא דִּלְהוֹן, וּמִמָּה הֲווֹ, אֶלָּא מֵאִינוּן עַמּוּדִין נַפְלִין תַּמָּן.

179. In the future to come they will burn incense daily from these spices in the presence of the Holy King. That incense will not be from ingredients crushed by humans. It is not known what the essence of these fragrances is nor what their ingredients are. They are just flowing in from those pillars.

180. תְּרֵין נִשְׁרִין בְּכָל עַמּוּדָא וְעַמּוּדָא, מִתְנַצְצָן וּמִתְלַהֲטִין בְּכָל גַּוְונִין. שְׁבַע מְאָה נִשְׁרִין. אִינּוּן, פַּרְחִין, אִלֵּין הָכָא וְאִלֵּין הָכָא, בְּגִלְגּוּלָא דְּעַמּוּדִין. כַּד אִסְתַּחֲרָן, לָא יַכְלִין עַיְינִין לְאִסְתַּכְּלָא, דּוּכְתָּא דִּבְהוּ.

180. Two eagles in every individual pillar sparkle and shine in all hues, so there are altogether seven hundred eagles IN ALL THE 350 PILLARS. They fly in all directions, those here and these there, with the revolutions of the pillars. And when they turn about, the eyes are incapable of watching their location.

181. תְּלַת אַתְוָון בַּלְטִין וּפַרְחִין, מִפּוּמָא דָּא לְפוּמָא דָּא. בְּגִלְגּוּלָא דְּעַמּוּדִין וְנִשְׁרִין. כָּל אִינּוּן אַתְוָון מְרֻקְּמָן בְּאֶשָּׁא חִוָּורָא, וְדַהֲבָא יְרוֹקָא. תְּרֵין אַלְפִין וּמְאָה מְנַרְתִּין, תַּלְיָין בֵּין אִינּוּן עַמּוּדִין. וּתְרֵין אַלְפִין וּמְאָה שְׁרָגִין, בְּכָל מְנַרְתָּא וּמְנַרְתָּא. דַּלְקִין בִּימָמָא, וּבְלֵילְיָא מִתְדַּעֲכֵי, עַל צַעֲרָא דְּיִשְׂרָאֵל. כַּד אָתֵי צַפְרָא, דַּלְקִין כֻּלְּהוּ מִגַּרְמַיְיהוּ.

181. Three letters protrude and fly from the mouth of this one to the mouth of that one, when the pillars and eagles circle. All the letters get embroidered in fire of white and gold and green. There are 2,100 lamps suspended between these pillars and 2,100 candles are in each individual lamp. They burn every day and are put out at night, because of the pain of Yisrael. When morning approaches, they light up spontaneously.

182. אַדְהֲווֹ יַתְבֵי, אַמְרֵי הָא רָמַשׁ לֵילְיָא. אָ"ל לְר"ש, אִי חֲסִידָא קַדִּישָׁא, נְהִירוּ דְּעָלְמָא, טוֹל פִּנְקְסָא דְּאַחְמָתָא דָּא, וְטוֹל שְׁרָגָא, וְכָתוּב מִלִּין אִלֵּין, דְּהָא מָטָא זִמְנָא דִּילָן, לְפַקְּדָא כָּל חַד וְחַד לְגוֹ קִבְרֵיהּ, עַד פַּלְגוּ לֵילְיָא, דְּקוּדְשָׁא בְּרִיךְ הוּא עָאל גּוֹ גִּנְתָּא לְאִשְׁתַּעְשְׁעָא בַּהֲדֵי צַדִּיקַיָּיא וּכְדֵין כָּל חַד וְחַד פָּרַח לְתַמָּן. וּלְמָחָר נֶהֱוֵי גַּבָּךְ, הוֹאִיל וְיָהֲבוּ לָן רְשׁוּ, לְאַשְׁלְמָא דּוֹרוֹנָא דְּקָא מְשַׁדְּרֵי לָךְ. פַּרְחֵי, בָּכָה ר"ש וְגָעָא.

182. While still seated, they mentioned that the night had fallen. He said to Rabbi Shimon, Oh, holy pious one, the light of the world. Take a scroll from this container, THAT IS A VESSEL IN WHICH WRITINGS ARE STORED, and take a candle and write these words. For our time has arrived, for each one to visit his grave until midnight. AND THEN the Holy One, blessed be He, enters the Garden of Eden to make merry with the just, and each one of us flies there. Tomorrow, we will be with you, since permission was granted us to complete the present that was sent to you, MEANING THE COMPLETION OF THE REVELATION OF THE SECRETS. They flew away. Rabbi Shimon cried and wailed.

23. "A loving hind"

A Synopsis

All night Rabbi Shimon writes what he has seen in the supernal realms. In the morning he sees the light of the Temple in the firmament. Two emissaries come from the head of the Yeshivah to reveal one thing to him.

183. פָּתַח וְאָמַר, אַיֶּלֶת אֲהָבִים וְיַעֲלַת חֵן דַּדֶּיהָ יְרַוֻּךָ בְכָל עֵת בְּאַהֲבָתָה תִּשְׁגֶּה תָמִיד. אוֹרַיְיתָא אוֹרַיְיתָא, נְהִירוּ דְּכָל עָלְמִין, כַּמָה יַמִּין, וּנְחָלִין, וּמְקוֹרִין, וּמַבּוּעִין, מִתְפַּשְּׁטֵי מִנָּךְ לְכָל סִטְרִין. מִנָּךְ כֹּלָא, עֲלָךְ קַיְימֵי עִלָּאִין וְתַתָּאִין, נְהִירוּ עִלָּאָה מִנָּךְ נָפְקָא. אוֹרַיְיתָא אוֹרַיְיתָא, מַה אֵימָא לְגַבָּךְ, אַיֶּלֶת אֲהָבִים אַנְתְּ, וְיַעֲלַת חֵן עֵילָא וְתַתָּא רְחִימִין דִּילָךְ. מַאן יִזְכֵּי לְיָנְקָא מִנָּךְ כַּדְקָא יֵאוֹת. אוֹרַיְיתָא אוֹרַיְיתָא שַׁעֲשׁוּעִים דְּמָארָךְ, מַאן יָכִיל לְגַלָּאָה, וּלְמֵימַר סִתְרִין וּגְנִיזִין דִּילָךְ. בָּכָה, וְאָעִיל רֵישֵׁיהּ בֵּין בִּרְכּוֹי, וְנָשַׁק לְעַפְרָא.

183. He opened the discussion saying, "A loving hind and a pleasant roe; let her breasts satisfy you at all times; and be you ravished always in her love" (Mishlei 5:19). O Torah, Torah, light of all worlds, how many seas and rivers and fountains and springs spread from you to all directions. From you comes everything, upon you are based higher and lower beings. The supernal light emanates from you. Torah, Torah, what shall I tell you? You are a loving hind and a pleasant roe. Those above and below are your admirers who would deserve to properly suckle from you. Torah, Torah, the delight of your Master, who is capable of revealing and speaking of the concealed and stored in you? He cried, placed his head between his knees and kissed the dust.

184. אַדְהָכִי חָמָא כְּמָה דְּיוֹקְנִין דְּחַבְרַיָּיא סַחֲרָנֵיהּ. א"ל, לָא תִּדְחַל בְּרֵיהּ דְּיוֹחַאי, לָא תִּדְחַל בּוּצִינָא קַדִּישָׁא, כְּתוֹב וַחֲדֵי גּוֹ חֶדְוָה דְּמָארָךְ. כָּתַב כָּל אִינּוּן מִלִּין דְּשָׁמַע בְּהַהוּא לֵילְיָא, וְלָעָא לוֹן, וְלָהַג לוֹן, וְלָא אַנְשֵׁי מִלָּה. וְהַהוּא שַׁרְגָּא נָהִיר קַמֵּיהּ כָּל הַהוּא לֵילְיָא, עַד דְּאָתָא צַפְרָא. כַּד אָתָא צַפְרָא, זָקַף עֵינוֹי, וְחָמָא חַד נְהִירוּ דַּהֲוָה נָהִיר

בִּרְקִיעָא, מָאִיךְ עֵינוֹי לְתַתָּא. אַהֲדָר כְּמִלְּקַדְמִין, וְחָמָא נְהִירוּ בְּכָל
רְקִיעָ, דְּנָהִיר וְסָלִיק בְּהַהוּא נְהִירוּ דִּיּוּקְנָא דְּבֵיתָא, בְּכַמָּה צִיּוּרִין. חֲדָא
ר"ש, וּלְפוּם רִגְעָא, אַגְנִיז הַהוּא נְהוֹרָא.

184. During this, RABBI SHIMON noticed several faces of his friends surrounding him. They told him, Do not fear, son of Yochai, do not be frightened, Holy Luminary, it is written that you shall rejoice in the happiness of your Master. He wrote all these things that he heard that night and he repeated them and studied them, and forgot nothing. The candle light illuminated for him all that night until the approach of the morning. When morning came, he raised his eyes and noticed a light that was bright in the sky. He lowered his eyes downwards, repeated again and saw light that was brightening the whole firmament. On that light emerged the form of the house, MEANING THE TEMPLE, SHOWING THAT THE UNION WAS ACHIEVED BETWEEN MALCHUT AND ZEIR ANPIN, pictured in several scenarios. Rabbi Shimon rejoiced and instantly the light was hidden away.

185. אַדְהָכִי, הָא אִינּוּן תְּרֵין שְׁלִיחָן אַתְיָין. אַשְׁכְּחוּהוּ רֵישֵׁיהּ בֵּין
בִּרְכּוֹי. אָמְרוּ לֵיהּ שְׁלָמָא עָלֵיהּ דְּמַר, שְׁלָמָא לְמַאן דְּעֵלָּאִין וְתַתָּאִין
בָּעָאן לְאַקְדְּמָא לֵיהּ שְׁלָם. קוּם. קָם ר"ש וַחֲדָא בְּהוּ. אָמְרוּ לֵיהּ, וְלָא
חָמֵית נַיְיחָא דְּרוּחָא דְּעָבֵד לָךְ מָארָךְ, חָמֵית נְהִירוּ דְּבֵיתָא בִּרְקִיעָא.
אָמַר לוֹן חֲמֵינָא, אָמְרוּ לֵיהּ בֵּיהּ שַׁעֲתָא, אַפִּיק תְּהוֹמָא בֵּי מַקְדְּשָׁא,
וְאַעְבְּרֵיהּ קוּדְשָׁא בְּרִיךְ הוּא בְּיַמָּא רַבָּא, וּמִנְּהִירוּ דִּילֵיהּ, הֲוָה נָהִיר
בִּרְקִיעָא.

185. Meanwhile, two emissaries arrived. They found him with his head between his knees. They told him, Peace be on you, my lord, peace to whom higher and lower beings wish to welcome. Rise. Rabbi Shimon rose and rejoiced with them. They said to him, Have you not seen the satisfaction that your Master had for you? You have beheld the light of the Temple in the firmament, MEANING THE ILLUMINATION OF THE UNION OF MALCHUT WITH ZEIR ANPIN THAT IS REFERRED TO AS FIRMAMENT. He told them, I have seen. They said to him, At the same time, the Holy One, blessed be He, removed the abyss of the Temple, WHICH IS MALCHUT, and transferred it through the great ocean, THAT IS BINAH. From its light, there was a shining

in the firmament – THE FORM OF THE TEMPLE, WHICH IS THE SECRET OF
THE UNION.

186. אָמְרוּ לֵיהּ, רַב מְתִיבְתָּא בָּעָא בִּשְׁלָמָךְ, וְהָא יָדַע דַּאֲנָן שְׁלִיחָן
לְגַבָּךְ. וְכַמָּה מִלִּין חַדְתִּין עַתִּיקִין, אִתְחַדָּשׁ בְּאוֹרַיְיתָא בְּהַאי לֵילְיָא.
אָמַר לוֹן, בְּמָטוּ מִנַּיְיכוּ, אִמְרוּ חַד מִלָּה מִנַּיְיהוּ. אָמְרוּ, לָא אִתְיְיהִיב
לָן רְשׁוּ לְמַאי דְּאָתֵינָן לְגַבָּךְ, אֲבָל מִלָּה חַדְתָּא הֲוָה לְגַבָּךְ הַשְׁתָּא.

186. They said to him, The head of the Yeshivah sends you greetings, since
he is aware that we are emissaries to you. Many new items from Atik
concerning the Torah were told this night. He said to them, I beg you please
say something from them. They said to him, We are not allowed TO REVEAL
TO YOU by the fact that we came here to you. However, we have one new
point for you at present.

24. He who has no merit in this place

A Synopsis

The emissaries are told things by the head of the Yeshivah that they had not been previously privileged to hear, because they were charged with revealing it to Rabbi Shimon. The topic has to do with God's admonition to Abram to leave his country; the head of the Yeshivah gives them the hidden meaning about the essence of the soul and why it does not shine in this place but is worthy to shine in a different place. He also tells them why levirate marriage allows a man's spirit to be rebuilt after he dies without having children. Rabbi Shimon asks the emissaries to find out if he can know whether women in the higher world get the opportunity to ascend higher.

187. פָּתַח רַב מְתִיבְתָּא וְאָמַר וַיֹּאמֶר יְיָ׳ אֶל אַבְרָם לֶךְ לְךָ מֵאַרְצְךָ וְגוֹ׳, דָּא בְּגִין דְּאִתְנַהֲרָא בֵּיה נְהִירוּ כְּגַוְונָא דָּא. מַאן דְּלָא זָכֵי בַּאֲתָר דָּא, יְהַךְ וְיִנְטַל גַּרְמֵיה לַאֲתָר אַחֲרָא, וְיִזְכֵּי בֵּיה. אָעָא דְּדָלִיק, וּנְהוֹרָא לָא סָלִיק וְנָהִיר בֵּיה, יְנַעְנְעוּן לֵיה, וְיִסְלַּק בֵּיה נְהוֹרָא, וְאַנְהִיר. וַהֲוֵינָן זְמִינִין לְמִשְׁמַע, אֲבָל בְּגִין לְמֵיתֵי גַּבָּךְ, לָא בָּעֵינָן לְאִתְעַכְּבָא, חַדֵּי ר׳ שִׁמְעוֹן.

187. THEY SAID TO HIM, The head of the Yeshivah opened the discussion saying, "Now Hashem said to Abram, 'Get you out of your country...'" (Beresheet 12:1). That is because the light shone to him in this manner, MEANING THAT THE HOLY ONE, BLESSED BE HE, TOLD HIM, "GET YOU OUT..." BECAUSE HE COULD NOT GET THE LIGHT IN ANOTHER MANNER, JUST IN THIS MANNER. Since he has no merit in this place, let him go and take himself to another place, and merit it there. If a piece of wood is lit and yet the light does not catch on and illuminate in it, let them shake it until the fire catches on and it shines. THE EMISSARIES said, We had been prepared to hear THE CONTINUATION OF THE TEACHINGS FROM THE HEAD OF THE YESHIVAH. However, since we have to come to you, we did not wish to tarry. Rabbi Shimon was glad.

188. אָמְרוּ לֵיה, אִי חֲסִידָא קַדִּישָׁא, כָּל מִלִּין דִּי בְּגַוְון בְּאוֹרַיְיתָא, מִלִּין זְעִירִין אִינוּן, בְּכָל מִלָּה וּמִלָּה. וְאִינוּן מִלִּין זְעִירִין, כַּמָּה אִינוּן

מִלִּין רַבְרְבִין וְעִלָּאִין, עַד דְּלֵית לוֹן שִׁיעוּרָא. דְּהָא לֵית בְּגַוְּון סְפֵקָא, אֶלָּא בְּרִירוּ דְּאוֹרַיְיתָא עַל בּוּרְיֵיהּ. וְהַשְׁתָּא רַב מְתִיבְתָּא פָּרִישׁ מִלִּין סְתִימִין עַל דָּא, בְּגִין דְּעִקָּרָא דְּנִשְׁמָתָא, אֲמַאי לָא נָהִיר בַּאֲתָר דָּא, וְזָכֵי לְאִתְנַהֲרָא בַּאֲתָר אַחֳרָא. וְעַד כְּעַן לָא זָכֵינָן בְּהוּ, בְּגִין לְמֵיתֵי גַּבָּךְ.

188. They said to him, Oh, holy pious one. All our matters in the Torah are short and to the point, MEANING THEY WERE SAID IN VERY CONCISE FORM. How great and supernal are these succinct teachings, so as to be immeasurable, since we have no doubts but only wish to establish the clarity of the Torah. Now the head of the Yeshivah explained matters that are concealed over this, about the essence of the soul and why it does not shine in this place but is worthy to shine in a different place. Until now, we have not been worthy of it, because WE HAD TO come to you.

189. וּמִלָּה אַחֳרָא זָכֵינָן לְמִשְׁמַע מִנֵּיהּ, רוּחָא דְּאָזְלָא בְּעַרְטוּרָא בְּהַהוּא עָלְמָא בְּלָא בְּנִין, אִנְתְּתֵיהּ יִתְעֲבִיד לֵיהּ מָאנָא לְאִתְבַּנָּאָה אִיהוּ. מַאי טַעְמָא. אִנְתְּתֵיהּ אִיהִי שְׁרָגָּא, דְּאִתְדְּלִיקַת מִנֵּיהּ, וְתַרְוַוייהוּ שְׁרָגָּא חֲדָא הֲווֹ, נְהוֹרָא דָּא נָפַק מִנְּהוֹרָא דָּא, אִתְדָּעָךְ דָּא, אִתְדְּלִיק מִגּוֹ נְהוֹרֵיהּ מַמָּשׁ, בְּגִין דַּחֲדָא נְהוֹרָא הֲווֹ.

189. We deserved to hear another thing from him. A spirit that goes naked in the world without children, his wife becomes a vessel, so he could be built up THROUGH LEVIRATE MARRIAGE. What is the reason for this? It is because his wife is like a candle that is lit from him and both were one candle, the one light coming out from this light. When this one is extinguished, MEANING HE DIED WITHOUT LEAVING ANY CHILDREN, it is lighted from the very light of his WIFE, since they were one light.

190. הַשְׁתָּא רִבִּי, נְהַדַּר לְמִלִּין קַדְמָאִין, וְכַד נְהַדַּר לְאַתְרִין, נְטוֹל רְשׁוּ מֵרַב מְתִיבְתָּא, בְּאִינּוּן מִלִּין דִּנְקַבֵּל מִנֵּיהּ, וְנֵימָא קַמָּךְ. זַכָּאָה חוּלָקָךְ, דְּאַתְּ זָכֵי לִנְהוֹרִין סְתִימִין, מִכָּל סִטְרִין, מֵעֵילָּא וּמִתַּתָּא, מֵהַאי עָלְמָא, וּמֵעָלְמָא אוֹחֳרָא. אָמַר ר' שִׁמְעוֹן, מִלָּה חֲדָא בָּעֵינָא לְמִנְדַע, אִי תֵּיכוּל

לְאוֹדָעָא לִי. נָשִׁין בְּהַהוּא עָלְמָא, אִי זַכָּאִין לְסַלְקָא לְעֵילָא, אוֹ הֵיךְ
אִינּוּן תַּמָּן. אָמַר לֵיהּ, אִי רִבִּי אִי רִבִּי, בְּדָא אִית לָן רָזָא יַקִּירָא. בְּגִין
דְּלָא לְגַלָּאָה סִתְרִין דְּתַמָּן, אֲבָל דָּא יְהַךְ וְיִטוֹל רְשׁוּ, וְנֵימָא לָךְ. אַדְהָכִי
פָּרַח חַד, וְאִתְכַּסֵי מִנַּיְיהוּ, וְאָזַל לֵיהּ.

190. Now, Rabbi, let's get back to OUR first points. When we return to our place, we will receive permission from the head of the Yeshivah about the information that we received from him, and we will tell you. Praised is your lot that you deserved the concealed lights from all directions, from above and from below, from this world and from another world. Rabbi Shimon said, I wish to find out one thing if you could inform me: if women in that world get the opportunity to ascend higher, or in what state they are there. He said to him, Oh, Rabbi. Oh, Rabbi. We have a precious secret about this. However, we are unable to reveal the hidden things of that place, but let this one go and get permission and we will tell you. Meanwhile, one flew off, disappeared from them and went away.

25. The judgment of one person that stood at the entrance to the Garden of Eden

25. The judgment of one person that stood at the entrance to the Garden of Eden

A Synopsis

The emissary returns with a letter for Rabbi Shimon, which the Rabbi reads all night until the letter flies away in the morning. The emissaries tell him about the judgment of a man standing at the entrance to the Garden of Eden, where the man is sentenced to remain outside in pain for forty days and then be tortured in Gehenom for an hour and a half. These punishments arose since the man put another friend to shame by not assisting him when he was trying to define some points in Torah.

191. וּלְפוּם שַׁעֲתָא תָּב לְגַבַּיְיהוּ, אָמַר לוֹן, זְמִינָא הֲוֵינָא לְמֵיעָאל, וַהֲווֹ כֻּלְּהוּ בְּעִטּוּרָא חֲדָא, דְּדַיְינֵי דִינָא דְּחַד בַּר נָשׁ, דְּקָאֵים עַל פִּתְחָא דְּגַן עֵדֶן, וְאִינּוּן כְּרוּבִין אֲחִידוּ בֵּיהּ, וְלָא שָׁבְקוּ לֵיהּ לְמֵיעָאל תַּמָּן, וַהֲוָה בְּצַעֲרָא בֵּינַיְיהוּ, וְצָוַוח צַוְוחִין עַל גַּבֵּי פִּתְחָא, וּשְׁמָעוּ כּוּלְּהוּ צַדִּיקַיָּיא דְּתַמָּן, וְהַשְׁתָּא הֲווֹ מִתְכַּנְּפֵי כָּל בְּנֵי מְתִיבְתֵּי, לְמֵיעָאל לְגַבֵּי מַלְכָּא מְשִׁיחָא, לְעַיְינָא בְּדִינֵיהּ. וַאֲתֵינָא לְאוֹדְעָא לְכוּ, וְדָא חַבְרַאי אִצְטְרִיךְ לְמֵהַךְ תַּמָּן, דְּכָרוֹזָא הֲוָה אַעֲבַר בְּכָל אִינּוּן בְּנֵי מְתִיבְתֵּי. דְּלִיהֱווֹן בְּנִישִׁין הַשְׁתָּא קַמֵּי מָשִׁיחַ. נָטַל פִּתְקָא חֲדָא, וְיָהַב לְרִבִּי שִׁמְעוֹן. אָמַר, טוֹל דָּא, וְעַיֵּין בְּמָה דְּתַמָּן, עַד דְּנֵיתֵי גַּבָּךְ, פַּרְחוּ תַּרְוַויְיהוּ.

191. Instantly, he returned to them and said to them, I was ready to enter and everyone was in one circle, MEANING THEY WERE SEATED IN A CIRCLE. They were in session judging a person that stood at the entrance to the Garden of Eden. The Cherubs grabbed him and did not allow him to enter there. He was in pain between them and was screaming loudly in the entrance. All the just that were there heard, and now all the members of that Yeshivah gathered to enter to Messiah, to give some thought about the judgment. And I came to inform you. And my associate here needs to go there, since a proclamation was passed among all the members of the Yeshivah that they should gather to welcome Messiah. He took a letter and presented it to Rabbi Shimon. He said, Take it and peruse what is WRITTEN in it, until we come back to you. Both flew away.

192. וְר׳ שִׁמְעוֹן נָטַל פִּתְקָא, וְחָמָא מַה דְּחָמָא, בְּרָזִין דְּתַמָּן, כָּל הַהוּא יוֹמָא. בְּלֵילְיָא חָמָא שְׁרָגָא, וְנָפִיל בֵּיהּ שֵׁינָתָא, וְדָמַךְ עַד צַפְרָא. כַּד נָהַר יְמָמָא, קָם וּפָרַח הַהוּא פִּתְקָא מִנֵּיהּ, וְהָא אִינּוּן תַּרְוַוייְהוּ אַתְיָין, אָמַר לֵיהּ, קוּם רִבִּי, זַכָּאָה חוּלָקָךְ, קוּם. בְּגִינָךְ חֲמֵינָן וְזָכֵינָן לְכַמָּה סִתְרִין עִלָּאִין, כַּמָּה חֶדְוָה אַחְזִיוּ לָן, כַּד יָהֲבוּ רְשׁוּ לְגַלָּאָה לָךְ, כָּל מַה דְּאַתְּ בָּעֵי. רֵישׁ מְתִיבְתָּא עִלָּאָה נָפַק לְגַבָּן, וְאָמַר, שָׁאִילוּ בִּשְׁלָמֵיהּ דְּבַר יוֹחָאי, אַתְרֵיהּ דְּבַר יוֹחָאי, הָא פָּנוּ לֵיהּ מִכַּמָּה יוֹמִין. לֵית מַאן דְּיִקְרַב לְגַבֵּיהּ, זַכָּאָה אִיהוּ.

192. Rabbi Shimon took the note and saw whatever he saw of the secrets that were in it all day long. At night, he saw a candle, sleepiness overcame him and he fell asleep until morning. When daylight broke, the letter rose and flew away from him. Behold, those two arrived. They told him, Get up, Rabbi. Blessed is your lot, rise. Due to you, we saw and deserved to know several supernal secrets. We were shown so much gladness when they permitted us to reveal to you all that you desire. The head of the highest Yeshivah came out to us and said, Give greetings to the son of Yochai. The son of Yochai's place has been waiting for him for several days and there is nobody that comes close to him. Happy is he.

193. רִבִּי רִבִּי, כַּד פַּרַחְנָא מִגַּבָּךְ, עָאלְנָא וַחֲמֵינָא כָּל בְּנֵי מְתִיבְתֵּי, דְּהָא מִתְכַּנְפֵי לְגוֹ הֵיכָלָא חֲדָא, דִּמְשִׁיחַ תַּמָּן, וְדַיְיְנוּ דִּינָא דְּהַהוּא בַּר נָשׁ, דְּקָאֵים עַל פִּתְחָא, שְׁמֵיהּ לֵית לָן רְשׁוּ לְגַלָּאָה. אִצְטָעַר ר׳ שִׁמְעוֹן עַל דָּא, אָמַר לֵיהּ, לָא תִּצְטָעַר רִבִּי עַל דָּא, אַנְתְּ תֵּדַע בְּדָא לֵילְיָא בְּחֶלְמָךְ. אֲבָל דִּינָא דַּיְינוּ עָלֵיהּ, דִּגְזַר מָשִׁיחַ, דִּלְהֱוֵי הַהוּא בַּר נָשׁ לְבַר בְּהַהוּא צַעֲרָא אַרְבְּעִין יוֹמִין. לְסוֹף אַרְבְּעִין יוֹמִין, יְצַעֲרוּן לֵיהּ בְּדִינָא, בְּצַעֲרָא דְּגֵיהִנָּם, שַׁעֲתָא וּפַלְגָּא.

193. Rabbi, Rabbi. When we flew away from you, we entered and saw all the members of the Yeshivah gathering to a certain sanctuary where Messiah was present. They were discussing the judgment of that man that stood at the entrance. We have no authority to reveal his name. Rabbi Shimon became sad about it. He told him, Do not feel sad about this, Rabbi, you will

get to know all about this, this night in your dream. However, they passed a judgment about him in accordance with the edict of Messiah, that this person shall remain outside with this pain for forty days. At the end of forty days, he will be tortured with the pain of Gehenom for an hour and a half.

194. וְכָל דָּא, בְּגִין דְּיוֹמָא חֲדָא, חַד מִן חַבְרַיָּיא הֲוָה פָּרִישׁ מִלִּין דְּאוֹרַיְיתָא, כַּד מָטָא לְחַד מִלָּה, יָדַע הַאי ב״נ דְּיִתְבְּשַׁל בֵּיה, וְאָמַר לְחַבְרַיָּיא שְׁתוֹקוּ, לָא תֵּימְרוּן מִדִי. וּבְגִין דְּשָׁתִיקוּ חַבְרַיָּיא אִתְבְּשַׁל בְּהַהוּא מִלָּה, וְאִכְסִיף. וְהַהוּא כְּסוּפָא. דְּגָרִים הַאי בַּר נָשׁ, דַּיְינִין לֵיה בְּהַאי דִּינָא קַשְׁיָא, בְּגִין דְּלָא בָּעֵי קוּדְשָׁא בְּרִיךְ הוּא לְשַׁבְקָא חוֹבָא דְּאוֹרַיְיתָא, אֲפִילוּ כִּמְלָא נִימָא.

194. All this is because one day, one of the friends was defining some points in the Torah. When he attempted one item, that person was aware that he would fail in it and told his friends to keep quiet and say nothing. Since the friends kept quiet, he stumbled on it and was put to shame. Due to causing that person shame, he was judged harshly, since the Holy One, blessed be He, does not allow inequities in the Torah, even as a hair's breadth.

26. The sanctuaries of the female souls

A Synopsis

The emissary tells Rabbi Shimon about the sanctuary where Batyah the daughter of Pharaoh lives, and how she goes out to see Moses' image three times a day. Batyah and the other women are clothed in light bodies and study the Torah. In another sanctuary there is Serach the daughter of Ashur, with many other women who study the Torah; she goes three times a day to see a light in the image of Joseph. In another sanctuary lives Yocheved the mother of Moses with many other women, and three times a day they all thank and praise God, and they sing the song of the sea. The fourth sanctuary of the Matriarchs is that of Deborah the prophetess. The emissary talks about the nightly coupling of the souls – soul to soul, light to light. Those unions produce the souls of those who get converted; this is the secret meaning of "The fruit of the righteous is a Tree of Life."

195. דַּיְינוּ דִּינֵיהּ, וְנַפְקוּ כָּל בְּנֵי מְתִיבְתָּא. וַאֲנָא שָׁאִילְנָא רְשׁוּ, דְּהָא בְּרֵיהּ דְּיוֹחָאי, שָׁאִיל שְׁאֶלְתָּא דָּא. וְעַל דָּא אַחֲזִיוּ לִי, מַה דְּלָא יְדַעֲנָא מִקַּדְמַת דְּנָא. אִי רַבִּי, שִׁית הֵיכָלִין אַחֲזִיוּ לִי, בְּכַמָּה עֲנוּגִין וְעִדּוּנִין, בַּאֲתַר דְּפָרוֹכְתָּא פְּרִישָׁא בְּגִנְתָּא. דְּהָא מֵהַהוּא פָּרוֹכְתָּא וּלְהָלְאָה, לָא עָאלִין דְּכוּרִין כְּלַל.

195. They passed his sentence and all the members of the Yeshivah left. I begged for permission, since the son of Yochai asked this question. Therefore, I was shown what I did not know before. Oh, Rabbi, I was shown six sanctuaries with a variety of delights and pleasures, in the place where the dividing curtain was unfurled in the Garden, since from that curtain and further on, no males can enter at all.

196. בְּהֵיכָלָא חֲדָא, אִית בַּתְיָה בַּת פַּרְעֹה, וְכַמָּה רִבּוֹא וְאַלְפֵי נָשִׁין, זַכְיָין בַּהֲדָהּ, וְכָל חֲדָא וַחֲדָא מִנַּיְיהוּ, דּוּכְתִּין דִּנְהוֹרִין וְעִדּוּנִין, בְּלָא דְּחַקָּא כְּלָל אִית לָהּ. תְּלַת זִמְנִין בְּכָל יוֹמָא, כָּרוֹזֵי אַכְרִיזוּ, הָא דִיּוּקְנָא דְּמֹשֶׁה נְבִיאָה מְהֵימָנָא אָתֵי, וּבַתְיָה נַפְקַת, לַאֲתַר דְּפַרְגּוֹדָא חֲדָא דְּאִית לָהּ, וְחָמְאַת דִּיּוּקְנָא דְּמֹשֶׁה, וְסָגִידַת לְגַבֵּיהּ, וְאָמְרָה, זַכָּאָה חוּלָקִי דִּרְבִיתִי נְהִירוּ דָא. וְדָא אִיהוּ עֲנוּגִין דִּילָהּ, יַתִּיר מִכֻּלְּהוּ.

196. In one sanctuary, Batyah the daughter of Pharaoh dwells, and many tens of thousands of virtuous women are with her. Each and every one of them occupies her place of brightness and pleasures very comfortably. Three times daily, a proclamation resounds, Here comes the image of Moses, the faithful prophet. Batyah goes out to her specified partition and observes Moses's image, bows before him and says, Praised is my part that I brought up this light. That is her SPECIAL pleasure more than all the others.

197. אַהֲדְרַת לְגַבֵּי נָשִׁין, וְאִשְׁתַּדְּלָן בְּפִקּוּדֵי אוֹרַיְיתָא. כֻּלְּהוּ בְּאִינּוּן דְּיוּקְנִין דַּהֲווֹ בְּהַאי עָלְמָא, בִּלְבוּשָׁא דִּנְהוֹרָא, כְּלבוּשָׁא דְּדְכוּרִין, בַּר דְּלָא נַהֲרֵי הָכִי, פְּקוּדִין דְּאוֹרַיְיתָא דְּלָא זָכוּ לְקַיְּימָא לוֹן בְּהַאי עָלְמָא, מִשְׁתַּדְּלֵי בְּהוּ, וּבְטַעֲמַיְיהוּ, בְּהַהוּא עָלְמָא. וְכָל הָנֵי נָשִׁין, דְּיַתְבִין בַּהֲדֵי בַּתְיָה בַּת פַּרְעֹה, אִקְרוּן נָשִׁים שַׁאֲנַנּוֹת, דְּלָא אִצְטַעֲרוּ בְּצַעֲרָא דְּגֵיהִנָּם כְּלַל.

197. Batyah returns to the women and they deal in the precepts of the Torah. All are in the form they were in this world, in a robe of light similar to the robes of the men, except that they are not quite as bright AS THE ROBES OF THE MEN. They study in that world the precepts of the Torah and their explanations that they did not deserve to fulfill in this world. All those women that dwell IN THE SAME SANCTUARY with Batyah, daughter of Pharaoh, are referred to as serene women, since they were not troubled at all in the pains of Gehenom.

198. בְּהֵיכָלָא אַחֲרָא, אִית סֶרַח בַּת אָשֵׁר, וְכַמָּה נָשִׁין רִבּוֹא וְאַלְפִין בַּהֲדָהּ. תְּלַת זִמְנִין בְּיוֹמָא מַכְרִיזִין קַמֵּהּ, הָא דְּיוּקְנָא דְּיוֹסֵף צַדִּיקָא אָתָא, וְאִיהִי חַדָּאת, וְנַפְקַת לְגַבֵּי פַּרְגּוֹדָא חֲדָא דְּאִית לָהּ, וְחָמָאת נְהִירוּ דְּדִיוּקְנָא דְּיוֹסֵף, וְחַדָּאת, וְסָגִידַת לְגַבֵּיהּ, וְאָמְרַת, זַכָּאָה הַאי יוֹמָא, דְּאִתְעֲרִית בְּשׂוֹרָה דִּילָךְ לְגַבֵּי סָבַאי. לְבָתַר אַהֲדְרַת לְגַבֵּי שְׁאַר נָשִׁין, וּמִשְׁתַּדְּלִין בְּתוּשְׁבְּחָן דְּמָארֵי עָלְמָא, וּלְאוֹדָאָה שְׁמֵיהּ. וְכַמָּה דּוּכְתִּין וַחֲידוּ, אִית לְכָל חֲדָא וַחֲדָא. וּלְבָתַר אַהֲדְרָן לְאִשְׁתַּדְּלָא בְּפִקּוּדֵי אוֹרַיְיתָא, וּבְטַעֲמַיְיהוּ.

198. In another sanctuary dwells Serah, the daughter of Asher, and thousands and thousands of women are with her. Three times daily, they proclaim in her presence, Here comes the image of Joseph the righteous. She is gladdened and goes out to her special partition, and sees a light in the image of Joseph. And she is glad and bows to him, saying, Praised is that day when I told your news to my grandfather. She then returns to the rest of the women, and they deal in the praises of the world's Master and give thanks to His name. How varied are the areas of happiness that each and every woman has. Then they return to deal with the precepts of the Torah and their reasons.

199. בְּהֵיכָלָא אַחֲרָא, אִית יוֹכֶבֶד, אִמֵּיהּ דְּמֹשֶׁה נְבִיאָה מְהֵימְנָא, וְכַמָּה אַלְפִין וְרִבְבָן בַּהֲדָהּ. בְּהֵיכָלָא דָּא, לָא מַכְרְזֵי כְּלַל, אֶלָּא ג׳ זִמְנִין בְּכָל יוֹמָא וְיוֹמָא, אוֹדֵת וּמְשַׁבַּחַת לְמָארֵי עָלְמָא, אִיהִי וְכָל אִינּוּן נָשִׁין דִּי בַּהֲדָהּ. וְשִׁירָתָא דְּיַמָּא מְזַמְּרִין בְּכָל יוֹמָא, וְאִיהִי בִּלְחוֹדָהָא אָמְרַת מֵהָכָא, וַתִּקַּח מִרְיָם הַנְּבִיאָה וְגוֹ׳, אֶת הַתּוֹף בְּיָדָהּ וְגוֹ׳. וְכָל אִינּוּן צַדִּיקַיָּיא דִּי בְּגַן עֵדֶן, צַיְּיתִין לְקַל נְעִימוּ דִּילָהּ. וְכַמָּה מַלְאָכִין קַדִּישִׁין אוֹדָאן וּמְשַׁבְּחָן עִמָּהּ לִשְׁמָא קַדִּישָׁא.

199. In another sanctuary dwells Jochebed, the mother of Moses, the faithful prophet, and several thousand and ten thousands are with her. In this sanctuary, there are no proclamations at all. However, three times daily, she thanks and praises the Master of the universe, she and all women with her. They also sing the song of the sea daily and she begins, on her own here: "And Miriam the prophetess...took a timbrel in her hand..." (Shemot 15:20). All the righteous in the Garden of Eden listen to her pleasant voice and many holy angels join her to thank and praise the Holy Name.

200. בְּהֵיכָלָא אַחֲרָא, אִית דְּבוֹרָה, אוֹף הָכִי וְכָל שְׁאַר נָשִׁין בַּהֲדָהּ, אוֹדָן וּמְזַמְּרָן בְּהַהִיא שִׁירָתָא דְּאִיהִי אָמְרַת בְּהַאי עָלְמָא. אִי רִבִּי, אִי רִבִּי, מַאן חָמֵי חֶדְוָה דְּצַדִּיקַיָּיא, וּדְנָשִׁין זַכְיָין דְּעַבְדִין לְגַבֵּי קוּדְשָׁא בְּרִיךְ הוּא. לְגוֹ לְגוֹ דְּאִינּוּן הֵיכָלִין, אִית אַרְבַּע הֵיכָלִין טְמִירִין, דְּאִמָּהָן קַדִּישִׁין דְּלָא אִתְמַסְרָן לְאִתְגַּלְּאָה, וְלֵית מַאן דְּחָמֵי לוֹן. בְּכוּלֵיהּ יוֹמָא

אִינּוּן בִּלְחוֹדַיְהוֹן, כְּמָה דַּאֲמֵינָא לָךְ, וְגוּבְרִין אוּף הָכִי.

200. In another sanctuary dwells Deborah, the prophetess. Likewise, all the women with her thank and chant the song that she composed in this world. Oh, Rabbi. Oh, Rabbi. Who observed the happiness of the righteous men and of the righteous women that serve the Holy One, blessed be He? In the inner sanctums of these temples, there exist four concealed sanctuaries of the holy Matriarchs that were not given to be divulged, and nobody ever saw them. Every day, they are themselves separate as I said to you and the men also ARE SEPARATE.

201. וּבְכָל לֵילְיָא אִתְכְּלִילָן כֻּלְּהוּ כַּחֲדָא, בְּגִין דְּשַׁעְתָּא דְּזִוּוּגָא אִיהוּ בְּפַלְגּוּת לֵילְיָא, בֵּין בְּהַאי עָלְמָא, בֵּין בְּהַהוּא עָלְמָא. זִוּוּגָא דְּהַהוּא עָלְמָא, אִתְדַּבְּקוּתָא דְּנִשְׁמָתָא בְּנִשְׁמָתָא נְהוֹרָא בִּנְהוֹרָא. זִוּוּגָא דְּהַאי עָלְמָא, גּוּפָא בְּגוּפָא. וְכֹלָּא כְּמָה דְּאִתְחֲזֵי, זִינָא בָּתַר זִינֵיהּ, זִוּוּגָא בָּתַר זִוּוּגָא, גּוּפָא, בָּתַר גּוּפָא זִוּוּגָא דְּהַהוּא עָלְמָא, נְהוֹרָא בָּתַר נְהוֹרָא. הֵיכָלִין דְּאַרְבַּע אִמָּהָן, אִקְרוּן הֵיכָלִין דִּבְנוֹת בּוֹטְחוֹת. וְלָא זָכֵינָא בְּהוּ לְמֶחֱמֵי. זַכָּאָה חוּלָקֵהוֹן דְּצַדִּיקַיָּיא, גּוּבְרִין וְנוּקְבֵי דְּאַזְלֵי בְּאֹרַח מֵישָׁר בְּהַאי עָלְמָא, וְזַכָּאִין לְכֻלְּהוּ עֲנוּגִין דְּהַהוּא עָלְמָא.

201. Every night they get together, since the time of coupling is at midnight, both in this world and that world. The coupling of that world is accomplished by the adherence of one soul to the other, light with light. The coupling in this world is body to body. Everything is as it should be, one kind with similar kind, a match with its equal, body to body, THAT IS IN THIS WORLD. In the other world, it is light with light. The sanctuaries of the four Matriarchs are referred to as the Sanctuaries of trusting daughters and I did not have enough merit to observe them. Praised is the lot of the righteous, males and females, that follow the straight path in this world and merit all the pleasures in the World to Come.

202. אִי רְבִּי, אִי רְבִּי, אִלְמָלֵא בַּר יוֹחָאי אַנְתְּ, לָא אִתְמְסַר לְגַלָּאָה. זִוּוּגָא דְּהַהוּא עָלְמָא, אִתְעֲבֵיד אִיבָּא יַתִּיר, מֵאִיבָּא דְּאִתְעֲבֵיד בְּהַאי עָלְמָא. בְּזִוּוּגָא דִּלְהוֹן, בְּזִוּוּגָא דְּהוּא עָלְמָא, בְּתִיאוּבְתָּא דִּלְהוֹן כַּחֲדָא,

כַּד מִתְדַּבְּקָן נִשְׁמָתִין דָּא עִם דָּא, עָבְדֵי אִיבִין, וְנַפְקֵי נְהוֹרִין מִנַּיְיהוּ, וְאִתְעֲבִדֵי שְׁרָגִין. וְאִינּוּן נִשְׁמָתִין, לַגִּיּוֹרִין דְּמִתְגַּיְירִין, וְכָל הָנֵי עַיְילִין לְהֵיכָלָא חֲדָא.

202. Oh, Rabbi. Oh, Rabbi. If you weren't the son of Yochai, it would not have been passed on to divulge this to you. The union in that world produces more fruit than the coupling in this world. When they pair up in the pairing in that world with their combined desire and when the souls cling one to another, they produce fruit. And lights emerge and candles are produced. These are the souls of those that get converted, and all those SOULS THAT WERE BORN FROM THESE CONNECTIONS enter a sanctuary.

203. וְכַד מִתְגַּיְירָא גִּיּוֹרָא חֲדָא, פַּרְחָא מֵהַהוּא הֵיכָלָא נִשְׁמָתָא, וְעָאלַת תְּחוֹת גַּדְפָהָא דִּשְׁכִינְתָּא, וְנָשְׁקַת לָהּ, בְּגִין דְּאִיהוּ אִיבָא דְּצַדִּיקַיָּיא, וּמְשַׁדְּרַת לָהּ לְגוֹ הַהוּא גִּיּוֹרָא, וְשַׁרְאַת בֵּיהּ. וּמֵהַהוּא זִמְנָא, אִקְרֵי גֵּר צֶדֶק. וְהַיְינוּ רָזָא דִּכְתִּיב, פְּרִי צַדִּיק עֵץ חַיִּים. מַה אִילָנָא דְּחַיֵּי אַפִּיק נִשְׁמָתִין, אוּף הָכִי צַדִּיק, אִיבָא דִּילֵיהּ עָבֵיד נִשְׁמָתִין.

203. When a foreigner gets converted, a soul flies from that sanctuary and enters under the wings of the Shechinah. AND THE SHECHINAH kisses it, since it is the fruit of righteous SOULS, and dispatches it into that proselyte and dwells within him. From that time on, he is referred to as a proselyte of righteousness. This is the secret meaning of what is written: "The fruit of is a Tree of Life" (Mishlei 11:30). Just as a Tree of Life, WHICH IS ZEIR ANPIN, produces souls, so too the righteous have similar fruits by producing souls.

204. רַב מְתִיבְתָּא אָמַר, כְּתִיב וַתְּהִי שָׂרַי עֲקָרָה אֵין לָהּ וָלָד. מִמַּאי דְּאָמַר וַתְּהִי שָׂרַי עֲקָרָה, לֵית אֲנָא יוֹדֵעַ דְּלֵית לָהּ וָלָד, מַאי אֵין לָהּ וָלָד. אֶלָּא הָכִי אָמַר רַב מְתִיבְתָּא, וָלָד לָא הֲוַת מוֹלִידָא, אֲבָל נִשְׁמָתִין הֲוַת מוֹלִידָא כְּאִתְדַּבְּקוּתָא דְּתִיאוּבְתָּא דְּאִינּוּן תְּרֵין זַכָּאִין, הֲוֹו מוֹלִידֵי נִשְׁמָתִין לְגִיּוֹרֵי כָּל הַהוּא זִמְנָא דַּהֲוֹו בְּחָרָן. כְּמָה דְּעָבְדִין צַדִּיקַיָּיא בְּגַן עֵדֶן. כְּמָה דִּכְתִּיב, וְאֶת הַנֶּפֶשׁ אֲשֶׁר עָשׂוּ בְחָרָן, נֶפֶשׁ עָשׂוּ וַדַּאי.

204. The head of the Yeshivah said, it is written: "But Sarai was barren; she had no child" (Beresheet 11:30). HE ASKED, From what it says, "But Sarai was barren," we understand that she had no child. Why write "she had no child"? This is what the head of the Yeshivah said, She wasn't giving birth to children. However, she did give birth to souls with the cleaving desire of these two righteous ones. They were producing souls for the proselytes during all the time that they were in Haran, as the just were producing in the Garden of Eden, as is written: "And the souls that they have acquired (lit. 'made') in Haran" (Beresheet 12:5). They definitely made souls.

205. חַדֵּי ר"ש, אָ"ל הַהוּא גַּבְרָא, אִי רִבִּי, מָה אֵימָא לָךְ, בְּכָל רֵיש יַרְחֵי וְשַׁבַּתֵּי וּמוֹעֲדַיָּיא וּזְמַנַיָּא, אִינּוּן דְּכוּרִין סַלְקִין לְאִתְחֲזָאָה קַמֵּי מַלְכָּא קַדִּישָׁא, דְּכוּרִין וְלָא נוּקְבִין, כד"א יֵרָאֶה כָּל זְכוּרְךָ. וְכַד אַהְדְרָן מְהַדְרָן בְּכַמָּה מִלֵּי חַדְתִּין, וְאַהְדְרָן מִלִּין קַמֵּי רַב מְתִיבְתָּא.

205. Rabbi Shimon rejoiced. That man said to him, Oh, Rabbi. What should I say to you? Every new moon, Shabbat, holidays and appointed days, the males go up to be seen in the presence of the Holy King, males and not females, as you indicated: "All your males shall appear" (Shemot 23:17). When they return, they come back with a variety of new topics, and they repeat them to the head of the Yeshivah.

27. The sanctuaries of the male souls

A Synopsis

We learn why it is possible that 'a wicked man that it is good with
him, and a just man that it is bad with him.' Through hardship and
punishment the soul is made to illuminate the body; when its light
is lit from the soul, the body praises God. It is impossible for the
wicked ones to illuminate however much they are hit because they
are incapable of illumination. The emissary tells Rabbi Shimon
that at night the righteous spirits enter the supernal Yeshivah and
are taught secret matters; when they ascend they leave their robes
of this world, and when they descend they again dress up in those
robes.

206. יוֹמָא דָּא אַהֲדְרָן מִלִּין חַדְתִּין קַמֵּי רַב מְתִיבְתָּא, עַל רָזִין עַתִּיקִין,
צַדִּיק וְטוֹב לוֹ, צַדִּיק וְרַע לוֹ. דְּכֻלְּהוּ סַלְקִין גּוֹ מַתְקְלָא דְּאִילָנָא, עַד
לָא יֵיתוּן לְעָלְמָא, וּכְפוּם טַקְלָא דְּמַתְקְלָא, הָכִי אִית לוֹן בְּהַאי עָלְמָא.
רַב מְתִיבְתָּא, נָחִית וְגַלֵּי מִמָּה דְּשָׁמַע לְעֵילָּא, מִלָּה חֲדָא גַּלֵּי וְלָא
יַתִּיר. אָעָא דְּלָא סָלִיק נְהוֹרֵיה, יִבָטְשׁוּן בֵּיה וְאַנְהִיר. גּוּפָא דְּלָא סַלְקָא
בֵּיה נְהוֹרָא דְּנִשְׁמָתָא, יְבָטְשׁוּן בֵּיה, וְיִסַלֵּק נְהִירוּ דְּנִשְׁמָתָא, וְיִתְאַחֲדוּן
דָּא בְּדָא לְאַנְהָרָא.

206. On these days, new matters were repeated to the head of the Yeshivah
about ancient secrets; 'a righteous man thrives', and 'a righteous man
suffers'. All the souls ascend into the weighing scale of that tree, WHICH IS
MALCHUT, prior to their descent into this world and according to the weight
they get in this world. The head of the Yeshivah came down and divulged
what he heard above. He revealed one point and nothing else. If wood
doesn't kindle, it is hit and struck and so it gives off light. If the light of the
soul does not come up in the body, the body is beaten until the light of the
soul will rise, and unite together THE BODY WITH THE SOUL to give off light.

207. בְּגִין דְּאִית גּוּפָא דְּנְהִירוּ דְּנִשְׁמָתָא לָא נָהִיר בֵּיה, עַד דְּיִבַטְשׁוּן
בֵּיה, כְּדֵין נָהִיר נְהִירוּ דְּנִשְׁמָתָא, וְאִתְאַחֲדַת בְּגוּפָא, וְגוּפָא אִתְאַחַד
בָּה. גּוּפָא כְּדֵין סָלִיק נְהִירוּ מִגּוֹ נִשְׁמָתָא, מְהַדַּר מְרוֹמֵם וּמְשַׁבַּח, מְצַלֵּי
צְלוֹתֵיה וּבְעוּתֵיה, מְבָרֵךְ לְמָארֵיה, הָא כְּדֵין כֹּלָּא נָהִיר. בְּגִין דְּאִית

גּוּפָא, דְּלָא יָכִילַת נִשְׁמְתָא לְאַנְהָרָא בֵּיהּ, עַד דִּיבַטְשׁוּן בֵּיהּ, כְּדֵין נָהִיר וְאִתְאֲחָד דָּא בְּדָא. אִית אָעָא דְּלָא אִתְאֲחָד בִּנְהוֹרָא, וְלָא סָלִיק נְהוֹרָא בֵּיהּ, עַד דִּיבַטְשׁוּן בֵּיהּ, וּכְדֵין נָהִיר.

207. A body exists but the light of the soul does not illuminate in it until they hit it. Then the light of the soul brightens and gets unified with the body, and the body is unified with it. When its light is lit from the soul, the body glorifies and exults and praises and lays out its prayer and request and blesses its Master. Behold, then everything is bright. AND THEREFORE THERE IS SUCH A THING AS A RIGHTEOUS MAN WHO SUFFERS.

208. סִטְרָא אָחֳרָא, בָּעֵי לְמֶעְבַּד הָכִי, וּבָטַשׁ בְּחַיָּיבַיָּא, וְכָל מַה דְּבָטַשׁ, כְּדֵין וְנֵר רְשָׁעִים יִדְעָךְ. מְחָרֵף וּמְגַדֵּף לְכָל סִטְרִין, וְלָא יָכִיל לְאַנְהָרָא כְּלָל, וּכְדֵין כְּתִיב כִּי מֶה הָאָדָם שֶׁיָּבֹא אַחֲרֵי הַמֶּלֶךְ. וּבָעֵי לְאִתְדַּמֵּי לֵיהּ, וְלָא יָכִיל. וְעַל דָּא יְיָ' צַדִּיק יִבְחָן, וּבָטַשׁ בֵּיהּ, וּכְדֵין נָהִיר וְאִתְתַּקַּף בִּנְהִירוּ. יִבְחָן, כד"א אֶבֶן בֹּחַן. גָּחִין ר' שִׁמְעוֹן, וְנָשִׁיק לְעַפְרָא. אָמַר, מִלָּה מִלָּה אֲבַתְרָךְ רְדִיפְנָא, מִיּוֹמָא דַּהֲוֵינָא, וְהַשְׁתָּא אִשְׁתְּמוֹדְעָא לִי מִלָּה, מִגּוֹ שָׁרְשָׁא וְעִקָּרָא דְּכֹלָּא.

208. The Other Side wishes to do the same thing and hits the wicked. As much as he punishes by hitting them, it is written: "But the candle of the wicked shall be put out" (Mishlei 13:9), since he blasphemes and curses in all directions and is incapable of illumination at all. It is then written: "For what can the man do who comes after the king?" (Kohelet 2:12), for he wishes to imitate him but is incapable of it. Therefore, "Hashem tries the righteous" (Tehilim 11:5) and hits him. Then he shines and gets strengthened with the light – "tries" is as it says in: "a tried stone" (Yeshayah 25:16). Rabbi Shimon bent over and kissed the dust. He said, Word, word, I have chased you since the day I became A MAN. And now this matter is revealed to me from the source and essence of everything.

209. אָ"ל, אִי רִבִּי, אִי רִבִּי, כַּד סַלְּקִין לְעֵילָּא, כָּל אִינּוּן רוּחִין דְּכוּרִין וְנוּקְבִין, בְּהַהוּא זִמְנָא, שַׁמְעִין מִלִּין חַדְתִּין וְעַתִּיקִין, נַחְתִּין וְעָאלִין לְגוֹ מְתִיבְתָּא, וְאַהְדְּרָן מִלֵּי קַמֵּי רַב מְתִיבְתָּא, וְאִיהוּ אוֹלִיף לוֹן מִלָּה

עַל קִיּוּמֵיהּ. כַּד סַלְקִין מִתְפַּשְּׁטִין מַלְּבוּשֵׁיהוֹן וְסַלְקִין. כַּד נַחְתֵּי, מִתְלַבְּשִׁין בִּלְבוּשֵׁיהוֹן דְּהַהוּא גּוּפָא.

209. He said to him, Oh Rabbi, oh Rabbi. When all the spirits, male and female, ascend, AT NIGHT DURING SLEEP, at that time they hear new and old matters. They descend and enter into the Yeshivah and the matters are repeated to the head of the Yeshivah, and he teaches them every matter well. When they leave, they undress from their robes OF THIS WORLD and ascend. When they descend, THEY AGAIN dress up in the robes of that body.

28. He who is small is great

A Synopsis
We hear that the head of the Yeshivah said that God made a person great only if he belittled himself, and that God belittled only those who are haughty. While Rabbi Shimon and the emissary are speaking they hear the song of the Sea in the most exquisite voice that was ever heard since the sweet voice of chanting was created.

210. אִי רִבִּי, אִי רִבִּי, כַּמָּה חַדְתִּין מִלִּין מִגּוֹ רַב מְתִיבְתָּא. זַכָּאָה אִיהוּ מַאן דְּאַזְעַר גַּרְמֵיהּ בְּהַאי עָלְמָא, כַּמָּה אִיהוּ רַב וְעִלָּאָה בְּהַהוּא עָלְמָא. וְהָכִי פָּתַח רַב מְתִיבְתָּא, מַאן דְּאִיהוּ זְעֵיר, אִיהוּ רַב. וּמַאן דְּאִיהוּ רַב, אִיהוּ זְעֵיר. דִּכְתִּיב, וַיִּהְיוּ חַיֵּי שָׂרָה מֵאָה שָׁנָה וְעֶשְׂרִים שָׁנָה וְשֶׁבַע שָׁנִים. מֵאָה דְּאִיהוּ חֶשְׁבּוֹן רַב, כְּתִיב בֵּיהּ שָׁנָה, זְעֵירוּ דִּשְׁנִין, חַד אַזְעִיר לֵיהּ. שֶׁבַע, דְּאִיהוּ חֶשְׁבּוֹן זְעֵיר, אַסְגֵּי לֵיהּ, וְרִבִּי לֵיהּ דִּכְתִּיב שֶׁבַע שָׁנִים. ת"ח, דְּלָא רַבֵּי קוּדְשָׁא בְּרִיךְ הוּא, אֶלָּא לְדְאַזְעִיר. לָא אַזְעִיר אֶלָּא לִדְרַבֵּי. זַכָּאָה אִיהוּ מַאן דְּאַזְעִיר גַּרְמֵיהּ בְּהַאי עָלְמָא, כַּמָּה אִיהוּ רַב בְּעִלּוּיָא בְּהַהוּא עָלְמָא.

210. Oh, Rabbi, oh Rabbi. How new are these matters of the head of the Yeshivah. Praised is he who humbles himself in this world. How great and lofty is he in that world. That is how the head of the Yeshivah began: He who is small is great, and he who is great is small, as it is written: "And Sarah was a hundred year and twenty year and seven years old: these were the years of Sarah's life" (Beresheet 23:1). "Hundred," since it is a large number is written with "year," the least number of years; it was diminished to one. "seven," that is a small number, is increased and made bigger, by writing "seven years," IN PLURAL. Come and see that the Holy One, blessed be He, made one great only if he had belittled himself. And THE HOLY ONE, BLESSED BE HE, belittled only he who is haughty. Praised is the one that humiliates himself in this world. How exultingly great is he in his elevation in that world.

211. אַדְהָכִי שָׁמְעוּ שִׁירָתָא דְּיַמָּא, בְּקַל נְעִימוּ דְּלָא שָׁמְעוּ מִיּוֹמָא דְּאִתְבְּרִיאוּ, קַל נְעִימוּ דְּשִׁירָתָא, כְּהַהוּא נְעִימוּ דַּהֲווֹ אָמְרֵי. וְכַד סִיּוּמוּ

יְיָ' יִמְלוֹךְ לְעוֹלָם וָעֶד. חָמוּ ד' דְּיוּקְנִין בִּרְקִיעַ. וְחַד מִנַּיְיהוּ רַב וְעִלָּאָה מִכֻּלְּהוּ. וְהַהוּא רַב וְעִלָּאָה מִנַּיְיהוּ, אִתְּעַר קָלָא וְאָמַר, כֹּה אָמַר יְיָ' זָכַרְתִּי לָךְ חֶסֶד נְעוּרַיִךְ אַהֲבַת כְּלוּלוֹתָיִךְ וְגוֹ'. שָׁאט בִּרְקִיעָא וְאַגְנִיז, קָם אַחֲרָא אֲבַתְרֵיהּ וְאָמַר, וְהוֹלַכְתִּי עִוְרִים בְּדֶרֶךְ לֹא יָדָעוּ בִּנְתִיבוֹת לֹא יָדָעוּ וְגוֹ'. סַיֵּים וְשָׁאט בִּרְקִיעָא וְאַגְנִיז.

211. While they were talking, they heard the song of the Sea in the most exquisite voice that was ever heard since the sweet voice of chanting was created, as this sweet sound in which it was said. When they finished, "Hashem shall reign for ever and ever" (Shemot 15:18). They noticed four images of men in the heavens and one of them was greater and higher above all of them; that greater and loftier of all raised his voice and said, "Thus says Hashem; I remember in your favor, the devotion of your youth, your love as a bride..." (Yirmeyah 2:2). He flew into the firmament and was hidden. And another one rose after him and said, "And I will bring the blind by a way that they know not; I will lead them in paths that they have not known..." (Yeshayah 42:16). He finished and flew into the firmament and was hidden.

29. The dead of the wilderness

A Synopsis
Four images of men in the heavens appear and say various things
and fly. In the morning the rabbis hear the sound of legions and
encampments praising God. The entire wilderness is covered in
clouds of glory shining and sparkling in a multitude of colors. The
rabbis say that the wilderness generation will be the first to arise
when King Messiah comes in the future.

212. פָּתַח אִידָךְ וְאָמַר, יְשׂוּשׂוּם מִדְבָּר וְצִיָּה וְתָגֵל עֲרָבָה וְתִפְרַח
כַּחֲבַצָּלֶת. וְשָׁאת בִּרְקִיעָא, וְאַגְנִיז. פָּתַח אִידָךְ וְאָמַר, כֹּה אָמַר יְיָ'
בּוֹרַאֲךָ יַעֲקֹב וְגוֹ', כֹּה אָמַר יְיָ' הַנּוֹתֵן בַּיָּם דָּרֶךְ וּבְמַיִם עַזִּים נְתִיבָה וְגוֹ'.
תְּכַבְּדֵנִי חַיַּת הַשָּׂדֶה תַּנִּים וּבְנוֹת יַעֲנָה וְגוֹ'. סִיֵּים וְשָׁאט בִּרְקִיעָא,
וְאַגְנִיז. כְּדֵין דְּחִילוּ סַגִּיא וְאֵמְתָנִי נָפַל עָלַיְיהוּ.

212. The other one opened with, "The wilderness and the arid land shall be
glad; and the desert shall rejoice, and blossom like the tulip" (Yeshayah
35:1). He flew into the firmament and was hidden. Another one opened the
discussion saying, "But now thus says Hashem that created you, O Jacob"
(Yeshayah 43:1). "Thus says Hashem, who makes a way in the sea, and a
path in the mighty waters..." (Ibid. 16). "The beast of the field shall honor Me,
the jackals and the owls..." (Ibid. 20). He concluded and flew into the
firmament and disappeared. Then they were overtaken with an awesome fear.

213. כַּד הֲוָה נָהִיר יְמָמָא, קָלָא אִתְּעַר כְּמִלְּקַדְמִין, וְאָמַר, עַמָּא תַּקִּיפָא
כְּאַרְיֵה, גֻּבְרִין כִּנְמֵרִין, הָבוּ יְקָר לְמָארֵיכוֹן. דִּכְתִּיב עַל כֵּן יְכַבְּדוּךְ עַם
עָז וְגוֹ'. שָׁמְעוּ קָל. חֵילִין וּמַשְׁרְיָין דַּהֲווֹ אַמְרֵי, לְךָ יְיָ' הַגְּדוּלָּה
וְהַגְּבוּרָה וְהַתִּפְאֶרֶת וְהַנֵּצַח וְהַהוֹד וְגוֹ', עַד וּמְרוֹמֵם עַל כָּל בְּרָכָה
וּתְהִלָּה. תַּוְוהוּ וְאַזְלוּ. אַדְּהָכִי נְהַר יְמָמָא, אַהֲדְרוּ רֵישָׁא, וְחָמוּ כָּל
מַדְבְּרָא חָפֵּי בַּעֲנָנֵי יְקָר, מְנַהֲרָן, מְנַצְצָן, בִּגְוָונִין סַגִּיאִין.

213. When the daylight broke, a voice arose again and said, A nation, strong
as a lion, powerful as tigers, give honor to your Master, as is written:
"Therefore shall the strong people glorify You..." (Yeshayah 25:3). They

heard the sound of legions and encampments that said, "Yours, Hashem, is the greatness, and the power, and the glory, and the victory, and the majesty..." (I Divrei Hayamim 29:11) until "which is exalted above all blessing and praise" (Nechemyah 9:5). They were filled with wonder, and left. During this time, the day became bright. They turned their heads and saw the entire wilderness covered in clouds of glory that shine and sparkle in a multitude of colors.

214. אָמְרוּ דָּא לְדָא, וַדַּאי קוּדְשָׁא בְּרִיךְ הוּא בָּעֵי לְאִשְׁתַּבְּחָא בְּתוּשְׁבַּחְתָּא דְּדָרָא דְּמַדְבְּרָא, דְּלָא הֲוָה בְּעָלְמָא, דָּרָא עִלָּאָה, כְּדָרָא דָּא. וְלָא יְהֵא עַד דְּיֵיתֵי מַלְכָּא מְשִׁיחָא וַדַּאי כָּל מַה דְּאַחְמֵי לָן קוּדְשָׁא בְּרִיךְ הוּא, לָא הֲוָה, אֶלָּא בְּגִין לְאוֹדָעָא לָן חֲבִיבוּ דְּמָארֵיהוֹן עֲלַיְיהוּ. לְאוֹדָעָא דְּאִית לוֹן חוּלָקָא טָבָא, וְאִינוּן בָּעֵי עָלְמָא דְּאָתֵי. וּלְזִמְנָא דְּאָתֵי כַּד יוֹקִים קוּדְשָׁא בְּרִיךְ הוּא מֵתַיָּיא, זְמִינִין אִלֵּין לְאַחֲיָיא בְּקַדְמֵיתָא. כד"א יִחְיוּ מֵתֶיךָ, וְאִלֵּין אִינּוּן דָּרָא דְּמַדְבְּרָא.

214. One said to the other, Certainly, the Holy One, blessed be He, wishes to be praised with praises of the generation of the wilderness, since there never existed such a lofty generation as that generation and there will not be until the coming of King Messiah. Certainly, all that we were shown by the Holy One, blessed be He, was only to inform us about their Master's great love for them, to let us know that they have a good portion and merit the World to Come. In the future, when the Holy One, blessed be He, will revive the dead, these, THE WILDERNESS GENERATION, will be destined to rise first, as it says, "The dead men of Your people shall live" (Yeshayah 26:19). That refers to the generation of the wilderness.

30. Three sounds that are never lost

A Synopsis

Rabbi Shimon wishes to know about the echo, and he is told about three sounds that never get lost besides the sounds of Torah and prayer. These are: 1) the sound of a woman in labor; 2) the sound of the person when the soul escapes its body; and 3) the sound of a snake when it sheds its skin. These sounds, which are all of pain, linger in the air and wander around the world. When a person raises his voice those sounds are awakened, although the voice of the snake can only be aroused when a person beats something. One kind of sound follows its own kind, so on the day of Rosh Hashanah the sound of the Shofar awakens the sound of another Shofar.

215. אָ"ל, אִי מִלָּה חַדְתָּא יָדְעַת, דַּאֲנָא עַרְטִירָא בָּהּ. אָ"ל אֵימָא. אָמַר קָלָא דְּהָדְרָא בָּעֵינָא לְמִנְדַּע. ב"נ יָהִיב קָלָא בְּחַקְלָא, אוֹ בַּאֲתָר אַחֲרָא, וְהָדְרָא קָלָא אַחֲרָא, וְלָא יְדִיעַ. אָ"ל, אִי חֲסִידָא קַדִּישָׁא, עַל מִלָּה דָּא, כַּמָּה קָלִין אִתְּעָרוּ, וְכַמָּה דִּקְדּוּקִין הֲווֹ קָמֵי רַב מְתִיבְתָּא, וְכַד נָחַת רַב מְתִיבְתָּא, אָמַר, הָכִי אוּקְמוּהָ מִלָּה בִּמְתִיבְתָּא דִּרְקִיעָא, וְרָזָא יַקִּירָא אִיהִי.

215. He said to him, Do you know something new that I am in want of knowing? He said to him, Speak. He said, I wish to understand the echo. A person sounds his voice in the field or in any other place. Another voice returns AFTER THAT and it is not known WHERE IT COMES FROM. He said to him, Oh, holy pious one. About this matter, many voices were raised and several concepts were placed in front of the head of the Yeshivah. When the head of the Yeshivah descended, he said, This is how they explained it in the heavenly Yeshivah, and it is a precious secret.

216. תָּא חֲזֵי, תְּלַת קָלִין אִינּוּן, דְּלָא אִתְאֲבִידוּ לְעָלְמִין, בַּר קָלִין דְּאוֹרַיְיתָא וּצְלוֹתָא, דְּאִלֵּין סַלְקִין לְעֵילָּא, וּבָקְעִין רְקִיעִין. אֲבָל קָלִין אַחֲרָנִין אִינּוּן דְּלָא סַלְקִין, וְלָא אִתְאֲבִידוּ.

216. Come and see: There are three sounds that are never lost; besides the sounds of Torah and prayer that ascend above and split the firmaments,

there are these other sounds that do not ascend and yet are not lost.

217. וְאִינּוּן תְּלַת: קוֹל חַיָּה בְּשַׁעֲתָא דְּאִיהִי עַל קַלְבִּיטָא, הַהוּא קָלָא מְשַׁטְטָא וְאָזְלָא בַּאֲוִירָא, מִסַּיְיפֵי עָלְמָא עַד סַיְיפֵי עָלְמָא. קוֹל דְּבַר נָשׁ, בְּשַׁעֲתָא, דְּנָפִיק נִשְׁמָתֵיה מִגּוּפֵיה, הַהוּא קָלָא מְשַׁטְטָא וְאָזְלָא בַּאֲוִירָא, מִסַּיְיפֵי עָלְמָא עַד סַיְיפֵי עָלְמָא. קוֹל נַחַשׁ, בְּשַׁעֲתָא דְּפָשִׁיט מַשְׁכֵיה, הַהוּא קָלָא מְשַׁטְטָא בַּאֲוִירָא, וְאָזְלָא מִסַּיְיפֵי עָלְמָא עַד סַיְיפֵי עָלְמָא.

217. These are the three sounds: 1) The sound of a woman in labor, when she stands on a footstool, goes about and wanders in the air from one end to the other end of the world; 2) The sound of the person, when the soul escapes his body, loiters and wanders in the air from one end of the world to the other end, and 3) The sound of the snake, when it sheds his skin, loiters in the air and wanders around the world from one end to the other.

218. אִי חֲסִידָא קַדִּישָׁא, כַּמָּה מִלָּה דָּא רַבָּא וְיַקִּירָא. אִלֵּין קָלִין, מַה אִתְעֲבֵיד מִנַּיְיהוּ, וּלְאָן אֲתַר עָאלִין וְשָׁרָאן. אִלֵּין קָלִין דְּצַעֲרָא אִינּוּן, וְאָזְלִין וּמְשַׁטְטֵי בַּאֲוִירָא, וְאָזְלֵי מִסַּיְיפֵי עָלְמָא, עַד סַיְיפֵי דְּעָלְמָא, וְעָאלִין גּוֹ נְקִיקִין וּמְחִילִין דְּעַפְרָא, וְאִתְטַמְּרָן תַּמָּן. וְכַד יָהִיב ב"נ קָלָא, אִינּוּן מִתְעָרִין לְגַבֵּי הַהוּא קָלָא. קָלָא דְּנָחָשׁ, לָא אִתְּעַר לְגַבֵּי קָלָא דב"נ. הֵיאַךְ יִתְּעַר. בִּמְחָאָה. כַּד מָחֵי ב"נ מָחָאָה אִתְּעַר קָלָא דְּנָחָשׁ, דְּאִתְטַמַּר לְגַבֵּיה הַהוּא קָלָא, וְלָאו קָלָא אַחֲרָא. קָלָא אִתְּעַר בָּתַר קָלָא, זִינָא בָּתַר זִינֵיה.

218. Oh, holy pious one, how great and important is this matter. What is produced by these sounds and whereto do they enter and dwell? These sounds are of pain. They roam and wander in the air and travel from one end of the world to the other, and enter into cracks and tunnels in the dust and lie hidden there. When a person sounds his voice, they are awakened toward that voice. ONLY the voice of the snake is not roused towards a human voice. How does it awaken then? By beating. That is, when a person beats AT SOMETHING, the sound of the snake that was hidden there, IN AN EMPTY PLACE OR IN THE FIELD, reverberates to the sound OF THAT BEATING, but

not towards another HUMAN voice. A sound reverberates to a sound; HOWEVER, a kind goes after its own kind. THIS IS TO SAY THAT THE FIRST TWO SOUNDS, WHICH ARE OF HUMANS, ARE AWAKENED TOWARDS OTHER HUMAN SOUNDS, AND THE THIRD SOUND, WHICH IS OF THE SNAKE, AWAKEN TOWARD A BEATING SOUND.

219. וְעַל דָּא בְּיוֹמָא דר"ה, קוֹל שׁוֹפָר, אִתְּעַר קוֹל שׁוֹפָר אַחֲרָא, זִינָא בָּתַר זִינֵיהּ אָזְלָא. אָרְחֵיהּ דְּנָחָשׁ לְבִישׁ אִיהוּ, לְקַטְלָא וּלְמִמְחָאָה, בְּהַהוּא קָלָא מַמָּשׁ, לָא אִתְּעַר קָלָא דְּהַאי נַחַשׁ, אֶלָּא בָּתַר זִינֵיהּ. וְדָא אִיהוּ, כַּד ב"נ מָחֵי בְּחוּטְרָא בְּאַרְעָא, וְקָרֵי לֵיהּ לְזִינֵיהּ, כְּדֵין אִתְּעַר הַהוּא קָלָא דְּנָחָשׁ, לְאָתָבָא לְזִינֵיהּ. וְרָזָא דָּא אִיהוּ טְמִירוּ.

219. Consequently, on the day of Rosh Hashanah (The Jewish New Year), the sound of the Shofar awakens the sound of another Shofar, THE SECRET OF THE SOUND OF BINAH. One sort follows its own sort. The way of the snake tends to evil, to kill and to beat. Thus, in the voice of a real PERSON, no snake sound gets stirred. It only follows its own type and this happens when a person hits the ground with a stick, which is a sound that calls its kind. Then the sound of the snake awakens to answer its own type. And this is a hidden secret.

220. אר"ש, וַדַּאי מִלָּה דָּא מִלָּה סְתִימָא הִיא. וְתַוְוהָנָא אֵיךְ שְׁלֹמֹה מַלְכָּא לָא יָדַע מִלָּה דָּא. א"ל, שְׁלֹמֹה מַלְכָּא מִנְדַּע יָדַע, וְלָא כ"כ. אֲבָל מַה דְּלָא יָדַע, הַהוּא קָלָא מַה תּוֹעַלְתָּא אִית בָּהּ, וְהֵיךְ יָתְבָא.

220. Rabbi Shimon said, Certainly this is a hidden matter. I wonder why King Solomon was not aware of this, SINCE HE SAID, "THERE ARE THREE THINGS...THE PATH OF A SNAKE UPON A ROCK" (MISHLEI 30:18-19). He said to him, King Solomon knew, but not that much. However, what he did not know was of that sound, what benefit it has and how it is settled.

221. וְרַב מְתִיבְתָּא הָכִי אָמַר, דְּקָדוּקָא דָּא לָא יָדַע שְׁלֹמֹה מַלְכָּא, דְּהָא הַהוּא קָלָא, אִיהִי כְּלִילָא רוּחָא וְנַפְשָׁא, וְהֶבֶל גַּרְמֵי מֵעַצְבוֹנָא דְּבִשְׂרָא, וּמְשַׁטְּטָא בַּאֲוִירָא, וְכָל חַד מִתְפְּרַשׁ דָּא מִן דָּא. וְכַד מָטָא

לְהַהוּא אֲתָר דְּעָאל בֵּיהּ, יָתְבָא כְּמֵיתָא. וְכָל אִינּוּן חַרְשִׁין וְקוֹסְמִין
יַדְעִין אַתְרִין אִלֵּין בְּחַרְשַׁיְיהוּ, וְגַחְנִין לְאַרְעָא, וְשַׁמְעִין קָלָא דָּא,
דְּמִתְחַבְּרוּן אִינּוּן רוּחָא וְנַפְשָׁא, וְהֶבֶל דְּגַרְמֵי, וְאוֹדְעִין מִלָּה וְדָא אִיהוּ
אוֹב מֵאֶרֶץ. וְעַל דָּא רָדִיף שְׁלֹמֹה, לְמִנְדַּע מַה דְּאִתְעָבֵיד מֵהַהוּא קָלָא,
וְלָא יָדַע. זַכָּאָה חוּלָקָךְ רִבִּי, דְּאִתְבְּרִיר לָךְ מִלָּה דִּקְשׁוֹט.

221. The head of the Yeshivah said it this way. King Solomon did not know this subtle point, that the sound is composed of the Ruach, the Nefesh, the breath of the bones and the composition of the flesh. AND THE SOUND hovers in the air and each one OF THOSE THREE separated from each other. When THE SOUND reaches that place where it entered, it sits as if dead. All the wizards and magicians are aware of these areas with their witchcraft; they bend themselves to the ground and hear these sounds, to which the Ruach, Nefesh and breath of the bones connect. They inform them of the matters THAT THEY INQUIRE ABOUT, and this is: "A medium, out of the ground" (Yeshayah 29:4). That is why Solomon pursued the knowledge of what happens with this sound, but could not find out. Praised is your lot, Rabbi, that you have discerned a matter of truth.

222. כַּד בַּ"נ אִתְּעַר קָלָא, מִיַּד אִתְּעַר הַהוּא קָלָא, וְלֵית לֵיהּ רְשׁוּ
לְאַרְכָּא יַתִּיר. אֶלָּא כְּעֵין הַהוּא קָלָא, דְּאִתְּעַר בַּ"נ, וְלָא יַתִּיר. וְאִי
אָרִיךְ בַּ"נ קָלֵיהּ, אִיהוּ לָא אֲרִיךְ כָּל כַּךְ בַּהֲדֵיהּ, אֶלָּא לְסוֹפָא דְקָלָא,
בְּגִין דְּלָא יָכִיל לְאַרְכָּא מַאי טַעֲמָא. בְּגִין דְּכַד נָפְקָא בְּקַדְמֵיתָא,
אִתְאָרִיךְ מִסַיְיפֵי עָלְמָא עַד סַיְיפֵי עָלְמָא, וְהַשְׁתָּא דְּעָאל תַּמָּן, לָא
יָכִיל לְאַרְכָּא קָלָא, דְּהָא לֵית לֵיהּ אֲתָר לְאִתְפַּשְּׁטָא תַּמָּן כִּדְבְקַדְמֵיתָא.

222. When a person raises a sound, that sound is instantly awakened, OF THE WOMAN GIVING BIRTH OR OF THE DEPARTURE OF THE SOUL. It is not authorized to be longer, just EQUAL TO the sound that the person aroused and not more. If a person prolongs his voice, it does not extend its sound as much with him, but rather it gets roused at the end of the voice OF THE PERSON, since it is incapable of being prolonged. What is the reason? It is because when it first left him, it was extended from one end of the world to the other end of the world. Now that it has entered there, it cannot extend the sound any more, since there is no more room there to extend it as before.

223. חַדֵּי ר"ש וְאָמַר, אִלְמָלֵי לָא זָכֵינָא לְמִשְׁמַע, אֶלָּא מִלָּה דָא, דִּי
לִי, לְמֶחֱוֵי חַדֵּי, דְּזָכֵינָא לְמִשְׁמַע מִלִּין דִּקְשׁוֹט, דְּהַהוּא עָלְמָא. אָ"ל,
אִי חֲסִידָא קַדִּישָׁא. אִלְמָלֵי יַדְעַת חֶדְוָה דְּמִלִּין בְּהַהוּא עָלְמָא קַמֵּי רַב
מְתִיבְתָּא, תְּהֵא חַדֵּי יַתִּיר.

223. Rabbi Shimon rejoiced and said, If I would have deserved to hear only this, it would have been sufficient to make me happy, since I managed to hear words of truth about that world. He said to him, Oh, holy pious one. If you would have known the rejoicing in these matters about that world in the presence of the head of the Yeshivah, you would have rejoiced even more.

31. "And Joseph shall put his hand on your eyes"

A Synopsis

We learn that we must close the eyes of a dead person because the eyes are the colors of this world, and the appearance and shape of this world is contained in them, so this world and its appearance must be closed off to him. It was Joseph who closed his father's eyes because he was so beloved, and with this action he was taking his father's sight now that his father's sight from this world is lost. From that point on his father is having a different sight of the other world prepared for him. During the time of the resurrection of the dead, not the tiniest thing will occur of the activities of this world; everything will first be destroyed and the person will be purified, and then his body will be made like a new creation. This is like it is now in the upper world even before the resurrection.

224. אָ"ל, מַאי חִדּוּשָׁא הֲוָה הַשְׁתָּא, כַּד אָתֵית לְגַבִּי. אָמַר, רַב מְתִיבְתָּא פָּתַח וְאָמַר, וְיוֹסֵף יָשִׁית יָדוֹ עַל עֵינֶיךָ. חֶדְוָה הוּא. אֲמַאי סְתִימוּ דְּעַיְינִין לְמֵיתָא. בְּגִין דְּעַיְינִין, גַּוְונִין דְּהַאי עָלְמָא אִינּוּן, וְחֵיזוּ וּדְיוּקְנָא דְּהַאי עָלְמָא בְּהוּ, אִיהוּ אַסְתִּים מִנֵּיהּ הַאי עָלְמָא, חֵיזוּ דְּהַאי עָלְמָא. אַסְתִּימוּ עֵינוֹי, כָּל חֵיזוּ דְּהַאי עָלְמָא, הָא אִתְחֲשָׁךְ מִנֵּיהּ. וְחֶשְׁכִין מִנֵּיהּ חֵיזוּ דְּעֵינוֹי, לֵית לֵיהּ חֵיזוּ בְּהַאי עָלְמָא, מִתַּמָּן וּלְהָלְאָה. אר"ש, יָאוּת תִּקּוּנָא דְּקַדְמָאֵי, וְחָכְמָתָא דִּלְהוֹן יַתִּיר מִמַּלְאָכִין קַדִּישִׁין.

224. He said to him, What new discovery was there now when you came to me? He said, The head of the Yeshivah opened the discussion saying, "And Joseph shall put his hand on your eyes" (Beresheet 46:4). That is A TIDING OF gladness. HE INQUIRES: Why is it required to close the eyes of a dead person? HE RESPONDS: Since the eyes are the colors of this world and the appearance and shape of this world is contained in them, IT FOLLOWS THAT WITH THE CLOSING OF THE EYES, he closes off to him this world and its appearance. When his eyes are closed, the entire world is dimmed to him AND IF they dim for him the sight of his eyes, he has no sight of this world from there onwards. Rabbi Shimon said, The expositions of those who went before us are beautiful; their wisdom surpasses those of the holy angels.

225. אָ"ל, יוֹסֵף אֲמַאי יָשִׁית יָדוֹ מִכָּל בְּנוֹי. וְאִי תֵּימָא עַל בְּשׂוֹרָה

דִּילֵיהּ, מִבָּעֵי לֵיהּ וְיוֹסֵף חַי תִּרְאֶה. אָ"ל יָשִׁית יָדוֹ בְּגִין דִּרְחִימוּ דִּילֵיהּ
הֲוָה, וּבג"כ דָּא אַסְתִּים מִנֵּיהּ נְהִירוּ דְּהַאי עָלְמָא, וְדָא נָטִיל לֵיהּ. מַאן
דְּאַסְתִּים עֵינוֹי, רְחִימָא דִּילֵיהּ אַחְזֵי הָכִי: חֵיזוּ דִּילָךְ דְּהַאי עָלְמָא
אִתְאֲבִיד, הָא אֲנָא חֵיזוּ דִּילָךְ בְּאַתְרָךְ. מִכָּאן וּלְהָלְאָה יַתְקְנוּן לָךְ
חֵיזוּ אַחֲרָא, דְּהַהוּא עָלְמָא.

225. He said to him: Why should it have been Joseph who placed his hand rather than all the other sons? If you think that he told him so as a result of his good tidings, THAT JOSEPH IS STILL ALIVE, then it should have said, 'You shall see Joseph alive'. WHY DID HE SAY: "AND JOSEPH SHALL PUT HIS HAND ON YOUR EYES"? He said to him: "put his hand" is because he was his beloved. Therefore, he closed from him the light of this world and he took it himself. Whoever closes the eyes of his beloved shows by that: Your sight of this world is lost, and I take your sight instead. From now on, they will prepare for you a different sight of that world. THIS IS THE REASON THAT THIS MATTER WAS GIVEN TO JOSEPH, SINCE HE WAS MORE BELOVED TO JACOB THAN ANY OF HIS SONS.

226. אר"ש, מַה אִתְהֲנֵי הַאי לְמֵיתָא, וּמַה תּוֹעַלְתָּא אִית לֵיהּ בְּהַאי.
מַאן דְּיִבְעֵי לְמִשְׁאַל יוֹמָא מַה דְּאִצְטְרִיךְ לְאַפְקָחָא עֵינוֹי, בְּגִין לְאַחֲזָאָה
דַּעֲדַיִין אִזְדַּמַן אִיהוּ, לְאָתָבָא לְחֵיזוּ דְּהַאי עָלְמָא כִּדְבְקַדְמִין.

226. Rabbi Shimon asked, What good will this provide to the dead and what benefit is there in it? Whoever will ask about this, IT IS NECESSARY to tell him that there is a need to open the eyes OF THE DEAD in order to show him that he will return to the sight of this world as before – MEANING, HE WILL BE RESURRECTED WITH THE DEAD TO LIFE.

227. אָ"ל אִי חֲסִידָא קַדִּישָׁא, וַדַּאי אִי לָא אַסְתִּים מִנֵּיהּ כָּל חֵיזוּ דְּהַאי
עָלְמָא, וְלָא אִתְאֲבִיד כֹּלָּא מִנֵּיהּ, לָא לֶהֱוֵי לֵיהּ חֵיזוּ וְחוּלָקָא דְּהַהוּא
עָלְמָא. עָלְמָא דָּא, בְּהִפּוּכָא אִיהוּ מֵהַהוּא עָלְמָא דַּאֲנָן בֵּיהּ, דְּבִזְמַנָא
דִּתְחַיַּית מֵתַיָּיא, אֲפִילוּ כְּחוּטָא דְּשַׂעֲרָא לָא הֲוָה מֵעוֹבָדָא דְּהַאי
עָלְמָא, דְּכֹלָּא אִתְאֲבִיד בְּקַדְמֵיתָא, בְּהַהוּא טַלָּא וְיִתְעֲבַר מִנֵּיהּ כָּל

זוּהֲמָא, וּלְבָתַר יִתְעֲבִיד כַּחֲמִירָא דָא, וּמִנֵּיה יִתְעֲבִיד גּוּפָא בְּרִיָה
חַדְתָּא, כַּךְ הָכָא.

227. He said to him, Oh, holy pious one. Certainly, if the sight of this world were not closed off to him entirely and he didn't lose it completely, he would have no sight and portion in that world, for this world has an opposite polarity from the world that we are in. During the time of the resurrection of the dead, even the tiniest thing will not occur of the activities of this world, since everything will first be destroyed by that dew, MEANING THE DEW OF RESURECTION. It will remove from him all the filth and then he will become like dough, and from it the body will be made like a new creation. So it is here, IN THE UPPER WORLD EVEN BEFORE THE RESURRECTION.

32. The garments of that world

A Synopsis

Rabbi Shimon knows that those he is speaking with are dressed with the dear robe of a purely holy body and wonders whether anything similar happens in this world. He is answered with the story of Esther who put on her royal apparel and went to see King Ahasuerus; he saw her clothed in a robe of light and he lost his soul for an instant. Mordechai too was enshrouded in the robes of that world. Rabbi Shimon understands that the just in this world get shrouded with the robe of Malchut. The Satan wants to prevent the righteous from being garbed in the pure and holy garment because as soon as they are so robed all the Evil Inclinations are removed. The spirits tell Rabbi Shimon why they visit the cemetery at the beginning of every night.

228. אָ"ל רִבִּי שִׁמְעוֹן, וַדַּאי יְדַעְנָא דְּאַתּוּן מְלוּבָּשִׁין תַּמָּן, בִּלְבוּשׁ יְקַר, דְּגוּפָא דַּכְיָא קַדִּישָׁא. אִי הֲוָה בְּגַוְונָא דָּא בְּהַאי עָלְמָא, ב"נ דְּאִתְחֲזֵי בְּהַהוּא גוּפָא, כְּגַוְונָא דְּאַתּוּן קַיְימִין בְּהַהוּא עָלְמָא.

228. Rabbi Shimon said to him, I certainly am aware that you are dressed there with the precious robe of a pure holy body. HE ASKS: Is there something similar in this world? IS THERE a person who appears here in that body, as you stand in that world?

229. אָ"ל, מִלָּה דָּא שָׁאִילוּ קַמֵּי רַב מְתִיבְתָּא, תְּרֵין עוּלֵימִין דְּאִתְלְבָּשׁוּ בֵּינָנָא, בָּתַר דְּסַבְלוּ צַעֲרָא עַל חוֹבָא, דְּלָא אִתְחֲזֵי לְגַלָּאָה, וְשָׁאִילוּ דָּא קַמֵּי רַב מְתִיבְתָּא. וְאִיהוּ אָמַר, דְּהָא הֲוָה בְּהַאי עָלְמָא הָכִי. מְנָלָן. דִּכְתִּיב וַיְהִי בַּיּוֹם הַשְּׁלִישִׁי וַתִּלְבַּשׁ אֶסְתֵּר מַלְכוּת, אִתְלְבָּשַׁת בְּהַהוּא דְּיוּקְנָא דְּהַהוּא עָלְמָא. מַלְכוּת: דָּא רוּחָא דְּקוּדְשָׁא, דְּהָא מַלְכוּת שְׁמַיָא, נָשִׁיב רוּחָא, מֵהַהוּא רוּחָא דַּאֲוִירָא דְּהַהוּא עָלְמָא, וְאִתְלַבְּשָׁא בֵּיהּ אֶסְתֵּר.

229. He said to him, This matter was asked by two youths, MEANING YOUNG MEN, in the presence of the dean of the Yeshivah. They were clothed among us after suffering pain about a sin that is improper to reveal, and this question was put to the head of the Yeshivah. He replied that

something similar happened in this world. How do we know? Since it is written: "Now it came to pass on the third day, that Esther put on her royal (lit. 'of Malchut') apparel" (Ester 5:1), MEANING THAT she was robed in the fashion of that world, Malchut, WHICH MEANS HERE, the Holy Spirit. For the Kingdom of Heaven, WHICH IS MALCHUT OF ZEIR ANPIN THAT IS CALLED HEAVEN, blows a wind (spirit) from the spirit of the air of that world, and Esther was robed in it.

230. וְכַד עָאלַת קַמֵּי מַלְכָּא אֲחַשְׁוֵרוֹשׁ, וְחָמָא הַהוּא לְבוּשָׁא דִּנְהוֹרָא, דִּיוּקְנָאָה אִדְמִי לְמַלְאַךְ אֱלֹהִים. פַּרְחָה מִנֵּיהּ נִשְׁמָתָא לְפוּם שַׁעֲתָא. מָרְדְּכַי אוֹף הָכִי, דִּכְתִיב וּמָרְדְּכַי יָצָא מִלִּפְנֵי הַמֶּלֶךְ בִּלְבוּשׁ מַלְכוּת. לְבוּשׁ מַלְכוּת, וַדַּאי, דִּיוּקְנָא דְּהַהוּא עָלְמָא. וְע"ד כְּתִיב, כִּי נָפַל פַּחַד מָרְדְּכַי עֲלֵיהֶם. פַּחַד מָרְדְּכַי, וְלָא פַּחַד אֲחַשְׁוֵרוֹשׁ. אָמַר רִבִּי שִׁמְעוֹן, כַּמָּה מְתִיקִין אִינּוּן מִלִּין, זַכָּאָה חוּלָקִי, וְהָא יְדַעֲנָא דְּצַדִּיקַיָּיא בְּהַאי עָלְמָא, מִתְלַבְּשָׁן בִּלְבוּשָׁא דְּאִקְרֵי לְבוּשׁ מַלְכוּת, וְהָכִי הוּא וַדַּאי.

230. When she entered into the presence of King Ahasuerus and he saw that robe of light, her form seemed to him like an angel of Elohim, and he lost his soul for an instant. Mordechai too WAS ENSHROUDED IN THE ROBES OF THAT WORLD, as is written: "And Mordechai went out from the presence of the king in royal (lit. 'of Malchut') apparel" (Ester 8:15), verily the apparel of Malchut that is the form of that world. Therefore, it is written: "Because the fear of Mordechai had fallen upon them" (Ester 9:3), the fear of Mordechai and not the fear of Ahasuerus, THAT IS, NOT BECAUSE AHASUERUS HAD MADE HIM GREAT, BUT RATHER BECAUSE OF HIS GARMENT OF THAT WORLD. Rabbi Shimon said, How sweet are these matters. Blessed is my lot. I am aware that the just in this world get shrouded with that robe that is called the robe of Malchut, and that is definitely so.

231. א"ל, אֲוֵירָא דְּג"ע, נְשִׁיבוּ דְּרוּחַ קוּדְשָׁא אִינּוּן, וּמִתְלַבְּשָׁן בֵּיהּ צַדִּיקַיָּיא, כְּגַוְונָא דַּהֲווֹ בְּהַאי עָלְמָא. וּלְבָתַר, רוּחַ קוּדְשָׁא שָׁרָאת, עַל רֵישָׁא דְּכָל חַד וְחַד. וְאִתְעַטַּר וְאִתְעֲבֵידָא לֵיהּ עֲטָרָא. וְכַךְ הֲוָה לְמָרְדְּכַי, דִּכְתִיב בִּלְבוּשׁ מַלְכוּת, דִּיוּקְנָא דְּהַהוּא עָלְמָא. וּלְבָתַר

וַעֲטֶרֶת זָהָב גְּדוֹלָה, דָּא עֲטֶרֶת, דִּשְׁרִיאַת עַל רֵישֵׁיהוֹן דְּצַדִּיקַיָּיא בְּהַהוּא עָלְמָא. כַּד קַבִּילוּ יִשְׂרָאֵל אוֹרַיְיתָא, כְּגַוְונָא דָּא הֲוָה לְהוֹן. עַד דְּחָבוּ, דִּכְתִיב בְּהוּ, וַיִּתְנַצְּלוּ בְנֵי יִשְׂרָאֵל אֶת עֶדְיָם מֵהַר חוֹרֵב. אִתְפְּשָׁטוּ מֵהַהוּא לְבוּשָׁא.

231. He said to him, The air of the Garden of Eden is the blowing of the Holy Spirit and the righteous are robed in it as they were in this world. Then, the Holy Spirit dwells upon the head of each individual. He is adorned with it and it becomes a crown to him. The same happened to Mordechai, as it is written: "in apparel of Malchut," WHICH MEANS in the form of that world, and then, "with a great crown of gold"; that is, in the crown that rests on the heads of the righteous in that world. When Yisrael received the Torah, they also had similar ones, MEANING ROBES OF THAT WORLD, until they sinned, as is written: "And the children of Yisrael stripped themselves of their ornaments by the Mount Horeb" (Shemot 33:6), THAT IS, stripping themselves of that garment.

232. וְכֵן כְּתִיב בִּיהוֹשֻׁעַ כַּהֲנָא רַבָּא, הָסִירוּ הַבְּגָדִים הַצּוֹאִים מֵעָלָיו. וּכְתִיב וַיַּלְבִּשׁוּהוּ בְּגָדִים, אִלֵּין לְבוּשִׁין דְּהַהוּא עָלְמָא. מֵהָכָא מִלִּין קַדְמָאִין. וּמֵהָכָא, דְּכָל זִמְנָא דְּגוּפָא דְּהַאי עָלְמָא קַיְּימָא בְּקַבְרָא בְּקִיּוּמָא, לָא אִתְלְבַּשׁ רוּחָא בִּלְבוּשָׁא דְּהַהוּא עָלְמָא. דִּכְתִיב וַיָּסִירוּ הַבְּגָדִים הַצּוֹאִים מֵעָלָיו בְּקַדְמֵיתָא. וּלְבָתַר וַיַּלְבִּשׁוּהוּ בְּגָדִים. וּמַלְאַךְ יְיָ' עוֹמֵד, מַהוּ עוֹמֵד. אֶלָּא דָּא הוּא עָטְרָא, דְּאִקְרֵי מַלְאַךְ יְיָ', דְּקַיְּימָא עַל רֵישֵׁיהוֹן דְּצַדִּיקַיָּיא וְדָא אִיהוּ עוֹמֵד. עוֹמֵד עַל רֵישָׁא לְעֵילָּא. לְבָתַר דְּאִתְלַבְּשָׁן בְּהַאי לְבוּשָׁא דִּיקָר.

232. Similarly, we find written about Joshua, the High Priest, "Take off the filthy garments from him...and clothed him with garments" (Zecharyah 3:4-5). These are the robes of that world. From here, WE DERIVE our earlier words THAT THERE IS A NEED TO FIRST CLOSE THE EYES FROM ALL SIGHTS OF THIS WORLD, WHICH ARE CONSIDERED AS FILTHY GARMENTS. THEN YOU COULD DESERVE TO SEE THE SIGHT OF THAT WORLD, WHICH ARE NEW ROBES, WITH WHICH THEY DRESSED JOSHUA. From here, we learn that during the entire period that the body of this world,

WHICH IS REFERRED TO AS "FILTHY GARMENTS," remains in the grave, the spirit does not acquire the robe of that world, since it is written first: "Take off the filthy garments from him," and then: "And clothed him with garments." AND IT IS WRITTEN: "And the angel of Hashem stood by" (Ibid. 5). HE INQUIRES: What is the meaning of "stood"? HE RESPONDS: Only that this is the crown, referred to as the angel of Hashem, that stands upon the heads of the righteous, AS MENTIONED BEFORE. That is WHAT IS WRITTEN: "stood," MEANING it stands above the head after they are adorned with this precious garment.

233. תְּרֵין גּוּפִין כַּחֲדָא, לָא יַכְלִין לְמֵיקַם, כָּל זִמְנָא דְּהַאי קַיָּים, רוּחָא לָא מְקַבְּלָא אַחֲרָא. אִתְעֲבַר דָּא, הָא אַחֲרָא זְמִינָא מִיַּד, וַדַּאי, דָּא נָפִיק, וְדָא עָאל. כְּגַוְונָא דְּיֵצֶר טוֹב וְיֵצֶר רָע. בְּהַאי עָלְמָא. לָא בָּעֵי קוּדְשָׁא בְּרִיךְ הוּא דְּתַרְוַוייהוּ יְקוּמוּן כַּחֲדָא.

233. Two bodies cannot exist together. As long as the one OF THIS WORLD exists, the spirit cannot accept another ROBE OF THAT WORLD. When this one, FROM THIS WORLD, passes away, the other one is instantly ready. Assuredly, this one leaves and that one enters. It is similar to the Good Inclination and Evil Inclination in this world, both of which the Holy One, blessed be He, does not wish to exist simultaneously in one BODY. IF THE EVIL INCLINATION DOMINATES, THE GOOD INCLINATION FLEES AND IF THE GOOD INCLINATION DOMINATES, THE EVIL INCLINATION FLEES.

234. אָמַר לֵיה, תַּוְוהְנָא עַל מַה דִּכְתִּיב וְהַשָּׂטָן עוֹמֵד עַל יְמִינוֹ לְשִׂטְנוֹ. וְכִי יְהוֹשֻׁעַ בֶּן יְהוֹצָדָק כַּךְ, שְׁאָר בְּנֵי עָלְמָא עַל אַחַת כַּמָּה וְכַמָּה. אָ"ל, חֲסִידָא קַדִּישָׁא, כַּמָּה טְמִירִין סְתִימִין מֵאִלֵּין אִלֵּין, אע"ג דְּחַבְרַיָּיא יַדְעִין בְּמִלִּין דְּהַהוּא עָלְמָא, לָא יַכְלִין לְמִנְדַּע בְּרָזִין אִלֵּין.

234. He said to him, I wonder about what is written: "And the adversary standing at his right hand to thwart him" (Ibid. 1). If it is this way with Joshua, the son of Josedech, it could most definitely happen to the rest of the people. He said to him, Holy pious one, how hidden and concealed those matters are. Although our friends are familiar with matters of that world, they are unable to comprehend such secrets.

235. אָ"ל, כֵּיוָן דְּבַר נָשׁ בְּהַהוּא עָלְמָא, מַה תּוֹעַלְתָּא אִית לְהַהוּא שָׂטָן לְאַסְטָאָה לֵיהּ, וְלָא דַּי לֵיהּ דְּאַפִּיק נִשְׁמָתֵיהּ מִנֵּיהּ, וְקָטִיל לֵיהּ. אָמַר לֵיהּ אִי חֲסִידָא קַדִּישָׁא, זַכָּאָה חוּלָקָךְ, ת"ח תִּיאוּבְתָּא דְּשָׂטָן לָא הֲוָה, אֶלָּא בְּגִין דְּלָא יִתְלַבַּשׁ הַהוּא זַכָּאָה בִּלְבוּשָׁא דַּכְיָא קַדִּישָׁא, דְּכֵיוָן דְּחָזֵי הַהוּא שָׂטָן, דִּלְבוּשָׁא דִּילֵיהּ אִתְדַּחְיָא, וְלָא אִתְחֲשִׁיב, עַל דָּא אַסְטֵי לֵיהּ. מַאי טַעֲמָא. בְּגִין דְּאִי אִתְלַבַּשׁ בְּהַהוּא לְבוּשׁ יְקָר, מִיָּד לְבוּשָׁא דְּזוּהֲמָא, וְעֲבִידְתָּא דְּהַהוּא שָׂטָן, יִתְבְּטַל וַיַּעֲבַר מֵעָלְמָא, וְלָא נִיחָא לֵיהּ לְשָׂטָן.

235. He said to him, Since a person is in that world, what benefit is there for the Satan to thwart him? Is he not satisfied that he already took his soul and killed him? He said to him, Oh, holy pious one, praised is your lot. Come and observe. The only desire that the Satan had was to prevent that righteous one, JOSHUA SON OF JOSEDECH, from being robed in this pure and holy garment. As soon as the Satan realized that his dress, THAT IS, THE SOILED GARMENTS, were pushed aside and were not considered worthy, he then tried to thwart him. What is the reason? Because once he is robed in that precious garment, instantly that soiled garment and the evil activity of the Satan would be voided and removed from the world. THAT IS WHY the Satan tried to prevent this.

236. וְתוּ, דִּבְכָל זִמְנָא דְּלָא אִתְלַבַּשׁ, פַּקְדָּא רוּחָא לְהַהוּא גּוּפָא דְּזוּהֲמָא דִּילֵיהּ, וְנִיחָא לֵיהּ לְשָׂטָן. וְכֵיוָן דְּאִתְלַבַּשׁ בְּהַהוּא לְבוּשׁ יְקָר, הָא אִתְבְּטַל גְּוָונֵי דְּיִצְרָא בִּישָׁא, וְגוּפָא דִּילֵיהּ, וְלֵית לֵיהּ דּוּכְרָנָא בַּהֲדֵיהּ לְעָלְמִין.

236. In addition, as long as he did not get dressed IN THE GARMENT OF THAT WORLD, the spirit visits that soiled body of his, and the Satan is pleased. However, as soon as he dressed up in that precious garment OF THAT WORLD, all types of the Evil Inclinations were voided, his body was gone and there was never any memory of it.

237. וְאִי תֵּימָא, דַּאֲנָן פַּקְדִין לְבֵי קִבְרֵי בְּרֵישׁ כָּל לֵילְיָא, לָאו עַל גּוּפָא

אֶלָּא עַל נַפְשָׁא. דְּהָא כָּל זִמְנָא דְּבִשְׂרָא קַיְּימָא, רוּחָא פָּקְדָא עָלָה
דְּנַפְשָׁא, וְנַפְשָׁא פָּקְדָא לְגוּפָא. אֲבָל הַשְׁתָּא, פִּקְדוֹנָא דִּילָן אִיהוּ
לְנַפְשָׁא, דְּאִיהִי מִשְׁתַּכְּבָא. וְאִשְׁתְּאָרַת בְּשִׁכּוּכֵי גּוֹ גַּרְמֵי. ובג"כ, בְּרֵישׁ
כָּל לֵילְיָא, פִּקְדוֹנָא דְּרוּחָא לְנַפְשָׁא, וְלָא עַל בִּשְׂרָא.

237. If you should ask here, we THE SPIRITS visit the cemetery at the beginning of each night, EVEN IF THE BODY HAS ALREADY BEEN REMOVED FROM THE WORLD. THE QUESTION MUST BE POSED AS TO WHY WE VISIT THE GRAVE. HE RESPONDS: This visit is not about the body, but rather about the Nefesh. As long as the flesh ON THE BODY is still in existence, the Ruach visits the Nefesh and the Nefesh visits the body. However, WHEN THE FLESH OF THE BODY WAS GONE FROM THE WORLD, our visiting is to the Nefesh that has quieted down and remained embedded in the bones OF THE BODY, SINCE A CERTAIN BONE WILL ALWAYS REMAIN IN THE GRAVE, FROM WHICH IT IS BUILT AT THE RESURRECTION OF THE DEAD. Therefore, at the beginning of each night, the visiting of the Ruach is for the Nefesh and not for the flesh.

33. Building the body of man

A Synopsis

Rabbi Shimon is told about the composition of a man's spirit and flesh; when the man dies only the part that was given by the Holy Spirit and its Chariots endures. The Satan stands by to thwart a person as long as his flesh is in existence but once the flesh is consumed he loses his authority to do this.

238. אִי חֲסִידָא קַדִּישָׁא, תָּא וְאַגְּלֵי לָךְ מִלָּה סְתִימָא. בִּנְיָינָא דְגוּפָא דְּבַר נָשׁ הָכִי הוּא, רוּחָא מֵעִם רוּחָא דְקוּדְשָׁא. נִשְׁמְתָא מִגּוֹ אִילָנָא דְחַיֵּי. כֵּיוָן דְּרוּחָא קַדִּישָׁא, יָהַב חֵילָא, מִיַּד רְתִיכִין דִּילֵיהּ. יָהֲבִין חֵילַיְיהוּ. חֵילָא דִּלְהוֹן, גַּרְמֵי וְשַׁיְיפִין. כֻּלְהוּ מִסִּטְרָא דִלְהוֹן, וְתִקּוּנַיְיהוּ דָּא עַל דָּא. סט״א יָהֲבַת בִּשְׂרָא, וּמִסִּטְרָא דִּילָהּ, אַתְיָא בִּשְׂרָא, וְלָא מִלָּה אַחֲרָא. רְתִיכִין דִּילָהּ, יָהֲבִין כָּל אִינּוּן גִּידִין וְעוֹרְקִין, לְאַמְשָׁכָא דְּמָא לְבִשְׂרָא. בָּתַר דְּאִלֵּין יָהֲבֵי חֵילַיְיהוּ, שְׁמַיָּא יַהֲבֵי חֵילַיְיהוּ, וּמַאן אִינּוּן. עוֹר דְּאִתְמְשָׁךְ עַל כֹּלָּא. כְּגַוְונָא דִלְהוֹן.

238. Oh, holy pious one. Rise and I will divulge to you a concealed matters. The composition of a man's spirit is this: HIS spirit is DRAWN from the Holy Spirit, WHICH IS MALCHUT. HIS Neshamah IS DRAWN from the Tree of Life. And since the Holy Spirit, WHICH IS MALCHUT, grants of its strength, its Chariots give of their power immediately. Their power is the bones and limbs; all are from the side of MALCHUT'S CHARIOTS, and construct each other, THAT IS, BONE OVER BONE AND LIMB OVER LIMB. The Other Side provides the flesh and from his side, only the flesh is provided and nothing else. His, THE OTHER SIDE'S, Chariots provide all the veins and arteries to carry the blood to the flesh. After these give their energy, the heavens, THAT ARE ZEIR ANPIN, provide their energies. What does this consist of? It is the skin that is spread over all of it, as they are, MEANING LIKE THE HEAVENS THAT SURROUND AND ENCOMPASS EVERYTHING.

239. לְבָתַר מִתְחַבְּרָן שְׁמַיָּא וְאַרְעָא כַּחֲדָא, וְיָהֲבֵי ד׳ יְסוֹדֵי אִלֵּין: אֶשָּׁא, וּמַיָּא וַאֲוִירָא, וְעַפְרָא. לְאַגָּנָא עַל אִלֵּין, וּלְחַפְיָא עַל כֹּלָּא. לְבָתַר, כָּל חַד נָטִיל חוּלָקֵיהּ דְּיָהַב, וְאִתְבַּטֵּל. רוּחָא דְקוּדְשָׁא, וּרְתִיכִין

דִּילֵיהּ, חוּלָקַיְיהוּ קַיְּימָא. רוּחָא דְּקוּדְשָׁא, רוּחָא דִּילֵיהּ קַיְּימָא
וְנִשְׁמָתָא סַלְקָא. רְתִיכִין דְּרוּחָא דְּקוּדְשָׁא, גַּרְמִין דִּלְהוֹן קַיְּימִין. וְע״ד
חָשִׁיבוּ דְּגוּפָא, גַּרְמִין הֲווֹ. וּבְג״כ כְּתִיב, וְעַצְמוֹתֶיךָ יַחֲלִיץ. וּבִשְׂרָא לָא
כְּתִיב בֵּיהּ הָכִי.

239. Following this, heavens and earth are joined together, THAT IS, ZEIR ANPIN AND MALCHUT, and provide these four foundations: fire, water, air and earth, to protect these and to cover everything. Then, WHEN IT DIES, each one takes back its part that it provided TO THAT BODY, and it becomes void. The part of the Holy Spirit and its Chariots THAT WAS PROVIDED TO THE PERSON endures. The Holy Spirit its spirit exists, and with the Neshamah they rise up. The Chariots of the Holy Spirit, their bones endure. Therefore, the importance of the body is the bones as it is written: "And make strong your bones" (Yeshayah 58:11), but flesh is not mentioned this way.

240. וְכָל זִמְנָא דְּבִשְׂרָא דְּסִטְרָא אַחֲרָא קַיְּימָא בְּקִיּוּמָא, הַהוּא שָׂטָן
קַיְּימָא לְאַסְטְנָא אִתְאֲבִיד בִּשְׂרָא, לֵית לֵיהּ רְשׁוּ לְאַסְטְנָא, דְּהָא לֵית
לֵיהּ עַל מַה דְּיִסְתְּמִיךְ. וְע״ד כְּתִיב, יִכֶל בְּשָׂרוֹ מֵרוֹאִי וְשֻׁפּוּ עַצְמוֹתָיו
לֹא רֻאוּ. מֵהַהוּא חֵיזוּ דְּשָׁטָן דְּקַיְּימָא לְאַסְטְנָא, דְּלָא יָכִיל, כֵּיוָן דְּיָכֵל
בִּשְׂרוֹ. וְשֻׁפּוּ עַצְמוֹתָיו לֹא רֻאוּ, לָא אִתְחֲזוּן לְקָרְבָא לְגַבֵּיהּ, דְּלֵית לֵיהּ
בְּהוֹן חוּלָקָא, כֵּיוָן דְּשָׁף כָּל חַד וְחַד מִדּוּכְתֵּיהּ, לָא תָּבַע עֲלַיְיהוּ, וְלָא
קָאִים לְאַסְטְנָא בְּגִינַיְיהוּ. לְבָתַר דְּבִשְׂרָא מִתְעַכְּלָא, הָא לָא יִתְבַּע
דִּינָא, וְלָא קָאִים לְאַסְטְנָא, דְּהָא לֵית לֵיהּ עַל מַה דְּיִסְתְּמִיךְ, וְלָא
אִדְכַּר לִב״נ בְּשׁוּם מִלָּה דְּעָלְמָא. א״ר שִׁמְעוֹן, הַשְׁתָּא יְדַעְנָא מִלִּין עַל
תִּקּוּנַיְיהוּ, וְדַאי יָאוּת הוּא לֵיהּ לְאַסְטְנָא.

240. As long as the flesh from the Other Side stays in existence, the Satan is standing there to thwart. Once the flesh is consumed, he loses his authority to thwart. Since he has no element of support, HE NO LONGER HAS A PART IN IT. About this, it is written: "His flesh is consumed away that it cannot be seen; and his bones that were not seen stick out" (Iyov 33:21). "THAT IT CANNOT BE SEEN" MEANS the Satan is ready to denounce, but cannot because "his flesh is consumed." "His bones that were not seen stick out" means that they are not seen by the Satan who would get close to him, since he has no part in him once each is detached, MEANING EVERY BONE from its place. He cannot prosecute them and be there to denounce them. After the flesh is consumed, no judgment can be obtained and he is not available to incriminate, since he has no support. And he does not mention that person in any way in the world. Rabbi Shimon said, Now I understand these things properly, MEANING WHAT IT IS WRITTEN, "AND THE ADVERSARY STANDING AT HIS RIGHT HAND TO THWART HIM." Certainly, he can incriminate him, AS LONG AS HE HAS NOT YET REMOVED HIS SOILED GARMENTS.

34. Women are light-minded

A Synopsis

Rabbi Shimon is told that his question about the lightness of women's minds is forbidden to ask. However, he can be told about the light cloud upon which Hashem rides, that is called Da'at of that bride, the fear of Hashem, and that is positioned in the center as the uppermost Da'at.

241. אָ"ל ר', חֲגוֹר זֵינָךְ, וְתַקִּין גַּרְמָךְ, אִי תִּבְעֵי לְמִנְדַּע מִלִּין דְּשָׁארִית. אוֹ אִי תִּשְׁאַל בְּהָנֵי מִלִּין, אֵימָא לִי. אָ"ל וַדַּאי, הָא יְדַעְנָא דְּבֵיתָאי שְׁכִיבַת, דְּלָא יְדַעְנָא מִנָּהּ כְּלוּם. וְחַבְרַיָּיא יַדְעִין. נָשִׁין מ"ט דַּעְתַּיְיהוּ קַלָּה.

241. He said to him, Rabbi, gird yourself with your weapon and prepare yourself. If you wish to understand the matters which you have started to study, or to ask anything about them, tell me. He said to him, Certainly, I know that my wife is dead, since I know nothing about her. But the friends do know ABOUT HER. What is the reason that women have a light mind (Heb. *da'at*)?

242. אָ"ל דַּעְתָּא אַתְיָא בְּשִׁית דַּרְגִּין, וְכָל חַד נָטִיל חוּלָקֵיהּ, מַה דְּאִשְׁתְּאַר, קַל אִיהוּ. אֲבָל יַקִּירָא דָּא, אִי לָאו דְּאֵשֶׁת כְּסִילוּת אִשְׁתַּתַּף בָּהּ. בְּמִלָּה דָּא לָא תִשְׁאַל, דְּהָא יְדַעְנָא דְּלָאו עַל דְּבֵיתָךְ שָׁאֶלְתָּ, אֶלָּא עַל מַה דִּכְתִיב, הִנֵּה יְיָ' רוֹכֵב עַל עָב קַל. וְהַהוּא עָב קַל אִקְרֵי דַעַת, מֵהַהִיא כַּלָּה יִרְאַת יְיָ', וְאִיהִי קַיְימָא בְּאֶמְצָעִיתָא כְּגַוְונָא דְּדַעַת עִלָּאָה, אֲבָל אִקְרֵי קַל. וְהָא יְדַעְנָא שְׁאֶלְתָּא דִּילָךְ מַאי הִיא.

242. He said to him, Da'at OF ZEIR ANPIN comes in six levels and each one takes its part. Whatever remains is light. But the precious one, were it not for the wife of foolishness that joined her... Do not inquire about this, SINCE IT IS FORBIDDEN TO ASK ABOUT THIS. I know, IN RELATION TO WHAT YOU SAID THAT YOUR WIFE IS DEAD, AND THAT YOU KNOW NOTHING WHATSOEVER ABOUT HER, that you did not ask about your wife. However, IT IS PERMITTED TO ASK about the verse: "Behold, Hashem rides upon a

swift cloud" (Yeshayah 19:1). That light cloud is called Da'at of that bride, the fear of Hashem, WHICH IS MALCHUT, and she is positioned in the center, like the uppermost Da'at. Yet she is considered light and I know what your question is.

35. Pillars and circles

A Synopsis

The spirit tells Rabbi Shimon about the inner hall of the court in the temple house and about its twelve entrances over each of which is marked the name of one of the twelve tribes. Each person must come in at the entrance of his own tribe. We hear about the living pillars and the song of praise that they sing, a new song. The spirit talks of Sarai and Abram and the renewal of their youth in their ability to have children. He tells Rabbi Shimon of great marvels to do with the pillars and the letters that move and roll, and he describes wonderful images of lions and apples and eagles and rings. At the end he says the eagles raise their voice and chant a lovely melody, then hide.

243. אֲבָל שָׁארִי וַחֲגוֹר זֵינָךְ, וְקָטִיר קִטְרָךְ, דְּהָא עִידָנָא הוּא לְגַלָּאָה, כְּמָה דְּשָׁארִית עוֹבָדָא. דְּעַל אַנְפֵּי רוֹחַב בֵּיתָא, אוּלָם הָעֲזָרָה לְגוֹ. בְּהַאי עֲזָרָה, אִית תְּרֵיסָר פִּתְחִין, לְפוּם חוּשְׁבָּן שִׁבְטַיָּא דְּיִשְׂרָאֵל. בְּפִתְחָא חֲדָא, כְּתִיב רְאוּבֵן. וּבְפִתְחָא אַחֲרָא, כְּתִיב שִׁמְעוֹן. וְכֵן כָּל שִׁבְטַיָּא דְּיִשְׂרָאֵל, רְשִׁימִין עַל אִינּוּן פִּתְחִין. בְּזִמְנָא דְּיִסַלְקוּן לְאִתְחֲזָאָה קַמֵּי מָארֵיהּ דְּעָלְמָא. מַאן דְּעָיֵיל בְּפִתְחָא דְּרָשִׁים בֵּיהּ רְאוּבֵן, אִי מִשִּׁבְטָא דִּרְאוּבֵן אִיהוּ, מְקַבְּלִין לֵיהּ פִּתְחִין, וְאִי לָא פַּלְטִין לֵיהּ לְבַר. וְכֵן בְּכֻלְּהוּ, דְּלָא יְקַבְּלוּן פִּתְחִין, אֶלָּא לְמַאן דְּאִיהוּ מֵהַהוּא שִׁבְטָא דְּרָשִׁים בְּהוֹן. וּבְדָא יִתְחַקְּקוּן וְיִשְׁתְּמוֹדְעָן כָּל חַד וְחַד.

243. However, start to gird your weapon and tie your knot, since it is time to divulge, as you started the matter. Upon the width of the temple house, there is the inner hall of the court. At that court are twelve entrances according to the number of the tribes of Yisrael. On one entrance, it is written Reuben. On the second entrance, it is written Shimon. Similarly, the rest of the tribes of Yisrael are marked on these entrances. During the period when they will come up to be seen in the presence of the Master of the world, whoever enters at the opening that is marked Reuben, the entrances accept him if he is from Reuben's tribe. If not, THE ENTRANCES expel him to the exterior. Similarly with all of them, the entrances do not accept anyone unless they are from the tribe that is marked on them. That way, each one is investigated and identified.

244 (1). תְּלַת מְאָה וְשִׁתִּין וְחָמֵשׁ עַמּוּדִין דִּנְהוֹרָא מְלַהֲטָא, אִית בְּכָל סְטְרָא, מֵאִינּוּן אַרְבַּע סְטְרִין. כָּל אִלֵּין עַמּוּדִין, אִקְרוּן עַמּוּדִים חַיִּים. בְּגִין דְּלָא קַיְּימָא נְהוֹרָא דִּלְהוֹן שָׁכִיךְ בְּאֲתָר חַד. וְכֻלְּהוּ, אִלֵּין סַלְקִין, וְאִלֵּין נַחְתִּין. יַהֲבֵי דוּכְתָּא דָּא לְדָא. אִלֵּין דְּסַלְּקִין בַּטְשִׁין דָּא בְּדָא, וּמְנַגְּנֵי נִגּוּנָא. וְאִלֵּין דְּנַחְתֵּי אוּף הָכִי.

244a. And 365 pillars of glowing light are on each side of the four sides IN THE COURT. All these pillars are called living pillars, since their light does not remain still in one position, since some of these PILLARS ascend and some descend, and make room for each other. Those ascending strike at each other and sing a tune and so also do those that descend.

244 (2). אִלֵּין דְּסַלְּקֵי דְּנַגְּנֵי, נִגּוּנָא, מַאי נִגּוּנָא מְנַגְּנֵי. שִׁיר יַתְמָא. מִזְמוֹר שִׁירוּ לַיְיָ' שִׁיר חָדָשׁ כִּי נִפְלָאוֹת עָשָׂה וְגוֹ'. שִׁיר חָדָשׁ, וְכִי אִית שִׁיר עַתִּיק. אֶלָּא שִׁיר, דְּעַד כְּעַן מַלְאָכִין קַדִּישִׁין לָא שַׁבְּחוּ לֵיהּ, בְּגִין דְּאִיהוּ חָדָשׁ. מַאי טַעֲמָא אִיהוּ חָדָשׁ. בְּגִין דְּהַהוּא דִּמְחַדֵּשׁ עוּלֵימוֹי, מְשַׁבַּח לֵיהּ, וְאָמַר לֵיהּ. וְהָכִי אָמַר רַב מְתִיבְתָּא, דָּא אִקְרֵי חָדָשׁ וְאִיהוּ חָדָשׁ. בְּגִין דְּדָבִיק בְּשִׁמְשָׁא, וְלָא אִתְפְּרַשׁ מִנֵּיהּ. לְאַפְּקָא סְטְרָא אַחֲרָא, דְּלֵית בֵּיהּ חִדּוּשָׁא, דִּכְתִיב בֵּיהּ וְאֵין כָּל חָדָשׁ. זָקֵן הוּא וְאִתְבְּלֵי, וְלָא אִתְחַדָּשׁ.

244b. Which tune do the ascending PILLARS sing? That is an anonymous tune, NO NAME IS MENTIONED AS TO WHO COMPOSED IT. "A psalm. O sing to Hashem a new song; for He has done marvelous things..." (Tehilim 98:1). HE INQUIRES: "A new song"? Is there such a thing as an old song? It is only that song through which, until the present, the angels have not praised Him yet, since it is new. What is the reason that it is new? It is because it is him that renews his youth, MEANING THE YOUTH METATRON, who praises Him and says it. So spoke the head of the Yeshivah. METATRON is considered new and he is new, BECAUSE HE REVITALIZES HIS YOUTH REGULARLY and it is because he is attached to the sun, THAT IS ZEIR ANPIN, and is not separated from it. This excludes the Other Side, which contains nothing new, as is written of it: "And there is nothing new" (Kohelet 1:9) since he is old and wilted and does not refresh.

245. תּוּ פָּתַח רַב מְתִיבְתָּא. שָׂרָה אִתְחַדְּשַׁת בְּעֶדּוּנָא, דַּרְגָּא דִּילָהּ
גָּרִים, דִּכְתִיב אַחֲרֵי בְלוֹתִי הָיְתָה לִי עֶדְנָה. מַאי עֶדְנָה, מְשִׁיכוּ דְּעֵדֶן
עִלָּאָה. וּבְגִין דְּאִתְמְשַׁךְ עָלָהּ מִסְטַר דְּנוּקְבָּא, כְּתִיב עֶדְנָה בְּהֵ"א וּבג"כ
כְּתִיב הָיְתָה, וְלֹא הָיָה.

245. Again, the head of the Yeshivah began. Sarah was rejuvenated with delight, as her level, THAT IS A FEMALE, brought it, as written: "After I am grown old shall I have pleasure (Heb. *ednah*) (lit. 'pleasure was to me')" (Beresheet 18:12). What is "*ednah*"? That is the continuation of the supernal Eden, WHICH IS CHOCHMAH. Since it was drawn upon her from the feminine aspect, it is written with Hei. Therefore, it is written "was," using a feminine and not a masculine suffix.

246. וַאדֹנִי זָקֵן. וְכִי אע"ג דְּאִיהוּ זָקֵן, לָא אִתְחֲזֵי לְאוֹלָדָא. אֶלָּא לָאו
מִלְתָא זְעֵירְתָא אָמְרָה לְגַבֵּיהּ, דִּבְגִין הַהוּא זָקֵן, לָא אִתְחַדָּשׁ וְלָא
עָבֵיד תּוֹלְדִין, דְּאִלְמָלֵא הֲוָה עָבֵיד תּוֹלְדִין הֲוָה מְטַשְׁטְשָׁא עָלְמָא. וְעַל
דָּא אַהֲדַר מִלִּין קוּדְשָׁא בְּרִיךְ הוּא, לָמָה זֶה צָחֲקָה שָׂרָה וְגו'. וְאִי
תֵּימָא וְהָא כְּתִיב וְאַבְרָהָם זָקֵן בָּא בַּיָּמִים. אֶלָּא בָּא בַּיָּמִים, בְּאִינוּן
יוֹמִין עִלָּאִין, דִּמְחַדְּשֵׁי עוֹלְמִין כְּנִשְׁרָא. וע"ד נִגוּנָא דָא נִגּוּנָא דְּהַהוּא
חָדָשׁ אִיהוּ. הוֹשִׁיעָה לּוֹ, לְמַאן. לְהַהוּא חָדָשׁ, הוֹשִׁיעָה יְמִינָא דְּמַלְכָּא
עִלָּאָה, וּדְרוֹעָא דִּילֵיהּ.

246. "My lord being old also" (Ibid.). HE ASKS: Because he is aged, is he not able to have children? WE FIND THAT OLD PEOPLE CAN ALSO HAVE CHILDREN. HE REPLIES: However, she said something significant IN SAYING, it is due to that old one, WHICH IS THE OTHER SIDE, THAT HAS NO REJUVENATION OR FECUNDITY AS MENTIONED. ABRAHAM is not rejuvenated and producing children, because if THE OTHER SIDE would have produced offspring, he would have made the world blurred. About this, the Holy One, blessed be He, replied, "Why did Sarah laugh..." (Ibid. 13). THAT IS TO SAY, SAYING THAT OLD ONE OF THE OTHER SIDE IS DOMINANT IN ABRAHAM. HE ASKS: You may wonder that it is written: "And Abraham was old, advanced in age (lit. 'coming with days')" (Beresheet 24:1), SO WE SEE THAT EVEN THE SCRIPTURE CONSIDERS ABRAHAM OLD. HE REPLIES: It is only because THE VERSE READS "coming with days," meaning that he is coming with days, the high days above OF ZEIR ANPIN, that renew their youthfulness like an eagle. Therefore, DUE TO THOSE HIGHER DAYS, this melody OF: "A PSALM. O SING TO HASHEM A NEW SONG" is the tune of that new one, METATRON, WHO IS ATTACHED TO THE HIGHER DAYS OF ZEIR ANPIN. "Have gained Him the victory" (Tehilim 98:1): Have gained whom the victory? That is, gain victory to the new one, WHO CONTAINS the right of the King up high, WHICH IS ZEIR ANPIN, and His arm, MEANING, ALSO THE LEFT. THEREFORE, IT IS WRITTEN: "HIS RIGHT HAND, AND HIS HOLY ARM" (IBID.).

247. אִינּוּן דְּנַחְתֵּי, אוֹף הָכִי מְנַגְּנֵי, וְאָמְרֵי שִׁירָה אַחֲרָא יַתְמָא. וּמַאן אִיהוּ. מִזְמוֹר לְתוֹדָה, דְּאִיהוּ יַתְמָא, אוֹף הָכִי.

247. UNTIL HERE, HE EXPLAINED THE SONG OF THE PILLARS THAT ARE ASCENDING UPWARDS. AND NOW HE EXPLAINS, Those PILLARS that descend FROM ABOVE DOWNWARDS also sing the music and chant another authorless song, MEANING THAT NO NAME IS ASCRIBED TO ITS COMPOSER. What is it? That is "a psalm of thanksgiving" (Tehilim 100:1), which is also authorless.

248. נְהוֹרָא דִּלְהוֹן חַד אִתְחֲזֵי. וְכַד מִתְגַּלְגְּלֵי, אִתְחֲזָן חָמֵשׁ גַּוְונִין דִּנְהוֹרִין. בְּכָל עַמּוּדָא וְעַמּוּדָא. עַמּוּדִין אִלֵּין כֻּלְּהוּ חֲלָלִין מִלְּגָאו. וְכַד סַלְקֵי וְנַחְתֵּי, נַפְקֵי מִנַּיְיהוּ שַׁלְהוֹבִין דְּנוּרָא, כְּגַוְונֵי חֵיזוּר וְשׁוּשַׁן. לְעֵילָא מִכָּל עַמּוּדָא וְעַמּוּדָא, אִית תְּלַת תַּפּוּחִין, דְּבַטְּשֵׁי בְּהוּ תְּלַת גַּוְונִין, סוּמָק יָרוֹק וְחִוּוּר. בְּכָל גָּוֶון וְגָוֶון מְלַהֲטָן אַתְוָון בִּלְטֵי, מִשַּׁלְהוֹבָא יְרוֹקָא דְּאֶשָּׁא, וְלָא מִשְׁתַּכְּחֵי לְעָלְמִין. וְלֵית מַאן דִּיְקוּם עֲלַיְיהוּ.

248. The light OF THE PILLARS appears as one light and when they roll around, five phases of light appear in each pillar. These pillars are all hollowed from the inside and, when they go up and down, flames of fire are spurting out similar to pomegranates and blossoms. Above each individual pillar are situated three apples, to which three colors are attracted – red, green and white. In each individual color glow prominently letters of green

flames of fire, which never rest. There is no one that will understand AND HAVE ANY CONCEPTION OF THEM.

249. אַרְבַּע גַּלְגַּלִּין מִתְחַמָּן עוֹבַד צִיּוּר, בְּכָל עַמּוּדָא וְעַמּוּדָא. בְּאִינּוּן גַּלְגַּלִין, אִית פְּלִיאָן רַבְרְבָן. כַּד מִסְתַּחֲרָן מַפְּקִין מִנַּיְיהוּ זַגִּין דְּדַהֲבָא וְאַבְנֵי יְקָר. וּמִיַּד מִתְכַּנְּשֵׁי בְּגַוַוייהוּ, וְלָא נָפְלֵי לְאַרְעָא. כַּד נָפְקִין אִינּוּן זַגִּין דְּדַהֲבָא, וְאִינּוּן אַבְנֵי יְקָר גּוֹ אִסְתַּחֲרוּתָא דְּגַלְגַּלִין, אִשְׁתְּמַע קָלָא דְּאָמְרֵי, זֹאת נַחֲלַת עַבְדֵי יְיָ׳ וְצִדְקָתָם מֵאִתִּי נְאֻם יְיָ׳.

249. Four embroidered circles expand and encircle each and every pillar OF THE 365 PILLARS MENTIONED ABOVE THAT ARE ON EACH SIDE OF THE COURT. In these circles, there are great marvels. When they turn, they exude tongues of gold and precious stones, which are instantly gathered back into them. They do not fall to the ground. During the period when these tongues of gold and precious stones are emerging, a sound is heard from within the turning of the circles that says, "'This is the heritage of the servants of Hashem and the recompense of their righteousness appointed by Me,' says Hashem" (Yeshayah 54:17).

250. תְּרֵין אַרְיָין בְּכָל גַּלְגַּלָא וְגַלְגַּלָא, אַרְיָא חֲדָא מִסְּטְרָא חֲדָא, וְאַרְיָא חֲדָא מִסְּטְרָא חֲדָא, וְכֻלְּהוּ מֵאֶשָּׁא יְרוֹקָא, וּבְגִלְגּוּלָא דְּקָא מִסְתַּחֲרָן גַּלְגַּלִין, מִתְחַבְּקָן אִלֵּין בְּאִלֵּין. וְאַזְלֵי כֻּלְּהוּ, בְּגִלְגּוּלָא מִתְדַּבְּקָן דָּא בְּדָא. כַּד סַלְּקִין עַמּוּדִין, מְנַהֲמָן אַרְיָין אִלֵּין בְּאִלֵּין, וְתַפּוּחִין פַּרְחִין בַּאֲוִירָא, וְסַלְּקִין לְעֵילָא, וּבַטְשֵׁי אִלֵּין בְּאִלֵּין בַּאֲוִירָא. וְתָבוּ לְאַתְרַיְיהוּ, וּמִתַּמָּן נָפְלֵי. וְאַרְיָין פַּשְׁטֵי יְדַיְיהוּ לְנַטְלָא לוֹן, וְסַלְּקִין אִלֵּין מִגַּרְמַיְיהוּ. אִי חֲסִידָא קַדִּישָׁא, מַאן חָמָא חָכְמְתָא דְּאוּמָנוּ, דְּצַיֵּיר קוּדְשָׁא בְּרִיךְ הוּא בְּעַמּוּדִין אִלֵּין.

250. There are two lions in each individual circle, one lion from one side and one lion from the other side. All are of green fire. THE LIONS embrace each other in the orbit in which the circles turn, and all go in a circle attached one to the other. When the pillars rise, the lions roar at each other and apples fly in the air ascending and knock each other in the air. Then they return to their spot and from there they drop. The lions extend their

paws to receive them AND THE APPLES rise on their own. Oh, holy pious one, who saw the wisdom of this craftsmanship that the Holy One, blessed be He, fashioned in those pillars!

251. בְּפַלְגּוּ יוֹמָא נָפְקֵי תְּרֵין נִשְׁרִין בְּכָל גַּלְגַּלָּא וְגַלְגַּלָּא, וְלָא יְדִיעַ אֲתָר דְּנָפְקֵי מִתַּמָּן, וְשַׁרְיָין עַל רֵישֵׁיהוֹן דְּאִלֵּין אַרְיָין. וּכְדֵין מִשְׁתַּכְּכֵי עַמּוּדִין וְגַלְגְּלִין, וְקַיְימֵי בְּקִיּוּמַיְיהוּ. וְתַפּוּחִין נָפְלֵי עַל פּוּמַיְיהוּ דְּנִשְׁרֵי, וּמְקַבְּלֵי לוֹן. וּמִיַּד פָּרְחִין מִפּוּמָא לְפוּמָא, וְאַזְלִין וּמְשַׁטְטֵי בֵּינַיְיהוּ, וְתָבוּ לְאַתְרַיְיהוּ, וְלָא יְדִיעַ מַאן הִיא. לְבָתַר שַׁעֲתָא וּפַלְגָּא, נִשְׁרִין אֲרִימִין קַלָא, וּמְנַגְּנִין נִגּוּנָא תָּאִיבָא, וְאִתְטַמְּרָן, וְלָא יְדִיעַ בְּהֵי אֲתָר.

251. At midday, two eagles leave in each individual ring. They rest on the heads of the lions. At that point, the pillars and the rings become still and stay in their position. Apples fall onto the eagles' mouths and they accept them, and instantly, THE APPLES fly from mouth to mouth. About an hour and a half later, the eagles raise their voice and chant a lovely melody, then hide.

36. "Half of them towards the eastern sea..."

A Synopsis

We hear that the teacher of Yeshivah explained the verse, "And on that day, living water shall go out from Jerusalem; half of them towards the eastern sea, and half toward the western sea," and then that a child's voice was heard questioning his explanation. The child was brought into the Yeshivah and expounded upon the verse, and then said 27 explanations in the Torah. We learn that the child had died because he openly embarrassed his teacher in front of everyone with argumentative questions. Lastly he speaks about two cherubim in the center of the court, underneath which all the children of Yisrael are destined to stand and receive their illumination.

252. סַחֲרָנַיְיהוּ דְּאִינּוּן עַמּוּדִין, אִית שְׁבָכִין עוֹבָד צִיּוּר. אֶשָּׁא סוּמָקָא, וּנְהוֹרָא חִוְּורָא, וְחוּטִין דְּדַהֲבָא, סְחוֹר סְחוֹר, סָחֲרִין לְכָל סְטָר. וּמַעְיָינָא דְּמַיָּא כד"א וְהָיָה בַּיּוֹם הַהוּא יָצְאוּ מַיִם חַיִּים מִירוּשָׁלַיִם חֶצְיָם אֶל הַיָּם הַקַּדְמוֹנִי וְחֶצְיָם אֶל הַיָּם הָאַחֲרוֹן.

252. Around the pillars, there exist network carpets of embroidery. IT IS KNITTED from red fire, WHICH IS THE ILLUMINATION OF THE LEFT, and from white fire, WHICH IS THE ILLUMINATION OF THE RIGHT, and gold strands, WHICH IS THE LEFT ILLUMINATION IN BINAH CALLED GOLD. It is encircled from all directions by a spring of water, as it says, "And on that day, living water shall go out from Jerusalem; half of them towards the eastern (also: 'primordial') sea, and half toward the western (last) sea" (Zecharyah 14:8).

253. הָכָא פָּרִישׁ רַב מְתִיבְתָּא קְרָא דָּא לְגוֹ, וְקַלֵּיהּ אִשְׁתְּמַע לְבַר. מִדַּהֲוָה פָּרִישׁ קְרָא דָּא. קָל יְנוֹקָא אִתְּעַר מִלְּבַר, הַהוּא יְנוֹקָא דַּהֲוָה פָּרִישׁ תַּלְמוּדֵיהּ, וְגָמִיר קַמֵּי חַד עַמּוּדָא דְּעָלְמָא, בְּרֵיהּ דְּרַבִּי יְהוּדָה, דְּרַבִּית אַנְתְּ. וַהֲווֹ אַחְדֵּי בֵּיהּ לְדִינָא, וְקַלֵּיהּ אִתְּעַר מִלְּבַר, בְּהַאי קְרָא, וְאָמַר, מַיָּא דְּאִינּוּן מִלְּרַע הֵיךְ סַלְּקִין לְעֵילָּא מִנֵּיהּ, לַאֲתָר עִלָּאָה יַתִּיר מִנֵּיהּ, בְּכַמָּה דַּרְגִּין, וּמַה אִצְטְרִיךְ לוֹן לְאִינּוּן מַיִין לְעֵילָּא. וּמָה אֲתָר דְּכָל מַבּוּעִין וּנְחָלִין נָפְקִין מִנֵּיהּ, וְלֵית פְּסִיקוּ לְמַבּוּעֵי וְנַחֲלֵי, אִתְשַׁקְיָא

-159-

מֵאֲתַר נָגִיב, מַאן חָמָא חֲפִירָא דְּבֵירָא, יָהִיב מַיִּין לְמַבּוּעָא דְּנָבִיעַ. וְכִי יְרוּשָׁלַם, יָהִיב מַיִּין אֶל הַיָּם הַקַּדְמוֹנִי, אֲתַר דְּכָל מֵימִין דְּעָלְמָא נָפְקֵי מִתַּמָּן, וְנַבְעִין מִנֵּיהּ. אִי חֲסִידָא קַדִּישָׁא, לְקָלָא דָּא אִשְׁתְּכָכוּ, וְצַיְּיתוּ כָּל קָלִין דִּבְנֵי מְתִיבְתֵּי דְּתַמָּן, וּבְג״כ לָא יָכִילוּ מָארֵי דְּדִינָא לְמִקְרַב גַּבֵּיהּ.

253. The head of the Yeshivah explained this verse inside and his voice was heard on the outside. When he finished explaining this verse, a child's voice was raised outside. THAT WAS the child that left his teaching and learned in the presence of a pillar of the world, the son of Rabbi Yehuda from Ravit Ant, WHICH IS A NAME OF A PLACE. He was being held BY PROSECUTING ANGELS to be judged and his voice was raised on the outside. WHEN HE HEARD of this verse FROM THE MOUTH OF THE HEAD OF THE YESHIVAH, he said, How could waters that are below IN JERUSALEM rise to a place that is higher from it by several steps, MEANING TO THE PRIMORDIAL SEA, WHICH IS BINAH? FURTHERMORE, what need is there for those waters above, IN BINAH? AND FURTHERMORE, how could a place that all the water springs and rivers leave from, and where there is no discontinuation to THOSE springs and rivers THAT EXIT FROM THERE WHICH IS THE PRIMORDIAL SEA, THAT IS BINAH, be irrigated from a dry place, WHICH IS JERUSALEM? Whoever saw a hole that has been dug giving water to a flowing water spring? Could Jerusalem give water to the primordial sea, which is a location from where all the waters come and flow? Oh, holy pious one, HE SAID TO RABBI SHIMON, to this voice everyone who was there from the members of the Yeshivah became quiet and listened. Therefore, the prosecutors could not approach him TO JUDGE HIM.

254. בָּכָה ר׳ שִׁמְעוֹן, אָ״ל לָא תִּבְכֵּי בּוּצִינָא קַדִּישָׁא, זַכָּאָה חוּלָקָךְ, דַּאֲפִילוּ יְנוּקֵי, מִנָּךְ אַמְרֵי רָזִין סְתִימִין דְּאוֹרַיְיתָא. תָּא, וְאֵימָא לָךְ, מַה דְּעַבְדוּ בְּנֵי מְתִיבְתֵּי עַל קָלֵיהּ דְּהַהוּא יְנוּקָא, כַּד עָאל קָלֵיהּ דְּהַהוּא יְנוּקָא, כְּגִירָא לְגוֹ, וְכֻלְּהוּ צַיְּיתֵי לֵיהּ. בְּהַהִיא שַׁעְתָּא אִזְדַּעְזַע רַב מְתִיבְתָּא, וְכָל אִינּוּן דַּהֲווֹ קַמֵּיהּ, וְאָמַר, מַאן אִינּוּן דְּלָא שַׁבְקִין לְהַהוּא בְּרָא דֶּאֱלָהָא חַיָּיא, לְמֵיעַל. קָמוּ וְאָחִידוּ בֵּיהּ תְּלָת עַמּוּדִין דְּקַיְימֵי קַמֵּי רַב מְתִיבְתָּא, וְעָאל. וְכָל בְּנֵי מְתִיבְתֵּי אִתְכְּנָשׁוּ לְגַבֵּיהּ,

אָמַר רַב מְתִיבְתָּא, אֵימָא קְרָאִיךְ בְּרָא קַדִּישָׁא.

254. Rabbi Shimon cried. He said to him, Do not cry, Holy Luminary. Praised is your lot that even children quote of you, THAT IS BECAUSE OF YOUR MERIT, in concealed secrets in the Torah. Come and I will tell you what the Yeshivah members did for the sake of that child's voice. When the voice of the child entered inside piercing like an arrow, everyone paid attention. At that time, the head of the Yeshivah was startled, as were all those that were in his presence, so he said, Who are those that do not allow this one, a son of a living Elohim, to enter? Three pillars, WHICH ARE THE SECRET OF ILLUMINATION IN THE THREE COLUMNS, that were standing in front of the head of the Yeshivah rose and held on to him, and he entered. All the members of the Yeshivah gathered around him. The head of the Yeshivah said, Speak your verse, holy son.

255. אָמַר, עַד כְּעַן דָּחִילְנָא, דְּהָא אֲנָא מִמְּתִיבְתָּא אַחֲרִינָא הֲוֵינָא, וְהָכִי אָמְרוּ לִי , כַּד מָארֵי דְּדִינָא הֲווֹ אֲחִדִין בֵּיהּ, א"ל, לָא תִּדְחַל בְּרָא קַדִּישָׁא, הָכָא תְּהֵא בֵּינָנָא שַׁבְעָה יוֹמִין, וְתִתְסְחֵי בְּכָל יוֹמָא מִטַּלָא קַדִּישָׁא. וּלְבָתַר יְסַלְּקוּן לָךְ. לְגוֹ הַהוּא מְתִיבְתָּא בִּשְׁאָר יְנוּקָא דְּהָכָא.

255. THAT CHILD said, Until now I was afraid, since I was from a different Yeshivah. That is what they told me when those prosecutors held on to me. He said to him, Do not fear, holy son. Here you will stay with us seven days and you will wash yourself with the holy dew every day. Then, they will take you up to that Yeshivah of the rest of the children here.

256. פָּתַח הַהוּא יְנוּקָא וְאָמַר, וְהָיָה בַּיּוֹם הַהוּא. הַהוּא, לָא יְדִיעַ מַאן הוּא. אֶלָּא בְּכָל אֲתָר בַּיּוֹם הַהוּא, יוֹמָא בַּתְרָאָה הוּא, אֲמַאי אִקְרֵי יוֹם הַהוּא. אֶלָּא דָּא הוּא יוֹמָא דְּאָחִיד סוֹפָא בְּשֵׁירוּתָא. שֵׁירוּתָא אִקְרֵי הוּא, כד"א וְעָבֵד הַלֵּוִי הוּא פֻּלְחָנָא דְּלֵוִי, לְדַרְגָּא דְּאִקְרֵי הוּא, טָמִיר וְגָנִיז. וְאִקְרֵי הַהוּא, לְאַחֲזָאָה סוֹפָא דְּכָל דַּרְגִּין, דְּאִיהוּ שֵׁירוּתָא, וְכֹלָּא חַד. וּבְגִין דְּאִיהוּ סוֹפָא, אִתּוֹסַף בֵּיהּ ה'.

256. That child opened the discussion saying, "And it shall come to pass, on

that day" (Zecharyah 14:9). HE ASKS: "That": It is not known which it is.
HE REPLIES: But wherever "that day" is mentioned, it is the last of days.
Why is it called "that (Heb. *hahu*) day"? It is only because it is a day in
which the end is connected to the beginning, WHICH IS BINAH. Its
beginning is referred to as "he (Heb. *hu*)," as it says: "But the Levites shall
do the service (lit. 'serve him')" (Bemidbar 18:23), since the performance of
the Levite is for the level that is called "he" that is concealed and hidden.
BECAUSE IT IS HIDDEN, IT IS THEREFORE CALLED "HE" IN THE THIRD
PERSON. When it is read '*Hahu*' WITH THE DEFINITE ARTICLE HEI,
WHICH IS MALCHUT, it comes to indicate that the end of all the levels,
THAT IS MALCHUT, is the beginning OF THE STEPS, WHICH IS BINAH,
since all is one. Since THE WORD *HAHU* is the end, MEANING MALCHUT,
Hei was added to it, MEANING THE HEI THAT IS MALCHUT WAS ADDED TO
THE WORD *HU*, WHICH IS BINAH, WHICH IS ENVELOPED WITHIN MALCHUT
WITH THE RESULT THAT THE WORD '*HAHU*' IS MALCHUT, BUT ONLY WHEN
BINAH IS ENVELOPED WITHIN HER.

257. זְמִינָא יְרוּשָׁלַם לְאַפָּקָא מַיִין, וּלְנַבְעָא נְבִיעוּ, הָכָא אִית לוֹמַר,
סוֹפָא דְּכָל דַּרְגִּין, לָאו אִיהוּ יְרוּשָׁלַם, אֶלָּא וַדַּאי יְרוּשָׁלַם וְיוֹמָא הַהוּא
כֹּלָּא חַד. מַה בֵּין הַאי לְהַאי. אֶלָּא יְרוּשָׁלַם, כָּל דַּרְגִּין קַדִּישִׁין דִּילָהּ,
כַּד אִסְתַּחֲרָן, אִקְרוֹן יְרוּשָׁלַם. וְהָכִי אִתְחֲמָאן. וְאִית דַּרְגִּין דְּסַחֲרָן,
וְאִקְרוֹן עֲזָרוֹת, אִלֵּין פְּנִימָאִין, וְאִלֵּין לְבַר. וְאִית דַּרְגִּין דְּאִקְרוֹן כַּד
אִסְתַּחֲרָן, לְשָׁכוֹת. וְאִית דַּרְגִּין דְּאִקְרוֹן כַּד אִסְתַּחֲרָן. הֵיכָל וּדְבִיר. לְגוֹ
מִכָּל אִינוּן דַּרְגִּין, אִית חַד נְקוּדָה, כְּבוּדָה בַּת מֶלֶךְ פְּנִימָה. נְקוּדָה דָּא,
אִקְרֵי יוֹם הַהוּא, וְסִימָנִיךְ הַהוּא יִקְרֵא אֶרֶץ.

257. Jerusalem is destined to produce water and to become a flowing spring.
Here it would be possible to say that the end of all steps, REFERRED TO BY
HAHU, is not Jerusalem. However, Jerusalem and "that day" are most
certainly all one, SINCE BOTH ARE MALCHUT. What is the difference
between them? It is only that when Jerusalem is surrounded by all her holy
steps it is called Jerusalem. That is the way they appear. There are steps that
surround, called the Temple courts. These are inner and some SURROUND IT
from outside. There are steps FURTHER WITHIN, which when they surround,
are called chambers. There are steps which when they surround, are called
the temple and the sanctuary. At the innermost of all these steps, there is one

point: "The king's daughter is all glorious within" (Tehilim 45:14). That point is called "that day." This is derived from "which (Heb. *hahu*) was called the land" (Devarim 3:13). THAT IS, MALCHUT IS CALLED LAND, BUT JUST HER HIDDEN POINT.

258. וְכַד יְקוּם יוֹמָא דָא, מִגּוֹ שְׁבָכִין דַּעֲזָרָה יְקוּם נְבִיעוֹ דְמַיָּא, וְהַהוּא נְבִיעוּ מִן הַיָּם הַקַּדְמוֹנִי לֶהֱוֵי. כְּגַוְונָא דְּאִמָּא, דִּבְרָהּ בֵּין דְּרוֹעָהָא, וּמִסְגִּיאוּ חֲלָבָא דְיָנִיק, אִתְמְלֵי פוּמֵיהּ, וְאִתְרַבֵּי בֵּיהּ, אָרִיק חֲלָבָא לְפוּמָא דְאִמֵּיהּ. כָּךְ חֶצְיָם אֶל הַיָּם הַקַּדְמוֹנִי.

258. When "that day" will be established, AT THE END OF CORRECTION, from the networks in the court, WHICH ARE THE SECRETS OF THE ILLUMINATION OF BINAH THAT IS ENVELOPED IN MALCHUT, a spring of water will rise. That spring will come from the primordial sea THAT IS BINAH, FROM WHICH IT CONTINUES TO MALCHUT, AND IS LIKE a mother that has her son between her arms. Due to the great amount of milk that he suckles, his mouth is filled up and overflowing, UNTIL he returns the milk to his mother's mouth. That is meant by "half of them towards the primordial sea" (Zecharyah 14:8)

259. נַטְלֵיהּ רַב מְתִיבְתָּא, וּנְשָׁקֵיהּ. אָמַר חַיֶּיךָ, הָכִי אוּקְמוּהָ בִּמְתִיבְתָּא דִּרְקִיעָא, וְהָכִי הוּא וַדַּאי. יָם הָאַחֲרוֹן: דַּרְגִּין בַּתְרָאִין דִּילָהּ. אִי חֲסִידָא קַדִּישָׁא, כַּמָּה חֶדְוָה עַל חֶדְוָה, אִתּוֹסַף בְּהַהוּא יְנוּקָא, גּוֹ בְּנֵי מְתִיבְתֵּי. כ"ז טַעֲמֵי דְאוֹרַיְיתָא, אָמַר הַהוּא יְנוּקָא. וְשַׁבְעִין כִּתְרִין אִתְעַטְּרוּהּ לַאֲבוּהּ בְּהַהוּא יוֹמָא. זַכָּאָה חוּלָקֵיהּ, מַאן דְּזָכֵי לְמֵילַף לִבְרֵיהּ. אָמַר רִבִּי שִׁמְעוֹן, לָא זָכָה אֲבוּהּ לְמֵילַף לֵיהּ. אָמַר, אֲבוּהּ שָׁבַק.

259. The head of the Yeshivah took him and kissed him. He said to him, On your life! That is the way they explained it in the heavenly Yeshivah. And that certainly is so. "The last sea" MEANS her last steps. Oh, holy pious one, SAID THE SOUL TO RABBI SHIMON, how much gladness upon happiness was added by that child between the members of the Yeshivah. The child said 27 explanations in the Torah, and seventy crowns were adorned to his father on that day. Praised is the lot of whoever deserved to teach his son. Rabbi Shimon inquired, Did not his father deserve to teach him? He replied that his father died.

260. וְרָזָא סְתִימָא הֲוָה בְּהַאי יְנוּקָא, עַל מַה דְּאִסְתַּלָּק מֵעָלְמָא, וְעַל דְּבָעוּ לְמֵידָן דִּינֵיהּ, וְאִשְׁתְּזִיב מִנֵּיהּ, דָּא הֲוָה בְּאִתְגַּלְּיָיא, דַּהֲוָה מַכְסִיף לְרַבֵּיהּ קַמֵּי כֹּלָּא, בִּשְׁאֶלְתִּין וְקוּשְׁיָין דִּילֵיהּ, וְלָא חָיִישׁ לְמֵהַךְ לְאַחֲרָא, לְאַתְקְנָא תַּלְמוּדוֹי, וְחָלִישׁ דַּעְתָּא דְּרַבֵּיהּ. וְעַ"ד בָּעוּ לְמֵידַן לֵיהּ בְּדִינָא תַּקִּיפָא. וּבְג"כ, אַף עַל גַּב דְּאִשְׁתְּזִיב מִמָּארֵיהוֹן דְּדִינָא, לָא אִשְׁתְּזִיב הָכָא. שִׁבְעָה יוֹמִין הֲוֵי דְּלָא אִשְׁתְּלִים דִּיוּקְנֵיהּ. וְכַד הֲוָה אֵסְתַּחֵי, בִּכְאֵבָא יַתִּירָא קַמֵּי כֹּלָּא כָּל אִינּוּן שִׁבְעָה יוֹמִין עַד דְּאִשְׁתְּלִים דִּיוּקְנֵיהּ. וְעַל דְּאִסְתַּלָּק מֵעָלְמָא לָא תִּבְעֵי לְמִנְדַּע. אִי רִבִּי, אִי רִבִּי, זַכָּאָה חוּלָקָךְ.

260. A hidden secret was with that child, why he departed from the world and why they wished to have him judged, and he was saved from it. That is because he openly embarrassed his teacher in front of everybody with the argumentative questions and difficulties that he posed to him, FOR HE WAS UNABLE TO SETTLE THEM IN RESPONSE. He was not afraid to go to another TEACHER to improve his studies and thereby his teacher was disconcerted. Consequently, they wished to judge him harshly. Therefore, even though he was saved from the court officials, he was not saved here, as seven days passed by before his image was perfected. When he washed, it was with great pain in front of everyone all these seven days, until his image was completed. Do not ask why he departed from the world. Oh, Rabbi, oh Rabbi. Praised is your lot.

261. ת"ח, תְּחוֹת עֲגוּלָא דְּאִינּוּן שְׁבָכִין, דְּתַמָּן בְּאִינּוּן מַיִין דְּהַהוּא נְבִיעוּ דְּמַעְיָינָא, אִתְרְשִׁים נְבִיעוּ חַד, וְאִתְפָּשַּׁט וְנָפִיק לְבַר, וְעָאל גּוֹ יַמָּא רַבָּא. וְרָשִׁים בֵּיהּ אָרְחָא בְּלִבָּא דְּיַמָּא, וּמִנֵּיהּ שָׁתֵי לִוְיָתָן, וְרַוֵּי, וְחַדֵי, וְאִתְרַבֵּי בְּרַבְוַויָיא. וְכַד נָפִיק נְבִיעוּ אַחֲרָא, הַהוּא נְבִיעוּ אִתְפָּשַּׁט וְאָזִיל בִּטְמִירוּ, תְּחוֹת תְּהוֹמָא, לְגוֹ יַמָּא בַּתְרָאָה. וְכָל אִינּוּן מַיִם זְדוֹנִים, וּמַיִין תַּקִּיפִין, מָאִיךְ לוֹן, וְכָפִיף לוֹן, דְּלָא יִפְּקוּן לְחַבְּלָא בְּנֵי

עָלְמָא. וְסִימָן הַנּוֹתֵן בַּיָּם דָּרֶךְ וּבַמַּיִם עַזִּים נְתִיבָה.

261. HE NOW RETURNS TO EXPLAIN IN ANOTHER MANNER AND IN OTHER WORDS, THE WORDS IN THE VERSE: "HALF OF THEM TOWARDS THE PRIMORDIAL SEA." Come and see, Under the ring of those networks that exist there. In these waters of the flowing spring THAT EXIST THERE, there is one distinct spring that expands and flows out and enters the great sea. It delineates in it a path to the heart of the sea. From it, the Leviathan drinks until he is happily satiated, and grows and enlarges greatly. THAT IS THE SECRET OF "HALF OF THEM TOWARDS THE PRIMORDIAL SEA," MEANING TO THE HEART OF THE SEA. When another spring flows out, that spring continues to expand secretly under the depths, into the last sea, THAT IS MALCHUT THAT IS HIDDEN. All these harsh and maligning waters it pushes and forces down, so they would not be able to harm the inhabitants of the world. This is derived from the verse: "Who makes a way in the sea, and a path in the mighty waters" (Yeshayah 43:16), NAMELY IN THE LAST SEA.

262. וּבְאֶמְצָעִיתָא דְּהַהִיא עֲזָרָה, אִית תְּרֵין כְּרוּבִים, עוֹבָדָא דְּאוּמָנָא דְּמַלְכָּא קַדִּישָׁא. וְלָא יַכְלִין לְקַיְּימָא בְּהוּ, עִלָּאִין וְתַתָּאִין. וּתְחוֹתַיְיהוּ זְמְנִין כָּל יִשְׂרָאֵל לְקַיְּימָא, דְּלָא יִפְּקוּן מִתְּחוֹת גַּדְפַיְיהוּ לְבַר, זַכָּאִין לֶיהֱווֹן, כָּל דְּעָאלִין תְּחוֹת גַּדְפַיְיהוּ. תְּלֵיסַר אַלְפֵי מִגְדָּלִין דְּשִׁמְשָׁא, דְּנָהִיר בְּצִצוּעָא, כְּדְקָא יָאוּת. רַב מְתִיבְתָּא בְּג״כ זָכָה לְהַהוּא יְקָר.

262. In the center of that court exist two Cherubs, a product of craftsmanship by the Holy King. The higher and lower beings are unable to stand on top of them. SINCE THEIR FIRST THREE SFIROT ARE COVERED WITH WINGS. But underneath them, THAT IS, IN THE ASPECT OF SIX EXTREMITIES OF THE FIRST THREE, all Yisrael are destined to stand, MEANING TO RECEIVE THEIR ILLUMINATION, PROVIDED that they will not leave to go out from under their wings, MEANING THAT THEY WON'T PEEK AT THE FIRST THREE SFIROT THAT ARE COVERED BY THE WINGS. All those that enter under the wings OF THE CHERUBS will be happy, since thirteen thousand towers of the sun, WHICH IS ZEIR ANPIN, MEANING TWELVE PERMUTATIONS OF YUD HEI VAV HEI AND THAT WHICH CONTAINS THEM, THAT IS THE SECRET OF CHOCHMAH AND BINAH, TIFERET AND MALCHUT, WHICH IS IN EACH OF THE THREE COLUMNS, illuminate upon the figures as required, MEANING THE CHERUBS. The head of the Yeshivah gained through this, BY ENTERING UNDER THE WINGS OF THE CHERUBS, to have all that glory.

37. Male and Female spirits rise up

A Synopsis

We hear that every Sabbatical year all members of the faith ascend to the Yeshivah above in heaven; Metatron tells them new and old things, and there is great rejoicing.

263. מַאן יָכִיל לְמֵימַר, מֵאִינּוּן מִלִּין דְּקָא מִתְחַדְּשָׁן בְּכָל יוֹמָא, מִקַּמֵּי רַב מְתִיבְתָּא, אִי רִבִּי, בְּכָל זִמְנָא דְּרוּחִין דְּכוּרִין סַלְּקִין לְעֵילָּא. נָשִׁין בְּהַהוּא זִמְנָא נָפְקֵי כֻּלְּהוּ, וּמִתְכַּנְּשֵׁי לְגוֹ הֵיכָלָא דְּבַתְיָה תַּמָּן, וְחַדְיָאן תַּמָּן, בְּכַמָּה מִלִּין עַתִּיקִין. וּמִתַּמָּן נָפְקִין, וְעָאלִין כֻּלְּהוּ. וְהִיא עִמְּהוֹן, לְגוֹ הֵיכָלָא דְּסֶרַח. וְחַדְיָאן בְּכַמָּה מִלִּין חַדְתִּין וְעַתִּיקִין, וּמִתַּמָּן נָפְקִין וְהִיא עִמְּהוֹן, וְעָאלִין לְגוֹ הֵיכָלָא דְּיוֹכֶבֶד. וְכֵן בְּכָל אִינּוּן הֵיכָלִין.

263. Who could speak of all those things that are daily discovered in the presence of the head of the Yeshivah? Oh, Rabbi. Every time the male spirits rise up, precisely then the women leave and gather at the sanctuary of Batyah, THE DAUGHTER OF PHARAOH, and they rejoice there with several ancient matters. From there, they all go out and enter together, AND BATYAH with them, to the sanctuary of Serah, DAUGHTER OF ASHER, to rejoice with several matters, old and new. From there, they leave, and SERAH is with them, and enter the sanctuary of Jochebed; likewise in all these sanctuaries.

264. הַשְׁתָּא ר' אֵימָא לָךְ רָזָא חֲדָא. ת"ח, בְּכָל שְׁמִטָּה וּשְׁמִטָּה, כָּרוֹזָא נָפִיק, אִתְכְּנִישׁוּ גּוּבְרִין וְנָשִׁין, וְכָל אִינּוּן בְּנֵי מְהֵימְנוּתָא, וּסְלִיקוּ. כְּדֵין כֻּלְּהוּ מִתְפַּשְׁטִין דְּכוּרִין וְנָשִׁין, וְסַלְּקִין. וְכָל אִינּוּן יַנּוּקֵי מֵחָלָב, עָאלִין לְגוֹ מְתִיבְתָּא דִּרְקִיעָא, וְחַדְיָאן חֶדְוָה, וְעִלּוּיָא דִּלְהוֹן, וְתַמָּן חֶדוּ עַל חֶדוּ. וְהַהוּא נַעַר דְּמַפְתְּחָן דְּמָארֵיהּ בִּידֵיהּ, קָם, וְאָמַר לוֹן כַּמָּה מִלִּין חַדְתִּין וְעַתִּיקִין, וְכֻלְּהוּ חָמָאן חֶדְוָה, דְּלֵית חֶדְוָה כְּהַהִיא חֶדְוָה.

264. Now, Rabbi, I will tell you a secret. Come and see: Each and every Sabbatical year, a proclamation is declared in the Garden of Eden: Gather together, men and women, and all the faithful people, and ascend. Then all are undressed and ascend, men, women and babies that stopped suckling, to

the heavenly Yeshivah, WHICH IS THE YESHIVAH OF METATRON, and rejoice about their ascension. And there is happiness upon happiness. The youth, MEANING METATRON, that has the keys of his Master in his hands, rises and tells them new and old things, and they all see gladness. There is no happiness such as that rejoicing.

265. לְבָתַר עָאלִין כֻּלְּהוּ לְגוֹ כַּמָּה פְּרוֹכְתִּין, וְכַמָּה הֵיכָלִין גְּנִיזִין תַּמָּן. דְּאִינּוּן נַהֲרִין בְּנֹעַם יְיָ׳, בְּגוֹ הֵיכָלָא דְּאַהֲבָה דְקוּדְשָׁא בְּרִיךְ הוּא. וְדָא הוּא דִכְתִּיב, לַחֲזוֹת בְּנֹעַם ה׳ וּלְבַקֵּר בְּהֵיכָלוֹ. לְבָתַר פַּרְחִין יַנוּקִין לְעֵילָּא וְאִינּוּן פַּרְחִין לְתַתָּא, וּמְהַדְּרִין לְדוּכְתַּיְיהוּ וּמִתְלַבְּשָׁן כִּדְבְקַדְמֵיתָא. זַכָּאָה עַמָּא דְּכָל טוּבָא דְּהַהוּא עָלְמָא מְחַכָּאן.

265. Following that, they all go inside. Many curtains and chambers are stored there, which illuminate in the pleasantness of Hashem within the chamber of love of the Holy One, blessed be He. This is what it is said: "To behold the beauty of Hashem, and to inquire in His temple" (Tehilim 27:4). Following this, the children WHO FINISHED SUCKLING MILK fly higher, MEANING TO A HIGHER YESHIVAH, and THE MEN AND WOMEN fly lower, SINCE THEIR PLACE IS THERE, to come back to their place IN THE LOWER GARDEN OF EDEN. AND THEY GET DRESSED THERE IN THEIR GARMENT as before. Praised is the nation for whom all the good of that world is waiting.

266. אר"ש, כַּמָּה מְתִיקִין מִלִּין דְּשָׁמַעְנָא. זַכָּאָה חוּלָקָא דִּידִי, דְּזָכֵינָא לְכָל הַאי לְמִשְׁמַע, זַכָּאָה יוֹמָא דְּנָפִיקְנָא הָכָא. אָמְרֵי לֵיהּ רִבִּי, תְּלַת יוֹמִין אִית לָן רְשׁוּ לְמֵיתֵי גַּבָּךְ, וּלְבָתַר חַד יוֹמָא חֶדְוָה דִּילָךְ.

266. Rabbi Shimon said, How sweet are these things which I have heard. Praised is my lot that I managed to hear all these. Praised is the day that I left to come here. They said to him, Rabbi, we have authorization for three days to come to you. And after one day. Your gladness... (THE REST IS MISSING).

38. The cry of the rooster

A Synopsis

The author says that after midnight Gabriel calls and then all the roosters of this world call, and we are told what words he calls out at each hour. Gabriel writes down all the activities of the world's inhabitants every day, and at night he reads everything he wrote during the day. We hear about the 365 sanctuaries in the inner part of the courtyard, and it is said that no one knows what is in those sanctuaries. The lights of the sanctuary on the east side are greater than those of the three other directions.

267. אִיהוּ מָשִׁיךְ מְשִׁיכוּ מִסִּטְרָא דִּילֵיהּ, וְאִתְטָמַּר וְאִתְחַפָּא תְּחוֹת אֲתָר דְּאִקְרֵי תָּא הָרָצִים, עַד פַּלְגוּ לֵילְיָא. מִבָּתַר פַּלְגוּ לֵילְיָא, שַׁלְהוֹבָא דְּעַמּוּדָא דְּיִצְחָק נָפִיק, וּבָטַשׁ בְּהַאי תַּרְנְגוֹלָא דְּאִקְרֵי גֶּבֶר, כְּגַוְונָא דִּגְבַר אַחֲרָא עִלָּאָה עָלֵיהּ. כֵּיוָן דִּבְטַשׁ בֵּיהּ הַאי גֶּבֶר, קָרֵי וְיָהִיב שִׁית קָלִין, וְכֻלְּהוּ בְּסָכְלְתָנוּ.

267. (THE BEGINNING IS MISSING) he stretched from his side and was hidden and covered under an area that is called the cell of the runners until midnight. After midnight, a flame emerged from the pillar of Isaac, THAT IS THE LEFT COLUMN, and struck at the rooster called Gever (Eng. 'male/rooster'), WHO IS GABRIEL, similar to another gever higher above him – WHO IS GVURAH OF ZEIR ANPIN, THE PILLAR OF ISAAC. Once THE FLAME IN THE LEFT COLUMN struck at the male, WHO IS GABRIEL, he called out and gave six sounds, all intelligent.

268. בְּשַׁעֲתָא דְּאִיהוּ קָרֵי, כָּל תַּרְנְגוֹלִין דְּהַאי עָלְמָא קָרָאן, וְנָפִיק מִנֵּיהּ שַׁלְהוֹבָא אַחֲרָא, וּמָטֵי לוֹן תְּחוֹת גַּדְפַיְיהוּ, וְקָרָאן. אִיהוּ מַה קָרֵי. בְּשַׁעֲתָא קַדְמָאָה קָרֵי וְאָמַר, קוֹל יְיָ׳ בַּכֹּחַ קוֹל יְיָ׳ בֶּהָדָר. וּבְשַׁעֲתָא תְּנְיָינָא קָרֵי וְאָמַר, קוֹל יְיָ׳ שׁוֹבֵר אֲרָזִים. בְּשַׁעֲתָא תְּלִיתָאָה קָרֵי וְאָמַר, קוֹל יְיָ׳ חוֹצֵב לַהֲבוֹת אֵשׁ. בְּשַׁעֲתָא רְבִיעָאָה קָרֵי וְאָמַר, קוֹל יְיָ׳ יָחִיל מִדְבָּר וְגוֹ׳. בְּשַׁעֲתָא חֲמִישָׁאָה קָרֵי וְאָמַר, קוֹל יְיָ׳ עַל הַמַּיִם וְגוֹ׳. בְּשַׁעֲתָא שְׁתִיתָאָה קָרֵי וְאָמַר, קוֹל יְיָ׳ יְחוֹלֵל אַיָּלוֹת וְגוֹ׳. לְבָתַר קָרֵי

וְאָמַר, קוֹל אוֹמֵר קְרָא וְאָמַר מָה אֶקְרָא וגו'. וְדָא אִיהוּ תַּרְנְגוֹלָא דְקָרֵי,
וְלָא שָׁכִיךְ וּלְבָתַר קָרֵי כְּמִלְקַדְּמִין.

268. At the time he, MEANING GABRIEL, calls, all the roosters of this world
call. Another flame emerges from him, FROM GABRIEL, reaches them under
their wings and they call. What does he, GABRIEL, call? In the first hour, he
calls and says: "The voice of Hashem is powerful; the voice of Hashem is
full of majesty" (Tehilim 29:3-9). In the second hour, he calls and says,
"The voice of Hashem breaks the cedars." In the third hour, he calls and
says: "The voice of Hashem divides the flames of fire." In the fourth hour,
he calls and says: "The voice of Hashem shakes the wilderness..." In the
fifth hour, he calls and says: "The voice of Hashem is upon the waters..." In
the sixth hour, he calls and says: "The voice of Hashem makes the hinds to
calve..." Then he says: "A voice says, 'Cry,' and he said, 'what should I
cry?'" (Yeshayah 40:6). That one is GABRIEL. He is the rooster that
continues calling and does not get quieted. After that, he calls again.

269. וּמַאי קָרֵי. כָּל עוֹבָדִין דִּבְנֵי עָלְמָא, בְּגִין דְּאִיהוּ מָארֵיהּ דְּאַחְמְתָא
וְקֶסֶת הַסּוֹפֵר בְּחַרְצוֹי. וְכָל עוֹבָדִין דִּבְנֵי עָלְמָא כָּתֵיב בְּכָל יוֹמָא.
וּבְלֵילְיָא, בָּתַר דְּקָרֵי כָּל קְרִיאָן אִלֵּין, קָרֵי כָּל מַה דְּכָתַב בְּיוֹמָא.

269. HE ASKS: What is GABRIEL crying AFTER THAT? HE REPLIES: He
calls out all the activities of people, since he is the keeper of the case,
MEANING THAT IN HIS AUSPICES IS THE CONTAINER THAT HOLDS ALL
THE SCRIPT LETTERS AND THE VERDICTS AND EDICTS. The inkwell of the
writer is at his waist and he writes down all the activities of the world's
inhabitants every day. At night, after he finishes reading out all these calls
MENTIONED ABOVE, he reads everything he wrote during the day.

270 (1). וְאִלְמָלֵא רַגְלוֹי אֶצְבְּעָאן דִּילֵיהּ, דְּאִינּוּן תְּרֵין דַּרְגִּין, חַד הַהוּא
דְּקַיְימָא בְּאֶמְצָעִיתָא. דְּאִיהוּ רַב. וְהַהוּא דְּקַיְימָא מֵאֲחוֹרָא, דְּאִיהוּ זְעֵיר,
דְּקָא מְעַכְּבִין לֵיהּ, יְהֵא מוֹקִיד עָלְמָא בְּשַׁלְהוֹבוֹי. וּמָה עַבְדֵּי. כֵּיוָן
דְּסָלִיק צַפְרָא, וְחוּטָא דִּנְהִירוּ נָפִיק מִסְטַר דָּרוֹם, כְּדֵין מִתְחַבְּרִין כֻּלְּהוּ,
וְאִתְעֲבָדִין תְּרֵין רַגְלִין תְּרֵין טַלְפִין כְּעֶגְלָא, לְקַיְימָא דִּכְתִיב וְכַף רַגְלֵיהֶם

בְּכַף רֶגֶל עֵגֶל, וְהָא יַדְעַת רָזָא דָא. שְׁאֵלַת עַנְפָּא דְּגוֹרֶן.

270a. If not for the fingers of his feet that contain IN THEM two steps, one IS THE FINGER standing in the middle, which is large AND ONE IS THE FINGER that stands behind, which is small, IF NOT FOR THESE TWO FINGERS that deter him, he would have burned the world with his flames. What do they do as soon as the morning light breaks and a thread of grace comes out of the south side? All join, MEANING THE MIDDLE FINGER WITH THE REAR FINGER, and they become two hoofs on EACH OF both legs, like a calf to uphold what is written: "And the sole of their feet was like the sole of a calf's foot" (Yechezkel 1:7). You already know this secret. You asked about the branch of the threshing ground... (THE REST IS MISSING).

270 (2). לְגוֹ בַּעֲזָרָה דָּא, אִית תְּלַת מְאָה וְשִׁתִּין וַחֲמִשָּׁה הֵיכָלִין, כְּחוּשְׁבָּן יוֹמֵי שַׁתָּא. וּבְכָל פִּתְחָא וּפִתְחָא כְּתִיב, יְהִי שָׁלוֹם בְּחֵילֵךְ שַׁלְוָה בְּאַרְמְנוֹתָיִךְ. לָא יְדִיעַ מַאי הוּא בְּהָנֵי הֵיכָלִין, אֶלָּא כֻּלְּהוּ, אִתְחֲמָן עוֹבָד צִיּוּר. שֶׁבַע סִדְרִין דְּמַרְגְּלָאן אִתְחֲמָן אַלֵּין בְּאַלֵּין, בְּכָל חַד וְחַד.

270b. In the inner part of this courtyard, WHICH IS THE SECRET OF MALCHUT, there are 365 sanctuaries, as the number of days in the year. At each and every entrance AT EACH SANCTUARY, it is written: "Peace be within your walls, and prosperity within your palaces" (Tehilim 122:7). It is not known what is in those sanctuaries, except that all encircle EACH OTHER in artistic tapestry; seven orders of gems ring within one another, in each and every one, MEANING IN EACH AND EVERY SANCTUARY.

271. אִי חֲסִידָא קַדִּישָׁא, כַּמָה מְשַׁבַּח רַב מְתִיבְתָּא הֵיכָלָא חֲדָא, דְּאִיהוּ בְּרֵישׁ סְטַר מִזְרָח דַּעֲזָרָה דָּא, בְּגִין דְּאַרְבַּע אִינוּן בַּד' סְטָרִין דְּעָלְמָא, אֲבָל הֵיכָלָא דְּסְטַר מִזְרָח, אַסְגֵּי נְהוֹרִין דִּילֵיהּ יַתִּיר מִכֻּלְּהוּ.

271. Oh, holy pious one. How much the head of the Yeshivah was praising a certain sanctuary that was situated at the top of the east side of this court, because there are four ASPECTS in the court, to the four corners of the world – WHICH ARE CHESED AND GVURAH ON THE RIGHT AND THE LEFT

WHICH IS SOUTH AND NORTH, AND TIFERET AND MALCHUT ON THE EAST AND WEST. But the lights of the sanctuary on the east side are greater than all of them.

39. Two tears, one to Sagdon and one to Gilba

A Synopsis

We are told about the gem called Sagdon that the Leviathan pulled up from the depths of the great sea; on the day the gem was pulled up the temple house was destroyed. The gem is one of the two tears of God that He sheds when He remembers His children; the other tear is sunk in the depth called Gilba.

272. יוֹמָא חַד, בְּיַמָּא רַבָּא, לְוְיָתָן נָפִיק, וְכָל יַמָּא אִזְדַּעְזָע, וְכָל נוּנֵי אָזְלִין לְכָאן וּלְכָאן, כַּד מָטֵי לְוְיָתָן בְּפִתְחָא דְּפַתְחָא דִתְהוֹמָא, שָׁארִי לְמֶחְדֵּי, וְאִשְׁתְּכַךְ תַּמָּן תְּהוֹמֵי, אֶלָּא הַהוּא כְּחֵיזוּ דְמַעְיֵּין, וְאִתְחַפְּיָין נְהוֹרִין, וְלָא אִתְחֲזוּן כָּל אִינּוּן נְהוֹרִין, בַּר נְהוֹרָא דְּהֵיכָלָא דִּבְסְטַר מִזְרָח דָּא.

272. One day, the Leviathan goes out on the great sea. The entire ocean trembles and all the fish scatter in every direction. When the Leviathan reaches the entrance of the depth, he begins to rejoice that the depths are stilled there…(THE REST IS MISSING)…except for that one, which is similar to a spring. The lights get dimmer and none of the lights is visible, except the light in that sanctuary on the eastern side.

273. הַהוּא מַרְגְּלָא דְּקָא אַפִּיק לְוְיָתָן, מִגּוֹ הַהוּא תְּהוֹמָא דְּאִקְרֵי סַגְדּוֹ"ן, מִמָּה אִתְעֲבֵיד. אֶלָּא יוֹמָא דָּא דְּקָא אַפִּיק לְוְיָתָן, דְּאִזְדַּעְזָע יַמָּא, יוֹמָא דְּאִתְחָרַב בֵּי מַקְדְּשָׁא, ט' בְּאָב אִיהוּ. וְהַהוּא מַרְגְּלָא, דְּכַד דְּכִיר קוּדְשָׁא בְּרִיךְ הוּא לִבְנוֹי, וְאוֹשִׁיד תְּרֵין דִּמְעִין לְגוֹ יַמָּא רַבָּא, חַד נָפִיל לְגוֹ תְּהוֹמָא דָּא דְּאִקְרֵי סַגְדּוֹ"ן, וְחַד נָפִיל לְגוֹ תְּהוֹמָא אַחֲרָא דְּאִקְרֵי גִּילְבָּ"א.

273. HE ASKS: The gem that the leviathan pulled out from that depth is called Sagdon. What is it made of? HE REPLIES: That day that the Leviathan pulled up THE GEM, and the ocean was shaking, was the day when the Temple was destroyed, Tish'ah B'Av (the Ninth of Av). About that gem, it is when the Holy One, blessed be He, remembers His children and spills two tears into the great ocean. One TEAR falls onto this depth called Sagdon and one TEAR drops into another depth called Gilba.

274. בְּגִין דְּחָמֵשׁ תְּהוֹמֵי אַחֲרָנִין אִינּוּן בְּיַמָּא רַבָּא. אֲבָל לָא חֲשִׁיבִין כְּהָנֵי אַחֲרָנִין, וְכֵיוָן דְּנַפְלֵי אִינּוּן דִּמְעִין, קָפָאן גּוֹ תְּהוֹמֵי חַד. וְחַד אַטְבַּע גּוֹ תְּהוֹמָא, דְּאִקְרֵי גִּילְבָּ"א.

274. Five other depths exist in the great ocean but are not as important as these others, WHICH ARE SAGDON AND GILBA. As soon as these tears drop, they are frozen within one depth and one TEAR is sunk into the depth called Gilba.

40. The first destroyer

A Synopsis

The author talks about the four sources that do damage to the world. These are the ox, the pit, the consumer and fire. Because some information is missing here from the text, the topic jumps to the observation of a person looking at a sanctuary, where it seems to change size until it has no measurements at all.

275. דְּתַתָּא גּוֹ שְׁמָרִים דְּחַמְרָא, דּוּרְדְּיָין בִּישִׁין, נָפִיק חַד עִרְעוּרָא מְקַטְרְגָא, מַזִיקָא קַדְמָאָה, וְאִיהוּ בְּרוּחָא דְּיוּקְנָא דְּאָדָם, כַּד קָרִיב לְגוֹ קוּדְשָׁא. כֵּיוָן דְּמִתְעֲבַר מִתַּמָּן, וּבָעֵי לְנַחְתָּא לְתַתָּא, לְאִתְלַבְּשָׁא בִּלְבוּשָׁא לְנַזְקָא עָלְמָא, נָחִית הוּא וּרְתִיכוֹי. וּלְבוּשָׁא קַדְמָאָה דְּקָא נָקִיט תַּבְנִית שׁוֹר, דְּיוּקְנָא דְּשׁוֹר. וְקַדְמָאָה לַנְזִיקִין מֵאִינוּן אַרְבַּע, שׁוֹר אִיהוּ. וְאִינוּן אַרְבַּע אָבוֹת לְנַזְקָא עָלְמָא. וְכֻלְּהוּ תְּלָתָא אָבוֹת נְזִיקִין, בַּר שׁוֹר, כֻּלְּהוּ דִּילֵיהּ.

275. On the bottom, within the wine's sediment, the bad sediments, emerges one who disrupts, the first destroyer IN THE WORLD. He is based on the principle of a human image that approached holiness. As soon as he was removed FROM SANCTITY and wished to go down, to dress up in a garment to harm the world, he came down with his Chariots. The first garment that he acquired was the likeness of an ox, the image of an ox, and the first of these four SOURCES OF DAMAGE is an OX, AS IS MENTIONED AT THE BEGINNING OF BABA KAMA, THE OX, THE PIT, THE CONSUMER AND FIRE. These are four sources of damage in the world and all the other three sources of damage, besides the ox, also belong TO THAT OX.

276. וע"ד כְּתִיב, וַיָּמִירוּ אֶת כְּבוֹדָם בְּתַבְנִית שׁוֹר אוֹכֵל עֵשֶׂב. מַהוּ אוֹכֵל עֵשֶׂב. הָא דַּרְשִׁינָן בֵּיהּ אֲבָל עִקָּרָא דְּמִלָּה, מִתַּמְצִית הַלֶּחֶם, וְלָא שִׂבְעַת זִינֵי דָּגָן, לֵית לֵיהּ בְּהוּ חוּלָקָא, וְלָא יָאוּת לֵיהּ לְמֶהֱוֵי תַּמָּן.

276. About this, it is written: "Thus they exchanged their glory for the likeness of an ox that eats grass" (Tehilim 106:20). HE ASKS: What is the meaning of: "That (he) eats grass"? HE REPLIES: We already dealt with it,

but the essence of it is that he has no part in the seven types of grains nor the essence of bread, WHICH ARE FROM MALCHUT, and it is improper for him to be there, MEANING TO SAY THAT HE IS NOT WORTHY TO SUCKLE FROM HUMAN FOOD, WHICH IS MALCHUT. AS A RESULT, IT SAYS: "THAT EATS GRASS."

277. מִדּוּכְתַּיְיהוּ, וְאִלֵּין יַתְבִין בְּדוּכְתַּיְיהוּ, עַד לָא נָפְקֵי אִלֵּין, זְמִינִין אִלֵּין, נְהִירוּ וּנְצִיצוּ דִּלְהוֹן, לָא יַכְלִין עַיְינִין לְמִסְבַּל. אַזְלִין בְּסָחֲרָנִין, לֵית לְהוֹן שְׁכִיכוּ לְעָלְמִין.

277. (THE BEGINNING OF THE SUBJECT IS MISSING)…from their location. These sit in their location, even before those that leave these are ready. The eyes cannot stand their light and sparkling. They circle around and never have any rest.

278. כַּד אֶסְתָּכַּל ב״נ בְּהַאי הֵיכָלָא, מִיַּד בְּאִסְתַּכְּלוּתָא קַדְמָאָה, אִתְחֲזֵי זְעֵיר וְלָא זְעֵיר, אֶסְתָּכַּל יַתִּיר, אִתְחֲזֵי רַב. תּוּ אֶסְתָּכַּל, אִתְחֲזֵי יַתִּיר רַב, כָּל מַה דְּאֶסְתָּכַּל, הָכִי אִתְחֲזֵי בְּאִתְפַּשְׁטוּתָא רַב וְעִלָּאָה, עַד דְּדָמֵי בְּאִסְתַּכְּלוּתָא כְּמִלָּא נִימָא, דְּלֵית לֵיהּ שִׁיעוּרָא.

278. When a person looks at this sanctuary, at his first observation, it seems to him somewhat small yet not that small. He looks a little longer and it seems large. He observes longer and it looks larger. The longer he stares at it, the more it seems to expand and the higher it gets, until his final gaze, AT THAT SANCTUARY, when a hair's breadth seems to him SO LARGE THAT it has no measurements any more.

279. עוֹבָדִין סַגִּיאִין לְגוֹ, דְּלָא יְדִיעַ אוּמָנוּ דִּלְהוֹן, מִנֵּיהּ נָהֲרָא עֲזָרָה, וְכָל מַה דְּאִית בָּהּ, בַּר כְּרוּבִים דִּנְהוֹרָא דִּלְהוֹן סַלְקָא עַד רוּם רְקִיעָא, בִּגְוָונִין סַגִּיאִין, וּנְהוֹרִין מְנַצְצָן. אֶלֶף וַחֲמֵשׁ מֵאָה וַחֲמִשָּׁה וְשַׁבְעִין גּוּפְנִין, עָבְדִין אֵיבִין בַּעֲזָרָה דָא.

279. Many works are inside whose craftsmanship is unknown, from which the court and all that is inside shines, besides the Cherubs, whose light rises to the lofty firmament in a variety of colors and sparkling brightness. There are 1,575 grapevines producing fruits in that courtyard. (BECAUSE THE BEGINNING AND END OF SUBJECT IS MISSING, I CAN'T EXPLAIN IT).

41. "Folds his hands together" and "eats his own flesh"

A Synopsis

We hear that after a person's death the evil one consumes his flesh but has no control over the Holy Spirit or the sanctified soul. The author says that the angel of death has no joy in killing a person; it's just that he is happy to do the will of God.

280. יַתִּיר חוֹבֵק אֶת יָדָיו, בִּמְרִירוּ וַאֲנִינוּ דִילֵיהּ, וּלְבָתַר אוֹכֵל אֶת בְּשָׂרוֹ בְּעַל כָּרְחֵיהּ, דְּלֵית לֵיהּ רְשׁוּ לְשַׁלְטָאָה עַל מִלָּה אַחֲרָא. מַה אִתְהֲנֵי לֵיהּ בְּכָל מַה דְּאַסְטֵי וְעָבֵיד וְעָמֵל, דִּלְבָתַר לֵית לֵיהּ רְשׁוּ, אֶלָּא עַל דִּילֵיהּ לְבָתַר מַרְקִיד וְחַדֵּי, כְּכְּסִיל בְּלָא דַעְתָּא כְּלָל, וְאָזִיל בְּלָא תּוֹעַלְתָּא, וְאָכִיל לִבְשָׂרָא. וּבַשְׁאָר לֵית לֵיהּ רְשׁוּ. מְרִירוּ דְעֵילָא וְתַתָּא, כַּד יִשְׂרָאֵל בְּעָאקוּ, וְאָכְלֵי לוֹן שַׂנְאֵיהוֹן וְלָא יַהֲבֵי חֵילָא בְּעוֹבָדִין טָבִין דִּלְהוֹן, לְאַפָּקָא מִנֵּיהּ.

280. (THE BEGINNING OF THE SUBJECT IS MISSING). More. THE FOOL, THAT IS THE OTHER SIDE, "folds his hands together" (Kohelet 4:5) in bitterness and mourning and then in spite of himself "eats his own flesh" (Ibid.), since THE OTHER SIDE has no permission to control anything else BESIDES FLESH. What pleasure he derives is from all that he has done and worked for, UNTIL HE KILLED HIM, because after that he has no permission TO ENJOY FROM HIM except what belongs to him, WHICH IS THE FLESH, SINCE THE OTHER SIDE PROVIDES MAN WITH HIS FLESH. He then dances and rejoices like a completely mindless fool. He goes without any purpose and consumes the flesh, and he has no authority over the rest. Bitterness prevails above and below, when Yisrael are in trouble and their enemies consume them, and Yisrael do not give power with their good deeds to extricate themselves FROM THE OTHER SIDE.

281. וַאֲפִילוּ מִבִּשְׂרֵיהּ דְּאִיהוּ מֵהַאי סְטָר, אַבְאִישׁ קַמֵּי מַלְכָּא קַדִּישָׁא, דְּאִיהוּ רַחוּם וְחַנּוּן. אֲבָל עַל דִּילֵיהּ, רוּחָא קַדִּישָׁא וְנִשְׁמָתָא קַדִּישָׁא, לֵית עִלָּאִין וְתַתָּאִין יַכְלִין לְשַׁלְטָא עֲלוֹי כְּלָל. וע"ד כָּל תַּסְקוּפִין, וְכָל מַה דְּאַסְטֵי הַהוּא רָע, דְּחָשִׁיב לְמִשְׁלַט עַל רוּחָא קַדִּישָׁא, וּלְבָתַר לָא

יָכִיל, וְיָשׁוּב וְאוֹכֵל אֶת בְּשָׂרוֹ. מַה תּוֹעַלְתָּא הֲוָה לֵיהּ. וְעוֹד דְּאִינּוּן חָפָאן כֻּלְּהוּ כְּעַרְטִירָאָה תַּקִּיף, וְלֵית שְׁכִיכוּ לְעֶלָאִין וְתַתָּאִין.

281. Even from the flesh of that side, the Holy King, is unhappy TO GIVE TO THE OTHER SIDE, since He is compassionate and merciful. However, as for what is His, OF THE HOLY ONE, BLESSED BE HE, that is the Holy Spirit and the holy soul, the upper and lower grades cannot have any power over it. As a result, at the end the evil one, THE OTHER SIDE, is unable to dominate the Holy Spirit which he meant to do by means of all his libelous plots and false accusations, so he must again "eats his own flesh." What benefit did he get FROM ALL HIS ACCUSATIONS …(SEVERAL WORDS ARE MISSING HERE). Furthermore, they cover everything like a heavy fog and the upper and lower beings have no rest.

282. תָּא וְאֵימָא לָךְ מִלָּה. אִי תֵּימָא, דְּחֶדוּ הוּא לְמַלְאָךְ הַמָּוֶת, כַּד קָטִיל בְּנֵי נָשָׁא. לָאו. אֶלָּא בְּגִין דְּחָמֵי דִּרְעוּתָא דְּמָארֵיהּ בְּכַךְ, אַחְזֵי גַּרְמֵיהּ בְּחֶדוּ, לְמֶעְבַּד רְעוּתֵיהּ דְּקוּדְשָׁא בְּרִיךְ הוּא, דִּכְתִיב רוּחַ סְעָרָה עוֹשָׂה דְבָרוֹ. אָ"ל ר"ש, וְהָא אִיהוּ אָזִיל וּמְרַקֵּד בְּחֶדְוָה קַמֵּי נָשִׁין. אָ"ל אִי חֲסִידָא קַדִּישָׁא, וַדַּאי הָכִי הוּא, לְאַחֲזָאָה קַמֵּי מַלְכָּא דְּנִיחָא לֵיהּ בִּרְעוּתֵיהּ דְּמַלְכָּא. אֲבָל נַיְיחָא דִּילֵיהּ בְּהֶסְפֵּדָא דְּנָשִׁין, אִיהוּ רָקִיד וְאוּדְנֵיהּ לְהֶסְפֵּדָא.

282. Come and I will tell you something. If you say that the Angel of Death feels joy when he kills a person, it is not true. It is only that he sees that this is his Master's wishes, so he seems happy to do the will of the Holy One, blessed be He, as is written: "Stormy wind fulfilling His word" (Tehilim 148:8). Rabbi Shimon said to him, yet he is going merrily along and dancing in front of the women? He said to him: Oh, holy pious one. It is most certainly so, in order to demonstrate before the King that it gives him pleasure to do the King's bidding. However, his satisfaction is at the women's eulogy, so he dances and listens to the eulogy.

283. אָ"ל אִי הָכִי, אֲמַאי אָזִיל וְאַסְטֵי עַל ב"נ לְעֵילָא, וְאַדְכַּר לְחוֹבוֹי. אָ"ל, בְּגִין דְּאִיהוּ זָקֵן וּכְסִיל, וְחָשִׁיב לְמִשְׁלַט עַל רוּחָא, וְכָל תּאוּבְתֵּיהּ

בְּגִינֵי כַּךְ אִיהוּ, לְסוֹף לָא שַׁלִּיט אֶלָּא עַל דִּילֵיהּ. בְּשָׂרָא דִּילֵיהּ. וע״ד כְּתִיב, יָשׁוּב עֲמָלוֹ בְרֹאשׁוֹ.

283. They said to him, If so, why does he go to accuse the person up high and mention his sins, IF HE TAKES NO JOY IN KILLING A PERSON? He said to him, Because he is an old fool and plans to control the spirit and dominate it. That is all he lusts after. However, eventually he has power only over what is his own. The flesh is his. Therefore, it is written: "His mischief shall return upon his own head" (Tehilim 7:17), MEANING THAT HE DOES NOT DERIVE ANY PLEASURE FROM HIS LABOR IN DENOUNCING BELOW AND DENOUNCING ABOVE.

42. Boiling tears

A Synopsis

We are told that the two tears that God weeps into the great ocean are boiling hot and that they congeal the water in the sea. The tears cause the waves to roar so loudly that they awaken the ancient patriarchs in the cave of Machpelah.

284. אָזִיל וּבְעֵי לְאַרְגְּשָׁא עָלְמָא, וּמַיָּא סְלִיקִין מִגּוֹ שְׁאַר תְּהוֹמִין, וּבְעָאן לְחַפְיָא עָלְמָא, אִינּוּן דִּמְעִין רְתִיחִין יַתִּיר מִכָּל אֶשָּׁא דְּעָלְמָא. וּמִגּוֹ תּוֹקֶף דִּרְתִיחוּ דִּלְהוֹן, אַקְפוּ מַיָּא, גּוֹ יַמָּא דְּנִקְפָּא. וְאִלְמָּלֵא דְּרָמַז קוּדְשָׁא בְּרִיךְ הוּא חַד נְשִׁיבוּ מִסִּטְרָא דְּאַבְרָהָם, מֵעַמּוּדָא דִּילֵיהּ, וְאַחְזֵי עַל עָלְמָא, לָא יָכִיל לְמֵיקָם אֲפִילּוּ רִגְעָא חֲדָא.

284. (THE BEGINNING IS MISSING) goes and wishes to disturb the world. And the waters rise from other depths and want to flood the world. These tears, MEANING THE TWO TEARS THAT THE HOLY ONE, BLESSED BE HE, DROPS INTO THE GREAT OCEAN, are boiling hotter than any fire in the world. From the energy of their boiling, they congeal the water in the gelled sea. If the Holy One, blessed be He, would not have hinted at the blowing of a wind from the side of Abraham, WHICH IS CHASSADIM, from his pillar, THAT IS THE RIGHT COLUMN, THAT WOULD COMBINE TO ONE WITH THE LEFT and show HIS ILLUMINATION over the world, the world could not withstand it even for an instant.

285. אִינּוּן דִּמְעִין כַּד נַפְלִין גּוֹ יַמָּא, אִשְׁתְּמַע קָלָא בֵּין יַמָּא, עַד מְעַרְתָּא דְּכַפֶּלְתָּא. מִקָל נְהִימוּ דִּלְהוֹן דְּקָא אִשְׁתְּמַע תַּמָּן, כַּד עָאלִין גּוֹ יַמָּא, מִתְעָרְן אֲבָהָן קַדְמָאֵי, וְקָמוּ, וְחָשְׁבוּ דְּקוּדְשָׁא בְּרִיךְ הוּא בָּעֵי לְאַהֲפָכָא עָלְמָא, עַד דְּקָלָא נָפִיק וְאָמַר לוֹן, לָא תִּדְחֲלוּ רְחִימִין קַדִּישִׁין, בְּגִינֵיכוֹן דָּכִיר קוּדְשָׁא בְּרִיךְ הוּא לִבְנֵיכוֹן, וְאִיהוּ בָּעֵי דְּמִפְרַק לוֹן, וְאַתּוּן תֶּחֱמוּן.

285. When these tears drop into the sea, the sound between the waves is heard up to the cave of Machpelah. From the roaring sounds of the waves that is heard there when they enter the sea, the ancient patriarchs are

awakened and rise, and think that the Holy One, blessed be He, wishes to turn the world upside down, until the voice comes out and tells them: Do not fear, holy beloved. Due to you, the Holy One, blessed be He, remembers your children and desires to redeem them, and you will see.

43. The Alphabets and the names

A Synopsis
We hear of the movement and permutation of the Alphabets as the letters fly in the air; no one can understand them except for Messiah.

286. אַלְפָא בֵּיתִין כֻּלְּהוּ, מְשַׁלְּבָן וּמִתְצָרְפָאן אִלֵּין בְּאִלֵּין, וְאִתְחַבְּרָן בְּצֵרוּפָא דִשְׁמָא קַדִּישָׁא. כֵּיוָן דְּאִתְחֲזוּן אַתְוָון בְּצֵרוּפָא דָא, אִלֵּין גְּנִיזִין, וְנָפְקִין אַחֲרָנִין, וְכֵן כֻּלְּהוּ. אִלֵּין גְּנִיזִין, וְאִלֵּין נָפְקִין, כֻּלְּהוּ לְגוֹ בְּחָלוּלָא דְּאִינּוּן כַּפְתּוֹרִים.

286. (THE BEGINNING OF THE SUBJECT IS MISSING) all the Alphabets fuse and interlock with each other to form the permutation of the Holy Name. After the appearance of the letters in this combination, these LETTERS are stored away and others emerge AND JOIN TO A DIFFERENT PERMUTATION. And this is how they are; these are hidden and these emerge, and all within the hollowness of these buttons.

287. תּוּ פַּרְחֵי תְּלַת זִמְנִין בְּיוֹמָא בַּאֲוִירָא וְנָפְקָא לְבַר, וְקַיְימָא שְׁמָא בְּאַרְבַּע אַתְוָון, תַּלְיָין בַּאֲוִירָא שַׁעֲתָא וּפַלְגָּא, לְבָתַר גָּנִיז דָּא, מִיָּד נָפִיק מִגּוֹ אֲוִירָא מֵחָלוּלָא דִילֵיהּ, שְׁמָא דִּתְרֵיסָר אַתְוָון, פָּרַח וְתַלְיָא בַּאֲוִירָא, שַׁעֲתָא חֲדָא, וְלָא יַתִּיר. לְבָתַר גָּנִיז דָּא, וְנָפְקָא מִיָּד צֵרוּפָא דְּאַתְוָון אַחֲרָנִין, שְׁמָא דכ"ב אַתְוָון, וְתַלְיָין בַּאֲוִירָא שַׁעֲתָא אַחֲרָא, וְאַגְנִיז. וּמִיָּד נָפְקֵי אַתְוָון מֵחָלוּלָא אַחֲרָא, שְׁמָא דִּתְמַנְיָא וְעֶשְׂרִין אַתְוָון, מִתְעַטְּרִין כֻּלְּהוּ בְּכִתְרַיְיהוּ, וְקַיְימֵי שַׁעֲתָא וּפַלְגָּא, וְאַגְנִיז דָּא. וּמִיָּד נָפְקֵי תַּלְיָא בַּאֲוִירָא, שְׁמָא דְּעֶשְׂרִין וַחֲמֵשׁ אַתְוָון בְּצֵרוּפַיְיהוּ, וְקַיְימָא שַׁעֲתָא וּתְלַת רִגְעֵי, נָפְקֵי אַתְוָון דְּאַרְבְּעִין וּתְרֵין אַתְוָון, לְעָלְמָא קַיְימָא.

287. THE LETTERS also fly three times a day in the air and make their exit, and the name is suspended in four letters in the air for an hour and a half. After that, this NAME gets hidden and immediately the name of twelve letters emerges from the air, from its hollowness. It flies suspended in the

air, one hour and not more. Then this NAME gets stored away and immediately, another combination of letters emerges. That is the name of 22 letters. They hang suspended in the air another hour, and become hidden. Immediately, other letters emerge from another empty space, the name of 28 letters. All get adorned with their crowns and stay for an hour and a half, and THIS NAME gets hidden. Immediately the name of 25 letters with their combinations emerges, hanging in the air, and remains an hour and three minutes...(MISSING HERE)...emerge letters with 42 letters...(THERE IS SOMETHING MISSING HERE)...stays forever...(THE REST IS MISSING).

288. שְׁמָהָן. אֶלָּא אַתְוָון כּוּלְּהוּ, לָא מִשְׁתַּכְּכֵי לְעָלְמִין, בַּלְטֵי וּמְנַצְצֵי לְבַר, וְסַלְקֵי וְנַחְתֵּי, לֵית מַאן דְּיָכִיל לְקַיְימָא בְּהוּ, בַּר מָשִׁיחַ בְּטוֹרַח סַגִּי. דָּא גָּנִיז, לְבָתַר דְּקַיְימָא תְּרֵין שַׁעְתִּין וְעֶשְׂרִין וּתְרֵין רִגְעִין, וְהַאי שְׁמָא גְּלִיפָא דְּע"ב אַתְוָון קָא נָפִיק. וְקַיְימָא וְתַלְיָא בַּאֲוִירָא, שַׁעְתָּא וּפַלְגָּא. כָּל הָנֵי שְׁמָהָן לָא נָפְקֵי, וְלָא אִתְחֲזוּן, אֶלָּא זִמְנָא חֲדָא בְּיוֹמָא, אֲבָל אִינּוּן אַלְפָא בֵּיתִין, אִתְחֲזוּן פַּרְחִין בַּאֲוִירָא, וּמִצְטְרְפִין אִלֵּין בְּאִלֵּין, תְּלַת זִמְנִין בְּיוֹמָא.

288. (THE BEGINNING IS MISSING) the names. All these letters never rest. They stand out and sparkle externally, and rise and descend. No one could understand anything about them, except for Messiah with great toil. That NAME gets hidden after staying around for two hours and 22 minutes and that name, which is engraved in 72 letters, emerges. It stays suspended in the air an hour and a half. All these names do not emerge and do not appear except once a day, but the letters of the Alphabet are visible flying in the air and combining LETTERS WITH LETTERS, three times a day.

289. כַּד פַּרְחָן אַתְוָון דְּאַלְפָא בֵּיתִין, אִלֵּין פַּרְחִין מִכָּאן, וְאִלֵּין מִכָּאן, וּמִתְצָרְפָן כֻּלְּהוּ. כַּד נָחִית תַּמָּן רַב מְתִיבְתָּא, שָׁארֵי, מָשִׁיחַ חָמָא בְּצֵרוּפָא דְּאַלְפָא בֵּיתָא, אַתְוָון כְּמָה דְּחָמָא דָּנִיאֵל, דְּאִינּוּן מַמְתוּס נַנְקְפִי אַאָלְרָן.

289. When the letters of the Alphabet fly, some of them fly from here and some FLY from here, and all combine. When the head of the Yeshivah

descended there, he said, Messiah saw in the permutations of the letters of the Alphabet, as Daniel saw in them, when he saw the letters, Mem Mem Tav Vav Samech, Nun Nun Kuf Pe Yud, Aleph Aleph Lamed Resh final Nun. HE KNEW TO COMBINE FROM THEM, "*MENE MENE TEKEL UFARSIN*" (DANIEL 5:25), FOR THE FIRST THREE LETTERS OF THESE THREE COMBINATIONS FORMS *MENE*. THE SECOND SET OF THREE LETTERS ALSO COMBINE TO *MENE*, THE THIRD SET COMBINE TO *TEKEL*, THE FOURTH SET OF THREE LETTERS COMBINE TO *UFAR* AND THE FIFTH SET COMBINE TO *SIN*.

44. Souls ascend and descend

A Synopsis

We are told about the great joy on each Shabbat eve when the Tree of Life is awakened and produces sanctified souls. When the Shabbat arrives the souls come down to rest on a holy nation and the souls of the righteous ascend to the higher Garden of Eden. When the Shabbat ends those additional souls that dwelt upon the children of Yisrael rise above and the souls of the just descend. The souls that rose stand in the presence of God who queries them about what new things in the Torah they learned in the world. When a soul says a new interpretation God gathers His entourage and tells them about it in both Yeshivot.

290. כָּל מַעֲלֵי שַׁבְּתָא, כַּד מְקַדְּשִׁין יִשְׂרָאֵל יוֹמָא לְתַתָּא, כָּרוֹזָא כָּרִיז לְאַרְבַּע סִטְרֵי עָלְמָא, אִתְכַּנָּשׁוּ מַשְׁרְיָין קַדִּישִׁין, אַתְקְנוּ כֻּרְסְיָין. מַאן חָמֵי חֶדְוָה, בִּתְלַת מְאָה וְתִשְׁעִין רְקִיעִין, כַּמָּה מְמָנָן, כַּמָּה שִׁלְטוֹנִין, מִתְכַּנְּשִׁין לְאַתְרַיְיהוּ. כֵּיוָן דְּיִשְׂרָאֵל לְתַתָּא מְקַדְּשִׁין, כְּדֵין אִתְּעַר אִילָנָא דְחַיֵּי, וְאָקִישׁ בְּאִינּוּן טַרְפִּין דִּילֵיהּ, רוּחַ נְשִׁיבוּ חַד מִגּוֹ עָלְמָא דְּאָתֵי, וְאִינּוּן עַנְפִּין דְּאִילָנָא מִתְנַעְנְעָן, וְסַלְקִין רֵיחִין דְּעָלְמָא דְאָתֵי.

290. Each Shabbat eve when Yisrael sanctify the day below, the proclamation goes out to the four corners of the world to assemble holy camps and prepare the thrones. Who saw such joy, WHEN in 390 firmaments many appointed ones and many rulers gather to their stations. As soon as Yisrael below sanctify THE DAY, the Tree of Life, THAT IS ZEIR ANPIN, gets awakened and a wind blows from the World to Come, WHICH IS BINAH, and beats at its leaves. The branches in the tree shake and exude fragrances from the World to Come. THE TREE IS ZEIR ANPIN, ITS BRANCHES ARE HIS SFIROT, ITS LEAVES ARE THE SOULS THAT IT PRODUCES. THE 390 FIRMAMENTS ARE THE SECRET OF CHOCHMAH AND BINAH, TIFERET AND MALCHUT, OF WHICH EACH IS COMPRISED OF ONE HUNDRED EXCEPT FOR MALCHUT THAT LACKS TEN LAST ONES, THESE BEING FROM MALCHUT OF MALCHUT WHICH ARE FROM THE ATRIBUTE OF JUDGMENT, AND ARE STORED AWAY, AND THEREFORE THEY ARE FOUR HUNDRED MINUS TEN.

291. הַהוּא אִילָנָא דְּחַיֵּי אִתְּעַר, וְאַפִּיק נִשְׁמָתִין קַדִּישִׁין, וּפָרִישׁ עַל

עָלְמָא. וְעִם כָּל דָּא, נִשְׁמָתִין נָפְקִין, וְנִשְׁמָתִין עָאלִין, אִלֵּין מִתְעָרֵי
אִלֵּין, אִלֵּין נָפְקִין וְאִלֵּין עָאלִין, וְאִילָנָא דְּחַיֵּי בְּחֶדְוָה.

291. The Tree of Life awakens and produces sacred souls, and spreads THEM over the world. Nevertheless, souls come and souls go, MEANING TO SAY THAT SOULS GO OUT TO BE DRESSED IN YISRAEL IN THIS WORLD AND THE SOULS OF THE RIGHTEOUS ASCEND FROM THE LOWER GARDEN OF EDEN AND ENTER ABOVE TO THE GARDEN OF EDEN UP HIGH. Those THAT LEAVE stir those TO ENTER. Therefore, these leave and these ascend and the Tree of Life, THAT IS ZEIR ANPIN, is joyful.

292. וּכְדֵין, יִשְׂרָאֵל כֻּלְּהוּ מִתְעַטְּרִין בְּעִטְרִין דְּאִינּוּן נִשְׁמָתִין קַדִּישִׁין,
כֻּלְּהוּ בְּחֶדְוָה בְּנַיְיחָא. וְכָל הַשַּׁבָּת, אִית לוֹן הַהוּא חֶדְוָה, וְהַהוּא
נַיְיחָא, וְכָל צַדִּיקַיָּיא דִּי בְּגִנְתָּא, כֻּלְּהוּ סַלְּקִין וּמִתְעַנְּגִין בְּעִנּוּגָא עִלָּאָה,
דְּעָלְמָא דְּאָתֵי. כֵּיוָן דְּנָפִיק שַׁבַּתָּא, כֻּלְּהוּ נִשְׁמָתִין פָּרְחִין וְסַלְּקִין.

292. Then all of Yisrael are adorned with the crowns of these sacred souls, THE SECRET OF THE ADDITIONAL SOULS, and all are in happiness and repose. And throughout the Shabbat, they enjoy that happiness and satisfaction. All the just that are in the Garden ascend and take pleasure in that uppermost pleasure of the World to Come, IN THE UPPER GARDEN OF EDEN. When Shabbat ends, all the souls fly away FROM YISRAEL and go up ABOVE.

293. ת"ח, כַּד עָיֵיל שַׁבַּתָּא נִשְׁמָתִין נַחְתִּין לְשַׁרְיָיא עַל עַמָּא קַדִּישָׁא.
וְנִשְׁמָתִין דְּצַדִּיקַיָּיא סַלְּקִין לְעֵילָּא. כַּד נָפִיק שַׁבַּתָּא, נִשְׁמָתִין סַלְּקִין,
אִינּוּן דְּשָׁארוּ עֲלַיְיהוּ דְּיִשְׂרָאֵל. וְנִשְׁמָתִין נַחְתִּין, אִינּוּן נִשְׁמָתִין
דְּצַדִּיקַיָּיא.

293. Come and see: When Shabbat arrives, the souls come down, MEANING THE ADDITIONAL SOULS, to rest on a holy nation. And the souls of the righteous, FROM THE LOWER GARDEN OF EDEN, ascend above TO THE HIGHER GARDEN OF EDEN. When Shabbat ends, those souls that dwelt upon Yisrael rise above, THAT IS, THE ADDITIONAL SOULS, and the souls of the just descend, THOSE THAT ROSE TO THE HIGHER GARDEN OF EDEN, AND ARE NOW RETURNING TO THE LOWER GARDEN OF EDEN.

294. כֵּיוָן דְּסַלְקִין כֻּלְּהוּ נִשְׁמָתִין דְּשָׁארוּ עֲלַיְיהוּ דְּיִשְׂרָאֵל. סַלְקִי וְקַיְימִין בְּדִיּוּקְנָא קַמֵּי מַלְכָּא קַדִּישָׁא, וְקוּדְשָׁא בְּרִיךְ הוּא שָׁאִיל לְכֻלְּהוּ, מַאי חִדּוּשָׁא הֲוָה לְכוּ בְּהַהוּא עָלְמָא בְּאוֹרַיְיתָא. זַכָּאָה אִיהוּ מַאן דְּחִדּוּשָׁא דְּאוֹרַיְיתָא אָמְרַת קַמֵּיהּ. כַּמָּה חֶדְוָה עָבֵיד קוּדְשָׁא בְּרִיךְ הוּא, כָּנִישׁ לְפָמַלְיָא דִּילֵיהּ, וְאָמַר, שִׁמְעוּ חִדּוּשָׁא דְּאוֹרַיְיתָא, דְּאָמְרַת נִשְׁמָתָא דָּא דִּפְלוֹנִי, וְכֻלְּהוּ מוּקְמֵי הַהִיא מִלָּה בִּתְרֵי מְתִיבְתֵּי. אִינּוּן לְתַתָּא, וְקוּדְשָׁא בְּרִיךְ הוּא לְעֵילָא, חָתִים לְהַהִיא מִלָּה.

294. As soon as all the souls that dwelt on Yisrael have risen above, they rise and stand, in form, in the presence of the Holy King. The Holy One, blessed be He, asks all of them, What new things in the Torah have you had in that world? Praised is the one that says in His presence a new interpretation in the Torah, as so much joy is produced by the Holy One, blessed be He. He gathers His entourage, MEANING THE HIGHER SOULS AND ANGELS, and says, Hear the new words of Torah, which that soul of so-and-so is recounting. All explain that point in the two Yeshivot, MEANING IN THE YESHIVAH OF THE HOLY ONE, BLESSED BE HE, AND THE YESHIVAH OF METATRON; they below, and the Holy One, blessed be He, above seals that item.

295. ת״ח, כַּד מִלָּה אִתְחֲדָשׁ בְּאוֹרַיְיתָא, וְנִשְׁמָתָא דְּנַחְתָּא בְּשַׁבַּתָּא אִתְעַסְקַת בְּאִינּוּן מִלִּין חַדְתִּין, וְסַלְקֵי לְעֵילָא. כָּל פָּמַלְיָא דִּלְעֵילָא, צַיְיתִין לְהַהוּא מִלָּה, וְחֵיוַות הַקֹּדֶשׁ מִתְרַבִּין בְּגַדְפִּין, וּמִתְלַבְּשָׁן בְּגַדְפִּין. וְכַד שָׁאִיל לוֹן קוּדְשָׁא בְּרִיךְ הוּא, וְלָא תָּבִין וְשָׁתְקִין, כְּדֵין חֵיוַות הַקֹּדֶשׁ מַה כְּתִיב, בְּעָמְדָם תְּרַפֶּינָה כַנְפֵיהֶם, כְּמָה דְאַתְּ אָמֵר כִּי עָמְדוּ לֹא עָנוּ עוֹד. וּכְפִתְחוֹ עָמְדוּ כָּל הָעָם.

295. Come and see: When some novel interpretation in Torah is discovered and the ADDITIONAL soul that came down in Shabbat was involved in this novel interpretation of the Torah, and ascends, AFTER SHABBAT, the entire

entourage above listen to that matter. The holy living creatures grow large with their outstretched wings and put on their wings. When He asks THE SOULS ABOUT THE TORAH'S NOVEL INTERPRETATIONS, they do not respond, but remain quiet. Then it is written about the sanctified holy living creatures: "When they stood still, they let down their wings" (Yechezkel 1:25). "STOOD STILL" MEANS IN THEIR SILENCE, as it says: "Because they stand there, and answer no more" (Iyov 32:16). "And when he opened it, all the people stood up" (Nechemyah 8:5), MEANING THEY WERE SILENT.

296. וְאִי תֵּימָא, שְׁתִיקָה אֲמַאי קָרוּ לֵיהּ עֲמִידָה. אֶלָּא, בְּדִבּוּרָא אִית ז' שַׁיְיפִין דְּמִתְנַעְנְעָן בַּהֲדֵיהּ, לִבָּא. רֵיאָה. קָנֶה. לָשׁוֹן. שִׁנַּיִם. שִׂפְוָון. בָּשָׂר. וּבִשְׁתִיקָה קַיְימוּ בְּקִיּוּמַיְיהוּ, בְּלָא נִעְנוּעָא. וע״ד קָרֵי לַשְׁתִּיקָה עֲמִידָה.

296. If you wonder why silence is referred to by standing, HE REPLIES it is because during speech, there are seven limbs that move WHILE TALKING, which are the heart, lung, voice pipe, tongue, teeth, lips and flesh. When silenced, they stay in their position without moving. Therefore, he calls silence standing.

297. דְּהָא רַב הַמְנוּנָא סָבָא אָמַר, יִשְׁלַח עֶזְרְךָ מִקֹּדֶשׁ וְגו'. מִקְדָּשׁ, דָּא קְדוּשׁ יָדַיִם. וּמִצִּיּוֹן יִסְעָדֶךָּ, דָּא הַמּוֹצִיא, דְּאִיהוּ סָעִיד לִבָּא דְּבַר נָשׁ. יִזְכֹּר כָּל מִנְחֹתֶיךָ, כָּל לְאַסְגָּאָה מִלָּה אַחֲרָא, דָּא נְטִילַת יָדַיִם בַּתְרַיְיתָא. וְעוֹלָתְךָ יְדַשְּׁנֶה סֶלָה, דָּא בִּרְכַּת הַמָּזוֹן בִּזְמוּן. וְאִי אַתְּ עָבֵיד כֵּן, יִתֵּן לְךָ כִלְבָבֶךָ וְכָל עֲצָתְךָ יְמַלֵּא. וּבְשַׁבָּת מִקְדָּשׁ, דָּא קְדוּשָׁא רַבָּא. וְעַל מִלָּה דָּא, אִתְעַטְּרוּ צַדִּיקַיָּיא בְּגַן עֵדֶן, מִשַּׁבָּת לְשַׁבָּת אַחֲרָא.

297. (THE BEGINNING IS MISSING...) because Rav Hamnuna Saba (the elder) said, "May He send you help from the sanctuary..." (Tehilim 20:4-5); the sanctuary is the sanctifying of the hands, MEANING THE FIRST WASHING BEFORE THE MEAL. "And strengthen you out of Zion": That is the blessing on the bread, which satisfies the heart of a person. "May He remember all your offerings": "All" indicates something else in addition, which is the washing of the hands at the end, MEANING THE LAST WATERS. "And accept

with favor your burnt offering": That is blessing after the meal in the company of the required quorum. If you do so, "May He grant you your heart's desire, and fulfill all your counsel" and on Shabbat, THE WORD "sanctuary" alludes to the great sanctification (Heb. *kiddush*) IN THE MORNING. About this matter, the righteous in the Garden of Eden were adorned with crowns, from one Shabbat to the next Shabbat...(THE END IS MISSING).

45. "Behold, His reward is with Him, and His hire before Him"

A Synopsis

The spirit talks about the future when the Shechinah will ascend from the mount of Avarim and proclaim the good tidings to the world. God will proclaim rewards for everyone according to their deeds, and all the idol worshipers will see the good reward of the righteous. When Jerusalem is raised the righteous in the Garden of Eden will have additional joy. The soul who has new interpretations of the Torah will be praised, and his father will be crowned for his sake.

298. תּוּ פָּתַח וְאָמַר, עַל הַר גָּבוֹהַ עֲלִי לָךְ מְבַשֶּׂרֶת צִיּוֹן וְגוֹ'. עַל הַר גָּבוֹהַ, הַאי וַדַּאי הַר הָעֲבָרִים, אֲתַר דְּמֹשֶׁה אִתְקְבַר. וְהָא אוּקְמוּהָ, דִּשְׁכִינְתָּא תִּסַלֵּק לְתַמָּן, וּתְבַשֵּׂר עָלְמָא. אֲבָל כֹּלָּא אִיהוּ, מְבַשֶּׂרֶת צִיּוֹן, דָּא אִיהִי חֶפְצִי בָּהּ, אִתְּתָא דְּנָתָן בַּר דָּוִד. אִימָא אִיהִי דִּמְשִׁיחָא, מְנַחֵם בַּ"ר עֲמִיאֵ"ל, וְאִיהִי תֵּיפוֹק וּתְבַשֵּׂר, וְאִיהִי בִּכְלָלָא דִּמְבַשֶּׂרֶת צִיּוֹן.

298. In addition, he opened the discussion saying, "You that bring good tidings to Zion, get you up into the high mountain..." (Yeshayah 40:9). "Into the high mountain" definitely means the mountain of Avarim, AT which Moses was buried. We have already explained that the Shechinah will ascend from there and will proclaim the good tidings to the world. However, she includes everything, MEANING THE EXPRESSION: "GOOD TIDINGS TO ZION" COMPRISES THE VARIETY OF LITERAL INTERPRETATIONS. "You that bring good tidings to Zion" is Hephzibah, the wife of Nathan son of David, who is the mother of Messiah, Menachem son of Amiel, WHO WAS HER DESCENDANT. She shall go out and bring the tidings ABOUT REDEMPTION and she is part of the general meaning of: "You that bring good tidings to Zion."

299. קָלָא יִשְׁתְּמַע בְּעָלְמָא, וּתְרֵין מַלְכִין יִתְּעָרוּן בְּעָלְמָא, לְאַגָּחָא קְרָבָא, וְיִפּוּק שְׁמָא קַדִּישָׁא עַל עָלְמָא. מַה תְּבַשֵּׂר וְתֵימָא. הִנֵּה יְיָ' אֱלֹהִים בְּחָזָק יָבֹא וּזְרֹעוֹ מֹשְׁלָה לוֹ. הִנֵּה שְׂכָרוֹ אִתּוֹ וּפְעֻלָּתוֹ לְפָנָיו. הִנֵּה שְׂכָרוֹ אִתּוֹ, דְּקוּדְשָׁא בְּרִיךְ הוּא כָּרִיז בְּכָל פָּמַלְיָא דִּלְעֵילָּא, וְיֵימָא

לוֹן, אִתְכְּנָשׁוּ וְדָאִינוּ דִינָא. מַאן דִּמְסַר נִשְׁמָתֵיהּ עַל קְדוּשַׁת שְׁמִי, אַגְרֵיהּ מַאי הוּא. וְאִינוּן יֵימְרוּן כַּךְ וְכַךְ. מַאן דִּסְבִיל כַּמָה חֵרוּפִין וְגִדּוּפִין בְּכָל יוֹמָא עֲלַי, מַהוּ אַגְרֵיהּ. אִינוּן אַמְרֵי כַּךְ. מַאן דְּאִתְעֲנָשׁ בְּכָל יוֹמָא עֲלַי, מַהוּ אַגְרֵיהּ. אִינוּן אַמְרֵי כַּךְ. הה״ד, הִנֵּה שְׂכָרוֹ אִתּוֹ וּפְעוּלָּתוֹ לְפָנָיו.

299. A voice will be heard around the world and two kings in the world will get aroused to wage battle. THEN, the Holy Name will emerge TO REIGN over the world. What tidings will she bear and declare? That is "Behold, Hashem Elohim, will come with might, and His arm shall rule for Him: behold, His reward is with Him, and His hire before Him" (Yeshayah 40:10). "Behold, His reward is with Him" means that the Holy One, blessed be He, will proclaim for the entire entourage above and command them to assemble and hold court. 'Whoever gave his soul for the sake of My name's sanctity, what is his reward? They will pronounce that much and so much. Whoever suffered so many disparaging remarks and curses for My sake, what is his reward? They will pronounce, it is this. Whoever was daily punished for My sake, what is his reward? And they will say, it is this.' That is the meaning of: "Behold, His reward is with Him, and His hire before Him."

300. מַהוּ וּפְעוּלָּתוֹ. אֶלָּא כְּמָה דִכְתִּיב, מָה רַב טוּבְךָ וְגוֹ׳. פָּעַלְתָּ לַחוֹסִים בָּךְ. דָּא הוּא פְּעוּלָּתוֹ. נֶגֶד בְּנֵי אָדָם מַהוּ. אֶלָּא נֶגֶד עכו״ם. אֲשֶׁר צָפַנְתָּ לִירֵאֶיךָ, מַהוּ אֲשֶׁר צָפַנְתָּ. וְכִי מַאן יִגְזוֹל וְיִטּוֹל מִן יְדוֹי, מַה דְּהוּא בָּעֵי לְמֵיהַב, דִּכְתִּיב צָפַנְתָּ.

300. HE INQUIRES: What is the meaning of: "And His hire (also: 'deed')"? HE REPLIES: It is as written: "Oh how great is Your goodness, which You have laid up for those who fear You; which You have performed for those who trust in You" (Tehilim 31:20). That is his deed. What is the meaning of: "In the sight of the sons of man"? (Ibid.). HE REPLIES: It means in the sight of those idol worshipers, THAT ALL OF THEM WILL SEE THE GOOD REWARD OF THE RIGHTEOUS. In "which You have laid up for those who fear You," what is the meaning of, "which You have laid up"? Who would want to rob and take away what He wishes to grant, as written "laid up"? AND WHY WOULD HE NEED TO HIDE IT?

301. אֶלָּא פּוּק וְחָמֵי עוֹבָדִין דְּרַחֲמָנוּ דְּעָבֵד קוּדְשָׁא בְּרִיךְ הוּא, בְּמַה דְּאִיהוּ מָחֵי, בֵּיהּ יָהִיב אַסְוָותָא. בְּמַה מָחֵי בִּשְׂמָאלָא, בִּימִינָא קָרִיב, וּבִשְׂמָאלָא מָחֵי. בְּמַה דְּמָחֵי, בֵּיהּ יָהִיב אַסְוָותָא לְעוֹלָם, כְּתִיב מִצָּפוֹן תִּפָּתַח הָרָעָה, וּבְצָפוֹן מָחֵי. דְּמִתַּמָּן נָפְקֵי כָּל דִּינִין וְכָל גְּזֵירֵי קַשְׁיָין. וּבֵיהּ שָׁרֵי כָּל אֲגַר טַב, וְכָל טִיבוּ, דְּזַמִּין קוּדְשָׁא בְּרִיךְ הוּא לְמֵיהַב לְיִשְׂרָאֵל. לִזְמִנָא דְּאָתֵי, קָרֵי קוּדְשָׁא בְּרִיךְ הוּא לַצָּפוֹן, וְיֵימָא לֵיהּ, בָּךְ יָהַבִית כָּל טִיבוּ, וְכָל אֲגַר טוֹב לִבְנַי, דְּסַבְלוּ כַּמָה בִּישִׁין בְּהַאי עָלְמָא, עַל קְדוּשַׁת שְׁמִי. הַב אַגְרִין טָבִין דְּיָהֲבִית בָּךְ.

301. HE REPLIES: Just go and see the compassionate action that the Holy One, blessed be He, takes, since, when He beats someone, He therein provides a remedy. How does He hurt? With the left, since He draws near with the right and through the left He inflicts blows. Behold: through that which He uses to hurt, He also brings the remedy, since it is written: "Out of the north the evil shall break forth" (Yirmeyah 1:14). THAT IS THE LEFT, since He hurls the blows at the left. From there, all the judgments and harsh edicts emanate and in it dwell all good recompense and kindness that the Holy One, blessed be He, has destined to grant Yisrael. In the future to come, the Holy One, blessed be He, will call on the north, THAT IS LEFT, and tell it, 'In you I have provided all benefits and good wages to My children who have suffered so many calamities in this world for the sake of the sanctity of My name. Pay out all the good wages that I have entrusted to you!'

302. הה"ד אוֹמַר לַצָּפוֹן תֵּנִי וּלְתֵימָן אַל תִּכְלָאִי וְגוֹ'. וְכִי אָרְחָא הָכִי הוּא דְּדָרוֹם, לְמִמְנַע בִּרְכָאן, וְהָא כָּל בִּרְכָאן מִסִּטְרָא דְּדָרוֹם, וְכָל טָבִין דְּעָלְמָא מִדָּרוֹם נָפְקֵי, וְאִיהוּ אָמַר לְתֵימָן אַל תִּכְלָאִי.

302. This is what it says: "I will say to the north, Give up; and to the south, Keep not back..." (Yeshayah 43:6). HE ASKS: Is this then the manner of the south, WHICH IS RIGHT, to deprive blessings? Aren't all the blessings from the south side, and good comes from the south? Yet He says to the south, "Keep not back."

303. אֶלָּא בְּהַהִיא שַׁעֲתָא, יִתְעַר קוּדְשָׁא בְּרִיךְ הוּא לְאַבְרָהָם, וְיֵימָא

לֵיהּ קוּם, דְּהָא מָטָא זִמְנָא דַּאֲנָא פָּרִיק לִבְנָךְ, לְמֵיהַב לוֹן אֲגַר טָב, עַל כָּל מַה דְּסָבְלוּ בְּגָלוּתָא. וּמִגּוֹ דְּאַבְרָהָם הֲוָה בִּזְבִינוּ דִּלְהוֹן, דִּכְתִּיב אִם לֹא כִּי צוּרָם מְכָרָם, דָּא אַבְרָהָם. הֲוָה לֵיהּ כְּמַאן דְּלָא טָב בְּעֵינוֹי, וְאַחֲמֵי גַּרְמֵיהּ, כְּמַאן דְּבָעֵי דְּיִלְקוּן עַל חוֹבֵיהוֹן יַתִּיר, וְיֵימָא גְּבוֹ מֵחוֹבֵיהוֹן, גְּבוֹ מֵחֲטָאֵיהוֹן. אָ"ל קוּדְשָׁא בְּרִיךְ הוּא לְאַבְרָהָם, יְדַעְנָא כֹּלָּא אִיהוּ מַה דְּאָמְרַת לְאַנְפִּין. אֲנָא אוֹף הָכִי לְאַנְפִּין. אַל תִּכְלָאִי, אֲנָא בָּעֵי לְפַיְּיסָא לָךְ עַל בְּנָךְ. לָא תִּמְנַע טִיבוּ מִנְּהוֹן, לָא תִּמְנַע אֲגַר טָב מִנְּהוֹן, כַּמָּה וְכַמָּה סָבְלוּ עַל חוֹבֵיהוֹן, וּבְגִינֵי כָּךְ אוֹמַר לַצָּפוֹן תֵּנִי. וְהַיְינוּ אֲשֶׁר צָפַנְתָּ, וְדָא הוּא מִלָּה דְּהַהִיא מְבַשֶּׂרֶת.

303. HE REPLIES: It is only that, at that period, the Holy One, blessed be He, will awaken Abraham and tell him, Rise, because the time has arrived in which I will redeem your children and grant them good compensation for all they suffered in the exile. This is due to the fact that Abraham was involved in their sale TO THE EXILE as is written: "Unless their Rock had sold them" (Devarim 32:30), which refers back to Abraham. He therefore acted as if this was not favorable in his eyes and showed himself as if he wished them to be hurt more for their iniquities, saying a payback should be collected for their iniquities and sins. The Holy One, blessed be He, said to Abraham, 'I am aware that whatever you said was just said on the surface, BUT NOT MEANT TRUTHFULLY OUT OF YOUR HEART. I too will be like that, I'LL DEAL WITH YOU on the surface AND SAY TO YOU, "Keep not back." I wish to please you for the sake of your children. Do not deprive them of kindness and do not deprive them of good compensation. They suffered so much for their iniquities. Therefore, "I will say to the north, Give up"', SO THE NORTH WILL PROVIDE GOOD WAGES. EVERYTHING ELSE, THE SOUTH WILL NOT KEEP BACK and that is the meaning of: "which You have laid up (Heb. *tzafanta*)," WHICH IS DERIVED FROM NORTH (HEB. *TZAFON*), WHICH PROVIDES EVERYTHING. This is the good tidings that she brings, MEANING WHAT IT SAYS ABOVE: "YOU THAT BRING GOOD TIDINGS TO ZION, GET YOU UP INTO THE HIGH MOUNTAIN..."

304. וְתוּ תְּבַשֵּׂר זִמְנָא תִּנְיָינָא, בְּשַׁעֲתָא דִּשְׁכִינְתָּא תִּסַּלֵּק עַל הַהוּא טוּרָא עִלָּאָה, וְתֵהַךְ וּתְבַשֵּׂר לַאֲבָהָן, מִיַּד תֵּהַךְ לִירוּשְׁלֵם, וְתֶחֱמֵי לָה

בְּחָרְבָּנָא. תֵּיעוֹל לְצִיּוֹן, וְתַמָּן תְּקַרְקֵר קִירָא כְּמִלְקַדְמִין, עַל אֲתָר בֵּי
מוֹתְבָהּ, וְעַל יְקָרָא דִּילָהּ בְּהַהוּא אֲתָר. וְתַמָּן אוֹמִיאַת, דְּלָא תִּיטוֹל
מִתַּמָּן, וְלָא תִּפּוֹק, עַד דְּקוּדְשָׁא בְּרִיךְ הוּא יִפְרוֹק לִבְנָהָא, וְדָא חֶפְצִי
בָהּ תְּבַשֵּׂר כְּמִלְקַדְמִין וְאָמְרַת, צַהֲלִי וָרֹנִּי יוֹשֶׁבֶת צִיּוֹן כִּי גָדוֹל בְּקִרְבֵּךְ
וְגוֹ'. מַאי גָדוֹל בְּקִרְבֵּךְ. דָּא קוּדְשָׁא בְּרִיךְ הוּא דְּאִיהוּ אָתֵי לְגַבָּהּ,
לְאָקָמָא לָהּ מֵעַפְרָא, וְיֵימָא לָהּ הִתְנַעֲרִי מֵעָפָר קוּמִי שְׁבִי יְרוּשָׁלָם.
יְרוּשָׁלַם אִיהִי, וִירוּשָׁלַם שְׁמָהּ וַדַּאי.

304. In addition, she will bring tidings for the second time when the Shechinah will be on that high mountain, and she will go with the tidings to the patriarchs. Swiftly, THE SHECHINAH will visit Jerusalem and see its destruction. She will enter Zion and there She will batter the wall as before, over Her original dwelling house and the glory SHE ENJOYED at that location. And she will swear that she will not leave there until the Holy One, blessed be He, redeems Her children. The same Hephzibah will bring tidings as before and declare, "Cry out and shout, you inhabitant of Zion: for great is the Holy One of Yisrael in the midst of you" (Yeshayah 12:6). What is "great...in the midst of you"? That is the Holy One, blessed be He, who comes to Her to raise her from the dust and say to Her, "Shake yourself from the dust; arise, and sit down, O Jerusalem" (Yeshayah 52:2). THE SHECHINAH is Jerusalem and Jerusalem is assuredly Her name.

305. וּבְדָא אוֹף הָכִי, כַּמָּה חֶדּוּ עַל חֶדּוּ הֲוֵי לְצַדִּיקַיָּיא בְּגַן עֵדֶן. וּבְגִ"כ
זַכָּאָה אִיהוּ, מַאן דְּנִשְׁמָתֵיהּ בְּשַׁבָּת אַסְהִידַת קַמֵּי מַלְכָּא, עַל חִדּוּשָׁא
דְּאוֹרַיְיתָא, דְּקוּדְשָׁא בְּרִיךְ הוּא, וְכָל פָּמַלְיָא דִּילֵיהּ, וְכָל אִינּוּן נִשְׁמָתִין
דְּצַדִּיקַיָּיא דַּהֲווֹ בְּגַן עֵדֶן, כֻּלְּהוּ מִתְעַטְּרִין בְּהַהוּא מִלָּה.

305. (THAT IS THE COMPLETION OF THE ABOVE ARTICLE FROM VERSES 290-296). By this too, how much additional joy will the righteous have in the Garden of Eden? As a result of this, praised is he whose soul bears witness on the Shabbat in the presence of the King with the new interpretations of the Torah IT SAID. Through this, the Holy One, blessed be He, and His entire entourage above and all these righteous in the Garden of Eden are adorned with that NOVEL INTERPRETATION.

306. תּוּ שְׁמַעֲנָא בּוּצִינָא קַדִּישָׁא, דְּכַמָּה יְקַר עַל יְקַר, וַעֲטָרָה עַל עֲטָרָה, מְעַטְּרָן לַאֲבוּהּ דְּהַהוּא ב"נ תַּמָּן, בְּשַׁעֲתָא דְּאָמַר קוּדְשָׁא בְּרִיךְ הוּא, אִתְכְּנָשִׁי לְמִשְׁמַע חִדּוּשָׁא וּמִלִּין חַדְתִּין דְּאוֹרַיְיתָא, מִשְּׁמֵיהּ דִּפְלוֹנִי בַּר פְּלוֹנִי, כַּמָּה אִינּוּן דְּנַשְׁקִין עַל רֵישֵׁיהּ. כַּמָּה צַדִּיקַיָּיא מְעַטְּרִין לֵיהּ, כַּד נַחְתִּין. זַכָּאָה חוּלְקֵיהוֹן דְּכָל אִינּוּן דְּמִשְׁתַּדְּלִין בְּאוֹרַיְיתָא, יוֹמָא דְּשַׁבְּתָא מִשְּׁאַר יוֹמִין.

עד כאן רב מתיבתא

306. Additionally, I heard from the Holy Luminary. How much glory upon glory and adornment upon adornment they crown the father of that man, WHOSE SOUL BEARS WITNESS ABOUT THE INNOVATIVE TORAH INTERPRETATIONS. During that time, the Holy One, blessed be He, says TO HIS ENTOURAGE, 'Gather to listen to new innovative matters in the Torah of so-and-so, son of so-and-so', BECAUSE AT THAT POINT, THE HOLY ONE, BLESSED BE HE, MENTIONS THE FATHER OF THE INNOVATOR. How many are they that kiss on the head OF THE INNOVATOR'S FATHER? How many righteous adorn him when they descend? Praised is the lot of all those who study and deal in the Torah, and especially on the Shabbat even more than the rest of the weekdays.

(up to here spoke the head of the Yeshivah).

46. "A cake of the first of your dough for a gift"

A Synopsis

We hear of the inner meaning of the offering of the cake (chalah) of the first of the dough. We are told that chalah is the Shechinah, and we learn that paternal merit ends for the wicked as they receive their reward in this world and they do not have Chassadim. The Shechinah indicates merit for her children when she receives from the right, where the 248 positive commandments are.

רעיא מהימנא

307. רֵאשִׁית עֲרִיסוֹתֵיכֶם חַלָּה תָּרִימוּ וְגוֹ', פִּקּוּדָא דָּא לְהַפְרִישׁ חַלָּה לַכֹּהֵן. חַלָּ"ה הָכִי חוּשְׁבָּנֵיהּ, מ"ג בֵּיצִים, וְחוֹמֶשׁ בֵּיצָה, חַד מֵחֲמֵשׁ. וְאִית חוֹמֶשׁ חַד מִן חַמְשִׁין, דְּאִיהוּ ן'. וְדָא סִימָן מָג"ן, דְּאִיהוּ מִיכָא"ל גַּבְרִיאֵ"ל נוּרִיאֵ"ל. חַלָּה, שְׁכִינְתָּא. דְּבַאֲתַר דְּאִלֵּין מַלְאָכִין תַּמָּן, אֲבָהָן תַּמָּן. וּבַאֲתַר דַּאֲבָהָן תַּמָּן, שְׁכִינְתָּא תַּמָּן. וּבָהּ וַיְחַל, בָּהּ צַלִּינָא, הה"ד וַיְחַל מֹשֶׁה אֶת פְּנֵי יְיָ' אֱלֹהָיו. אֲדֹנָי יֱדֹוִד אַתָּה הַחִלּוֹתָ לְהַרְאוֹת אֶת עַבְדְּךָ. וּבָהּ חַלָּה זְכוּת אָבוֹת. וּבָהּ תָּמָה זְכוּת אָבוֹת לָרְשָׁעִים. דַּהֲווֹ מְקַבְּלִים אַגְרַיְיהוּ בְּהַאי עָלְמָא.

Ra'aya Meheimna (the Faithful Shepherd)

307. "You shall offer up a cake (Heb. *chalah*) of the first of your dough for a gift" (Bemidbar 15:20). This commandment is to separate a piece of dough for the priest. *Chalahs'* numerical value is *Mem Gimel* (= 53). THIS INDICATES THAT DOUGH DOES NOT ACQUIRE THE SIZE WHEN *CHALAH* IS TO BE REMOVED FROM IT, UNLESS IT CONTAINS 43 and 1/5 of an eggs's size OF AN EGG. There are times when fifth means one of fifty, which is final *Nun* (= 50). This is derived from *Mem Gimel final Nun*, which is the initials of Michael, Gabriel and Nuriel, WHO CORRESPOND TO CHESED, GVURAH AND TIFERET OF ZEIR ANPIN. *Chalah* is the Shechinah, for wherever these angels *MEM GIMEL FINAL NUN*, are, there are the patriarchs, WHO ARE CHESED, GVURAH AND TIFERET. Wherever the patriarchs are, THAT IS, CHESED, GVURAH AND TIFERET, there the Shechinah is found, SINCE CHESED, GVURAH AND TIFERET ARE THE SECRET OF THREE COLUMNS AND MALCHUT RECEIVES FROM THEM. And in her, IN

MALCHUT, one beseeches, foin her one prays. SHE IS REFERRED TO AS PRAYER, as written: "And Moses besought (Heb. *vayechal*) Hashem his Elohim..." (Devarim 3:24) and "O Hashem Elohim, You have begun (Heb. *hachilota*) to show Your servant..." (Shemot 32:11). In her *Chalah*, NAMELY, the paternal merits begin, WHICH IS DERIVED FROM *HACHILOTA*. In her, paternal merit ends for the wicked, SINCE PATERNAL MERIT DOES NOT STAND FOR THEM as they receive their reward in this world.

308. דְּמִסְטְרָא דִּימִינָא, דְּתַמָּן י' דְּאִיהוּ חָכְמָה, שְׁרוּתָא דִּשְׁמָא דִּידְוָד, דְּאִיהוּ אַחְזֵי זְכוּתָא עַל בְּנָהָא מִימִינָא, דְּתַמָּן רמ"ח פִּקּוּדִין דַּעֲשֵׂה. מִסְטְרָא דְּאָת ה' בַּתְרָאָה, דְּאִיהִי לִשְׂמָאלָא דִּגְבוּרָה, דְּתַמָּן לֹא תַעֲשֶׂה, דְּאִינּוּן שס"ה, דְּתַמָּן נְדוֹנִין רְשָׁעִים גְּמוּרִים, תַּמָּה לוֹן זְכוּת אָבוֹת, וְאִתְהַפָּךְ לוֹן שֵׁם יְהֹוָ"ה, הֹוֵ"י. וְאוֹלִיפְנָא מֵהָמָן הָרָשָׁע, וְכָל זֶה אֵינֶנּוּ שֹׁוֶה לִי.

ע"כ רעיא מהימנא

308. Since from the right side, where the Yud is, that is Chochmah, BECAUSE CHOCHMAH IS AT THE RIGHT AND BINAH IS AT THE LEFT, THAT ARE *YUD-HEI*, which is the beginning of the Name Yud Hei Vav Hei, THE SHECHINAH indicates merit for Her children WHEN SHE RECEIVES from the right, where the 248 positive commands are, THAT IS THE SECRET OF CHASSADIM, and from the side of the last Hei OF HEI VAV YUD HEI, that is to the left of Gvurah, SINCE MALCHUT IS ERECTED FROM THE LEFT SIDE. PRIOR TO THAT, SHE RECEIVES FROM THE RIGHT, where the negative commands exist, which total 365 THAT ARE ON THE LEFT, where the totally wicked are sentenced. FOR THEM, paternal merit has ended, BECAUSE THEY STILL DO NOT HAVE CHASSADIM FROM CHESED, GVURAH AND TIFERET, WHO ARE CALLED FATHERS. The name of Yud Hei Vav Hei is reversed to Hei Vav Hei Yud, MEANING BACKWARDS, INDICATING JUDGMENT. We learn this from the wicked Haman, BECAUSE HE SAID, "Yet all this avails me nothing" (Ester 5:13). THE LETTERS AT THE END OF THE WORDS FORM HEI VAV HEI YUD, WHICH IS AN INDICATION OF JUDGMENTS.

End of Ra'aya Meheimna

47. Moses' birth

A Synopsis

Rabbi Chizkiyah says that God gave Yisrael the Torah and also faithful prophets to lead them. All the prophets beheld God's glory from a high place, but not as near as Moses, who was closer to God than any of them. Rabbi Chizkiyah interprets the scripture beginning "And there went a man of the house of Levi, and took to wife the daughter of Levi," as meaning that Zeir Anpin joined with Malchut. We learn that the Shechinah hid Moses for three months because he was present above in the higher realm before he descended to this world. She allowed Moses to sail among the angels because he was later destined to go up among them to receive the Torah. We are told that the daughter of Pharaoh came from the left aspect of harsh judgment, and that she saw the child Moses stamped with the signature of Zeir Anpin and Malchut when she found him in the box of papyrus. From all this Rabbi Shimon derives that the souls of the righteous come from a high place, and that the soul has a father and a mother. Everything comes from and exists from male and female; Malchut is seen to be the mother of the soul of the first man.

309. וַיֹּאמֶר יְיָ׳ אֶל מֹשֶׁה לֵּאמֹר דַּבֵּר אֶל בְּנֵי יִשְׂרָאֵל וְגוֹ׳ וְעָשׂוּ לָהֶם צִיצִת עַל כַּנְפֵי בִגְדֵיהֶם לְדֹרוֹתָם וְגוֹ׳. ר׳ חִזְקִיָּה פָּתַח, וַיַּרְאֵנִי אֶת יְהוֹשֻׁעַ הַכֹּהֵן הַגָּדוֹל וְגוֹ׳. כַּמָּה זַכָּאִין אִינּוּן יִשְׂרָאֵל, דְּקוּדְשָׁא בְּרִיךְ הוּא בָּעֵי בִּיקָרְהוֹן עַל כָּל בְּנֵי עָלְמָא, וְיָהַב לוֹן אוֹרַיְיתָא קַדִּישָׁא, וְיָהַב לוֹן נְבִיאֵי מְהֵימְנֵי, דִּמְדַבְּרֵי לְהוּ בְּאוֹרַיְיתָא, בְּאֹרַח קְשׁוֹט.

309. "And Hashem spoke to Moses, saying, 'Speak to the children of Yisrael, and bid them that they make them fringes in the corners of their garments throughout their generations...'" (Bemidbar 15:37-38). Rabbi Chizkiyah opened the discussion saying, "And He showed me Joshua the High Priest..." (Zecharyah 3:1). How happy are Yisrael that He desires their glory above all the people, has granted them the Holy Torah and given them faithful prophets that lead them according to the Torah on the true path.

310. תָּא חֲזֵי, כָּל נְבִיאֵי וּנְבִיאֵי דְּאוֹקִים קוּדְשָׁא בְּרִיךְ הוּא לְיִשְׂרָאֵל, כֻּלְּהוּ אִתְגְּלֵי קוּדְשָׁא בְּרִיךְ הוּא עֲלַיְיהוּ, בְּדַרְגִּין עִלָּאִין קַדִּישִׁין, וְחָמוּ

זִיו יְקָרָא קַדִּישָׁא דְּמַלְכָּא מֵאֲתַר עִלָּאָה, אֲבָל לָא קָרִיב כְּמֹשֶׁה, דַּהֲוָה
קָרִיב לְמַלְכָּא יַתִּיר מִכֹּלָּא, דְּהָא זַכָּאָה חוּלָקֵיהּ יַתִּיר מִכָּל בְּנֵי עָלְמָא,
דְּעָלֵיהּ כְּתִיב, פֶּה אֶל פֶּה אֲדַבֶּר בּוֹ וּמַרְאֶה וְלֹא בְחִידוֹת. וּשְׁאָר נְבִיאֵי,
הֲווֹ חָמָאן מֵאֲתַר רְחִיקָא, כְּמָה דְּאַתְּ אָמַר מֵרָחוֹק יְיָ' נִרְאָה לִי.

310. Come and see all the various groups of prophets that the Holy One, blessed be He, set up for Yisrael. The Holy One, blessed be He, revealed Himself to them all on the highest holy levels and they beheld the King's holy radiance of Glory from a lofty location – but not as near as Moses, who was closer to the King than any of them since his lot was more blessed than that of any other man. About him, it is written: "With him I speak mouth to mouth, manifestly, and not in dark speeches" (Bemidbar 12:8). The rest of the prophets saw from a distant place, as you say, "Hashem appeared of old (also: 'from afar') to me" (Yirmeyah 31:2).

311. א"ר חִזְקִיָּה, הָכִי אוֹלִיפְנָא, כְּתִיב וַיֵּלֶךְ אִישׁ מִבֵּית לֵוִי וַיִּקַּח אֶת
בַּת לֵוִי. וַיֵּלֶךְ אִישׁ: דָּא קוּדְשָׁא בְּרִיךְ הוּא כד"א יְיָ' אִישׁ מִלְחָמָה.
מִבֵּית לֵוִי: דָּא קוּדְשָׁא בְּרִיךְ הוּא, אֲתַר דְּחָכְמָה עִלָּאָה, וְהַהוּא זֹהַר
מִתְחַבְּרָן כַּחֲדָא, דְּלָא מִתְפָּרְשָׁן לְעָלְמִין. מִבֵּית לֵוִי: דְּאַשְׁרֵי לִוְיָתָן כָּל
חִידוּ בְּעָלְמָא, הה"ד לִוְיָתָן זֶה יָצַרְתָּ לְשַׂחֶק בּוֹ. וַיִּקַּח אֶת בַּת לֵוִי, דָּא
קוּדְשָׁא בְּרִיךְ הוּא, אֲתַר דִּנְהִירוּ דְּסִיהֲרָא נָהִיר.

311. Rabbi Chizkiyah said, This is how I learned it. It is written: "And there went a man of the house of Levi, and took to wife the daughter of Levi" (Shemot 2:1). "And there went a man": That is the Holy One, blessed be He, THAT IS ZEIR ANPIN, as it says, "Hashem is a man of war" (Shemot 15:3). "The house of Levi" is the Holy One, blessed be He, WHO WENT FROM the area where supernal Chochmah and that bright radiance, WHICH IS SUPERNAL BINAH, join together and never separate. HE INTERPRETS "LEVI" AS DERIVED FROM ATTACHMENT, AS IN 'LIVYUT' (ENG. 'ACCOMPANIMENT'). ANOTHER EXPLANATION OF: "Of the house of Levi" is that the Leviathan, THAT IS YESOD OF ZEIR ANPIN, has inspired all enjoyment in the world AND HE INTERPRETS "LEVI" AS DERIVED FROM LEVIATHAN, as is written: "There is the Leviathan, whom You have made to play therein" (Tehilim 104:26). "And took to wife the daughter of Levi": That is the Holy One, blessed be He, which is the place where the moon is bright, THAT BEING MALCHUT.

312. וַתַּהַר הָאִשָּׁה וַתֵּלֶד בֵּן. הָאִשָּׁה וַדַּאי, כד"א לְזֹאת יִקָּרֵא אִשָּׁה. בְּקַדְמֵיתָא בַּת לֵוִי, הָכִי הוּא וַדַּאי. וְכִי בַּת לֵוִי בְּקַדְמֵיתָא, וְהַשְׁתָּא אִשָּׁה. אֶלָּא הָכִי אוֹלִיפְנָא, אִתְּתָא עַד לָא אִזְדַּוְּוגַת, אִתְקְרִיאַת בַּת פְּלוֹנִי, בָּתַר דְּאִזְדַּוְּוגַת. אִתְקְרֵי אִשָּׁה, וְהָכָא, בַּת וְאִשָּׁה, כֹּלָּא בְּחַד דַּרְגָּא הִיא.

312. "And the woman conceived, and bore a son" (Shemot 2:2). Surely, "the woman" IS MALCHUT, as it says, "she (Heb. zot) shall be called woman" (Beresheet 2:23) AND "ZOT" IS THE NAME OF MALCHUT. At first, SHE IS CALLED "the daughter of Levi" and certainly it is so. Why did he first CALL HER the daughter of Levi and now a woman? HE RESPONDS: This is what we have learned. Before she is married, a woman is referred to as the daughter of so-and-so, but after she is married, she is referred to as a woman. Here too, daughter and woman pertain to the same level, MEANING MALCHUT. HOWEVER, BEFORE HE TOOK HER IN MARRIAGE, SHE WAS REFERRED TO AS THE DAUGHTER OF LEVI, AND AFTER THAT, A WOMAN.

313. וַתִּצְפְּנֵהוּ ג' יְרָחִים, אִלֵּין תְּלַת יַרְחִין דְּדִינָא קַשְׁיָא שַׁרְיָא בְּעָלְמָא. וּמַאי נִינְהוּ. תַּמּוּ"ז וְאָ"ב וְטֵבֵ"ת. מַאי קָא מַשְׁמַע לָן. דְּעַד דְּלָא נָחַת מֹשֶׁה לְעָלְמָא, שְׁכִיחַ הֲוָה הוּא לְעֵילָּא, וְעַל דָּא אִזְדַּוְּוגַת בֵּיהּ שְׁכִינְתָּא מִן יוֹמָא דְּאִתְיְלִיד. מִכָּאן אָמַר רַבִּי שִׁמְעוֹן, רוּחֵיהוֹן דְּצַדִּיקַיָּיא שְׁכִיחִין אִינּוּן לְעֵילָּא, עַד לָא יֵחֲתוּן לְעָלְמָא.

313. "She hid him three months" (Shemot 2:2): These are the three months when heavy Judgment rests in the world. Which ones are they? Tamuz, Av and Tevet. AND THEREFORE, THE SHECHINAH HID HIM. HE ASKS: What is it trying to tell us by this? HE REPLIES: IT LETS US KNOW that before Moses went down to the world, he was above. Therefore, the Shechinah joined him since the day he was born, AND PROTECTED HIM. From here, Rabbi Shimon took it to say that the spirits of the righteous are above before they descend into this world.

314. וְלֹא יָכְלָה עוֹד הַצְּפִינוֹ וַתִּקַח לוֹ וְגוֹ' מַאי וַתִּקַח לוֹ תֵּיבַת גֹּמֶא. דְּחָפַת לֵיהּ בְּסִימָנָהָא, לְמֶהֱוֵי נָטִיר מֵאִינּוּן נוּנֵי יַמָּא, דְּשָׁאטִין בְּיַמָּא רַבָּא, כְּמָה דִּכְתִיב שָׁם רֶמֶשׂ וְאֵין מִסְפָּר. וְהִיא חָפַת לֵיהּ לְמֶהֱוֵי נָטִיר מִנַּיְיהוּ בְּחָפּוּ דְּסִטְרָא דְּיוֹבְלָא יַקִּירָא בִּתְרֵי גַּוְונִין, בְּחִיוָור וְאוּכָם, וְאָנַח לֵיהּ לְמֹשֶׁה לְמֵישַׁט בֵּינַיְיהוּ, לְאִשְׁתְּמוֹדַע בֵּינֵיהוֹן, בְּגִין דִּזַמִּין הוּא לְסַלְקָא בֵּינַיְיהוּ, זִמְנָא אַחֲרָא, לְקַבְּלָא אוֹרַיְיתָא.

314. "And when she could no longer hide him" (Ibid. 3). HE ASKS: What is the meaning of: "She took for him a box made of papyrus"? (Ibid). HE REPLIES: She coated it with conserving ingredients to keep it safe from these sea fish, MEANING HIGH ANGELS, that swim in the great ocean, as is written: "Wherein are creeping things innumerable" (Tehilim 104:25). She coated it so that he should be kept from them, with a coat from the precious Jubilee, THAT IS BINAH, in two colors, white and black. THAT IS THE SECRET OF CLAY AND TAR, WHICH CORRESPONDS TO THE TWO COLUMNS, RIGHT AND LEFT, SINCE TAR IS THE SECRET OF THE LEFT, EXCEPT THAT IT IS BLENDED WITH MALCHUT OF THE ATTRIBUTE OF JUDGMENT. THEREFORE, THE RED IN THE LEFT TURNS TO BLACK; THAT IS THE SECRET OF THAT BLACK IS ACTUALLY RED, EXCEPT THAT IT IS DEFECTIVE. She allowed Moses to sail among them, THE ANGELS, and to become known among them, because he was destined to go up among them at a later date to receive the Torah.

315. וַתֵּרֶד בַּת פַּרְעֹה. דָּא הִיא, דְּאַתְיָא מִסִּטְרָא שְׂמָאלָא דְּדִינָא קַשְׁיָא, כְּמָה דְּאִתְּמַר לִרְחוֹץ עַל הַיְאוֹר. עַל הַיְאוֹר דַּיְיקָא, וְלָא עַל הַיָּם. וְאִי תֵּימָא, הָא כְּתִיב וּמַטֶּךָ אֲשֶׁר הִכִּיתָ בּוֹ אֶת הַיְאוֹר. וּמֹשֶׁה לָא הִכָּה אֶלָּא בַּיָּם, וְקַרְיֵיהּ קְרָא יְאוֹר. אֶלָּא יְאוֹר הֲוָה דִּמְחָא אַהֲרֹן עַל יְדָא דְּמֹשֶׁה, וְשַׁוְוַיֵּיהּ קְרָא דְּאִיהוּ עֲבַד.

315. "And the daughter of Pharaoh came down to wash herself at the River" (Shemot 2:5). This DAUGHTER OF PHARAOH came from the left aspect of harsh Judgment, as is written: "To wash herself at the River." "At the River" is exact, instead of "at the sea," SINCE THE SEA INDICATES MALCHUT. HOWEVER, THE RIVER IS HARSH JUDGMENT FROM THE

LEFT SIDE, WHICH THE EGYPTIANS HAVE MADE THEIR DEITY. If you wonder about this, that it is written: "And your rod, with which you smote the river" (Shemot 17:5), although Moses never struck the river but rather the sea. The verse refers to it as river INDICATING THAT THE TERM RIVER IS NOT ACCURATE. HE REPLIES: It is indeed the River which Aaron struck under Moses direction, and the scripture assigned it as if Moses himself did the striking.

316. כְּהַאי גַּוְונָא וַיִּמְלֵא שִׁבְעַת יָמִים אַחֲרֵי הַכּוֹת יְיָ' אֶת הַיְאוֹר, וְאַהֲרֹן הִכָּה, אֶלָּא עַל דָּא דְּאָתָא מִסְּטְרָא דְּקוּדְשָׁא בְּרִיךְ הוּא, קַרְיֵיהּ קְרָא הַכּוֹת יְיָ', לְבָתַר קַרְיֵיהּ בִּשְׁמָא דְּמֹשֶׁה. וְנַעֲרוֹתֶיהָ הוֹלְכוֹת, אִינּוּן שְׁאַר מַשִׁרְיָין דְּאַתְיָין מִסְּטְרָא דָּא.

316. Similarly, "And seven days were completed, after Hashem had smitten the River" (Shemot 7:25). EVEN THOUGH Aaron struck it, it is only because it came from the Holy One, blessed be He, WHO COMMANDED HIM, that the scripture referred to it as: "Hashem had smitten." Later on, it was referred to in the name of Moses, FOR THE SAME REASON. "And her maidens walked along" (Shemot 2:5): These are the rest of the camps that came from that LEFT side.

317. וַתִּפְתַּח וַתִּרְאֵהוּ אֶת הַיֶּלֶד. וַתִּרְאֵהוּ, וַתֵּרֶא מִבָּעֵי לֵיהּ, מַאי וַתִּרְאֵהוּ. וְהָא אָמַר רִבִּי שִׁמְעוֹן לֵית לָךְ מִלָּה בְּאוֹרַיְיתָא, אוֹ אָת חַד בְּאוֹרַיְיתָא, דְּלָא אִית בֵּיהּ רָזִין יַקִּירִין וְעִלָּאִין. אֶלָּא הָכִי אוֹלִיפְנָא, רְשִׁימָא דְּמַלְכָּא וּמַטְרוֹנִיתָא אִשְׁתְּכַחַת בֵּיהּ, וְאִינּוּן רְשִׁימָא דְּוָא"ו הֵ"א, מִיַּד וַתַּחְמוֹל עָלָיו וְגוֹ'. עַד כָּאן לְעֵילָּא. מִכָּאן וּלְהָלְאָה לְתַתָּא, בַּר הַאי קְרָא, דִּכְתִיב וַתֵּתַצַּב אֲחוֹתוֹ מֵרָחוֹק. אֲחוֹתוֹ דְּמַאן. אֲחוֹתוֹ דְּהַאי אִיהוּ, דְּקָרָא לִכְנֶסֶת יִשְׂרָאֵל אֲחוֹתִי, כד"א פִּתְחִי לִי אֲחוֹתִי. מֵרָחוֹק: כד"א, מֵרָחוֹק יְיָ' נִרְאָה לִי.

317. "And when she had opened it, she saw him, the child" (Ibid. 6). HE INQUIRES: What is: "she saw him"? "She saw" was the proper way to use. Why "she saw him"? Didn't Rabbi Shimon say that there was nothing in the Torah, or even one letter in the Torah, that does not contain highly valuable secrets? HE RESPONDS: That is how we have learned. The impression of

the King and the Matron, THAT ARE ZEIR ANPIN AND MALCHUT, THE
SECRET OF VAV-HEI OF YUD HEI VAV HEI, was found upon him, and that
is the impression of Vav-Hei THAT WERE ADDED TO "SHE SAW (HEB.
VATERE)." THEREFORE, IT IS SPELLED "*VATIR'EHU* (ENG. 'SHE SAW
HIM')." Instantly, "she had compassion on him..." (Ibid.). Up to here it
relates to the higher, TO HIGHER REALMS. From here on, IT DISCUSSES
THIS WORLD below, except for this verse, in which is written: "And his
sister stood afar off" (Ibid. 4). HE INQUIRES: Whose sister, AND REPLIES:
The sister of the one, MEANING ZEIR ANPIN, who called the Congregation
of Yisrael my sister, as it says, "Open to me, my sister" (Shir Hashirim 5:2).
"afar off" MEANS as in, "Hashem appeared from afar to me" (Yirmeyah 31:2).

318. מַאי מַשְׁמַע. מַשְׁמַע דְּאִינּוּן זַכָּאִין, עַד דְּלָא נַחְתּוּ לְעָלְמָא,
אִשְׁתְּמוֹדְעָן אִינּוּן לְעֵילָּא לְגַבֵּי כֹּלָּא, וכ״ש מֹשֶׁה. וּמַשְׁמַע דְּנִשְׁמַתְהוֹן
דְּצַדִּיקַיָּיא, אִתְמְשַׁךְ מֵאֲתָר עִלָּאָה, כְּמָה דְּאוֹקִימְנָא. וְרָזָא דְּמִלָּה
אוֹלִיפְנָא, דְּמַשְׁמַע דְּאָב וְאֵם אִית לְנִשְׁמְתָא, כְּמָה דְּאִית אָב וְאֵם
לְגוּפָא, בְּאַרְעָא.

318. HE INQUIRES: What is to be derived FROM THIS PASSAGE? HE
REPLIES: It means that all these righteous, prior to their descent to the
world, are made known to all above. THAT APPLIES TO ALL THE
RIGHTEOUS, and most certainly to Moses. It means that the souls of the
righteous are derived from a lofty place, SINCE "of the house of Levi"
ALLUDES TO SUPERNAL CHOCHMAH AND BINAH, as we have explained.
We learned the secret of the matter, which means that there are a father and
a mother to the soul, as there are a father and mother to the body on earth,
SINCE A MAN IS ZEIR ANPIN AND "DAUGHTER OF LEVI" IS MALCHUT.
AND FROM THEIR UNION, THE SOUL OF MOSES WAS BORN.

319. וּמַשְׁמַע דְּבָכָל סִטְרִין, בֵּין לְעֵילָּא, בֵּין לְתַתָּא, מִדְכַר וְנוּקְבָּא
כֹּלָּא אַתְיָא וְאִשְׁתְּכַח. וְהָא אוּקְמוּהָ רָזָא דִּכְתִיב, תּוֹצִיא הָאָרֶץ נֶפֶשׁ
חַיָּה. הָאָרֶץ, דָּא כְּנֶסֶת יִשְׂרָאֵל. נֶפֶשׁ חַיָּה, נַפְשָׁא דְּאָדָם קַדְמָאָה
עִלָּאָה, כְּמָה דְּאִתְּמַר. אָתָא רִבִּי אַבָּא וּנְשָׁקֵיהּ, אָמַר וַדַּאי שַׁפִּיר קָא
אֲמָרַת, וְהָכָא הוּא כֹּלָּא.

319. It seems on all sides, both above, THE MALE AND FEMALE PRINCIPLES, and below, FATHER AND MOTHER OF THIS WORLD, that is comprised of male and female. That is how the secret of the scripture was explained: "Let the earth bring forth living creatures (Heb. *Nefesh*)" (Beresheet 1:24). "The earth" refers to the Congregation of Yisrael THAT IS MALCHUT; the living Soul (lit. 'Nefesh') IS the Soul (lit. 'Nefes') of supernal Adam, as we have learned, SINCE MALCHUT IS THE MOTHER OF THE SOUL (LIT. 'NEFESH') OF THE FIRST MAN. Rabbi Aba approached him and kissed him. He said, You certainly spoke properly, and it is as you say.

320. זַכָּאָה חוּלָקֵיה דְּמֹשֶׁה נְבִיאָה מְהֵימָנָא, עַל כָּל שְׁאַר נְבִיאֵי עָלְמָא. בְּגִין כָּךְ, לָא אִשְׁתְּדַּל בֵּיה כַּד אִסְתַּלָק מֵעָלְמָא, בַּר קוּדְשָׁא בְּרִיךְ הוּא, דְּאַעֲלֵיה לְפַרְגוֹדֵיה. וְעַל דָּא סָלִיק מֹשֶׁה בִּנְבוּאָה עִלָּאָה, וּבְדַרְגִּין יַקִּירִין, מִכָּל נְבִיאֵי עָלְמָא, וּשְׁאַר נְבִיאֵי חָמָאן בָּתַר כּוֹתָלִין סַגִּיאִין.

320. Moses, the faithful prophet, is praised above all the rest of the prophets. Therefore, when he departed, no one else dealt with him besides the Holy One, blessed be He, who raised him to His presence. Therefore, Moses has surpassed in his lofty prophecy and glorious levels all the prophets, while the other prophets saw as if behind many walls.

48. The Tzitzit (fringed garment)

A Synopsis

Rabbi Yitzchak says that any person not fortunate enough to become adorned in this world with the covering of a good deed stands in a soiled garment and stands trial for it in the next world.

321. וַיַּרְאֵנִי אֶת יְהוֹשֻׁעַ הַכֹּהֵן הַגָּדוֹל, מַאי קָא חָמָא, דַּהֲוָה קָאֵים קַמֵּי מַלְאָכָא, וּמִתְלַבַּשׁ בִּלְבוּשִׁין מְלוּכְלְכִין, עַד דִּכְרוֹזָא נָפִיק, וְאָמַר הָסִירוּ הַבְּגָדִים הַצּוֹאִים מֵעָלָיו. אָמַר רִבִּי יִצְחָק, כְּתִיב הָכָא וְעוֹמֵד לִפְנֵי הַמַּלְאָךְ, מַאי לִפְנֵי הַמַּלְאָךְ. דַּהֲוָה דָּאֵין דִּינוֹי, הַהוּא דִּכְתִיב בֵּיהּ, וְאַל תֹּאמַר לִפְנֵי הַמַּלְאָךְ כִּי שְׁגָגָה הִיא. מַאי קָא מַשְׁמַע לָן. דְּכָל בַּר נָשׁ דְּלָא זָכֵי בְּהַאי עָלְמָא, לְאִתְעַטְּפָא בְּעִטּוּפָא דְּמִצְוָה, וּלְאִתְלַבְּשָׁא בִּלְבוּשָׁא דְּמִצְוָה. כַּד עָיֵיל בְּהַהוּא עָלְמָא, קָאֵים בִּלְבוּשָׁא טְנוּפָא, דְּלָא אִצְטְרִיךְ, וְקָאֵים בְּדִינָא עָלֵיהּ.

321. "And He showed me Joshua the High Priest..." (Zecharyah 3:1). HE ASKS: What did he see? HE RESPONDS that he was standing in the presence of the angel dressed in filthy clothes until the proclamation came forth and said, "Remove the soiled clothes from him" (Ibid. 4). Rabbi Yitzchak said that it is written here: "And he stood in the presence of the angel" (Ibid 3). What is the meaning of: "In the presence of the angel"? It means that he was judging him, he about whom it is written: "Nor say before the angel, that it was an error" (Kohelet 5:5). What is this telling us? That whoever did not merit in this world to be wrapped with a spiritual covering, and dressed with a spiritual garment, MEANING WITH THE TZITZIT, has a soiled garment that must not be SO, and is judged for it.

322. ת"ח, כַּמָה לְבוּשִׁין מְזְדַּמְנִין בְּהַהוּא עָלְמָא, וְהַהוּא בַּר נָשׁ דְּלָא זָכֵי בְּהַאי עָלְמָא בִּלְבוּשִׁין דְּמִצְוָה, כַּד עָיֵיל לְהַהוּא עָלְמָא, מַלְבִּשִׁין לֵיהּ בְּחַד לְבוּשָׁא דְּאִשְׁתְּמוֹדַע לְגַבֵּי מָארֵיהוֹן דְּגֵיהִנָם, וְהַהוּא לְבוּשָׁא, וַוי לְמַאן דְּאִתְלַבָּשׁ בֵּיהּ. דְּהָא כַּמָה גַּרְדִּינֵי נִמוּסִין, זְמִינִין לְאַחֲדָא בֵּיהּ, וְעָיְילֵי לֵיהּ לַגֵּיהִנָם. וּשְׁלֹמֹה מַלְכָּא צָוַוח וְאָמַר בְּכָל עֵת יִהְיוּ בְגָדֶיךָ לְבָנִים.

322. Come and see the variety of garments available in that world. That person that did not merit in this world spiritual garments, MEANING THE TALIT AND TZITZIT, when he enters that world, he is dressed with a certain dress that is known to the masters of Gehenom. Woe to him who is dressed in that garb, since many legal investigators will seize him and usher him into Gehenom. King Solomon cried out and said, "Let your garments be always white" (Kohelet 9:8).

323. תָּאנָא בְּרָזָא דְסִפְרָא דִצְנִיעוּתָא, אַרְבַּע מַלְכִין נָפְקִין לְקַדְמַת אַרְבַּע. בְּהוּ תַּלְיָין כַּעֲנָבִים בְּאִתְכְּלָא, צְרִירָן בְּהוּ ז' רְהִיטִין, סָהֲדִין סַהֲדוּתָא. וְלָא קַיְימִין בְּדוּכְתַּיְיהוּ.

323. We learned in the secret of Safra Det'zniuta (the Concealed Book) that four kings come out AND EMANATE in the presence of four. They come out from them like grapes in a cluster. Seven runners are incorporated in them, and they testify. They never stand still WHEN THEY TESTIFY.

A Synopsis
We learn about the reason for wearing the tzitzit, and for the plate of pure gold that must be gazed at. We are told that there is blue in the tzitzit to remind people to fear God and we learn about the strands on the tzitzit.

רעיא מהימנא

324. צִיצִית, פִּקּוּדָא דָא אִיהוּ, לְאַדְכְּרָא כָּל פִּקּוּדֵי אוֹרַיְיתָא בְּגִינָה. כד"א וּרְאִיתֶם אוֹתוֹ וּזְכַרְתֶּם אֶת כָּל מִצְוֹת יְיָ' וַעֲשִׂיתֶם אוֹתָם. דָא אִיהוּ סִימָנָא דְמַלְכָּא, לְאַדְכְּרָא וּלְמֶעְבַּד.

Ra'aya Meheimna (the Faithful Shepherd)

324. The Tzitzit: This command is to remember all the precepts of the Torah through it, as it says, "That you may look upon it, and remember all the commandments of Hashem, and do them" (Bemidbar 15:39). That is the sign of the King to remember and do.

325. כְּתִיב וְעָשִׂיתָ צִיץ זָהָב, וְהָא אוֹקִימְנָא רָזָא דְּצִיץ לְאִתְעַטְּרָא בֵּיהּ כַּהֲנָא רַבָּא. וְדָא אִיהוּ צִיץ, לְאִסְתַּכְּלָא בֵּיהּ עַיְינִין, דְּאִיהוּ סִימָן דְּעָלְמָא עִלָּאָה, דְּאִתְעֲטָר בֵּיהּ כַּהֲנָא רַבָּא.

325. It is written: "And you shall make a plate of pure gold" (Shemot 28:36). We have already explained that the secret of the plate (Heb. *tzitz*) is to adorn the High Priest with it. It is REFERRED TO AS *Tzitz*, WHICH MEANS SEEING, DERIVED FROM HE PEEPED (HEB. *HETZITZ*) AND WAS HURT. So the eyes will gaze at it, for it is a sign of the world above, THAT IS ZEIR ANPIN, WHERE THE SECRET OF BESTOWING THE ILLUMINATION OF CHOCHMAH IS INFERRED BY GAZING OF THE EYES, with which the High Priest was adorned.

326. וּבְגִין כַּךְ אִסְתַּכְּלוּתָא דִּילֵיהּ מְכַפְּרָא עַל עַזּוּת פָּנִים, דְּלָא קַיְימָא לְקַמֵּיהּ, אֶלָּא פָּנִים דִּקְשׁוֹט, רָזָא דְּכָל אִינּוּן פָּנִים עִלָּאִין, דְּאִינּוּן פָּנִים דִּקְשׁוֹט, פָּנִים דֶּאֱמֶת. דִּכְלִילָן בֶּאֱמֶת דְּיַעֲקֹב.

326. Because of this, looking UPON THE GOLD PLATE serves as absolution from insolence (lit. 'impudence of face'), since nothing prevails in its presence except a face of truth, which is the secret of every supernal face. THAT IS THE SECRET OF THE ILLUMINATION OF CHOCHMAH CLOTHED WITH CHASSADIM, WHICH IS REFERRED TO AS FACE, which is true face, MEANING the true face that is incorporated in the truth of Jacob THAT IS ZEIR ANPIN, IN ACCORDANCE WITH THE SECRET OF THE SCRIPTURE: "YOU WILL SHOW TRUTH TO JACOB" (MICHAH 7:20).

327. צִיצִית אִיהוּ נוּקְבָא, רָזָא בְּעָלְמָא תַּתָּאָה. אִסְתַּכְּלוּתָא לְאַדְכְּרָא. צִיץ דְּכַר, צִיצִית נוּקְבָא, וְדָא לְכָל בַּר נָשׁ. צִיץ לְכַהֲנָא.

327. Tzitzit is feminine, which is the secret of the lower world, MEANING MALCHUT, that is a look for the purpose of remembering, MEANING AS IT SAYS, "THAT YOU MAY LOOK UPON IT, AND REMEMBER" (BEMIDBAR 15:39). Tzit is masculine, MEANING ZEIR ANPIN, and Tzitzit is feminine, WHICH IS MALCHUT. That TZITZIT is for every man, while Tzit is just for the priest.

328. וְתָנֵינָן, אָסוּר לְאִסְתַּכְּלָא בִּשְׁכִינְתָּא, בג״כ אִית תְּכֵלָא, בְּגִין דְּתִכֵלֶת, אִיהוּ כֻּרְסְיָיא לְבֵית דָּוִד, וְתִקּוּנָא דִּילֵיהּ. וְדָא אִיהוּ דַּחֲלָא מִן קֳדָם יְיָ׳ לְדַחֲלָא מֵהַהוּא אֲתָר. וְעַל דָּא וּרְאִיתֶם אוֹתוֹ וּזְכַרְתֶּם אֶת כָּל מִצְוֹת יְיָ׳, וְדָא כֻּרְסְיָיא דְּדַיְינִין בָּהּ דִּינֵי נְפָשׁוֹת, כְּמָה דְּאוֹקִמוּהָ, דְּכָל גְּווֹנִין טָבִין לְחֶלְמָא, בַּר תְּכֵלָא, דְּאִיהוּ כֻּרְסְיָיא דְּסָלִיק בְּדִינָא דְּנְפָשׁוֹת.

328. We have learned that it is forbidden to gaze at the Shechinah. Therefore, there is blue IN THE TZITZIT (LIT. 'FRINGED GARMENT'), since blue is a throne for the house of David, THAT IS MALCHUT, and its restoration. That is in order to have fear of the presence of Hashem, to fear that area. Therefore, "That you may look upon it, and remember all the commandments of Hashem, and do them." AND BLUE is the throne at which criminal law is judged, as was explained, that all colors are good in a dream except blue, since that throne rises to judge criminal law.

329. כְּתִיב וְנָתְנוּ עַל צִיצִת הַכָּנָף פְּתִיל תְּכֵלֶת. וְנָתְנוּ עַל הַכָּנָף לָא כְּתִיב, אֶלָּא וְנָתְנוּ עַל צִיצִת. דְּדָא אִיהוּ דְּחָפֵי עַל שְׁאַר חוּטִין.

329. It is written: "And that they put upon the fringe of each corner a thread of blue" (Ibid. 38). It is not written: 'They shall put upon the corner', but rather "They put upon the fringe," since it covers over the rest of the threads, MEANING THAT TZITZIT ALLUDES TO THE ILLUMINATION OF CHOCHMAH. THEREFORE, ONLY THEY REQUIRE A COVER AND PROTECTION FROM THE BLUE THREAD. THAT IS WHY IT IS WRITTEN: "AND THAT THEY PUT UPON THE FRINGE."

330. וּרְאִיתֶם אוֹתוֹ וּזְכַרְתֶּם, וּכְתִיב, זָכוֹר אֶת אֲשֶׁר עָשָׂה לְךָ עֲמָלֵק. מ״ט דָּא. אֶלָּא לְבָרָא דְּפָרִיץ גְּדְרָא, וּנְשַׁכְיֵהּ כַּלְבָּא. כָּל זִמְנָא דְּאָבוֹי בָּעֵי לְאוֹכְחָא לִבְרֵיהּ, הֲוָה אָמַר הֲוֵי דָּכִיר כַּד נָשִׁיךְ לָךְ כַּלְבָּא. אוֹף הָכָא וּרְאִיתֶם אוֹתוֹ וּזְכַרְתֶּם, דְּדָא אִיהוּ אֲתָר דְּסַלְקִין נִשְׁמָתִין לְמֵידָן.

330. "And you shall see it and remember": IT IS AS WHAT is written: "Remember what Amalek did to you" (Devarim 25:17). What is the reason?

It is SIMILAR to a son that breaches a fence and gets bitten by a dog. Every time the father wants to reprove his son, he says to him, Remember when the dog bit you? Here too, "you shall see it and remember," since THE BLUE is the area where the souls ascend to be judged. THEREFORE, IT IS ALSO SIMILAR TO WHAT IS WRITTEN: "REMEMBER WHAT AMALEK DID TO YOU."

331. כְּגַוְונָא דָא, וְהָיָה כָּל הַנָּשׁוּךְ וְרָאָה אוֹתוֹ וָחָי, אֲמַאי. אֶלָּא כַּד סָלִיק לְעֵינוֹי, וְחָמֵי הַיּוּקְנָא הְּהַהוּא הְּנָשִׁיךְ לֵיהּ, הֲוָה דָחִיל, וְצַלֵּי קֳדָם יְיָ', וַהֲוָה יָדַע הְּאִיהוּ עוֹנָשָׁא הְּחַיָּיבַיָּא. כָּל זְמַן הְּבָרָא חָמֵי רְצוּעָה הַּאֲבוֹי, הָחִיל מֵאֲבוֹי. אִשְׁתְּזִיב מֵרְצוּעָה, אִשְׁתְּזִיב מִכֹּלָּא. מָאן גָּרִים לֵיהּ לְאִשְׁתְּזָבָא. הַהוּא הְּחָמֵי בְּעֵינוֹי הַהוּא רְצוּעָה, הַהוּא רְצוּעָה גָּרִים לֵיהּ לְאִשְׁתַּזָבָא. וְע"ד וְרָאָה אוֹתוֹ וָחָי, חַמֵי רְצוּעָה הְּאַלְקֵי לֵיהּ, וְאִיהוּ עָבֵיד לֵיהּ לְאִשְׁתְּזָבָא. אוֹף הָכָא וּרְאִיתֶם אוֹתוֹ וּזְכַרְתֶּם, וַעֲשִׂיתֶם וַדַּאי. וְאִי לָאו, הָא רְצוּעָה, הְּהַאי יִגְרוֹם לְכוֹן, לְמֶהֱוֵי תָּבִין לְפוּלְחָנָא הִּילִי תָּדִיר, וּכְדֵין וַעֲשִׂיתֶם.

331. Similarly, "and it shall come to pass that every one that is bitten, when he looks upon it, shall live" (Bemidbar 21:8). Why is this? It is only when he raised his eyes and saw the form of that which bit him, he was afraid and prayed to Hashem, and knew that this was punishment for the wicked. As long as a son sees his father's strap, he fears his father. If he is saved from the strap, so is he saved from everything. Who caused him to be saved? His seeing the strap with his own eyes. SO the strap caused him to be saved. Hence, "when he looks upon it, shall live." He saw the strap that beat him, and it caused him to be saved. Here too, "that you may look upon it, and remember all the commandments of Hashem, and do" certainly. If not, here is the strap, MEANING THE BLUE that will cause you to return always to My service. Then, "do."

332. וְלֹא תָתוּרוּ אַחֲרֵי לְבַבְכֶם, יִמְנַע מִנְכוֹן בִּישִׁין אָרְחִין אַחֲרָנִין, וַדַּאי, לֹא תָתוּרוּ, וְלָא תַעַבְדוּ בִּישִׁין. וְעַל הָא סַלְקָא גָּוֶון הְּכֵלָא. הָא הְּכֵלֶת, הַּמְיָא לְכֻסֵּא הַכָּבוֹד, מַה כֻּסֵּא הַכָּבוֹד, עָבֵיד לְבַר נָשׁ לְמֵהַךְ לְאָרְחָא הְּמֵישָׁר, לְהַכָּאָה לֵיהּ. אוֹף הַאי הְּכֵלֶת, עָבֵיד לב"נ לְמֵהַךְ בְּאֹרַח מֵישָׁר, וַדַּאי הְּכֵלָא אִית לְדַחֲלָא מֵהַאי אֲתָר, לְמֵיהַךְ בְּמֵישָׁר.

332. "And that you seek not after your own heart" (Bemidbar 15:39). ONCE YOU SAW THE BLUE, it prevented you from other evil ways. Assuredly, "you seek not" and commit no evil. Therefore, blue is seen over THE TZITZIT. This blue is similar to the Throne of Glory. Just as the Throne of Glory causes a person to follow the upright path to purify him, so too this blue causes him to walk the straight path. Certainly every person should have fear of this place, thus walking in the straight path.

333. כְּתִיב מִכְּנַף הָאָרֶץ זְמִירוֹת שָׁמַעְנוּ צְבִי לַצַּדִּיק וָאוֹמַר רָזִי לִי וְגוֹ'. מִכְּנַף הָאָרֶץ, דָּא כְּנָף דְּצִיצִית, דְּאִיהוּ כְּנַף הָאָרֶץ. זְמִירוֹת שָׁמַעְנוּ, אִלֵּין שְׁאָר חוּטִין, דְּנָפְקִין וְתַלְיָין מֵאֲתַר עִלָּאָה, גּוֹ אִינּוּן שְׁבִילִין עִלָּאִין, דְּנָפְקִין מֵחָכְמָה עִלָּאָה. צְבִי לַצַּדִּיק, דָּא צַדִּיק חַי הָעוֹלָמִים, דְּאִינּוּן חוּטִין אִינּוּן שְׁפִירוּ דִּילֵיהּ, דְּהָא מִנֵּיהּ נָפְקִין, וְכָל חוּטָא כְּלִילָא בִּתְרֵין סִטְרִין. וְכַד אִסְתַּכַּלְנָא, אֲמֵינָא רָזִי לִי רָזִי לִי, דְּהָא מִגּוֹ רָזָא עִלָּאָה דְּכָל מְהֵימְנוּתָא נָפְקִין. וְכַד אִסְתַּכַּלְנָא בִּתְכֵלֶת, וַחֲמֵינָא רְצוּעָה לְאַלְקָאָה, אֲתַר דְּחִילוּ לְמִדְחַל, אֲמֵינָא אוֹי לִי, דִּבְנֵי נָשָׁא לָא יַדְעֵי לְאַשְׁגָּחָא וּלְאִסְתַּכְּלָא עַל מַה מִתְעַנְּשִׁין לְשַׁקְרָא, בְּהַאי בּוֹגְדִים בָּגָדוּ, דְּהָא קוֹרִין ק"ש בְּלָא צִיצִית, וְסָהֲדִין סַהֲדוּתָא דְּשִׁקְרָא, וְאִלֵּין אִינּוּן בּוֹגְדִים דְּבָגָדוּ, מְשַׁקְרֵי דְּגַרְמַיְיהוּ.

333. It is written: "From the uttermost part of the earth have we heard songs, glory to the righteous. But I said, 'my leanness (also: 'secret')...'" (Yeshayah 24:16). "From the uttermost part of the earth" refers to the corner of the Tzitzit, which is the edge of the earth, MEANING THE CORNER OF MALCHUT CALLED EARTH. "Have we heard songs": These are all the threads that come out and hang from a high place, within those lofty paths that emerge from supernal Chochmah. "Glory to the righteous": That is the Righteous that lives forever, WHICH IS YESOD OF ZEIR ANPIN, since the threads of the Tzitzit are His beauty. From Him, they emanate AND ARE GIVEN TO MALCHUT, and each thread is comprised of two aspects, MEANING CHASSADIM AND CHOCHMAH, WHICH ARE RIGHT AND LEFT. When I gaze, I say: "my secret, my secret" (Ibid.), since they come out from the high principle of the whole Faith AS THEY ARE THE WHOLE OF THE LIGHTS OF MALCHUT, REFERRED TO AS FAITH. And when I gaze at the blue and see a strap for beating, which is the place of awe that inspires fear,

I say, "Woe to me" (Ibid.), because people do not know enough to watch and observe why they are punished for lying. "Traitors have dealt treacherously" (Ibid.), since they read Kriat Sh'ma without the Tzitzit and give false evidence. These are the traitors who have dealt treacherously, since they are false to themselves.

334. וּבֶגֶד בּוֹגְדִים בָּגָדוּ, לְבוּשָׁא דִלְהוֹן בְּלָא צִיצִית, אִקְרֵי בֶּגֶד בּוֹגְדִים. לְבוּשָׁא דְּאִינּוּן בּוֹגְדִים דְּבָגְדוּ, דִּמְשַׁקְרֵי וְסָהֲדִין סַהֲדוּתָא דְשִׁקְרָא בְּכָל יוֹמָא. וַוי לוֹן, וַוי לְנַפְשֵׁיהוֹן, דְּסַלְקֵי בְּהַהוּא כֻּרְסְיָיא דְּתִכְלָא לְמֵידָן. וַעֲלַיְיהוּ כְּתִיב, דּוֹבֵר שְׁקָרִים לֹא יִכּוֹן לְנֶגֶד עֵינָי, הַהוּא בֶּגֶד דִּלְהוֹן אִשְׁתְּמוֹדַע לְגַבֵּי כָּל מָארֵיהוֹן דְּדִינִין. וַוי לוֹן, דְּלֵית לוֹן חוּלָקָא בְּעָלְמָא דְאָתֵי. זַכָּאִין אִינּוּן צַדִּיקַיָּיא, דְּמַלְבּוּשֵׁיהוֹן וְתִקּוּנֵיהוֹן אִשְׁתְּמוֹדְעָן לְעֵילָּא, לְאוֹטָבָא לוֹן בְּהַאי עָלְמָא וּבְעָלְמָא דְאָתֵי.

334. "Traitors have dealt very treacherously" (Ibid.): their garment when without Tzitzit is considered "traitors (Heb. *beged*) have dealt very treacherously," that is, a garment (Heb. *beged*) of those traitors who are treacherous, who lie and give false testimony every day. Woe to them and woe to their souls, since they will ascend to that blue throne to HAVE THEM judged. About them, it is written: "He that tells lies shall not remain in My sight" (Tehilim 101:71). That garment of theirs is known to all the prosecutors. Woe to them that they have no part in the World to Come. Praised are the righteous, whose garments and works are known above to benefit them in this world and in the World to Come.

335. פִּקּוּדָא דָא מִצְוַת צִיצִית, כָּלִיל תְּכֵלֶת וְלָבָן, דִּינָא וְרַחֲמֵי בְּנוּרָא. אֶשָּׁא חִוָּורָא לָא אָכִיל, תְּכֵלָא אָכִיל וְשָׁצֵי. וְתֵאכַל הָעוֹלָה, חִוָּור מִימִינָא, תְּכֵלֶת מִשְּׂמָאלָא. עַמּוּדָא דְּאֶמְצָעִיתָא יִחוּד בֵּין תַּרְוַויְיהוּ, יָרוֹק. וּבְג"ד אוּקְמוּהָ מָארֵי מַתְנִיתִין, מֵאֵימָתַי קוֹרִין אֶת שְׁמַע בְּשַׁחֲרִית, מִשֶּׁיַּכִּיר בֵּין תְּכֵלֶת לְלָבָן. וּבְג"ד תַּקִּינוּ פָּרָשַׁת צִיצִית לְמִקְרֵי לֵהּ בְּיִחוּדָא.

ע"כ רעיא מהימנא.

335. This commandant is the precept of Tzitzit, which is comprised of blue and white, MEANING FOUR WHITE THREADS AND ONE THREAD OF BLUE, that are Judgment and Mercy in fire. White fire does not consume, but the blue consumes and destroys everything. "And consumed the burnt offering" (II Divrei Hayamim 7:1), MEANING the white FIRE on the right and the blue FIRE from the left. The Central pillar, MEANING THE CENTRAL COLUMN THAT UNITES RIGHT AND LEFT, is the union between the two, and is green FIRE. Therefore, the masters of the Mishnah have established: 'When does one read the Sh'ma in the morning: when one can distinguish between blue and white'. THAT IS, WHEN ONE CAN DISCRIMINATE BETWEEN JUDGMENT AND CHESED, BECAUSE THEN ONE WILL ADHERE TO CHESED, WHICH IS THE SECRET OF KRIAT SH'MA. Therefore, it has been established to recite the passages about Tzitzit in union... (THE ENDING IS MISSING).

End of Ra'aya Meheimna

A Synopsis

Rabbi Yehuda tells us that God has many witnesses to testify for a person, all of whom provide counsel for the person. If he listens to them all is well, but if not they testify about his iniquities above. Rabbi Yehuda tells us what a person is reminded of when he dons the Tefilin and the tzitzit. He reminds us of the precept to remember all the commandments of God. Rabbi Shimon says that God is destined to extricate the children of Yisrael from the exile, and in that day His name will be praised throughout the earth. God will perform signs and miracles in the world, and His name will be One.

336. אָמַר רִבִּי יְהוּדָה, כַּמָּה סַהֲדֵי עָבֵיד קוּדְשָׁא בְּרִיךְ הוּא לְאַסְהֲדָא בְּהוּ בִּבְנֵי נָשָׁא, וְכֻלְּהוּ בְּעֵיטָא וּבְסַהֲדוּתָא קַיְימִין לְקַבְּלֵיהּ. קָם בְּצַפְרָא אוֹשִׁיט רַגְלוֹי לְמֵהַךְ, סָהֲדַיָּיא קַיְימִין לְקַבְּלֵיהּ, מַכְרִיזִין וְאָמְרִין, רַגְלֵי חֲסִידָיו יִשְׁמוֹר וְגוֹ'. שְׁמוֹר רַגְלְךָ כַּאֲשֶׁר תֵּלֵךְ. פַּלֵּס מַעְגַּל רַגְלֶךָ. אַפְתַּח עֵינוֹי לְאִסְתַּכְּלָא בְּעָלְמָא, סָהֲדַיָּיא אָמְרֵי, עֵינֶיךָ לְנֹכַח יַבִּיטוּ. קָם לְמַלְלָא, סָהֲדַיָּיא אָמְרֵי נְצוֹר לְשׁוֹנְךָ מֵרָע וְגוֹ'. אוֹשִׁיט יְדוֹי בְּמִלֵּי עָלְמָא, סָהֲדַיָּיא אָמְרֵי סוּר מֵרָע וַעֲשֵׂה טוֹב.

336. Rabbi Yehuda said, How many witnesses has the Holy One, blessed be

He, set up to testify about people. All are in counsel and testify about him.
When he gets up in the morning and stretches his leg forward to start
walking, the witnesses stand before him and declare and say, "He will keep
the feet of His pious ones..." (I Shmuel 2:9) as well as "Keep your feet when
you go" (Kohelet 4:17) and "Make even the path of your foot" (Mishlei
4:26). When he opens his eyes to look around the world, the witnesses say,
"Let your eyes look right on" (Ibid. 25). He starts to talk and the witnesses
say, "Keep your tongue from evil..." (Tehilim 34:14). He extends his hands
to worldly things and the witnesses say, "Depart from evil, and do good"
(Ibid. 15).

337. אִי צַיֵּית לְהוּ, יָאוּת. וְאִי לָא, כְּתִיב וְהַשָּׂטָן עוֹמֵד עַל יְמִינוֹ
לְשִׂטְנוֹ. כֻּלְּהוּ סָהֲדִין עָלֵיהּ בְּחוֹבוֹי לְעֵילָא. אִי בָּעֵי ב״נ לְאִשְׁתַּדְּלָא
בְּפוּלְחָנָא דְקוּדְשָׁא בְּרִיךְ הוּא, כֻּלְּהוּ סָהֲדִין סַנֵּיגוֹרִין קַמֵּיהּ, וְקָיְימִין
לְאַסְהֲדָא עָלֵיהּ טָבָאן, בְּשַׁעֲתָא דְּאִצְטְרִיךְ לֵיהּ.

337. If he obeys them it is well, and if not, it is written: "And the adversary
standing at his right hand to thwart him" (Zecharyah 3:1) All testify about
him and his iniquities above. If a person wishes to strive in the service of the
Holy One, blessed be He, all the witnesses become good advocates for him
and are ready to give a good TESTIMONY for him when he needs it.

338. קָם בְּצַפְרָא, מְבָרֵךְ כַּמָּה בִּרְכָאן. אֲנַח תְּפִילִין בְּרֵישֵׁיהּ בֵּין עֵינוֹי.
בָּעֵי לְזַקְפָּא רֵישֵׁיהּ, חָמֵי שְׁמָא קַדִּישָׁא עִלָּאָה, אָחִיד וְרָשִׁים עַל
רֵישֵׁיהּ. וּרְצוּעִין תַּלְיָין מֵהַאי גִּיסָא וּמֵהַאי גִּיסָא עַל לִבֵּיהּ. הָא אֶסְתָּכַּל
בִּיקָרָא דְּמָארֵיהּ. אוֹשִׁיט יְדוֹי, חָמֵי יְדָא אַחֲרָא, מִתְקַשְּׁרָא בְּקִשּׁוּרָא
דִּשְׁמָא קַדִּישָׁא. אַהְדַּר יְדֵיהּ וְאִסְתָּכַּל בִּיקָרֵיהּ דְּמָארֵיהּ. אִתְעֲטַף
בְּעִטּוּפָא דְמִצְוָה, בְּאַרְבַּע זִיוְיָין דִּכְסוּתֵיהּ, אַרְבַּע מַלְכִין נָפְקִין לְקַדְמוּת
אַרְבַּע. אַרְבַּע סַהֲדֵי קְשׁוֹט דְּמַלְכָּא, תַּלְיָיא מֵאַרְבַּע זִיוְיָין, וְתַלְיָין בְּהוּ
כַּעֲנָבִים בְּאִתְכְּלָא.

338. When he rises in the morning, he recites several blessings, puts on
Tefilin on his head between his eyes. When he wishes to raise his head, he
sees the supernal Holy Name attached to and marked over his head, and

straps hanging from each side over his heart. He thereby observes the glory of his Master. He extends his hands and sees the other hand tied with the knot of the Holy Name. He returns his hand and gazes at the glory of his Master. He wraps himself in a Tzitzit, with the four corners of his garment. Four kings come before four, MEANING four true witnesses of the King, WHICH ARE THE FOUR THREADS OF THE TZITZIT hanging from the four corners, like grapes on a cluster.

339. מָה אִתְכְּלָּא, דְּאִיהוּ חַד, וְתַלְיָין בֵּיהּ כַּמָּה עֲנָבִים, מֵהַאי סְטָר וּמֵהַאי סְטָר. כָּךְ הַאי, מִצְוָה חֲדָא, וְתַלְיָין בֵּיהּ כַּמָּה עֲנָבִים, וְזַגִּין וּזְמוֹרִין צְרִירִין בְּהוּ, שַׁבְעָה רְהִיטִין אִלֵּין אִינּוּן שִׁבְעָה צְרִירִין דִּתְכֶלְתָּא, דְּבָעֵי לְכַרְכָא בֵּיהּ בְּכָל חַד וְחַד, אוֹ לְאַסְגָּאָה עַד תְּלֵיסַר, מַאן דְּיוֹסִיף, לָא יוֹסִיף עָלַיְיהוּ עַל תְּלֵיסַר. מַאן דְּיִמְעַט, לָא יִמְעַט מִשִּׁבְעָה.

339. Just like a grape cluster is one cluster but has several grapes hanging on each side, so too this TZITZIT is one commandment, with grapes, grapeskin and little branches coming out of it, MEANING SEVERAL DIFFERENT LEVELS. Seven runners are entwined in them. They are the seven bands of the blue that one has to bind to each or to add up to thirteen BUNCHES. If adding, one must not add beyond thirteen and if decreasing one must not make less than seven.

340. וְתָאנָא, הַאי תְּכֵלֶת, הוּא רָזָא דְּדָוִד מַלְכָּא. וְדָא חוּטָא דְּאַבְרָהָם, דְּזָכָה בֵּיהּ לִבְנוֹי בַּתְרוֹי. מַאי תְּכֵלֶת. תַּכְלִית דְּכֹלָּא. רִבִּי יְהוּדָה אוֹמֵר, כֻּסֵּא הַכָּבוֹד אִקְרֵי.

340. We have learned that this blue is the secret of King David, THAT IS MALCHUT. It is the thread of Abraham, which he merited for himself and his descendants after him. What is the meaning of blue (Heb. tchelet)? It is the ending (Heb. tachlit) of everything, SINCE ITS AIM IS THE ENDING OF ALL THE WORLDS. Rabbi Yehuda says it is called the Throne of Glory, WHICH IS MALCHUT.

341. רִבִּי יִצְחָק אָמַר, שִׁבְעָה כְּרִיכָן דְּאִיהִי שְׁכִינְתָּא שְׁבִיעָתָא דְּכֹלָּא

וַדַּאי. דְּהָא הִיא מִתְבָּרְכָא מְשִׁיתָא אַחֲרָנִין, עַל יְדָא דְּצַדִּיק. וְאִי תְּלַת עֶשָׂר, תְּלַת עֶשָׂר אִינּוּן, כְּמָה דְּאוּקְמוּהָ בִּתְלַת עֶשָׂר מְכִילָן. וְהַאי הִיא פִּתְחָא דְכֻלְּהוּ.

341. Rabbi Yitzchak said: Seven wraps THAT ARE BOUND OVER THE TZITZIT are the Shechinah, which is the seventh of everything definitely, since She is blessed from the other six SFIROT, CHESED, GVURAH, TIFERET, NETZACH, HOD AND YESOD, through the Righteous, WHO IS YESOD. THEREFORE, SHE COMPRISES ALL SEVEN. If thirteen WRAPS are done, then the thirteen are as was set in the thirteen attributes of Mercy. MALCHUT is the entrance to all AND, THEREFORE, CONTAINS THIRTEEN.

342. וְהִיא חוּטָא חַד, וּרְשִׁימָא בִּגְוָונָהָא, וּגְוָונָא דִּילָהּ נָפִיק, מֵחַד נוּנָא דְּאָזִיל בְּיַם כְּנֶרֶת. וְכִנֶּרֶת עַל שְׁמָהּ אִתְקְרֵי. וְעַל דָּא, כִּנּוֹר הֲוָה תָּלוּי לְעֵילָּא מֵעַרְסָא דְּדָוִד, דְּהָא וַדַּאי אִיהוּ כִּנּוֹר דְּדָוִד, מְנַגֵּן מֵאֵלָיו לְמַלְכָּא קַדִּישָׁא עִלָּאָה. וּבְג"כ, גְּוָונוֹי עָיֵיל עַד רְקִיעָא, וּמֵרְקִיעָא עַד כּוּרְסָיָיא.

342. This BLUE is one thread marked in her color. Her color is produced from a certain fish in the sea of Kineret (Galilee) called Kineret after her, MALCHUT. Because of that, there is a violin (Heb. *kinor*) hanging above David's bed, THE VIOLIN BEING THE SECRET OF MALCHUT, which is surely David's violin that played on its own to the supernal Holy King, THAT IS, ZEIR ANPIN. Therefore, the colors OF BLUE rise to the firmament, THAT IS ZEIR ANPIN, and from the firmament to the throne, THAT IS BINAH.

343. וְהָכָא כְּתִיב מִצְוָה, כד"א מִצְוַת הַמֶּלֶךְ הִיא. מַדּוּעַ אַתָּה עוֹבֵר אֶת מִצְוַת הַמֶּלֶךְ. כִּי מִצְוַת הַמֶּלֶךְ. וְתָאנָא, יְסוֹדָא וְשָׁרְשָׁא בְּמַלְכָּא מִתְעַטְּרִין כַּחֲדָא. וְהַאי הוּא דּוּכְרָנָא וּפִתְחָא לְכָל שְׁאָר כִּתְרִין. דִּכְתִיב, פִּתְחוּ לִי שַׁעֲרֵי צֶדֶק. וּכְתִיב, זֶה הַשַּׁעַר לַיְיָ'. וע"ד כְּתִיב, וּרְאִיתֶם אוֹתוֹ וּזְכַרְתֶּם אֶת כָּל מִצְוֹת יְיָ', לְאַכְלְלָא בְּהַאי כָּל שְׁאָר כִּתְרִין. וע"ד אִינּוּן סַהֲדֵי סַהֲדוּתָא, וְלָא קַיְימֵי בְּדוּכְתַּיְיהוּ בְּגִין דְּאִיהִי מִצְוָת.

343. Here a precept is written, MEANING: "AND YOU SHALL REMEMBER ALL THE COMMANDMENTS OF HASHEM," BECAUSE MALCHUT IS CALLED PRECEPT, as is written: "For the king's commandment was" (II Melachim 18:36). THAT ALLUDES TO MALCHUT; "Why do you transgress the king's commandment" (Ester 3:3), "For it was the king's commandment" (Nechemyah 11:23) – ALL THESE ALLUDE TO MALCHUT, WHICH IS CALLED THE KING'S COMMANDMENT. We learned that Yesod, WHICH IS THE LAST SFIRAH IN ZEIR ANPIN, and the root, WHICH IS KETER, THE SOURCE OF EVERYTHING, get adorned together in Malchut. This, MALCHUT, is the memory and the opening to all the rest of the Sfirot, as is written: "Open to me the gates of righteousness" (Tehilim 118:19), WHICH IS MALCHUT THAT IS CALLED RIGHTEOUSNESS. It is written IN THE FOLLOWING VERSE: "This is the gate of Hashem" (Ibid. 20), HER BEING THE GATE TO ALL THE SFIROT. Therefore it is written: "that you may look upon it, and remember all the commandments of Hashem," SINCE THE SCRIPTURE COMES to include in it, IN MALCHUT, all the rest of the Sfirot. FOR IN MALCHUT THAT IS REFERRED TO AS COMMANDMENT, ALL THE SFIROT INCLUDED IN HER ARE CALLED COMMANDMENTS. Therefore, WE LEARNED they give their testimony but do not stay in place, BECAUSE THE SFIROT OF ZEIR ANPIN GIVE TESTIMONY BY REVEALING THE ILLUMINATION OF CHOCHMAH THAT IS CALLED TESTIMONY, AND DO NOT REMAIN IN THEIR PLACE IN ZEIR ANPIN. For she is a commandment, SINCE THE TZITZIT IS THE SECRET OF MALCHUT CALLED COMMANDMENT AND THE SFIROT OF ZEIR ANPIN THAT ARE INCLUDED IN HER ARE CALLED COMMANDMENTS. AND THEREFORE THEY ARE NOT IN THEIR PLACE, IN ZEIR ANPIN, BUT RATHER IN MALCHUT.

344. וְתָנֵינָן, תַּשְׁמִישֵׁי מִצְוָה, נִזְרָקִין. וְאִי תֵּימָא, הָא לוּלָב וַעֲרָבָה וְכוּ', תַּשְׁמִישֵׁי קְדוּשָׁה אִינוּן, אֲמַאי נִזְרָקִין. אֶלָּא תַּשְׁמִישֵׁי קְדוּשָׁה, בְּגִין דִּרְשִׁימִין בִּכְתִיבָה דִּשְׁמָא קַדִּישָׁא.

344. We have learned that ritual articles, THAT BELONG TO MALCHUT, can be thrown away. If you wonder about the Lulav and willow twigs, WHERE THE LULAV ALLUDES TO YESOD OF ZEIR ANPIN, AND THE WILLOW TWIGS TO NETZACH AND HOD OF ZEIR ANPIN, FOR WHICH REASON THEY ARE NOT RITUAL ARTICLES, BUT RATHER sacred articles, MEANING IN ZEIR ANPIN, so why are they discarded? HE ANSWERS: That is because sacred articles are marked with the writing of the Holy Name. HOWEVER,

LULAV AND THE WILLOW TWIGS, EVEN THOUGH THEY ALLUDE TO ZEIR ANPIN, ARE NEVERTHELESS AS RITUAL ARTICLES AND CAN BE THROWN AWAY.

345. א"ר יִצְחָק, אִינוּן חוּטִין, לְאַחֲזָאָה הֵיךְ תַּלְיָין מִכָּאן וּמִכָּאן, לְד' סִטְרֵי עָלְמָא, מֵהַאי אֲתָר. וְאִיהִי שַׁלְטָא עַל כֹּלָּא. בְּרָזָא דְלֵב, דְּאִיהִי לִבָּא דְכָל הַאי עָלְמָא, וְלִבָּא דְעֶלָאֵי, וְתַלְיָא בַּלֵב עֶלָאָה. וְכֹלָּא הוּא בַּלֵב, דְּנָפַק מֵחָכְמָה עֶלָאָה. א"ר יִצְחָק, שִׁעוּרָא דְּהַאי, וְאוֹרְכָּא דְּהַאי, אִתְּמַר בְּאַתְוָון גְּלִיפָן דְּר' אֶלְעָזָר.

345. Rabbi Yitzchak said, The purpose of the threads OF THE TZITZIT is to show how they are suspended from this and that place, and from here to the four corners of the world, and she, MALCHUT, rules over them all in the secret of the heart (Heb. *lev – Lamed Bet*), being the heart of the whole world, and the heart of the higher beings, MEANING IN THE THREE WORLDS OF BRIYAH, YETZIRAH AND ASIYAH, and originates in the highest heart OF ZEIR ANPIN. Everything is in THE SECRET OF the heart that emerges from the highest wisdom, INDICATING THE *LAMED BET* (= 32) PATHS OF WISDOM THAT SHINE IN IT. Rabbi Yitzchak said, We have learned its measure and length, OF THE TZITZIT, in the engraved letters of Rabbi Elazar.

346. א"ר יְהוּדָה, אָמַר קוּדְשָׁא בְּרִיךְ הוּא, מַאן דְּבָעֵי לְמֵהַךְ בָּתַר דְּחַלְתִּי, יְהַךְ בָּתַר לִבָּא דָא, וּבָתַר עַיְינִין דְּקַיְימִין עֲלָה. מַאן אִינוּן עַיְינִין. כד"א, עֵינֵי יְיָ' אֶל צַדִּיקִים אֲבָל אַתֶּם לֹא תָתוּרוּ אַחֲרֵי לְבַבְכֶם וְאַחֲרֵי עֵינֵיכֶם. מ"ט בְּגִין דְּאַתֶּם זוֹנִים אַחֲרֵיהֶם.

346. Rabbi Yehuda said, The Holy One, blessed be He, says, 'Whoever wishes to follow the awe of Me should follow this heart, WHICH IS MALCHUT, and the eyes that are over it.' Who are these eyes? It is as in, "The eyes of Hashem are towards the righteous" (Tehilim 34:16). THESE ARE ZEIR ANPIN'S EYES. However, "you seek not after your own heart and your own eyes." What is the reason for this? It is because "after which you go astray" (Bemidbar 14:39).

347. אָמַר ר' חִיָּיא, מַאי טַעֲמָא הָכָא יְצִיאַת מִצְרַיִם, דִּכְתִיב אֲשֶׁר

הוֹצֵאתִי אֶתְכֶם מֵאֶרֶץ מִצְרָיִם. אֶלָּא, בְּגִין דְּכַד נַפְקוּ מִמִּצְרַיִם, בְּהַאי
חוּלָקָא עָאל. וּבְהַאי, קָטִיל קוּדְשָׁא בְּרִיךְ הוּא קְטוּלָא דְּמִצְרָיִם. וע״ד
בְּאַתְרֵיהּ אִתְדְּכַר, וּבְאַתְרֵיהּ אִזְדְּהַר לְהוּ בְּדָא. מַאי בְּאַתְרֵיהּ. בְּגִין
דְּהַאי מִצְוָה, הִיא אֲתַר דִּילָהּ.

347. Rabbi Chiya said, What is the reason that the exodus from Egypt is MENTIONED here, as it says: "Who brought you out of the land of Egypt" (Shemot 20:2). HE REPLIES: It is only because, when they left Egypt, they entered this part, WHICH IS MALCHUT, and through it, IN MALCHUT, the Holy One, blessed be He, slaughtered those killed in Egypt. Therefore, THE EXODUS FROM EGYPT is mentioned in its rightful place. At that place, He has warned them about it, AS IT IS WRITTEN: "I AM HASHEM YOUR ELOHIM, WHO BROUGHT YOU OUT…" Why is it in its place? It is because this precept OF THE TZITZIT is its place OF MALCHUT.

348. תָּאנֵי ר׳ יֵיסָא, כְּתִיב כִּימֵי צֵאתְךָ מֵאֶרֶץ מִצְרַיִם אַרְאֶנּוּ נִפְלָאוֹת.
כִּימֵי, כַּיּוֹם מִבָּעֵי לֵיהּ, דְּהָא בְּחַד זִמְנָא נַפְקוּ וְלָא אִתְעַכְּבוּ. אֶלָּא
כְּאִינּוּן יוֹמִין עִלָּאִין, דְּאִתְבָּרְכָא בְּהוּ כְּנֶסֶת יִשְׂרָאֵל. כַּךְ זַמִּין קוּדְשָׁא
בְּרִיךְ הוּא לְאַפָּקָא לְהוּ לְיִשְׂרָאֵל מִן גָּלוּתָא, וּכְדֵין כְּתִיב וַאֲמַרְתֶּם בַּיּוֹם
הַהוּא הוֹדוּ לַיְיָ׳ קִרְאוּ וְגוֹ׳, זַמְּרוּ יְיָ׳ כִּי גֵאוּת עָשָׂה מוּדַעַת זֹאת בְּכָל
הָאָרֶץ. מַאי מוּדַעַת זֹאת. בְּגִין דְּהַשְׁתָּא אִשְׁתְּמוֹדְעָא זֹאת בְּעֵטוּפָא
דְּמִצְוָה. בְּהַהוּא זִמְנָא אִשְׁתְּמוֹדְעָא זֹאת, בְּכַמָּה נְמוּסִין דִּילָהּ, דְּיַעֲבֵיד
קוּדְשָׁא בְּרִיךְ הוּא אָתִין וְנִסִּין בְּעָלְמָא, כְּדֵין כְּתִיב בַּיּוֹם הַהוּא יִהְיֶה יְיָ׳
אֶחָד וּשְׁמוֹ אֶחָד.

348. Rabbi Yesa taught that it is written: "As in the days of your coming out of the land of Egypt I will show him marvelous things" (Michah 7:15). HE INQUIRES: It says, "As in the days," but it should have said, 'As in the day', since they left at once and did not tarry. HE RESPONDS: THE EXPLANATION IS as in these lofty days, CHESED, GVURAH, TIFERET, NETZACH, HOD AND YESOD OF ZEIR ANPIN, the Congregation of Yisrael was blessed with. So will the Holy One, blessed be He, extricate Yisrael from exile THROUGH THE DAYS OF ZEIR ANPIN. Then it is written: "And in that day shall you say, Praise Hashem, call upon His name... Sing to Hashem; for He has done excellent things: this is known in all the earth" (Yeshayah 12:4-5). What is "this (Heb. *zot*) is known"? HE RESPONDS: Now, *Zot*, WHICH IS MALCHUT, is known by THE SPIRITUAL GARMENT, MEANING BY TZITZIT. At that time, *Zot* will be renowned in its various ways when the Holy One, blessed be He, will perform signs and miracles in the world. Then it is written: "On that day Hashem shall be one and His Name One" (Zecharyah 14:9).

בָּרוּךְ יְיָ׳ לְעוֹלָם אָמֵן וְאָמֵן. יִמְלוֹךְ יְיָ׳ לְעוֹלָם אָמֵן וְאָמֵן.

Blessed is Hashem for evermore. Amen and Amen. May Hashem reign for evermore. Amen and Amen.

KORACH

Names of the articles

1. "Now Korah..."

A Synopsis

Rabbi Yitzchak tells us that if the children of Yisrael had followed the Torah they would not have been exiled, because whoever deals in the Torah has freedom from everything including death. The Torah is the power of the right, and whoever exchanges the left for the right is as if he destroys the world. Rabbi Yitzchak says that Aaron is right and the Levites are left, and that Korah wanted to exchange them in that he desired the priesthood; this is why he was punished. Korah had an evil tongue, he took bad counsel, he chased after something that was not his, and he turned to disagreement which brought conflict instead of peace. The Shabbat is the peace of the upper and lower grades, and by this peace the world endures; whoever creates dissension in this peace will be destroyed.

1. וַיִּקַּח קֹרַח בֶּן יִצְהָר בֶּן קְהָת בֶּן לֵוִי וְגוֹ'. רִבִּי אַבָּא פָּתַח הַנֶּחֱמָדִים מִזָּהָב וּמִפַּז רַב וּמְתוּקִים מִדְּבַשׁ וְנוֹפֶת צוּפִים. כַּמָּה עִלָּאִין פִּתְגָּמֵי אוֹרַיְיתָא, כַּמָּה יַקִּירִין אִינּוּן, תְּאִיבִין אִינּוּן לְעֵילָא, תְּאִיבִין אִינּוּן לְכֹלָּא. בְּגִין דְּאִינּוּן שְׁמָא קַדִּישָׁא. וְכָל מַאן דְּאִשְׁתָּדַל בְּאוֹרַיְיתָא, אִשְׁתָּדַל בִּשְׁמָא קַדִּישָׁא, וְאִשְׁתְּזִיב מִכֹּלָּא, אִשְׁתְּזִיב בְּעָלְמָא דֵּין, וְאִשְׁתְּזִיב בְּעָלְמָא דְּאָתֵי. ת"ח, כָּל מַאן דְּאִשְׁתָּדַל בְּאוֹרַיְיתָא, אָחִיד בְּאִילָנָא דְּחַיֵּי. כֵּיוָן דְּאָחִיד בֵּיהּ, בְּכֹלָּא אָחִיד, דִּכְתִיב עֵץ חַיִּים הִיא לַמַּחֲזִיקִים בָּהּ וְגוֹ'.

1. "Now Korah, the son of Izhar, the son of Kohath, the son of Levi took..." (Bemidbar 16:1). Rabbi Aba opened the discussion with the verse: "more to be desired are they than gold, even much fine gold: sweeter also than honey and the honeycomb" (Tehilim 19:11). How supreme are matters of Torah, and how precious they are. They are desired above and they are desired by all, because they constitute the Holy Name. Whoever toils in the Torah strives for the Holy Name and is saved from all EVIL; he is saved in this world and rescued in the World to Come. Come and behold: whoever deals in the Torah is attached to the Tree of Life and, since he is attached to the Tree of Life, he is part of everything, as is written: "she is a tree of life to those who lay hold on her..." (Mishlei 3:18).

2. רִבִּי יִצְחָק אָמַר, כָּל מַאן דְּיִשְׁתְּדַּל בְּאוֹרַיְיתָא, חֵירוּ אִית לֵיהּ מִכֹּלָּא, חֵירוּ מִמִּיתָה, כְּמָה דְּאָמָרָן. בְּגִין דְּחֵירוּ עֲלֵיהּ שַׁרְיָא, וְאָחִיד בֵּיהּ. אִילוּ יִשְׂרָאֵל מִתְעַטְּרִין בְּאוֹרַיְיתָא, יִשְׁתְּזָבוּ מִכֹּלָּא, וְלָא יִשְׁתַּכְּחוּ בְּגָלוּתָא, וְדָא הוּא דִּכְתִיב חָרוּת עַל הַלֻּחוֹת, אַל תִּקְרֵי חָרוּת אֶלָּא חֵירוּת. וְחֵירוּת דָּא בְּאוֹרַיְיתָא אִשְׁתְּכַח, אוֹרַיְיתָא אִיהִי חֵילָא דִּימִינָא, כְּד"א מִימִינוֹ אֵשׁ דָּת לָמוֹ, וּשְׂמָאלָא אִתְכְּלִיל בִּימִינָא, מַאן דְּעָבֵיד יְמִינָא שְׂמָאלָא, וּשְׂמָאלָא יְמִינָא, הָא אִיהוּ כְּאִילוּ חָרִיב עָלְמָא.

2. Rabbi Yitzchak said: Whoever deals in the Torah is free from everything, even free from death, as mentioned, since liberty, WHICH IS BINAH, dwells upon him and is attached to him. If Yisrael had adorned themselves with Torah, they would have been saved from everything and would not have found themselves in exile. This is what is written: "engraved (Heb. *charut*) upon the tablets" (Shemot 32:16). Do not read it WITH AN 'A', but rather WITH AN 'E', as "*Cherut*," since this freedom (Heb. *cherut*) is available in the Torah. The Torah is the power of the right, as it is written: "from His right hand went a fiery law for them" (Devarim 33:2), and the left is included in the right. Whoever makes the right left and the left right is as if he destroys the world.

3. ת"ח, אַהֲרֹן יְמִינָא. לֵיוָאֵי שְׂמָאלָא, קֹרַח בָּעֵי לְמֶעְבַּד חֲלוּפָא דִּימִינָא לִשְׂמָאלָא, בְּג"כ אִתְעֲנַשׁ. וְלָא עוֹד אֶלָּא דְּאִשְׁתְּכַח בֵּיהּ לִישָׁנָא בִישָׁא, וְאִתְעֲנַשׁ בְּכֹלָּא. רִבִּי יְהוּדָה אָמַר, שְׂמָאלָא אִתְכְּלִיל תָּדִיר בִּימִינָא, קֹרַח בָּעָא לְאַחְלָפָא תִּקּוּנָא דִּלְעֵילָּא וְתַתָּא, בְּג"כ אִתְאֲבִיד מֵעֵילָּא וְתַתָּא.

3. Come and behold: Aaron is right, WHICH IS CHESED, and the Levites are left, WHICH IS GVURAH. Korah wanted to exchange the right for left; HE DESIRED THE PRIESTHOOD, WHICH IS RIGHT, FOR THE LEVITES, WHO ARE LEFT; therefore, he was punished. Furthermore, he had the evil tongue, BY SPEAKING OUT AGAINST MOSES, and was punished for everything. Rabbi Yehuda said: The left is always contained in the right, BECAUSE THAT IS HOW THE LEFT IS CORRECTED. Korah wished to substitute the correction of above and below, SINCE HE ASPIRED TO THE

DOMINATION OF THE LEVITES, WHICH ARE LEFT, SO THAT THEY SHOULD NOT BE INCLUDED IN THE PRIESTS, WHICH ARE RIGHT. Therefore, he was annihilated from above and below.

4. וַיִּקַּח קֹרַח, מַאי וַיִּקַּח. נָסִיב עֵיטָא בִּישָׁא לְגַרְמֵיהּ, כָּל דְּרָדַף בָּתַר דְּלָאו דִּילֵיהּ, אִיהוּ עָרִיק מִקַּמֵּיהּ. וְלֹא עוֹד, אֶלָּא מַה דְּאִית בֵּיהּ אִתְאֲבִיד מִנֵּיהּ. קֹרַח רָדִיף בָּתַר דְּלָאו דִּילֵיהּ, דִּילֵיהּ אָבִיד, וְאַחֲרָא לָא רָוַוח.

4. "Now Korah...took" (Bemidbar 16:1). HE ASKS: What is the meaning of "took"? HE RESPONDS: He took faulty counsel for himself. If one chases after something that does not belong to him, it escapes from him and he even loses what he has. Korah chased after something that was not his. Therefore, he lost his own and no one else gained.

5. קֹרַח אָזִיל בְּמַחֲלוֹקֶת. מַאי מַחֲלוֹקֶת. פְּלוּגְתָּא. פְּלוּגְתָּא דִּלְעֵילָּא וְתַתָּא. וּמַאן דְּבָעֵי לְאַפְלְגָא תִּקּוּנָא דְּעָלְמָא, יִתְאֲבִיד מִכֻּלְּהוּ עָלְמִין. מַחֲלוֹקֶת, פְּלוּגְתָּא דִּשְׁלוֹם. וּמַאן דְּפָלִיג עַל שָׁלוֹם, פָּלִיג עַל שְׁמָא קַדִּישָׁא, בְּגִין דִּשְׁמָא קַדִּישָׁא, שָׁלוֹם אִקְרֵי.

5. Korah turned to disagreement. What is the meaning of disagreement? Distancing and repulsion; the distancing and repulsion of what is above and below, and whoever wishes to postpone the restoration of the universe will become lost from all the worlds. Conflict is a distancing of peace, and whoever is in conflict about peace is in disagreement with His Holy Name, because His Holy Name is called 'Peace'.

6. ת"ח, לֵית עָלְמָא קָאִים אֶלָּא עַל שָׁלוֹם, כַּד בָּרָא קוּדְשָׁא בְּרִיךְ הוּא עָלְמָא, לָא יָכִיל לְאִתְקַיְּימָא, עַד דְּאָתָא וְשָׁרָא עֲלַיְיהוּ שָׁלוֹם. וּמַאי הוּא. שַׁבָּת, דְּאִיהוּ שְׁלָמָא דְּעֶלְאֵי וְתַתָּאֵי, וּכְדֵין אִתְקַיִּים עָלְמָא. וּמַאן דְּפָלִיג עֲלֵיהּ, יִתְאֲבִיד מֵעָלְמָא.

6. Come and behold: the world does not exist except through peace. When the Holy One, blessed be He, created the world, it could not endure until He

came and made peace dwell upon them. What is it? It is the Shabbat, which is the peace of the upper and the lower grades. And then the world endured. THEREFORE, whoever creates dissension about this PEACE will be lost from the world.

7. צְלָפְחָד פָּלִיג עַל שַׁבָּת, דַּהֲוָה מְקוֹשֵׁשׁ עֵצִים. וּמַאן אִינּוּן עֵצִים. אִינּוּן אִילָנִין אַחֲרָנִין כִּדְאַמָּרָן. וְאִינּוּן מִלִּין דְּחוֹל, וְחוֹל בַּקֹּדֶשׁ לָא שַׁרְיָיא, דְּפָלִיג עַל שְׁלָמָא דְּעָלְמָא.

7. Zelophehad was in dissension with the Shabbat because he was gathering wood (or: 'trees'). What were these trees? These were the other trees OF THE SEVENTY CHIEFTAINS, as we mentioned. These were secular matters and secular concerns do not prevail in sanctity. HENCE, he was in conflict with the world peace, WHICH IS SHABBAT, BECAUSE HE BLENDED THE SECULAR WITH THE SHABBAT.

8. רִבִּי יוֹסֵי אָמַר, כְּתִיב שָׁלוֹם רָב לְאוֹהֲבֵי תוֹרָתֶךְ וְגוֹ'. אוֹרַיְיתָא הוּא שָׁלוֹם, דִּכְתִיב וְכָל נְתִיבוֹתֶיהָ שָׁלוֹם. וְקֹרַח אָתָא לְאַפְגְּמָא שָׁלוֹם דִּלְעֵילָא וְתַתָּא, בְּג"כ אִתְעֲנִישׁ הוּא מֵעֵילָא וְתַתָּאה.

8. Rabbi Yosi says that it is written: "great peace have they who love Your Torah" (Tehilim 119:165). The Torah is peace, as is written: "and all her paths are peace" (Mishlei 3:17). And Korah came to blemish that peace of above – WHICH IS THE TORAH, MEANING THE CENTRAL COLUMN THAT IS CALLED 'TORAH' THAT PRODUCES PEACE BETWEEN THE RIGHT AND LEFT, and of below, OF MOSES. Therefore, he was punished from the higher and the lower aspects BY FIRE AND BY THE OPENING OF THE EARTHLY CHASM.

2. "Summoned to the congregation"

A Synopsis

Rabbi Shimon explains how the higher world is like the lower one, so that when the Congregation of Yisrael are gathered together for festivals, the higher Sfirot are summoned by the Upper Temple. He says that the men of renown who came against Moses and Aaron were not men of God, since they emerged from the aspect of Gvurah, and that those men created dissension.

9. וַיָּקוּמוּ לִפְנֵי מֹשֶׁה וְגוֹ'. הַאי קְרָא אוֹקְמוּהָ חַבְרַיָּיא. ר' שִׁמְעוֹן אָמַר, קְרִיאֵי מוֹעֵד קְרָאֵי כְּתִיב, חָסֵר יוֹ"ד, אֲמַאי קְרָאֵי. אֶלָּא הָכִי הוּא, מַלְכוּתָא דְּאַרְעָא כְּעֵין מַלְכוּתָא דִּרְקִיעָא. וְרָזָא דָא, כָּל אִינּוּן כִּתְרִין עִלָּאִין, דִּשְׁמָא קַדִּישָׁא אִתְאֲחִיד בְּהוּ, כֻּלְּהוּ זְמִינִין מֵאֲתַר דְּאִקְרֵי קֹדֶשׁ, הה"ד מִקְרָאֵי קֹדֶשׁ. וְאֵימָתַי בְּשַׁעֲתָא דְּמוֹעֵד זַמִּין בְּעָלְמָא, כְּגַוְונָא דְּאִינּוּן כִּתְרִין עִלָּאִין, דְּזְמִינִין מִקְדָּשׁ עִלָּאָה, ה"נ קֹדֶשׁ תַּתָּא זַמִּין לְחֵילוֹי, לְאַטְטְרָא וּלְאַעֲלָאָה לְהוּ.

9. "And they rose up before Moses..." (Bemidbar 16:2). This verse has been explained by the friends. Rabbi Shimon says: "regularly summoned (Heb. *kri'ei*) to the congregation (Heb. *mo'ed*)" (Ibid.), is missing a *Yud*. Why is it written *"Kriei"*? HE RESPONDS: It is only that the earthly kingdom is like heavenly kingdom, MEANING THAT MALCHUT BELOW IS LIKE MALCHUT ABOVE. That is the secret meaning of all these higher Sfirot onto which the Holy Name holds. All are summoned from the place that is called 'Holiness', THAT IS THE SECRET OF SUPERNAL ABA AND IMA, as it is written: "which you shall proclaim to be (also: 'summoned from') holy gatherings" (Vayikra 23:37). When is this? When *mo'ed* prevails in the world, THAT IS, DURING FESTIVALS AND APPOINTED TIMES (HEB. *MO'ED*). Just as these higher Sfirot are summoned by the Upper Temple, SO AS TO SANCTIFY THEM, similarly the Lower Sanctity summons its legions to adorn and uplift them. THESE ARE THREE WORLDS BRIYAH, YETZIRAH AND ASIYAH, WHICH ARE THE LEGIONS OF MALCHUT THAT ADORNS THEM AND UPLIFTS THEM TO ATZILUT.

10. קֹדֶשׁ עִלָּאָה יְדִיעָא, קֹדֶשׁ תַּתָּאָה חָכְמַת שְׁלֹמֹה, ה"נ אִיהִי זְמִינַת

לְכָל חֵילָהָא. וְאִינּוּן חַיָּילִין כּוּלְהוּ, זְמִינִין לְאִתְעַטְּרָא בְּהַאי קֹדֶשׁ
תַּתָּאָה, בְּזִמְנָא דְּמוֹעֵד שַׁרְיָיא בְּעָלְמָא. וּכְגַוְונָא דְּחֵילָהָא קַיְימִין
לְעֵילָּא, ה"נ קַיְימֵי מְמָנָן דְּעַמָּא, כְּדוּגְמָא דִּילָהּ לְתַתָּא, וע"ד אִקְרוֹן
קְרָאֵי מוֹעֵד. וּבְגִין דְּאִנּוּן לְתַתָּא, קְרָאֵי מוֹעֵד חָסֵר, אֲבָל בִּשְׁלִימוּ יַתִּיר
אִינּוּן.

10. The higher Holiness is known AS ABA AND IMA ABOVE, and the lower Holiness is the wisdom of Solomon, MEANING MALCHUT, which also summons all her legions TO SANCTIFY THEM WITH HER HOLINESS. These legions are all invited to be adorned in this lower Holiness at a time when a festival prevails in the world. As her legions are standing above IN ATZILUT SUMMONED BY MALCHUT, so are the appointed of the nation, MEANING THE CHIEFTAINS OF YISRAEL, according to her example below, IN THIS WORLD. Therefore, it is written as: "summoned to the congregation (Heb. mo'ed)," and of those below it is written, "summoned (Heb. kri'ei) to the congregation"; "Kriei" is missing a Yud. However, they are then in increased wholeness.

11. אַנְשֵׁי שֵׁם וַדַּאי, וְלָא אַנְשֵׁי יְיָ. וְדָא הוּא רָזָא, בְּנָקְבוֹ שֵׁם יוּמָת,
וְאוֹקִימְנָא. וְעַל דָּא אִקְרֵי הָכָא, אַנְשֵׁי שֵׁם וַדַּאי, כֵּיוָן דְּמִסִּטְרָא דִּגְבוּרָה
קָא אַתְיָין, אַנְשֵׁי שֵׁם אִינּוּן, הָא שְׁבָחָא דִּלְהוֹן יַתִּיר, אֲבָל אִינּוּן נַטְלוּ
לְגַרְמַיְיהוּ. וְאִתְאַחֲדוּ בְּמַחֲלוֹקֶת.

11. "…men of renown (also: 'name')…" (Bemidbar 16:2) is most certainly said and not 'men of Hashem' – MEANING THE PEOPLE OF MALCHUT CALLED 'NAME', but not 'men of Hashem', THAT IS ZEIR ANPIN. That is the secret of: "and he who blasphemes the Name of Hashem shall be put to death" (Vayikra 24:16). We established THAT IT ALLUDES TO MALCHUT THAT IS CALLED 'NAME' and, therefore, they were certainly considered men of name, since they emerged from the aspect of Gvurah, WHICH IS MALCHUT CALLED 'THE LOWER GVURAH'. They are men of name and that WAS SAID to increase their praise. However, they took HER for themselves, MEANING THEY SEPARATED MALCHUT FROM ZEIR ANPIN, and held on to a dissension WITH MOSES, WHO IS THE SECRET OF ZEIR ANPIN.

3. Holy, pure

A Synopsis

Rabbi Shimon says that Moses asked Korah and the others to come
before him in the morning because morning is the time of holiness,
of Chesed, and therefore of the priests. Essentially Moses was
saying to them that if they remained on the side of Judgment the
morning would not tolerate them and they would not be found holy
and worthy of the priesthood. The matter would be tested by the
offering of the incense, and the man who God chooses must be
holy and not pure: the priest is holy and the Levite is pure.

12. בֹּקֶר וְיוֹדַע יְיָ' אֶת אֲשֶׁר לוֹ. אֲמַאי בֹּקֶר, וַאֲמַאי קָדוֹשׁ וְלָא טָהוֹר.
אֶלָּא אִינוּן מִסִּטְרָא דְּטָהוֹר קָא אַתְיָין, וְקָדוֹשׁ כַּהֲנָא. אָמַר מֹשֶׁה, בֹּקֶר,
דִּכְדֵין כִּתְרָא דְּכַהֲנָא אִתְּעַר בְּעָלְמָא, אִי אַתּוּן כַּהֲנֵי, הָא בֹּקֶר, פַּלְחוּ
עֲבוֹדָה דְּבֹקֶר, וּכְדֵין וְיוֹדַע יְיָ' אֶת אֲשֶׁר לוֹ וְאֶת הַקָּדוֹשׁ. אֶת אֲשֶׁר לוֹ
סְתָם, דָּא לֵיוָאֵי. וְאֶת הַקָּדוֹשׁ, דָּא כַּהֲנָא, כְּדֵין וְהִקְרִיב אֵלָיו. וְלֵית
מַאן דְּאַבְחִין מִלָּה, אֶלָּא בֹּקֶר, אִי תִּתְחֲזוּן לְאִשְׁתַּאֲרָא בְּסְטַר דִּינָא,
בֹּקֶר לָא סָבִיל לְכוּ, דְּהָא לָאו זִמְנֵיהּ הוּא. וְאִי תִּתְחֲזוּן לְאִשְׁתַּאֲרָא
בְּחֶסֶד, הָא זִמְנֵיהּ הוּא, וְתִשְׁתַּאֲרוּן גַּבֵּיהּ, וִיקַבֵּל לְכוּ.

12. "Tomorrow morning Hashem will show who is His" (Bemidbar 16:5).
HE INQUIRES: Why in the morning, PRECISELY, and why "holy" and not
pure, MEANING "AND WHO IS HOLY; AND WILL CAUSE HIM TO COME NEAR
TO HIM" (IBID.)? IT SHOULD HAVE SAID, 'AND WHO IS PURE'. HE
REPLIES: For they, THE CONGREGATION OF KORAH, came from the pure
side, SINCE THE LEVITES ARE IN THE ASPECT OF PURE, AND NOT HOLY,
and the priest is holy. Moses said in the morning when the Sfirah of the
priest, WHICH IS CHESED, gets awakened in the world: 'If you are priests,
here is the morning. Let them perform the service of the morning,' WHICH
IS CHESED. Then, "Hashem will show who is His, and who is holy."
"…who is His…" is unspecific, which is the Levi. "…and who is holy…" is
the priest. Then, "and will cause him to come near to Him," HE WHO IS
HOLY. There is no one who can discern the matter except the morning.
THUS, HE SPOKE TO THEM: 'If you find yourself remaining on the side of
Judgment, the morning, WHICH IS CHESED, will not tolerate you, since that

is not the time of Judgment. But if you see yourselves remaining in Chesed, then here is its time. And you will stay with it, and it will accept you'.

13. בְּמָה. בַּקְטֹרֶת. דְּהָא קְטֹרֶת בָּעֵי לְשׁוּשְׁבִינָא, לְאִתְקַטְּרָא עַל יְדֵיהּ בְּכֹלָּא, וּלְאִתְקַשְּׁרָא. מַאן שׁוּשְׁבִינָא. דָּא כַּהֲנָא. וּבג״כ, וְהָיָה הָאִישׁ אֲשֶׁר יִבְחַר יְיָ׳ הוּא הַקָּדוֹשׁ, וְלָא הַטָּהוֹר. תְּרֵין דַּרְגִּין אִינּוּן: קָדוֹשׁ. וְטָהוֹר. כֹּהֵן, קָדוֹשׁ. לֵוִי, טָהוֹר. וע״ד הַקָּדוֹשׁ כְּתִיב.

13. In what WILL THE MATTER BE TESTED? In the offering of the incense, since the incense must be brought through the groom's best man in all OF THE LEVELS and be connected THROUGH THEM, SINCE THE SCENT OF THE INCENSE RISES AND BINDS ALL THE LEVELS INTO ONE. Who is that groom's man? It is the priest, WHO IS CHESED. Therefore, the man whom Hashem chooses shall be holy and not pure, since holy and pure are two distinct levels: the priest is "holy" and the Levite is "pure." Therefore, it is written: "and who is holy."

4. "El, the Elohim of the spirits"

A Synopsis

We read how when Moses and Aaron fell on their faces they gave themselves up to death. Rabbi Yehuda says that men are repaid with the deeds that they do, but if they repent God will gather them back to Himself. Rabbi Yosi draws an analogy with Levirate marriage where the brother must set his heart upon the redemption of his brother in order to build him back up; his motives must not be lust for the brother's wife. We hear that the Ruach and Neshamah are in the hands of God and He has compassion on human beings so that they shall not be lost from this world or the next.

14. וַיִּפְּלוּ עַל פְּנֵיהֶם וַיֹּאמְרוּ אֵל אֱלֹהֵי הָרוּחוֹת לְכָל בָּשָׂר. ת״ח, מֹשֶׁה וְאַהֲרֹן מָסְרוּ גַרְמַיְיהוּ לְמִיתָה. בְּמָה, בְּגִין דִּכְתִיב וַיִּפְּלוּ עַל פְּנֵיהֶם וַיֹּאמְרוּ אֵל אֱלֹהֵי הָרוּחוֹת, רוּחַת כְּתִיב, חָסֵר וָא״ו. ובג״כ אִילָנָא דְּמוֹתָא הוּא, וּבְכָל אֲתָר נְפִילַת אַנְפִּין לְהַהוּא אֲתָר הֲוֵי. וע״ד אֵל אֱלֹהֵי, אֵל: הה״ד וְאֵל זוֹעֵם בְּכָל יוֹם. אֱלֹהֵי הָרוּחוֹת, דְּאִיהוּ אֲתָר צְרוֹרָא דְּנִשְׁמָתִין דְּעָלְמָא, וְכָל נִשְׁמָתִין תַּמָּן סַלְּקִין, וּמִתַּמָּן אַתְיָין.

14. "And they fell upon their faces, and said, 'El, Elohim of the spirits of all flesh'" (Bemidbar 16:22). Come and behold: Moses and Aaron gave themselves up to death. How? It is written: "and they fell upon their faces, and said, 'El, Elohim of the spirits (Heb. *ruchot*)'." *Ruchot* is spelled with the *Vav* missing. Therefore, that is the Tree of Death, WHICH IS MALCHUT, and the falling on the face is always to that side. Therefore, IT IS WRITTEN, "El, Elohim of," as is written: "and El Who has indignation every day" (Tehilim 7:12), WHICH REFERS TO MALCHUT. "…Elohim of the spirits…" is the source where all the world's souls are bound together and all the souls ascend there. From there they come, THAT IS, MALCHUT.

15. רִבִּי יְהוּדָה פָּתַח, שִׁמְעוּ חֲכָמִים מִלַּי וְיוֹדְעִים הַאֲזִינוּ לִי. הַאי קְרָא אֵלִיהוּא אֲמָרוֹ. ת״ח, מַה כְּתִיב וּבִשְׁלֹשֶׁת רֵעָיו חָרָה אַפּוֹ עַל אֲשֶׁר לֹא מָצְאוּ מַעֲנֶה וְגוֹ'. דְּהָא אִינוּן הֲווֹ אַמְרִין מִלִּין, וְאִיּוֹב לָא הֲוָה אִתְנְחִים עֲלַיְיהוּ. מֵהָכָא אוֹלִיפְנָא, מַאן דְּעָאל לְנַחֲמָא לְאָבֵל, בָּעֵי לְיַסְדָא מִלִּין בְּקַדְמֵיתָא, דְּהָא חַבְרַיָיא דְּאִיּוֹב הֲווֹ אַמְרֵי מִלֵּי קְשׁוֹט, אֲבָל לְנַחֲמָא

לֵיהּ לָאו, בְּגִין דְּבָעֵי מִלִּין דְּאִיהוּ יוֹדֵי עֲלַיְיהוּ, וּכְדֵין יְקַבֵּל עָלֵיהּ דִּינָא, וְיוֹדֵי לְמַלְכָּא קַדִּישָׁא עָלֵיהּ. מַה כְּתִיב, וֶאֱלִיָּהוּ חִכָּה אֶת אִיּוֹב בִּדְבָרִים וְגוֹ'. דְּאוֹדֵי לְבָתַר לְקוּדְשָׁא בְּרִיךְ הוּא, וְקַבִּיל עָלֵיהּ דִּינָא דִּשְׁמַיָּא.

15. Rabbi Yehuda opened the discussion with the verse: "hear my words O wise men; and give ear to me, you who have knowledge" (Iyov 34:2). Elihu spoke this verse. Come and behold: it is written, "also against his three friends did his anger burn, because they had found no answer" (Iyov 32:3), since they did speak but Iyov was not consoled by them. From here we take a lesson that whoever comes to console the mourner must structure his speech first, SO THAT THEY ARE WORTHY TO CONSOLE HIM. Job's friends spoke words of truth but not to console him, and since it requires words that THE MOURNER will acknowledge, then he will accept upon himself the Judgment. And he acknowledged the Holy King, as is written: "now Elihu had waited to speak to Iyov" (Ibid. 4), since he acknowledged himself afterward to the Holy One, blessed be He, and accepted upon himself the sentence of heaven.

16. ת"ח, כְּתִיב לָכֵן אַנְשֵׁי לֵבָב שִׁמְעוּ לִי חָלִילָה לָאֵל מֵרֶשַׁע וְשַׁדַּי מֵעָוֶל. לָכֵן אַנְשֵׁי לֵבָב שִׁמְעוּ לִי, שְׁלֵימִין בְּכֹלָּא, לְאַבְחֲנָא מִלִּין. חָלִילָה לָאֵל מֵרֶשַׁע, הה"ד וְאֵל זוֹעֵם בְּכָל יוֹם. וְשַׁדַּי מֵעָוֶל, דָּא סָמִיךְ לְקַבְלָא דָּא, וְהָא אוּקְמוּהָ אֵל שַׁדָּי. כִּי פֹעַל אָדָם יְשַׁלֶּם לוֹ, הָא ב"נ אָזִיל בְּהַאי עָלְמָא, וְעָבֵיד עֲבִידְתּוֹי וְחָטֵי קַמֵּי מָארֵיהּ, הַהוּא עוֹבָדָא תַּלְיָא עָלֵיהּ, לְשַׁלְּמָא לֵיהּ דִּינָא, הה"ד כִּי פֹעַל אָדָם יְשַׁלֶּם לוֹ, הַהוּא עוֹבָדָא יְשַׁלֶּם לוֹ.

16. Come and behold: it is written, "therefore hearken to me, you men of understanding: far be it from El, that He should do wickedness; and from Shadai, that He should commit iniquity" (Iyov 34:10). "Therefore hearken to me, you men of understanding" (Ibid.); these are the most perfected who can discern the matters. And "far be it from El that He should do wickedness." This is what is written: "and El Who has indignation every day" (Ibid.); THAT REFERS TO MALCHUT THAT IS CALLED 'EL'. "...and from Shadai, that He should commit iniquity" (Ibid.); this one is close to that one, SINCE SHADAI IS YESOD THAT IS NEAR EL, WHICH IS

MALCHUT. It was already explained that in, "El Shadai," EL REFERS TO
MALCHUT AND SHADAI REFERS TO YESOD. "For the work of a man shall
He pay back to him" (Ibid. 11). If a person walks about in this world
performing deeds and sins before his Master, that deed impends upon Him
to reward him with Judgment. This is what it says: "that the man's deed will
pay him," as that particular act THAT HE PERFORMED will pay him.

17. וְעִם כָּל דָּא, אִם יָשִׂים אֵלָיו לִבּוֹ, כֵּיוָן דְּבַר נָשׁ שַׁוֵּי לִבֵּיהּ וּרְעוּתֵיהּ
לְאִתָּבָא קַמֵּי מָארֵיהּ, כְּדֵין אֵל אֱלֹהֵי הָרוּחֹות רוּחוֹ וְנִשְׁמָתוֹ אֵלָיו
יֶאֱסוֹף לְאִתְצַרְרָא בִּצְרוֹרָא דְּחַיֵּי, וְלָא שָׁבִיק לְנַפְשֵׁיהּ לְבַר, לְאִתְדָּנָא
בְּדִינָא אַחֲרָא.

17. With all this, "if he set his heart upon Him" (Ibid. 14). As soon as a
person places his heart and will to return to his Master, then El, the Elohim,
will "gather to Himself his spirit and his breath (Heb. neshamah)" (Ibid.).
He will gather to him to bind them in the bundle of life and he does not
leave his Nefesh out to be judged in another Judgment.

18. רִבִּי יוֹסֵי אָמַר, הַאי מִלָּה רָזָא הוּא, בְּדִינִין טְמִירִין דְּקוּדְשָׁא בְּרִיךְ
הוּא. כִּי פוֹעַל אָדָם יְשַׁלֶּם לוֹ, לְאִתְדָּנָא בְּדִינֵיהּ, וּבְאִינוּן עוֹבָדִין דְּבַר
נָשׁ עָבִיד בְּהַאי עָלְמָא, וְסָלִיק לֵיהּ לְאִתְדָּנָא כְּעוֹבָדוֹי, וְיִתְאֲבִיד
מֵעָלְמָא, מַה כְּתִיב בַּתְרֵיהּ, מִי פָקַד עָלָיו אָרְצָה וּמִי שָׂם תֵּבֵל כֻּלָּהּ. מִי
פָקַד עָלָיו אָרְצָה, דָּא הוּא אָחוּהּ דְּפָרִיק לֵיהּ. וּמִי שָׂם תֵּבֵל כֻּלָּהּ,
דְּבָאנֵי בֵּיתָא, וּבְנֵי בִנְיָין עָלְמָא, וְתִקּוּנָא וְיִשׁוּבָא. מַה כְּתִיב בַּתְרֵיהּ,
אִם יָשִׂים אֵלָיו לִבּוֹ. הַאי בַּר נָשׁ, דְּפָקִיד עָלֵיהּ לְמִבְנֵי בִּנְיָינָא, בָּעֵי
לְכַוְּונָא לִבָּא וּרְעוּתָא לְגַבֵּיהּ דְּהַהוּא מִיתָא. מִכָּאן, בַּר נָשׁ דְּאָתֵי עַל
הַהִיא אִתְּתָא, בְּגִין שְׁפִירוּ וְתִיאוּבְתָּא דִּילָהּ, הָא בִּנְיָין עָלְמָא לָא
אִתְבְּנֵי, דְּהָא רְעוּתָא וְלִבָּא לָא אִתְכַּוְּון לְגַבֵּי מִיתָא.

18. Rabbi Yosi said: That matter is a secret among the concealed Judgments
of the Holy One, blessed be He, since, "for the work of a man shall He pay
back to him," means to be sentenced in his Judgment, according to the
activities he performed in this world. He raises him to be judged

accordingly and he is lost from the world. The following verse says: "who has given Him charge over the earth? Who has disposed the whole world?" (Ibid. 13). "Who has given Him charge over the earth?" is the one WHO APPOINTED IN CHARGE OVER HIM his brother that redeems him. "Who has placed the whole world under Him?" means THAT HIS BROTHER constructs a house, BY PERFORMING LEVIRATE MARRIAGE WITH HIS WIFE, and builds an everlasting structure and restoration and inhabitation OF THE WORLD. Following that, it is written: "if he set his heart upon Him," since that person that was appointed AS THE REDEEMER to erect the structure needs to have an attentive heart and desire for that dead person, IN ORDER TO ERECT HIS NAME FOR HIM. The lesson from here is that if a person takes that woman in levirate marriage for her beauty and his lust, then the everlasting edifice does not get built, since his desire and heart were not directed for the sake of the one who died.

19. וּבְגִין כַּךְ כְּתִיב, אִם יָשִׂים אֵלָיו לִבּוֹ, בִּרְעוּתָא דְלִבָּא דִיכַוֵּין לְגַבֵּיהּ, כְּדֵין רוּחוֹ וְנִשְׁמָתוֹ אֵלָיו יֶאֱסוֹף, וְאִתְמְשַׁךְ גַּבֵּיהּ, לְאִתְבַּנָּאָה בְּהַאי עָלְמָא, מַה כְּתִיב בַּתְרֵיהּ, יִגְוַע כָּל בָּשָׂר יָחַד וְאָדָם עַל עָפָר יָשׁוּב, יִגְוַע כָּל בָּשָׂר יָחַד, הַהוּא גוּפָא יִתְבְּלֵי בְּעַפְרָא, וְכָל הַהוּא בִּשְׂרָא. וְהַשְׁתָּא, אָדָם עַל עָפָר יָשׁוּב, הָא חַדְתּוּתִין דְּבִנְיָנָא כְּמִלְקַדְמִין, וְיֵתוּב עַל עַפְרָא דְבִנְיָינָא דְּגוּפָא אַחֲרָא, כְּמָה דַּהֲוָה בְּקַדְמֵיתָא. וְעַל דָּא, רוּחָא וְנִשְׁמְתָא בִּידוֹי דְקוּדְשָׁא בְּרִיךְ הוּא, וְחָיֵיס עָלַיְיהוּ דִּבְנֵי נָשָׁא, דְּלָא יִתְאֲבִידוּ מֵהַאי עָלְמָא, וּמֵעָלְמָא אַחֲרָא, בְּגִין כַּךְ אֵל אֱלֹהֵי הָרוּחוֹת לְכָל בָּשָׂר.

19. Therefore, it is written: "if he set his heart upon him." It must be in the desire of the heart that the intention is towards THE DEAD one. Then, "gather to Himself his spirit and his breath," because he continues through him to be built up in this world. It is then written: "all flesh shall perish together, and man shall return to dust" (Ibid. 15). "All flesh shall perish together," so that his body and flesh will rot in the dust. Now, AFTER THIS, "man shall return to dust," so there will be the REVIVAL of the structure as before. "…and it will return the dust…" (Ibid. 15) in the composition of another body, as it first was. For the Ruach and Neshamah are in the hands of the Holy One, blessed be He, and He has compassion on human beings,

so that they shall not be lost from this world nor the other world. Therefore, it is written: "El, Elohim of the spirits of all flesh."

5. "Take a censer"

A Synopsis
Rabbi Chiya interprets the title verse by saying that people must be careful not to be sinful because their deeds are all recorded before God; if during the time of judgment a righteous person is in the world to plead for the sinful, God relents of His anger and uses compassion.

20. וַיֹּאמֶר מֹשֶׁה אֶל אַהֲרֹן קַח אֶת הַמַּחְתָּה וְגוֹ'. רַבִּי חִיָּיא פָּתַח חֲמַת מֶלֶךְ מַלְאֲכֵי מָוֶת וְאִישׁ חָכָם יְכַפְּרֶנָּה. כַּמָּה אִית לְהוּ לִבְנֵי נָשָׁא, לְאִסְתַּמְּרָא מֵחוֹבַיְיהוּ, וּלְנַטְרָא עוֹבָדַיְיהוּ, דְּהָא בְּכַמָּה זִמְנִין עָלְמָא אִתְדָּן, וּבְכָל יוֹמָא וְיוֹמָא עוֹבָדִין בְּמַתְקְלָא סַלְּקִין, וּמַשְׁגִּיחִין עֲלַיְיהוּ לְעֵילָא, וְאַכְתִּיבוּ קַמֵּיהּ. וְכַד עוֹבָדַיְיהוּ דִּבְנֵי נָשָׁא, לָא מִתְכַּשְׁרָן קַמֵּי מַלְכָּא, סָלִיק רוּגְזָא, וְדִינָא אִתְּעַר, הֵהַ"ד חֲמַת מֶלֶךְ מַלְאֲכֵי מָוֶת, וע"ד בְּכָל יוֹמָא וְיוֹמָא בָּעֵי ב"נ לְאִזְדַּהֲרָא מֵחוֹבוֹי.

20. "And Moses said to Aaron, 'Take a censer...'" (Bemidbar 17:11). Rabbi Chiya opened the discussion with the verse: "the wrath of a king is as messengers of death: but a wise man will pacify it" (Mishlei 16:14). How particular people need to be to prevent themselves from giving in to their iniquities and to be careful with their activities. At various occasions, the world is judged. And on a daily basis, their deeds are entered upon the scale of Justice, are monitored from above, and are recorded before Him. When a person's acts are not fit for the King, anger rises and Judgment is stirred. This is what is written: "the wrath of a king is as messengers of death." Therefore, a person must be on watch for his iniquities each and every day.

21. וְאִישׁ חָכָם יְכַפְּרֶנָּה, בְּשַׁעֲתָא דְּמָארֵיהוֹן דְּדִינִין קַיְימִין עַל עָלְמָא, וְרוּגְזָא תָּלֵי, אִי אִשְׁתְּכַח בְּדָרָא זַכָּאָה דְּרָשִׁים לְעֵילָא, קוּדְשָׁא בְּרִיךְ הוּא אַשְׁגַּח בֵּיהּ, וְאִשְׁתְּכַךְ רוּגְזָא. לְמַלְכָּא דְּאִתְרְגַז עַל עַבְדּוֹי, וַהֲוָה תָּבַע עַל סַנְטִירָא לְמֶעְבַּד דִּינָא, אַדְהָכִי עָאל רְחִימָא דְּמַלְכָּא, וְקָם קַמֵּיהּ, כֵּיוָן דְּחָמָא לֵיהּ מַלְכָּא, אִתְנְהִירוּ אַנְפּוֹי. שָׁארֵי הַהוּא רְחִימָא דְּמַלְכָּא לְאִשְׁתָּעֵי בַּהֲדֵיהּ, וּמַלְכָּא חַדֵּי. לְבָתַר כַּד אֲתָא סַנְטִירָא, חָזָא

אַנְפּוֹי דְּמַלְכָּא חַדְאָן, אִסְתַּלָּק וְאָזִיל לֵיהּ, וְלָא עָבֵיד דִּינָא. וּכְדֵין, הַהוּא רְחִימָא בָּעֵי לְמַלְכָּא עַל עַבְדּוֹי, וּמְכַפֵּר לְהוּ. וּבְג״כ, וְאִישׁ חָכָם יְכַפְּרֶנָּה.

21. "But a wise man will pacify it," during the time when prosecutors prevail on the world and anger impends. If the righteous man is at hand in that generation who is distinguished above, the Holy One, blessed be He, looks at him and the anger subsides. This is SIMILAR to a king who is angry at his servants and demands the officer that carry out justice. In the meantime, the beloved of the king arrives and stands in front of him and, as soon as the king sees him, his face shines. When that friend of the king begins to speak with him, the king is glad. After this, when the police official arrives and sees the king's face in happiness, he departs and no longer carries out the sentence. Then that beloved of the king beseeches the king on behalf of his servants and the king forgives them. As a result of this, "a wise man will pacify it."

22. אוּף הָכָא, כַּד חָמָא מֹשֶׁה דְּרוּגְזָא הֲוָה תָּלֵי, מִיַּד וַיֹּאמֶר מֹשֶׁה אֶל אַהֲרֹן, בְּגִין דְּאִיהוּ שׁוּשְׁבִינָא דְּמַטְרוֹנִיתָא, וּקְטֹרֶת לָא סַלְקָא אֶלָּא בִּידוֹי, דְּאִיהוּ אַסְגֵּי שְׁלָמָא בְּעָלְמָא, וְקָשִׁיר קִשְׁרָא דִמְהֵימְנוּתָא. קְטֹרֶת, הָא אוּקְמוּהָ, חֶדְוָותָא דִּלְעֵילָּא וְתַתָּא, קְשׁוּרָא דִמְהֵימְנוּתָא, סְלִיקוּ דְּרוּגְזָא, הה״ד שֶׁמֶן וּקְטֹרֶת יְשַׂמַּח לֵב, וּכְדֵין וְאִישׁ חָכָם יְכַפְּרֶנָּה, יְנַקֵּי וִידַכֵּי לְהַהוּא רוּגְזָא, וְרַחֲמִין מִתְעָרִין.

22. Here too, when Moses saw the anger pending, Moses immediately said to Aaron: 'He is the groom, MEANING THAT FRIEND, of the Queen, and the incense does not rise except through his hands, since he increases peace in the world and ties the knot of Faith,' THAT IS MALCHUT. Incense was already set and explained. That is the joy above and below, the tie of Faith and the disappearance of anger. This is what is written: "ointment and perfume rejoice the heart" (Mishlei 27:9). Then, "a wise man will pacify it," will clean and purify that anger and compassion will be stirred.

6. "Do not cut off the tribe of the families of the Kohathites"

A Synopsis

Rabbi Elazar says that the Levites can approach the Holy only through the priest, and that the priest hides and covers anything that they are not permitted to see. This is because everything of the priest is done in a whisper, secretly, while the Levites' speech and activities are in the raising of song and revelation of secrets. The priest's words are not spoken openly because he is of the right, Chesed. Rabbi Elazar tells us that when judgment prevails on the world from the left aspect, the right draws near by the burning of incense that is done quietly in secret. When Aaron ran into the midst of the congregation to stop the plague that was killing them he stood between the dead and the living, that is, between the Tree of Life and the Tree of Death. Thus the Tree of Life that is from the right came close to the priest, who was from the right, and the plague was stopped. Rabbi Elazar says that the priest has power above and below, and he is the cause of peace above and below; at all times the left serves the right.

23. רִבִּי אֶלְעָזָר אָמַר, אַל תַּכְרִיתוּ אֶת שֵׁבֶט מִשְׁפְּחוֹת הַקְּהָתִי מִתּוֹךְ הַלְוִיִם, בְּגִין דְּאִינוּן גִּזְעָא וְשָׁרְשָׁא דְּלֵיוָאֵי. וְזֹאת עֲשׂוּ לָהֶם וְחָיוּ וְלֹא יָמוּתוּ, דְּבָעֵי כַּהֲנָא לְאַתְקָנָא לְהוּ, דְּאַע״ג דְּקְרִיבִין אִינוּן לְקוּדְשָׁא, לָא יֵיעֲלוּן אֶלָּא בְּתִקוּנָא דְּכַהֲנָא, דְּהוּא יָדַע סִימָנָא דְּימָטוּן לְגַבֵּיה, וְלָא יַתִּיר. וְכַד מְכַסְיָא לְמָאנֵי קוּדְשָׁא, כְּדֵין כִּסוּיָא אַחֲרָא שָׁרֵי, וְאָסִיר לוֹן לְקַרְבָא לְמֶחֱמֵי, דְּהָא מִלָּה בַּחֲשַׁאי לָא אִית לְגַבַּיְיהוּ, אֶלָּא לְכַהֲנָא, דְּמִלָּה דִּלְהוֹן וְעוֹבָדָא דִּלְהוֹן בְּרָזָא וּבַחֲשַׁאי וְלֵיוָאֵי לְאַרָמָא קָלָא.

23. Rabbi Elazar said: "Do not cut off the tribe of the families of the Kohathites from among the Levites" (Bemidbar 4:18), since they are the trunk and root of the Levites. "…but thus do to them, that they may live, and not die…" (Ibid.). The priest must establish that for them; even though they are nearing to the Holy, they should only approach with the amendment of the priest, since he is aware of the signal, UP TO WHERE he can reach and not further. When they cover the holy vessels, another coverage prevails from above and it is forbidden FOR THE LEVITES to approach and look, since anything that is in a whisper, THAT IS, A SECRET, applies only to the priests, since their speech and activities are in secret and they whisper. The Levites' speech and activities are in the raising of the voice IN SONG.

24. בג״כ כַּהֲנֵי בַּחֲשַׁאי וּבְרָזָא, וע״ד אָסִיר לוֹן חַמְרָא, דְחַמְרָא לְאַרְמָא קָלָא, וּלְגַלָּאָה רָזִין אִיהוּ. בג״כ לֵיוָאֵי אִתְמְסָרוּ לְאַרְמָא קָלָא, דְהָא בְּדִינָא אִתְאַחַד, דִּינָא בְּאִתְגַלְיָיא אִיהוּ, וּלְפַרְסְמָא מִלָּה קַמֵּי כֹּלָא. אֲבָל כַּהֲנָא, כָּל מִלּוֹי בְּרָזָא וּבַחֲשַׁאי, וְלָאו בְּאִתְגַלְיָיא. בְּגִין דְּאִיהוּ יְמִינָא, כַּד דִּינִין שַׁרְיָין בְּעָלְמָא מִסִּטְרָא דִשְׂמָאלָא, יְמִינָא יְהֵא מִקָרְבָא, וּבַמָה. בִּקְטֹרֶת, דְּאִיהוּ בַּחֲשַׁאי, בְּרָזָא דָקִיק, וּפְנִימָאָה מִכֹּלָא.

24. Therefore, all the activities of the priests are performed quietly and secretively. Consequently, wine is forbidden to them, since wine is for raising the voice, FOR SONG, and revelation of secrets. The Levites are given to attend the raising of voice because they are connected to Judgment and Judgment is open in order to publicize it to all. However, all the priest's words are secretive and in a whisper, they are not spoken openly because he is of the right, THAT IS CHESED. When Judgments prevail on the world from the left aspect, the right draws near. By means of what? By the burning of incense, which is done quietly in secret, more subtle and refined than anything, THAT IS BINAH.

25. ת״ח, כַּד הַאי מַדְבְּחָא אַחֲרָא, שָׁארֵי לְאַתְעָרָא אִתְעָרוּתָא, כַּד לָא יִשְׁתַּכְחוּ זַכָּאִין, מַדְבְּחָא פְּנִימָאָה אִתְעַר לְגַבֵּיה, וְקָאִים לָקֳבְלֵיה, וְדִינִין מִשְׁתַּכְּכֵי. וע״ד קַיְימָא לָקֳבֵל דָא, וּכְדֵין דִּינָא אִסְתַּלָּק.

25. Come and behold: when this other altar, THE EXTERNAL ALTAR, WHICH IS MALCHUT, begins to stir the awakening OF JUDGMENT, and no righteous people are around TO PROTECT it, the inner altar, BINAH, awakens to him and stands up against him, and the Judgments are subdued. Therefore, THIS one stands opposite the other one and then Judgment departs.

26. ר' אֶלְעָזָר אָמַר, זֹאת עֲבוֹדַת בְּנֵי קְהָת בְּאֹהֶל מוֹעֵד קֹדֶשׁ הַקֳּדָשִׁים, בְּשַׁעֲתָא דִּבְנֵי קְהָת נַטְלִין קֹדֶשׁ קָדָשִׁים, כְּדֵין אָתֵי כַּהֲנָא, וְחָפֵי כֹּלָא, עַד לָא יְקָרְבוּן לְנַטְלָא לֵיה, וְלָא הֲווֹ חָמָאן לְעָלְמִין מַה דְּאִינּוּן נַטְלִין, אֶלָּא כֹּלָא בְּכִסּוּיָיא מִנַּיְיהוּ. כְּמָה דִכְתִיב וּבָא אַהֲרֹן וּבָנָיו בִּנְסֹעַ הַמַּחֲנֶה וְהוֹרִידוּ אֵת פָּרוֹכֶת הַמָּסָךְ. וְרוֹב כִּסּוּיָיא דְמָאנֵי מַקְדְּשָׁא,

תְּכֵלֶת אִיהוּ, בְּגִין דִּתְכֵלֶת הָא אוּקְמוּהָ וְאִתְּמַר. בָּתַר דְּאִתְכַּסְיָיא כֹּלָּא, מְקָרְבִין בְּנֵי קְהָת דְּנַטְלִין, וְלָא מְקָרְבִין אֶלָּא בְּאִינוּן בַּדִּים דְּנָפְקִין לְבַר. הה"ד, וְכִלָּה אַהֲרֹן וּבָנָיו לְכַסֹּת אֶת הַקֹּדֶשׁ וְגוֹ', בִּנְסֹעַ הַמַּחֲנֶה וְאַחֲרֵי כֵן יָבֹאוּ בְנֵי קְהָת לָשֵׂאת וְגוֹ'.

26. Rabbi Elazar says: "This shall be the service of the sons of Kohath in the Tent of Meeting, namely, the most holy thing" (Ibid. 4). During the period of time that the sons of Kohath came to take the Holy of Holies, the priest approached and covered everything prior to their approach, and they never saw what they carried. Instead, everything was covered from them, as it says, "and when the camp sets forward, Aaron shall come, and his sons, and they shall take down the veil of the screen" (Ibid. 5). Most of the casings for the Temple's utensils were colored blue. The significance of blue was already explained and taught. After everything was covered, the children of Kohath, who carried it, came near. They did not get any closer than the poles that extended out, as it is written: "and when Aaron and his sons have made an end of covering the Sanctuary...as the camp is to set forward; after that, the sons of Kohath shall come to bear it..." (Ibid. 15).

27. בג"כ קְטֹרֶת דְּאִיהִי פְּנִימָאָה, וְכָל מַה דִּי בְּרָזָא, לְכַהֲנָא אִתְמְסַר. וע"ד וַיִּקַּח אַהֲרֹן כַּאֲשֶׁר דִּבֶּר מֹשֶׁה וַיָּרָץ אֶל תּוֹךְ הַקָּהָל וַיִּתֵּן אֶת הַקְּטֹרֶת, דְּאִיהִי פְּנִימָאָה, רָזָא דִּכַהֲנָא, כְּדֵין וַיְכַפֵּר עַל הָעָם וַיַּעֲמוֹד בֵּין הַמֵּתִים וּבֵין הַחַיִּים, בֵּין אִילָנָא דְּחַיֵּי, וּבֵין אִילָנָא דְּמוֹתָא, כְּדֵין יְמִינָא קָרִיב דָּא בְּדָא, וַתֵּעָצַר הַמַּגֵּפָה, זַכָּאָה חוּלָקָא דְּכַהֲנָא, דְּכַהֲנָא אִית לֵיהּ חֵילָא לְעֵילָא, וְאִית לֵיהּ חֵילָא לְתַתָּא, וְהוּא גָּרִים שְׁלָמָא לְעֵילָא וְתַתָּא, וּבְכָל זִמְנָא, שְׂמָאלָא פָּלַח לִימִינָא, הה"ד וְיִלָּווּ עָלֶיךָ וִישָׁרְתוּךָ, וִימִינָא בִּשְׂמָאלָא מִשְׁתַּכְּחֵי בְּמִקְדָּשׁ.

27. Therefore, burnt incense, which is inward, and all that is in secret is given over to the priest. Therefore, "Aaron took as Moses commanded, and ran into the midst of the congregation...and he put on incense" (Bemidbar 17:12), because it is of the innermost, the secret of the priest WHO IS ALSO WITHIN. Then, "and made atonement for the people. And he stood between the dead and the living..." – that is, between the Tree of Life and the Tree of Death. Then the right causes one to approach the other, MEANING THE TREE OF LIFE, THAT IS RIGHT, COMES CLOSE TO THE PRIEST, WHO IS RIGHT, "and the plague was stayed." Praised is the priest's lot, since the priest has power above and power below, and he is the cause of peace above and below. And at all times, the left serves the right. This is what it says: "that they may be joined to you, and minister to you" (Bemidbar 18:2); and the right THAT IS INCLUDED in the left is prevalent in the Temple.

7. "Whatever your hand finds to do, do it with your strength"

A Synopsis

Rabbi Shimon explains to his son that a person must include life from the Tree of Life in his life here, because life, the secret of illumination of wisdom, prevails only here, in Malchut. All the words of King Solomon were spoken in the secret of Wisdom, and his verses mean that a person must always include the left in the right; when his actions are on the right side God will dwell with him in this world and will gather him to Himself in the World to Come. A person cannot decide to ask for mercy after death because "there is no work, nor device, nor knowledge, nor wisdom" after he leaves this world. All his deeds here must be done for the sake of God. Rabbi Shimon says that every night a person must account for his actions that day, repent of them and ask for compassion for them. Whoever strives through knowledge and wisdom to know God will not be among the wicked who are judged in Gehenom at Sheol; he will instead be raised higher and higher to the place of many lights.

‏28. רְבִּי אֶלְעָזָר הֲוָה קָאֵים קַמֵּיהּ דְּרִבִּי שִׁמְעוֹן אֲבוּהַ, א"ל, כְּתִיב רְאֵה חַיִּים עִם אִשָּׁה אֲשֶׁר אָהַבְתָּ כָּל יְמֵי חַיֵּי הֶבְלֶךָ. א"ל, ת"ח, רְאֵה חַיִּים עִם אִשָּׁה אֲשֶׁר אָהַבְתָּ דָּא הוּא רָזָא, דְּבָעֵי בַּר נָשׁ לְאַכְלְלָא חַיִּים בַּאֲתָר דָּא, דָּא בְּלָא דָּא לָא אָזְלָא. וּבָעֵי ב"נ לְאַכְלְלָא מִדַּת יוֹם בַּלַּיְלָה, וּמִדַּת לַיְלָה בַּיּוֹם. וְדָא הוּא רְאֵה חַיִּים עִם אִשָּׁה אֲשֶׁר אָהַבְתָּ מַאי טַעֲמָא כִּי הִיא חֶלְקְךָ בַּחַיִּים, דְּחַיִּים לָא שַׁרְאָן אֶלָּא עַל דָּא. וּבַעֲמָלְךָ אֲשֶׁר אַתָּה עָמֵל תַּחַת הַשָּׁמֶשׁ, כְּמָה דְּאָמַר בְּכָל דְּרָכֶיךָ דָעֵהוּ וְהוּא יְיַשֵּׁר אֹרְחוֹתֶיךָ.‏

28. Rabbi Elazar was standing in the presence of his father, Rabbi Shimon. He told him that it says: "live joyfully with the wife whom you love all the days of the life of your vanity" (Kohelet 9:9). WHAT IS THE EXPLANATION? He said to him: Come and behold. The verse: "live joyfully with the wife whom you love," is the secret that a person must include life, FROM THE TREE OF LIFE, THAT IS ZEIR ANPIN, in this place, WHICH IS MALCHUT REFERRED TO AS 'WOMAN'. One does not go without the other, ZEIR ANPIN WITHOUT MALCHUT. A person must include the measure of the day at night; THAT IS, A MEASURE OF ZEIR ANPIN, REFERRED TO AS 'DAY' IN

MALCHUT, REFERRED TO AS 'NIGHT', AND VICE VERSA, the measure of night in the day. That is the meaning of: "live joyfully with the wife whom you love all the days of the life of your vanity." What is the reason? "For that is your portion in life," since life, THAT IS, THE SECRET OF ILLUMINATION OF CHOCHMAH, does not prevail except on this, ON MALCHUT, SINCE THE ILLUMINATION OF CHOCHMAH DOES NOT BECOME REVEALED IN ANY OTHER PLACE THAN HER. "And in your labor in which you do labor under the sun" (Ibid.) is as you say: "in all your ways acknowledge (Heb. *da'ehu*) Him, and He shall direct your paths" (Mishlei 3:6). *DA'EHU* INCLUDES THE LETTERS OF KNOW (HEB. *DA*) AND VAV-HEI, WHICH ARE ZEIR ANPIN AND MALCHUT.

29. ות״ח כָּל מְלוֹי דִּשְׁלֹמֹה מַלְכָּא, כֻּלְּהוּ סְתִימִין לְגוֹ בְּחָכְמְתָא, וְהָנֵי קְרָאֵי אִתְחֲזוּן דְּהוּתְרָה רְצוּעָה, כְּמָה דִּכְתִיב בַּתְרֵיה, כֹּל אֲשֶׁר תִּמְצָא יָדְךָ לַעֲשׂוֹת בְּכֹחֲךָ עֲשֵׂה כִּי אֵין מַעֲשֶׂה וְחֶשְׁבּוֹן וְגוֹ'. הַאי קְרָא אִית לְאִסְתַּכְּלָא בֵּיה, כֹּל אֲשֶׁר תִּמְצָא יָדְךָ לַעֲשׂוֹת בְּכֹחֲךָ עֲשֵׂה, וְכִי שְׁלֹמֹה דְּחָכְמְתָא עִלָּאָה בֵּיה, יַתִּיר עַל כָּל בְּנֵי עָלְמָא, אָמַר הָכִי.

29. Come and behold: all the worlds of King Solomon are deeply concealed in Wisdom. These verses seem as if the restriction has been removed, since it says following that: "whatever your hand finds to do, do it with your strength, for there is no work, nor device..." (Kohelet 9:10). This verse must be studied carefully. Did Solomon, who had higher wisdom than any world inhabitants, indeed say this?

30. אֶלָּא כָּל מְלוֹי דִּשְׁלֹמֹה מַלְכָּא עַל רָזָא דְּחָכְמְתָא אִתְּמָרוּ. ת״ח, כֹּל אֲשֶׁר תִּמְצָא יָדְךָ לַעֲשׂוֹת בְּכֹחֲךָ עֲשֵׂה, דָּא הוּא דְּבָעֵי בַּר נָשׁ לְאַכְלְלָא שְׂמָאלָא בִּימִינָא, וְכָל מַה דְּהוּא עָבֵיד, מִבָּעֵי לֵיה דְּלָא יְהוֹן אֶלָּא כְּלִילָן בִּימִינָא. כֹּל אֲשֶׁר תִּמְצָא יָדְךָ, דָּא שְׂמָאלָא. לַעֲשׂוֹת בְּכֹחֲךָ: דָּא הוּא יְמִינָא, כד״א יְמִינְךָ יְיָ' נֶאְדָּרִי בַּכֹּחַ. וְכֵיוָן דְּבַר נָשׁ יִזְדָּהַר דְּכָל עוֹבָדוֹי יְהוֹן לְסִטְרָא דִּימִינָא, וְיַכְלִיל שְׂמָאלָא בִּימִינָא, כְּדֵין קוּדְשָׁא בְּרִיךְ הוּא שָׁארֵי בְּגַוְּוֵיה בְּהַאי עָלְמָא, וְיַכְנִישׁ לֵיה לְגַבֵּיה לְהַהוּא עָלְמָא דְּאָתֵי.

30. HE RESPONDS: It is only that all the words of Solomon, the king, were spoken in the secret of Wisdom. Come and behold: "whatever your hand finds to do, do it with your strength." That means that a person needs to include the left in the right, and everything he does should only be composed of the right. "whatever your hand finds to do," is the left, WHICH IS CALLED 'HAND', and, "to do...with your strength," is right, as it is written, "Your right hand, Hashem, is glorious in power" (Shemot 15:6). As soon as a person is careful so that all his actions are on the right side, he will gather the left into the right, and the Holy One, blessed be He, will dwell within him in this world and will gather him to be with Him in the World to Come.

31. וְלָא יֵימָא בַּר נָשׁ בְּשַׁעֲתָא דְּאַתְיָנָא לְהַהוּא עָלְמָא, כְּדֵין אֶתְבַּע מִן מַלְכָּא רַחֲמֵי, וְאֵיתוּב קַמֵּיהּ, אֶלָּא כִּי אֵין מַעֲשֶׂה וְחֶשְׁבּוֹן וְדַעַת וְחָכְמָה, בָּתַר דְּיִסְתְּלַק בַּר נָשׁ מֵהַאי עָלְמָא, אֶלָּא אִי בָּעֵי בַּר נָשׁ, דְּמַלְכָּא קַדִּישָׁא יַנְהִיר לֵיהּ לְהַהוּא עָלְמָא, וְיִתֵּן לֵיהּ חוּלָקָא לְעָלְמָא דְּאָתֵי, יִשְׁתַּדֵּל בְּהַאי עָלְמָא, לְאַכְלְלָא עוֹבְדוֹי בִּימִינָא, וְכָל עוֹבְדוֹי יֶהֱווֹן לִשְׁמָא דְּקוּדְשָׁא בְּרִיךְ הוּא, דְּהָא לְבָתַר כַּד יִתְכְּנִישׁ מֵהַאי עָלְמָא, לְאִתְדָּנָא בְּדִינָא תַּקִּיפָא, בְּדִינָא דְּגֵיהִנָּם, לֵית תַּמָּן עֵיטָא וְחָכְמָה וְסָכְלְתָנוּ לְאִשְׁתְּזָבָא מִן דִּינָא.

31. A person should not say, 'When I get to that world, then I will ask the King for mercy and I will repent in His presence,' because IT IS FOR THIS THAT IT IS SAID: "for there is no work, nor device, nor knowledge, nor wisdom" after the person departs from this world. However, if a person desires the Holy King to illuminate him in this world and grant him a part in the World to Come, he should toil in this world to gather his activities to the right. All his deeds should be for the sake of the Holy One, blessed be He, for after departing this world to be judged in harsh Judgment and to be punished in Gehenom, there is no recourse to counsel, wisdom or understanding to be saved from that sentence.

32. ד"א כִּי אֵין מַעֲשֶׂה וְחֶשְׁבּוֹן וְדַעַת וְחָכְמָה בִּשְׁאוֹל. בְּגֵיהִנָּם, אִית בֵּיהּ מָדוֹרִין עַל מָדוֹרִין. מָדוֹרָא תַּתָּאָה שְׁאוֹל. מָדוֹרָא תַּתָּאָה מִנֵּיהּ, אֲבַדּוֹן. וְדָא סָמִיךְ לְדָא. מַאן דְּנָחִית לִשְׁאוֹל, יְדוּנוּן לֵיהּ וּמִתַּמָּן

יִצְפְצֵף וְעוֹלֶה. הה"ד מוֹרִיד שְׁאוֹל וַיָּעַל. וּמַאן דְּנָחִית לַאֲבַדּוֹן, תּוּ לָא
סָלִיק לְעָלְמִין.

32. Another explanation of: "for there is no work, nor device, nor
knowledge, nor wisdom, in Sheol." There are levels upon levels in
Gehenom, and the lowest level is "Sheol." An even lower level is
"Avadon," and one is near the other. Whoever descends to Sheol will be put
on trial. From there he can rise in a whistle, as it is written: "He brings down
to Sheol, and brings up" (I Shmuel 2:6). Whoever is lowered to "Avadon"
never rises FROM THERE.

33. מַאן דְּאִית בֵּיה עוֹבָדָא טָבָא, אוֹ דְּאִיהוּ מָארֵי דְחוּשְׁבָּנָא, הָא
אוּקְמוּהָ דִּבְכָל לֵילְיָא וְלֵילְיָא עַד לָא יִשְׁכַּב, וְעַד לָא נָאִים, בָּעֵי בַּר נָשׁ
לְמֶעְבַּד חוּשְׁבָּנָא מֵעוֹבָדוֹי דְּעָבַד כָּל הַהוּא יוֹמָא, וְיֵתוּב מִנַּיְיהוּ, וְיִבְעֵי
עָלַיְיהוּ רַחֲמֵי. מ"ט בְּהַהִיא שַׁעֲתָא. בְּגִין דְּהַהִיא שַׁעֲתָא אִילָנָא דְמוֹתָא
שָׁרֵי בְּעָלְמָא, וְכָל בְּנֵי עָלְמָא טַעֲמִין טַעֲמָא דְמוֹתָא, וּבָעֵי בְּהַהִיא
שַׁעֲתָא לְמֶעְבַּד חוּשְׁבָּנָא מֵעוֹבָדוֹי, וְיוֹדֵי עָלַיְיהוּ, בְּגִין דְּאִיהִי שַׁעֲתָא
דְמוֹתָא, וְאִלֵּין אִקְרוּן מָארֵי דְחוּשְׁבָּנָא.

33. For whoever has a good deed or is of those who do reckoning, it was
already explained that each and every night, before he sleeps, he must make
an accounting of the actions that he did all that day, repent for them, and ask
for compassion for them. What is the reason THAT HE MUST DO THE
ACCOUNTING at that time? Because during that period, the Tree of Death
prevails on the world and all the world's inhabitants get a taste of death.
THEREFORE, at that time, a person must make an accounting of his deeds
and confess them, since it is a time of death. And they are called 'those who
do reckoning'.

34. וְכֵן מַאן דְּאִשְׁתְּדַל בְּדַעַת וּבְחָכְמָה לְמִנְדַע לְמָארֵיה, כַּד יַעַבְרוּן
לֵיה לְאִסְתַּכָּאָה וּלְאִסְתַּכְּלָא בְּאִינּוּן חַיָּיבִין דְּאִתְטְרִידוּ בְּגֵיהִנָּם,
וּבְדַרְגָּא דִּשְׁאוֹל, וְכֻלְּהוּ צַוְוחִין מֵאִינּוּן דַּרְגִּין, הוּא לָא יִשְׁתְּאַר תַּמָּן,
וְלָא יִשְׁתְּכַח בֵּינַיְיהוּ, וְעַל דָּא אֵין מַעֲשֶׂה וְחֶשְׁבּוֹן וְדַעַת וְחָכְמָה

בִּשְׁאוֹל, וְלָא יִשְׁתְּכַח אֶלָּא לְעֵילָא לְעֵילָא, בַּאֲתָר דְּכַמָּה נְהוֹרִין וּבוֹצִינִין, וְכַמָּה כְּסוּפִין שָׁארָן בֵּיה, וְקוּדְשָׁא בְּרִיךְ הוּא אָתֵי לְאִשְׁתַּעְשְׁעָא עִם שְׁאָר צַדִּיקַיָּיא דִּי בְּגַן עֵדֶן. זַכָּאָה חוּלָקֵהוֹן דְּצַדִּיקַיָּיא בְּהַאי עָלְמָא, וּבְעָלְמָא דְּאָתֵי, עָלַיְיהוּ כְּתִיב אַךְ צַדִּיקִים יוֹדוּ לִשְׁמֶךְ יֵשְׁבוּ יְשָׁרִים אֶת פָּנֶיךָ.

34. Similarly, this is the case for whoever strives in knowledge and wisdom to know his Master. AFTER HIS DEATH, WHEN THEY WILL BYPASS HIM to look and gaze at these wicked that are being judged in Gehenom at the level "Sheol," where all scream from these levels, he will not remain there and not be among them. About this, IT IS WRITTEN: "for there is no work, nor device, nor knowledge, nor wisdom, in Sheol." THERE IS NO ONE THERE WHO HAS A GOOD DEED, NOR ANYONE WHO HAS DEVICE, RECKONING, OR KNOWLEDGE, NAMELY, ONE WHO STRIVES TO KNOW, BECAUSE ALL THESE ARE NOT IN "SHEOL." And he will be found higher and higher, where many lights and candles and delightful things are present. And the Holy One, blessed be He, comes to be merry with the rest of the righteous in the Garden of Eden. Praised is the lot of the Righteous in this world and the World to Come. About them, it is written: "surely the righteous shall give thanks to Your Name: the upright shall dwell in Your presence" (Tehilim 140:14).

8. "But the Levites shall do the service"

A Synopsis

Rabbi Aba tells us that when God wanted to create the world He did so with the Torah, and through it the world became perfected. When Adam emerged into the world the world was perfected, but when the spirits and demons emerged the world seemed to be faulty and lacking. However, when the children of Yisrael were sanctified the Levites were placed on the left side to restore the left. For this reason the Levites must be cleansed, for they who completed the perfection of the left side ended the flaw of the world. Rabbi Aba says that if judgment had not existed in the world people would not have followed the Torah nor would they have performed the entire service that has to be done for God, and which is done by the Levites. Rabbi Yitzchak tells us that in the future God will brighten the light of the moon to be as bright as the sun, and that He will brighten the sun seven times what it is now.

35. וְעָבַד הַלֵּוִי הוּא אֶת עֲבוֹדַת אֹהֶל מוֹעֵד וְגוֹ'. רִבִּי אַבָּא פָּתַח, הַיּוֹשֵׁב עַל חוּג הָאָרֶץ וְגוֹ'. ת"ח, כַּד בָּעָא קוּדְשָׁא בְּרִיךְ הוּא לְמִבְרֵי עָלְמָא, סָלִיק בִּרְעוּתָא קַמֵּיהּ, וּבָרָא לֵיהּ בְּאוֹרַיְיתָא. וּבָהּ אִשְׁתַּכְלַל. הה"ד בַּהֲכִינוֹ שָׁמַיִם שָׁם אָנִי. וּכְתִיב וָאֶהְיֶה אֶצְלוֹ אָמוֹן. וְהָא אוּקְמוּהָ, אַל תִּקְרֵי אָמוֹן, אֶלָּא אוּמָן.

35. "But the Levites (lit. 'Levite, he') shall do the service of the Tent of Meeting..." (Bemidbar 18:23). Rabbi Aba opened the discussion with the verse: "it is he that sits upon the circle of the earth" (Yeshayah 40:22). Come and behold: when the Holy One, blessed be He, wanted to create the world, it rose in His wish and He created it with the Torah, and through it, it became perfected. This is what is written: "when He established the heavens, I was there" (Mishlei 8:27), and it is written, "then I was by Him, as a nursling (Heb. *amon*)" (Ibid. 30). It was explained that we should not pronounce it '*amon*', but rather, '*oman* (lit. 'craftsman')'; SHE WAS FOR HIM THE CRAFTSMAN OF THE UNIVERSE.

36. כַּד אֲתֵי לְמִבְרֵי אָדָם, וְהָא אִתְּמַר, אָמְרָה תּוֹרָה וְכִי לְמַגָּנָא אִתְקְרִיאַת אֶרֶךְ אַפַּיִם וְרַב חֶסֶד. בְּהַהִיא שַׁעֲתָא דְּנָפִיק אָדָם לְעָלְמָא,

-247-

הֲוָה זִיו פַּרְצוּפָא דִּילֵיהּ מֵעֵילָא וּמִתַּתָּא, וַהֲווֹ דַחֲלִין מִנֵּיהּ כָּל בִּרְיָין, וְאוֹקְמוּהָ. תָּ"ח, לָא אִתְקַיַּים עָלְמָא, וְלָא אִשְׁתְּלִים, עַד הַהִיא שַׁעֲתָא דְּנָפַק אָדָם בִּשְׁלִימוּ דְכֹלָּא, וְאִתְקַדָּשׁ יוֹמָא, וְאִתְתְּקַן כֻּרְסְיָיא קַדִּישָׁא לְמַלְכָּא, כְּדֵין אִשְׁתְּלִימוּ עִלָּאֵי וְתַתָּאֵי, וְאִשְׁתְּכָחוּ חֶדְוָון בְּכֻלְּהוּ עָלְמִין.

36. When He came to create Adam, we were taught that the Torah said, 'is it in vain, that You are called long suffering and abundant in love?' AND IF THERE WILL BE NO MAN WHO WILL SIN, FOR WHOM WILL YOU RESTRAIN ANGER? At the time that Adam emerged into the world, the luster of his face was from above and from below. All the creatures were fearful of him, as it was explained. Come and behold: the world had no endurance and was not perfected until that time when Adam emerged in total perfection and that day was sanctified. A Holy Throne was prepared for the King, WHICH IS MALCHUT. Then the upper and the lower grades were considered complete, and joy was attained in all the worlds.

37. בְּהַהִיא שַׁעֲתָא דְּבָעָא יוֹמָא לְאִתְקַדְּשָׁא, הֲווֹ נָפְקֵי רוּחֵיהוֹן דְּשֵׁדִין לְאִתְבְּרֵי גּוּפָא דִלְהוֹן, וְאִתְקַדָּשׁ יוֹמָא, וְלָא אִתְבְּרִיאוּ, וְאִשְׁתְּאַר עָלְמָא כְּמָה דְּאִתְפְּגִים מֵעֲבִידָתָא וְאִתְחֲסַר, כֵּיוָן דְּאִתְקַדָּשׁוּ יִשְׂרָאֵל, וְאִשְׁתְּלִימוּ בְּדַרְגֵּיהוֹן, וְאִשְׁתְּכָחוּ לֵיוָאֵי בְּסִטַר שְׂמָאלָא, כְּדֵין אִשְׁתְּלִים הַהוּא פְּגִימָא דְעָלְמָא, דְּמִסְטַר שְׂמָאלָא.

37. At the moment when the day wished to be sanctified, spirits and demons emerged to have a body created for them. However, the day was sanctified and they were not created. The world appeared to be left as if faulty in its work and lacking, BECAUSE OF THE PRESENCE OF THESE SPIRITS AND DEMONS. However, as soon as Yisrael were sanctified and perfected in their level, the Levites were placed on the left side. Then that flaw of the world was perfected, WHAT WAS DONE on the left, DUE TO THE EXISTENCE OF THE SPIRITS AND DEMONS, BECAUSE THROUGH THE LEVITES, THE LEFT WAS GATHERED INTO THE RIGHT AND THE LEFT WAS THEREBY RESTORED.

38. וע"ד בָּעָאן לְאִתְדַּכְּאָה לֵיוָאֵי, וּכְדֵין כֹּלָּא אִתְכְּלִיל בִּימִינָא, וְעָלְמָא לָא אִתְפְּגִים, וּבג"כ כְּתִיב, וְעָבַד הַלֵּוִי הוּא. הוּא אַשְׁלִים לְסִטַר

שְׂמָאלָא. הוּא אַשְׁלִים לִפְגִימוּ דְּעָלְמָא. וַאֲפִילוּ הַהוּא סִטְרָא דְּצָפוֹן,
דְּאִשְׁתְּאַר חָסֵר בְּעָלְמָא, כַּד בָּרָא קוּדְשָׁא בְּרִיךְ הוּא עָלְמָא. לֵיוָאָה
בַּאֲרוֹנָא אַשְׁלִים לְכֹלָּא. מַאי בַּאֲרוֹנָא. בְּהַהוּא מָטוּלָא דְּהֲווֹ נַטְלֵי
בְּמַשְׁכְּנָא, אִשְׁתְּלִים כָּל הַהוּא פְּגִימוּ עַל יְדֵיה.

38. Therefore, the Levites must be cleansed and everything must be
gathered into the right so that the world is not flawed. Due to this, it is
written: "but the Levite, he shall do the service." He who completed the
perfection of the left side ended the flaw of the world. Even that northern
side that was missing in the world when the Holy One, blessed be He,
created the world, THE LEVITES ALSO COMPLETED, SINCE the Levites at
the Ark completed everything. What is the meaning of 'at the Ark'? It
means with that burden they carried at the Tabernacle, DURING THE TRAVEL
PERIOD OF THE TABERNACLE, all that was flawed was restored to
perfection.

39. הוּא: לְעֵילָא לִשְׂמָאלָא. הוּא: אִתְכְּלִיל בִּימִינָא, תּוּ הוּא: דָּא
עַתִּיקָא. אִלְמָלֵי דִּינָא לָא אִשְׁתְּכַח בְּעָלְמָא, לָא הֲווֹ יַדְעֵי בְּנֵי נָשָׁא
מְהֵימְנוּתָא עִלָּאָה, וְלָא יִשְׁתַּדְּלוּן בְּנֵי נָשָׁא בְּאוֹרַיְיתָא, וְלָא יִתְקַיְימוּ
פִּקּוּדֵי אוֹרַיְיתָא, פּוּלְחָנָא שְׁלֵימוּתָא דְּיִשְׁתְּכַח בְּעָלְמָא לְגַבֵּי מַלְכָּא
קַדִּישָׁא, מַאן עָבֵיד לֵיה. הֲוֵי אוֹמֵר דָּא לֵיוָאָה.

39. "BUT THE LEVITE, HE SHALL SERVE"; "he" alludes to the left above,
meaning THAT HE RESTORES THE LEFT ABOVE. The pronoun "he"
indicates that it is included in the right. In addition, "he" is the Ancient One,
THAT IS, KETER. FOR HIS SERVICE AND RESTORATION REACHES ALL
THE WAY TO KETER, SINCE "HE" INDICATES THE HIDDEN. If Judgment,
WHICH IS THE SECRET OF THE AMENDMENT OF THE LEVITES, had not
existed in the world, people would not have been aware of the highest Faith.
And people would not have engaged in the Torah, and the commandments
of the Torah would not have been kept, nor would people have performed
the entire service that is to be done in this world for the Holy King. Who
performs it? One says: The Levites.

40. וְתוּ וְעָבַד הַלֵּוִי הוּא, כד״א כִּי יְיָ' הוּא הָאֱלֹהִים. הוּא אַשְׁלִים

שְׁלֵימוּתָא, לְמֶיהֱוֵי כֹּלָּא חַד. הוּא: פְּשִׁיטָא לְקַבְּלָא לִכְנֶסֶת יִשְׂרָאֵל,
כד"א, שְׂמָאלוֹ תַּחַת לְרֹאשִׁי, בְּגִין לְחַבְּרָא זִווּגָא כַּחֲדָא. מָאן אִתְּעַר
רְחִימוּתָא. הֲוֵי אוֹמֵר הוּא. תּוּ הוּא כד"א הוּא עָשָׂנוּ וְלֹא אֲנַחְנוּ עַמּוֹ.
בג"כ הוּא: לְתַתָּא. הוּא: לְעֵילָא. הוּא: אִתְגַּלְיָיא. הוּא סָתִים. הוּא
אֱלֹהִים.

40. "But the Levite, he shall serve"; "he" is as it is written, "Hashem, He is the Elohim" (Devarim 4:35), SINCE THROUGH HIM THIS UNIFICATION IS ACCOMPLISHED. He finalizes that perfection so that all shall be one, so THAT ALL THE LEVELS WILL COMBINE AND UNIFY TO BECOME ONE. "He" INDICATES the extension OF THE LEFT towards the Congregation of Yisrael, WHICH IS MALCHUT, as it says, "His left hand is under my head" (Shir Hashirim 2:6), in order to connect AFTERWARDS. This mating together IS THE SECRET MEANING OF, "AND HIS RIGHT ARM EMBRACES ME." Who awakens this love OF, "HIS LEFT HAND IS UNDER MY HEAD," WHICH IS THE SECRET OF MARITAL LOVE? One says that it is "he," THE LEVI and also, "He," as it is written, "it is He who made us, and we belong to Him" (Tehilim 100:3), WHICH ALLUDES TO THE HOLY ONE, BLESSED BE HE. Therefore, "He" POINTS downward TO REPAIR THE FLAW THAT IS IN THE WORLD, and "He" is above TO RESTORE THE LEFT UP HIGH. "He" openly REVEALS FAITH AND SERVICE IN THE WORLD, and "He" is concealed, WHICH POINTS TO THE ANCIENT ONE. "He is the Elohim," WHICH POINTS TO UNIFICATION OF YUD HEI VAV HEI. HE IS THE ELOHIM AS MENTIONED.

41. ר' יִצְחָק אָמַר, זַמִּין קוּדְשָׁא בְּרִיךְ הוּא לְאַנְהָרָא לְסִיהֲרָא, כִּנְהוֹרָא
דְשִׁמְשָׁא. וּנְהוֹרָא דְשִׁמְשָׁא יְהֵא עַל חַד שְׁבַע זִמְנִין. הה"ד וְהָיָה אוֹר
הַלְבָנָה כְּאוֹר הַחַמָּה וְגו'. וּכְתִיב לֹא יָבֹא עוֹד שִׁמְשֵׁךְ וִירֵחֵךְ לֹא יֵאָסֵף.
וּכְתִיב לֹא יִהְיֶה לָךְ עוֹד הַשֶּׁמֶשׁ וְגו'.

41. Rabbi Yitzchak said: In the future, the Holy One, blessed be He, is destined to brighten the light of the moon to be as bright as the sun. The light of the sun will be seven times brighter, as it is written: "moreover the light of the moon shall be as the light of the sun..." (Yeshayah 30:26). It is also written: "your sun shall no more go down; nor shall your moon withdraw itself" (Yeshayah 60:20), and it is further written: "the sun shall be no more..." (Ibid. 19)

A Synopsis

Moses talks about the command to redeem the firstling, and that if one does not redeem his Nefesh and Ruach and Neshamah in the Torah he is destined to reincarnate again. He also speaks about the three times of exile and the last redemption.

רעיא מהימנא

42. כָּל פֶּטֶר רֶחֶם לְכָל בָּשָׂר וְגוֹ', וְאֶת בְּכוֹר הַבְּהֵמָה הַטְּמֵאָה תִּפְדֶּה. פִּקּוּדָא דָּא לִפְדּוֹת פֶּטֶר חֲמוֹר, לִפְדּוֹת לְעָלְמָא דְּאָתֵי. וְאִי קוֹדֶם דְּאָזִיל לְהַהוּא עָלְמָא, לָא יִפְדֶּה נַפְשֵׁיהּ וְרוּחֵיהּ וְנִשְׁמָתֵיהּ בְּאוֹרַיְיתָא, עָתִיד לְאַחְזְרָא לְהַאי עָלְמָא כְּדְבְקַדְמֵיתָא. יָשׁוּב לִימֵי עֲלוּמָיו, וְלָקַבֵּל נַפְשָׁא וְרוּחָא וְנִשְׁמָתָא.

Ra'aya Meheimna (the Faithful Shepherd)

42. "Everything that opens the womb in all flesh...and the firstling of unclean beasts shall you redeem" (Bemidbar 18:15). This commandment is to redeem the firstling of a mule, that is, to redeem HIMSELF for the World to Come. If prior to going to that world he does not redeem his Nefesh and Ruach and Neshamah in Torah, he is destined to return back AND REINCARNATE in this world as originally, AS IT SAYS: "he shall return to the days of his youth" (Iyov 33:25), and receive Nefesh, Ruach and Neshamah.

43. כְּתִיב הֵן כָּל אֵלֶּה יִפְעַל אֵל פַּעֲמַיִם שָׁלֹשׁ עִם גָּבֶר, וְיִשְׂרָאֵל. בְּגִין דְּפִדְיוֹן דִּלְהוֹן הֲוָה בְּלָא תּוֹרָה, דְּאִיהוּ כֶּסֶף כְּסוּפָא דְּעָלְמָא דְּאָתֵי, אַהְדְּרוּ תְּלַת זִמְנִין אַחֲרָנִין בְּגָלוּתָא, וּבְפוּרְקָנָא בַּתְרַיְיתָא דְּפוּרְקָנָא דִּלְהוֹן יְהֵא בְּאוֹרַיְיתָא, לָא יְהַדְּרוּן לְעָלַם בְּגָלוּתָא. אָתוּ רַבָּנָן וּבְרִיכוּ לֵיהּ, וְאָמְרוּ רַעְיָא מְהֵימָנָא, קוּדְשָׁא בְּרִיךְ הוּא יִפְדֶּה לָךְ, וְכָל יִשְׂרָאֵל יִפְדּוּן עַל יְדָךְ, וְתִתְחַדֵּשׁ עִמְּהוֹן, וְאִינּוּן עִמָּךְ.

43. It is written: "lo, El does all these things twice or three times with a man" (Iyov 33:29). THAT IS the children of Yisrael, since their redemption takes place without Torah, which is like silver (Heb. *kesef*) that is "*Kisufa*" (lit. 'delight') of the World to Come. They returned three other times to the exile and, at the last redemption when they will be redeemed through Torah, they will never ever return to exile. The rabbis came and gave him their blessings, saying, 'Faithful Shepherd, the Holy One, blessed be He, will redeem you and all the children of Yisrael will be redeemed through you, and you will be renewed with them and they with you.'

9. Household arrangements

A Synopsis

Moses compares a virtuous wife to the Shechinah, saying that whoever does kindness by Her will receive invaluable recompense but that whoever is sinful to Her will receive punishment beyond measure. He tells us that anyone who inherits a Neshamah or Ruach or Nefesh from the Shechinah does not require redeeming. The Shechinah's redemption is dependent on God, and that redemption is drawn by the Tefilin, the keeping of the Shabbat, the marking of the festival days, the mark of circumcision, the Torah and with several precepts.

44. פִּקּוּדָא בָּתַר דָּא, לָדוּן בְּעֶרְכֵּי בַּיִת. וּבְרָזָא דְחָכְמְתָא, בַּיִת דב"נ, דָּא אִתְּתָא. אִי אִיהִי אִתְּתָא דְטוֹב וָרָע, וּבָעֵי לְהַמִיר רָעָה בְּטוֹבָה, יִפְדֶּה לָה מֵהַהוּא רָע, וְיָהִיב לֵיהּ עֶרֶךְ דִּילָהּ. אֲבָל אִתְּתָא דְּאִילָנָא דְחַיֵּיא, אִתְּמַר בָּהּ לֹא יַעַרְכֶנָּה זָהָב וּזְכוֹכִית וּתְמוּרָתָהּ כְּלִי פָז, וְאֵין לָהּ עֶרֶךְ. כְּמָה דְּאִתְּמַר, אֵשֶׁת חַיִל עֲטֶרֶת בַּעְלָהּ. וְאִתְּמַר אֵשֶׁת חַיִל מִי יִמְצָא וְגוֹ'. וְדָא שְׁכִינְתָּא. מַאן דְּגָמִיל חֶסֶד עִמָּהּ, לֵית עֶרֶךְ לְאַגְרָא דִּילֵיהּ. וּמַאן דְּחָאב לְגַבָּהּ, לֵית עֶרֶךְ לְעָנְשָׁא דִּילֵיהּ.

44. The precept following this is the dealing in household arrangements. In the secret of wisdom, a man's house is his wife. If she is a woman of good and evil and he wishes to exchange a bad WOMAN for a good one, he should redeem her from that evil one and give her her worth. However, it says about a woman of the Tree of Life, THAT IS MALCHUT: "gold and glass cannot equal it: and the exchange of it shall not be for vessels of fine gold" (Iyov 28:17). She is invaluable, as it says, "a virtuous woman is a crown to her husband" (Mishlei 12:4), and it also says, "who can find a woman of worth..." (Mishlei 31:10). That is the Shechinah. Whoever does kindness by Her shall receive invaluable recompense, and whoever is sinful to Her shall receive punishment beyond measure.

45. כַּמָה שְׁפָחוֹת אִית לָהּ דִּמְשַׁמְּשִׁין לָהּ, וְכָל חֲדָא וַחֲדָא מִנַּיְיהוּ, אִית לָהּ עֶרֶךְ. וְכָל חַד וְחַד צָרִיךְ פִּדְיוֹן. אֲבָל מַאן דִּירִית נִשְׁמָתָא, אוֹ רוּחָא, אוֹ נַפְשָׁא מִשְּׁכִינְתָּא, לָא צָרִיךְ פִּדְיוֹן, דִּשְׁכִינְתָּא עֲלָהּ אִתְּמַר אֲנִי יְיָ'

-253-

הוּא שְׁמִי וּכְבוֹדִי לְאַחֵר לֹא אֶתֵּן. דְּפִדְיוֹן דִּילָהּ בְּקוּדְשָׁא בְּרִיךְ הוּא
תַּלְיָא. דְּאִמְשְׁכָן לָהּ יִשְׂרָאֵל, בְּקִשּׁוּרָא דִּתְפִלִּין, בְּאוֹת דְּשַׁבָּת, בְּאוֹת
דְּיוֹמִין טָבִין, בְּאוֹת דִּבְרִית, וְתוֹרָה, בְּכַמָּה פִּקּוּדִין. דְּפִדְיוֹן דִּילָהּ תַּלְיָא
בְּקוּדְשָׁא בְּרִיךְ הוּא, הה"ד וָאַעַשׂ לְמַעַן שְׁמִי, וּבְגִינָהּ וְאַף גַּם זֹאת.
הָכִי כַּמָּה פִּקּוּדִין אִינּוּן דְּעַבְדִין בְּנֵי נָשָׁא עַל מְנָת לְקַבֵּל פְּרָס. וְכַמָּה
חוֹבִין. וּלְכָל פִּקּוּדָא אִית לֵיהּ עֵרֶךְ בְּהַהוּא עָלְמָא. אֲבָל עוֹנְשָׁא לְמַאן
דְּאַעְבָּר עֲלַיְיהוּ, אֵין לֵיהּ עֵרֶךְ וְשִׁיעוּר.

45. She has many maidservants who serve her. Each and every one of them has value and each one needs a ransom, MEANING TO RANSOM HER FROM THE HOLD OF THE OTHER SIDE. However, a Neshamah or Ruach or Nefesh inherited from the Shechinah does not require redeeming, since it is said about the Shechinah, "I am Hashem, that is My Name, and My glory will I not give to another" (Yeshayah 42:8). Her redemption is dependent on the Holy One, blessed be He, which Yisrael draw to Her by the knot of the Tefilin, with the Shabbat sign, with the marking of the festival days, with the mark of circumcision, with Torah, and with many precepts. Since Her ransom is dependent on the Holy One, blessed be He, this is what it says, "but I acted for My Name's sake," (Yechezkel 20:9) and for her: "and yet for all that (Heb. *zot*)..." (Vayikra 26:44). In this manner, people perform many precepts in order to receive recompense. Each precept has a value in that world. However, the punishment for someone who transgresses them has no value.

10. Devoting one's possessions to the priest

A Synopsis

Moses speaks about anger, saying that there is deadly poison in rage, and that when one is angry it is the same as if he is an idol worshipper. Therefore the person who sins in anger must give his offering to the priest because the priest is compassion and blessing and will cause the anger in the left to be subdued and replaced with mercy.

46. פְּקוּדָא בָּתַר דָּא, לָדוּן בְּמַחֲרִים נִכְסָיו לַכֹּהֵן, הה״ד כָּל חֵרֶם בְּיִשְׂרָאֵל לְךָ יִהְיֶה. וְרָזָא דָּא כָּל פֶּטֶר רֶחֶם לְכָל בָּשָׂר אֲשֶׁר יַקְרִיבוּ לַיְיָ׳ בָּאָדָם וּבַבְּהֵמָה. רֶחֶם: בְּהִיפּוּךְ אַתְוָון כְּחוּשְׁבַּן רמ״ח אֵבָרִים דב״נ, עֲלַיְיהוּ אִתְּמַר בְּרֹגֶז רַחֵם תִּזְכּוֹר. בָּתַר דְּכָעִיס ב״נ, וּמַחֲרִים הַהוּא בְּעִירָא לְגַבֵּיהּ, הָא שַׁרְיָא אֵל אַחֵר נָחָשׁ, דְּאִתְּמַר בֵּיהּ, אָרוּר אַתָּה מִכָּל הַבְּהֵמָה, וְאִיהוּ לִשְׂמָאלָא דב״נ. בְּגִין דָּא מְנֵי קוּדְשָׁא בְּרִיךְ הוּא, לְמֵיהַב לְכַהֲנָא, דְּאִיהוּ רַחֲמֵי בִּרְכָה, לְאִתְכַּפְיָיא רֹגֶז, דְּאִתְּעַר בְּהַהוּא ב״נ מָרָה, חַרְבָּא דְּמַלְאָךְ הַמָּוֶת, וְאִתְּעַר יְמִינָא לְגַבֵּיהּ בְּרַחֲמֵי, וְאִתְכַּפְיָיא רוּגְזָא דִּשְׂמָאלָא, וְהַאי אִיהוּ בְּרֹגֶז רַחֵם תִּזְכּוֹר.

46. The next precept after this one relates to someone who devotes his possessions to the priest. This is what is written: "everything devoted in Yisrael shall be yours" (Bemidbar 18:14). That is the secret meaning of: "everything that opens the womb in all flesh, which they bring to Hashem, whether it be of men or beasts" (Ibid. 15). Womb (*Rechem; Resh-Chet-Mem*) AMOUNTS TO *RESH-MEM-CHET* (= 248) by resetting the letters, like the number of 248 limbs and organs of a man, about whom it is said: "in wrath remember mercy (Heb. *rachem*)" (Chavakuk 3:2). After a person sins in anger and dedicates this beast to Him, another El, a serpent, dwells ON IT, as it says, "you are cursed above all cattle" (Beresheet 3:14), and he is to the left of man. Therefore, the Holy One, blessed be He, commanded that IT be given to the priest, who is compassion and blessing, in order to subdue the anger, SINCE in that person the bitterness is stirred, which is the sword of the Angel of Death. THEREFORE, the right is awakened toward him with compassion, and the anger in the left is subdued. And so when angry, have compassion; "in wrath remember mercy."

‫47. מַאן דְּכָעֵיס, דְּאִית לֵיהּ בְּכַעַס סַם הַמָּוֶת, דְּעָלֵיהּ אוֹקְמוּהָ מָארֵי‬
‫מַתְנִיתִין, כָּל הַכּוֹעֵס כְּאִילוּ עוֹבֵד ע"ז. בְּגִין דְּסִטְרָא אַחֲרָא אִתּוֹקְדַת‬
‫בב"נ. וּבְהַהִיא בְּעִירָא דְּיָהִיב לְכַהֲנָא אִתְפְּרַשׁ חֵרֶם מִנֵּיהּ, וְסָמָאֵל אֵל‬
‫אַחַר חֵרֶם, וְנוּקְבָּא דִּילֵיהּ קְלָלָה, כְּלוּלָה מִכֹּל קְלָלוֹת שֶׁבַּמִּשְׁנֶה תּוֹרָה.‬
‫וְקוּדְשָׁא בְּרִיךְ הוּא בָּרִיךְ בְּכָל אוֹרַיְיתָא כֹּלָּא, וְכָל בִּרְכָאן מִיְּמִינָא,‬
‫דְּאָחִיד בָּהּ כֹּהֵן. וּבְגִין דָּא כָּל חֵרֶם צָרִיךְ לְמֵיהַב לֵיהּ לְכַהֲנָא, דְּאִיהוּ‬
‫אָכִיל לֵיהּ בְּנוּרָא, וְשֵׁצֵי לֵיהּ מֵעָלְמָא, וְשָׁכִיךְ אֶשָּׁא מִשְׂמָאלָא בִּיְמִינָא,‬
‫דְּאִיהוּ מַיָּיא, וּבֵיהּ וַחֲמַת הַמֶּלֶךְ שָׁכָכָה.‬

47. When one is angry, there is deadly poison in his rage. About him, the masters of the Mishnah have stated: Whoever is angry, it is as if he is an idol-worshipper, since the Other Side burns the person and by giving that beast to the priest, that possession separates from him. Samael, a strange El, consecrated destruction, and his female is a curse that is contained in all the curses mentioned in the book of Devarim. The Holy One, blessed be He, granted blessings throughout the Torah and all the blessings are from the right, to which the priest holds on. Due to this, any consecration needs to be given to the priest, who burns it in fire and destroys it from the world. The fire of the left gets calmed in the right, which is water, and "then the king's wrath was pacified" (Ester 7:10) through it.

11. Two out of one hundred

A Synopsis

We hear from the Faithful Shepherd about the next precept, that is to set aside a great offering, two out of one hundred. This means to unify God twice a day with the morning prayer and the evening prayer. We learn the gematria that explain the one hundred from the name Yud Hei Vav Hei and the ten Sfirot and the word Tzadi or Righteous. Moses also mentions the hundred blessings that a person is required to do every day to bless God. He refers to several offerings and emphasizes the importance of the mating of Zeir Anpin and Malchut.

48. פְּקוּדָא בָּתַר דָּא לְהַפְרִישׁ תְּרוּמָה גְּדוֹלָה, וְאוֹקְמוּהָ תְּרֵי מִמְּאָה, מַאי תְּרוּמָה. רַבָּנָן דִּמְתִיבְתָּא, הַאי תְּרוּמָה דִּצְרִיכִין לְאַפְרָשָׁא תְּרֵי מִמְּאָה, בְּסִתְרֵי תּוֹרָה מַאי נִיהוּ. מַאן דְּבָעֵי לְמִטְעַם, אִי הוּא זָר יוּמַת וְהַיְינוּ אֵל זָר סָמָאֵ"ל. דְּקוּדְשָׁא בְּרִיךְ הוּא אָמַר וְיִקְחוּ לִי תְּרוּמָה, תְּרֵי מִמְּאָה, לְיַחֲדָא לֵיהּ תְּרֵין זִמְנִין בְּיוֹמָא, דְּהַיְינוּ תְּרֵי מִמְּאָה, בְּמ"ט אַתְוָון דִּשְׁמַע וּבָרוּךְ שֵׁם כְּבוֹד מַלְכוּתוֹ לְעוֹלָם וָעֶד דְּעַרְבִית, וּבְמ"ט אַתְוָון דְּשַׁחֲרִית, חַסְרִין תְּרֵין מִמְּאָה, אִינּוּן שְׁכִינְתָּא עִלָּאָה, וְתַתָּאָה, בְּתַרְוַוייְהוּ צָרִיךְ לְיַחֲדָא לְקוּדְשָׁא בְּרִיךְ הוּא, אַמָּה דְּתַרְוַוייְהוּ. מִדָּה דְּתַרְוַוייְהוּ. מֵאָה בָּאַמָּה. אַמָּ"ה בְּאַתְווֹי מֵא"ה אִיהוּ וְאִיהוּ בְּהִפּוּךְ אַתְוָון, הַא"ם.

48. The precept after this is to separate aside a great offering, and it was set at two out of one hundred. HE INQUIRES: What is an offering? HE RESPONDS: The rabbis in the Yeshivah SAID, 'This offering requires the setting aside two out of one hundred.' According to Sitrei Torah (lit. "the hidden Torah'), what DOES IT ALLUDE TO? It means that whoever wishes to taste OF HER shall be killed if he is a stranger. That means the strange El, Samael, since the Holy One, blessed be He, said, "that they bring Me an offering (Heb. *trumah*)" (Shemot 25:2) two (Heb. *tri*) out of a hundred (Heb. *me'ah*). THIS MEANS to unify Him twice a day, which is two out of a hundred, THAT ARE 49 letters of Sh'ma, and, 'blessed is the glorious Name of His kingdom forever and ever', of the evening prayer Arvit, and the 49 letters of the morning prayer. Two are missing HERE for THE COMPLETION

of one hundred and they are the higher Shechinah, WHICH IS BINAH, and the lower Shechinah, WHICH IS MALCHUT. With both combined, they must be unified with the Holy One, blessed be He, that is, the cubit, the measurement of both. AND TOGETHER WITH THEM, IT IS a hundred. *Amah* (Eng. 'cubit') has the same letters of *Me'ah* (Eng. 'hundred'). In changing the letters, it forms *Ha'em* (Eng. 'the mother'), WHICH ALLUDES TO BINAH.

49. וְעוֹד וְהָיָה בַּאֲכָלְכֶם מִלֶּחֶם הָאָרֶץ תָּרִימוּ תְרוּמָה לַיְיָי, תָּרִימוּ, כְּגוֹן רוּם יָדֵיהוּ נָשָׂא וְאִינּוּן עֶשֶׂר אֶצְבְּעָן, דְּסַלְּיקוּ דִלְהוֹן לַעֲשַׂר סְפִירָן, דְּאִינּוּן יוֹ״ד הֵ״א וָא״ו הֵ״א, דְּסַלְּיקוּ מ״ה. וּבְאַתְוָון דְּאַלְפָא בֵּיתָא, מָה סַלִיק מֵא״ה, י״ם ה״צ. וְהַאי אִיהוּ דְּאוּקְמוּהָ רַבָּנָן מָארֵי מַתְנִיתִין, וְעַתָּה יִשְׂרָאֵל מָ״ה יְיָ׳ אֱלֹהֶיךָ שׁוֹאֵל מֵעִמָּךְ, וְאָמְרוּ, אַל תִּקְרֵי מָה אֶלָּא מֵאָה, לְקַבֵּל מֵאָה בִּרְכָאן דְּמִחַיָּיב ב״נ לְבָרְכָא לְמָארֵיהּ בְּכָל יוֹמָא, וְהַאי אִיהוּ דְּצָרִיךְ ב״נ לְמַטְעַם בְּכָל יוֹמָא לְמָארֵיהּ, ובג״ד וְיִקְחוּ לִי תְּרוּמָה.

49. In addition, "then it shall be that when you eat of the bread of the land, you shall offer up a gift to Hashem" (Bemidbar 15:19). "…offer up…" is as is written: "and lifted up its hands on high" (Chavakuk 3:10), BECAUSE, "LIFTED UP ITS HANDS," IS EXPLAINED AS THE TEN FINGERS ON HIS HANDS. This refers to the ten fingers. Lifting them, THAT IS, ACCORDING TO THE MEANING OF, "LIFT UP YOUR HANDS IN THE SANCTUARY" (TEHILIM 134:2), is to the ten Sfirot that are Yud-Vav-Dalet, Hei-Aleph, Vav-Aleph-Vav, Hei-Aleph. The numerical values equal 45, Mem-Hei, by EXCHANGING letters of the alphabet USING THE SYSTEM IN WHICH *ALEPH =TAV, BET=SHIN*, Mem-Hei amounts to one hundred. This is because THE *MEM* IS SUBSTITUTED WITH *YUD* ACCORDING TO THE COMBINATION Yud =*Mem*. IN *ALEPH=TAV, BET=SHIN* AND THE *HEI* CHANGES WITH THE *TZADI* ACCORDING TO THE COMBINATION OF Hei=Tzadi. *TZADI* PLUS *YUD* TOTALS ONE HUNDRED. This is why it has been explained by the rabbis, the sages of the Mishnah, that, "and now Yisrael, what (Heb. *mah, Mem-Hei*) does Hashem your Elohim require of you" (Devarim 10:12). Do not pronounce it '*Mah',* but rather, 'hundred' or 'Meah'. That corresponds to the hundred blessings that a person is required to bless his Master with daily. That is because a person needs to taste daily FOR THE SAKE OF his Master. Therefore, IT IS WRITTEN, "that they bring Me an offering."

50. וְכַמָּה תְּרוּמוֹת אִינּוּן, אִית תְּרוּמָה מִדְאוֹרַיְיתָא, תּוֹרָה מ׳. וְהַאי אִיהוּ תְּרוּמָה, תּוֹרָה דְּאִתְיְהִיבַת בְּאַרְבָּעִים יוֹם. וְאִי תֵּימְרוּן דְּאָכִילְנָא מִנָּהּ, הָא כְּתִיב וַיְהִי מֹשֶׁה בָּהָר אַרְבָּעִים יוֹם וְאַרְבָּעִים לַיְלָה לֶחֶם לֹא אָכַל וּמַיִם לֹא שָׁתָה. נְטִירַת הֲוָה עַד הַשְׁתָּא הַאי תְּרוּמָה לְקוּדְשָׁא בְּרִיךְ הוּא. וְכֵיוָן דְּמַלְכָּא לָא אָכַל, אֵיךְ אַכְלִין עַבְדֵּי, דְּהָא לְבָתַר דְּאָמַר אָרִיתִי מוֹרִי עִם בְּשָׂמִי, לְבָתַר אִכְלוּ רֵעִים, יֵיכְלוּן עַבְדּוֹי.

50. There are several offerings there. There is an offering mentioned in the Torah, SINCE TRUMAH (ENG. 'OFFERING') CONSISTS OF TORAH AND THE LETTER MEM. That is an offering, which is the Torah, given in *Mem* (= 40) days. If you say that yet I ate from her IN THOSE FORTY DAYS, does it not say: "and he was there with Hashem forty days and forty nights; he did neither eat bread, nor drink water" (Shemot 34:28)? It was kept until this time, MEANING UNTIL THE ERECTION OF THE TABERNACLE. This was an offering to the Holy One, blessed be He, and if the King did not eat, THAT IS, THERE WAS NO MATING OF ZEIR ANPIN AND MALCHUT REFERRED TO AS 'EATING', how could his servants eat? Following that, AFTER THE TABERNACLE WAS ERECTED, it says, "I have gathered my myrrh with my spice" (Shir Hashirim 5:1) – THAT THERE WAS A MATING OF ZEIR ANPIN AND MALCHUT. Following that, it is written, "eat, O dear ones" (Ibid.), and the servants could eat; THAT IS, THEY WILL RECEIVE FROM THE ILLUMINATION OF THIS MATING.

12. To set aside tithe

A Synopsis

Moses speaks about the next precept, that is to set aside a tithe for
the Levites. This offering comes from the left, Gvurah and is given
to the right, Chesed. Again Moses elaborates on the numerical
values of many letters and words as derived from the amounts of
offerings prescribed in scripture.

51. פְּקוּדָא בָּתַר דָּא לְהַפְרִישׁ מַעֲשֵׂר לְלֵוִי, וְאִיהִי שְׁכִינְתָּא מִסְטַר
הַיְמִינָא דְּאִיהוּ חֶסֶד, תְּרוּמָה גְּדוֹלָה לַכֹּהֵן. מִסְטְרָא דִשְׂמָאלָא, דְּאִיהוּ
גְּבוּרָה, תְּרוּמַת מַעֲשֵׂר לְלֵוִי, דְּאִיהִי שְׁכִינְתָּא.

51. The precept after this is to set aside a tithe for the Levi. Thus is the
Shechinah from the right side, which is Chesed. The great offering IS GIVEN
to the priest, WHO IS CHESED. From the left side, Gvurah, the tithe offering
IS GIVEN, REFERRING TO THE OFFERING OF TITHE belonging to Levi,
which is the Shechinah ON THE LEFT SIDE.

52. יוֹ״ד הֵ״י וָא״ו הֵ״י, שְׁלֹשֶׁת עֶשְׂרוֹנִים לַפָּר, מִסְטְרָא דְּהַהוּא דְּאִתְּמַר
בֵּיהּ, וּפְנֵי שׁוֹר מֵהַשְּׂמֹאל, וְדָא גְבוּרָה. וְעִשָּׂרוֹן לַכֶּבֶשׂ, וְדָא יוֹ״ד הֵ״א
וָא״ו הֵ״א, דְּסָלִיק לְעֶשֶׂר אַתְוָון, הַאי עִשָּׂרוֹן. וְעֶשֶׂר לְמ״ה וּמ״ה
לְמֵאָה.

52. THE YUD HEI VAV HEI OF THE NUMERICAL VALUE OF 63, WHICH IS
Yud-Vav-Dalet, Hei-Yud, Vav-Aleph-Vav, Hei-Yud, IS THE SECRET OF
IMA, WHICH IS LEFT IN RELATION TO ABA, WHO IS YUD HEI VAV HEI OF
NUMERICAL VALUE OF 72, SINCE 72 AND 63 ARE RIGHT AND LEFT. It is
"three tenth measures shall you offer for a bullock" (Bemidbar 28:28), THAT
IS, THE THREE YUD'S OF THE NAME OF THE FULL SPELLING OF 63,
CALLED THE 'THREE TENTH MEASURES'. THIS IS SAID OF AN OX
BECAUSE IT IS of that side about which is said, "and they four had the face
of an ox on the left side" (Yechezkel 1:10). That is Gvurah, MEANING THE
LEFT COLUMN. "…a tenth measure for one lamb…" That totals ten letters
–Yud-Vav-Dalet-Hei-Aleph-Vav-Aleph-Vav-Hei-Aleph, and that is a tenth
measure. THE TEN LETTERS and these ten LETTERS AMOUNT NUMERICALLY

to *Mem-Hei* (= 45), and *Mem-Hei* is one hundred (Heb. *meah*), AS
EXPLAINED ABOVE.

53. אֲבָל שְׁלֹשָׁה עֶשְׂרוֹנִים י׳ י׳ י׳, וְסַלְקִין לְל׳, וְי׳ סְפִירָן בְּהוֹן, סַלְקִין
מ״ג בֵּיצִים וְכֻלָּא יוֹ״ד, חוֹמֶשׁ בֵּיצָה, תּוֹסֶפֶת מִצַּד ה׳, וְהָכִי מַעֲשֵׂר,
דְּאִיהוּ פְּקוּדָא לְהַפְרִישׁ יִשְׂרָאֵל מַעֲשֵׂר, מִסִּטְרָא דְאָת י׳, מַעֲשֵׂר מִן
הַמַּעֲשֵׂר, חַד מֵחֲמֵשׁ מִסִּטְרָא דְאָת ה׳. כָּל עֶשׂוּרִין דְּאָת י׳, וְאִיהִי
שְׁכִינְתָּא חַד מֵעֲשַׂר סְפִירָן. א׳ מֵחֲמֵשׁ, אִיהוּ מִסִּטְרָא דְתִפְאֶרֶת, דְּאִיהוּ
חֲמִשָּׁה מִכֶּתֶר. וְכַד תַּחְשׁוֹב מִמַּלְכוּת עַד תִּפְאֶרֶת, תִּשְׁכַּח תִּפְאֶרֶת
חָמֵשׁ מִתַּתָּא לְעֵילָא. וּשְׁכִינְתָּא חֲמִשָׁאָה לְגַבֵּיהּ.

53. Three tenth measures ALLUDE TO THE SETTING ASIDE OF THE DOUGH
OFFERING, WHICH IS APPLICABLE TO A DOUGH OF THE SIZE OF FORTY
THREE AND ONE FIFTH OF AN EGG'S SIZE. The three *Yuds* OF THE YUD
HEI VAV HEI OF 63 ARE THREE LETTERS amounting to THE NUMERICAL
VALUE OF THIRTY AND TOGETHER TOTAL 33, AND WITH the ten Sfirot in
them – IN THE THREE *YUD'S* – totaling 43, WHICH IS THE SECRET OF 43
eggs. All this is *Yud*, SINCE THE NUMBER 43 IS DERIVED FROM THAT
YUD, WHICH ARE THE THREE LETTERS OF *YUD* IN THE FULL SPELLING OF
YUD HEI VAV HEI OF 63, AND THEIR AMOUNT IS THIRTY PLUS THE TEN
SFIROT. The fifth of an egg's size that is added TO THE MEASURE OF 43
EGGS' SIZE, is due to the *Hei*, SINCE MALCHUT HAS THE ASPECT OF *YUD*
AND THE ASPECT OF *HEI*. So the tithe, of the commandment that Yisrael
are required to set aside a tithe, is due to the letter *Yud* IN MALCHUT, which
is tithe of a tithe, MEANING THAT MALCHUT IS ONE OF TEN SFIROT AND
NINE OF THE SFIROT ARE PART OF HER. THEREFORE, IT IS THE SECRET
OF *YUD* and it is one of five SFIROT from the aspect of *Hei*. Anywhere it
says ten, it is from the letter *Yud*, which is the Shechinah, which is one of
ten Sfirot. One of five is from the aspect of Tiferet, due to the fact THAT
TIFERET is the fifth of Keter, WHICH IS CHOCHMAH AND BINAH,
CHESED, GVURAH AND TIFERET. When you count from Malchut to
Tiferet, you will find that Tiferet is the fifth from bottom upwards. THAT IS,
MALCHUT, YESOD, HOD, NETZACH AND TIFERET and the Shechinah is
the fifth to it, TO TIFERET, AND ALL THESE FOUR – TIFERET, NETZACH,
HOD AND YESOD, ILLUMINATE IN HER. THEREFORE, SHE IS THE

SECRET OF *Hei* (= 5), SINCE FROM THIS HEI, THE ADDITION COMES OF
ONE FIFTH OF THE EGG SIZE, AS EXPLAINED ABOVE.

‎54. וּמִסִּטְרָא אַחֲרָא אִיהִי שְׁנֵי עֶשְׂרוֹנִים לָאַיִל, וּכְלִילַת י' י' הַכַּף
‎בְּשֶׁקֶל הַקֹּדֶשׁ, עֲשָׂרָה עֲשָׂרָה י' ה"ה, לָאַיִל דָּא ו', דְּאִיהוּ שֶׁקֶל הַקֹּדֶשׁ,
‎וְהַאי אִיהוּ עֲשָׂרָה עֲשָׂרָה הַכַּף בְּשֶׁקֶל הַקֹּדֶשׁ. וְעוֹד, שְׁנֵי עֶשְׂרוֹנִים, י' י'
‎מִן וַיִּיצֶר. לָאַיִל ו' מִן וַיִּיצֶר. וְכֹלָּא א', י' לְעֵילָא, י' לְתַתָּא, ו'
‎בְּאֶמְצָעִיתָא.

54. From the aspect OF MALCHUT, there are "two tenth measures for one
ram" (Bemidbar 28:28) SINCE, "TWO TENTHS MEASURES" ARE TWO
YUD'S and she is included in, "the golden spoons...weighing ten shekels
apiece" (Bemidbar 7:86). Ten apiece is *Yud* FROM THE RIGHT, *Hei-Hei*,
WHICH ARE A FULLY SPELLED HEI, FROM THE LEFT, THAT IN NUMERICAL
EQUIVALENT TOTALS YUD (= 10) "...for one ram..." is *Vav*, which is the
shekel of the sanctuary, WHICH IS THE CENTRAL COLUMN THAT
BALANCES (HEB. *SHOKEL*) AND OUTWEIGHS THEM. That is the meaning
of "the golden spoons...weighing ten shekels apiece (lit. 'ten ten')" SINCE
THE SPOON, WHICH IS MALCHUT, IS COMPRISED OF YUD (TEN) FROM
THE RIGHT AND YUD (TEN) FROM THE LEFT. "THE SHEKEL OF THE
SANCTUARY" IS THE CENTRAL COLUMN THAT IS THE VAV. "...two tenth
measures for one ram..." are the *Yud-Yud* of "*Vayyitzer* (Eng. 'formed')"
(Beresheet 2:19). "...for one ram..." is that *Vav* of "*Vayyitzer*." All this is in
THE FORM OF an *Aleph*, WHOSE FORM IS a *Yud* above and a *Yud* below,
WHICH INDICATES TO THE RIGHT AND LEFT, while the *Vav* in the middle
INDICATES THE Central Column.

13. Setting aside a thank offering

A Synopsis

We hear about the precept to set aside a thanks offering and are told the appropriate amounts and values, and we learn the secret meaning of why it must never be less than ten remembrances.

55. וְעוֹד שְׁלֹשָׁה עֶשְׂרוֹנִים אִינּוּן י׳ י׳ י׳. פְּקוּדָא בָּתַר דָּא, לְהַפְרִישׁ תּוֹדָה. וְרַבָּנָן מָארֵי מַתְנִיתִין אוּקְמוּהָ, דְּתוֹדָה עֶשְׂרִים עֶשְׂרוֹנִים, וּמִתְפַּלְגִין י׳ עֶשְׂרוֹנִין לְחָמֵץ, וְי׳ לְמַצָּה. וּמִי׳ שֶׁל מַצָּה, עוֹשִׂים ל׳ מַצּוֹת. וּמֵעֲשָׂרָה שֶׁל חָמֵץ, עוֹשִׂים י׳ חַלּוֹת. וְדָא אִיהוּ סֹלֶת חַלּוֹת מַצּוֹת בְּלוּלֹת בַּשֶּׁמֶן. מֵי׳ עֶשְׂרוֹנִים, דְּאִינּוּן יֹו״ד הֵ״י וָא״ו הֵ״י, הֲווֹ עַבְדִין ל׳ מַצּוֹת, דְּאִינּוּן י׳ י׳ י׳. הַאי שְׁמָא, זִמְנִין אִיהוּ לִימִינָא, וְזִמְנִין אִיהוּ לִשְׂמָאלָא, וְזִמְנִין בְּאֶמְצָעִיתָא. רַחֲמֵי מִכָּל סִטְרָא, לִימִינֵיהּ וְלִשְׂמָאלֵיהּ.

55. Also, three tenth measures are THREE TIMES *YUD, YUD* AND *YUD* IN YUD HEI VAV HEI WHEN FULLY SPELLED OUT, TOTALING TO 63. They are the precepts after this one to set aside a thanks offering. And the rabbis, the sages of the Mishnah set it that a thanking is equal to twenty tenth measures, and they are divided into ten tenth measures for leavened bread and ten for unleavened. From the ten of unleavened, they produce thirty Matzot and, from the ten of leavened bread, they produce ten *challot* (lit. 'dough cakes'). That is the meaning of: "unleavened cakes of fine flour mingled with oil" (Vayikra 2:4). From the ten tenth measures – WHICH ARE THE TEN LETTERS OF YUD HEI VAV HEI FULLY SPELLED TO THE NUMERICAL VALUE OF 63, which are *Yud-Vav-Dalet, Hei-Yud, Vav-Aleph-Vav, Hei-Yud*, they made thirty Matzot that are *Yud, Yud* and *Yud*, THAT IS, IN THE *YUD HEI VAV HEI* OF 63. THIS IS BECAUSE IN NUMERICAL VALUE THEY ARE THIRTY, THE SECRET OF THE THREE TENTH MEASURES, AS EXPLAINED ABOVE. This Name – YUD HEI VAV HEI IN THE FULL SPELLING OF '63' – is sometimes to the right, CHESED, and sometimes it is to the left, GVURAH. Sometimes, it is in the center, which is Mercy from every direction, both to the right and left, SINCE THE CENTRAL COLUMN INCLUDES THE RIGHT AND LEFT.

56. וְזִמְנִין י׳ לִימִינָא, וְאֵין פּוֹחֲתִין בֵּיה מֵעֲשָׂרָה מַלְכִיּוֹת. וּלְזִמְנִין יו״ד לִשְׂמָאלָא, וְאֵין פּוֹחֲתִין בֵּיה מֵעֲשָׂרָה שׁוֹפָרוֹת. וּלְזִמְנִין יו״ד בְּאֶמְצָעִיתָא, וְאֵין פּוֹחֲתִין בֵּיה מֵי׳ זִכְרוֹנוֹת.

56. Sometimes, the *Yud*, WHICH REPRESENTS MALCHUT, is in the right, and THAT IS THE SECRET OF why it must never be less than ten Malchuts, SINCE TEN IS THE SECRET OF *Yud*. Sometimes the *Yud*, WHICH IS MALCHUT, is on the left, AND THIS IS THE SECRET OF why it must never be less than ten blows of the Shofar, SINCE AT THAT TIME, IT IS CONSIDERED A SHOFAR, LIKE IMA WHO IS ON THE LEFT, AS MENTIONED. Sometimes the *Yud*, THAT IS, MALCHUT, is in the center, BETWEEN THE RIGHT AND LEFT, WHEN IT IS REFERRED TO AS 'REMEMBRANCE', CORRESPONDING TO THE NAME ZEIR ANPIN THAT IS THE CENTRAL COLUMN. THAT IS THE SECRET MEANING OF why it must never be less than ten remembrances.

14. "At the commandment of Hashem they remained encamped"

A Synopsis

Here Moses emphasizes strongly the number twelve, as manifested in the twelve boundaries, the twelve countenances and the twelve tribes. He talks about the three living creatures, lion, ox and eagle, each with its four aspects. We learn that for whoever produces merits in order to receive a reward, God comes down in the Chariot of the servant Metatron and with His four guards, the archangels. But for whoever produces merits not for the sake of receiving a reward, He descends in His own Chariot. Finally Moses says that God descends upon the wicked with their deeds, with demons, harmful spirits and destructive angels with the Chariot, in order to take revenge on them.

57. עַל פִּי יְיָ' יַחֲנוּ וְעַל פִּי יְיָ' יִסָּעוּ אֶת מִשְׁמֶרֶת יְיָ' שָׁמָרוּ. דְּכָל י' אִית לָהּ ד' אַנְפִּין, ג' חֵיוָון אִינוּן, לָקֳבֵל תְּלַת יוֹדִין, וְד' אַנְפִּין לְכָל חַיָּה, לָקֳבֵל ד' אַנְפִּין דִּיהֹוָ"ה, עַל פִּי יְיָ' יַחֲנוּ וְיִסָּעוּ.

57. "At the commandment of Hashem they remained encamped, and at the commandment of Hashem they journeyed: they kept the charge of Hashem." (Bemidbar 9:23). THIS VERSE CONTAINS THREE NAMES OF YUD HEI VAV HEI, IN ACCORDANCE WITH THE THREE YUD'S MENTIONED ABOVE, since each Yud has four faces, MEANING FOUR LETTERS OF YUD HEI VAV HEI. THIS IS THE SECRET OF THE TWELVE BOUNDARIES THAT CONTAIN ALL PERFECTION, WHICH ARE THE FOUR LETTERS OF YUD HEI VAV HEI, CHESED, GVURAH, TIFERET AND MALCHUT. WITHIN EACH ONE, THERE ARE THREE YUD'S; THAT IS, THREE COLUMNS FOR A TOTAL OF TWELVE. HE EXPLAINS FURTHER: There are three living creatures corresponding to the three Yud's, MEANING THE THREE COLUMNS CALLED 'LION', 'OX' AND 'EAGLE'. And there are four aspects to each living creature, THAT IS, TO EACH COLUMN in accordance with the four aspects of Yud Hei Vav Hei, MEANING IN ACCORDANCE WITH THE FOUR LETTERS OF YUD HEI VAV HEI, WHICH ARE CHESED, GVURAH, TIFERET AND MALCHUT, THE TWELVE BOUNDARIES. "At the commandment of Hashem they remained encamped, and at the commandment of Hashem they journeyed," THAT IS, IN HARMONY WITH THE PERFECTION OF THE TWELVE BOUNDARIES.

58. שָׁמָרוּ, דָּא שְׁכִינְתָּא, דְּנָטְרָא לְאִינוּן דִּשְׁמָרֵי שַׁבָּתוֹת וְיָמִים טוֹבִים,

דרבג״כ לָא זָזָה שְׁכִינָה מִיִשְׂרָאֵל בְּכָל שַׁבָּתוֹת וִיו״ט, וַאֲפִילוּ בְּשַׁבָּתוֹת
דְּחוֹל, אֶלָּא דְּאִיהוּ סוֹגֶרֶת וּמְסוּגֶרֶת בְּהוֹן.

58. AFTER THE THREE YUD HEI VAV HEI: "AT THE COMMANDMENT OF
HASHEM...AT THE COMMANDMENT OF HASHEM...THE CHARGE OF
HASHEM." IT SAYS, "they kept," which is the Shechinah THAT RECEIVES
FROM THESE THREE COLUMNS THAT ARE THE SECRET OF THE TWELVE
BOUNDARIES. IT IS INDICATED IN THE WORDS "THEY KEPT," SINCE She
keeps all those who keep the Shabbatot and holidays. Therefore, the
Shechinah has not moved from Yisrael all the Shabbatot and holidays. This
is true even on Shabbatot that are not on festive days, only She is shut up
and closed in them, MEANING THAT SHE DOES NOT BESTOW PLENTY ON
THE LOWER BEINGS. THAT IS NOT THE CASE ON SHABBATOT THAT
OCCUR ON HOLIDAYS, WHEN HER PLENTY IS POURED IN GREAT
ABUNDANCE.

59. וּבְכָל צְלוֹתָא, אִיהוּ עוֹלָה לַיְדוֹ״ד, עַד דְּמָטָאת לְמֶרְכַּבְתָּא דַּאֲבָהָן
עִלָּאִין, דְּאִינוּן: גְּדוּלָ״ה, גְּבוּרָ״ה, תִּפְאֶרֶ״ת, דְּאִית לְהוֹן תְּרֵיסַר אַנְפִּין,
לָקֳבֵל תְּרֵיסַר שְׁבָטִין. וּכְפוּם דְּאִיהִי אוֹלִיפַת זְכוּת, עַל אִלֵּין מָאֵרֵי
צְלוֹתִין, וּמָאֵרֵי זַכְוָון, בְּכָל פִּקוּדָא וּפִקוּדָא דְּאוֹרַיְיתָא, הָכִי יַחֲנוּ עַל
זַכְוָון דִּלְהוֹן וְכֵן יִסְעוּ לְגַבַּיְיהוּ. וְהָכִי נַחֲתָא שְׁמִירָה לְגַבַּיְיהוּ.

59. At every prayer, she, MALCHUT, ascends to Yud Hei Vav Hei, THAT IS
ZEIR ANPIN, until it reaches the Chariot of the Supreme Patriarchs, who are
Chesed, Gvurah and Tiferet, which contain the twelve countenances
corresponding to the twelve tribes. This is BECAUSE EACH ONE OF CHESED,
GVURAH, AND TIFERET INCORPORATES FOUR COUNTENANCES, CHESED,
GVURAH, TIFERET AND MALCHUT, TOTALING TWELVE. According to her,
MALCHUT advocates merits for all those who pray and have earned merits
in each and every precept in the Torah. So they "remained encamped" over
their merits and so they "journeyed" to their merits. Thus the "charge" is
going down to them.

60. אִינּוּן דְּעַבְדִין זַכְוָון עַל מְנָת לְקַבֵּל פְּרָס, נָחִית קוּדְשָׁא בְּרִיךְ הוּא
בְּמֶרְכַּבְתֵיה דְּעֲבַד, וּבַד׳ שׁוֹמְרִין דִּילֵיה, וּמַאן דְּעָבֵיד זַכְוָון שֶׁלֹּא עַל

מְנָת לְקַבֵּל פְּרָס, נָחִית עֲלַיְיהוּ בְּמֶרְכַּבְתָּא דִילֵיהּ. וּלְרַשִׁיעַיָא נָחִית עֲלַיְיהוּ בְּעוֹבָדַיְיהוּ, בְּאִינּוּן שֵׁדִין וּמַזִּיקִין וּמַלְאֲכֵי חַבָּלָה בְּמֶרְכַּבְתָּא דִלְהוֹן, לְאִתְפָּרְעָא מִנְּהוֹן. פָּתְחוּ מָארֵי מַתְנִיתִין וְאָמְרוּ. וַדַּאי הָכִי הוּא, זַכָּאָה חוּלָקָךְ רַעְיָא מְהֵימָנָא.

ע״כ רעיא מהימנא

60. HE EXPLAINS HIS WORDS: For those who produce merits in order to receive a reward, MEANING WAGE RECOMPENSE, the Holy One, blessed be He, comes down in the Chariot of the servant, THAT IS METATRON, and with His four guards, THAT ARE MICHAEL, GABRIEL, URIEL AND RAPHAEL. But for whoever produces merits not for the sake of receiving a reward, He descends in His own Chariot. To the wicked, He descends upon them with their deeds, with demons, harmful spirits, and destructive angels with the Chariot, in order to have revenge upon them. The scholars of the Mishnah said: Certainly it is so. Praised is your lot, Faithful Shepherd.

End of Ra'aya Meheimna (the Faithful Shepherd)

בָּרוּךְ יְיָ׳ לְעוֹלָם אָמֵן וְאָמֵן. יִמְלוֹךְ יְיָ׳ לְעוֹלָם אָמֵן וְאָמֵן.

Blessed is Hashem for evermore. Amen and Amen. May Hashem reign for evermore. Amen and Amen.

CHUKAT

1. "This is the ordinance of the Torah"

A Synopsis

Rabbi Yosi draws a distinction between the Torah itself, that is Zeir Anpin, and the law of the Torah, that is Malchut. Rabbi Yehuda says that the verse, "and this is the Torah," means a union of total perfection, including male and female, but the verse, "this is the ordinance of the Torah," means Malchut without Zeir Anpin.

וְיָדַבֵּר יְיָ אֶל מֹשֶׁה וְאֶל אַהֲרֹן לֵאמֹר זֹאת חֻקַּת הַתּוֹרָה אֲשֶׁר צִוָּה .1
יְיָ לֵאמֹר וְגוֹ'. ר' יוֹסֵי פָּתַח, וְזֹאת הַתּוֹרָה אֲשֶׁר שָׂם מֹשֶׁה לִפְנֵי בְּנֵי
יִשְׂרָאֵל. ת"ח, מִלִּין דְּאוֹרַיְיתָא קַדִּישִׁין אִינּוּן, עִלָּאִין אִינּוּן, מְתִיקִין
אִינּוּן. כְּמָה דִכְתִיב, הַנֶּחֱמָדִים מִזָּהָב וּמִפָּז רָב וּמְתוּקִים מִדְּבַשׁ וְגוֹ'.
מַאן דְּאִשְׁתַּדַּל בְּאוֹרַיְיתָא, כְּאִלּוּ קָאִים כָּל יוֹמָא עַל טוּרָא דְּסִינַי וְקַבִּיל
אוֹרַיְיתָא. הה"ד, הַיּוֹם הַזֶּה נִהְיֵיתָ לְעָם. וְהָא אוּקְמוּהָ חַבְרַיָיא.

1. "And Hashem spoke to Moses and Aaron, saying, 'This is the ordinance of the Torah which Hashem has commanded'" (Bemidbar 19:1-2). Rabbi Yosi opened the discussion saying: "and this is the Torah which Moses set before the children of Yisrael" (Devarim 4:44). Come and behold: the words of the Torah are holy, lofty, and sweet, as it is written: "more to be desired are they than gold, and much fine gold: sweeter also than honey..." (Tehilim 19:11). It is as if whoever studies the Torah stands every day at Mount Sinai and receives the Torah. This is what it says: "this day you are become a people" (Devarim 27:9). And the friends have already set the explanation.

כְּתִיב הָכָא זֹאת חֻקַּת הַתּוֹרָה, וּכְתִיב וְזֹאת הַתּוֹרָה, מַה בֵּין הַאי .2
לְהַאי. אֶלָּא רָזָא עִלָּאָה הוּא, וְהָכִי אוֹלִיפְנָא, וְזֹאת הַתּוֹרָה: לְאַחֲזָאָה
כֹּלָּא בְּיִחוּדָא חַד, וּלְאַכְלְלָא כנ"י בְּקוּדְשָׁא בְּרִיךְ הוּא, לְאִשְׁתַּכְּחָא
כֹּלָּא חַד. בְּגִינֵי כָּךְ וְזֹאת הַתּוֹרָה. אֲמַאי תּוֹסֶפֶת וָא"ו. אֶלָּא הָא אִתְּמַר,
לְאַחֲזָאָה דְּכֹלָּא חַד, בְּלָא פֵּרוּדָא. וְזֹאת: כְּלָל וּפְרָט כַּחֲדָא, דְּכַר
וְנוּקְבָא. ובג"כ וְזֹאת הַתּוֹרָה וַדַּאי. אֲבָל זֹאת בְּלָא תּוֹסֶפֶת וָא"ו, חֻקַּת
הַתּוֹרָה וַדַּאי, וְלָא הַתּוֹרָה, דִּינָא דְּאוֹרַיְיתָא, גְּזֵרָה דְּאוֹרַיְיתָא.

2. It is written here: "this is the ordinance of the Torah," and it is also, "and

this is the Torah," BUT IT IS NOT WRITTEN, 'THE ORDINANCE'. What is the difference between this and that? HE RESPONDS: It is a lofty secret and that is what we learned. The words, "and this is the Torah," are to show that all is in one unison and to unite the Congregation of Yisrael, THAT IS MALCHUT, with the Holy One, blessed be He, THAT IS ZEIR ANPIN, so that all will be one. Therefore, "and this is the Torah." Why is there the addition of "and" (Heb. *Vav*), TO "this"? It is only to show that as we are taught, all is one without division. The words, "and this," indicate the general and the particular, NAMELY male and female combined together, SINCE VAV IS MALE, THAT IS ZEIR ANPIN, WHICH IS GENERAL – AND "THIS" IS FEMALE, MEANING MALCHUT, WHICH IS PARTICULAR. Therefore, it is assuredly WRITTEN: "and this is the Torah," TO INDICATE ZEIR ANPIN AND THE NUKVA IN ONE UNISON. However, "this," without the additional Vav is specifically the ordinance of the Torah, WHICH IS MALCHUT THAT IS CONSIDERED THE ORDINANCE. AND it EMANATES FROM ZEIR ANPIN, WHICH IS CONSIDERED THE TORAH, but is not the Torah ITSELF, WHICH IS ZEIR ANPIN. It is ONLY the law of the Torah, the decree of Torah, WHICH IS MALCHUT.

3. ת"ח, זֹאת אֲשֶׁר לַלְוִיִּם, וְלָא וְזֹאת. דְּהָא מִסִּטְרָא דְּדִינָא קָא אַתְיָין, וְלָא מִסִּטְרָא דְּרַחֲמֵי. א"ר יְהוּדָה, וְהָא כְּתִיב וְזֹאת עֲשׂוּ לָהֶם וְחָיוּ. וְדָא בִּלְוִיאֵי אִתְּמַר, וְאַתְּ אַמְרַת זֹאת וְלָא וְזֹאת. אָ"ל, וַדַּאי הָכִי הוּא, וּקְרָא מוֹכַח, מַאן דְּאָחִיד סַמָּא דְּמוֹתָא, אִי לָא יְעָרַב בֵּיהּ סַמָּא דְּחַיֵּי, הָא וַדַּאי יְמוּת. וע"ד, וְזֹאת עֲשׂוּ לָהֶם וְחָיוּ, וְלֹא יָמוּתוּ, בְּגִין דְּסַמָּא דְּחַיֵּי מְעָרַב בַּהֲדֵיהּ, וְזֹאת עֲשׂוּ וְחָיוּ וְלֹא יָמוּתוּ, וַדַּאי וְזֹאת אִצְטְרִיךְ לְהוּ, וְלָא זֹאת. בְּגִינֵי כָּךְ וְזֹאת הַתּוֹרָה מַמָּשׁ, בְּיִחוּדָא חַד, בְּיִחוּדָא שְׁלִים, כְּלָלָא דִּדְכַר וְנוּקְבָּא. ו"ה. זֹאת: ה' בִּלְחוֹדוֹי, וע"ד זֹאת חֻקַּת הַתּוֹרָה.

3. Come and behold: IT IS WRITTEN, "this is that which belongs to the Levites" (Bemidbar 8:24). It is not WRITTEN, 'and this,' WITH A *VAV*, since they emerge from the side of Judgment, WHICH IS FROM THE LEFT SIDE AND FROM THE SIDE OF MALCHUT THAT IS ERECTED FROM THE LEFT, and not from the angle of Compassion, WHICH IS ZEIR ANPIN. THEREFORE, "THIS" IT IS WRITTEN WITHOUT A VAV, MEANING MALCHUT WITHOUT ZEIR ANPIN. Rabbi Yehuda said: Yet it is written, "and this do to them, that they may live" (Bemidbar 4:19). Here, "THIS" IS WITH A VAV, and it is said

about the Levites, and yet you say THAT THE LEVITES ARE THE ASPECT OF "this," and not of, "and this." He said to him: It is most certainly so, THAT THEY ARE IN THE ASPECT OF, "AND THIS." The scripture proves that whoever holds on to deadly poison spices but does not blend into it life-giving spices will certainly die. Therefore, IT IS WRITTEN: "And this do to them, that they may live," MEANING THAT "THIS," WHICH IS THE SECRET OF MALCHUT, CONSIDERED THE TREE OF DEATH, SHOULD JOIN WITH VAV, WHICH IS ZEIR ANPIN, THE TREE OF LIFE. "...and not die..." (Ibid.) This is because the spice of life is mixed with it. THEREFORE, "and this do to them, that they may live, and not die," since they require, "and this," and not 'this'. THEREFORE, the verse: "and this is the Torah," INDICATES that it really is actually in one union, a union of total perfection, male and female in one inclusion; THAT IS THE SECRET OF Vav-Hei. However, "this," ALONE WITHOUT THE VAV, is a Hei alone WITHOUT A VAV, THAT IS, MALCHUT WITHOUT ZEIR ANPIN. About this, it IS WRITTEN: "this is the ordinance of the Torah."

2. "A man pulled off his shoe"

A Synopsis

The rabbis discuss the preceding verse and also the verse that speaks about redeeming and exchanging and sealing the bargain by means of the removal of the shoe. Rabbi Elazar cites God's commandment to Moses to take off his shoes, meaning that he commanded him to separate from his wife and join the Shechinah instead. He says that whoever takes the shoe sends the one who gave him the shoe to another world, and that whenever someone draws off his shoe and gives it to another in order to seal a transaction, he is doing this by a decree from above. Rabbi Elazar mentions the drawing off of the sandal at the time of levirate marriage as well, and explains that the widow accepts the shoe to indicate that her dead husband returns among the living. The conclusion to be drawn is that the exchange of the shoe is not just an agreed concensus but is in fact indicating support from the higher grades.

4. רִבִּי שִׁמְעוֹן וְר' אַבָּא וְר' אֶלְעָזָר וְר' יִצְחָק, הֲווֹ שְׁכִיחֵי בְּבֵי ר' פִּנְחָס בֶּן יָאִיר, אָמַר ר' פִּנְחָס לְר' שִׁמְעוֹן, בְּמָטוּתָא מִנָּךְ אַנְתְּ דְּאוּקְמֵי עֲלָךְ לְעֵילָא, וּמִילָךְ בְּאִתְגַּלְיָיא, מַה דְּלָא אִתְיְהִיב רְשׁוּתָא לב"נ אַחֲרָא. בְּפָרְשָׁתָא דָּא אֵימָא מִלָּה חַדְתָּא, א"ל וּמַאי הִיא. א"ל זֹאת חֻקַּת הַתּוֹרָה. א"ל הָא הָא שְׁאַר חַבְרַיָּיא יֵאמְרוּ. אָמַר לְר' אֶלְעָזָר בְּרֵיהּ, אֶלְעָזָר קוּם בְּקִיּוּמָךְ, וְאֵימָא מִלָּה חַד בְּפָרְשָׁתָא דָּא, וְחַבְרַיָּיא יֵימְרוּן אֲבַתְרָךְ.

4. Rabbi Shimon, Rabbi Aba, Rabbi Elazar and Rabbi Yitzchak were in the house of Rabbi Pinchas ben Yair. Rabbi Pinchas spoke to Rabbi Shimon saying: I beg of you, you who are appointed from above, to speak openly about that which no other person was permitted to speak. Say something new about this passage. He said to him: Which passage is it? He said to him: "This is the ordinance of the Torah" (Bemidbar 19:2). He said to him: Here are the other friends, let them speak. He told his son, Rabbi Elazar: Elazar, stand up and say something about this passage. Then the friends will speak after you.

5. קָם ר' אֶלְעָזָר וְאָמַר, וְזֹאת לְפָנִים בְּיִשְׂרָאֵל עַל הַגְּאוּלָּה וְעַל הַתְּמוּרָה לְקַיֵּים וְגוֹ'. הַאי קְרָא אִית לְאִסְתַּכְּלָא בֵּיהּ, וְאִי אִינּוּן קַדְמָאֵי

עָבְדֵי הַסְכָּמָה דָּא בְּדִינָא דְּאוֹרַיְיתָא, וְאָתוּ בַּתְרָאֵי וּבְטְלוּהָ, אֲמַאי בִּטְלוּהָ. וְהָא מַאן דְּבָטִיל מִלָּה דְּאוֹרַיְיתָא. כְּאִילּוּ חָרִיב עָלְמָא שְׁלִים. וְאִי לָאו אִיהוּ בְּדִינָא דְּאוֹרַיְיתָא, אֶלָּא הַסְכָּמָה בְּעָלְמָא, אֲמַאי נַעַל הָכָא.

5. Rabbi Elazar stood up and spoke: "Now this was the custom in former times in Yisrael concerning redeeming and concerning exchanging, to confirm..." (Rut 4:7). This scriptural verse must be studied carefully. If the earlier ones have made this consensual agreement, TO BUY EVERYTHING THROUGH A SHOE, according to the law of Torah, and the latter ones came and voided it, WE MUST INQUIRE why it was made void. Is not one who abrogates any matter in the Torah considered as if he destroys the whole world? If it is not a Torah law but merely an agreed consensus, THE QUESTION IS why SPECIFICALLY a shoe was used here, AND NOT ANY OTHER METHOD.

6. אֶלָּא וַדַּאי בְּדִינָא דְּאוֹרַיְיתָא הֲוָה, וּבְרָזָא עִלָּאָה אִתְעֲבֵידַת מִלָּה, וּבְגִין דַּהֲווֹ קַדְמָאֵי חֲסִידֵי זַכָּאֵי, מִלָּה דָּא אִתְגַּלְיָיא בֵּינַיְיהוּ, וּמִדְּאַסְגִיאוּ חַיָּיבֵי בְּעָלְמָא, אִתְעֲבֵידַת הַאי מִלָּה בְּגַוְונָא אַחֲרָא, בְּגִין לְאִתְכַּסָּאָה מִלִּין דְּאִינּוּן בְּרָזָא עִלָּאָה.

6. HE RESPONDS: It was most certainly according to the law of the Torah, and it was done with a lofty secret. Because the earlier were pious and just, this matter was revealed and known among them. And when the wicked increased in the world, this matter was accomplished in a different manner, in order to cover these matters which are in accordance with a lofty secret.

7. ת״ח, וַיֹּאמֶר אַל תִּקְרַב הֲלוֹם שַׁל נְעָלֶיךָ מֵעַל רַגְלֶיךָ וְגוֹ'. וְכִי אֲמַאי נַעַל הָכָא. אֶלָּא אִתְּמַר, דְּפָקִיד לֵיהּ עַל אִתְּתָא, לְאִתְפָּרְשָׁא מִנָּהּ, וּלְאִזְדַּוְּוגָא בְּאִתְּתָא אַחֲרָא, דְּנְהִירוּ קַדִּישָׁא עִלָּאָה, וְאִיהִי שְׁכִינְתָּא.

7. Come and behold: it is written, "and he said, 'Do not come near: put off your shoes from off your feet...'" (Shemot 3:5). HE ASKS: Why is the shoe specifically mentioned here? HE RESPONDS: It is the way we were taught,

that He commanded him to separate from his wife and join another woman of the light of the holy up high, which is the Shechinah.

‎8. וְהַהוּא נַעַל אוקִים לֵיה בַּאֲתָר אַחֲרָא, אַעֲבָּר לֵיה מֵהַאי עָלְמָא, וְאוֹקִים לֵיה בְּעָלְמָא אַחֲרָא. וע"ד, כָּל מַה דְיָהִיב מִיתָא לְבַר נָשׁ בְּחֶלְמָא טַב. נָטִיל מָאנֵיה מִן בֵּיתָא בִּישׁ, כְּגוֹן סַנְדָּלֵיה. מ"ט. בְּגִין דְאַעֲבָּר רַגְלֵיה, דְּאִינוּן קִיוּמָא דְבַר נָשׁ, מֵהַאי עָלְמָא, וְכָנִישׁ לוֹן לְעָלְמָא אַחֲרָא, אֲתָר דְּמוֹתָא שָׁארֵי בֵּיה, דִּכְתִיב מַה יָפוּ פְּעָמַיִךְ בַּנְּעָלִים בַּת נָדִיב. וְרָזָא דְמִלָּה בֵּין חַבְרַיָּיא אִיהוּ.

8. That shoe is explained in another place; it is explained THAT WHOEVER TAKES IT passes THE ONE WHO GIVES IT from this world and installs him in another world. Consequently, everything that the dead one grants to a person in his dream is beneficial. However, if he takes any utensil from the house, it is harmful, for example, if he takes his shoe. What is the reason, since THAT INDICATES that he passed his foot, which gives standing support to the person, from this world and gathered him to another world to the place where the dead one dwells. A SHOE ALLUDES TO HIS LEG, WHICH GIVES HIM DURABLE SUPPORT, as is written: "how beautiful are your feet in the sandals, O prince's daughter" (Shir Hashirim 7:3). The secret of the matter is among the friends.

‎9. וְדָא כַּד מִיתָא נָטִיל לוֹן, אֲבָל בְּזִמְנָא דְחַיָּיא שָׁלִיף מָסָאנֵיה, וְיָהִיב לְבַר נָשׁ אַחֲרָא, בְּגִין לְקַיְימָא קַיָּים, קָא עָבֵיד בִּגְזֵרָה דִּלְעֵילָא. נַעַל דַּחֲלִיצָה, כְּגַוְונָא דִּלְעֵילָא נַעַל אַחֲרָא, וְכֹלָּא רָזָא חֲדָא.

9. That is so, that when the dead one takes it, IT INDICATES THAT HE PASSES HIM ON TO THE PLACE OF DEATH. However, when the living one draws off his shoe and gives it to another person in order to maintain a transaction, he carries this out by the decree of the above, WHICH MEANS THAT IT WAS DECREED THAT THE POSSESSION SHOULD PASS ON FROM THIS ONE'S PROPERTY TO THAT ONE'S PROPERTY. The removal of the shoe in the ritual of Chalitzah (removal of the sandal in the law of levirate marriage) is another shoe in the likeness of the above, THAT IS, AS HE EXPLAINS FURTHER, all is one secret meaning.

10. ת״ח, הַהוּא מִיתָא דְּאִסְתַּלָּק מֵעָלְמָא בְּלָא בְּנִין, הַאי בַּת נָדִיב לָא כְּנִישַׁת לֵיה לְהַהוּא בַּר נָשׁ לְגַבָּה, וְאָזִיל לְאִתְטַרְדָּא בְּעָלְמָא, דְּלָא אַשְׁכַּח אֲתָר, וְקוּדְשָׁא בְּרִיךְ הוּא חָיֵיס עֲלֵיה וּפָקִיד לְאָחוּהִי לְמִפְרַק לֵיה, לְאָתָבָא וּלְאִתְתַּקְנָא בְּעַפְרָא אַחֲרָא. כְּמָה דִּכְתִיב, וְאָדָם עַל עָפָר יָשׁוּב וְאוֹקְמוּהָ.

10. Come and behold: when this dead one departs from the world without children, this prince's daughter, WHICH IS MALCHUT, does not gather that person to her. He goes about loitering and wandering in the world, because he cannot find a place. The Holy One, blessed be He, has mercy on him and commands his brother to redeem him, so that he shall return and be restored in other dust, MEANING THAT HE SHALL INCARNATE, as is written: "and man shall return to dust" (Iyov 34:15). And this has already been explained.

11. וְאִי הַהוּא פָּרוּקָא לָא בָּעֵי לְקַיְּימָא לְאָחוּהִי בְּהַאי עָלְמָא, בָּעֵי לְמִקְטַר חַד נַעַל בְּרַגְלֵיה, וְהַהוּא אִתְּתָא דְּתִשְׁרֵי לֵיה וּמְקַבְּלָא לְהַהוּא נַעַל לְגַבָּה. אֲמַאי נַעַל. אֶלָּא בְּגִין דְּהַהוּא נַעַל בְּגִין מִיתָא הוּא, וְאִתְיְהִיב בְּרַגְלֵיה דְּחַיָּיא אָחוּהִי, וְאִתְּתָא מְקַבְּלָה לְהַהוּא נַעַל לְגַבָּה, לְאַחֲזָאָה דְּהָא הַהוּא מִיתָא בֵּין חַיָּיא אַהֲדָר בְּעוֹבָדָא דָא.

11. If this redeemer does not wish to revive his brother in this world, MEANING TO MARRY HIS WIFE IN ORDER THAT HE MAY INCARNATE THROUGH THE BIRTH OF A SON, it is required to tie a shoe to his foot. That woman will take off the shoe and receive that sandal for herself. And why the sandal? It is only because this shoe is for the dead one, THAT IS, IT IS CONSIDERED AS BELONGING TO THE DEAD ONE, and he places it on the foot of his living brother. The woman, THE WIDOW, accepts that shoe to indicate that this dead one returns among the living through this ritual.

12. וְהוּא בְּהִפּוּכָא מֵהַהוּא נַעַל דְּנָטִיל מִיתָא מֵחַיָּיא, וְהַשְׁתָּא הַאי נַעַל נָטִיל חַיָּיא מִמִּיתָא, וּבְהַהוּא נַעַל הַהוּא מִיתָא אָזִיל בֵּין חַיָּיא, וְאִתְּתָא

נַטְלָא לֵיהּ לְגַבָּהּ, לְאַחֲזָאָה דְּהַהִיא אִתְּתָא עֲטֶרֶת בַּעֲלָהּ, נַטְלָא לֵיהּ וּמְקַבְּלָא לֵיהּ לְגַבָּהּ.

12. That is the opposite of the shoe that the dead takes IN A DREAM from the living, THAT WE MENTIONED ABOVE. THROUGH THE TAKING OF THE SHOE, HE PASSES ON THE LIVING FROM THIS WORLD TO THE OTHER WORLD OF THE DEAD. Now the living man takes this shoe OF CHALITZAH from the dead one. THEREFORE, the dead one walks among the living in that shoe. FOR IN THAT CASE THE LIVING WIFE WOULD HAVE LED THE DEAD FROM THE OTHER WORLD TO THIS WORLD AMONG THE LIVING, FOR HE WHO WOULD HAVE INCARNATED IN THE SON THAT WOULD HAVE BEEN BORN FROM THAT MARRIAGE. BUT NOW THAT HE DOES NOT WANT TO MARRY HER and the wife takes him to her, to indicate that the woman is the crown of her husband, WHICH IS THE SHECHINAH, she accepts him and takes him to her.

13. וּבָעֵי לְבַטְּשָׁא לֵיהּ לְהַהוּא נַעַל בְּאַרְעָא, לְאַחֲזָאָה דְּשָׁכִיךְ גּוּפֵיהּ דְּהַהוּא מֵיתָא. וְקוּדְשָׁא בְּרִיךְ הוּא לְזִמְנָא דָּא, אוֹ לְבָתַר זִמְנָא, חָיֵיס עֲלֵיהּ, וִיקַבֵּל לֵיהּ לְעָלְמָא אַחֲרָא. תּוּ בְּטִישׁוּתָא דְּהַהוּא נַעַל מִידָא דְּאִתְּתָא לְאַרְעָא לְאַחֲזָאָה, דְּהָא יִתְבְּנֵי הַהוּא מֵיתָא בְּעַפְרָא אַחֲרָא דְּהַאי עָלְמָא, וְהַשְׁתָּא יְתוּב לְעַפְרֵיהּ דַּהֲוָה מִתַּמָּן בְּקַדְמֵיתָא, וּכְדֵין הַהִיא אִתְּתָא תִּשְׁתְּרֵי לְמֶעְבַּד זַרְעָא אַחֲרָא, וְאוֹקְמוּהָ.

13. There is a requirement to throw that shoe on the ground, to indicate that the body of the dead one has calmed. And the Holy One, blessed be He, will have compassion for him and accept him into the other world at this time or sometime later. In addition, the striking of the sandal from the hands of the wife to the ground comes to show that this dead one will be resurrected from the dust of another body in this world, MEANING HE WILL REINCARNATE. But he will first return to the dust whence he came. Then, that woman is permitted to produce other children, as has been explained.

14. ת"ח, ע"ד מַאן דְּבָעֵי לְקַיְּימָא קָיָּים, נָטִיל נַעֲלֵיהּ, וְיָהַב לְחַבְרֵיהּ, לְקַיְּימָא עֲלֵיהּ קַיָּימָא. הה"ד, וְזֹאת לְפָנִים בְּיִשְׂרָאֵל עַל הַגְּאוּלָה. מַאי

וְזֹאת. קַיְּימָא שְׁלִים בְּכֹלָּא. לְפָנִים בְּיִשְׂרָאֵל, כַּד הֲווֹ צְנוּעִין קַדִּישִׁין. לְקַיֵּים כָּל דָּבָר, כָּל דָּבָר מַמָּשׁ, דְּהָא דָּא הוּא קִיּוּמָא. וּכְדֵין וְזֹאת הַתְּעוּדָה בְּיִשְׂרָאֵל, וַדַּאי. דְּלָא תֵּימָא דְּהַסְכָּמָה בְּעָלְמָא הִיא, וּמִדַּעְתַּיְיהוּ עַבְדֵי לָהּ, אֶלָּא קִיּוּמָא עִלָּאָה הֲוָה, לְמֶחֱוֵי עוֹבָדֵיהוֹן בְּרָזָא דִלְעֵילָּא.

14. Come and see: for this reason, whoever wishes to maintain a lasting deal takes his sandal and gives it to his associate to perform through it a lasting deal. This is what is written, "now this was the custom in former times in Yisrael concerning redeeming." What is, "and that (lit. 'this')"? IT MEANS THAT, "AND THIS," WHICH IS MALCHUT, stood perfect in everything; "in former times in Yisrael," when they were modest and holy, "to confirm all manner of transactions (lit. 'all thing')," meaning everything, ALLUDING TO THE LOFTY COUPLING OF YESOD AND MALCHUT, SINCE "ALL" IS YESOD AND "THING" IS MALCHUT. This gives endurance and therefore, "this was the manner of attesting in Yisrael" (Ibid.), assuredly. FOR YOU SHOULD NOT SAY that it was merely an agreed consensus TO PERFORM A DEAL WITH A SANDAL and it was done through their own idea. But rather, you should perceive that it was a support of the grades up high, so that their performance BELOW would be similar to the secret above, SINCE IT ALLUDES TO THE COUPLING OF YESOD AND MALCHUT, AS MENTIONED, WHICH IS THE SECRET OF THE UPPERMOST DURABILITY.

15. כֵּיוָן דְּאַסְגִּיאוּ חַיָּיבִין בְּעָלְמָא, כָּסִיאוּ מִלָּה בְּגַוְונָא אַחֲרָא, בְּכַנְפָא דְמַלְבּוּשָׁא, וְהַאי מַלְבּוּשָׁא הִיא תִּקּוּנָא עִלָּאָה, וְרָזָא דְמִלָּה, וְלֹא יְגַלֶּה כְּנַף אָבִיו כְּתִיב.

15. As soon as the wicked increased in the world, they concealed the matter in a different manner, THAT IS, THE PERFORMANCE OF A DEAL, with the corner of a garment. That dress is a lofty emendation, WHICH IS ZEIR ANPIN, AND THE CORNER (LIT. 'WING') OF THE DRESS IS MALCHUT CALLED 'WING', WHICH ALSO INDICATES THE JOINING OF ZEIR ANPIN AND MALCHUT, SIMILAR TO THE SHOE. The secret meaning of this is: "nor uncover his father's skirt (lit. 'wing')" (Devarim 23:1). SO WE SEE THAT THE WIFE IS CALLED 'WING'.

3. "This is the ordinance of the Torah," part two

A Synopsis

Rabbi Elazar says that 'keep' and 'remember', the secret of the male and female, are connected together by the covenant. We are told the inner meaning of 'chukat' or ordinance.

16. זֹאת חֻקַּת הַתּוֹרָה. זֹאת: דָּא אָת קַיָּימָא, דְּלָא אִתְפְּרַשׁ דָּא מִן דָּא דְּאִקְרֵי זֶה. וּמֵנוּקְבָּא עָיֵיל לִדְכַר. וע"ד, שָׁמוֹ"ר וְזָכוֹ"ר כַּחֲדָא מִתְחַבְּרָן. חֻקַּת הַתּוֹרָה, חֹק הַתּוֹרָה מִבָּעֵי לֵיהּ, מַאי חֻקַּת.

16. "This is the ordinance of the Torah" (Bemidbar 19:2). The word "this (Heb. *zot*, fem.)" is the sign of the Covenant, SINCE THE SIGN OF THE COVENANT IS CALLED *'ZEH'* (LIT. 'THIS', MASC.), and they have not parted from each other. THAT IS, IN THE WORD *ZOT*, WHICH IS MALCHUT, THE WORD *ZEH* IS INCLUDED, WHICH ALLUDES TO YESOD, AND THAT INDICATES THAT YESOD AND MALCHUT DO NOT SEPARATE FROM EACH OTHER. From the female we enter into the male. Therefore, 'keep' and 'remember', THE SECRET OF THE MALE AND FEMALE, are connected together. HE ASKS: In the verse, "the ordinance (Heb. *chukat*) of the Torah," it should have said *'Chok* (Eng. 'law')' of the Torah. What is *chukat*?

17. אֶלָּא חֻקַּת וַדַּאי, וְאוֹקִימְנָא, ה' ד' הֲוַת וְהָא אִתְּמַר. אֲבָל ת', הוּא ד' וְנ' מְחַבֵּר כַּחֲדָא. וְנו"ן הָא אִתְּמַר, נו"ן אֲמַאי אִקְרֵי הָכִי בְּנו"ן. אֶלָּא, כד"א וְלֹא תוֹנוּ אִישׁ אֶת עֲמִיתוֹ. דְּהַשְׁתָּא הִיא בְּאַנְפָּהָא נְהִירִין וְעוֹבְדָא אוֹנָאָה לִבְנֵי נָשָׁא, לְבָתַר מַחְיָא כְּחִוְיָא, וְשָׁצֵי וְקָטִיל וְאָמְרָה לֹא פָעַלְתִּי אָוֶן. וְעַל דָּא הָכִי אִקְרֵי בְּנו"ן, דְּאִתְּמַר עֲלֵיהּ. ת' כֹּלָּא כַּחֲדָא דָּלֶ"ת נו"ן. ד' נו"ן נו"ן רֵי"שׁ, רֵי"שׁ וְדָלֶ"ת חַד מִלָּה הוּא. וּבְאַתְוָו"ן גְּלִיפִין אִינּוּן חֹק וְת' וְכֹלָּא חַד מִלָּה.

17. HE RESPONDS: MALCHUT IS assuredly *chukat*. And we explained that *Hei* is *Dalet*, and we were already taught THE MEANING OF THE *DALET*. However, *Tav* is a combination of *Dalet* and *Nun*, and we were taught why *Nun* is called this way, MEANING SPELLED WITH THE LETTERS *NUN-VAV-*

NUN. HE RESPONDS: It is only as it says, "you shall not therefore defraud one another" (Vayikra 25:17), SINCE *NUN* IS FROM THE LINGUISTIC DERIVATIVE OF 'FRAUD' (HEB. *ONA'A*, ALEPH-VAV-NUN-ALEPH-HEI). Now she seems to be with a happy, delightful face. HOWEVER, she defrauds human beings SINCE, following this, she hits like a snake, destroys, kills, and says, "I have done nothing wrong (Heb. *aven, Aleph-Vav-Nun*)" (Mishlei 30:20). Therefore, she is spelled *Nun-Vav-Nun*, DERIVED FROM FRAUD, which is ascribed to her, THE *NUN.* The *Tav* is altogether composed of *Dalet* and *Nun. Dalet* and *Nun* are ALSO SIMILAR TO *Nun* and *Resh*, SINCE *Resh* and *Dalet* are the same thing; BOTH MEAN POVERTY. And with engraved letters, *CHUKAT* is composed of THE LETTERS *Chet-Kof* (lit. 'law') and *Tav.* And all is the same thing.

4. A red heifer

A Synopsis

We learn that the offering of a cow is to purify the unclean, and that red means a sentence of law. The cow must be without defect to indicate soft judgment, and without blemish since all blemishes are healed through the illumination of Wisdom. Rabbi Elazar explains why the offering was taken to the adjutant to Aaron and not directly to the high priest, saying that this would be improper because Aaron approaches from the holy side not the pure side. We hear about the seven washings, the seven years of Shmitah and the seven Sfirot. Rabbi Elazar says that throwing cedar wood on the burnt ashes weakens the energy of the unclean aspect, so the people become cleansed. We hear about the "water of sprinkling" that is for purification when the world dwells in Judgment, and Rabbi Elazar concludes by saying that defilement and purification are the most important rules of the Torah.

18. דַּבֵּר אֶל בְּנֵי יִשְׂרָאֵל וְיִקְחוּ אֵלֶיךָ פָרָה, הַאי פָּרָה לְדַכְיוּתָא קָא אַתְיָיא. לְדַכְּאָה לִמְסָאֲבֵי. פָּרָה דְּקַבִּילַת מִן שְׂמָאלָא. וּמַאן הוּא לְשְׂמָאלָא. שׁוֹר. כד״א, וּפְנֵי שׁוֹר מֵהַשְּׂמֹאל. אֲדוּמָה, סוּמָקָא כְּוַורְדָּא. דִּכְתִּיב, כְּשׁוֹשַׁנָּה בֵּין הַחוֹחִים. אֲדוּמָה: גְּזֵרַת דִּינָא.

18. "Speak to the children of Yisrael, that they bring you a red heifer..." (Bemidbar 19:2). This cow is for the purpose of cleansing to purify the unclean, WHICH IS MALCHUT that receives from the left. Who is on that left? It is the ox THAT IS GVURAH IN ZEIR ANPIN, as it says, "the face of the ox from the left side" (Yechezkel 1:10). Red means red as a rose, as written: "like the rose among thorns" (Shir Hashirim 2:2). RED MEANS a sentence of law, SINCE THE LAWS OF THE LEFT COLUMN ARE CONSIDERED RED.

19. תְּמִימָה, מַאי תְּמִימָה. כְּמָה דִּתְנֵינָן, שׁוֹר תָּם וְשׁוֹר מוּעָד. שׁוֹר תָּם דִּינָא רַפְיָיא. שׁוֹר מוּעָד דִּינָא קַשְׁיָא. אוּף הָכָא תְּמִימָה דִּינָא רַפְיָיא, גְּבוּרָה תַּתָּאָה, דָּא הִיא תְּמִימָה. גְּבוּרָה עִלָּאָה, דָּא הִיא דִּינָא קַשְׁיָא, וְהִיא יַד הַחֲזָקָה תַּקִּיפָא.

19. "...without defect (Heb. *temimah*)..." (Bemidbar 19:2). HE ASKS: IT IS WRITTEN, "WITHOUT DEFECT." What is the meaning? HE RESPONDS: It is

as we were taught about a bull that has not gored (Heb. *tam*) and the bull that has gored thrice. The bull that has not gored MEANS lax, soft Judgment. The bull that has gored thrice is harsh Judgment. Here too, *temimah* MEANS a lax sentence that is lower Gvurah, MEANING MALCHUT, since one that is as such is without defect. Gvurah up high, THAT IS THE GVURAH IN ZEIR ANPIN, is the severe and mighty hand.

20. אֲשֶׁר אֵין בָּהּ מוּם, כד״א כֻּלָּךְ יָפָה רַעְיָתִי וּמוּם אֵין בָּךְ. אֲשֶׁר לֹא עָלָה עָלֶיהָ עוֹל. עַל כְּתִיב, כד״א וּנְאֻם הַגֶּבֶר הוּקַם עָל. מ״ט. בְּגִין דְּהִיא שְׁלוּמֵי אֱמוּנֵי יִשְׂרָאֵל, וְעָלֶיהָ לָאו הִיא אֶלָּא עִמָּהּ. אֲשֶׁר לֹא עָלָה עָלֶיהָ עֹל, הַיְינוּ דִּכְתִיב בְּתוּלַת יִשְׂרָאֵל, בְּתוּלָה וְאִישׁ לֹא יְדָעָהּ.

20. "…in which there is no blemish…" (Ibid.) is as it is written, "you are all fair, my love; there is no blemish in you" (Shir Hashirim 4:7). SHE SHINES WITH THE ILLUMINATION OF CHOCHMAH, AND SHE IS CONSIDERED BEAUTIFUL SINCE ALL BLEMISHES ARE HEALED THROUGH THE ILLUMINATION OF CHOCHMAH. "…and upon which never came a yoke (Heb. *ol*, Ayin-Lamed)…" (Bemidbar 19:2). The word "*ol*" is spelled WITHOUT A *VAV*, which is as it is written: "and the man who was raised up on high (Heb. *al*, Ayin-Lamed)" (II Shmuel 23:1). What is the reason? It is because she is "the peaceable and faithful in Yisrael" (II Shmuel 20:19), and he is not above her but rather with her. "…and upon which never came a yoke…" is as it is written: "the virgin of Yisrael" (Amos 5:2), and, "a virgin, neither had any man known her" (Beresheet 24:16).

21. וּנְתַתֶּם אוֹתָהּ אֶל אֶלְעָזָר, מִצְוָותָהּ בַּסְּגַן, וְאוּקְמוּהָ. מ״ט לֵיהּ וְלָא לְאַהֲרֹן. אֶלָּא אַהֲרֹן שׁוֹשְׁבִינָא דְּמַטְרוֹנִיתָא. וְעוֹד דְּאַהֲרֹן לָא אָתֵי מִסִּטְרָא דְּטָהוֹר, אֶלָּא מִסִּטְרָא דִּקְדוֹשׁ, וּבְגִין דְּדָא אַתְיָיא לְטַהֲרָה, לָא אִתְיְיהִיב לֵיהּ.

21. "And you shall give her to Elazar" (Bemidbar 19:3). THAT IS BECAUSE the prescribed performing of the ritual is through the adjutant to the High Priest AND NOT BY THE HIGH PRIEST HIMSELF, and they established it that way. What is the reason? It is for ELAZAR and not for Aaron. HE RESPONDS: It is only because Aaron is the best man of the Queen.

THEREFORE, HE WOULD BE IMPROPER FOR THE RITUAL OF THIS COW, WHICH IS HARSH JUDGMENT, and furthermore, he would be improper because Aaron does not approach this from the pure side but rather from the holy side. Since the primary function of the red cow is for purification, it is therefore not given to him.

22. כָּל מִלָּה דְּהַאי פָּרָה, הִיא בְּשֶׁבַע, ז' כְּבוּסִים וְכוּ', וְהָא אִתְּמַר, מ"ט. בְּגִין דְּהִיא שֶׁבַע שְׁנֵי שְׁמִטָּה, וּבַת שֶׁבַע אִתְקְרֵי, וע"ד כָּל עוֹבָדוֹי בְּשֶׁבַע. ת"ח, כָּל מַאי דְּאִתְעֲבֵיד מֵהַאי פָּרָה, בְּגִין לְדַכְאָה, וְלָא לְקַדְּשָׁא, ואע"ג דְּאִתְיְיהִיב לַסְּגָן, הוּא לָא שָׁחִיט וְלָא שָׂרִיף, בְּגִין דְּלָא יִשְׁתְּכַח דִּינָא בִּסְטְרוֹי, וכ"ש אַהֲרֹן דְּאִיהוּ בְּדַרְגָּא שְׁלִים יַתִּיר, דְּלָא בָּעֵי לְאִשְׁתַּכְּחָא תַּמָּן, וּלְאִזְדַּמְּנָא תַּמָּן.

22. Every item that pertains to this cow, WHICH IS MALCHUT, is in seven, seven washings. And we were already taught that. What is the reason? It is because MALCHUT is the seven years of the Sabbatical year THAT CONTAINS SEVEN SFIROT – CHESED, GVURAH, TIFERET, NETZACH, HOD, YESOD AND MALCHUT, and is called 'Bathsheba' (lit. 'Daughter of Seven'). Therefore, all her rituals are in seven. Come and behold: all that is made from this cow is for the purpose of purification and not for sanctification. Although it was given to an aid OF THE PRIEST, THAT IS, ELAZAR, he does not perform the slaughtering or the burning so that no Harsh Judgment will be at his aspect. Even more so for Aaron, who is in a more perfected level THAN ELAZAR. He need not present himself or be available there.

23. הַאי פָּרָה, כֵּיוָן דְּאִתְעֲבֵיד אֵפֶר, בָּעֵי לְמִשְׁדֵּי בֵּיהּ עֵץ אֶרֶז, וְאֵזוֹב, וּשְׁנֵי תוֹלַעַת, וְהָא אִלֵּין אִתְּמָרוּ. וְאָסַף אִישׁ טָהוֹר, וְלָא קָדוֹשׁ. וְהִנִּיחַ מִחוּץ לַמַּחֲנֶה בְּמָקוֹם טָהוֹר, דְּהָא טָהוֹר לָא אִקְרֵי, אֶלָּא מִן סִטְרָא דִּמְסָאֵב בְּקַדְמֵיתָא.

23. As soon as this cow turns into ashes, there is a requirement to throw into it "cedar wood, and hyssop, and scarlet" (Bemidbar 19:6) as we have already learned. "And a man that is clean shall gather up" (Ibid. 9) and not a holy man. "...and lay them outside the camp in a clean place..." (Ibid.)

since nothing is called 'clean' except from the aspect that he was first unclean.

24. רָזָא דְּכֹלָּא, הַאי דִּכְתִּיב לְמֵי נִדָּה חַטָּאת הִיא, בְּגִין דְּכָל דִּינִין תַּתָּאִין, וְכָל אִינּוּן דְּאָתוּ מִסִּטְרָא דִּמְסָאֲבָא, כַּד אִיהוּ יַנְקָא מִסִּטְרָא אַחֲרָא, וְיָתִיבַת בְּדִינָא, כד"א מָלְאָה דָם הוּדַשְׁנָה מֵחֵלֶב. כְּדֵין כֻּלְּהוּ מִתְעָרֵי וּמִסְתַּלְּקֵי וְשָׁרָאן בְּעָלְמָא. כֵּיוָן דְּעַבְדֵי הַאי עוֹבָדָא דִּלְתַתָּא, וְכָל הַאי דִּינָא בַּאֲתַר דָּא דְּהַאי פָּרָה, וְרָמָאן עָלָה עֵץ אֶרֶז וְגו'. כְּדֵין אִתְחַלָּשׁ חֵילָא דִּלְהוֹן, וּבְכָל אֲתַר דְּשָׁרָאן אִתְּבָּרוּ וְאִתְחַלָּשׁוּ וְעַרְקִין מִנֵּיהּ, דְּהַאי חֵילָא דִּלְהוֹן אִתְחֲזֵי כְּגַוְונָא דָּא לְגַבַּיְיהוּ, כְּדֵין לָא שָׁרָאן בְּבַר נָשׁ, וְאִתְדַּכֵּי.

24. The secret of all this is written: "for the water of sprinkling, it is a purification offering" (Ibid.). That is because all the lower Judgments and all that come from the aspect of Defilement RECEIVE THEIR STRENGTH FROM MALCHUT AT THE TIME when she sucks from the Other Side and dwells in Judgment, as it says: "filled with blood, it is made fat with fatness" (Yeshayah 34:6). At that moment, all THE SENTENCES FROM THE ASPECT OF DEFILEMENT are stirred up to rise and dwell in the world. As soon as they perform that ritual OF BURNING THE COW down below and the sentence is carried out in this place, in this cow, they throw on her the cedar wood. Then their energy is weakened, OF THE UNCLEAN ASPECT, and wherever they prevail, they break down and become weak and escape from there, since they see their might BROKEN AND SUPRESSED, AS IT WAS PERFORMED IN THE RITUAL OF BURNING THE COW. Then, they do not prevail on man and he becomes cleansed.

25. וע"ד אִתְקְרֵי מֵי נִדָּה, מַיָּיא לְדַכְּאָה. כַּד עָלְמָא שָׁארֵי בְּדִינָא, וְסִטְרָא מְסָאֲבָא אִתְפְּשַׁט בְּעָלְמָא, הָכָא אִתְכְּלִילָן כָּל זִינִין מְסָאֲבָא, וְכָל זִינֵי דַכְיוּ, וּבְגִין כַּךְ טוּמְאָה וְטָהֳרָה, כְּלָלָא עִלָּאָה דְּאוֹרַיְיתָא, וְאוֹקְמוּהָ חַבְרַיָּיא. אר"ש, אֶלְעָזָר, עֲבַדְתְּ דְּלָא יֵימְרוּן חַבְרַיָּיא מִלָּה אֲבַתְרָךְ.

25. Therefore, it is called "water of sprinkling (Heb. nidah)." THAT MEANS water for purification when the world dwells in Judgment and the defiled

aspect expands in the world, AS BY THE UNCLEANNESS OF A MENSTRUATING WOMAN (HEB. *NIDAH*). Here are gathered together a variety of unclean things and a variety of methods of purification. Consequently, defilement and purification are the most important rules of the Torah, and the friends have already explained this. Rabbi Shimon said: Elazar, you have accomplished so much that your friends will not be speaking of anything following you, SINCE FROM THE GREAT WISDOM AND WHOLESOMENESS OF YOUR SPEECH THEY WILL BE SHY TO GIVE THEIRS.

A Synopsis

Moses says that it is forbidden to plow during the Shabbat with an ox. He says that the lower Shechinah is a red cow from the aspect of Gvurah, and he goes on to talk about the aspect of the higher Shechinah that is liberty. The result of the offering is that there is no authority for the Other Side to rule.

רעיא מהימנא

26. פָּרָה אֲדוּמָה תְּמִימָה אֲשֶׁר אֵין בָּה מוּם וְגוֹ', אָסוּר לַחֲרוֹשׁ בְּשַׁבָּת חֲרִישָׁה דְּשׁוֹר, דְּאִתְּמַר עַל גַּבִּי חָרְשׁוּ חוֹרְשִׁים. וּשְׁכִינְתָּא תַּתָּאָה, אִיהִי פָּרָה אֲדוּמָה, מִסִּטְרָא דִּגְבוּרָה. תְּמִימָה מִסִּטְרָא דְּחֶסֶד, דְּאִיהוּ דַּרְגָּא דְּאַבְרָהָם, דְּאִתְּמַר בֵּיהּ הִתְהַלֵּךְ לְפָנַי וֶהְיֵה תָּמִים. אֲשֶׁר אֵין בָּהּ מוּם, מִסִּטְרָא דְּעַמּוּדָא דְּאֶמְצָעִיתָא. אֲשֶׁר לֹא עָלָה עָלֶיהָ עוֹל, מִסִּטְרָא דִּשְׁכִינְתָּא עִלָּאָה, דְּאִיהִי חֵירוּ. בַּאֲתָר דְּאִיהִי שַׁלְטָא, וְהֲזָר הַקָּרֵב לֵית רְשׁוּ לְסִטְרָא אַחֲרָא לְשַׁלְטָאָה. לָא שָׂטָן, וְלָא מַשְׁחִית, וְלָא מַלְאָךְ הַמָּוֶת, דְּאִינּוּן מִסִּטְרָא דְּגֵיהִנָּם.

ע"כ רעיא מהימנא

Ra'aya Meheimna (the Faithful Shepherd)

26. "A red heifer without defect, in which there is no blemish..." It is forbidden to plow during the Shabbat with an ox and plow, as it says, "the plowers plowed upon my back" (Tehilim 129:3), and the lower Shechinah, WHICH IS MALCHUT, is a red cow from the aspect of Gvurah. She is

without defect from the aspect of Chesed, which is a level of Abraham, of whom it says, "walk before Me, and be perfect (Heb. *tamim*)" (Beresheet 17:1). "...In which there is no blemish..." She is from the aspect of the Central Column, WHICH IS ZEIR ANPIN THAT UNITES HER LEFT AND RIGHT. The verse continues, "and upon which never came a yoke," which is from the aspect of the higher Shechinah, which is liberty, MEANING BINAH at the location where she dominates, WHICH IS MALCHUT THAT IS COMPRISED OF EVERYTHING MENTIONED ABOVE. "And the stranger that comes near SHALL BE PUT TO DEATH." There is no authority for the Other Side to rule, not for Satan, not for the Destroyer, and not for the Angel of Death, all of which are from the side of Gehenom.

End of Ra'aya Meheimna (the Faithful Shepherd)

5. "He sends the springs into the valleys"

A Synopsis

Rabbi Shimon examines the title verse, speaking about the flow of higher wisdom, the river that emanates from Eden, the deep stream of Yisrael Saba and Tevunah, and the higher sanctified rivers of Zeir Anpin. We learn that after Zeir Anpin and Malchut drink they give drink to every wild beast, and we are told of the four creatures – lion, ox, eagle and man – in the vision of Ezekiel. Rabbi Shimon talks about the uniting at different levels and how the blessings prevail from the watering of the stream. We learn about the time of judgment and the Spirit of Defilement that dwells upon someone who sinned. The Spirit of Defilement is removed through the purification of the offering, and the sprinkling of clean water is part of the purification and sanctification required in order to deserve the World to Come.

27. פָּתַח ר"ש וְאָמַר, הַמְשַׁלֵּחַ מַעְיָנִים בַּנְּחָלִים וְגוֹ'. יַשְׁקוּ כָּל חַיְתוֹ שָׂדָי וְגוֹ'. הָנֵי קְרָאֵי דָוִד מַלְכָּא בְּרוּחָא קַדִּישָׁא אַמְרָן, וְאִית לְאִסְתַּכְּלָא בְּהוּ. ת"ח, בְּשַׁעֲתָא דְחָכְמְתָא עִלָּאָה בָּטַשׁ בְּגְלִיפוֹי, אע"ג דְּהִיא טְמִירָא בְּכָל סִטְרִין, פָּתַח וְאִתְנְגִיד מִנֵּיהּ חַד נַהֲרָא, מַלְיָא בְּתַרְעִין עִלָּאִין.

27. Rabbi Shimon opened the discussion with the verse: "He sends the springs into the valleys...they give drink to every wild beast..." (Tehilim 104:10-11). These verses were uttered by King David in the Holy Spirit, and they require studying. Come and behold: there was a time when the higher wisdom imprinted its engravings, MEANING AT THE MOMENT WHEN THE HIGHER CHOCHMAH AND BINAH UNITED TOGETHER, even though THE HIGHER CHOCHMAH is the most hidden of all the hidden, SINCE IN HIGHER CHOCHMAH AND BINAH, WHICH ARE ABA AND IMA ABOVE, THE YUD DOES NOT EMERGE FROM THE AIR. It is an opening from which flows a river full of higher gates, THAT IS BINAH.

28. כְּמַבּוּעָא וּמְקוֹרָא דְּמַיָּא דְּמָלֵי קוֹזְפָא רַבָּא מִנֵּיהּ, וּמִתַּמָּן אִתְמַשְׁכָן מַבּוּעִין דְּנַחֲלִין וְנַהֲרִין בְּכָל סְטַר, כָּךְ הַאי, בְּחַד שְׁבִיל דָּקִיק דְּלָא אִתְיְידַע, מָשִׁיךְ וְנָגִיד הַהוּא נָהָר דִּנְגִיד וְנָפִיק, וּמְמַלֵּי לְהַהוּא נַחֲלָא

עֲמִיקָא, וּמִתַּמָּן אִתְמַשְׁכָאן מַבּוּעִין וּנְחָלִין, וְאִתְמַלְיָין מִנֵּיהּ. הה"ד, הַמְשַׁלֵּחַ מַעֲיָנִים בַּנְּחָלִים וְגוֹ'. אִלֵּין נַהֲרֵי עִלָּאֵי קַדִּישָׁא דְּאֲפַרְסְמוֹנָא דַּכְיָיא, וְכֻלְּהוּ אִתְשַׁקְיָין כְּחַד מֵהַהוּא נְבִיעָא דְּנַחֲלָא עִלָּאָה קַדִּישָׁא דְּנָפִיק וְנָגִיד.

28. HE COMPARES THIS SUBJECT MATTER OF ABA AND IMA ABOVE AND YISRAEL-SABA AND TEVUNAH to a spring and source of water that fills up a huge lake. From there, FROM THE LAKE, flow springs, streams and rivers in every direction, TO THE RIGHT AND TO THE LEFT. Similarly, this ABA AND IMA AND YISRAEL-SABA AND TEVUNAH flows through a certain narrow path that is not known, MEANING AT THE UNION OF YESOD'S ABA AND IMA ABOVE, WHO ARE NOT REVEALED, IN WHOM THE YUD DOES NOT EMANATE FROM THE AIR. That river emerges continuously and emanates FROM EDEN. THROUGH THIS EXITING AND ENTERING, it fills that deep stream – MEANING YISRAEL-SABA AND TEVUNAH, SIMILAR TO THE HUGE LAKE OF WATER THAT IS FILLED UP FROM THE SPRING AND SOURCE THAT ARE ABA AND IMA ABOVE. From there, springs and streams continue TO ZEIR ANPIN AND MALCHUT, and from it they are filled up WITH CHOCHMAH AND CHASSADIM. This is what it is written: "He sends the springs into the valleys" (Ibid.). These are the higher sanctified rivers OF ZEIR ANPIN of pure balsam, SINCE IT IS THE SECRET OF THE PURE AIR THAT CHESED, GVURAH AND TIFERET OF ZEIR ANPIN RECEIVE FROM ABA AND IMA ABOVE. THAT IS THE SECRET OF THE PURE BALSAM AND THAT IS WHAT IS MEANT BY: "THEY FLOW BETWEEN THE HILLS," WHICH ARE CHESED, GVURAH AND TIFERET OF ZEIR ANPIN, CALLED 'MOUNTAINS'. AND FROM IT MALCHUT RECEIVES. And all, ZEIR ANPIN AND MALCHUT, drink together from that spring of the higher sanctified stream that continues to flow, WHICH IS YISRAEL-SABA AND TEVUNAH.

29. לְבָתַר, יַשְׁקוּ כָּל חַיְתוֹ שָׂדָי, הַיְינוּ דִּכְתִיב וּמִשָּׁם יִפָּרֵד וְהָיָה לְאַרְבָּעָה רָאשִׁים. הָנֵי ד' רָאשִׁין, אִלֵּין אִינּוּן חַיְתוֹ שָׂדָי, כְּלָלָא דְּכָל אִינּוּן מַשִׁרְיָין, וְכָל אִינּוּן חַיָּילִין, דַּאֲחִידָן בְּהוּ שָׂדָי, אַל תִּקְרֵי שָׂדָי, אֶלָּא שַׁדַּי. דְּהוּא נָטִיל, וְאַשְׁלִים שְׁמָא מִיְּסוֹדָא דְּעָלְמָא.

29. AFTER ZEIR ANPIN AND MALCHUT DRINK, "they give to drink to every wild beast" that which is written: "and from thence it was parted, and branched into four streams (lit. 'heads')" (Beresheet 2:10). These four heads are "every wild (lit. 'field', Heb. *sadai*) beast," WHICH ARE FOUR CREATURES, LION, OX, EAGLE AND MAN, WHICH ARE THE CHARIOT OF MALCHUT. They are the inclusion of all the camps and legions THAT ARE IN BRIYAH, YETZIRAH AND ASIYAH to which Shadai, THAT IS METATRON THAT IS CALLED 'SHADAI', is attached, WHO IS ABOVE ALL OF THEM. Do not pronounce it Sadai WITH SIN, but rather Shadai, WITH SHIN, which is METATRON that receives and perfects IN HIMSELF the Name from Yesod, the Foundation of the world. This is SINCE THE NAME SHADAI IS IN YESOD OF ZEIR ANPIN, AND METATRON, BEING A CHARIOT TO YESOD OF ZEIR ANPIN, RECEIVES THIS NAME.

30. יְשַׁבְּרוּ פְרָאִים צְמָאָם, אֵלֵּין אִינּוּן דִּכְתִיב בְּהוּ, וְהָאוֹפַנִּים יִנָּשְׂאוּ לְעוּמָּתָם כִּי רוּחַ הַחַיָּה בָּאוֹפַנִּים, מַאן חַיָּה. אֶלָּא אֵלֵּין חַיְתוֹ שָׂדָי, אַרְבַּע אִינּוּן, וְכָל חַד וְחַד לְחַד סִטְרָא דְּעָלְמָא. וְהַהוּא אִקְרֵי חַיָּה, וְאוֹפַנִּים לָקֳבֵיל כָּל חַד וְחַד. וְלָא אַזְלִין אֶלָּא מֵרוּחַ דְּהַהִיא חַיָּה דְּאָזִיל עָלַיְיהוּ וְכַד אֵלֵּין מִתְשַׁקְיָין מֵהַהוּא שַׁקְיוּ עִלָּאָה, כָּל שְׁאַר חַיָּילִין אַחֲרָנִין אִשְׁתַּקְיָין, וְאִתְרַוְוֹן, וּמִשְׁתָּרְשָׁן בְּשָׁרְשַׁיְיהוּ, וְאִתְאַחֲדָן אֵלֵּין בְּאֵלֵּין, בְּדַרְגִּין יְדִיעָן. הה"ד, עֲלֵיהֶם עוֹף הַשָּׁמַיִם יִשְׁכּוֹן וְגוֹ'. מַשְׁקֶה הָרִים מֵעֲלִיּוֹתָיו וְגוֹ'. אֵלֵּין שְׁאַר דַּרְגִּין עִלָּאִין.

30. "The wild asses quench their thirst" (Tehilim 104:11). These are the ones about whom it is written: "and the wheels were lifted up along with them: for the spirit of the living creature was in the wheels" (Yechezkel 1:20). What is "the living creature"? These are the wild beasts, which are four, and each one of them is in one direction OF THE FOUR DIRECTIONS of the world, and is called a 'living creature'. There are FOUR wheels to each one OF THE FOUR CREATURES, and none OF THE WHEELS move except from the spirit of the living creature that goes over it, MEANING EACH ONE OF THE WHEELS FROM THE CORRESPONDING SPIRIT IN THE CREATURES. When these LIVING CREATURES AND WHEELS are imbued with that higher drinking liquid, all the rest of the legions are fed and saturated and are rooted in their sources, and they unite with each other at certain levels. This is what is written: "beside them dwell the birds of the sky...He waters the hills from His upper chambers..." (Tehilim 104:12-13). These are the rest of the higher levels.

31. לְבָתַר כָּל דָּא, מִפְּרִי מַעֲשֶׂיךָ תִּשְׂבָּע הָאָרֶץ, אַרְעָא עִלָּאָה קַדִּישָׁא.
וְכַד אִיהִי מִתְבָּרְכָא, כָּל עָלְמִין כֻּלְּהוּ חַדָּאן, וּמִתְבָּרְכָאן. דָּא בְּשַׁעֲתָא
דְּבִרְכָּאן מִשְׁתַּכְּחֵי, מִשַּׁקְיוּ דְּנַחֲלָא עֲמִיקָא דְּכֹלָּא.

31. After all this, WHEN ALL THE HIGHER AND LOWER GRADES WERE
FILLED WITH ABUNDANCE FROM ABA AND IMA, IT SAYS: "the earth is
satiated with the fruits of Your works" (Ibid.); that is, the sanctified land up
high, MEANING MALCHUT. When it is blessed, all the worlds are gladdened
and are blessed, and that happens when the blessings prevail from the
watering of the stream, WHICH IS THE SPRING MENTIONED ABOVE, THAT
IS ABA AND IMA, the deepest of all.

32. וּבְשַׁעֲתָא דְּבִרְכָאן לָא מִשְׁתַּכְּחֵי לְנַחְתָּא בְּעָלְמָא, כְּדֵין עָלְמָא
יָתִיב בְּדִינָא, וּמִסִּטְרָא דִּשְׂמָאלָא רוּחָא אִתְּעַר וְאִתְפָּשַׁט בְּעָלְמָא וְכַמָּה
חֲבִילֵי טְרִיקִין מִשְׁתַּכְּחֵי בְּעָלְמָא, וְשַׁרְיָאן עַל בְּנֵי נָשָׁא, וּמְסָאַב הַהוּא
רוּחָא לְהוּ, כְּבַר נָשׁ דְּגָוַע וְרוּחַ מְסָאֲבָא שַׁרְיָא עֲלֵיהּ. הָכִי נָמֵי שַׁרְיָא,
לְמַעַן דְּיִקְרַב בַּהֲדֵיהּ.

32. At the time when the blessings are not available to descend upon the
world, WHICH ARE CHASSADIM, AND MALCHUT RECEIVES CHOCHMAH
FROM THE LEFT WITHOUT THE CHASSADIM, the world, THAT IS MALCHUT,
sits in Judgment. From the left side stirs a spirit that extends over the world,
and many regiments of harmful angels dwell in the world and rest over the
people, SINCE WHEN CHOCHMAH IS WITHOUT CHASSADIM, ALL THE
HARSH JUDGMENTS EMANATE FROM HER. And that spirit defiles them,
similar to a person who dies and has a Spirit of Defilement dwell upon him.
This is true for whoever comes near that SPIRIT FROM THE LEFT.

33. הה"ד, תַּסְתִּיר פָּנֶיךָ יִבָּהֵלוּן וְגוֹ'. הַאי קְרָא מַאי קָא מַיְירֵי. אֶלָּא
תַּסְתִּיר פָּנֶיךָ יִבָּהֵלוּן, דְּהָא לָא אִתְשַׁקְיָין לְאִשְׁתַּכְּחָא בִּרְכָאן לְעָלְמִין.
תּוֹסֵף רוּחָם יִגְוָעוּן, וְאִתְּעַר רוּחָא אַחֲרָא מִסִּטְרָא שְׂמָאלָא, וְרוּחַ
מְסָאֲבָא שַׁרְיָא עַל בְּנֵי נָשָׁא, עַל אִינוּן דְּמֵיתִין, וּמַאן דְּקָאִים בַּהֲדַיְיהוּ,
וְעַל שְׁאַר בְּנֵי נָשָׁא, מַאי אַסְוָתָא דִּלְהוֹן. הָא דִּכְתִיב וְאֶל עֲפָרָם

וְשׁוּבוּן. דָּא עָפָר שְׂרֵיפַת הַחַטָּאת, בְּגִין לְאִתְדַּכְּאָה בֵּיהּ. וְהַיְינוּ רָזָא הַכֹּל הָיָה מִן הֶעָפָר, וַאֲפִילוּ גַּלְגַּל חַמָּה.

33. That is what is meant when it says: "You hide Your face, they are troubled" (Ibid. 29). What does this verse mean? It is only, "You hide Your face, they are troubled." That is because THOSE LEVELS were not watered so that blessings would prevail in the world, SINCE "YOUR FACE" MEANS CHASSADIM AND BLESSINGS. THEN, "You take away their breath (also: 'spirit'), they die" (Ibid.), because another spirit stirs from the left direction, WITHOUT THE RIGHT. The Spirit of Defilement dwells upon people, upon those who died, those who were with them, and on the rest of humanity, MEANING THAT THE SPIRIT OF DEFILEMENT EXPANDS OVER THE WHOLE WORLD. What is its remedy? This is what is written: "and return to their dust" (Ibid.). That means the dust of the burning of this offering in order to have purification, and that is the secret meaning of, "all are of the dust" (Kohelet 3:20), even the sun's circle.

34. לְבָתַר דִּמְהַדְּרָן לְהַאי עָפָר, בְּגִין לְאִתְדַּכְּאָה בֵּיהּ, מִתְעֲבַר רוּחָא מְסָאֲבָא, וְאִתְּעַר רוּחָא אַחֲרָא קַדִּישָׁא, וְשָׁארֵי בְּעָלְמָא. הֲדָא הוּא דִּכְתִיב, תְּשַׁלַּח רוּחֲךָ יִבָּרֵאוּן, יִבָּרֵאוּן, וְיִתְּסוּן בְּאַסְוָותָא עִלָּאָה, דְּרוּחָא אַחֲרָא. וּתְחַדֵּשׁ פְּנֵי אֲדָמָה, דְּהָא אִתְדַּכְּיַאת, וְחַדְתּוּתֵי דְּסִיהֲרָא אִשְׁתְּכַח, וְעָלְמִין כֻּלְּהוּ מִתְבָּרְכָאן. זַכָּאָה חוּלָקֵהוֹן דְּיִשְׂרָאֵל, דְּקוּדְשָׁא בְּרִיךְ הוּא יָהִיב לוֹן עֵיטָא, דְּכֹלָּא אַסְוָותָא, בְּגִין דְּיִזְכּוּן לְחַיֵּי עָלְמָא דְּאָתֵי, וְיִשְׁתַּכְּחוּ דַּכְיָין בְּהַאי עָלְמָא, קַדִּישִׁין לְעָלְמָא דְּאָתֵי, עָלַיְיהוּ כְּתִיב וְזָרַקְתִּי עֲלֵיכֶם מַיִם טְהוֹרִים וּטְהַרְתֶּם.

34. After returning to this dust in order to be purified through it, AS MENTIONED NEARBY, the Spirit of Defilement is removed. And another Holy Spirit is aroused, which prevails upon the world. This is what it says: "You send forth your breath (also: 'spirit'), they are created" (Ibid. 30); they are created and healed with the loftier remedy of another spirit. "And You renew the face of the earth" (Ibid.); since it was purified, the moon is renewed and all the realms are blessed. Praised is the lot of Yisrael, since the Holy One, blessed be He, gave them counsel. All of it is a remedy in order to gain life in the World to Come, and for them to be considered purified in this world and sanctified for the World to Come. About them, it is written: "then will I sprinkle clean water upon you, and you shall be clean" (Yechezkel 36:25).

6. Moses, Aaron and Miriam

A Synopsis

Rabbi Shimon tells Rabbi Yehuda that Miriam died because the death of righteous atones for the world; when she departed the well that accompanied the children of Yisrael in the desert was gone. At that time the right was weakened and the sun was dimmed, and when Aaron died the right was broken and the sun was darkened. Rabbi Shimon says there has never been a generation like the one in which Moses, Aaron and Miriam all lived. Even in the generation of Solomon they drew from the moon, that was full, rather than the sun, as in Moses' time. Rabbi Shimon talks about Joshua, who labored to inherit the land of Yisrael but did not attain the full completion of the moon; he toiled for Yisrael under the sun, Moses, for he did not have light of his own. We learn that every place where Solomon mentions "under the sun," he is speaking about his own level, Malchut. Rabbi Shimon says that whoever is attached to the moon without the sun reflects the first sin in the world, the sin of the Tree of Knowledge of Good and Evil.

35. וַיָּבֹאוּ בְנֵי יִשְׂרָאֵל כָּל הָעֵדָה מִדְבַּר צִין וְגוֹ'. ר' יְהוּדָה אָמַר, אֲמַאי פַּרְשָׁתָּא דְפָרָה, סְמִיכָה לְמִיתַת מִרְיָם. הָא אוּקְמוּהָ. אֶלָּא כֵּיוָן דְּאִתְעֲבֵיד דִּינָא בְּהַאי פָּרָה, לְדַכְּאָה לִמְסָאֲבֵי, אִתְעֲבֵיד דִּינָא בְּמִרְיָם, לְדַכְּאָה עָלְמָא, וְאִסְתַּלְּקַת מִן עָלְמָא. כֵּיוָן דְּאִסְתַּלְּקַת מִרְיָם, אִסְתַּלָּק הַהוּא בְּאֵר, דַּהֲוָה אָזִיל עִמְּהוֹן דְּיִשְׂרָאֵל בְּמַדְבְּרָא וְאִסְתַּלָּק בֵּירָא בְכֹלָּא.

35. "Then came the children of Yisrael, the whole congregation into the desert of Zin..." (Bemidbar 20:1). Rabbi Yehuda said: Why is the passage about the laws of the red cow near to the death of Miriam? The explanation was already established. HE RESPONDS: However, since the Judgment was executed upon this cow in order to purify the unclean, Judgment was executed upon Miriam for the purpose of cleansing the world, SINCE THE DEATH OF THE JUST ATONES FOR THE WORLD, and she departed from this world. When Miriam departed, the well that accompanied the children of Yisrael in the desert was gone. And the well of everyone was gone; THAT IS THE SECRET OF MALCHUT.

36. א"ר אַבָּא, כְּתִיב וְאַתָּה בֶן אָדָם שָׂא קִינָא עַל בְּתוּלַת יִשְׂרָאֵל, וְכִי

עָלָה בִּלְחוֹדָהָא. לָא. אֶלָּא בְּגִין דְּכֹלָא אִתְּבַּר בְּגִינָה. בְּגִינָה אִתְּבַּר
יְמִינָא אֲבַתְרָה, דַּהֲוָה מְקָרֵב לָה גַּבֵּי גוּפָא. וְגוּפָא דְּאִיהוּ שִׁמְשָׁא,
אִתְחֲשָׁךְ בְּגִינָה. וְדָא הוּא רָזָא דִּכְתִיב הוֹשִׁיעָה יְמִינְךָ וַעֲנֵנִי. גוּפָא
דִּכְתִיב אַלְבִּישׁ שָׁמַיִם קַדְרוּת, דְּהָא שִׁמְשָׁא אִתְחֲשָׁךְ בְּגִינָה. כְּגַוְונָא דָא
וַתָּמָת שָׁם מִרְיָם וְגוֹ'.

36. Rabbi Aba said that it is written: Now, you "son of man, take up a lamentation" (Yechezkel 28:12), about the virgin of Yisrael, THAT IS MALCHUT. HE ASKS: Is it about her alone? HE RESPONDS: No. It is only that everyone was broken because of her, since it was for her that the breaking of the right OF ZEIR ANPIN followed, THAT IS THE SECRET OF THE DEPARTURE OF CHESED DUE TO THE SEPARATION OF MALCHUT. FOR CHESED was bringing her near to the body, WHICH IS ZEIR ANPIN. And the body, which is the sun, MEANING ZEIR ANPIN THAT INFLUENCES MALCHUT, was dimmed for her, SINCE IT HAD NOBODY TO INSPIRE. This is the secret of: "save with Your right hand, and answer me" (Tehilim 60:7), MEANING SAVE THE RIGHT HAND THAT WAS SEVERED BY THE SEPARATION OF MALCHUT. ALSO, this affected the body, as is written: "I clothe the heavens with blackness" (Yeshayah 50:3), since the sun, THAT IS ZEIR ANPIN, was darkened because of her. Similar to this is the verse: "And Miriam died there" (Bemidbar 20:1), BECAUSE THAT INDICATES THE DEPARTURE OF MALCHUT. AS MENTIONED ABOVE, THE WEAKENING OF THE RIGHT ALSO OCCURRED AND ZEIR ANPIN WAS DARKENED.

37. וְלֹא הָיָה מַיִם לָעֵדָה, דְּהָא אִסְתַּלַּק בֵּירָא דְּעֵילָא וְתַתָּא לְבָתַר
אִתְּבַר יְמִינָא, דִּכְתִיב וַיֵּאָסֵף אַהֲרֹן אֶל עַמָּיו. וּלְבָתַר אִתְחֲשָׁךְ שִׁמְשָׁא,
דִּכְתִיב וּמוּת בָּהָר וְגוֹ'. וְהֵאָסֵף אֶל עַמֶּךָ וְגוֹ'. הָא דְּרוֹעָא יְמִינָא אִתְּבַר,
וְגוּפָא דְּאִיהוּ שִׁמְשָׁא אִתְחֲשָׁךְ.

37. "And there was no water for the congregation" (Ibid. 2), since the well of above departed, WHICH IS MALCHUT, as well as the lower, WHICH IS MIRIAM. Then the right was broken, as is written: "Aaron shall be gathered to his people" (Ibid. 24). HE IS THE SECRET OF CHESED, WHICH IS THE RIGHT. Following that, the sun dimmed, as is written: "and die in the mount...and be gathered to your people" (Devarim 32:50), AND MOSES WAS

THE CHARIOT TO ZEIR ANPIN, REFERRED TO AS 'SUN'. We see here that the right arm was broken and the body, which is the sun, became darkened.

38. וְת״ח, לָא אִשְׁתְּכַח דָּרָא בְּעָלְמָא, כְּדָרָא דְּמֹשֶׁה קַיְּימָא בְּעָלְמָא, וְאַהֲרֹן וּמִרְיָם. וְאִי תֵּימָא בְּיוֹמוֹי דִּשְׁלֹמֹה הָכִי נַמֵּי. לָאו. דְּהָא בְּיוֹמוֹי דִּשְׁלֹמֹה שַׁלִּיט סִיהֲרָא, וְשִׁמְשָׁא אִתְכְּנִישׁ. וּבְיוֹמוֹי דְּמֹשֶׁה, אִתְכְּנִישׁ סִיהֲרָא, וְשִׁמְשָׁא שַׁלְטָא.

38. Come and behold: there was no generation in the world similar to the generation when Moses as well as Aaron and Miriam lived in the world. If you say that the times of Solomon were similar, it is not so. In the times of Solomon, the moon was dominant, SINCE THAT GENERATION WAS RECEIVING FROM THE MOON, WHICH IS MALCHUT, and the sun was gathered, BECAUSE THEY DID NOT RECEIVE FROM ZEIR ANPIN, REFERRED TO AS 'SUN'. During the time of Moses, the moon was gathered, so THAT THEY DID NOT RECEIVE FROM MALCHUT, and the sun was dominant, AS THEY WERE RECEIVING FROM ZEIR ANPIN, REFERRED TO AS 'SUN'.

39. תְּלַת אַחִין הֲווֹ: מֹשֶׁה, אַהֲרֹן, וּמִרְיָם. כד״א וָאֶשְׁלַח לְפָנֶיךָ אֶת מֹשֶׁה אַהֲרֹן וּמִרְיָם. מִרְיָם, סִיהֲרָא. מֹשֶׁה, שִׁמְשָׁא. אַהֲרֹן, דְּרוֹעָא יְמִינָא. חוּר, דְּרוֹעָא שְׂמָאלָא. וְאָמְרֵי לָהּ, נַחְשׁוֹן בֶּן עֲמִינָדָב. בְּקַדְמֵיתָא מִיתַת מִרְיָם, אִסְתַּלְּקַת סִיהֲרָא, אִסְתַּלַּק בְּאֵר. לְבָתַר אִתְּבַּר דְּרוֹעָא יְמִינָא, דִּמְקָרֵב תָּדִיר סִיהֲרָא, בְּאַחֲוָה, בְּחֶדְוָה. וְע״ד כְּתִיב, וַתִּקַּח מִרְיָם הַנְּבִיאָה אֲחוֹת אַהֲרֹן. אֲחוֹת אַהֲרֹן וַדַּאי, דְּאִיהוּ דְּרוֹעָא, דִּמְקָרֵב לָהּ בְּאַחֲדוּתָא, בְּאַחֲוָה עִם גּוּפָא.

39. There were three siblings, Moses, Aaron and Miriam, as it says: "and I sent before you Moses, Aaron, and Miriam" (Michah 6:4). Miriam is the moon, MALCHUT, Moses is the sun, ZEIR ANPIN, Aaron is the right arm, CHESED, and Hur is the left arm, GVURAH. Some say that Nahshon, the son of Amminadab WAS THE LEFT ARM. At first Miriam died, and the moon departed and the well disappeared. Afterward, the right arm that always brings near the moon, WHICH IS MALCHUT, joyfully and with friendship, broke. Therefore, it is written: "and Miriam the prophetess, the sister of

Aaron, took..." (Shemot 15:20). Surely she is Aaron's sister, for he is the arm that brings her near in unity and brotherhood with the body, WHICH IS ZEIR ANPIN.

40. לְבָתַר אִתְכְּנִישׁ שִׁמְשָׁא וְאִתְחֲשַׁךְ, כְּמָה דְּאוֹקִימְנָא דִּכְתִיב וְהֵאָסֵף אֶל עַמֶּךָ גַּם אַתָּה וְגו'. זַכָּאָה חוּלָקֵהוֹן דְּמֹשֶׁה אַהֲרֹן וּמִרְיָם, דְּאִשְׁתְּכָחוּ בְּעָלְמָא. בְּיוֹמוֹי דִּשְׁלֹמֹה, שַׁלְטָא סִיהֲרָא, בְּתִקּוּנָהָא, וְאִתְחֲזֵי בְּעָלְמָא. וְאִתְקְיַּים שְׁלֹמֹה בְּחָכְמְתָא דִּנְהִירוּ דִּילָהּ, וְשָׁלִיט בְּעָלְמָא. כֵּיוָן דְּסִיהֲרָא נַחְתָּא בְּחוֹבוֹי, אִתְפְּגִים יוֹמָא בָּתַר יוֹמָא, עַד דְּאִשְׁתְּכַח בְּקֶרֶן מַעֲרָבִית, וְלָא יַתִּיר, וְאִתְיְהִיב שִׁבְטָא חַד לִבְרֵיהּ. זַכָּאָה חוּלָקָא דְּמֹשֶׁה נְבִיאָה מְהֵימְנָא.

40. Afterward, the sun was gathered in and it was darkened, as we explained that it is written: "and be gathered to your people..." Happy is the generation in which Moses, Aaron, and Miriam existed in the world. During the era of Solomon, the moon was dominant, WHICH IS MALCHUT, in her correction, IN HER FULLNESS, and was visible in the world. Solomon was established in the wisdom of her light, SINCE THE REVELATION OF THE LIGHT OF CHOCHMAH IS ONLY POSSIBLE IN MALCHUT. And he ruled the world. As soon as the moon set, due to his sins, she became flawed day after day until she was located in the western sector, WHICH IS THE LOCATION OF MALCHUT ITSELF, and nothing more. Then, just one tribe was given to his son, SOLOMON, AND THE REST TO JEROBOAM. Happy is the lot of Moses, the faithful prophet.

41. כְּתִיב וְזָרַח הַשֶּׁמֶשׁ וּבָא הַשֶּׁמֶשׁ וְגו'. הַאי קְרָא אוֹקִימְנָא. אֲבָל וְזָרַח הַשֶּׁמֶשׁ, כַּד נַפְקוּ יִשְׂרָאֵל מִמִּצְרַיִם, דְּנָהִיר שִׁמְשָׁא וְלָא סִיהֲרָא. וְאֶל מְקוֹמוֹ שׁוֹאֵף וְגו', הָא כְּתִיב וּבָא הַשֶּׁמֶשׁ, בְּמַדְבְּרָא, עִם שְׁאַר מֵתֵי מַדְבְּרָא. כֵּיוָן דְּעָאל שִׁמְשָׁא, לְאָן אֲתַר אִתְכְּנִישׁ, בְּגִין לְאַנְהָרָא לְסִיהֲרָא. הֲה"ד שׁוֹאֵף זוֹרֵחַ הוּא שָׁם. דְּאע"ג דְּאִתְכְּנִישׁ, זוֹרֵחַ הוּא שָׁם וַדַּאי. דְּהָא לָא אַנְהִיר סִיהֲרָא, אֶלָּא מִנְהוֹרָא דְּשִׁמְשָׁא. וְדָא הוּא רָזָא דִּכְתִיב, הִנְּךָ שׁוֹכֵב עִם אֲבוֹתֶיךָ וְקָם. אע"ג דְּתִתְכְּנֵשׁ, הִנְּךָ קַיָּים לְאַנְהָרָא לְסִיהֲרָא. דָּא הוּא יְהוֹשֻׁעַ.

41. It is written: "the sun also rises, and the sun goes down" (Kohelet 1:5), and we have explained this verse. However, "the sun also rises," refers to the time when Yisrael left Egypt, when the sun, WHO IS MOSES, was shining, and not the moon, WHICH IS MALCHUT. "...and hastens to its place..." since it is written: "and the sun goes down," BECAUSE MOSES WAS GATHERED in the desert with the rest of those who died in the desert. When the sun set, to which location was it gathered? "To its place"; that is, so it would illuminate the moon. This is what it says: "hastens...where it rises again"; and even though it was gathered, it assuredly "rises again," since the moon has no illuminating brightness except that which it receives from the sun. This is the secret of that which is written: "You shall sleep with your fathers...will rise up..." (Devarim 31:16). Even though you will be gathered, you will rise up to illuminate to the moon, which refers to Joshua, SINCE JOSHUA WAS A CARRIAGE TO MALCHUT.

42. וְעָלֵיהּ כְּתִיב הַאי קְרָא, מַה יִּתְרוֹן לָאָדָם בְּכָל עֲמָלוֹ וְגוֹ'. מַה יִּתְרוֹן לָאָדָם בְּכָל עֲמָלוֹ, דָּא יְהוֹשֻׁעַ, דְּאִשְׁתַּדַּל לְאַחֲסָנָא אַרְעָא דְּיִשְׂרָאֵל, וְלָא זָכָה לְאַשְׁלְמָא לְסִיהֲרָא כַּדְקָא יָאוּת, דְּהָא אִיהוּ אַעֲמַל בְּהוּ בְּיִשְׂרָאֵל, תַּחַת הַשֶּׁמֶשׁ תְּחוֹתֵיהּ דְּמֹשֶׁה. ת"ח, וַוי לְהַהוּא כְּסוּפָא, וַוי לְהַהוּא כְּלִימָה, בְּגִין דִּפְלַח, וְלָא נָטַל אַתְרֵיהּ מַמָּשׁ, אֶלָּא תְּחוֹת שִׁמְשָׁא, וְלָא הֲוָה לֵיהּ נְהִירוּ מְדִילֵיהּ, אֶלָּא נְהִירוּ דְּנָהִיר לֵיהּ. וְאִי הָכִי, מַאי תּוּשְׁבַּחְתָּא הֲוָה לֵיהּ, הוֹאִיל וְלָא אַשְׁלִים לְהָכָא וּלְהָכָא.

42. And about him, OF JOSHUA, this verse is written: "what profit has a man of all his labor..." (Kohelet 1:3). That is Joshua, who strove to inherit the land of Yisrael, WHICH IS MALCHUT, and did not attain the full completion of the moon, WHICH IS MALCHUT, AS would have been proper. He toiled for Yisrael under the sun, MEANING under Moses, WHO IS THE SECRET OF ZEIR ANPIN, REFERRED TO AS 'SUN'. Come and behold: woe for that embarrassment, woe for that shame, that he worked UNDER MOSES and did not actually take his place, WHICH IS THE SUN, but rather he only had a place under the sun, for he had no light of his own, except the brightness OF THE SUN that was illuminating on him. What praise is then upon him if he could not fulfill completely either way, TO THE SUN OR THE MOON, FOR SINCE HE COULD NOT PERFECT HIMSELF IN THE LEVEL OF THE SUN, HE THEREFORE COULD NOT PERFECT THE MOON.

‫43. וּבְכָל אֲתָר דְּאָמַר שְׁלֹמֹה תַּחַת הַשֶּׁמֶשׁ, עַל דַּרְגָּא דִּילֵיהּ קָאָמַר.‬
‫רָאִיתִי תַּחַת הַשֶּׁמֶשׁ. וְעוֹד רָאִיתִי תַּחַת הַשֶּׁמֶשׁ. שַׁבְתִּי וְרָאֹה תַּחַת‬
‫הַשֶּׁמֶשׁ. וְכֵן כֻּלְּהוּ. וּבְגִין דַּרְגָּא דִּילֵיהּ קָאָמַר. וְדָא הוּא רָזָא דְּמִלָּה‬
‫וַדַּאי.‬

43. In every place where Solomon mentions, "under the sun," he speaks about his own level, THAT IS MALCHUT. For example: "I have seen under the sun" (Kohelet 5:12), and, "moreover I saw under the sun" (Kohelet 3:16), and finally, "I returned, and saw under the sun" (Kohelet 9:11). It is the same in everything that he spoke of his own level, and that definitely is the secret of the matter.

‫44. רש"א, וַדַּאי מַאן דְּנָטִיל סָמָא דְּמוֹתָא בִּלְחוֹדוֹי, עֲלֵיהּ כְּתִיב בְּכָל‬
‫עֲמָלוֹ שֶׁיַּעֲמוֹל תַּחַת הַשֶּׁמֶשׁ וַדַּאי. וּמַאן הוּא תַּחַת הַשֶּׁמֶשׁ. הֲוֵי אֵימָא‬
‫דָּא סִיהֲרָא. וּמַאן דְּאָחִיד סִיהֲרָא בְּלָא שִׁמְשָׁא, עֲמָלוֹ תַּחַת הַשֶּׁמֶשׁ‬
‫וַדַּאי. וְדָא הוּא חוֹבָא קַדְמָאָה דְּעָלְמָא. וְעַל דָּא מַה יִּתְרוֹן לָאָדָם בְּכָל‬
‫עֲמָלוֹ, לָאָדָם קַדְמָאָה, וְכֵן לְכֻלְּהוּ דְּאַתְיָין בַּתְרֵיהּ, דְּחָבוּ בַּאֲתָר דָּא.‬

44. Rabbi Shimon says that HE DISAGREES WITH THE ABOVE MENTIONED: Certainly, the scripture writes about one who takes deadly poison alone, MEANING MALCHUT EXCLUSIVELY, WITHOUT ZEIR ANPIN: "of all his labor wherein he labors under the sun" (Kohelet 1:3). Who is under the sun? One says that is the moon, WHICH IS MALCHUT, and whoever is attached to the moon without the sun, DEFINITELY FINDS his labor to be "under the sun." That was the first sin in the world, MEANING THE SIN OF THE TREE OF KNOWLEDGE OF GOOD AND EVIL THAT CARRIED DOWN THE LIGHT OF CHOCHMAH IN MALCHUT FROM ABOVE TO BELOW. BY THIS, IT SEPARATED HER FROM ZEIR ANPIN, HER HUSBAND, AND TOOK MALCHUT ALONE. Therefore, THE SCRIPTURE SAYS: "what profit has a man (Heb. *Adam*) of all his labor wherein he labors under the sun." THAT IS SAID about Adam, and the same applies to all those who come after him who sin in that location.

7. "Round and round goes the wind"

A Synopsis

Rabbi Shimon says that in the title verse it means the wind is the Holy Spirit that circles in two directions to adhere to the body. He refers to the three Patriarchs who are the holy Chariot and says that David is the spirit that was attached to them so that they are a perfectly complete holy Chariot. Rabbi Shimon concludes by saying that all of King Solomon's words are recited in the innermost recesses of the holy chamber because they conceal a much deeper wisdom than people realize.

45. הוֹלֵךְ אֶל דָּרוֹם וְסוֹבֵב אֶל צָפוֹן, הַיְינוּ דִּכְתִּיב, מִימִינוֹ אֵשׁ דָּת לָמוֹ. יְמִינוֹ, זֶה דָּרוֹם. אֵשׁ דָּת, דָּא צָפוֹן. וְדָא כָּלִיל בְּדָא.

45. "…goes toward the south, and veers to the north…" (Kohelet 1:6). This is what is written: "from His right hand went a fiery law for them" (Devarim 33:2); "His right hand," is south, CHESED; "a fiery law," is north, GVURAH – and one is included in the other. THEREFORE, IT IS WRITTEN: "GOES TOWARD THE SOUTH, AND VEERS TO THE NORTH."

46. סוֹבֵב סוֹבֵב הוֹלֵךְ הָרוּחַ, הַאי קְרָא קַשְׁיָא, סוֹבֵב סוֹבֵב הוֹלֵךְ הַשֶּׁמֶשׁ מִבָּעֵי לֵיהּ, מַאי הוֹלֵךְ הָרוּחַ. מַאן רוּחָא דָא, דָּא הוּא תְּחוֹת הַשֶּׁמֶשׁ, דְּאִקְרֵי רוּחַ הַקֹּדֶשׁ. וְדָא רוּחַ הוֹלֵךְ וְסוֹבֵב לְאִלֵּין תְּרֵין סִטְרִין לְאִתְחַבְּרָא בְּגוּפָא. וע"ד כְּתִיב הָרוּחַ, הַהוּא דְּאִשְׁתְּמוֹדַע. חוּלָקָא דְיִשְׂרָאֵל.

46. "Round and round goes the wind" (Kohelet 1:6). This verse is difficult. It should have said, 'Round and round goes the sun'. What is, "goes the wind"? HE REPLIES: Who is that wind (also: 'spirit')? It is under the sun and is called the 'Holy Spirit', MEANING MALCHUT. And that spirit, MALCHUT, follows and circles in those two directions, SOUTH AND NORTH, WHICH ARE THE RIGHT COLUMN AND THE LEFT COLUMN, to adhere to the body, THAT IS ZEIR ANPIN CALLED 'SUN'. Therefore, "the wind," is spelled out WITH THE *HEI* OF THE DEFINITE ARTICLE, TO INDICATE that which is obvious, which is the portion of Yisrael, MEANING MALCHUT, WHICH IS THE PART OF ZEIR ANPIN CALLED 'YISRAEL'. SIMILARLY,

YISRAEL BELOW COUNT IN ACCORDANCE WITH THE MOON CYCLE, WHICH IS THEIR LOT, ONLY IT IS TOGETHER WITH ZEIR ANPIN.

47. וְעַל סְבִיבוֹתָיו שָׁב הָרוּחַ, מַאן סְבִיבוֹתָיו. אַלֵּין אֲבָהָן, דְּאִינּוּן רְתִיכָא קַדִּישָׁא, וְאִינּוּן תְּלַת, וְדָוִד דָּא הוּא רוּחָא רְבִיעָאָה, דְּאִתְחַבָּר בְּהוּ הָא אִינּוּן רְתִיכָא קַדִּישָׁא שְׁלֵימָתָא, וְעַל דָּא כְּתִיב, אֶבֶן מָאֲסוּ הַבּוֹנִים הָיְתָה לְרֹאשׁ פִּנָּה.

47. "And on its circuits the wind returns" (Ibid.). HE INQUIRES: What are "its circuits"? HE REPLIES: These refer to the Patriarchs, who are the holy Chariot. They are three and David is the spirit, that fourth who was attached to them so that they are a perfectly complete holy Chariot. ABOUT DAVID WHO ROSE TO BE INCLUDED IN THE HIGHER CHARIOT, it is written: "the stone which the builders rejected has become the head stone of the corner" (Tehilim 118:22).

48. בְּגִין דְּכָל מִלּוֹי דִּשְׁלֹמֹה מַלְכָּא סְתִימִין כֻּלְּהוּ בְּחָכְמָתָא, וְכֻלְּהוּ לְגוֹ בְּגוֹ דְּהֵיכָלָא קַדִּישָׁא, וּבְנֵי נָשָׁא לָא מִסְתַּכְּלֵי בְּהוּ, וְחָמָאן מִלּוֹי כְּמִלִּין דב"נ אַחֲרָא. אִי הָכִי, מַה שְׁבָחָא הוּא לִשְׁלֹמֹה מַלְכָּא בְּחָכְמָתֵיהּ, מִשְּׁאַר בְּנֵי נָשָׁא. אֶלָּא וַדַּאי כָּל מִלָּה וּמִלָּה דִּשְׁלֹמֹה מַלְכָּא סְתִים בְּחָכְמָתָא.

48. Because all of King Solomon's words are concealed in wisdom, all ARE RECITED in the innermost recesses of the holy chamber. People do not pay attention to observe them and they simply see his words as the same as the sayings of any other person. And if this is so, what is the praise to King Solomon with his wisdom over any other person? Assuredly, every word and saying of Solomon, the King, is concealed in wisdom.

8. "Wisdom is good with an inheritance"

A Synopsis

Rabbi Shimon tells us that the title verse means that it is good when Wisdom, Chochmah, dwells with the children of Yisrael so they will be attached to her. We hear that "the excellency of knowledge" is the Tree of Life, the secret of Da'at and Zeir Anpin. In another explanation, Rabbi Shimon says that it is the Righteous of the world that is the brightness of the sun, and he goes on to talk about those who become attached to the Tree of Life.

49. פָּתַח וְאָמַר, טוֹבָה חָכְמָה עִם נַחֲלָה וְיוֹתֵר לְרוֹאֵי הַשָּׁמֶשׁ, אִי לָאו דְּהָא אִתְגַּלְיָיא מִלָּה דָּא, לָא יְדַעְנָא מַאי קָאָמַר. טוֹבָה חָכְמָה, דָּא הִיא חָכְמָה, דְּהִיא תַּחַת הַשָּׁמֶשׁ, כּוּרְסְיָיא מִתְתַּקְנָא לֵיהּ. טוֹבָה חָכְמָה עִם נַחֲלָה, יָאָה וְשַׁפִּירָא כַּד אִיהִי שַׁרְיָיא עִמְּהוֹן דְּיִשְׂרָאֵל, דְּאִינּוּן נַחֲלָה וְעַדְבָּא דִּילָהּ, לְאִתְקַשְּׁרָא בָּהּ.

49. He opened the discussion with the verse: "wisdom is good with an inheritance: and by it there is [more] profit to them that see the sun" (Kohelet 7:11). If this matter had not been revealed TO ME, I would have no idea of its meaning. "Wisdom is good," refers to Chochmah that is underneath the sun, which is a Throne that is prepared FOR THE SUN THAT IS ZEIR ANPIN, WHICH IS CHOCHMAH IN MALCHUT, MEANING THE LOWER CHOCHMAH REFERRED TO AS "UNDER THE SUN," AND CALLED THE 'THRONE'. "Wisdom is good with an inheritance," means it is well and good when CHOCHMAH, WHICH IS MALCHUT, dwells with Yisrael so they will be attached to her, since they are the inheritance and lot OF MALCHUT.

50. אֲבָל תּוּשְׁבַּחְתָּא יַתִּיר לְרוֹאֵי הַשָּׁמֶשׁ, לְאִינּוּן דְּזָכוּ לְאִתְחַבְּרָא בְּשִׁמְשָׁא, וּלְאִתְקַשְּׁרָא בֵּיהּ, דְּהָא אָחִיד בְּאִילָנָא דְּחַיֵּי, וּמַאן דְּאָחִיד בֵּיהּ, בְּכֹלָּא אָחִיד, בַּחַיִּין דְּהַאי עָלְמָא, וּבְחַיֵּי דְּעָלְמָא דְּאָתֵי, וְדָא הוּא דִּכְתִּיב, וְיִתְרוֹן דַּעַת הַחָכְמָה תְּחַיֶּה בְעָלֶיהָ. מַאי וְיִתְרוֹן דַּעַת. דָּא אִילָנָא דְּחַיֵּי. יִתְרוֹן דִּילֵיהּ מַהוּ, הַחָכְמָה וַדַּאי, דְּהָא תּוֹרָה, מֵחָכְמָה עִלָּאָה נָפְקָא.

50. However, more profit is for those "that see the sun," because they merit to be attached to the sun, WHICH IS ZEIR ANPIN, and to be connected with him. This one is attached to the Tree of Life, and whoever is attached to the Tree of Life is attached to everything, to the life of this world, WHICH IS MALCHUT, and life of the World to Come, WHICH IS BINAH, SINCE ZEIR ANPIN IS ATTACHED IN MALCHUT AND BINAH. This is what is written: "but the excellency of knowledge is that wisdom gives life to those who have it" (Ibid. 12). The meaning of, "but the excellency of knowledge" is the Tree of Life, WHICH IS THE SECRET OF DA'AT AND ZEIR ANPIN. What is its excellency? It is definitely Chochmah, since the Torah, WHICH IS ZEIR ANPIN, certainly emanated from higher Chochmah, WHICH IS ABA AND IMA.

51. תּוּ טוֹבָה חָכְמָה עִם נַחֲלָה, טוֹבָה חָכְמָה, וַדַּאי עִם נַחֲלָה, דָּא צַדִּיקָא דְּעָלְמָא, דְּאִיהוּ נְהוֹרָא דְּשִׁמְשָׁא, דְּהָא תְּרֵין דַּרְגִּין אִלֵּין כַּחֲדָא יַתְבֵי, וְדָא הוּא שְׁפִּירוּ דִּלְהוֹן, אֲבָל וְיוֹתֵר לְרוֹאֵי הַשָּׁמֶשׁ, לְאִינּוּן דְּמִתְאַחֲדִין בְּשִׁמְשָׁא, תּוּקְפָּא דְּכֹלָּא, שְׁבָחָא דְּכֹלָּא.

51. Another EXPLANATION FOR: "wisdom is good with an inheritance." Assuredly, "wisdom is good," WHICH IS THE LOWER CHOCHMAH, "with an inheritance." It is the Righteous of the world, MEANING YESOD IN ZEIR ANPIN, which is the brightness of the sun, SINCE YESOD OF ZEIR ANPIN IS THE LIGHT OF ZEIR ANPIN CALLED 'SUN'. Those two levels, YESOD AND MALCHUT, dwell together, and that is their beauty. However, "more profit to them that see the sun," NAMELY to those that unite with the sun ITSELF, WHICH IS ZEIR ANPIN, the strength of all and the praise of all.

52. וְדָא הוּא דַּעַת, אִילָנָא דְּחַיֵּיא, וְהָא אוּקְמוּהָ גַּם בְּלֹא דַעַת נֶפֶשׁ לֹא טוֹב. מַאן נֶפֶשׁ. דָּא נֶפֶשׁ טוֹב דְּדָוִד מַלְכָּא. וְדָא חָכְמָה דְּקָאמְרָן. וּבְגִינֵי כַּךְ יִתְרוֹן דַּעַת הַחָכְמָה, דְּמִתַּמָּן אִשְׁתְּרְשָׁא אִילָנָא וְאִתְנְטַע לְכָל סִטְרִין, וְכֵן לְכָל אִינּוּן דַּאֲחִידָן בֵּיהּ בְּהַאי אִילָנָא, וְעַל דָּא שְׁלֹמֹה מַלְכָּא לָא אִשְׁתְּכַח אֶלָּא בְּהַהוּא דַּרְגָּא דִּילֵיהּ, וּמִתַּמָּן יָדַע כֹּלָּא, וַהֲוָה אָמַר עוֹד רָאִיתִי תַּחַת הַשָּׁמֶשׁ, וְשַׁבְתִּי וְרָאִיתִי וְגו'. וְכֵן כֻּלְּהוּ. זַכָּאִין אִינּוּן צַדִּיקַיָּיא, דְּמִשְׁתַּדְּלֵי בְּאוֹרַיְיתָא, וְיָדְעִין אוֹרְחוֹי דְּמַלְכָּא קַדִּישָׁא,

וּסְתִימִין עִלָּאִין דִּגְנִיזִין בְּאוֹרַיְיתָא, דִּכְתִיב כִּי יְשָׁרִים דַּרְכֵי יְיָ' וְגוֹ'.

52. THE SUN is Da'at OF ZEIR ANPIN, which is the Tree of Life, as has already been explained: "Also, that the soul be without knowledge is not good" (Mishlei 19:2). Whose is this "soul"? It is the good soul of King David, THAT IS MALCHUT, and that is the Chochmah we mentioned, THAT AT THE TIME THAT THE SOUL, WHICH IS MALCHUT, IS ATTACHED TO DA'AT OF ZEIR ANPIN, IT IS CALLED 'LOWER CHOCHMAH'. Therefore, "the excellency of knowledge (Heb. *da'at*) is...wisdom." From there, FROM DA'AT, the tree is rooted, WHICH IS MALCHUT, and is planted in all directions, TO RIGHT AND LEFT, in all those who become attached to this tree. Therefore, Solomon the king was established only in his level, THAT IS MALCHUT. From there, he was aware of everything and he used to say: "and moreover I saw under the sun" (Kohelet 3:16); THAT IS MALCHUT THAT IS CALLED "UNDER THE SUN," AND ALSO, "I returned, and saw under the sun" (Kohelet 9:11). The same applies to all. Happy are the just who study the Torah and know the ways of the Holy King and the highly sealed things that are stored and hidden in the Torah, as it is written: "for the ways of Hashem are right..." (Hoshea 14:10).

9. "Aaron shall be gathered to his people"

A Synopsis

From Rabbi Chiya we learn that when Solomon said, "So I praised the dead that are already dead more than the living that are yet alive," he meant those who had already been reincarnated more than once and have returned from the dead to redeem their earlier actions. We are told that the just deserve to reach a level higher than all the holy angels and their levels, that is the Upper Eden. Those who have less merit occupy a place below, the lower Eden that is located over the terrestrial garden. We hear about the difference between the higher Eden and the lower Eden. King Solomon said that the spirit that has not come down and is still in its original state is better than the dead or the living because it has not yet sinned and needs to receive no punishment. "But better than both of them," is the person who are innocently righteous that keep all the precepts of the Torah and stay attached always to God. Rabbi Chiya talks about Moses removing Aaron's garments and giving them to his son Elazar, and about God preparing a bed for Aaron at his death. Rabbi Shimon says that Miriam, Aaron and Moses each died in the place that was appropriate for them, and he describes some details about this. He concludes by saying that when punishment is decreed over the children of Yisrael it is voided by the righteous who are in God's presence above.

53. יֵאָסֵף אַהֲרֹן אֶל עַמָּיו וְגו'. רִבִּי חִיָּיא פָּתַח, וְשַׁבֵּחַ אֲנִי אֶת הַמֵּתִים שֶׁכְּבָר מֵתוּ וְגו'. הַאי קְרָא אִתְּמַר וְאוּקְמוּהָ. ת"ח, כָּל עוֹבָדוֹי דְּקוּדְשָׁא בְּרִיךְ הוּא, בְּדִינָא וּקְשׁוֹט, וְלֵית מַאן דְּאַקְשֵׁי לָקֳבְלֵיהּ, וְיִמְחֵי בִּידֵיהּ, וְיֵימַר לֵיהּ מַה עַבְדַת, וְכִרְעוּתֵיהּ עָבֵד בְּכֹלָּא.

53. "Aaron shall be gathered to his people" (Bemidbar 20:24). Rabbi Chiya opened the discussion with the verse: "so I praised the dead that are already dead..." (Kohelet 4:2). We have learned this verse and it has been explained. Come and behold: all the deeds of the Holy One, blessed be He, are according to Justice and Truth. There exists no one that can present Him with ANY DIFFICULTIES, and object to it, and say to Him: 'What are you doing?' And He accomplished everything as He wished.

54. וְשַׁבֵּחַ אֲנִי אֶת הַמֵּתִים. וְכִי שְׁלֹמֹה מַלְכָּא מְשַׁבֵּחַ לְמֵתַיָּיא יַתִּיר מָן

חַיָּיא, וְהָא לָא אִקְרֵי חַי אֶלָּא מַאן דְּאִיהוּ בְּאֹרַח קְשׁוֹט בְּהַאי עָלְמָא, כְּמָה דְאַתְּ אָמֵר וּבְנָיָהוּ בֶן יְהוֹיָדָע בֶּן אִישׁ חַי, וְהָא אוּקְמוּהָ חַבְרַיָּיא, וְרָשָׁע דְּלָא אָזִיל בְּאֹרַח קְשׁוֹט אִקְרֵי מֵת, וְאִיהוּ מְשַׁבֵּחַ לַמֵּתִים מִן הַחַיִּים.

54. "So I praised the dead." HE ASKS: Does King Solomon then praise the dead more than the living? Here, nobody is considered living unless he is on a true path in this world, as it says, "And Benaiah ben Jehoiada, the son of a valiant (lit. 'living') man" (II Shmuel 23:20). The friends have explained this. The wicked one who does not follow the true path is considered dead, YET KING SOLOMON praises the dead more than the living ones.

55. אֶלָּא, וַדַּאי כָּל מִלּוֹי דִּשְׁלֹמֹה מַלְכָּא, בְּחָכְמְתָא אִתְּמָרוּ, וְהָא אִתְּמַר, וְשַׁבֵּחַ אֲנִי אֶת הַמֵּתִים, אִילּוּ לָא כְּתִיב יַתִּיר, הֲוָה אֲמֵינָא הָכִי, אֲבָל כֵּיוָן דִּכְתִיב שֶׁכְּבָר מֵתוּ, אִשְׁתְּכַח מִלָּה אַחֲרָא בְּחָכְמְתָא. שֶׁכְּבָר מֵתוּ: זִמְנָא אַחֲרָא אִסְתְּלָקוּ מִן עָלְמָא, וְאִתְתַּקַּן בְּעַפְרָא, כ״שׁ דְּהָא קַבִּיל עוֹנָשָׁא זִמְנָא וּתְרֵין, וְדָא וַדַּאי, אַתְרֵיהּ אִתְתַּקַּן בְּשַׁבְחָא יַתִּיר מֵאִינּוּן חַיֵּי, דְּעַד לָא קַבִּילוּ עוֹנָשָׁא.

55. Most definitely, all the words of King Solomon were said with wisdom and here we were taught, "so I praised the dead." If nothing more had been written, I would have said so, THAT HE PRAISES THE DEAD ONES MORE THAN THE LIVING, but since it is already written, "that are already dead," we find here another gem of wisdom. "…that are already dead…" MEANS that they have already died at a different time and that they have already departed from the world and were mended by the dust. THEY HAVE ALREADY RETURNED, INCARNATED, AND REVISITED THIS WORLD, and most certainly received their punishment once or twice, SINCE THEY WERE ALREADY HERE IN THIS WORLD TWICE. It is certain that their station has been more profitably prepared than those living and that they have not yet received the punishment OF REINCARNATION.

56. וע״ד כְּתִיב וְשַׁבֵּחַ אֲנִי אֶת הַמֵּתִים שֶׁכְּבָר מֵתוּ, דַּיְיקָא, אִלֵּין אִינּוּן חַיִּין, וְאִקְרוּן מֵתִים. מ״ט אִקְרוּן מֵתִים, בְּגִין דְּהָא טַעֲמוּ טַעֲמָא

דְּמוֹתָא, וְאע״ג דְּקַיְימֵי בְּהַאי עָלְמָא, מֵתִים אִינוּן, וּמְבֵּין מֵתַיְיא אַהֲדְרוּ. וְעוֹד עַל עוֹבָדִין קַדְמָאִין קַיְימִין לְאַתְקָנָא, וְאִקְרוּן מֵתִים. מִן הַחַיִּים אֲשֶׁר הֵמָּה חַיִּים, דְּעַד לָא טָעֲמוּ טַעֲמָא דְּמוֹתָא, וְלָא קַבִּילוּ עוֹנְשַׁיְיהוּ, וְלָא יַדְעֵי אִי זַכָּאן בְּהַהוּא עָלְמָא וְאִי לָאו.

56. Therefore, it is written: "so I praised the dead that are already dead," AND "THAT ARE ALREADY DEAD" is precise, MEANING those that are alive now, but are considered dead. What is the reason that they are considered dead? It is because they have already felt the taste of death and, although they exist in this world, they are dead and they were returned here from the dead. In addition, they are ready to repair the earlier activities THAT THEY PERFORMED PRIOR TO DYING. THEREFORE, they are considered dead, SINCE THEY ARE IN THE PROCESS OF CORRECTING THE DEEDS OF SOMEONE WHO ALREADY DIED. "...from these living that are alive..." (Kohelet 4:2). Since they have not yet tasted the taste of death and have not received their punishment, they do not know if they are worthy of that world or not.

57. ת״ח, זַכָּאִין דְּזַכָּאן לְאִתְקַשְּׁרָא בִּצְרוֹרָא דְּחַיֵּי, אִינוּן זַכָּאִין לְמֶחֱמֵי בִּיקָרָא דְּמַלְכָּא עִלָּאָה קַדִּישָׁא, כְּמָה דְּאַתְּ אָמֵר, לַחֲזוֹת בְּנֹעַם יְיָ׳ וּלְבַקֵּר בְּהֵיכָלוֹ. וְאִינוּן מְדוֹרְהוֹן, יַתִּיר וְעִלָּאָה מִכָּל אִינוּן מַלְאָכִין קַדִּישִׁין, וְכָל דַּרְגִּין דִּלְהוֹן. דְּהָא הַהוּא אַתְרָא עִלָּאָה, לָא זַכָּאִין עִלָּאִין וְתַתָּאִין לְמֶחֱמֵי לֵיהּ, הה״ד עַיִן לֹא רָאָתָה אֱלֹהִים זוּלָתְךָ וְגו׳.

57. Come and behold: the just merit to be bound in the bundle of Life, THAT IS YESOD IN ZEIR ANPIN. They are worthy of seeing the glory of the Holy King up high, as it is written: "to behold the beauty of Hashem, and to inquire in His Temple" (Tehilim 27:4). Their dwelling is higher than all the holy angels and all their levels, since neither the upper nor the lower grades merit seeing this highest location. This is what is said: "neither has the eye seen that Elohim, besides You..." (Yeshayah 64:3). THAT IS THE SECRET OF THE UPPER EDEN.

58. וְאִינוּן דְּלָא זַכָּאן לְסַלְּקָא כ״כ כְּאִינוּן, דּוּכְתָּא, אִית לוֹן לְתַתָּא כְּפוּם אוֹרְחַיְיהוּ, וְאִלֵּין לָא זַכָּאן לְהַהוּא אֲתָר, וּלְמֶחֱמֵי כְּמָה דְּחָמָאן

אִינּוּן דִּלְעֵילָּא, וְאִלֵּין קַיְימֵי בְּקִיּוּמֵי דְּעֵדֶן תַּתָּאָה וְלָא יַתִּיר. וְאִי תֵּימָא מַאן עֵדֶן תַּתָּאָה. אֶלָּא דָּא עֵדֶן דְּאִקְרֵי חָכְמָה תַּתָּאָה, וְדָא קַיְימָא עַל גַּן דְּבְאַרְעָא, וְאַשְׁגָּחוּתָא דְּהַאי עֵדֶן עָלֵיהּ, וְאִלֵּין קַיְימֵי בְּהַאי גַּן, וְאִתְהַנּוּן מֵעֵדֶן דָּא.

58. Those who do not merit to rise as much as these occupy a place below, according to their deeds. They do not merit that location and to see what those above see; they merit ONLY to remain in the lower Eden and not more. If you wonder what the lower Eden is, it is the Eden that is considered lower Chochmah, WHICH IS MALCHUT, and is located over the terrestrial garden. This Eden watches over THIS GARDEN, and the righteous remain in the Garden of Eden, THAT IS ON EARTH, and enjoy this Eden, WHICH IS THE LOWER CHOCHMAH.

59. מַאי בֵּין עֵדֶן תַּתָּאָה לְעִלָּאָה. כִּיתְרוֹן הָאוֹר מִן הַחֹשֶׁךְ, עֵדֶן תַּתָּאָה, אִקְרֵי עֶדְנָא נוּקְבָּא. עֵדֶן עִלָּאָה, אִקְרֵי עֵדֶן דְּכַר, עָלֵיהּ כְּתִיב עַיִן לֹא רָאָתָה אֱלֹהִים זוּלָתְךָ. הַאי עֵדֶן תַּתָּאָה, אִקְרֵי גַּן לְעֵדֶן דִּלְעֵילָּא, וְהַאי גַּן אִקְרֵי עֵדֶן, לְגַן דִּלְתַתָּא. וְאִלֵּין דְּמִשְׁתַּכְּחֵי בְּגַן תַּתָּאָה, אִתְהַנּוּן מֵהַאי עֵדֶן דְּעָלַיְיהוּ, בְּכָל שַׁבָּת וְשַׁבָּת, וּבְכָל יַרְחָא וְיַרְחָא, הה"ד וְהָיָה מִדֵּי חֹדֶשׁ בְּחָדְשׁוֹ וּמִדֵּי שַׁבָּת בְּשַׁבַּתּוֹ.

59. What is the difference between the lower Eden and the higher Eden? It is: "as far as light excels darkness" (Kohelet 2:13). The lower Eden is called 'pleasure (Heb. *ednah*)', which is female, and the higher Eden is considered 'delight (Heb. *eden*)', which is masculine. About this it is written: "neither has the eye seen that Elohim, besides you." This lower Eden is considered a garden in comparison to the Eden above, and that garden is considered Eden in comparison to the garden below. Those who exist in the lower garden, WHICH IS THE GARDEN OF EDEN ON EARTH, receive pleasure from that Eden that is above them, WHICH IS THE LOWER CHOCHMAH, every single Shabbat and every new moon, as it is written: "And it shall come to pass, that every new moon, and every Shabbat" (Yeshayah 66:23).

60. וְעַל אִלֵּין אָמַר שְׁלֹמֹה, מִן הַחַיִּים אֲשֶׁר הֵמָּה חַיִּים עֲדֶנָה, דְּהָא

אִלֵּין בְּדַרְגָּא עִלָּאָה יַתִּיר מִנַּיְיהוּ. מַאן אִינוּן. אִינוּן שֶׁכְּבָר מֵתוּ,
וְקַבִּילוּ עוֹנָשָׁא תְּרֵי זִמְנֵי, וְאִלֵּין אִקְרוּן כֶּסֶף מְזוּקָק, דְּעָאל לְנוּרָא
זִמְנִין וּתְרֵין, וְנָפִיק מִנֵּיהּ זוּהֲמָא, וְאִתְבָּרַר וְאִתְנְקֵי. וְטוֹב מִשְּׁנֵיהֶם אֶת
אֲשֶׁר עֶדֶן לֹא הָיָה. הַהוּא רוּחָא דְּקָאֵים לְעֵילָא, וְאִתְעַכָּב לְנַחְתָּא
לְתַתָּא, דְּהַאי קָאֵים בְּקִיּוּמֵיהּ, וְלֵית לֵיהּ לְקַבְּלָא עוֹנָשָׁא, וְאִית לֵיהּ
מְזוֹנָא מֵהַהוּא מְזוֹנָא עִלָּאָה דִּלְעֵילָא לְעֵילָא.

60. About these, Solomon said: "...from these living that alive..." since these are in a level higher than them. Who are they? This refers to those who have already died before and received their punishment twice. They are considered like refined silver that has entered the oven once or twice and has had the impurities sorted out, picked clean. "But better than both of them is he who has not yet been" (Kohelet 4:3). That is the spirit that remains above and is restrained from coming down, since that one is still in its original state AND HAS NOT SINNED YET. It does not need to receive punishment and obtains sustenance from that sustenance that is up very high.

61. טַב מִכֻּלְּהוּ, מַאן דְּלָא אִתְפְּרַשׁ, וְלָא אִתְגַּלְיָיא, וְכָל מִלּוֹי בִּסְתִימָא
אִינוּן. דָּא הוּא זַכָּאָה חֲסִידָא, דְּנָטַר פִּקּוּדֵי אוֹרַיְיתָא, וְקַיֵּים לוֹן,
וְאִשְׁתָּדַּל בְּאוֹרַיְיתָא יְמָמָא וְלֵילֵי. דָּא אִתְאַחִיד וְאִתְהֲנֵי בְּדַרְגָּא עִלָּאָה
עַל כָּל שְׁאָר בְּנֵי נָשָׁא, וְכֻלְּהוּ אִתּוֹקְדָן מֵחוּפָּה דְּהַאי.

61. "But better than both of them" is he WHO ARRIVES IN THIS WORLD and does not part FROM THE HOLY ONE, BLESSED BE HE, and is not known. All his words are covert. That is the innocent pious that kept the precepts of the Torah and upheld them, and dealt in the Torah day and night. Such a person is united and enjoys the higher level above all other people, and all the rest are burned from GAZING AT this one's canopy.

62. ת״ח, בְּשַׁעֲתָא דְּאָמַר קוּדְשָׁא בְּרִיךְ הוּא לְמֹשֶׁה יֵאָסֵף אַהֲרֹן אֶל
עַמָּיו, אִתְחַלָּשׁ חֵילָא דִּילֵיהּ, וְיָדַע דְּהָא אִתְבַּר דְּרוֹעָא יְמִינָא דִּילֵיהּ,
וְאִזְדַּעְזָעָא כָּל גּוּפֵיהּ, כֵּיוָן דְּאָמַר קַח אֶת אַהֲרֹן וְאֶת אֶלְעָזָר בְּנוֹ, אָ״ל
קוּדְשָׁא בְּרִיךְ הוּא, מֹשֶׁה, הָא דְּרוֹעָא אַחֲרָא אוֹזִיפְנָא לָךְ, וְהַפְשֵׁט אֶת

אַהֲרֹן וְגוֹ', וְאַהֲרֹן יֵאָסֵף, הָא אֶלְעָזָר יְהֵא לְגַבָּךְ, יְמִינָא דָא תְּחוֹת
אֲבוֹי. וְעִם כָּל דָּא לָא אַשְׁלִים אֲתָר בְּהַהוּא זִמְנָא כַּאֲבוֹי, דְּהָא עֲנָנֵי
יְקָר אִסְתַּלָּקוּ, וְלָא אָהַדְרוּ אֶלָּא בִּזְכוּתָא דְּמֹשֶׁה, וְלָא בִּזְכוּתָא
דְּאֶלְעָזָר.

62. Come and behold: at the time the Holy One, blessed be He, said to
Moses, "Aaron shall be gathered to his people," his strength was weakened
and he knew that his right arm, WHICH IS CHESED, broke and his entire
body trembled. As soon as he said: "Take Aaron and Elazar his son," the
Holy One, blessed be He, said to him: 'Here, I will lend you another arm.'
"And strip Aaron...and Aaron shall be gathered." Elazar shall serve as the
right hand for you instead of his father. In spite of all this, he did not
entirely fill the place of his father, since the clouds of glory departed and
would not have returned if not for the merit of Moses, but not because of
Elazar's merit.

63. וַיַּעַשׂ מֹשֶׁה כַּאֲשֶׁר צִוָּה וְגוֹ'. אַמַּאי לְעֵינֵי כָּל הָעֵדָה. אֶלָּא, בְּגִין
דְּאַהֲרֹן הֲוָה רְחִימָא דְּעַמָּא, יַתִּיר מִכֹּלָּא, וְלָא יֵימְרוּן דְּהָא אִתְנְגִיד עַל
יְדָא דְּמֹשֶׁה. וּמֹשֶׁה מָשִׁיךְ לְאַהֲרֹן בְּמִלִּין, עַד דְּסָלִיקוּ לְטוּרָא, וְכָל
יִשְׂרָאֵל הֲוֹו חָמָאן, בְּשַׁעֲתָא דְּאַפְשִׁיט מֹשֶׁה לְבוּשֵׁי דְּאַהֲרֹן, וְאַלְבִּישׁ
לוֹן לְאֶלְעָזָר.

63. "And Moses did as Hashem commanded..." (Bemidbar 20:27). HE
ASKS: Why, "in the sight of all the congregation" (Ibid.)? HE RESPONDS:
This was because Aaron was the most beloved by the nation and they should
not say that he died through Moses. Moses drew Aaron with words until
they ascended the mountain, and all of Yisrael watched while Moses
undressed the garments of Aaron and robed Elazar with them.

64. מַאי טַעֲמָא מֹשֶׁה. אֶלָּא מֹשֶׁה אַלְבִּישִׁנּוּן לְאַהֲרֹן כַּד סָלִיק לִכְהֻנָּא,
הה"ד וְיַּלְבֵּשׁ מֹשֶׁה אֶת אַהֲרֹן אֶת בְּגָדָיו, וּכְתִיב וַיַּלְבֵּשׁ אוֹתוֹ אֶת
הַמְּעִיל. הַשְׁתָּא. מֹשֶׁה אַעֲדֵי מִנֵּיהּ, מַה דְּיָהַב לֵיהּ. וְקוּדְשָׁא בְּרִיךְ הוּא
אַעֲדֵי מִנֵּיהּ, מַה דְּיָהַב לֵיהּ. וְתַרְוַויְיהוּ אַפְשִׁיטוּ לֵיהּ לְאַהֲרֹן מִכֹּלָּא,

וּמֹשֶׁה אַעְדֵּי לְבַר, וְקוּדְשָׁא בְּרִיךְ הוּא לְגוֹ. וְעַד דְּאַעְדֵּי מֹשֶׁה, קוּדְשָׁא בְּרִיךְ הוּא לָא אַעְדֵּי, זַכָּאָה חוּלָקָא דְּמֹשֶׁה.

64. HE ASKS: What is the reason that Moses REMOVED HIS GARMENTS? HE REPLIES: It is because Moses was the one that put them on Aaron when he was elevated to the priesthood. It says that Moses clothed Aaron with the garments, and it is written: "and clothed him with the robe" (Vayikra 8:7). THEREFORE, Moses then removed what he gave him and the Holy One, blessed be He, removed that which He granted him, MEANING HIS SOUL. Both of them undressed Aaron completely, Moses removed what was external, and the Holy One, blessed be He, removed what was internal. As long as Moses did not complete his removal, the Holy One, blessed be He, did not complete His own. Happy is the lot of Moses.

65. זַכָּאָה חוּלָקְהוֹן דְּצַדִּיקַיָּיא, דְּקוּדְשָׁא בְּרִיךְ הוּא בָּעֵי בִּיקָרֵיהוֹן. אַתְקִין קוּדְשָׁא בְּרִיךְ הוּא לְאַהֲרֹן, עַרְסָא וּמְנַרְתָּא דְּדַהֲבָא דְּנַהֲרָא. וּמִדִּידֵיהּ נָטִיל, מֵהַהוּא מְנַרְתָּא דַּהֲוָה דָּלִיק בְּכָל יוֹמָא תְּרֵי זִמְנֵי וְאַסְתִּים פּוּם מְעַרְתָּא וְנַחְתּוּ.

65. Happy is the lot of the just, since the Holy One, blessed be He, desires their honor. The Holy One, blessed be He, prepared for Aaron a bed and candelabra of gold that gives light, and took it from him, from that lamp that he used to light twice every day. AND AFTER THAT, He sealed the opening of the cave and they went down.

66. רִבִּי יְהוּדָה אָמַר, פּוּם מְעַרְתָּא הֲוָה פְּתִיחָא, דְּכָל יִשְׂרָאֵל הֲווֹ חָמָאן לְאַהֲרֹן שָׁכִיב, וּבוּצִינָא דִּמְנַרְתָּא דָּלִיק קַמֵּיהּ, וְעַרְסֵיהּ נָפִיק וְעָיֵיל, וַעֲנָנָא חַד קָאִים עֲלֵיהּ. וּכְדֵין יָדְעוּ יִשְׂרָאֵל דְּהָא אַהֲרֹן מִית. וְחָמוּ דְּהָא אִסְתַּלְּקוּ עַנְנֵי כָּבוֹד, הַהַ"ד וַיִּרְאוּ כָּל הָעֵדָה כִּי גָוַע אַהֲרֹן וְגוֹ', וְהָא אוּקְמוּהָ. וְעַ"ד בָּכוּ לְאַהֲרֹן כָּל בֵּית יִשְׂרָאֵל, גּוּבְרִין וְנָשִׁין וְטָף, דְּהָא רְחִימָא מִכֻּלְּהוּ הֲוָה.

66. Rabbi Yehuda said: The entrance of the cave was wide open; all of Yisrael observed Aaron dead. The candle of the lamp was lit before him, his bed was coming in and out, SO THAT ALL OF YISRAEL COULD SEE THAT HE WAS DEAD, and one cloud remained OVER THE BED. At that point, Yisrael knew that Aaron was dead. They noticed that the clouds of glory departed FROM YISRAEL, as it is written: "and when all the congregation saw that Aaron was dead..." (Bemidbar 20:29). And this was previously explained. Therefore, "they mourned for Aaron...all the house of Yisrael," men, women and children, since he was beloved by all.

67. רִבִּי שִׁמְעוֹן אָמַר, הָנֵי תְּלָתָא אָחִין עִלָּאִין קַדִּישִׁין, אֲמַאי לָא אִתְקַבְּרוּ בְּאֲתַר חַד, וְשַׁיְיפִין אִתְבַּדְּרוּ, חַד הָכָא, וְחַד הָכָא, וְחַד בְּאֲתַר אָחֲרָא. אֶלָּא אִית דְּאָמְרֵי, בַּאֲתַר דְּבָעָאן יִשְׂרָאֵל לְאִסְתַּכְּנָא בֵּיהּ, מִית כָּל חַד וְחַד, בְּגִין לְאַגָּנָא עָלַיְיהוּ, וְאִשְׁתְּזִבוּן, אֲבָל כָּל חַד וְחַד מִית כַּדְקָא חֲזֵי עָלַיְיהוּ. מִרְיָם בְּקָדֵשׁ, בֵּין צָפוֹן לְדָרוֹם. אַהֲרֹן לְסִטַר יְמִינָא. מֹשֶׁה כַּדְקָא חֲזֵי לֵיהּ. אָחִיד הַהוּא טוּרָא לְטוּרָא דְּאַהֲרֹן, וְכָנִישׁ לִקְבוּרָתָא דְּמִרְיָם לְגַבֵּי הַהוּא טוּרָא, אָחִיד לִתְרֵי סִטְרֵי. וְעַל דָּא אִתְקְרֵי הַר הָעֲבָרִים, דִּתְרֵי סִטְרֵי טוּרָא דִּמְעַבְרֵי, וְאָחִיד לְסִטְרָא דָּא וּלְסִטְרָא דָּא.

67. Rabbi Shimon said: Why were these three holy elevated siblings not buried in a single area? And why were the limbs spread about, one here and one in another place? There are some who say that each one died at a location where Yisrael were destined to be in danger in the future in order to defend Yisrael, so that they would be saved. However, THE EXPLANATION IS that each one died as appropriate. Miriam died in Kadesh and was in the location between North and South, SINCE MIRIAM WAS THE CHARIOT TO MALCHUT, WHICH IS BETWEEN THE RIGHT AND LEFT OF ZEIR ANPIN, REFERRED TO AS SOUTH AND NORTH. Aaron, WHO WAS THE CHARIOT FOR CHESED, DIED IN MOUNT HOR, and was to the right direction. Moses, WHO DIED IN THE MOUNTAIN OF AVARIM, WAS IN THE CENTER, as was appropriate for him, SINCE MOSES WAS THE CARRIAGE TO THE CENTRAL COLUMN, THAT IS, TIFERET. This was WHERE MOSES WAS pulled onto the mountain where Aaron was, and he collected Miriam's burial ground to that mountain OF MOSES, which was held on both sides, FROM THE RIGHT AND FROM THE LEFT, SINCE THE CENTRAL COLUMN COMBINES THE RIGHT AND THE LEFT. Therefore, it is called the

'Mountain of Avarim' IN ORDER TO COMMEMORATE THE PASSAGE THAT EXISTS BETWEEN the two sides of the mountain that allow crossings (Heb. *ma'avarim*). THAT PASSAGEWAY is attached to this side and to that side, TO THE RIGHT AND TO THE LEFT.

68. זַכָּאָה חוּלָקֵהוֹן דְּצַדִּיקַיָּיא בְּעָלְמָא דֵּין וּבְעָלְמָא דְּאָתֵי. וְאע"ג דְּאִינּוּן בַּאֲתָר אַחֲרָא, בְּעָלְמָא אַחֲרָא עִלָּאָה, זְכוּתְהוֹן קַיְּימָא בְּעָלְמָא דָּא, לְדָרֵי דָּרִין. וּבְשַׁעֲתָא דְּיִשְׂרָאֵל תַּיְיבִין בְּתִיוּבְתָּא קַמֵּי קוּדְשָׁא בְּרִיךְ הוּא, וּגְזֵירָה אִתְגְּזַר עֲלַיְיהוּ, כְּדֵין קָארֵי קוּדְשָׁא בְּרִיךְ הוּא לְצַדִּיקַיָּיא דְּקַיְימֵי קַמֵּיהּ לְעֵילָּא, וְאוֹדַע לוֹן, וְאִינּוּן מְבַטְּלֵי הַהִיא גְּזֵרָה, וְחָיֵיס קוּדְשָׁא בְּרִיךְ הוּא עֲלַיְיהוּ דְּיִשְׂרָאֵל. זַכָּאִין אִינּוּן צַדִּיקַיָּיא, דְּעֲלַיְיהוּ כְּתִיב וְנָחֲךָ יְיָ' תָּמִיד וְגוֹ'.

68. Happy is the portion of the righteous in this world and the World to Come. Even though they are in another world, in another higher world, their merit endures in this world for generations to come. During the period that Yisrael return to repent in the presence of the Holy One, blessed be He, some punishment is decreed over them. Then the Holy One, blessed be He, calls upon the righteous, who remain in His presence above, and informs them. They void that decree and the Holy One, blessed be He, has Mercy on Yisrael. Happy are the just, about whom it is written, "and Hashem will guide you continually..." (Yeshayah 58:11).

10. "And the people spoke out against Elohim, and against Moses"

A Synopsis

Rabbi Yitzchak informs us that "Now it came to pass on the third day, that Esther put on her royal apparel" means she was enveloped by the Holy Spirit after three days of fasting that made her body weak. She merited this blessing because she guarded her words and did not speak evil. We are assured that anyone who speaks with an evil tongue will be harmed by his own actions in some way, and then Rabbi Yitzchak talks about the title verse – in which the masses say slanderous things about God and also quarrel with Moses. It was, we learn, for this reason these people were burned in the fire.

69. וַיְדַבֵּר הָעָם בֵּאלֹהִים וּבְמֹשֶׁה וְגוֹ'. פָּרְשְׁתָּא דָא, בַּאֲתָר אַחֲרָא אִסְתָּלִיק, עִם אִינּוּן מֵי מְרִיבָה דְּמֹשֶׁה וְאַהֲרֹן.

69. "And the people spoke out against Elohim, and against Moses..." (Bemidbar 21:5). This passage was explained in another place, with THOSE SCRIPTURE PASSAGES RELATING TO the waters of Merivah (Eng. 'dispute') against Moses and Aaron.

70 (1). רִבִּי יִצְחָק פָּתַח, וַיְהִי בַּיּוֹם הַשְּׁלִישִׁי וַתִּלְבַּשׁ אֶסְתֵּר מַלְכוּת וְגוֹ'. מְגִלַּת אֶסְתֵּר בְּרוּה"ק נֶאֶמְרָה, וּבְגִין כָּךְ כְּתוּבָה בֵּין הַכְּתוּבִים. וַיְהִי בַּיּוֹם הַשְּׁלִישִׁי, דְּאִתְחַלָּשׁ חֵילָא דְּגוּפָא, וְהָא קַיְּימָא בְּרוּחָא בְּלָא גוּפָא, כְּדֵין וַתִּלְבַּשׁ אֶסְתֵּר מַלְכוּת. מַאי מַלְכוּת. אִי תֵּימָא בִּלְבוּשֵׁי יְקָר וְאַרְגְּווָנָא, הָא לָאו הָכִי אִקְרֵי. אֶלָּא וַתִּלְבַּשׁ אֶסְתֵּר מַלְכוּת, דְּאִתְלַבְּשַׁת בְּמַלְכוּת עִלָּאָה קַדִּישָׁא, וַדַּאי לָבְשָׁה רוּחַ הַקֹּדֶשׁ.

70a. Rabbi Yitzchak opened the discussion with the verse: "Now it came to pass on the third day, that Esther put on her royal apparel (Heb. *malchut*)" (Esther 5:1). The scroll of Esther was said in the Holy Spirit and, therefore, it is written among the scriptures. "Now it came to pass on the third day." When the body energy was low and weak, DUE TO THE FASTING, she remained in her spirit without the body. Then, "that Esther put on Malchut." What is the meaning of Malchut? If you think it is glorious and purple garments, these are not called so, BY THE NAME OF MALCHUT. "Esther put on Malchut," MEANS that she was clothed in the supernal Holy Malchut. She was assuredly enveloped in the Holy Spirit, SINCE MALCHUT IS CONSIDERED THE HOLY SPIRIT.

70(2). מַאי טַעֲמָא זָכְתָה לְהַאי אֲתָר. בְּגִין דְּנַטְרָא פּוּמָה דְּלָא לְחַוָּואָה מִדֵּי. הַה"ד אֵין אֶסְתֵּר מַגֶּדֶת מוֹלַדְתָּה. וְאוֹלִיפְנָא כָּל מַאן דְּנָטִיר פּוּמֵיה וְלִישָׁנֵיה, זָכֵי לְאִתְלַבְּשָׁא בְּרוּחַ דְּקוּדְשָׁא. וְכָל מַאן דְּסָטֵי פּוּמֵיה לְמִלָּה בִּישָׁא, הָא וַדַּאי הַהוּא מִלָּה בִּישָׁא עֲלֵיה. וְאִי לָאו, הָא נְגָעִים, אוֹ צָרַעַת, דְּמוֹקְדָן כְּחִוְיָא עֲלֵיה, וְהָא אוּקְמוּהָ.

70b. What is the reason that she merited this stature, MEANING MALCHUT? It is because she guarded her lips so as not to reveal anything. This is what is written: "Esther had not yet made known her kindred or her people" (Ester 2:20). We were taught that whoever guards his lips and tongue is worthy of clothing himself with the Holy Spirit. And anybody who curves his lips to speak evil will be harmed by that matter of which he speaks, MEANING THAT IF HE SPEAKS THE EVIL TONGUE, LIKE THE PRIMORDIAL SNAKE, THEN THAT SNAKE DOMINATES HIM. AND THAT IS WHY WHEN YISRAEL SPOKE AGAINST ELOHIM AND MOSES, HE SET SNAKES AND VIPERS UPON THEM. If he does not, he is afflicted by diseases or leprosy, which is burning like a snake, as we have already explained.

71. וַיְדַבֵּר הָעָם בֵּאלֹהִים וּבְמֹשֶׁה. דְּאָמְרוּ מִלָּה בִּישָׁא בְּקוּדְשָׁא בְּרִיךְ הוּא, וּכְתַרְגּוּמוֹ. וְעִם מֹשֶׁה נָצוּ. לָמָּה הֶעֱלִיתוּנוּ, שָׁוּוּ כָּל אַפַּיָּיא שַׁוְיָין בג"כ אִזְדְּמַן לְגַבַּיְיהוּ חִוְיָין, דְּמוֹקְדָן לוֹן כְּאֶשָׁא, וְעַיֵּיל אֶשָׁא לִמְעַיְיהוּ וְנַפְלִין מֵתִין, כד"א וַיְשַׁלַּח יְיָ' בָּעָם אֵת הַנְּחָשִׁים הַשְּׂרָפִים.

71. "And the people spoke out against Elohim, and against Moses." They said slanderous things about the Holy One, blessed be He, according to the ARAMAIC translation of "MURMUR," and they quarreled with Moses. "Why have you brought us up?" (Bemidbar 21:5). They treated all aspects equally, BECAUSE THEY EQUATED ELOHIM TO MOSES, AND SAID TO THEM: "WHY HAVE YOU BROUGHT US UP?" This is why snakes that burned them like fire were sent upon them. The fire entered their internals and they dropped dead, as is written: "and Hashem sent venomous serpents among the people" (Ibid. 6).

‏72. ר' חִיָּיא אָמַר, חִוְיָין הֲווֹ אַתְיָין, מְלַחֲשָׁן בְּפוּמַיְיהוּ, וְנַשְׁכִין וּמֵתִין. מַאי מְלַחֲשָׁן. כד"א אִם יִשׁוֹךְ הַנָּחָשׁ בְּלֹא לָחַשׁ. אֶשָּׁא הֲווֹ מְלַהֲטָן בְּפוּמַיְיהוּ, וְנַשְׁכִין, וְשַׁדְיָין אֶשָּׁא בְּהוּ, וְאִתּוֹקְדָאן מֵעַיְיהוּ וּמֵתִין וְהָא מִלִּין אִלֵּין אִסְתְּלָקוּ לַאֲתָר אַחֲרָא.

72. Rabbi Chiya said: Snakes would approach and their lips would whisper, and they would bite and die. What is whispering? It is as it says, "if the serpent bites and cannot be charmed (also: 'without a whisper')" (Kohelet 10:11). A fire would glow from their mouths, and they would bite and inject the fire into them. Their internal organs were burned and they died, and these items were defined somewhere else.

11. The well

A Synopsis

We hear an elaboration of the letters of 'she' and 'he' and the places where masculine and feminine are referred to in regard to the well. Rabbi Shimon says that the spirit in the water is the Holy Spirit that elevates Mayin Nukvin so that the waters will flow. The important point is that in everything there is a requirement to arouse something from below by action or speech, or to indicate and display some similarity to the act, and then the arousal from above will take place. Rabbi Shimon talks about the well being divided into thirteen streams and overflowing in all directions so that all of Yisrael could be sustained. We learn that most people do not know how to call upon God in Truth and arouse actions above, and that God is only near to those who do. The children of Yisrael said things which were matters of Truth in order to arouse the well; even sorcerers have to say some truth in order to awaken actions. Rabbi Shimon says the difference between most people and the Righteous is that the Righteous know the essence of words and actions, and they know how to direct their hearts and desires to God more than those who are not as knowledgeable; they draw blessings from the area of thought, that is Chochmah. When they call on God He is ready for them, and when they are in distress He is with them. He honors them in this world and in the World to Come.

73. וּמִשָּׁם בְּאֵרָה הוּא הַבְּאֵר. מ"ש דְּהָכָא בְּאֵרָה, וּלְבָתַר בְּאֵר. אֶלָּא בְּאֵרָה, לְבָתַר דְּמִתְכַּנְשֵׁי מַיָּיא לְגוֹ יַמָּא, וְנַחְתֵּי לְתַתָּא. בְּאֵר, בְּשַׁעֲתָא דְּיִצְחָק מַלְּיָיא לֵיהּ. הִיא הַבְּאֵר, הוּא כְּתִיב וְרָזָא דָּא, כְּמָה דִּכְתִיב וְעָבַד הַלֵּוִי הוּא.

73. "And from thence they went to Be'er (Eng. 'well') that is the well" (Bemidbar 21:16). HE ASKS: What is the change – why does it first say, Be'erah (Eng. 'to the well') and immediately after that, Be'er (Eng. 'well')? HE RESPONDS: It is only that Be'erah IS HOW MALCHUT WAS CALLED after all the waters converged into the sea and flowed down TO THE AREA OF MALCHUT. MALCHUT IS CALLED Be'er when Isaac, WHO IS THE LEFT COLUMN OF ZEIR ANPIN, fills it up. SINCE THE BE'ER IS STILL ENACTED UPON BY ZEIR ANPIN, IT IS THEREFORE CALLED BE'ER WITHOUT HEI, INDICATING MASCULINE LANGUAGE. THEREFORE, "she (Heb. hi) is the well," is spelled, "he (Heb. hu) is the well," WITH THE VAV, INDICATING

THAT IT IS MASCULINE LANGUAGE. The secret is as we explained. "But the Levite, he shall do the service" (Bemidbar 18:23), SINCE HE INDICATES THE LEFT SIDE OF ZEIR ANPIN.

74. ר' אַבָּא אָמַר, בְּכָל אֲתָר הוּא, וְקַרֵינָן הִיא, דְּכַר וְנוּקְבָּא כַּחֲדָא. וּכְלָלָא עִלָּאָה, ה' נוּקְבָּא, ו' דְּכַר, א' כְּלָלָא דְּכֹלָּא. דְּהָא א' בִּשְׁלִימוּ שַׁרְיָא. זַכָּאִין אִינוּן יִשְׂרָאֵל, אע"ג דְּאִינּוּן לְתַתָּא, אִינּוּן אֲחִידָן בִּכְלָלָא עִלָּאָה דְּכֹלָּא, ובג"כ כְּתִיב הוּא עָשָׂנוּ וְלֹא אֲנָחְנוּ, בְּאָלֶף כְּתִיב. כְּלָלָא דְּו"ה וְא' דְּכָלִיל כֹּלָּא.

74. Rabbi Aba said: Anyplace WHERE IT IS SPELLED "he" and pronounced "she," AS IT IS HERE AT THE WELL, IT INDICATES male and female combined, AND THE THREE LETTERS OF "HE" (*HEI-VAV-ALEPH*) is an overall high principal. *Hei* is female, MALCHUT, *Vav* is male, ZEIR ANPIN, and *Aleph* IS BINAH THAT IS inclusive of all, SINCE ZEIR ANPIN AND THE FEMALE EMERGE FROM HER. *Aleph*, WHICH IS BINAH, is the perfection of everything, SINCE ALL THE MOCHIN FLOW FROM HER. Happy are the children of Yisrael. Although they are down, they are grasped in the highest principle of all – THAT IS, IN THE THREE LETTERS OF *HEI, VAV, ALEPH*. Therefore, it is written: "it is He who made us, and we belong to Him" (Tehilim 100:3). The word *lo* is spelled with an *Aleph* INSTEAD OF A *VAV*, INDICATING, "AND NOT (HEB. *LO*) WE," as it is the inclusion of *Vav-Hei*, WHICH ARE ZEIR ANPIN AND THE FEMALE. And the *Aleph* includes everything.

75. ר"ש אָמַר, רוּחַ דְּמַיָּא, דָּא הוּא רוּחַ הַקֹּדֶשׁ, דְּנָשַׁב בְּקַדְמֵיתָא. כד"א הָפִיחִי גַנִּי, לְבָתַר נַזְלִין מַיָּא לְמַלְיָא לָה, ההד"ד יַשֵּׁב רוּחוֹ יִזְּלוּ מָיִם. יַשֵּׁב רוּחוֹ בְּקַדְמֵיתָא, וּלְבָתַר יִזְּלוּ מָיִם. וְעַד לָא נָשִׁיב הַאי רוּחָא, לָא נַזְלִין מַיָּא. מַאי קָא מַשְׁמַע לָן, מַשְׁמַע דְּבָעֵי בְּכֹלָּא לְאִתְּעָרָא מִלָּה, בְּעוֹבָדָא אוֹ בְּמִלָּה, אוֹ לְאִתְחֲזָאָה כְּחֵיזוּ דְּעוֹבָדָא. וְהָכָא, עַד דְּרוּחָא לָא נָשִׁיב, לָא נַזְלִין מַיָּא לְגַבֵּיהּ דְּהַהוּא רוּחַ.

75. Rabbi Shimon said: The spirit (also: 'wind') in the water is the Holy Spirit, MEANING THE SPIRIT OF MALCHUT THAT IS REFERRED TO AS 'HOLY

SPIRIT' that blows in the beginning, as it says, "blow upon My garden" (Shir Hashirim 4:16). This MEANS THAT IT ELEVATES MAYIN NUKVIN (FEMALE WATERS), and then waters will flow, WHICH ARE THE UPPER MAYIN DUCHRIN (MALE WATERS) to fill her. This is what is written: "He causes His wind to blow: they run as water" (Tehilim 147:18). At first, "He causes His wind to blow," and then, "waters will flow." As long as He does not cause His wind to blow, the waters will not flow. What does this teach us? From this, it is apparent that in everything there is a requirement to arouse something FROM BELOW, THAT IS AN ASPECT OF FEMALE WATER, by action or speech, or to indicate and display some similarity to the act, AND THEN COMES THE AROUSAL FROM ABOVE. THEREFORE, until the wind does not blow, the water, WHICH IS THE SECRET OF ABUNDANT FLOW, does not flow towards the wind, WHICH IS MALCHUT.

76. הוּא הַבְּאֵר, הִיא הַבְּאֵר קָרֵינָן, מ"ש בְּקַדְמֵיתָא בְּאֵרָה, וְהַשְׁתָּא בְּאֵר, אֶלָּא בְּקַדְמֵיתָא נוּקְבָּא בִּלְחוֹדָהָא, וְהַשְׁתָּא דְקָאמַר הוּא, כְּלָלָא דִּדְכַר וְנוּקְבָּא, אִקְרֵי בְּאֵר. וּבַאֲתַר דְּאִשְׁתְּכַח דְּכַר, אֲפִילוּ מְאָה נוּקְבָּא, דְּכַר קָרֵינָן לְכֹלָּא.

76. "…that (lit. 'he') is the well," IS SPELLED, but we pronounce it as: "She is the well." ALSO, what changes so that it is written "Be'erah" at first and then, "Be'er"? HE REPLIES: It is only because the female, THAT IS MALCHUT, was alone in the beginning AND THEREFORE IT WAS SAID IN FEMININE LANGUAGE, "BE'ERAH." When it says "he," it indicates the inclusion of both male and female, so it is called "Be'er" in MASCULINE LANGUAGE. ALTHOUGH IT ALSO INCLUDES THE FEMALE, IT IS IN THE MASCULINE FORM, since all are called in the masculine form in the area where a male exists, even if he has WITH HIM a hundred females.

77. אֲשֶׁר אָמַר יְיָ' לְמֹשֶׁה אֶסוֹף אֶת הָעָם, בְּגִין דְּהַאי בְּאֵר לָא אַעְדֵּי מִנַּיְיהוּ. וְאִי תֵּימָא, הֵיךְ יַכְלִין לְשָׁאֲבָא מִנֵּיהּ כֹּלָּא, אֶלָּא אִיהוּ נָפִיק לְתְלֵיסַר נַחֲלִין, וּנְבִיעַ אִתְמַלֵּי וְנָפִיק לְכָל סִטְרִין, וּכְדֵין הֲווֹ יִשְׂרָאֵל בְּשַׁעֲתָא דְּשָׁאֲרָן וּבָעְיָין מַיָּיא, קַיְימִין עָלֵיהּ, וְאָמְרֵי שִׁירָתָא. וּמַה אָמְרֵי, עֲלִי בְאֵר. סַלְקִי מֵימִיךְ, לְאַנְפָּקָא מַיִין לְכֹלָּא, וּלְאִתְשַׁקְאָה מִנָּךְ.

וְכֵן אַמְרֵי תּוּשְׁבַּחְתָּא דְּהַאי בְּאֵר, בְּאֵר חֲפָרוּהָ שָׂרִים וְגוֹ'. מִלָּה קְשׁוֹט
הֲווֹ אַמְרֵי, וְכַךְ הוּא.

77. IT IS WRITTEN: "THAT IS THE WELL of which Hashem spoke to Moses saying, 'Gather the people together'" (Bemidbar 21:16). This is because that well was not missing from them. If you wonder how all of them could possibly draw from that one, it is because it divided into thirteen streams. This is SINCE MALCHUT DIVIDES INTO THIRTEEN, IN THE SECRET OF THE TWELVE, WHICH IT RECEIVES FROM THE TWELVE BOUNDARIES IN ZEIR ANPIN, AND ONE IS COMPOSED OF ALL OF THEM. The flowing spring in the well is filled and overflows in all directions. Then, at the time the children of Yisrael were singing and desired water, the children of YISRAEL would stand about her, OVER THE WELL, and sing. What did they say? "'Spring up, O well" (Ibid. 17), and raise your water to produce water for everyone to drink.' That is the way to praise this well, and THAT IS "the well that the princes dug out." They spoke words of truth. And so it is.

78. מֵהָכָא אוֹלִיפְנָא, כָּל מַאן דְּבָעֵי לְאִתְעָרָא מִלִּין דִּלְעֵילָא, בֵּין
בְּעוֹבָדָא בֵּין בְּמִלָּה. אִי הַהוּא עוֹבָדָא, אוֹ הַהוּא מִלָּה, לָא אִתְעָבֵיד
כַּדְקָא יָאוּת, לָא אִתְּעַר מִדֵּי. כָּל בְּנֵי עָלְמָא אַזְלִין לְבֵי כְּנִישְׁתָּא
לְאִתְעָרָא מִלָּה דִּלְעֵילָא, אֲבָל זְעֵירִין אִינּוּן דְּיַדְעִין לְאִתְעָרָא, וְקוּדְשָׁא
בְּרִיךְ הוּא קָרִיב לְכֹלָּא דְּיַדְעֵי לְמִקְרֵי לֵיהּ וּלְאִתְעָרָא מִלָּה כַּדְקָא יָאוּת,
אֲבָל אִי לָא יַדְעֵי לְמִקְרֵי לֵיהּ, לָאו אִיהוּ קָרִיב, דִּכְתִיב קָרוֹב יְיָ' לְכָל
קוֹרְאָיו וְגוֹ'. מַאי בֶּאֱמֶת. דְּיַדְעֵי לְאִתְעָרָא מִלָּה דִּקְשׁוֹט כַּדְקָא יָאוּת,
וְכֵן בְּכֹלָּא.

78. From here, we were taught that for whoever desires to arouse matters above, either by deed or speech, if that deed or speech is not performed properly, then nothing gets aroused. All the inhabitants of the world go to the synagogue to arouse something above, but few are those who know how to arouse. The Holy One, blessed be He, is near those who know how to call on Him and arouse properly. However, if they do not know how to call on Him, He is not near, as is written: "Hashem is near to all those who call upon Him, to all who call upon Him in truth" (Tehilim 145:18). What is, "in truth"? That is that they know how to arouse the truthful thing appropriately, and it applies to all THINGS as well.

79. אוֹף הָכָא, הֲוֹו אַמְרֵי יִשְׂרָאֵל הָנֵי מִלִּין, מִלִּין דִּקְשׁוֹט, בְּגִין לְאִתְעָרָא לְהַאי בֵּירָא, וּלְאַשְׁקָאָה לוֹן לְיִשְׂרָאֵל, וְעַד דְּאַמְרֵי הָנֵי מִלֵי לָא אִתְּעַר. וְכֵן אֲפִילוּ בְּאִינּוּן חֲרָשֵׁי עָלְמָא, דְּמִשְׁתַּמְּשֵׁי בְּזִינִין בִּישִׁין, עַד דְּעַבְדֵּי עוֹבָדוֹי דִּקְשׁוֹט לְגַבַּיְיהוּ, אִי לָא אָמְרוּ מִלֵי דִּקְשׁוֹט, בְּגִין לְאַמְשָׁכָא לוֹן בְּהָנֵי גְוְונָא דְּבַעְיָין, לָא מִתְעָרִין לְגַבַּיְיהוּ, וַאֲפִילוּ דְּצַוְוחֵי כָּל יוֹמָא בְּמִלִּין אַחֲרָנִין, אוֹ בְּעוֹבָדָא אַחֲרָא, לָא מַשְׁכִין לוֹן לְגַבַּיְיהוּ לְעָלְמִין, וְלָא מִתְעָרִין לְקַבְלַיְיהוּ.

79. ABOUT THE WELL, Yisrael said these things which are matters of truth in order to arouse this well, WHICH IS MALCHUT, and to give drink to Yisrael. If they had not said these things, THE WELL would not have been aroused. Likewise, even the world's sorcerers who use evil things would not be awakened for them until they performed for them some veritable acts; they would not awaken if they did not say some truths in order to draw them in the manners they desire. Even if they had screamed all day long with other words and different acts, they would never have been capable of drawing them, and they would not have been awakened towards them.

80. ת"ח, כְּתִיב, וַיִּקְרְאוּ בְּשֵׁם הַבַּעַל וְגוֹ'. מַאי טַעְמָא. חַד דְּלָאו רְשׁוּ בְּהַהוּא בַּעַל בְּהַאי. וְעוֹד דְּמִלִּין לָא מִתְכַּשְּׁרָן בֵּינַיְיהוּ, וְאַנְשֵׁי לוֹן קוּדְשָׁא בְּרִיךְ הוּא מִנְּהוֹן. הה"ד וְאַתָּה הֲסִבּוֹתָ אֶת לִבָּם אֲחוֹרַנִּית. זַכָּאִין אִינּוּן צַדִּיקַיָּיא, דְּיַדְעֵי לְמִקְרֵי לְמָארֵיהוֹן כַּדְקָא יָאוֹת.

80. Come and behold: it is written, "and called on the name of the Ba'al..." (I Melachim 18:26) What is the reason THAT THEY WERE NOT ANSWERED? HE RESPONDS: First, it was not within the Ba'al's authority TO BRING DOWN FIRE FROM HEAVEN. In addition, since the wording was not the right one among them, the Holy One, blessed be He, made them forget them. That is what is written: "and that You have turned their hearts back again"(Ibid. 37). Praised are the righteous who know how to call upon their Master properly.

81. אָמַר רִבִּי שִׁמְעוֹן, הָכָא בָּעֵינָא לְגַלָּאָה מִלָּה. ת״ח, כָּל מַאן דְּיָדַע לְסַדְרָא עוֹבָדָא כַּדְקָא יָאוֹת, וּלְסַדְרָא מִלִּין כַּדְקָא יָאוֹת, הָא וַדַּאי מִתְעָרֵי לקוּדְשָׁא בְּרִיךְ הוּא, לְאַמְשָׁכָא מִלִּין עִלָּאִין דְּמִתְכַּשְׁרָן. וְאִי לָא, לָא אִתְכְּשַׁר לְגַבַּיְיהוּ. אִי הָכִי כָּל עָלְמָא יַדְעֵי לְסַדְרָא עוֹבָדָא, וּלְסַדְרָא מִלִּין, מַאי חָשִׁיבוּ דִּלְהוֹן דְּצַדִּיקַיָּיא, דְּיַדְעֵי עִקָּרָא דְּמִלָּה וְעוֹבָדָא, וְיַדְעֵי לְכַוְּונָא לִבָּא וּרְעוּתָא, יַתִּיר מֵאִלֵּין אַחֲרָנִין, דְּלָא יַדְעֵי כָּל כָּךְ.

81. Rabbi Shimon said: Here I wish to reveal something. Come and behold: anyone who is capable of preparing his deed as is proper and sets his speeches as is proper, definitely arouses the Holy One, blessed be He, to extend forth high matters that are upright. And if not, he is not propitious to them. If this is so, does not the whole world know how to prepare in an orderly manner the necessary performances and speeches? What then is the special value of them, the righteous? The righteous know the essence of words and actions, and they know how to direct their heart and desire more than those who are not as knowledgeable.

82. אֶלָּא אִלֵּין דְּלָא יַדְעֵי עִקָּרָא דְּעוֹבָדָא כּוּלֵי הַאי, אֶלָּא סִדּוּרָא בְּעָלְמָא וְלָא יַתִּיר, מַשְׁכִין עָלַיְיהוּ מְשִׁיכוּ דְּבָתַר כַּתְפוֹי דקוּדְשָׁא בְּרִיךְ הוּא, דְּלָא טָס בַּאֲוִירָא דְּשִׁגְחוּ אִקְרֵי.

82. HE RESPONDS: It is only that those who are not as knowledgeable of the essence of actions, but simply know their orderly set up and nothing more, draw to themselves from behind the shoulders of the Holy One, blessed be He. THEIR PRAYER does not soar in the air, which is considered providence, MEANING TO SAY THAT IS THE PROVIDENCE OF THE FACE AND THEY ARE ONLY WORTHY OF THE ASPECT OF BEHIND THE SHOULDERS.

83. וְאִלֵּין דְּיַדְעֵי וּמְכַוְּונֵי לִבָּא וּרְעוּתָא, מַפְּקֵי בִּרְכָאן מֵאֲתָר דְּמַחֲשָׁבָה, וְנָפְקֵי בְּכָל גִּזְעִין וְשָׁרְשִׁין בְּאֹרַח מֵישָׁר כַּדְקָא יָאוֹת, עַד דְּמִתְבָּרְכָן עִלָּאִין וְתַתָּאִין, וּשְׁמָא קַדִּישָׁא עִלָּאָה מִתְבָּרַךְ עַל יְדֵיהוֹן. זַכָּאָה חוּלָקֵהוֹן. דְּהָא קוּדְשָׁא בְּרִיךְ הוּא קָרִיב לְגַבַּיְיהוּ, וְזַמִּין

לְקָבְלֵיהוֹן, בְּשַׁעֲתָא דְּקָארוֹן לֵיהּ, הוּא זַמִּין לוֹן. בְּשַׁעֲתָא דְּאִינוּן בְּעָאקוּ, הוּא לְגַבַּיְיהוּ, הוּא אוֹקִיר לוֹן בְּעָלְמָא דֵּין וּבְעָלְמָא דְּאָתֵי, הה"ד כִּי בִי חָשַׁק וַאֲפַלְּטֵהוּ אֲשַׂגְּבֵהוּ כִּי יָדַע שְׁמִי.

83. Those that are knowledgeable and direct the heart and desire extricate blessings from the area of the thought, WHICH IS CHOCHMAH. They emerge in all the branches and roots OF THE LEVELS in a straightforward manner as called for, until the higher and lower grades receive their blessings and the Holy Name is blessed through them. Happy is their lot, since the Holy One, blessed be He, is close to them and available to them. When they call on Him, He is ready for them, and at the time of their distress, He is with them. He honors them in this world and in the World to Come. This is what is written: "because he has set his delight upon Me, therefore will I deliver him: I will satisfy him, and show him My salvation" (Tehilim 91:14).

12. "Fear him not"

A Synopsis

Rabbi Yehuda informs us that when Yisrael gather together they receive nourishment sometimes from Compassion and sometimes from Judgment, and that no divine influence prevails until there is a place for it to dwell down in the world of matter. Rabbi Yehuda says that God told Moses not to be afraid of king Og, because Og had defiled the sign of his covenant, and would therefore, by reason of his very own deeds, be uprooted and undone on earth. We hear that the children of Yisrael were blessed to have Moses as the prophet among them, since it was for his sake alone that God performed many miracles; and, lastly, we're reminded that God's Covenant was made only with the children of Abraham.

84. וַיֹּאמֶר יְיָ' אֶל מֹשֶׁה אַל תִּירָא אוֹתוֹ וְגוֹ'. רִבִּי יְהוּדָה פָּתַח, לֹא תִּירָא לְבֵיתָהּ מִשָּׁלֶג כִּי כָל בֵּיתָהּ לָבוּשׁ שָׁנִים. ת"ח, כְּנֶסֶת יִשְׂרָאֵל יַנְקָא מִתְּרֵי סִטְרֵי, הַשְׁתָּא בְּרַחֲמֵי, הַשְׁתָּא בְּדִינָא. כַּד בַּעְיָא לְיַנְקָא בְּרַחֲמֵי, אִשְׁתְּכַח אֲתָר לְאִתְיַשְׁבָא בֵיהּ. כַּד בָּעֵי לְיַנְקָא בְּדִינָא, אֲתָר אִשְׁתְּכַח לְאִתְיַשְׁבָא בֵּיהּ, וּלְמִשְׁרֵי עָלוֹהִי, דְּהָכִי הוּא בְּכָל אֲתָר, לָא שָׁארֵי מִלָּה דִּלְעֵילָּא, עַד דְּאִשְׁתְּכַח אֲתָר לְמִשְׁרֵי עֲלוֹי. וע"ד, כְּנֶסֶת יִשְׂרָאֵל לֹא תִּירָא לְבֵיתָא מִשָּׁלֶג, מ"ט, בְּגִין דְּכָל בֵּיתָא לָבוּשׁ שָׁנִים. לָא שַׁרְיָא הַאי, אֶלָּא בְּהַאי חִוָּור בְּסוּמָק, וְסוּמָק בְּחִוָּור. וְהָא אוֹקִמוּהָ.

84. "And Hashem said to Moses, 'Fear him not'" (Bemidbar 21:34). Rabbi Yehuda opened the discussion with the verse: "she is not afraid of the snow for her household: for all her household are clothed with scarlet" (Mishlei 31:21). Come and behold: the assembled Congregation of Yisrael nourishes from both sides, sometimes from Compassion and sometimes from Judgment. When it wishes to nourish from Compassion, there is a place WHERE COMPASSION will dwell. When it wishes to nourish from Judgment, there is room so THAT JUDGMENT will dwell and prevail on him. This is always the case. Nothing prevails from above until the room exists for it to dwell upon. Therefore, the Congregation of Yisrael "is not afraid of the snow for her household." What is the reason? It is because "all her household are clothed in scarlet." That one does not dwell only in that one, white in red, and red in white. And that was already established.

85. וַיֹּאמֶר יְיָ' אֶל מֹשֶׁה אַל תִּירָא אוֹתוֹ, תְּרֵין אוֹתוֹ אִינּוּן שְׁלֵימִין בְּאוֹרַיְיתָא בִּתְרֵין וָוִי"ן, חַד דָּא, וְחַד, עַד דְּרוֹשׁ אָחִיךָ אוֹתוֹ. מַ"ט. בְּגִין דְּאִינּוּן אוֹת מַמָּשׁ. עַד דְּרוֹשׁ אָחִיךָ אוֹתוֹ, דְּבָעֵי לְפָרְשָׁא הַהוּא אוֹת, דְּהַהוּא אֲבֵידָה.

85. "And Hashem said to Moses, 'Fear him (Heb. *oto*) not'." Twice IN THE TORAH IS FOUND, "*OTO* (*ALEPH-VAV-TAV-VAV*)," which is spelled out fully, with two *Vavs*. Once here and once in the verse: "until your brother seek after it (Heb. *oto*)" (Devarim 22:2). What is the reason? It is because THEIR MEANING IS an actual letter (Heb. *ot*) and they ARE NOT DERIVED FROM THE PARTICLE ET. "…until your brother seeks after it…" MEANS that he is required to define and spell out the SIGN AND mark (Heb. *ot*) of that lost item.

86. אוֹף הָכָא דֵּין אוֹתוֹ, דָּא עוֹג, דְּאִתְדַּבַּק בְּאַבְרָהָם, וּמֵאַנְשֵׁי בֵּיתֵיהּ הֲוָה, וְכַד אִתְגְּזַר אַבְרָהָם מַה כְּתִיב, וְכָל אַנְשֵׁי בֵיתוֹ וְגוֹ'. דָּא עוֹג דְּאִתְגְּזַר עִמֵּיהּ, וְקַבִּיל הַאי אָת קַדִּישָׁא, כֵּיוָן דְּחָמָא עוֹג דְּיִשְׂרָאֵל מִקָרְבִין גַּבֵּיהּ, אָמַר הָא וַדַּאי אֲנָא אַקְדִּימְנָא זְכוּתָא דְּקָאֵים לוֹן, וְדָא שַׁוִּי לְקַבְלֵיהּ.

86. Here too, it is Og who joined Abraham and he is from the people of his household. When Abraham was circumcised, it was written: "and all the men of his house" (Beresheet 17:26). That is Og, who was also circumcised with him and received that Holy Sign (Heb. *ot*). As soon as Og saw Yisrael approaching him, he thought to himself, 'I have certainly performed that precept that stands up for them,' SINCE HE WAS ALREADY CIRCUMCISED BEFORE OUR PATRIARCH ISAAC. And he placed this before him, AS SECURITY.

87. בֵּיהּ שַׁעֲתָא דָּחִיל מֹשֶׁה, הֵיךְ יָכִיל לְאַעְקְרָא רְשִׁימָא דְּרָשִׁים אַבְרָהָם. אָמַר, וַדַּאי הָא יְמִינָא דִּילִי מִית, דְּהָא יְמִינָא בַּעְיָא לְהַאי. אִי נֵימָא הָא אֶלְעָזָר, יְמִינָא דְּסִיהֲרָא הוּא, וְלָא דִּילִי. וְהַאי אָת לִימִינָא הוּא, דְּאַבְרָהָם לִימִינָא הוּא.

87. At that moment, Moses was afraid. How could he uproot the impression that Abraham made? He thought: 'Assuredly, my right hand, WHICH IS AARON, is dead, since the right is necessary TO WIN this.' It may be said that Elazar is here, who is the right of the moon, NAMELY, OF MALCHUT, but not mine, SINCE HE IS NOT THE RIGHT OF ZEIR ANPIN, WHICH IS THE SECRET OF MOSES, AS WAS AARON. That sign OF OG is to the right OF ZEIR ANPIN, since Abraham is the right OF ZEIR ANPIN.

88. מִיָּד אָמַר קוּדְשָׁא בְּרִיךְ הוּא, אַל תִּירָא אוֹתוֹ, לָא תִּדְחַל לְהַהוּא אָת דִּילֵיה, וַאֲפִילוּ לִימִינָא לָא אִצְטְרִיךְ. כִּי בְיָדְךָ נָתַתִּי. שְׂמָאלָא דִּילָךְ יַעֲקַר לֵיה מֵעָלְמָא, דְּהָא הוּא פָּגִים רְשִׁימָא דִּילֵיה, וּמַאן דְּפָגִים לְהַאי אָת, אִתְחֲזֵי לְאִתְעַקְּרָא מֵעָלְמָא, כ"ש שְׂמָאלָא דִּילָךְ, דְּאִיהוּ יָדְךָ, יֶעֱקָר לֵיה מֵעָלְמָא, בְּגִין כַּךְ אִתְעֲקַר מֵעָלְמָא, וַאֲפִילוּ דְּאִיהוּ תַּקִּיפָא מִבְּנֵי גִּבָּרַיָּיא, וּבָעָא לְשֵׁיצָאָה לְהוּ לְיִשְׂרָאֵל, נָפַל בִּידֵיה דְּמֹשֶׁה וְאִשְׁתְּצֵי.

88. Immediately, the Holy One, blessed be He, said, "Fear him not." Do not fear his sign, and even for the right there is no need. "For I have delivered him into your hand" (Ibid.). Your left will uproot him from the world, since he, OG, defiled the sign of his Covenant, and whoever makes a flaw in the sign of the Covenant is fit to be uprooted from this world ON HIS OWN. Of course, your left, that is, "your hand," will uproot him from the world. That is why he was uprooted from the world. Even though he was mighty from the sons of the mighty, and THOUGH he wanted to destroy Yisrael, he fell into the hands of Moses and was annihilated.

89. בְּגִין כַּךְ כֹּלָּא כָּךְ שֵׁצִיאוּ יִשְׂרָאֵל בְּנוֹי וְכָל עַמֵּיה, וְכָל דִּילֵיה. כְּמָה דִּכְתִיב, וַיַּכּוּ אוֹתוֹ וְאֶת בָּנָיו וְאֶת כָּל עַמּוֹ וּכְתִיב, וַנַּךְ אוֹתוֹ וְאֶת בָּנוֹ. בְּנוֹ כְּתִיב חָסֵר יוֹ"ד, וְקָרֵינָן בָּנָיו, וְהָא אוּקְמוּהָ חַבְרַיָּיא.

89. That is why Yisrael have annihilated all of them, his children, his people and everything belonging to them, as is written: "so they smote him, and his sons, and all his people" (Bemidbar 21:35). It is also written: "and we smote him, and his sons (Heb. *banav*)" (Devarim 2:33). It is written, "*banav*," without a *Yud*, INDICATIVE OF PLURALITY, yet it is pronounced *Banav* (plur.). This has already been explained by the friends.

90. זַכָּאִין אִינוּן יִשְׂרָאֵל, דְּמֹשֶׁה נְבִיאָה הֲוָה בֵּינַיְיהוּ, דִּבְגִינֵיהּ עֲבֵיד לוֹן קוּדְשָׁא בְּרִיךְ הוּא כָּל הָנֵי אַתְוָון, וְאוֹקִמוּהָ. וְקוּדְשָׁא בְּרִיךְ הוּא לָא גָּזַר קַיּוּמֵיהּ עִם שְׁאַר עַמִּין לְאִתְקַשְּׁרָא בֵּיהּ, אֶלָּא עִם יִשְׂרָאֵל, דְּאִינוּן בְּנוֹי דְּאַבְרָהָם, דִּכְתִּיב בּוֹ וּבֵין זַרְעֲךָ אַחֲרֶיךָ לְדֹרֹתָם בְּרִית עוֹלָם. וּכְתִיב וַאֲנִי זֹאת בְּרִיתִי אוֹתָם אָמַר יְיָ׳ רוּחִי אֲשֶׁר עָלֶיךָ וְגוֹ׳. לֹא יָמוּשׁוּ מִפִּיךָ וְגוֹ׳.

90. Happy are the children of Yisrael that Moses the prophet was among them, since the Holy One, blessed be He, performed all these signs for his sake, as we have explained. The Holy One, blessed be He, did not make His Covenant with the rest of the nations to be connected to them, only with Yisrael, who are the children of Abraham. About the children of Yisrael, it is written: "between...your seed after you in their generations for an everlasting Covenant" (Beresheet 17:7), and: "'as for Me, this is My Covenant with them,' said Hashem; 'My spirit that is upon you...shall not depart out of your mouth...'" (Yeshayah 59:21).

בָּרוּךְ יְיָ׳ לְעוֹלָם אָמֵן וְאָמֵן.

Blessed be Hashem for evermore. Amen and Amen.

End of Parashat Chukat

NOTES

NOTES

NOTES

NOTES

NOTES

NOTES